Child of Mine

FEEDING WITH LOVE AND GOOD SENSE

ELLYN SATTER, MS, RD, CICSW, BCD

Child of Mine

FEEDING WITH LOVE AND GOOD SENSE

COMPLETELY REVISED AND UPDATED

BULL PUBLISHING COMPANY
PALO ALTO, CALIFORNIA

Child of Mine: Feeding with Love and Good Sense
Copyright © 2000 Ellyn Satter

Bull Publishing Company
P.O. Box 208
Palo Alto, CA 94302-0208
Phone 650-322-2855
Fax 650-327-3300
www.bullpub.com

ISBN 0-923521-51-8

Library of Congress Cataloging-in-Publication Data

Satter, Ellyn.
    Child of mine: feeding with love and good sense / Ellyn Satter.
        p. cm.
    "Completely revised and updated."
    Includes bibliographical references and index.
    ISBN 0-923521-51-8
        1. Children–Nutrition. 2. Toddlers–Nutrition. 3. Child rearing.
        I. Title

    RJ206 .S24 2000
    613.2'083–dc21

Printed in the U.S.

Distributed in the United States by:
Publishers Group West
1700 Fourth Street
Berkeley, CA 94710

Publisher: James Bull
Editor: Mary Ray Worley
Cover design: Lightbourne Images
Interior design: Karen Foget
Compositor: Sherpe Advertising Art

10 9 8 7 6 5 4 3 2

Dedicated to my children,
Kjerstin,
Lucas, and
Curtis,
and to my grandchildren,
Emma,
Adele, and
Marin

CONTENTS

vii

FIGURES

PREFACE

WHEN I BEGAN WRITING *Child of Mine* back in 1979, I intended it as a farewell gift to a part of my life that had meant great deal to me. My three children were no longer babies or even toddlers—my youngest child was 8 years old. Not only that, but I was in graduate school preparing to be a psychotherapist, and I was closing my practice as a pediatric dietitian. I had learned a great deal about child nutrition and feeding in my personal and professional lives, and I wanted to write it down and share it with other parents before I forgot it. Imagine my surprise to find myself 20 years later still in the field, still writing, talking and puzzling about feeding babies and children. Readers of the first *Child of Mine* remember my stories about my children as infants and toddlers and are continually surprised that they haven't been frozen in time. My children are adults now, and I am a grandmother.

We have all changed, and it shouldn't be surprising that I return to this revision—and this topic—changed. Actually, the surprise has been that I stayed with the issue at all. Rather than closing the door on child nutrition as I had expected, I found that more and more possibilities and challenges emerged as I began developing ways of helping parents not only with choosing food for children but with feeding relationships as well. I discovered that writing a book is much like having a child. You don't just produce it and walk away. You have a responsibility to raise it, in a sense, and to be raised *by* it. Like a beloved child, a book provides opportunities for growth and change. *Child of Mine* catapulted me into the field of feeding dynamics—of understanding the social, emotional, behavioral, and parenting aspects of feeding. While I have become a psychotherapist, I have specialized in feeding and eating problems. I have used my background in mental health to more fully understand the complexity of feeding and to help parents and children with that complexity. I am now ready to weave together all that I have learned in the 20 years since I began to prepare what I thought was my parting gift.

My motives for writing the first edition of *Child of Mine* weren't totally altruistic—I was at least partly fueled by anger. I was angry about all the bad feeding advice I had been given, angry to hear that same bad advice being passed along to other young parents, and angry at myself for having bought it. As a young mother who was a dietitian, I had been appalled that I knew so little about feeding my first baby. I vaguely assumed I would breastfeed and then someday start solid foods. I had observed that while I didn't know much about *dealing* with babies, my newborn daughter seemed to know a good bit about *being* a baby, so I followed her lead and did what she seemed to need. I know now that my plans were sound enough, she was a competent and intelligible baby, and we were both fortunate that breastfeeding went well. The one big flaw in my plan was my naïveté: I had absolutely no way to defend against the advice I was being given in the health care setting.

I had been trusting my daughter, but feeding advice seemed to be built on the assumption that what she was telling me was wrong. When she was 1 month old, I was told to begin feeding her infant cereal on the grounds that if I didn't, my newborn infant would get "too opinionated" to eat it later and that unless I began supplementing breastmilk immediately she "would turn into a fat little milk baby." Both of these reasons turned out to be ridiculously unfounded, but at the time I didn't know that. I disliked foisting cereal onto my cuddly month-old baby who was doing so well on breastfeeding, but I did it anyway. By the time she was 10 weeks old I had so slavishly followed advice that I had her on cereal, fruits, vegetables, and mixed dinners. I remember it well, because part of our freight for a 4-week camping trip was jars and jars of baby food. You can imagine what a hassle it was to feed her, and the irony is that it was all so unnecessary. Kjerstin was doing great on breastfeeding, and breastfeeding alone would have worked *so* well with camping and traveling.

I was so dismayed about my ignorance and about those feeding guidelines that I set out to find a better way. It was heavy going. At first, everything I found was somebody's opinion, presented as if it was a rule set in stone. I became interested in the history of child feeding, and that was helpful, mostly because it demonstrated that there was no real logic or reasoning behind infant feeding recommendations. The only consistency was in attitude: advisors about infant feeding were convinced that they were right and extremely plausible—if poorly founded—in their reasoning. The need to control—and in the process ignore children's needs, behaviors, and capabilities—is a theme that came up again and again in my research and, unfortunately, remains prominent today. In the early part of this century, infants were kept on breastmilk until they were about a year old. People were afraid to feed their babies solid foods: they thought the babies would get sick, or at least not do as well on anything but breastmilk. They were right, to begin with.[1] At that time many had an erratic food supply and unreliable sanitation and refrigeration. Depending on solid foods could be dangerous for babies. Infant infectious diarrhea was a scourge that caused many deaths, as it still does in developing countries. The problem was that the feeding pattern outlived its usefulness; the pattern persisted although sanitation and refrigeration improved.

Over the years, health professionals began to get more adventurous about earlier introduction of infants to solid food as they looked for a substitute and a supplement for breastfeeding. Nutrition was a developing science, bringing with it an awareness of the importance of a diversified diet. Beginning in the late 1920s one vitamin after another was identified as having a role in preventing nutritional deficiency illnesses and food sources were identified. Taking science to its excruciating extreme, it became common practice for pediatricians to dictate precisely the types and frequencies of foods children were to be given during the transition from suckling to adult food between age 7 months to 3 or 4 years of age. The belief was rigidly held that infants and young children lacked the ability to regulate

food intake, and rules were handed down for giving them prescribed amounts of foods. The historical accounts don't report
the emotional consequences of these feeding patterns, but we
can guess. Children were undoubtedly forced to eat certain
amounts and types of food, regardless of whether they retched
in protest at one extreme or begged for more at the other.
Parents likely had to harden their hearts to successfully feed in
this fashion and to regard their children's suffering as defiance.
Since the conviction of the times was that sparing the rod led to
spoiling the child, parents who were more sympathetic and
softhearted would likely have been branded as being delin-
quent in their duties.

Physician Clara Davis questioned these high-handed feeding practices, and in 1928 she first published her now-famous
infant feeding studies done at New York's Mt. Sinai Hospital. In
feeding experiments starting with infants around 8 months old
and lasting up to 1 year, she and her team demonstrated that
infants could be healthy and grow well on self-selected diets
offering a variety of natural, healthy foods.[2] Davis's studies
broke the spell, and in 1937 an article in the *Journal of the
American Medical Association* recommended the introduction of
solid foods by age 4 to 6 months to provide vitamins, iron, and
"possible other factors," and because of "psychological benefits
on food habits."[3]

During the early thirties, breast- and formula-feeding of
infants changed as well. A formula based on evaporated milk
was perfected. Supplemented with vitamin C in some form, it
finally solved the age-old problem of babies' getting diarrhea
from artificial feedings and opened the door to formula-feeding.
Formula-feeding was "modern," people switched from breast-
to formula-feeding in increasing numbers, but nobody knew
how to do it. Once again, nobody asked the babies. Formula-
feeding became as arbitrary as solids-feeding had been, and
babies were given an allotment of formula divided into six
equal feedings at 4-hour intervals. If parents failed to follow the
regimen, there were dire warnings about physical and emotional consequences, all of them hypothetical. Those rigid guidelines made it miserable for babies and parents alike. Babies did-
n't get hungry every 4 hours. They asked to be fed after every 1
or 2 or 3 hours, and parents either let them cry and felt terrible
or fed them and felt terrible. That time, the people who went

riding in on white horses to save babies and parents were
Arnold Gesell and Frances Ilg.[4] In their series of experiments,
they formula-fed babies when they were hungry, let them eat as
much as they were hungry for, and let them sleep when and
how much they wanted to. The babies grew consistently and
well, and demand feeding slowly began to be accepted, an
acceptance that is by no means complete today.

Unfortunately, from overprotecting infants with respect to
feeding, the pendulum swung to the opposite extreme of
expecting them to grow up early. In 1943, a physician searching
for ways to supplement breastfeeding created a sensation when
he successfully fed 4- to 8-week-old babies sardines in oil,
creamed tuna fish, salmon, shrimp, and mashed peas and carrots. A 1956 professional journal article recommended solid
foods on the second or third day of life and encouraged omitting the night feeding by age 15 days. After that, the infants
were to continue on three meals per day.[1] This nutritional
underprotection extended to the milk feeding as well, with
many professionals recommending infants be shifted at 3 or 4
months from formula or breastmilk to 2 percent milk. The dual
misconceptions were that babies no longer needed the nutritional support of formula and that putting them on low-fat milk
would keep them from being fat in later life. Health professionals were not averse to early weaning from breastfeeding as they
tended to regard it as eccentric and troublesome.

The trend to early introduction of solid foods was so energetic that the Committee on Nutrition of the American
Academy of Pediatrics issued a position paper in 1958 caution-
ing against early supplementation with solid foods and giving
3 months as the earliest starting date.[5] For the first time, feeding
recommendations were based on research about nutrition and
physiology. The committee argued that feeding solids before
that time had no clear advantage—or disadvantage. While they
cited Virginia Beal's Colorado observations that mothers and
infants engaged in serious feeding struggles when solids were
introduced before age 4 months, they failed to recognize those
struggles as indicating a significant shortcoming of early introduction of solid foods.[6] But even that 3-month starting date,
which seems so early today, was viewed by parents and professionals as calling for an incredible delay. It was ignored until
the 1970s, when the trend shifted in the opposite direction, and

in 1980 the committee reinforced the stand that had been taken—and ignored—years before.[7] In 1992 the Committee on Nutrition strongly recommended breastmilk or iron-fortified formula for the whole first year and stressed avoiding pasteurized milk until that time.[8] Keep that sequence in mind when you run across advice about starting babies very early on solid food or switching them early to 2 percent or even whole milk. It's old-fashioned advice that was never grounded in any clear understanding of infants' nutritional or developmental needs.

The upshot of all this historical spelunking for me was—and is—the observation that a good bit of pain has been created by the need to be controlling of infants' and children's eating. From that grew my conviction that to avoid inflicting that pain the only legitimate guidelines about infant and child feeding must be based on the children themselves. That meant I could ignore arbitrary and old-fashioned feeding regimens that I was being given by my health care providers and feed my children in a logical way that made both them and me happy. When my second child, Lucas, was a baby, I was more tuned in and responsive to his capabilities than I had been with Kjerstin, and with Curtis I did better still. Not only had I started Kjerstin on solid food too early, but I had compounded my error by keeping her on baby food too long. She got so stuck on commercial baby food that at age 1 year she was reluctant to eat regular applesauce.

With Lucas I started solid food later and shortened his tenure on puréed food. With Curtis I dispensed with the baby food altogether, and by the time he was 8 months old he was sitting in his high chair finger-feeding himself soft table food with great gusto. The message I hope you will take from this historical discourse is that if you are being given arbitrary feeding advice, it is by definition logically unfounded and as a consequence it will only by chance be right for your child and supportive of your relationship. Children will survive and seemingly even thrive on a variety of foods and feeding regimens, but it doesn't necessarily follow that those regimens are best for them—or for their parents.

While I made some miscues and followed some bad advice with my children, I didn't do anything to make either my children or me downright miserable. However, the parents I began to see in my outpatient pediatric nutrition clinic were another story. By that time, control tactics in feeding primarily took the form of managing growth. Parents were admonished to get their small babies to eat more and grow faster; their big babies to eat less and grow more slowly. Early solid food introduction was still being encouraged, and for some reason that I was not ever able to unearth, mothers were panicked about the need to get vegetables into their children. Feeding schedules were still being pushed as highly desirable, and most parents staved babies off to get them to wait longer between feedings or woke them up to eat when they weren't ready or hungry. In short, there was a great deal of well-meaning abuse going on in the name of feeding.

In the first edition of *Child of Mine*, I told the stories of those parents and children who weren't getting their needs met with respect to feeding, and I related how much more effective and rewarding feeding was when parents lightened up on the rules and trusted children to do their share with feeding. That first edition was a nutrition book with a relatively small amount of feeding advice thrown in—in the entire book there were references to only seven articles dealing with parent-child feeding interactions. It was the feeding stories that hit a nerve. After the book was first published I began getting phone calls from reporters and program planners all over the country wanting me to tell them more, not about food selection but about child *feeding*. At my first speaking engagement in Lafayette, Louisiana, it was abundantly clear that my audiences didn't want to hear about child nutrition—they had read *Child of Mine* and they understood that. They wanted to know about child *feeding*. They found my principle of the division of responsibility in feeding to be revolutionary and freeing, and they wanted to be reassured that it was all right to apply it with their children. You will hear much about this principle. In brief, it states that parents are responsible for the *what, when,* and *where* of *feeding,* and children are responsible for the *how much* and *whether* of *eating.* At the time, it was revolutionary to insist that children know how much they needed to eat and that all children, even "too thin" or "too fat" children, must be allowed to eat as little or as much as they want.

It was only after *Child of Mine* readers guided me with their questions and interest that it began to dawn on me that the feeding relationship was a topic that needed to be addressed.

There was much to be done with understanding and supporting the complexity of the interactions that go on between parents and children around feeding. The topic of feeding dynamics had hooked my audience, and it hooked me. I have made
feeding dynamics my niche and stayed in the area of child
nutrition, understanding, writing, and teaching about feeding
dynamics. To understand the feeding relationship, I have had to
weave together seemingly incompatible elements. In my 1986
article on the feeding relationship, I depended on the observations of Mary Ainsworth, a psychologist who is well known for
her work with infant attachment; Hilde Bruch, Maria Palazzoli,
and Salvadore Minuchin, all clinicians who worked with adolescents who had eating disorders; nutritionist Ernesto Pollitt
and physician Peter Wright, both of whom observed the impact
of parent-child feeding dynamics on growth; Suzanne Evans
Morris, a speech pathologist who worked with acquisition of
oral feeding skills; and child development specialists Arnold
Gesell and Frances Ilg, who emphasized children's innate capabilities with eating.[4]

By the time I wrote on the topic of feeding dynamics in *How
to Get Your Kid to Eat . . . But Not Too Much,* which was published in 1987, I had found a considerable network of knowledgeable researchers and clinicians. That process has continued.
In this revised edition of *Child of Mine,* the selected references
read like a who's who listing of the feeding dynamics world. I
hesitate to name anyone in particular because there are so many
who have done so much, but I have found especially empowering the sharing and insights on child psychosocial development
and feeding of Irene Chatoor, child psychiatrist at Children's
Hospital Medical Center in Washington, D.C. I have also
depended on reading the extensively published research of
Leanne Birch, psychologist at Pennsylvania State University, for
testing my clinical observations and hypotheses. In the chapters
to come I have also told you stories about the some of the clinicians who have seen the possibilities of working with the feeding relationship as a way of truly helping parents do a good job
raising their children.

In contrast to when I first started writing *Child of Mine,* most
food selection recommendations made today for infants and
children up to age 2 years are reasonably consistent and are
based on clear logic about child development, nutrition, and

behavior. I would like to think that I made a contribution to
that consistency and logic. There are advisors and even writers
who still pass along poor advice and teach counterproductive
food selection and feeding, but those are the ones who haven't
studied the issue. They go by their biases and inherited misconceptions. The feeding relationship has now become a routine
consideration in child nutrition. Concern about the feeding relationship seemed far-fetched to many back when I first started
writing and talking about it, but now it has become mainstream. That's a pretty fast turnaround for such a major change
in thinking and practice, and I credit dietitians for leading the
way. I think particularly of Charlie Slaughter, public health
nutritionist with the Oregon WIC program, who immediately
recognized in the principles and practices of the feeding relationship the possibilities for enhancing quality of life for parents
and the nutritionists who serve them. Charlie—and many others—have taken considerable leadership, and as a result, programs devoted to child nutrition include considerations of the
feeding relationship as part of their service and educational
mission. Books written about child nutrition include discussions
of feeding dynamics and considerations of developmental
aspects of feeding. Early childhood professionals have been
pleased to set aside rigid feeding guidelines. They recognize
that the principles of the feeding relationship are consistent
with philosophies of optimum parenting and child development that state that children are entitled to a full share of
respect and as much responsibility as they are capable of exercising. The physicians are running behind, but the nurses, nurse
practitioners, dietitians, and parents are bringing them along.

However, that is not to say that negative influences on children's eating have disappeared. Nowadays, policy makers' and
advisors' need to control takes the form of making parents
responsible for raising a child who is slim, smart, healthy, and
resistant to degenerative disease. The nutritional watchword
seems to be *avoid:* avoid fat, avoid getting fat. Like Hercules of
Greek mythology, who battled the many-headed Hydra, it
seems that no sooner have we lopped off one controlling head
than two others grow in its place! Now the dangers to feeding
relationships are fat restriction[9] and weight restriction.[10] Getting
caught by either will put parents in the same old miserable
adversarial position with their children around feeding. As with

all of the other ill-considered feeding regimens, to follow the advice parents have to harden their hearts and assume that what their children are telling them is wrong. As a consequence, there is suffering and loss on both sides. In *Child of Mine: Feeding with Love and Good Sense,* I am doing my best to prevent that and instead help and support parents in taking wise leadership and being understanding and accepting of their children.

Others feel the same way and have dedicated themselves to the same ends. Earlier I compared writing a book with raising a child. Children—and books—help you to establish relationships with other people, and the people I have just named and alluded to have made rich contributions to my life. I have also felt enriched by working with people in the fine agencies that directly support child nutrition and feeding, including the WIC program (Special Supplemental Nutrition Program for Women, Infants, and Children), CACFP (the Child and Adult Care Food Program), the School Nutrition Program, University Extension (especially through the Expanded Foods and Nutrition Education Program and the food stamp education programs), Head Start, the federally funded, state-sponsored, and multiply named early childhood programs for children with special needs, and the myriad state, locally, and privately funded parent education and support programs.

The first edition of *Child of Mine* took me four years to write. This edition took me less than a year, and it is a bigger and more inclusive book. My supportive attitude toward parents and the nutrition information is still there, but otherwise it is all new. This *Child of Mine* goes far beyond the other by weaving together nutrition and food selection; feeding dynamics; child physical, emotional, and social development; and parenting. A few months was a remarkably short time for writing this book, but I felt I had to move quickly to capture all those disparate elements. Furthermore, unlike the first *Child of Mine,* which was pretty much a solo job, I now have a network of people I can depend on to help me. I wrote and revised (and revised and revised) the copy and gave it all I had. Then I sent it around to people whom I respected who were willing to give it their scrutiny, question fuzzy thinking, and catch my gaps and errors. I drew on their multiple areas of expertise, and I thank them for their generosity. Know as you read that their contributions have enriched this edition of *Child of Mine*. My reviewers were Ines Anchondo, Edie Applegate, Christine Berman, Susan Clark, Pam Estes, Jane Fowler, Gretchen Hanna, Joanne Tatum Hattner, Marsha Dunn Klein, Betty Lucas, Paulette Sharkey, Barbara Turner, Karen Webber, and Donald Williams. They represent agencies, populations, and areas of expertise that are important to children. I also want to thank the group of readers who reviewed the first edition of *Child of Mine* ahead of time and told me what they thought needed to be kept and changed: Ines Anchondo, Christine Berman, Holly Hudson Bobyn, Jane Dahlhauser, Kristina Elsaesser, Jennifer Parker, Martha Rabin-Widman, Kjerstin Satter, and Barbara Turner.

Constructing this revision of *Child of Mine* has been a celebration of sharing tasks with talented and splendid people in addition to all the ones I have named already. I am thinking particularly of designer and commercial artist Karen Foget and Howard Sherpe, who contributed so much to the attractiveness and accessibility of *Child of Mine*; Clio Marsh, my associate and administrative assistant, who read every word more than once, offered excellent suggestions time and time again, and acted as a splendid sounding board on our daily walks in the University of Wisconsin Arboretum; Matthew O'Brien, who had my bibliography in such good shape that compiling references was a dream of convenience and efficiency; Mary Ray Worley, a grand and perceptive editor who supports, understands, and extends my message and can tell when my quirky and conversational writing goes over the line to being unintelligible; Paulette Sharkey who did her usual splendid work with indexing; and Water Treatment Engineer Chris Bellovary who helped me decipher the mysteries of water chemistry.

Finally, I would like to honor my long-standing association with Bull Publishing. David Bull gave me my first chance in the writing world. He was fond of talking about how my book proposal for *Child of Mine* had come in "through the transom," which I understand is publishing talk for "unsolicited." Dave liked my writing because it was entertaining and not preachy, and I liked Bull Publishing because I respected the company's commitment to accurate and responsible information about nutrition and health. Unlike most larger publishers, Bull Publishing kept my books on their list year after year, while it— and I—found our niche in the child care and parenting world.

That original *Child of Mine* continued to be available and remarkably up-to-date and has sold well until now—when it will be replaced by this edition. David and his wife, Mary Lou, became my respected friends over the years, as did many of the other authors of the Bull Publishing family. Dave's death in 1994 was a considerable loss to us all. David and Mary Lou's son, James Bull, has taken over the business. Jim brought his own extensive publishing experience and innovative approaches to Bull Publishing, and he continues with the tradition of accessible, responsible, mainstream information on nutrition and health.

It's not too fashionable these days to be responsible, but I am sure as you read *Child of Mine* you will find that being *responsible* doesn't mean being *boring*. Knowing and understanding children is exciting, revealing, and healing. Given the long-standing negativity in child-feeding advice, almost all of us have been more or less poorly parented with regard to eating. *Child of Mine* will help you understand your child and yourself, show you what healthy and normal eating is all about, and help you heal from your own eating and growing-up history.

CHAPTER 1

FEEDING *IS* PARENTING

WHEN FEEDING IS GOING WELL, it's like a smoothly flowing conversation. The parent offers food skillfully, and the child takes it willingly. Parent and child are in sync, each taking pleasure and reward from being together and from the feeding process. It looks so easy and natural that it's hard to detect how much goes into it. In my experience, if children are fed in an age-appropriate way that respects their feeding cues, they eat to the limits of their ability, and you have every reason to expect that you and your child will be able to establish a positive and rewarding feeding relationship.

For many parents, feeding goes so well that when I tell them about my work and writing, they seem puzzled and ask, "what's to know? I didn't ever have any trouble with my child's eating." I certainly applaud that. Such parents may have such good intuitive senses that they were able to establish a positive feeding relationship with their child. On the other hand, they may have just been lucky in the child they got! A child may be born competent, and we can do well by following her lead and playing a supportive role. However, even with a competent child, feeding is hard to do well in today's culture. There is much negative and unhelpful information floating around out there—much of it controlling, telling parents that it is their job to *get* their child to eat and telling them they are responsible for raising a child who is

1

slim, smart, healthy, and resistant to degenerative disease. Although I have written a book called *How to Get Your Kid to Eat . . . But Not Too Much* (Bull, 1987), please understand that the message of that book is this: "the way to get a kid to eat is not to try" (page 31), and that's what I still recommend.

When it comes to feeding, common sense isn't common any more. Feeding practice and advice is so negative and controlling that it causes struggles between parents and children, and much of it is misguided and even detrimental to your child. Putting infants on feeding schedules is wrong. Starting infants on solid foods at 3 months—or even 4 months for many—is wrong. Putting children on low-fat diets is wrong. Letting toddlers graze for food or providing them with special foods to get them to eat is wrong. Making preschoolers eat their vegetables in order to earn dessert is wrong. I will explain more about why these practices are wrong in the upcoming chapters.

Our attitudes and behaviors about *feeding* reflect our behaviors and attitudes about *eating*. Given all the concern with weight control and avoidance of dietary fat, it begins to seem that *not* eating is far more respectable than *eating*. As a consequence, this most basic of human needs, supported by the most powerful and compelling of drives, gets treated as an afterthought. Feeding our children and ourselves is no longer a priority, and eating and feeding become an offhand endeavor that one turns to when driven by hunger. Social trends and attitudes, work demands, and community scheduling patterns make it hard for us to remember that *children* are our priority and that nurturing our children is simply the most important thing we do.

Some of my data are old and hard to come by, but it is still clear that feeding problems are common. According to parents' complaints in health care settings, at least 25 percent of children have feeding problems, and the figure rises to 33 percent of children in specialized centers dealing with children who have developmental disabilities. Problems include bizarre food habits, mealtime tantrums, delays in self-feeding, difficulty in accepting various foods and food textures, and multiple food dislikes, as well as other feeding disorders such as infant rumination, childhood obesity, and eating disorders.[1] Half of mothers complained about their toddler's and preschooler's poor food acceptance, preference for "junk" food, and poor behavior at the table.[2] Almost half of parents said they offer alternative

foods to their toddlers when they don't eat enough, and 10 percent said they force or bribe them to eat.[3] A third of surveyed
parents of preschool-aged children described their child's
appetite as fair, with vegetable and meat items most frequently
reported as disliked by children.[4] These are serious problems,
not only because of the distress they cause right now, but also
because of the distress and incapacity they cause in the future.
Children want and need to feel competent with their eating. To
be comfortable in the world, they have to be able to eat the food
there. To relegate eating to its proper place as one of life's great
pleasures, they have to be successful at it.

Indications from my clinical work, consulting, and teaching
are that the situation isn't getting any better. Family meals are
eroding, and children absolutely depend on family meals to do a
good job with their eating. Children learn to eat a variety of food
and take responsibility for their own eating when they are regularly offered a variety of nutritious food in a no-pressure environment. No pressure means getting a meal on the table and *eating with* a child rather than *feeding* her. Generating food especially for a child makes pressure an unavoidable part of the equa-
tion. Pressured family mealtimes are not rewarding for children
or parents. In many cases parents have come to dread them and
complain that they are a struggle in which nobody has any fun.
What is the problem? There are many problems, really, and to
identify them and head them off will require the rest of this
book. The short version, however, is that parents and children
are crossing the lines of division of responsibility in feeding.

MAINTAIN A DIVISION OF RESPONSIBILITY IN FEEDING

Successful feeding demands a division of responsibility. Parents
are responsible for the *what, when,* and *where* of *feeding;* children
are responsible for the *how much* and *whether* of *eating.* Put
another way, parents are responsible for what food they serve to
their children, and when and where they serve it; children are
responsible for how much of that food they eat and whether
they eat any of it at all. That division of responsibility plays out
in different ways at different ages and for different children, but
the principle is the same. Parents provide the food, children eat
it. Parents get into trouble with feeding—and children get into

trouble with eating—when parents take over the child's respon- sibility, like trying to get children to eat certain types or amounts of food, or when parents don't fulfill their own responsibility, like failing to regularly and reliably provide their child with appropriate food.

Knowing what you are doing with feeding and applying positive feeding principles does make a difference. Many peo- ple have written to me about their experiences applying the advice I gave in my earlier books. To encourage you that what you read here can make a difference to your feeding relation- ship with your child, let me tell you about a few of those letters. "I have raised my children according to Ellyn Satter's guide- lines, and their eating habits are so good my coworkers com- ment on them," wrote one young mother of a toddler and a pre- schooler. Another said she had used the same principles with equally good results. She added, "My daughter's eating has always been wonderful. She has learned to like many foods, and now, at age 4 years, she likes almost everything. She even likes her vegetables, and her favorite is spinach!" Another had had a few more challenges. "My son is cautious in all things, and offering him new foods wasn't much fun at first. If I am careful not to push him, however, I have found he ever so slow- ly pushes himself along to learn to like new foods. He is so proud when he tries something new!"

Some parents know what a difference it can make when they have crossed the lines, gotten into trouble, and then changed their approach to feeding. Parents who are worn out and fed up with generating three or four meals to get their child to eat comment about what a relief it is to them to realize that it *isn't their job* to get food into their child. They also are surprised at how much better their children eat when they stop their short-order cooking. One mother wrote that she had two tod- dlers with what she saw as two growth problems—one wouldn't eat enough and grew poorly, and the other ate too much and was too fat. She had tried to overfeed the first and underfeed the second, and her life had been one long struggle of trying to manage her children's eating and dreading feeding times. Then she had read about the principle of the division of responsibility in feeding, and it made sense to her. Applying it was helping. "Today I provided my children with good food and company and a pleasant atmosphere, and I believe it is paying off. I feel better knowing that I did my part and have fulfilled my responsibility to them. And they ate! Not a lot, but enough to satisfy my worries. And they certainly seem happier."

Another mother wrote of her struggles getting her fully breastfed daughter to start eating solid foods. "She was growing and doing well, but beginning at 5 1/2 months, I was anxious because she wasn't interested in solid foods. She sensed this, and when I offered food she sealed her lips and looked away. Mealtimes became a struggle for me to get her to eat a couple of mouthfuls of cereal or fruit while she resisted or gagged on whatever I was able to slip past her defenses. Finally I discovered your principle of the division of responsibility in feeding. It was *such* a relief! I wasn't a failure for not getting her to eat! As a matter of fact, I could have caused future problems if I had kept on forcing her. So I relaxed and waited for her to tell me what she wanted. I discovered that I had to be careful not to put the spoonful of food too far into her mouth, because she didn't like it. Now she eats as much or as little as she wants, and I stop feeding her when she closes her mouth and looks at me."

One more story, and we will move on. A mother of a 2-year-old was exhausted and frustrated with power battles over food. The division of responsibility made sense to her, and she could see how her child's fighting back had become more important to him than eating. She wrote, "We have stopped trying to force our son to eat and have been practicing letting him eat by himself. Sometimes he eats a lot and sometimes he doesn't eat much. But that's okay. We don't put pressure on his eating anymore. He seems to enjoy his meals, and he likes to try new foods, especially vegetables. My husband and I are very happy now, especially at mealtime."

Why the Division of Responsibility in Feeding. With my own children, I knew and practiced the division of responsibility intuitively, but I wasn't able to *say* what I was doing. In feeding my children, I had observed that there were some things I could control and some I couldn't. While I could choose nutritious food, cook well, and make our mealtimes pleasant, there was no way I could get my children to eat when they didn't want to. Nor could I restrict their food intake. I had, in fact, greatly enjoyed the enthusiasm and delight with which my chubby sons approached their eating, and I was thankful that I didn't feel I had to restrict them. Even back in the heyday of sounding the alarm about fat babies and predicting they would be fat for life, I didn't worry about it. I had fed them well, and they had done the eating. Since I have always assumed that my children knew more about their eating than I did, I felt curious, amazed, and delighted as I watched the pleasure they took in their eating. Restricting them would have taken the joy out of it for all of us.

I first put my feeding intuition into words in the midst of a difficult nutrition counseling session 30 years ago, back in my dietitian-in-a-medical-clinic days. I was struggling to help a mother of a child who continued to be chubby despite her attempts to restrict his food intake and get him to slim down. I was giving her food selection and menu-planning information. To her credit, she knew there was more to it than that. Finally, exasperated, she burst out, "I am already doing all that! What am I supposed to do?" she demanded. "I have one at home who is too thin, and this one is too fat. How am I supposed to get that one to eat more and this one to eat less?" Well, she had me there. What in the world could I say? After a pause that seemed to go on forever, I blurted, "You don't have to worry about how much either one of them eats." The mother looked startled, and I rushed on. "That's not your job. Your job is to put the meals on the table. After that, they are the ones to decide how much to eat." The mother glared. Her little boy, who until that moment had been slumping over in his chair and looking perfectly miserable, smiled and straightened. I gulped. "Holy smokes," I thought. "Where did that come from? That is pretty revolutionary. Is it really true?" But it was better than anything else I had said that day, so I let it stand.

I don't think I helped that mother and child as much as they helped me and helped other people. The part that I didn't say, the part that would have made it come together, was this: "You don't have to take responsibility for how your sons' bodies turn out. That is up to them and mother nature. Do your job with feeding and the rest is up to them." By the way, that session, and others like it, also taught me to do a careful evaluation before I start giving such specific advice.

Since then, I have tested the division of responsibility with all kinds of families with children of all ages and applied it to a variety of feeding problems. I have taught it to many professionals, and they, in turn, have used it to work with parents and children to enhance feeding rather than just applying rules of food selection or using their ingenuity to try to get children to eat. I have written about it in three books and heard from parents like the ones I just quoted, who say that applying it has completely changed their relationship with their child around food. I have taught the division of responsibility to lots of professionals who work with children and their eating in lots of settings. I have held my breath while I read the careful research that people in universities have done with children and their eating—and seen the principles confirmed. The principle is widely accepted and widely quoted—sometimes with the recognition of my authorship, sometimes not. And I have seen it enter the public consciousness. "It is a traditional principle of feeding well-known in the child development world," said one government publication, "to observe a division of responsibility in feeding."

Applying the Division of Responsibility at Different Stages.
Feeding demands a division of responsibility. This deceptively simple principle incorporates what we know and understand about children, parent/child relationships, feeding, and nutrition. You will discover as you read *Child of Mine* that the division of responsibility in feeding applies no matter the age of your child, but the way you *play it out* varies. With the infant, the division of responsibility is simple: You are responsible for *what* your child is offered to eat, she is responsible for *how much* she eats. From there on, you follow your child's lead in feeding and do what she needs to keep her comfortable and happy. However, if you try to keep your toddler comfortable and happy, you will be treating her like a baby and not giving her the structure and limits that she needs to grow and develop properly. Feeding on demand is no longer appropriate, because in the hands of the toddler feeding on demand turns into *panhandling* for food. To learn to eat a variety of food and to join in with the sociability of family meals, a toddler needs regular and structured meals and snacks and limits on her between-time food begging. Mastering the food and sociability of the family table as a toddler allows the preschooler to get ever better at eating as she learns to like an increasing variety of food and eat comfortably in more and more settings.

The division of responsibility in feeding is based on the assumption that if you do your tasks with feeding, your child will be competent with eating. When your child is an infant, your tasks are the moment-to-moment reading of your baby's cues, being responsive to her and feeding on demand. When your child is a toddler, preschooler, and older, your tasks are to choose and prepare food, provide regular meals and snacks, make eating times pleasant, and provide your child with the opportunities she's ready for and the expectation that she will learn. Your child comes equipped with certain capabilities with regard to eating, and if you do your job with feeding by giving her opportunities to learn, structure, and limits, she will hang on to those capabilities as she gets older. She *will* eat, she knows *how much* to eat, she will eat a *variety* of food, she will *grow* predictably, and she will *mature* with regard to eating.

A child's eating capabilities are based on everything that has gone before. In the data I quoted earlier, most parents complained about problems feeding toddlers or preschoolers. Parents assume that the problems started at that age, and professionals who work with parents often make the same mistake. The toddler and preschool ages bring their own challenges in feeding, but problems that appear at those ages typically have started long before. When I evaluate a toddler or preschooler with eating problems, I usually find a child who was particularly challenging in some way as an infant. She may have been temperamentally perplexing, seemed vulnerable, or was difficult to feed from the first. I generally also find a parent who for some reason from early on has taken over the child's prerogative with eating. That parent might have been particularly anxious about the child's welfare, been alarmed that the child seemed small or ill, had difficulty coping with the child's temperament, or may have had some agendas about feeding and growth. Struggles with feeding have gotten started early and remain at a low and irritating level until they become heightened in the older child to the point that they have to be attended to. But in most cases they don't *start* there.

FEEDING TEACHES YOU ABOUT YOUR CHILD

Learning to feed effectively can be extraordinarily helpful in learning to parent, because feeding provides such a concrete laboratory for the parent-child relationship overall. To do a good job with feeding—and with parenting—you need to understand feeding dynamics, nutrition, child development, and positive family interaction. It's all woven together in *Child of Mine.* Applying principles from all these areas to feeding makes them understandable and gives you a clear basis for the choices you make in parenting. The principles of child development provide a particularly good example. Understanding that your newborn's task is establishing homeostasis—an unflustered and tuned-in approach to the world—will guide you in helping her get settled down and awake enough to do a good job with eating. After homeostasis, her next developmental stage is attachment—learning to love and be loved in return and to communicate back and forth with you. To help you succeed with your baby and help her with homeostasis and attachment, in chapter 4, "Understanding Your Newborn," you will learn about sleep states, reading your baby's cues, and understanding your baby's temperament. Next she moves on to separation and individuation: discovering autonomy and demonstrating to herself—and you—that you and she are no longer one. The first evidence of separation and individuation appears in the older baby's burning need to do it *herself.* She *needs* you to pay attention to her cues with spoon feeding, and she *needs* you to support her increasing ability to touch her food, put it in her mouth, and feed herself. As we'll cover in chapter 7, "Feeding Your Older Baby," you support her needs by offering her developmentally appropriate food and then feeding in a way that keeps her in control of the process.

From these early explorations with autonomy, your baby soon blooms into what we recognize as the exploring and sometimes oppositional toddler. Your parenting tasks change at that point, because rather than supporting and gratifying as you have before, you must begin providing structure and limits. In feeding you get a concrete demonstration of how important it is to your child to provide her with structure and opportunities to learn, and to give her limits that keep her world small enough to be safe and manageable for her. Chapter 8, "Feeding Your Toddler," gives you a primer on parenting a toddler through the moves and countermoves you will participate in when your child is between ages 1 to 3 years. If all goes well, your toddler will emerge as a cooperative preschooler who wants to get better at all that she does, including eating. Then it's time for you to develop a philosophy of parenting. As you will learn in chapter 9, "Feeding Your Preschooler," children do best with eating—and with everything else—when parents are able to be decisive and reliable, when they are able to give leadership on the one hand and remain respectful and tuned in with the child on the other.

At each stage, certain tasks take center stage, but the tasks that come before and after are still there in the wings, being worked on. To be able to move smoothly to the next stage, children have to have at least minimally achieved the stage before. The newborn works on homeostasis, the 2- to 3-month-old works on attachment, and the older baby works on autonomy. The toddler works on separation and individuation, and the preschooler works on initiative. However, at each age the child gets better at mastering and integrating the stage that has gone before and begins working on the ones that come after. For instance, in treating the infant with respect and feeding in accordance with her signals, we begin treating her as an individual. That means we have already begun working on autonomy as a developmental task, and when she is a toddler that task takes center stage. She will have already laid a lot of the groundwork and won't have to be as defiant. The toddlers who are the most compliant with parental limits are the ones whose have been complied with by their parents when they were infants.[5] To work it the other way around, in her learning, defying, and exploring, the toddler provides herself with a lot of stimulation. Rather than letting that stimulation get her too worked up and out of control, she continues to build on what she intuitively learned about homeostasis in her first few months to control her excitement. While these principles may seem somewhat mysterious to you in the abstract, they will be played out so concretely in feeding that they will soon become clear to you.

NUTRITION AND FOOD SELECTION

An important part of your job as parent is food selection. You have to know enough about nutrition and about your child's oral-motor capabilities with eating to choose food that is nutritionally and developmentally appropriate for her. In this case, the word *developmentally* broadens to include not only social and emotional development but also your child's developing ability to consciously control her body. Knowing what to look for as your baby's swallowing and then chewing develops, along with her ability to control her hands, arms, and whole body, will guide you in your feeding decisions. Waiting for her capabilities to emerge, respecting her timetable, and setting aside your own agenda will give you a good lesson in respecting your baby's developmental tempo. When it comes to motor development, some babies move along quickly, others progress more slowly. You can't rush development by pushing it. You can only wait for it to unfold.

Being able to identify and observe your baby's increasing ability will also make your baby's achievements more fun for you. It is simply magic how those capabilities unfold, and it is fun and exciting to watch the matter-of-fact delight of a child as she struggles to get her muscles going. For an adult, such struggles would be wildly frustrating. For a child, they are wonderfully gratifying and, moreover, all in a day's work! Your task is to provide backup and support, not to do it for her. Throughout the early months and years, you make your feeding decisions based on what your child can do, not on how old she is.

Starting somewhere around the middle of the first year, your child will start her transition from the breast- or formula-feeding of the early months, through the introduction of semi-solid foods, to learning to eat thick and lumpy food to picking up and finger-feeding herself pieces of soft table food. From there it is an easy step to the family table. Again, children develop at all different tempos, and you have to know what you are doing in moving your child along, but it isn't uncommon for a child to be able to finger-feed herself many foods from the family table and join in with family meals by the time she is 8 to 10 months old! For a sneak preview of that whole process, take a look at Figure 7.1, "What Your Baby Can Do and How and What to Feed Him," on pages 250-251. While your child won't enthusiastically take to most foods the first time you offer them, over time her eating skills will develop and she will learn to like a variety of wholesome food, provided you keep her in control of what actually goes into her mouth.

As your child moves from being an infant to a toddler and then a preschooler, her becoming competent with eating absolutely depends on your having regular, appealing, and satisfying family meals. While you must be considerate of your child and adapt family meals so she can be successful eating them, you must not prepare special menus for her or limit menus to food that she will readily accept. She is growing up to join you at your family table; you are not learning to eat off the high-chair tray. You know more about the food that is in the world than she does. Unless you go to negative and puritanical extremes with your own food selection, she will learn to like the food *you* enjoy.

However, offering your child good meals and a healthful assortment of food does not—and must not—mean that it has to be the dreary or unappealing food that many think of when they think "healthy." To raise a child well nutritionally, you must be committed to the day-in-day-out of family meals. For you to carry through on that commitment, it must be more than a chore. It must be intrinsically rewarding. The reward is good eating. Your meals have to be satisfying to plan, cook, serve, and eat. Your child will take more pleasure in eating if the food tastes good, and you will take more pleasure in feeding her if she is not the sole reason for getting a meal on the table. First, you have to feed yourself. If getting the reward of good eating and feeding means you have to break a few nutritional rules, so be it. You will do better nutritionally in the long run if you are able to be consistent about planning and cooking.

HOW TO READ THIS BOOK

This is a book to go back to again and again as your child moves through her ages and stages. Before your baby comes, I particularly recommend that you read chapters 3 through 6, "Your Feeding Decision," "Understanding Your Newborn," "Breastfeeding Your Baby," and "Formula-Feeding Your Baby." Those chapters give you the basics of what you need to know to get started feeding your baby. Just as important, reading them now will give you enough familiarity with me and the subject matter so you won't be wary about going back to the information when you need it. It's hard to anticipate how vulnerable you will feel when you have a new baby. Being able to know ahead of time that I am friendly and supportive will help you turn to those chapters when you need information, encouragement, and propping up.

Most of the chapters are fairly long. I have organized each

one around a particular age or stage of your child, and I've given you enough detail to empower you to understand your child and make informed decisions about what is best for her and for you. As I said earlier, feeding well demands a working understanding of nutrition, feeding, child development, and parenting. Covering all that subject matter takes time. Read the longer chapters in more than one sitting. If a topic is upsetting for you, put it away and give it time to soak in, and give your feelings time to resolve themselves before you move on. Readers of the first edition of *Child of Mine* have told me that it is bedside table reading for them. They keep it handy and refer to it again and again. I have seen some of those copies, and they are wonderfully dog-eared, marked-up, and falling apart. I am sure that you will find as I do that going back to the child development information deepens your understanding of these sometimes-complex topics. You will have "a-ha" moments as you observe your child and then explain from your reading what you have seen.

To help you find what you need in the midst of the detail, I have given you lots of subheadings, a detailed table of contents, and a detailed index. Many topics are dealt with over and over again within the age-related chapters. I have handled that repetition by putting a detailed discussion in one chapter only, then summarized and referred back—or forward—to the place where I have discussed the topic in greater detail. I have also made liberal use of appendixes to give you extra tools without overwhelming you with too much detail. The information in those appendixes is optional. It is there to give you background or more depth on a particular topic, but you can understand the information in the chapters perfectly well without it. Since *Child of Mine* is a crossover book—meaning that it is read by professionals as well as parents—some of my appendixes and references to source material may be most helpful to professionals. The references are cited with superscripts in the text, and you can find them in the back of the book.

CHILDREN WANT TO GROW UP WITH REGARD TO EATING

Your child wants to learn and grow and be successful. That is what it means to be a child. You do not have to force that desire or put it into her. In fact, the more you push, the more slowly she will learn. But if you don't offer, she won't get the opportunity to learn. Eating is a complex set of skills that your child will learn slowly over time. Each stage builds on the ones before. The infant's ability to remain calm and alert, build trust, and give and take during feeding provides the foundation for the toddler's striving for autonomy and the preschooler's desire to please you and get better at all that she does, including eating. In *Child of Mine,* we are working toward the time your preschooler has mastered the following competencies. At that time, you will observe that your child

- Likes eating and feels good about it
- Is interested in food
- Likes being at the table
- Can wait a few minutes to eat when she is hungry
- Relies on internal cues of hunger and fullness to know how much to eat
- Relies on variations in appetite to know what to eat
- Enjoys many different foods
- Can try new foods and learn to like them
- Can politely turn down foods she doesn't want to eat
- Can be around new or strange food without getting upset
- Can "make do" with less than favorite food
- Has reasonably good table manners
- Can eat comfortably in places other than home

As you look over the list, you may get the uneasy feeling that you haven't mastered all of these competencies yourself. That's not surprising, but it's still good information for you and you may discover that you have some work to do. Becoming more competent with your own eating will be rewarding for you. Aside from that, you do have to become competent with eating if you want your child to grow up with positive eating attitudes and behaviors. None of us can take another person where we haven't gone ourselves. Almost all parents today have some anxiety and ambivalence about eating that affect the way they feed their children. Rather than being joyful and rewarding, eating and feeding have become thankless chores—a drab business of forcing down dreary food in the name of health and avoiding appealing food in the name of weight control. You can change your negative eating attitudes and behaviors. In *Secrets of Feeding a Healthy Family* (Kelcy Press, 1999), I share how to do just that, and how to plan, purchase, and cook satisfying and rewarding food.

The life lesson to be learned from this eating and feeding dilemma is that with our children we have a window of opportunity to learn a better way. We all grow and change because we want life to be better for our children than it has been for us.

HOW I KNOW ABOUT FEEDING

In *Child of Mine,* I will weave together what I have learned and experienced as a nutritionist, mental health professional, mother, and grandmother. On these pages I will tell you stories from my own family and from my several careers. During the first part of my career I worked as an outpatient dietitian in a group medical practice, then I earned another degree, this one in clinical social work, which allowed me to become a mental health professional. After that, I combined my backgrounds in nutrition and mental health to work as a specialist in eating disorders. I now work in a private mental health clinic and evaluate and do treatment with distorted eating attitudes and behaviors in children and adults.

I will tell you lots of stories about my own children and about children and parents in my various practices. Although I have changed the names and descriptions to protect privacy, the stories are true. They are stories of the families I have encountered in my clinical practice, in my consulting and teaching of professionals from around the country, and in the many presentations I have made to parents. Throughout my professional career I have worked with people of all ages—infants through the elderly. My patients have provided me with a fascinating and unfolding story. In the young I see where it starts; in adults I see where it ends up. As I attempt to understand feelings, attitudes, and behaviors that seem puzzling in an adult, I find that sooner or later I meet a child who teaches me where those patterns come from. When I evaluate distorted eating attitudes and behaviors in children, I can see all too clearly where those distortions are headed unless they are corrected.

The approach I take to feeding and eating is accurate and sound theoretically. It is based on my own experience and is backed up by a careful reading of the literature as well as checking my perceptions with those of other professionals who work with feeding and eating issues. I realize that it's possible to become almost as attached to *brain* children as to *real* children, so I am ruthless about testing my assumptions against the research and writings of the others I will tell you about. I must admit that often I have held my breath as I have done my reading, but my clinical observations have held up. One of my strongest professional attributes is the willingness to be wrong. Without it, I wouldn't be able to stick my neck out to write books, teach, or, for that matter, raise children.

Let me share a bit of philosophy that I think will be helpful to you as a parent. I have found that choosing a clear course of action is always based on a contradiction. On the one hand, you must think, read, observe, evaluate, and question yourself, but on the other hand, you must take a firm and clear course of action. Then, rather than being convinced once and for all about the rightness of your way, you must maintain a healthy skepticism. You must be open to the possibility that you are on the wrong track without undermining yourself so that your leadership suffers. Usually life offers opportunities for healthy skepticism. In chapter 5, "Breastfeeding Your Baby," I relay the story of some new parents who had a visitor so critical that she cast serious doubts in their minds about the wisdom of breastfeeding. Those parents had to go back to the drawing board and decide all over again whether they were on the right track. For a more positive example, my daughter tells me that visits with extended family help her parent because she sees other people expecting capabilities from her infants that she didn't know they had. Since life, after all, is a learning experience, it is not surprising that we must repeatedly go through the same process. It is only the extremes that are wrong: being too wishy-washy to take a clear course of action at the one extreme or too pigheaded to question yourself at the other.

OTHER PROFESSIONALS ARE OUT THERE

Finding advice about feeding is easy, but finding *good* advice is more difficult. If you go looking for well-informed help with feeding your child, chances are good that you will be able to find a health professional with *Child of Mine* or one of my other books, *How to Get Your Kid to Eat . . . But Not Too Much* or *Secrets of Feeding a Healthy Family* on the shelf. You may even be able to find someone who has taken my intensive workshop, *Feeding with Love and Good Sense*. Many dietitians and nutritionists have been particularly receptive to the concepts of the feeding relationship. They have worked long enough with teaching nutrition and diets to know that imposing shoulds and oughts on eating simply doesn't help parents, either with feeding themselves or feeding their children.

My methods and approaches have become known in a variety of professional circles from my books, professional articles, lecturing, teaching, and consulting. My major contribution has been the concept of the feeding relationship and, growing out of that, the *trust* model of feeding and eating (*Child of Mine*, 1st ed., 1983).[6-12] That is based on the idea that, given an appropriate context for our eating, we all have *within* us the capability of knowing what and how much to eat. We don't have to be so controlling with ourselves or our children.

I have made it my professional mission to revolutionize feeding and eating. To achieve that mission, I have written and published teaching materials for parents[13,14] and training materials for professionals,[15] and I have established professional workshops on feeding and eating.[16,17] Dietitians, nutritionists, child care workers, nurse practitioners, speech pathologists, occupational therapists, and mental health professionals representing a variety of early childhood programs attend the workshops. We have learned from each other, and some of the stories I tell are from those workshops. I have been impressed by the degree to which these professionals respect parents and want to help them do the best possible job of raising children. My trainees are encouraged by the possibilities of integrating effective feeding management into improving clinical practice, and they have gone on to work creatively with feeding relationships in their own professional settings. I talk about many of them in the pages of *Child of Mine*.

YOU ARE SPECIAL

You are reading this to become the best parent that you can possibly be. If you are like most parents, most of the time you will feel inspired, encouraged, and excited by the possibilities of being sensitive and wise in feeding your child. You will be able to tell whether feeding is going well because you will be having a good time, and so will your child. You will be working smoothly together, having the kinds of feeding conversations I talk about in chapter 7, "Feeding Your Older Baby," each of you confident that the other will do the next thing to move the conversation along. For feeding conversations to go well, both partners have to play their part. Throughout *Child of Mine,* I will talk a lot about feeding in a way that allows your child to take her part—reading and following her cues, holding back, and seeing to it that she takes the lead, not feeding unless she clearly indicates that she wants to eat, and feeding her only as much or as little as she wants.

Beyond the contribution that the child makes to feeding, I have found that feeding goes well when parents carry out the feeding tasks mentioned earlier—when they support without taking over and give autonomy without abandoning their child. I have found that feeding goes poorly when parents offer too little support or exert too much pressure. Too little support might be not tuning in to an infant's feeding cues or not providing the toddler with the structure and limits she needs. Too much pressure might be trying to get a child to eat more or different food than she wants or, conversely, trying to get a child to eat *less* food than she wants. When we cover your own behaviors and attitudes, you may find that occasionally what I say hits so close to home that you feel hurt or even threatened. Try not to get down on yourself, but don't set the issue aside either. Feeling upset may be the first step in growing and changing so that feeding can turn out well for you and your child. You can grow, and you can change. That is what parenting is all about. When you change, your child will change right along with you.

How to Tell Whether You Are on the *Wrong* Track. I have found that parents know when something is the matter, and they appreciate clues as to what that *something* might be. They keep seeking a solution until they find it. My intent here is to offer you some clues without criticizing or judging. There *are* times when feeding doesn't go well because of characteristics, life circumstances, or agendas of the parent. If you are too busy, are stressed by internal or external pressures, or are making your priority something other than your family, you will have trouble being successful with feeding. If you are overactive or under-responsive, it will be hard for you to get on the same wavelength as your child. If you have a fixed idea of what your child should do or be, it will be hard for you to empathize with her and see her point of view. Since finding the middle ground is so much harder than finding than the extremes, it may be helpful for you to take a look at what counterproductive extremes in parenting might look like. Here are a few examples:

- Parents may be overactive and so stimulating that it's hard for them to compute information coming from the child. They may be working far too hard and not giving their child credit for being able to do her part.
- They may be underactive and not engaging. They may be overwhelmed or depressed or for some reason not very interested in or responsive to the child.
- They may be chaotic or disorganized. To read an infant's cues and feed responsively, it's necessary to be reasonably organized. Older children need order and predictability to do well.
- Parents may be so rigid or overcontrolling that they find it hard to relax and let a child do her part in feeding—let her eat what and how much she wants of what has been put before her. Their interfering reflex produces an overly compliant or rebellious child.
- Parents may be overly concerned about eating, diet, weight, or growth. These are culturally based issues, but if parents are so concerned that they offer drab and uninteresting meals or regularly ignore the division of responsibility and cross into the child's area of *whether* and *how much* to eat, their concern is counterproductive.
- Parents may be overly concerned about their *own* eating, diet, or weight. Nobody can take another person anywhere they haven't gone themselves. Parental overconcern will be reflected sooner or later in feeding.
- Parents may not be concerned *enough* about their child's eating, diet, weight, or growth. They may brush significant problems aside and fail to take appropriate remedial action.

You will be on the right track if you and your child are having fun. You will be on the wrong track if one or both of you are *not* having fun. If you aren't enjoying feeding, and if the same problems keep coming up again and again despite your best efforts to solve them, get help. You can't expect to know all the answers. We are raising children in a world we didn't grow up in, and there are no clear answers and no absolute rules or even traditions to guide us. Early problems with feeding and parenting are relatively easy to turn around. Young children are wonderfully adaptable, and they adjust if we do. The best parents are not those who know all the answers, are convinced of the rightness of their way, and never swerve from it. They are the ones who are sufficiently tuned in to their child so they know when something they are doing isn't working.

YOU NEED SUPPORT

The logical topic that emerges from the discussion of the challenges of parenting is keeping yourself going as a parent. Unfortunately, while parenting advice is plentiful, *good* advice and true support for good parenting are scarce. By way of encouraging you, let me treat you to another bit of my own cosmic philosophy and life experience: The help is out there if you look for it. Whatever your need or your issue, if you are willing to keep looking and not settle for less than what you need, you will find someone who can be helpful to you. It is worth seeking advisors whom you trust and sources of positive support. To parent successfully, you need to be reasonably steady, relaxed, and flexible. Those qualities allow you to tune in moment-by-moment on what is going on with yourself and your child; they allow you to go with the flow and act in a way that is appropriate for a given time and place. People who are overstressed and overwhelmed by their circumstances tend to become insensitive to information coming from themselves and their child. As a consequence, they tend to apply the same negative and unproductive solutions again and again, and the situation with the child becomes worse and worse. I describe one such situation in the story of Mary on pages 41-44 in chapter 2, "Your Child Knows How to Eat and Grow."

No matter how competent you are, you will benefit from having appropriate backup and support. In fact, you will benefit from the same warm, consistent, and caring response that is so important to your child. If you are lucky enough to have parents, older friends, siblings, or peers who are in a position to be supportive of you in raising your child, help them to be helpful to you. Appreciate what they do for you. If they are interested, encourage them to read this book so they can be knowledgeable and helpful with feeding. In trusting your child's eating and taking the risk of letting your child grow up to get the body that is constitutionally right for her, you may alarm the people who are closest to you. It will help them to be helpful to you if they can clearly understand your approach to feeding.

Keep in mind that there are many ways to give support. Support can be washing dishes or baby-sitting to give you an evening off. Support can be saying "yes, you're right; you're doing it just right," but not if it isn't true. Support can involve looking carefully at your child and your situation, helping to figure out what's going on, offering observations, and even at times offering negative feedback. Negative feedback offered in a loving and supportive way can be helpful. As a parent, you are not going to do everything just right the first time you try it. If you are sensitive to your child, she can let you know when you are on the wrong track. However, we all have blind spots, and other adults in your life can help you to see around them.

Your child's other parent, having had an upbringing different from yours, will be able to see issues and offer solutions that you are not able to see. However, to be a true partner in raising your child, that person has to be willing to become informed, think about the issues, observe your child and the situation, and participate in the solution—to take responsibility for the course of action. Reserving the right to criticize and veto is not truly partnering in raising a child.

Parenting Help. Parenting groups can be helpful, but be sure to check out the philosophy and focus of the group. The most helpful group will assist you in knowing and accepting your child, taking leadership, and providing firm limits. Many self-help parenting groups seem to be organized around a particular parenting problem. That is great, if the goal is to *solve* the problem. However, if the goal of the group is to play *ain't it awful* and swap war stories, then the group won't be helpful. A group of parents who make problems their currency for social interaction have a good chance of being permissive parents. They feel they can't solve their problems, because they are unclear and inconsistent in their expectations, they don't see themselves as being able to take a real leadership role, and they fail to set firm limits with their children. Their children are likely to behave aggressively, lack self-control, disobey the parents, and be disrespectful. At the other extreme are parenting groups that are based on authoritarian parenting principles—parents who are overly strict and too controlling, who think the only way to prevent "spoiled" children is to enforce immediate and unquestioning compliance. Although such parents are to be commended for *thinking* about their parenting and giving it their best shot, such methods are not productive. Children raised by authoritarian parents tend to be belligerent, anxious, withdrawn, and distrustful. For the research and further discussion about parenting styles, see chapter 9, "Feeding Your Preschooler."

Therapists, child development specialists, child care providers, and day care teachers can be helpful as well. They have a broader perspective, are not as hooked in emotionally to your child, and can give you information and model constructive parenting for you. Let me remind you once again: if you seek help with your child, it doesn't mean that you are a not a good parent. In many cases parents who seek help are those who for some reason have a child who is challenging for them. If you are the mild-mannered parent of a headstrong child, you likely would benefit from some good parenting help.

TODAY'S PARENTS HAVE THEIR OWN SPECIAL CHALLENGES

Setting aside agendas and enjoying your child for who she is is not easy in today's parenting world. At the same time as our culture provides precious little help with parenting, it lays on lots of prescriptions and expectations. Not only that, but in contrast to earlier times, we are now for the most part having children as a choice—because we want to. It is no longer a matter of being *expected* to have children or having them for economic security—because we need them to help us make a living or to support us in our old age. As a consequence, we find ourselves putting our energy and concern into parenting as never before. To justify our choice, we feel duty-bound to do a great job. If you take the job too seriously, you can end up with a crushing list of responsibilities. How are you responsible? Let me count the ways:

- To raise a child who is happy and successful
- To raise a child with a high IQ
- To raise a child who is healthy and well nourished
- To raise a child who will not get heart disease or cancer
- To raise a child who is not fat

Before you become so alarmed by this list that you stop reading altogether, let me reassure you that I find these expectations unreasonable, and in naming them, I hope to take some of the power out of them. You must, of course, provide a good environment for your child's little bundle of constitutional capabilities and help her to grow up to be all she can be. However, you can't change mother nature, and if you try, the result may be the opposite of what you intend.

Raising a Happy and Successful Child. Loving your child as you do, you will want to protect her from frustation and pain. Perhaps in your own childhood, you were exposed to too much frustration and pain, and you would like to spare your child that, if you could. It is an admirable goal to keep frustration and pain from being *overwhelming,* but keep in mind that it is a matter of degree. Completely sheltering your child is not realistic or even desirable. Frustration and pain are a part of life, and your child needs to learn how to handle it. Your job as parent is not to make your child's way smooth, but rather to help her develop inner resources so she can cope. Life will provide plenty of opportunities to learn. Your job is to set limits that keep your child's world to a size she can comfortably manage. The issue is not to protect her from life at the one extreme or to contrive frustration at the other, but to protect her from circumstances that are more than she can handle at her stage in development. Children don't expect to have carefree lives. In fact, they take pleasure and build self-esteem from facing challenges and overcoming them.

Poignantly enough, your job as a parent is to make yourself obsolete. However, getting to the point that your child is ready to go out into the world is an extremely gradual, long-term building, back-and-forth process. This can seem like a daunting job for an inexperienced parent, but take heart. The process of growth and development is more one of unfolding than putting-in-place. Your job as parent is not to install your child's capabilities, but rather to support, cultivate, and preserve them. This interplay between internal capability and external support is easy to see in the concrete interactions of feeding. You provide the food, the structure, and the positive social and emotional environment for feeding. Your child knows how much to eat, and she knows how to grow in the way nature intended. Once you have done your job—and it is a considerable one— you can't determine what or how much your child will eat, and you can't control how her body will turn out. That is up to her, and you simply have to let go and accept the outcome.

Raising an Optimally Nourished Child. In the pages of this book we will cover nutrition in detail, and I will give you guidance about choosing appropriate food. I encourage you to learn and take responsibility, but I discourage you from making it an obsession. There is no doubt that it is vitally important to offer children a nutritionally adequate diet. There is no doubt that eating enough of the right kind of foods is essential for children be as healthy, strong, and energetic as they can possibly be. It is unquestionably true that doing a good job of parenting with food throughout a child's growing-up years can make an enormous difference in her nutritional status and overall health and well-being. For instance, consistently making milk the regular mealtime beverage is essential for your child's lifelong bone health. It's as much the parents' role to say "milk for meals, soda only once in a while," as it is to say "you can't play in the street." It's as much the parents' role to keep up the day-in and day-out of nutritious family meals as it is to send a child to school. More so, even, because food is more basic. However, good nutrition is optimizing, providing, and celebrating; it is *not* restricting, controlling, and avoiding. Good nutrition is not a dreary and anal-retentive chore of getting all the shoulds and oughts to fit together. It is a robustly cheerful and flexible business of cooking, serving, and eating rewarding food.

Today's parents appear to be grappling with a peculiar problem. They have gotten the message about good nutrition, and they want their children to eat well. But somehow standard parenting practice seems to have extended beyond simply get-

ting food on the table to also getting it *into* the child. Family
meals are spoiled as parents plead, threaten, bribe, and short-
order cook to get children to eat. These practices are so contrary
to effective feeding that I am not entirely sure why they persist.
Part of the problem may be that parents are *feeding* children
rather than *eating with* them. I dedicated one of my earlier
books, *Secrets of Feeding a Healthy Family,* to getting families back
to the table, and there I identified part of the problem as being
the loss of cooking skills and a lack of family meal traditions.
Housework is regarded as scut work, couples argue over who
has to do it, and somehow cooking has gotten tarred with the
same brush. However you feel about housework, keep in mind
that *cooking* is *nurturing.* Whoever gets to do the cooking gets
the best job.

If you offer regular, enjoyable, nutritious meals, then put
your energies into making mealtimes enjoyable—for yourself
as well as for your child. This is what it takes for your child to
eat well.

Raising a Child Who Won't Get Heart Disease or Cancer.
Despite all the hoopla about eating to prevent degenerative disease, we really don't know what causes it or how to prevent it.
All we are sure about is that early susceptibility to degenerative
disease is inherited and that life and the aging process sooner or
later give us all degenerative diseases. The evidence that diet
accelerates the process is certainly not firm enough to risk your
child's nutritional health. With feeding children to prevent disease, the task is to *optimize,* it is not to restrict, manipulate, or
control. The best way to help your child avoid disease is to help
her to be healthy in the first place. It naturally follows that it is
far more important nutritionally to *eat* than to *avoid* eating. The
primary nutritional task in feeding a child is to support normal
growth and development, not to restrict food intake in order to
keep a child slim or to ward off disease.

Currently the nutritional culprit in degenerative disease is
identified as dietary fat in general and saturated fat in particular, although the research that makes this connection is inadequate and contradictory. For more about this topic, see appendix K, "Children, Dietary Fat, and Heart Disease—You Don't
Have to Panic." The public health policy of fat avoidance and
the resulting media and food manufacturer hoopla has so iden-

tified fat-as-enemy in our thinking that fat avoidance has become the number one nutritional priority for almost two-thirds of consumers. Eating an overall healthy diet, which is a far more important consideration for children as well as for adults, is identified as a priority by less than 5 percent of consumers.[18] There are so many rules and prescriptions about food selection that it is little wonder that consumers find "eating for health" to be too difficult, confusing, expensive, and boring. Today's consumer feels obligated to avoid pleasure in the name of health. As a consequence, the way adults feed themselves— and their children—becomes inconsistent, guilt-ridden, and permeated with conflict and anxiety.

Getting away from the automatic negatives about eating is tremendously difficult. In writing *Secrets of Feeding a Healthy Family* I had to be excruciatingly careful to use language that was elaborately encouraging and permissive. People are so accustomed to nutritional finger-wagging that even the most positive messages can come off as sounding negative and forbidding. I have encountered the same dilemma in working with magazine and newspaper writers, as they have inserted their own shoulds and oughts in paraphrasing my advice. Even the enduring middle-ground food selection message of variety, moderation, and balance has been spoiled by today's negativity about food. Fundamentally, it is a good message: Eat a variety of food, do so in moderation, and balance foods to make it all add up to good nutrition. Unfortunately, people today feel so guilty and negative about eating that even these seemingly neutral guidelines come across as judgmental and withholding. Variety means "eat a lot of food you don't like." Moderation means "don't eat as much as you are hungry for." Balance means "put together meals you'd rather not eat." It's all very dreary.

However, a new day is dawning in our thinking about nutrition and disease. Currently, the absolute conviction about the fat-disease connection is weakening, and emerging research indicates that dietary folate, antioxidants, and phytochemicals, all found in fruits and vegetables, and even unknown factors in (gasp) butter and animal fat may be helpful. At long last the much-maligned egg, such a mainstay in feeding children, is being given a clean bill of health. If all goes well, public health policy will revert to emphasizing food *seeking* and variety rather than food avoidance. However, it is equally possible that the emphasis on variety will be framed in a way to turn eating fruits and vegetables into medicine and make it the same chore as avoiding fat has been in the past. It need not be so. My best recommendation is to enjoy your food—*all* your food. There is no magical food that will protect you and your child against disease, nor is there any food that will kill you. Hedge your bets against disease by eating a variety of truly enjoyable foods, prepared in appealing and tempting ways. The key to eating for health is to truly enjoy all food so you can eat it without feeling self-sacrificing.

Raising a Child Who Is Not Fat. It's ridiculous to assume that you could keep your child from being fat, but it's hard to see why. We are accustomed to assuming for ourselves—or others—that we can choose and attain a particular body size and shape through dieting and exercise. As a consequence, it has escaped us that body dimensions are almost totally genetically determined. Even though so few achieve their weight goal, the assumption persists. Why? Because we believe that it is *us* and not the assumption that is at fault; it is our lack of will power or our inability to stay the course. For most people, weight-reduction dieting is more of a hobby than anything else—something to talk about at coffee break. But for some people it is dead serious and even an organizer for life. Achieving weight loss is the grand hope—the way to accomplish personal, social, and vocational goals and have a happy and satisfying life.

If adults want to make food restriction and striving for a lower body weight a part of life, that is up to them. For children, however, the process is invariably destructive. In her book *Eating Disorders: Anorexia Nervosa and Obesity,* Hilde Bruch, a Texas child psychiatrist and respected specialist in eating disorders, talks about emotional health and fatness in a way that vividly describes my own observations of my patients. Bruch reported that in her many years of clinical practice she had come in contact with two kinds of obese* people: the emotionally healthy and the emotionally unhealthy. The unhealthy obese

---

* Issues of semantics and political correctness that I discuss in the next chapter have led me to generally substitute the term *fat* for the presumed euphemism *obese.* However, I have kept Bruch's usage. She was talking about people who were *very* fat.

person saw weight as being the single most salient feature about
him. He hated it and was dedicated to getting rid of it. In his
view, he had to do that, because until he got thin he would not
be able to do, be, or acquire anything he wanted in life. He
essentially had life on hold until he could get thin. On the other
hand, the emotionally healthy obese person felt good about himself. He was well aware of his obesity and would probably prefer to be thinner and may even have tried at some point to be
thinner. But it hadn't worked out, and it didn't dominate his life.
He was living his life, achieving, had friends and lovers, and
generally did fine.

The difference between the two groups, said Bruch, was
parental attitude. In the first case, parents had been vehemently
preoccupied with their child's weight and had gone to extreme
measures to get rid of it. And, commented Bruch with chagrin,
"the greater the number of helpers the more negative the outcome." Today's "helpers" are health workers, teachers, commercial weight-loss businesses, YMCA workers, coaches, extended
family, and neighbors—anybody who is trying to get a child to
eat less and lose weight. As one of my patients said, "all the
help didn't really help; it just made me feel worse and worse
about myself." I might add from my own observations that the
presumed help may very likely have also made the person fatter than she otherwise would have been.

Clearly, with children and weight—and with children and
anything else—if we do too much we will harm. How can we
help without harming? We can help preserve children's abilities
to eat in a positive and healthful way, we can help preserve
their joy in moving their bodies, we can love them without
reservation or criticism, and we can thereby support them in
feeling good about themselves. But we can't make them thin.
Some children will be slim, some children will be average, and
some children will be fat, and there is nothing we do about it.
For more on this topic, read chapter 2, "Your Child Knows How
to Eat and Grow."

For the child who is naturally fat—who maintains a consistent and predictable pattern of growth—there is no problem.
There is a *challenge*, because raising an emotionally healthy
child in today's fat-phobic culture is tremendously difficult. The
fat child, like any child who is in any way different from the
norm, requires better-than-average social and emotional skills

in order to be successful. A heavier-than-average child will present you with challenges in parenting. You may need help. If you can't be accepting of your child's size and shape and are vehement about trying to change her weight, if you blame yourself for your child's weight, or if you feel sorry for her and are over-protective, get help.

In brief, the message of this chapter—and this book—is *settle down*. Throughout, I strive to help you be positive, confident, encouraged, and supported. I haven't always said you are on the right track, because I have seen enough parenting to predict common errors. I have tried to head you away from making those errors and to help you detect them when you make them. In my experience, parents don't feel overly upset or over-whelmed by their errors as long as they can generate another approach that works better. I have offered that other, better approach as well.

Throughout, my goal is to help you feel comfortable in your role as parent so you can enjoy feeding and eating with your child. Rather than getting bogged down with your sense of responsibility or carried away by your agenda, remind yourself of why you decided to have a child in the first place. I hope a major reason is for the sheer joy of it. It is a grand privilege to have a front-row seat on someone else's life. If you let your child surprise you and keep your own ego out of it, she will provide the leavening for your concern about doing the right thing as a parent. Certainly do your homework, but then set the homework aside and pick up your sense of wonder and your sense of humor. Relax and enjoy your child.

CHAPTER 2

YOUR CHILD KNOWS
HOW TO
EAT AND GROW

IF YOU DO A GOOD JOB of feeding, the chances are very good that your child will grow up to have the size and shape body that is right for him and that he will have a stable and appropriate weight as an adult. However, like no other topic in child nutrition, food regulation and growth is permeated with misunderstanding and pitfalls. We have been informed again and again about the alarming increase in the incidence of child and adult obesity. Obesity has been targeted as the number one child nutritional problem, and parents who have a child who is chubby—or who just has a family history of fatness—try to take evasive action by restricting their child's food intake.

Parents who fear their child is growing "too slowly" will find the issue just as troublesome as those whose child is supposedly growing "too fast." As with restricting a child who presumably eats "too much," trying to "get" a slow-growing child to eat more is an uphill battle that can be extraordinarily unpleasant for everyone concerned. Given our culturally weird eating attitudes and behaviors, however, we are all too ready to interfere with our children's eating and growth, simply because we are accustomed to interfering with our own.

Consider the $30 billion a year weight-loss industry. In 1999 one-third to one-half of Americans surveyed said they were diet-

ing either to lose or maintain weight.[1] Consider that most people
say they are dieting only when they are frankly restricting food
intake. The majority, for whom restraint has become the usual
eating practice, don't see themselves as dieting but only as
eating normally. Consider that 40 percent of Americans feel conflicted and anxious about their food choices, and they are upset
that they aren't living up to today's stringent nutritional standards.[2] Restrained eating—that is, regular attempts to eat less
than we are really hungry for or to settle for less appealing food
than we really want—has become such a fixed part of our relationship with food that it is hard for most people to see that the
negativity and restraint are anything but normal. They are not. It
is harder still to see how *our* restrained eating could complicate
and even contaminate our attempts to feed our children. It does.

Appropriate feeding is built on trust—trust in your child's
ability to eat and in his ability to grow in the way nature
intended. Once you have done your job with feeding, it is up to
your child to eat what and how much he needs, and then both
you and your child can trust his body to grow and develop
appropriately. Given today's concern with health, size, and
shape, a child who grows "too fast" or "too slowly" may tempt
you to restrain what he eats or force him to eat more. It won't
work. If you try to take evasive action with your child's growth,
you can cause the very problem you fear. If you restrict your
chubby child and try to make him be thinner, he can become
preoccupied with food and may be prone to overeat whenever
he gets the chance. If you try to get your slender child to eat
more and fill out, he may become revolted by food and be
prone to undereat whenever he gets the chance. A chubby child
doesn't necessarily grow up to be a fat adult, and a thin child
doesn't necessarily grow up to be a thin adult. Interfering, however, frequently produces the very result it is meant to prevent.
Moreover, interference inevitably causes lasting damage to the
parent's relationship with the child. If you interfere, you will
give your child the message that your love is conditional—that
you can truly approve of him only if and when he is different.
Since you won't want to make your child feel so bad, your path
is clear: you can only wait, enjoy your child, keep a healthy
curiosity, and enjoy watching him grow up. You won't know
how it will turn out until your child is grown. As so aptly put
by Yogi Berra, "It ain't over till it's over."

MAINTAIN A DIVISION OF RESPONSIBILITY

Instead of trying to control and manage your child's eating and weight, think in terms of optimizing. By optimizing, I mean feeding your child in the most helpful and supportive way possible, doing your job to provide food and supporting your child in doing his. Throughout *Child of Mine*, I will encourage you to observe a division of responsibility in feeding.

The Division of Responsibility
Parents are responsible for the *what, when,* and *where* of *feeding.*
Children are responsible for the *how much* and *whether* of *eating.*

I will elaborate more in the coming chapters on how that division of responsibility is played out with children of different ages and in different circumstances. For now, it is enough to say that you provide your child with the food and feeding environment he needs, and then you let go. You trust that as long as you are doing your job, your child will eat what he needs and will grow appropriately. Optimizing is far different from doing nothing at all. As you can see from the list below, optimizing means that you actually do a great deal.

To go into more detail, *you* are responsible for

- Controlling what food comes into the house.
- Making and presenting meals.
- Insisting that children show up for meals.
- Making mealtimes pleasant.
- Teaching children to behave at the table.
- Regulating timing and content of snacks—no running with food, no food right before dinner.
- And a few nuggets of your grandmother's wisdom: no fanning the refrigerator door, no candy before dinner, and saying "yes, please" and "no, thank you."

However, you the parent are *not* responsible for

- How much your child eats.
- Whether he eats.
- How his body turns out.

Your child knows how much to eat, and he has within him the genetic blueprint for his growth. In order to build on that blueprint and make the most of it, however, he needs your help, support, and acceptance. You must do your part in feeding by reliably and lovingly providing him with appropriate food. You must limit his sedentary activities and give him opportunities to be active. And you must do it year after year, in a loving and consistent fashion. Once you have done all of that, you must trust the outcome. You must keep your nerve and resist the impulse to interfere. Your child may be fatter or thinner, shorter or taller than you are comfortable with, but you have to assume that his size and shape are right for him. Then you must be accepting and supportive. Even if your child's body turns out not to be as fashionable as you would like, your love and support will help him to be comfortable and to accept himself.

WHAT IS NORMAL GROWTH?

Your child has a natural way of growing that is right for him, and he knows how much he needs to eat to grow that way. If you do your jobs in feeding and let him decide how much he wants to eat, you generally don't need to worry about normal growth—it will happen. There are many different normal body shapes and sizes. Some children are short and stocky, some are tall and slender. Some are fat and some are thin. Your child's shape and size are determined mostly by heredity: the size and shape of his mother and father. Expect him to grow according to your genes, not your wishes.

To understand normal growth, it helps to understand growth charts. When you take your child to a health clinic for regular checkups, he is weighed and measured, and those numbers are plotted on a standard growth chart. Figure 2.1 is a standard weight chart for boys aged 0 to 36 months. There are more growth charts in appendix A, "What Is Normal Growth?" that plot height for age and weight for height. Figure 2.1 is a weight for age growth chart for boys, and the ones in the appendix are charts for girls. As you can see, the chart is set up like a graph with age in months along the bottom, weight in pounds along the side. The curves drawn on it are standard growth curves, or reference curves, compiled from averages of thousands of children. The graph has a plot on it, as if a child has been weighed time after time: as a newborn, age 1 week, 1 month, 2 months, 4 months, and so on. As you can see by the example, this fictional child's weight follows along near the 75th percentile. His height will be plotted on a separate curve, and it might be at the same percentile, or higher or lower. His weight for height might come out the same, or, again, be higher or lower. The actual percentile doesn't matter so much as your child's showing a consistent

FIGURE 2.1 BOYS' WEIGHT FOR AGE GROWTH CHART

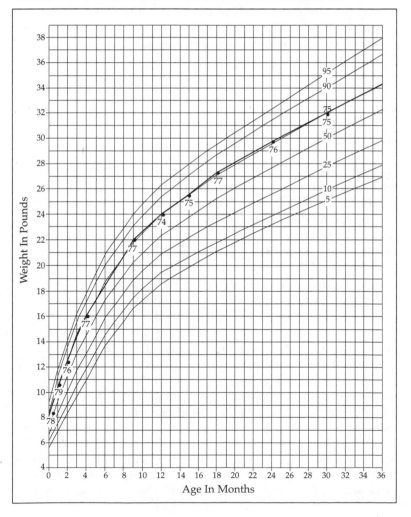

pattern of growth as it is plotted over several months or years.

Statistically, our boy whose weight is around the 75th percentile is heavy relative to other boys—75 out of 100 boys will weigh less than he does at this age. But comparing a child with other children is not the important point of the charts—it is more important to compare a child with himself. Does he grow consistently and smoothly? Sometimes a child's true growth pattern doesn't appear until about age 12 months. It's not uncommon for an infant to have a period of "catch-up" growth during the early months if he was small to begin with, or "slow-down" growth if he was big to begin with. Over the first 7 years, a child's height tends to adjust toward the average of his parents' heights. Don't ask me to explain it—it's all done with percentiles. Slowly crossing percentiles can even be normal as long as the growth is *smooth* and that it is consistent with the previous pattern. Once a child's growth levels off and establishes itself on a given percentile, however, that is where it is likely to stay as he gets older and moves from this growth chart to the one for boys up to 18 years old.

Growth Reflects Your Child's World. Growth plots give one of the best overall indicators that things are going well for your child—medically, nutritionally, emotionally, and in terms of the feeding relationship. From my perspective, investigating an upward or downward blip in the growth chart often reveals that food selection or feeding have gotten a bit derailed. I think, for instance, of the boy whose weight at 12 to 15 months bumped up from the 50th percentile to the 75th percentile. His parents were still feeding him on demand rather than providing him with the structure and limits he needed as a toddler, and he had predictably become a tyrant with food. I also think of the girl whose weight fell off her usual curve about that same time—her parents were giving her only very low fat food and she wasn't able to eat enough to satisfy her calorie needs. Still another child the same age comes to mind. This little boy was still predominantly breastfed and had no interest in eating table food or even semisolid foods. Another girl gained a considerable amount of weight at that age when she got the upper hand with her mother, who had been restricting her food intake from the time she was born. These are all toddler examples, but we see these growth blips at other ages as well. The child under age 6 months might diverge downward because she doesn't suck well, for instance. Eight to nine months is a frequent age for downward growth blips, when the child begins wanting desperately to feed himself and the parent thinks he's still a baby.

Medical professionals follow children's growth looking for confirmation that a child is doing well medically. A medical worker who sees these kinds of blips in growth curves will be likely to mentally review your child's history to look for indicators that something is *medically* amiss. Not finding anything to be concerned about, she will reassure you that everything is fine. What she means is that everything is fine *medically*. However, seeing such a blip in your child's growth, it would be legitimate for you to ask to see the dietitian to rule out any problems with nutrition or feeding. A word of reassurance: if you catch such problems early, they are likely to be small and easily resolved.

Growth Extremes Are Not a Problem. The weight of a child who grows consistently at the 5th percentile or the 95th percentile is just as appropriate and trustworthy as that of the child growing closer to the mean—the 50th percentile. However, since that growth is statistically unusual, and since the child whose measurements are at the outer fringes of the growth chart is relatively small or large in size, health workers tend to be more vigilant to be sure growth progresses well. Parents may pick up on that vigilance and compound it with their own natural uneasiness about any extreme feature or behavior in their child, growth included. The problem that emerges is that parents of large children may unconsciously hold back with feeding, and parents of small children may unconsciously try to feed past children's fullness cues. Be aware of the tendency, and resist the impulse. Your large or small child is just as trustworthy about regulating his food intake as is the child whose size is closer to the average. Trying to change the amounts your child normally eats will only make feeding miserable for both you and your child, and is highly likely to exaggerate the very pattern you are concerned about.

Some few health professionals misinterpret extremes in growth. On a public health level, in fact, children who are above the 95th percentile are classified as obese, and children below the 5th percentile are classified as showing growth failure.

Guidelines for children growing at the outer percentiles vaguely recommend that a child "should be checked, followed up and possibly referred."[3] The issue gets really ticklish when you realize that children are certified for WIC (Special Supplemental Nutrition Program for Women, Infants, and Children) if they are above the 95th percentile or below the 5th, which tends to automatically label the child, at least in the parents' eyes, as being somehow abnormal. He is not. He is not obese; he is just big. His growth is not faltering; he's just small. The child growing consistently on his own growth curve, even if it is *above* the 95th percentile or *below* the 5th percentile, is likely to be regulating very well and growing in accordance with his constitutional endowment. Again, the real growth issue for any child on any percentile curve is whether his growth follows along his usual growth curve. If it follows along, it is appropriate growth. If it diverges abruptly upward or downward, there could be something wrong. That divergence needs to be carefully investigated to determine whether everything is still all right medically, nutritionally, emotionally, and in terms of the feeding relationship.

For more about the principles of growth curves, see appendix A, "What Is Normal Growth?" There I have given you examples of other growth curves and of how children's growth is plotted on those curves. I will also cover growth characteristics in the age-related chapters (chapters 7 through 9).

RESTRICTING CALORIES

I am absolutely opposed to putting children on weight-reduction diets. In my view, no person has the right to impose food restriction on another, even if that person is your child. Withholding food profoundly interferes with a child's autonomy, and you will both pay the price for that interference. Your restricted child will grow up feeling angry with you; he will feel bad about himself, and he will depend on you to provide controls on his eating and will be unable to tap into those controls within himself.

You will be pressured from the outside to do something about your large or small child. "He doesn't look like he ever missed a meal," family and friends will say, or "what a little peanut! Don't you feed that child?" Of course they intend to be funny or clever, but for a parent who is at all sensitive about a child's size and shape, such comments can be hurtful. Particularly with a fat child, outsiders feel duty-bound to express their opinions. This bit of cultural weirdness is given periodic encouragement by public health pronouncements. The Centers for Disease Control and other government agencies warn us that child obesity is our number one health concern and register the opinion that the reasons children—and adults as well—are fat are (1) too much food and (2) too little activity. Such announcements are likely to make the most enlightened parent withhold second helpings or declare trips to the ice cream shop—every child's basic entitlement—as off limits.

One cannot argue with the statistics and with the self-evident assessment of the problem as disruption in energy balance. However, we still need to answer a fundamental question. *Why* are children eating too much? Children are excellent regulators. They know how much they need to eat, and they are highly likely to grow in a predictable fashion. Even when food is very good, children get filled up on it and eat only as much as they are hungry for.

It seems to me that a good bit of the problem lies in the solution. That problem, and the solution, are food restriction. Most health professionals today have gotten the message that "diets don't work" and will not ostensibly put your child on a "diet." They are afraid that restricting a child's food intake will precipitate eating disorders in later life. It's rare for a parent of a child who grows "too fast" or "too slowly" to be given a calorie prescription or told how much their child should eat. More often external control of a child's calorie intake comes about indirectly. Parents—often on the advice of health professionals—may attempt to restrict a child's fat intake as a way of keeping him slim. I talked with a very sad mother the other day who was reflecting on how upsetting it had been for her chubby 8-year-old son to be admonished at every checkup to restrict his dietary fat to keep himself "healthy." The boy knew it wasn't "health" that was being talked about but "weight," and he had learned to feel bad about his ever-chubbier size and shape. Outside restrictions can take the form of anything from behavioral modification to labeling foods as good, bad, or indifferent. It's the *attitude* that makes the difference. If the intent of an approach to feeding is to reduce the child's weight, it is outside control and it is destructive.

Whether or not you call it a diet, general advice about how much a child "should" eat or clothing that advice in weaselly words won't stop this approach from having negative effects. "He's gaining pretty fast—see if you can get him to eat less." "His growth is slow—see if you can get him to eat more." Other times the outside control comes in the form of a feeding schedule. "Don't let him eat so often—he's getting too much." Even the seemingly permissive message "let your child have his treats—just don't let him eat too much" is weaselly because it undermines trust. You manage the menu; your child will get enough—you don't have to make it happen. Any such messages can lead you to ignore your child's feeding cues and, instead, impose some outside prescription on how much he "should" eat. That will turn you into a police officer rather than a parent, and it can have long-lasting consequences for your child's psyche, his size and shape, and the way he feels about himself and the world. Let me give you an example.

Amanda Nagle and her daughter, 3-month-old Sena, stopped by my office one day to talk about breastfeeding and food restriction. Amanda was struggling with her pediatrician's advice and she wanted a second opinion. Sena was growing very quickly—she had gained 7 pounds since birth and had done it all on breastmilk. At their last appointment, the doctor had advised Amanda to restrict her chubby daughter to five rather than seven breastfeedings a day to try to hold down her rate of gain. Amanda had tried to follow the advice and not feed her daughter so often, but the result was disastrous. "She would ask to be fed, and I felt it was wrong to feed her. I would try to stave her off, play with her, entertain her. She would get more and more unhappy and upset until eventually I would give in and feed her. She would just wolf down her breastfeeding and look around for more. The whole time I felt bad because I felt I was doing something wrong by even feeding her as little as I was. So I gave it up. I decided that I couldn't do it. It was making her unhappy and certainly making me unhappy. In fact, I felt that the only way I could really follow the doctor's advice was to put her on the bottle because this infrequent nursing was drying up my milk supply. I guess if my feeding Sena this way will make her fat, she will just have to be fat. I feel bad about that, but I'm not willing to spoil our time together."

Amanda did some very healthy parenting. She went down a wrong path, knew it, and found another way. Getting it right the first time is not the point—knowing whether you are getting it *wrong* and then tinkering is the point. The real misfortune of this story is that the mother was made to feel so bad about doing the right thing for her baby and for herself. Fortunately, that pediatrician, like a lot of others, has discovered the error of his ways and no longer gives that sort of advice. However, just the other day a lactation consultant told me the same story about another baby, mother, and doctor, only this time the mother persisted in following the doctor's advice until her breastmilk dried up and she had to wean her baby to formula.

Since indirect controls on children's food regulation can be as destructive as more direct controls, it is important to be able to see that such controls are really weight-reduction dieting by another name. Amanda wasn't told to put her daughter on a diet, but she was instructed to feed some vaguely defined "less" than her daughter wanted. The parents of the chubby 8-year-old were not told to put their son on a diet, but the low-fat food instructions were actually intended to control his eating and weight. Parents of a large child or one with a robust appetite generally don't see themselves as putting their child on a diet, but nevertheless they often hesitate to gratify his appetite for fear he will eat too much and get too fat. Direct or indirect, outside pressures on food intake can lead to struggles about eating and have truly disastrous consequences.

Since *Child of Mine* is about getting things to go *right* with your child, I will emphasize what to do and generally stay away from horror stories about what can go wrong. You are in a position to enjoy your child and to have the fun and satisfaction of watching him grow and develop, and you can expect your feeding relationship to be a positive one. However, since our culture is so full of such truly distorted and destructive attitudes about feeding and body weight, I am going to tell you a couple of horror stories. Think of them as an opportunity to raise your consciousness. You will benefit from knowing what it looks like when things *really* go wrong.

Distorted Eating—Mary's Story. Seventeen-year-old Mary was suffering from bulimia; she was obsessed with food and with dieting, she disliked and distrusted her body, and she ate in a bizarre and extreme fashion. She would diet severely, so severely that she virtually starved herself and ate only when she couldn't stand the pain of hunger any longer. When she finally gave in to her hunger and ate, she wouldn't just eat enough to satisfy her hunger. As far as she was concerned, even eating at all was bad, and once she had started eating she might as well go the whole way and eat as much as she could hold. She would go on eating binges, stuffing herself in a frantic fashion, eating whole cakes and butter by the spoonful and virtually depleting the family food supply. Then when her stomach became so bloated and painful that she could hardly stand it, she would vomit. She used her finger, pushing it far down her throat so she could retch again and again until she had no more left to throw up. Sometimes that would be the end of it. Other times she would repeat the pattern, stuffing and purging herself repeatedly in the course of a day.

Mary perceived herself as being fat, although she was not. She had a nicely proportioned medium build and an attractive figure. The problem was that she was heavier than the model thinness that she thought was ideal and that her parents seemed to have in mind for her. Mary thought she was ugly, and she was so ashamed of her size and shape that she stayed home, avoiding her friends and their activities. Part of her distress about her body came from high school standards of body shape and size and standards of thinness. Part of her distress came from the modeling school her parents were sending her to in hopes that it would "make her feel better about herself." In reality it just made her feel worse to be around all those skinny women with all that emphasis on appearance. But the most powerful pressure came from home. Mary's mother was thin, the kind of disciplined-looking thinness you get only when you work on your weight, and work hard. She had the model look about her—starved. That is a different kind of look than the one of people who are constitutionally thin, because naturally thin people look for the most part like their flesh covers their bones and like they are strong and healthy. Mary's mother looked fragile, and there was a quality of being forced about her, as if she constantly had to drive herself, physically and emotionally.

Mary's father was thin, too, but not excessively so. However, he was the one who voiced their concern about

Mary's "overeating." He said that Mary had always eaten a lot, and he wondered how much it was normal for someone of her age to eat. In fact, he said, Mary had eaten a lot ever since she was born. When she was still in the hospital, the nurse had brought her into the room and said "Your little girl certainly eats a lot—she had two whole bottles." Of course they thought eating a lot meant Mary would get fat, so they set out to prevent that. Actually, I wondered whether Mary was hungry when she was born—had her mother gained enough weight during pregnancy? I never heard a word from them about growth curves—whether Mary was even big to start with. The whole tragedy of Mary's feeding seemed to be based on those two bottles and that nurse's chance comment.

From that day on, Mary and her parents struggled over her eating. From observing other parents with their supposedly overweight babies, I can guess what that struggle was like. I would guess that when Mary's parents tried to feed her less than she really wanted, the spirited Mary fussed and cried until she got more to eat. How long she had to fuss probably depended on how able her parents were on any given day to tolerate her fussiness. Her crying was no doubt upsetting, and the only way they could stop it was to do the one thing they didn't want to do—feed her.

Mary grew into what they perceived as being a chubby toddler, and by the time she was three years old she was sneaking extra food from wherever she could get it. Her first memory of mealtime was of her mother dishing up her plate for her with a limited amount of carefully selected food. And Mary cried at the memory of never getting enough to eat unless she sneaked to do it. For Mary, not getting enough food felt very much like not getting enough love. Her parents said they were doing it for her own good, but I wondered how much their own egos were involved—how important it was for them to have a thin and what they perceived as being a more beautiful daughter.

Comparing Mary's parents with Amanda Nagle teaches a lot about the contrast between effective and ineffective parenting. Amanda tried restricting Sena, saw that it was hurtful, and quit. Mary's parents never saw their tactics as hurtful or even ineffective. They did the same thing, year after year. They saw Mary's lack of cooperation and out-of-control eating as being the problem, rather than being able to see that what they were doing was contributing. It didn't bother them that Mary was so unhappy—it bothered them only that Mary was giving them so much trouble.

Despite their rigid determination, Mary's parents had not been successful in getting her to undereat and weigh less. Other parents are successful, and as a result children are smaller or thinner than they might otherwise be. Which it is depends on who is more determined and resourceful: the parents or the child. Now let's turn to a story about a parent who got the upper hand.

Deliberate Underfeeding. A psychologist at a professional meeting told me about a young mother in his neighborhood whom he had heard about from his daughter, who had baby-sat for the children. All of this rigamarole starts to sound like an urban rumor, but it is not. Rather than telling another underfed child story that I know about first-hand, I have included this one because its extremes illustrate such important points. The mother was so determined that her children were not going to get fat that she frankly underfed them, and the children appeared to be thin and short, and they were *certainly* preoccupied with food. The psychologist's daughter was so distressed about the children's plight that she had refused to baby-sit them again.

According to the baby-sitter, the mother's strategy was to restrict anything that might put weight on her children. She used only low-fat recipes and would not allow her children to have butter, margarine, or salad dressings. She was very stingy with breads and other starchy foods, and she certainly would not let them eat candy or anything sweet. She would let them eat only so much at mealtimes, even if they said they were still hungry and begged for more, and she absolutely forbade their eating between meals. She left instructions with all the baby-sitters she hired that they were not to feed the children. It was hard on the sitters, because they felt bad for the children, and the children were so hungry they couldn't get their minds off of food. But the sitters didn't dare feed them, because the mother could tell by the satisfied way the children behaved if they had been fed. Most sitters wouldn't work for her any more because they felt so sorry for the kids.

This is an extreme case. So extreme, in fact that I called it child abuse and advised the psychologist to report it to the

proper authorities. Failing to give a child enough food is fundamental neglect. Once again, this mother is an example of a
not-good parent. The children were clearly in distress, but the
mother was so invested in her agenda that she was not sensitive
to their plight. I don't know if there was a father in the picture,
but if there was, he wasn't doing his job either. He was failing
to challenge her on behalf of the children. Good parents are not
the ones who say, "yes, dear, you're right, anything you say."
They are the ones who help each other by challenging and
disagreeing when parenting is going down a wrong path.

However, even though this case is extreme, elements of it
are not that unusual. There are many reports in the pediatric
literature and at clinical meetings about nutritional growth
retardation due to parents' adherence to health beliefs currently
in vogue and recommended by the scientific community.[4] Most
of those cases of poor growth are caused by parents' adherence
to a low-fat diet. Given today's emphasis on low-fat eating, it is
an understandable error. Parents think restricting fat is the right
thing to do. Often a child, rather than putting up a fuss or acting starved like the children I just described, simply quietly
loses interest in eating. The problem becomes apparent when
the child is weighed and measured and is discovered not to be
growing well. Parents are shocked and appalled—and often
angry—that their honest efforts to do the right thing have been
so destructive. For guidelines on managing the fat in your
child's diet, see the section called "Enjoy Fats and Oils" in
chapter 8 (pages 351-354).

I hope you get the point: these are stories of extreme behaviors that cause eating disorders and growth distortions, and *you*
are not going to go there.

A Compulsive Eater Who Was Just Normal. Before we move
on, let's neutralize those horror stories. Hearing about the
extremes is helpful for recognizing negative patterns, but going
to the extremes is not an immediate threat for you. Most people
are good enough parents—not perfect, but at least within the
ballpark. All parents make mistakes. The effective parents are
the ones who are sensitive enough to their child to realize when
their tactics are not working and do something to remedy them.
Young children change rapidly. If you change what you do with
feeding, and keep it changed, your child will change right along

with you. Let me tell you a happier story to illustrate my point.

Todd's parents, like Mary's, feared that their 2 1/2-year-old was a compulsive overeater. Unlike Mary's parents, Todd's parents sensed that something was wrong and sought help. As the parents told it, Todd always wanted second helpings or even thirds, although it seemed that he had eaten quite a lot. In fact, the minute he came to the table he began begging for more food than his parents were giving him. Even with such big meals, between times he hung around and begged for food handouts. Todd regularly embarrassed his parents at birthday parties by pining so much over the cake that he wasn't interested in going off to play with the other children. At home, when the parents put out a plate of cheese and crackers for company, Todd was right there, eating steadily as long as the supplies held out.

Todd's weight was going up, not down. But to his parents, his weight pattern was beside the point. They saw his eating as being so abnormal that they labeled him a compulsive eater, and that was their major concern. What was the problem? Restrained feeding. Todd's parents were trying to restrict him to only one helping at mealtimes and no snacks between times. But Todd was tougher and more resourceful than they were, and he regularly wore them down. Since he was so afraid that he was going to have to go without, once he had access to food he ate as much as he could hold, not knowing when he would be able to wear them down again. Both parents were surprised when I told them that they didn't have to control the amounts that Todd ate because he was capable of doing that himself. They didn't know that internal regulation even existed, as they had not experienced it for themselves. Todd's mother was bulimic—her way of regulating her food intake was to try to follow a 1,200-calorie diet and then throw up if she ate more than her allotment of food. The father was uninterested in food and regulated his eating by giving himself a food quota and then eating it as if it were like doing any other chore.

My assessment was that Todd's food preoccupation and overeating were growing out of his fear that he would not get enough to eat. I encouraged the parents to establish a division of responsibility in feeding, to have regular meals and snacks, and to let Todd eat as much as he wanted at those times. They were not to give in to his food-panhandling between times. At all times, they were to reassure him. At meals and snacks, they were to say, "you may eat as much as you want" and then *let* him eat as much as he wanted. When he begged for food between times, they were to say "snack time is coming soon and you can eat as much as you want then." Todd's parents were worried about the plan. If Todd's eating was so out of control when they were restricting him, what would it be like when they withdrew the controls?

At first, Todd confirmed their worst fears. He ate like there was no tomorrow. But after 2 to 3 weeks, he started to trust that his parents really meant it when they said he could eat as much as he wanted, and his eating started to settle down. He began eating like any other toddler. He would eat a lot on one day and hardly anything the next. Sometimes he forgot all about his snack, which pleased his parents, but I told them they had to offer snacks anyway. Todd needed to trust that this parents would remember to feed him. To help Todd, his parents had to be trustworthy about doing their part in feeding; then they had to trust him to regulate his food intake. Since none of us can take our children where we haven't gone ourselves, the parents had to learn to trust their own food-regulation processes as well. I treated the mother's eating and coached both parents in experiencing their own ability to regulate food intake.

The treatment succeeded. Within 6 to 8 weeks, Todd's "compulsive eating" had gone away. He was no longer so preoccupied with food, and he was relaxed and casual about meals and snacks. He was able to have fun playing with the other kids at birthday parties. But the proof of the treatment came when I last saw the family. They had put out a plate of cheese and crackers for company and Todd had eaten a couple of crackers and gone off to play.

How Food Restriction Feels to the Child. It is clear from the previous discussion that appropriate food regulation depends on a positive and accepting feeding relationship between parent and child. The impact of this relationship becomes more clear if we imagine what it must be like for a child, who is, after all, essentially a captive audience in the feeding situation. He is absolutely dependent on his parents and other adults to satisfy his food needs, and those needs make themselves insistently apparent. Hunger is a powerful, potentially gratifying, and potentially painful drive. Whether a child learns to fear or accommodate hunger depends on his early experience with feeding. If he asks to be fed and someone feeds him promptly and lets him eat until he is satisfied, he associates hunger with pleasure and he looks forward to what happens next. But if his parents try to get him to eat less than he is hungry for and stop feeding him before he is really full, then hunger becomes very unpleasant. In my videotape *Feeding with Love and Good Sense*, 8-month-old Andrew is so excited to eat that he can't sit still in his chair. But his excitement is tinged with anxiety, and it isn't long before the viewer knows why. Andrew's child care provider has been instructed by the parents not to let Andrew eat as much as he is hungry for, on the grounds that he "has no stopping place." Of course, the assumption is an incorrect one, because every child has a stopping place.*

Andrew is chubby, but that's all right, because many children are naturally chubby toward the end of the first year. The chubby infant has no greater risk of growing up fat than the thin infant. In fact, there is no significant correlation between fatness in childhood and in later life until a child gets to be at least 6 years old and perhaps older.[5] Most fat adults become fat as adults, and only about a quarter of preschoolers appear to retain their fatness.[6] Given our previous discussion about the tendency of a child's growth to follow consistently along a particular percentile, the wonder is that not all children in the upper percentiles retain that pattern as adults. These figures on longitudinal patterns in growth are often used to sound the alarm that childhood fatness is retained into later life. In reality, the data makes the point that most young children slim down. However, Andrew's chances of slimming down as he gets older are being decreased before our very eyes, because his child care provider follows directions and stops feeding him before he is really full. Andrew cries and looks around for more food, but no more is forthcoming. This has happened enough that even at 8 months of age, Andrew approaches eating knowing that it is not going to turn out well for him. He will be hungry and dis-

---

*The only exception to this statement is the child with Prader Willi syndrome, a developmental disability that often includes cognitive impairment but always includes an extremely thrifty metabolism combined with excessive appetite and preoccupation with food. Unless their food intake is restricted, children with Parder Willi eat more than their extremely limited needs and gain far too much weight.

appointed at the end of the meal. To understand what it is like for Andrew, imagine that you are on an ocean cruise or a raft trip without enough food to go around. How relaxed and capable of enjoying the trip would you be? Hunger becomes a harsh master if there is no way to make it go away.

Andrew's child care provider might have been helpful to him and to his parents if she had said, "no way am I going to make a child go hungry." A good child care provider is more valuable than rubies, and those parents might have listened to her. However, that provider didn't become enlightened until after she saw the videotape, and she felt bad when she came to understand why it wasn't good to underfeed Andrew. My favorite fantasy about Andrew is that when he got to be a toddler he turned into a little cupboard raider like Todd, our "compulsive eater," and made himself such a nuisance to his parents that they sought some help to straighten out their approach to feeding. Sometimes situations have to get worse before parents can see that there is a problem.

It's hard for a child to settle for less than he wants, but it is also difficult for a child to eat more than he wants. If you have ever had to eat when you really weren't hungry, or experienced the nauseated, too-full feeling that comes from having overdone it, you know that it is not a pleasant experience. A mother who approached me wanting advice about her too-small child, whom she had been force-feeding, said it best: "When you don't want the food, it feels like it grows in your mouth." Despite her sensitivity to his feelings, this mother was so desperate about her son's very survival that she was putting food in his mouth and holding his lips shut until he swallowed. If you find yourself forcing your child to eat, know that it is the wrong solution and that you must have help in finding another way. Forcing is miserable and extremely costly emotionally for both you and your child.

EVEN BIG AND SMALL CHILDREN REGULATE

Terminology fails me when I try to talk about the large child. *Chubby* works for some children, but the large child may not be chubby but only *solid* or *stocky*, as my mother accurately said about me when I was in the fourth and fifth grade. *Chubby* to me means a high proportion of body fat, *solid* or *stocky* means strong muscles and heavy bones and maybe a blocky (another word) silhouette. A stocky child might plot out high on the weight-to-height percentile charts but still have a pretty low percentage of body fat. *Fat* is a word that is usually considered a derogatory term, but people in the size acceptance movement are trying to take the word back and neutralize it as a simple descriptive term. They see the word *obese* as being inappropriate because it makes fatness a medical condition. Despite all the flap about health consequences of elevated body weight, it is only for the few people in the far upper ranges of weight who suffer clearly identifiable health consequences. Talking about the *thin* child is easier, because the terms are not so negative or pejorative. However, the child who is taunted by his schoolmates for being *skinny* or a *beanpole* has a social challenge similar to the one faced by a child who is taunted for being fat.

Why do I need a word? Because I have to tell you that despite your best efforts your child might be fat—or thin—and there is nothing you can do about it. Your child is highly likely to grow up to resemble your body size and shape. That may mean that your child's normal pattern of growth will be at one of the extremes on the weight-to-height charts. That extreme plotting may come from a relatively high proportion of body fat. Or it may mean that your child may be particularly thin and slight and have not only low body fat but low muscle mass as well. *Your task as parent is not to try to change your child's size and shape but to support him and accept him just the way he is.*

Even the fat child is entitled to eat as much as he is hungry for. Even the small and slight child is entitled to eat as little as he is hungry for. The division of responsibility in feeding, and the parts about not being responsible for how much a child eats and how his body turns out, apply just as much to the fat child and the thin child as to the child who is closer to the average. Your job is to feed your child, see how he grows, and love whatever he turns out to be. Your job is *not* to try to get him to grow any differently than his constitutional blueprint dictates.

Because of your own struggles with weight, you may be tempted to try to control or modify your child's weight. Don't. It won't work and it is likely to make the problem worse, not better. Do a stellar job of feeding, then let nature take its course.

You can't tell at this age how your child's body will turn out. Your control efforts can make the problem worse, not better. Rather than trying to change your child's natural body, it's much better to put your efforts into feeling good about your child and helping him to develop good character, common sense, problem-solving skills, the ability to get along well with others, and good ways to cope with his emotions. Children who are unusual—whether they are relatively fat or relatively thin— like children with other characteristics that make them different, need better-than-average social skills in order to succeed.

HOW MUCH DO CHILDREN EAT?

General or specific, we don't say what quantity an infant or child *should* eat. There are too many variables: activity level, calories required for growth, the ability of the body to squander or conserve calories in response to changes in food intake, and behavioral and psychological consequences of manipulation of food intake. Nor do we *need* to know how much a child should eat. Children have finely tuned mechanisms for determining how much they need to eat, mechanisms that automatically take into account variations in the food they eat as well as in activity, growth, body metabolism, and body chemistry. In a very few cases we make a rough beginning guess of how much a child might need and then fine-tune that guess on the basis of the child's growth. We need to do that, for instance, with children who are tube-fed, but even those children have hunger and fullness cues that can help guide the tube-feeding process.

Children Vary Child-to-Child. Every five years a committee of the National Research Council publishes the Recommended Dietary Allowances.[7] The committee is made up of respected nutritionists who summarize current nutritional knowledge and make estimates about levels of nutrients required for health. Over the years they have had a hard time making recommendations for calories because calorie requirement is so variable. Currently, they are finding their way out of their dilemma by giving ranges. Generally speaking, they give an average calorie requirement and then follow it with a "coefficient of variability of plus or minus 20%." That means that once an average figure has been arrived at, a child might actually eat 20 percent fewer calories or 20 percent more than that average. Figure 2.2, "Range of Calorie Intake for the Average Infant," and Figure 2.3, "Range of Calorie Intake for the Average Child," show the calculated medium, low, and high intake of a boy or girl growing at the 50th percentile for height. In other words, the graphs illustrate the range of calories that a child *might* eat. A taller or shorter child may eat more or less. Once again, keep in mind that in most cases knowing how many calories an infant or child is consuming is unimportant and is just a matter of curiosity. Two children may be the identical size and shape and appear to have the same level of physical activity, but one may need to eat twice again as much as the other.

Children Vary Day-to-Day. Not only do children vary child-to-child, they vary day-to-day as well. Allow me to illustrate. Back in the thirties, when people were first beginning to bottle-feed, they tried very hard to learn how. This was the "scientific age of feeding." A formula based on evaporated milk had just been

FIGURE 2.2 RANGE OF CALORIE INTAKE FOR THE AVERAGE INFANT

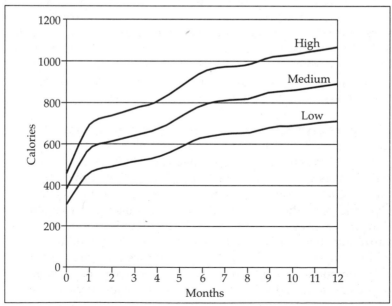

FIGURE 2.3 RANGE OF CALORIE INTAKE FOR THE AVERAGE CHILD

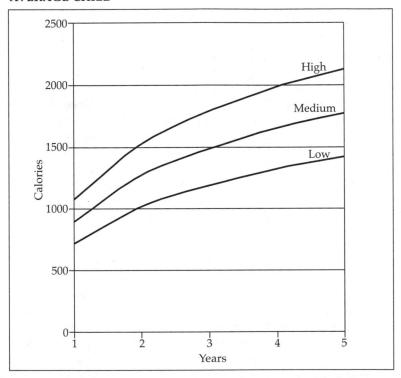

perfected. Supplemented with vitamin C in some form, it finally solved the age-old problem of babies' getting diarrhea from artificial feedings and opened the door for bottle-feeding. And people switched from breast- to bottle-feeding in increasing numbers. Bottle-feeding was "modern," but nobody really knew how to do it.

Unfortunately, to begin with, nobody asked the babies. The then new professions of pediatrics and nutrition attempted to fill the gap with scientific reasoning. They figured out how many calories babies "should" be having per pound of body weight, weighed and measured them, and calculated their total allotment. Then they divided that allotment into six equal feedings (every 4 hours, you know) and instructed parents to give the babies just that, no more, no less, at exactly those intervals around the clock. If parents failed to follow the regimen, there

were dire warnings about the physical and emotional distortions that would result. Like the feeding recommendations,
these were largely the product of someone's imagination and
had very little to do with knowledge of how babies really oper-
ate. It was miserable for babies and parents alike, because
babies didn't get hungry every 4 hours. They asked to be fed
after ever 2 or 3 hours, and parents either let them cry and felt
terrible or fed them and felt terrible.

But at the Gesell Institute, Arnold Gesell and Frances Ilg
challenged these assumptions.[8] They said, essentially, wait a
minute, that's not what works with babies! If feeders are that
controlling and ignore information coming from babies, it is
going to cause a lot of problems, and both parents and babies
are going to suffer. By way of backing up their contention, they
did a series of bottle-feeding experiments with babies in which
researchers fed them when they were hungry and let them eat as
much as they were hungry for. Babies were allowed to go to
sleep when they wanted to and to sleep as long as they wanted
to. And when they woke up, they were fed whenever they asked
for it, even if they wanted to eat twice in a row after a long nap.

Researchers kept track of how much the babies ate and
weighed them every day. Figures 2.4 and 2.5 show what happened with one little boy, Baby "J."

The only thing that was consistent about J's intake was his
inconsistency. One day he ate a lot, the next day not so much.
His intake from day to day varied by about 20 to 30 percent.
During the third week of the study, when he was 8 weeks old,
he had a cold and his intake varied even more. One day, for
example, it was only 20 ounces, the next day it was 32. But his
growth was smooth, even during that third week when his food
intake varied so widely. Little "J" knew what he was doing.

You Can't Tell by Looking How Much a Child Eats. Some
children require a lot of food and some don't require so much,
and you can't tell by looking, or even weighing and measuring,
how much your child is likely to need. The common assumption, of course, is that people are fat because they overeat. This
assumption represents an extravagant level of nutritional snob-
bery and metabolic ignorance. Such a distorted assumption can
lead you to attempt to underfeed your chubby baby—or even
your slim baby with a strong family history of obesity—or

FIGURE 2.4 FORMULA INTAKE OF BABY "J"

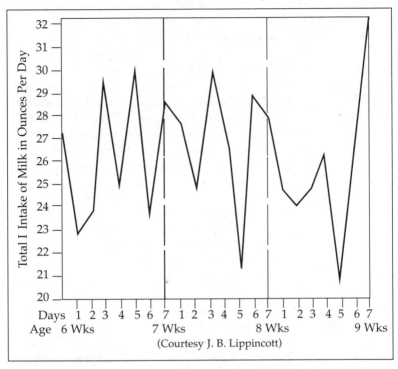

(Courtesy J. B. Lippincott)

FIGURE 2.5 GROWTH OF BABY "J"

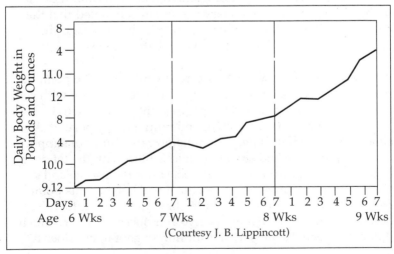

(Courtesy J. B. Lippincott)

attempt to overfeed your thin baby. Such attempts would not only be profoundly disruptive of the feeding relationship with your child, they would also be extraordinarily misguided. In reality, slim babies do not undereat and fat babies do not overeat. In a 1979 food intake survey, Michigan researchers talked to the mothers of 650 children up to 1 year old to find out how much children ate. The researchers then separated off from the full group of 650 children the 35 who ate the most and the 34 who ate the least. The contrast was startling. The lightest-eating children, who consumed only 550 calories per day, were the heaviest—they weighed on the average 20 pounds. The heaviest-eating children ate 1,100 calories per day and weighed an average of 14 $^1/_2$ pounds.[9]

It is legitimate to question this study because the researchers got their data from mothers' reports of infant food intake, and mothers could have unconsciously distorted the information. If a mother was self-conscious about having a thinner-than-average or fatter-than-average baby, she could have fudged the information a bit to make it look like her baby was eating more or less than he really was. I'm not accusing the mothers of lying—in most cases this fudging is done unconsciously. But there was another, more carefully controlled study done by two Harvard nutritionists that showed essentially the same thing. The researchers actually recorded and measured what the babies ate. They also found out how much they exercised, by strapping tiny pedometers to their arms and legs. As in the Michigan study, the Harvard researchers noted that the fattest babies were the least active and ate the least, and the leanest babies were the most active and ate the most.[10]

A Low Metabolism Won't Make Your Child Fat. The point of the research we just examined is that children are *born* with certain tendencies for size and shape, food intake, and activity. Those tendencies are interactive and mutually supportive. A child is born with the energy regulation capabilities to support his distinctive size and shape. A child is born with the tendency to be active or inactive, and that, too, supports his size and shape—and his hunger and appetite. I will belabor this point, because there is so much misunderstanding about it. Just because a baby is relatively inactive and doesn't eat very much it doesn't mean it will be easier for him to get fat, nor does it mean that he is somehow deprived or going without if he eats as little as he needs. He will be as good at regulating as any other baby, and he will eat as much as he is hungry for. When he gets as much food as he needs, he will be full and satisfied. Food will no longer taste good to him, and he will stop eating without feeling deprived. All three of my children looked average in size and shape but plotted relatively tall and heavy on their growth charts. All three ate relatively small amounts of food. They were all good regulators and as adults have continued to be good regulators and have continued to be about average in size and shape. None of them felt deprived because they couldn't eat as much as their big-eating friends. Even sturdy Curtis, who had a small appetite, seemed to have no envy of his slender friend Jason, who ate at least twice as much. In fact, I was the only person who really noticed how much Jason ate, and that was because I am a nutritionist who takes an interest in such things.

Small-eating adults who look with envy at their big-eating friends are missing one important point: Once you have had enough to eat, food stops tasting good. If you are a small-eating person, you might be wise to choose food carefully and eat the good stuff first, but there is no reason to feel deprived simply because you can't eat a ton. Think of the expense! Big-eating people *do* have a nutritional advantage, because in eating all that food their chances are increased of getting the nutrients they need. However, a little care in food selection can make up the difference.

Food Selection Doesn't Distort How Much Children Eat.
A 16-year longitudinal study conducted at the University of California–Berkeley, illustrated that children who became fat when they were teenagers ate no more—at any stage of their upbringing—than children who remained thin. In fact, children who later became fat ate somewhat less. This study also found that children's tendency to be fat or thin was no different whether they were breast- or bottle-fed; whether they were given whole, 2 percent, or skim milk; whether they were started early or late on solid foods; whether they ate a lot of "junk" foods, and whether their parents used certain feeding practices like withholding desserts to compel eating meals. Two feeding-relationship factors appeared to be correlated with adolescent

obesity. The risk of childhood obesity increased (1) with increased parental concern about obesity and (2) with increased incidence of early childhood feeding problems.[5] The explanation? When children and parents struggle about feeding, children lose track of their internal regulators and make mistakes in the amount they eat. One other factor that appeared to be correlated with adolescent obesity was that children who later became fat had a slightly decreased level of activity compared with children who stayed slim. We will talk on pages 72-76 about the role of physical activity in food regulation.

THE FEEDING RELATIONSHIP AFFECTS FOOD REGULATION

Not only does your child know how much to eat, but he is also capable of making up for his errors in regulation. We all overeat at times. We all undereat at times. The same is true for your baby. You will overfeed him at times, possibly with his enthusiastic cooperation, at other times you may underfeed him. He will make up for it—by eating less or more the next time, by getting hungry not so soon or sooner. To overfeed or underfeed your child in a way that has a significant and lasting impact on his weight, you have to be relentless about it. You have to do it again and again, time after time. Eventually, your baby could learn to overfeed himself, but only after the errors in feeding go on for a long, long time. I worked with a man who had learned to overeat and tune out his internal regulators because his mother, who was a dreadful cook, put a great deal on his plate and made him eat all she gave him. She fed him this way from when he was little until he was old enough to leave home, and over time he learned to consistently eat until he was way too full. With careful treatment, he was able to discover that *good* food was worth tuning into and that he truly preferred stopping when he had had enough rather than too much.

Feeding Distortion Starts Early. Feeding interactions that distort children's food regulation can start very early. Mary Ainsworth, who was a pioneer in attachment studies of infants and parents, observed 26 mothers and their babies in the feeding situation. Her observations give us some clues to types of feeding interactions that can either support or undermine children's abilities to eat the right amount of food. As you read them, keep in mind that my intent is to *reassure* you. You will make mistakes in feeding, but you will be able to compensate for those mistakes. You are not going to make the extreme and persistent mistakes in feeding that Ainsworth observed some of the mothers making.

Seven of Ainsworth's mothers were sensitive to their babies' signals and skillful in their feeding. They presented food so the baby could take it easily, and mother and child enjoyed each other in the feeding situation. Three mothers were eager to get their babies on a schedule. To achieve that, they ignored their children's hunger and delayed feeding so long that the babies became overly hungry and upset. As a consequence, the feedings were tense and unhappy. Four mothers were impatient at feeding times. They said they were feeding on demand, but they seemed so eager to be finished caring for their babies that they put them down whenever the babies paused or smiled or fussed during the feeding. Perhaps because the mothers wanted to get the feedings over with in a hurry, the nipple holes were too big, so the babies coughed and gagged and paused in the feeding. When they paused, the mothers assumed they were full and terminated the feedings. Five of the mothers overfed their babies, some to gratify them and some to fill them up so they would sleep a long time. In the latter case, the babies spit out the nipple, struggled, and tried to avert their heads. But the mothers were determined to get the food in, and they did. Needless to say, the feedings were also tense and anxious.

In five of the cases, the feeding was absolutely arbitrary in timing, pacing, or both. In each case, the mother was having personal problems such as depression or anxiety that made her detached and insensitive to the baby's signals. These mothers put their babies away for long periods and either tuned out the crying or failed to perceive it as a sign of hunger. Feeding times were erratic, as were feeding styles. Sometimes the mothers forced their babies to eat long past the point when they indicated they were full, and sometimes these mothers interpreted any pause as satiety and stopped feeding. Feeding was at the mother's whim and showed little consideration of the baby's wishes. Ainsworth commented in one case that a mother's determined stuffing of her baby "had to be seen to be believed."[11]

As long as the mothers were responsive to their infant's signals, the feedings were positive. However, when the mothers went to either extreme of being controlling or neglectful, the infants ate poorly and mistakes were made in food regulation. Feeding doesn't have to be perfect, but it does have to avoid the extremes. Although she did not measure how much the babies ate, Ainsworth did note that the overfed babies were heavier, and the babies who were fed erratically and whose feedings were terminated too soon were underweight. For more discussion about this topic, see appendix J, "Children and Food Regulation: The Research."

INTERNAL MECHANISMS DEFEND BODY WEIGHT

The body will regulate if you let it—or, much of the time, in spite of what you do to it. Put another way, body weight is not that easy to disrupt. The body has powerful built-in regulatory systems that maintain more-or-less stable weight. There are systems of regulating food intake as well as systems for conserving or squandering calories metabolically, in response to deficits or excesses in calorie intake. If you look at yourself a moment, you will realize that in the last year, in spite of all the different ways that you have lived, eaten, drunk, and exercised, your weight has probably stayed pretty stable. You may not have liked the regulation, because even if you have tried to lose or gain weight you probably will have found that once you relaxed your efforts to modify your food intake, your weight returned to very near its original level. Even if you are 10 pounds heavier or lighter than you were a year ago, you will have missed an exact balance of calorie output and input by an average of only about 100 calories per day. You can hardly call that gluttony—or starvation.

The way growing children regulate is even more remarkable. Not only do they need calories for their general bodily maintenance, as do adults, they also need the right amount of calories for growth. They get taller and heavier, and usually weight increases proportionally to height. Generally, once children are established on a smooth pattern of growth for height and weight, they adhere to that pattern very well. Their level of food intake will support their growth pattern. Children grow faster or slower from time-to-time, and as growth velocity

varies, their food intake varies to match it. The same thing happens with a variation in exercise levels. It is all automatic; the
child can do it all himself with his own feelings of hunger and
satiety. All you have to do is provide the food.

I have repeated to a point of rigor that to a considerable
extent body weight is constitutionally determined. Because
physical, behavioral, and metabolic processes defend that constitutionally determined body weight, achieving a body weight
other than what is genetically appropriate will be accomplished
only at considerable cost. Figure 2.6, "Regulation of Body
Weight," gives an overview of the complex and interactive
processes that maintain body weight. Preferred body weight is
maintained both by adjustments in hunger and appetite, on the
in side, and by adjustments in energy usage, on the *out* side.
The body can either conserve or squander calories and defend a
stable body weight. You can support and enhance your child's
ability to regulate well by helping him to be tuned in to eating
on the *in* side or supporting his getting enough activity on the
out side. However, Figure 2.6 makes clear what I said before: if
you try to overwhelm your child's ability to regulate you can
end up distorting the balance and causing the very problem
you fear. Restricting a child's food intake could make him less
active and more metabolically efficient as well as preoccupied
with food and prone to overeat. Making a child eat more than
he wants can make him squander calories in the form of extra
body heat or sped-up metabolism, and it can make him feel
revolted by food and prone to undereat whenever he has the
opportunity.

If you are able to accept and support your child's constitutionally determined size and shape, you will provide him with
the best possible help with his lifelong food and body weight
regulation. However, that is not the only benefit. Accepting
your child's size and shape honors him and strengthens your
relationship with him.

MAINTAIN A POSITIVE ATTITUDE ABOUT YOUR CHILD'S EATING

If your feeding relationship with your child is positive and
accepting, it is likely to affect your whole relationship and have

FIGURE 2.6 REGULATION OF BODY WEIGHT

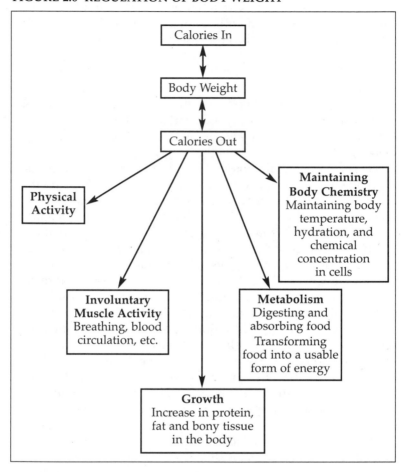

a far-reaching impact on your child. Your attitude about your child is reflected in the way you feed him. If you have an attitude of curiosity, relaxation, and trust, you will watch for his cues and respond to them. You will depend on information coming from him and be willing to let him develop the body that's right for him. On the other hand, if you are overly responsible and controlling, you will not be able to be trusting. You will have to supervise your child's eating closely and monitor his growth, being ready at all times to step in and curb or boost his growth pattern.

Your child learns about himself and about the world from the way he is fed. Can he be trusting? Is the world trustworthy? If he asks in a moderate way for food and you are able to respond promptly in a supportive and consistent fashion, then it is likely that the world is trustworthy and he can, in turn, allow himself to depend on others. If, on the other hand, he has to fight and struggle for every mouthful of food, then it is likely the world is not very trustworthy at all. In these feeding interactions your child will learn whether he has the capability to influence others. If other people respond to him in a prompt and appropriate fashion, he learns that what he wants and needs matters and that other people take an interest. It naturally follows that he thinks, on whatever level babies think, that he must be a fine fellow that people go to such trouble for him. On the other hand, if he has to fuss and fight and struggle mightily to get his needs met, or if what he gets has little or nothing to do with what he wants, then he is likely to think of himself as not having much importance to other people or clout in the world.

The way health professionals teach you to feed your child will have an impact on your attitude about your child. If we use growth charts to label your child's growth as being good or bad and suggest to you that you get your child to eat more or less, we are teaching you to be controlling. From your control, your child learns that he is not all right the way he is. A child can outgrow a diet that is less than optimally chosen, as long as it is offered supportively and lovingly. However, outgrowing deeply embedded attitudes about self and the world is devilishly difficult.

The task that presents itself, then, is to find the middle ground. What can you do with feeding that is helpful and productive for your child? What can you do to help your child to get the body that is right for him—without doing any harm?

SUPPORT THE REGULATION PROCESS

People regulate their food intake by getting hungry, by eating, by becoming full and satisfied, and by stopping eating. Your child's body will regulate if you let it. Your job is to support that process; to help set things up for your child so that regulation works as well as possible. Your guide to how much your child needs to eat will be his signals of hunger and fullness. Children must be allowed to rely on their internal regulation or they will lose the ability to be tuned in, and they will be forced to rely on outside sources of regulation instead. Of course, internal regulation is far superior to external.

Make Eating Times Significant. From the very first, it is important for you to give your time and attention to feeding your child: paying attention to him, observing and solving problems to fashion a feeding interaction that is as supportive and constructive as it can be. For the infant, that means using a system of trial and error to find out why he pulls off the nipple, or fusses, or spits up, or seemingly terminates feeding too soon. For the older child, it means providing the structure and support that promote good eating and providing the guidelines and the environment so he can eat well. We will cover this at length in later chapters. Your willingness to feed appropriately can have a big impact on how much your child eats.

For children to eat well—not too much and not too little—they must have their emotional needs met. A newborn needs help being quiet and alert and tuning in on feeding and on what goes on around him. An older baby needs connection and responsiveness in order to take an interest in food and to regulate properly. Sometimes food gets used as a substitute for quieting or connecting with a baby, and the child can eat too much. Older babies and toddlers need to be allowed to feed themselves, and they need the structure and limits of regular meals and snacks without being allowed to panhandle for food between times. Giving a defiant toddler a cookie instead of a clear limit can teach him to eat instead of working through conflict with other people. Making food available at all times can teach a child to use food for entertainment or for staving off boredom. Children who are bored or lonely at the table, or exposed to a lot of stress, may under- or overeat.

Be Reliable about Feeding Your Child. Your child has to be so sure that he will be fed that he doesn't even have to think about it. To give him that kind of security, you have to be absolutely reliable in feeding him. Make family meals and regular, predictable snacks a priority. Children are a captive audience when it comes to feeding. We can work through lunch and not worry about it because we know that we can raid the refrigerator or, if worse comes to worse, we can get in the car and whip through the closest drive-through. Children can't do that. They completely depend on us to feed them. Of course, you will at times feed your child by making arrangements for someone else to do it, like the child care provider or the pre-school. That is fine. The issue is that feeding has to be a priority, and you have to be thoroughly reliable about seeing to it that your child gets fed—consistently and well.

Beyond the reliability of regular feeding, think about the *quality* of feeding. You want your child to enjoy mealtime, pay attention to his food, and enjoy it thoroughly at eating time. Then you want him, as much as possible, to forget about it the rest of the time. That means mealtime has to be a pleasant time when you can concentrate on sociability and companionship. Don't *feed* your child, sit down and *eat* with him. It's not your job to get food into your child, so avoid urging, rewarding, and encouraging him to eat. Then put away the food until snack time, and do it all over again.

Maintain Structured Feedings. Your child will do the best job of eating the right amount for him if he comes to the table hungry, so he is eager to eat and so his appetite heightens his interest in and awareness of food. We do not want him to come to the table overly hungry to the point that he is either too cranky to eat or so famished that he just wolfs down his food and gets a stomachache. Which it is to be depends on how often he eats. Set regular times for meals, and offer food to your child at those times whether he asks or not. Between meals, have planned snacks, and, again, offer the food whether your child asks for it or not. Restricting your child's between-times panhandling for food and beverages (except water) keeps him from coming to the table already filled up from nibbling on little bits and pieces of food. Maintaining the structure of meals and snacks is essential to enabling him to do a good job with food acceptance as well as regulation.

Some children who are allowed to eat all the time eat too little and grow poorly. Some children who eat all the time eat too much and get too fat. Some children who eat all the time regulate just fine and grow well and predictably. However, since children panhandle for candy and not for broccoli, the nutritional quality of the diet will suffer if a child is allowed to graze. Here's the point: you don't know which kind of child you have, so you would be well advised to set up his environment so he can regulate as well as possible. That means regular meals, planned snacks, and no panhandling for either food or beverages between times.

Have Good-Tasting Food. Throughout *Child of Mine* I encourage you to set up feeding times so they are emotionally, socially, and aesthetically supportive and rewarding for your child. Use the same principles for choosing food. To help your child (and yourself) eat well, you must provide food that is rewarding to cook, serve, share, and eat. Austerity doesn't cut it with children. Making eating a nutritional chore that has to be done doesn't cut it with children. For children to eat well, food has to be tasty and well prepared. To be tasty and well prepared, food has to contain fat.

Children are extremely tuned in to hunger and appetite. If they are hungry, they will eat. If food tastes good to them, they will eat it. Fat with food helps it to taste good, and gives it a slippery quality that makes it easier for a young child to chew and swallow. Children will push themselves along to learn to like new foods, but they will not eat a food because it is "good for you." They will eat only what tastes good. The extreme and overblown concern adults have about eating fat has trickled down into the younger set and interfered with the pleasure and reward of the family meal. Some food guides for toddlers dictate limits on the amount of fat children should have at meals. Whether that amount is 1, 2, or even more tablespoons, it is still a prescription and, as such, will distort feeding. Children can regulate their fat intake—they don't need us to do it for them. Children need fat in their diets to provide for their energy needs. They need fat to make food taste good and to give them staying power. For guidelines on managing the fat in your child's diet, see the section "Enjoy Fats and Oils" in chapter 8 (pages 351-354).

Select Foods That Help Regulation. In chapter 8 we will talk about what I call the *Mother Principle:* A meal needs to have some protein, and it needs a starch (different cultures have dif-

ferent starches, like grits or potatoes or plantain or rice), a vegetable (or fruit, or both), bread (or tortillas or biscuits), a good
source of calcium, like milk, and some fat. At breakfast, milk
may do double duty as a source of both protein and calcium,
and the fruit/vegetable may be orange juice. Here, I will go into
a little more detail about the biochemistry of meal planning, but
don't forget, meal planning and eating are more than chemistry.
A vital part of the Mother Principle is enjoyment.

A well-selected meal, with a good distribution of protein,
fat, and carbohydrate, can help your child regulate his food
intake. Each of these nutrients has a role to play in inducing
some of the many satiety factors that let your child know that
he has had enough to eat and give him sustained energy
between eating times. The pattern of satisfaction derived from
consuming each separately appears to be different from the pattern of satisfaction from all of them consumed together. Figure
2.7, "Satisfaction from Consuming Sugar, Starch, Protein, and
Fat," shows the pattern of energy release your child gets from
consuming each of the major nutrients.

As you can see from the first curve in the figure, sugar, or
simple carbohydrate, provides quick energy but doesn't have
much staying power. A glass of orange juice in the morning
will give quick energy, but your child will be hungry soon. The

FIGURE 2.7 SATISFACTION FROM CONSUMING SUGAR, STARCH, PROTEIN, AND FAT

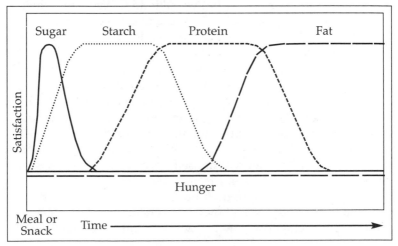

second curve, for starch, or complex carbohydrate, takes longer to move up but stays up longer because starch has to be digested and then is gradually absorbed. For the same reasons, starch satisfies hunger longer. A bagel, toast, or crackers with the juice give breakfast or a snack more staying power. The bagel, toast, and crackers are also chewy and good tasting. Your child needs both chewing and good taste to feel satisfied.

As you can see, the protein curve is even slower and longer. Since protein takes longer to digest than carbohydrate, that energy kicks in after the carbohydrate energy gives out—and lasts longer, too. A glass of skim milk makes the breakfast or snack last longer. So does an egg or some cheese, but when you include those foods you also add fat. The fat curve is the slowest and longest of all. Fat gives food staying power. It slows down the emptying time of the stomach and makes everything in the meal break down more slowly. Food tastes better if it has fat in it or with it, because fat in food carries the flavor.

See appendix B, "Select Foods That Help Regulation," for more detail about satiety curves and a table that shows what foods have protein, fat, and carbohydrate in them.

Your Child Can Savor High-Calorie Foods. Before we leave the topic of food composition and food regulation, we need to discuss the regulation of foods with very high caloric density: the foods that are high in sugar, high in fat, or both. These foods are harder to regulate. They are delicious, and they are concentrated in calories. Studies show that we all tend to eat faster when something is very good. Nowadays, the idea is very well implanted that those are *forbidden* foods—foods we can eat only when we are being *bad.* As a consequence, we tend to throw away control when we eat high-sugar, high-fat foods, and our assumption is that to truly enjoy them is to have a *lot* of food— huge portions, unlimited quantities. We go overboard on both ends, keeping ourselves on a tight rein and then cutting loose. We'll discuss this pattern of eating more in chapter 9 (pages 422-423).

Your child won't deprive himself only to overeat later, unless he learns this behavior from you or other adults. Children are so tuned in to their hunger and appetite that they will stop in the middle of a bowl of ice cream when they get enough. Children know how to savor—to tune in to the taste of good food to get its rewards. Your job is to preserve what is there and not teach bad habits. It's a tricky job. Let's take potato chips, for instance. They do have the nutrients of the potato, but because they are fried and salty to boot, many parents classify them as forbidden foods for themselves and for children. Or visualize, if you will, Oreo cookies, a sugary and low-nutrient snack if there ever was one. Parents try to keep children from eating these questionable goodies, and both children and parents get into a starve-and-stuff mentality. Parents sneak off to crunch their chips or scrape the frosting off the Oreo cookies with their teeth, and so do children when they get a chance. We have a pretty good idea that the sneaking isn't working, but for proof we can look at actual university research, which shows that, particularly for girls, the more mothers restricted access to palatable snack foods, the more snacks children ate when they got the opportunity.[12] The fatter the girls, the more the mothers restrained both themselves and the girls *and* the more they both disinhibited, which means letting go after a period of restraint. Disinhibition and overweight were not related in fathers and sons, fathers and daughters, or mothers and sons.[13]

So what are you to do? It doesn't work to banish the food, and clearly you will be abdicating your food-managing responsibility if you just throw open the cupboard doors and let your child eat whatever he wants and whenever he wants. Here is the middle ground: Have chips periodically at mealtimes, and make sure there are plenty to go around more than once so you even have some left over. Have chips often enough so they don't become a forbidden fruit or even a special treat. Have sweets at snack time, and do the same. Although it hurts me to say it, for the occasional snack put a plate of Oreo cookies on the table along with a glass of milk and let your child eat as many as he is hungry for. I know kids love Oreos, but the nutritionist in me says, "but they don't have anything in them but a little bit of enriched flour!" So be it. Children's nutritional and calorie requirements are such that there is plenty of room for high-calorie low-nutrient food, so not everything they eat has to be high in nutrition. I don't recommend giving unlimited cookies at mealtime because they will replace the meal, but snack time gives a good opportunity to let your child eat as many cookies as he wants. Again, have the sweets often enough so they aren't a forbidden fruit.

Candy is a little trickier—why I don't know. Probably because my mother would let me have only one piece of her wonderful brown sugar candy at a time. Probably because generations of parents have taught us that you don't fill up on candy—except on Halloween of course (see pages 427-428). But from my mother's doling out I learned to savor—I could make a piece of candy last for half an hour. Why not teach your child that candy is special and something to be savored? While you are at it, learn to savor your special treats as well. When you have that cheesecake—or even that Oreo cookie—tune in to it. Get yourself a cup of tea, and sit down to give it your full attention. Take a bite, and close your eyes so you can *taste* and *feel* that food in your mouth. *Celebrate* that treat, don't just wolf it down. Eat until you truly feel like stopping. You don't have to wolf down delicious food to get as much as you want, and you don't have to settle for a small amount if you are going to savor. Pay attention, and eat the food until it no longer tastes good to you. "Eat," as one of my patients said, "until your *mouth* is finished as well as your stomach."

Give yourself—and your child—room to make some errors in food regulation, and trust your internal regulators to make up for those errors. With a particularly delicious food it is easy to enjoy too much and end up eating more than usual. You do it, and your child will do it. Overeating at times is not all that bad. Even people who are what I consider "normal" eaters occasionally eat until they feel quite full. It appears that the body's process of food regulation is flexible enough to compensate for this; it regulates food intake on a daily basis as well as on the basis of weeks or even months. Children may seem to overeat at times to provide for high-energy needs for activity or growth, and then settle down and eat less for a while. They are such good regulators that they work well with their bodies to account for calorie excesses and deficits and balance the energy ledger.

Make Wise Social and Emotional Use of Food. This section is for you. Your child will take on your attitudes and behaviors. The problem is not that we eat—or feed our children—when we are celebrating or depressed or lonely. The problem is that we do it poorly. Eating well can be wonderfully satisfying and relaxing. As the ad for the current weight-loss abomination, a fat blocker, trumpets, *"We do our best work after a good meal."* Of course, the advertisers want you to take their product to block a third of that good meal's fat from being absorbed, thereby presumably allowing you to lose a little weight. Never mind that it gives you gas and diarrhea and so interferes with absorption of fat-soluble vitamins that you are advised to take a supplement. The philosophy behind the medication is that the way to regulate food intake is to eat and then flush yourself out, a primitive method when compared with attending to hunger and appetite. It is all crazy, but they are right on one account: We *do* do our best work when we are feeding ourselves well. We are energized, organized, and soothed by eating well. But somehow in today's world that is not all right. "It used to be that having a good meal was a great stress-reliever," laments comedienne Loretta LaRoche during one of her routines on *The Joy of Stress*, "but that was before the food Nazis got hold of us."

For eating to be anything but a chore, it *has* to be gratifying emotionally. It has to be exciting, rewarding, sensual, nurturing. Little wonder that eating well can be encouraging and give us a way of lightening an otherwise humdrum day. *There is nothing wrong with that!* The problem is that we do it guiltily, impulsively, and unconsciously, and we get none of the benefit out of it. To allow food to be helpful for you emotionally, you have to tune in and enjoy it. Celebrating with food makes it clear that eating is joyful and rewarding. Soothing with food does the same. When you need encouragement and support, it is all right to make food part of that support. Find something you really like to eat, put yourself in an environment that you find pleasant, and be aware of letting the pleasure of the food raise your spirits. Eating can relax you if you will slow yourself down, concentrate, and allow the rhythm of the eating process to smooth out your nervous tension. If you make good emotional use of food, you may even be able to stop in the middle of a bowl of ice cream when you get enough!

This is not to imply that you should give your child a cookie every time he scrapes his knee or is bored. Eating is *one* way of emotional coping, but by no means the *only* way. It is certainly more appropriate to offer your child some comfort or your calm expectation that he can get interested in doing something else. However, once you sort the feelings out, it is okay to use food for comfort. It is a problem only if you reach for food as an automatic reflex without sorting things out first, and if you get stuck on food as your only way of offering support.

ACTIVITY SUPPORTS BODY WEIGHT REGULATION

While it is generally assumed that people get too fat because they eat too much and exercise too little, the research is no better at proving that point for activity than it is for food intake. Fat people are no more or less active than people who are thin. It appears that larger people move less than smaller ones, but when you figure that the energy cost of moving is greater for a larger person than for a smaller one, it comes out about the same. Fat or thin, there are natural variations in activity levels. One child will be very active, another will be not as active. However, the least active child will be more active than the most active adult. Being active, moving his body, and being physically capable are an important part of your child's health, his physical self-esteem, and self-esteem overall.

Supporting your child in being active depends on a division of responsibility: you provide the opportunities and your child partakes or doesn't partake in the activity. Develop your tolerance for noise and movement, inform yourself about reasonable levels of physical risk, find your child a safe place to play, and let him do what comes naturally. Above all, turn off the television. Don't try to force your child to be active, or you will experience the same kind of whiplash you would if you tried to manage your child's eating. Encourage your child to enjoy activity for its own sake—don't make the mistake of encouraging activity as a way of slimming down, bulking up, or being "healthy." That will take all the fun out of it. Joyful activity is sustainable—it has a chance of developing into a lifelong habit of movement.

Activity Fine-Tunes Food Regulation. While activity may or may not make your child fat or thin, maintaining a certain minimum level of activity appears to be necessary for the body's food regulation mechanisms to work well. I have to extrapolate from adults, however, to talk about this. In 1956 Harvard nutritionist Jean Mayer and his group did a series of observations in a jute factory in Bengal, India. They chose the setting because it was a self-contained environment, because everyone ate the same type of food, and because the men engaged in different occupations with widely varying levels of physical activity. The more sedentary men were stall holders and supervisors, who sat most of the time. The most active people were the load carriers, coal workers, and blacksmiths, who kept the fires going and moved huge and heavy bales. The people between the two extremes of physical activity were the clerks and mechanics, who moved around during their days' activities but, most significantly, walked long distances to work or who took part in sports.

Figure 2.8 illustrates that, with the exception of the people in the sedentary range, the more active people became, the more they ate. However, their weights remained stable. They were able to automatically balance energy intake with output and maintain a consistent body weight. However, the people in the sedentary range, rather than eating less to match their energy requirements, actually ate more and gained weight.[14] This is an old study but by no means an outdated one. The group set out to test in humans well-established observations in animals. The way to fatten an experimental rat or mouse is to immobilize it. Farmers restrict the activity of cows or pigs in order to fatten them.

Even though I have used data for *adults*, there's good reason to believe they are applicable to children. If you want your child to regulate well, let him get his exercise. Children of all ages benefit physically from being allowed to roam about in as large an area as they can safely handle. They also benefit from a family recreation pattern that includes moderate, pleasurable exercise—and from parents who are capable of turning off that antiexercise machine, the television set.

Limit Sedentary Activities. The equivalent of that Bengalese jute factory for today's child may be the TV room. Population studies find that the more television children watch, the heavier they tend to be. An analysis of the 1988 to 1994 National Health and Nutrition Examination Survey found that one-quarter of U.S. children ages 8 through 16 watched 4 or more hours of television each day. Furthermore, boys and girls who watched 4 or more hours of television each day had greater body fat and had a higher weight for height than those who watched less than 2

FIGURE 2.8 THE RELATIONSHIP OF FOOD INTAKE, PHYSICAL ACTIVITY, AND BODY WEIGHT

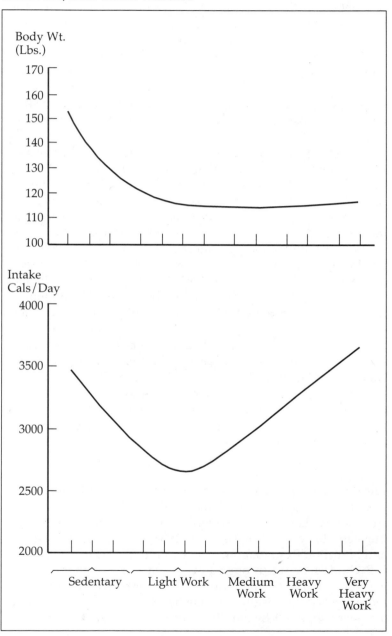

hours per day.[15] There is, of course, a logic to this, especially if we remember the associations from the Bengalese study. Children who watch too much television may not have the opportunity to get themselves out of the sedentary range of physical activity, and they may therefore eat disproportionately to their actual needs. And there may be more to it than that. Studies in a Memphis metabolic laboratory of 8- to 12-year-old children showed that while they watched television their metabolic rate was roughly 15 percent lower than when they were awake but at rest. Extrapolated over a day, the decrease in expenditure was 211 calories.[16]

Studies that have attempted to increase children's activities in the name of weight management have indirectly demonstrated television watching to be significant in children's activity—or lack of it. The greatest impact on children's overall activity level was produced by restricting sedentary activity, not by encouraging or even rewarding children for being more active. In fact, children who were not allowed to watch television appeared to increase their activity level and energy expenditure, even when they turned to other sedentary pursuits.[17]

Don't Be Your Child's Entertainment Committee. Based on the evidence we examined above, and based on my own convictions about good parenting in general, I strongly encourage you to limit your child's television time. A 2-hour limit is fairly good, a 1-hour limit is far better. I further encourage you that turning off the television need not—in fact, must not—mean that you will become your child's entertainment committee. Your child can entertain himself. Teach your child to play by himself and to be responsible for himself. Certainly you will take an interest and be companionable and set aside regular time to play. However, once you have done that, it is up to your child to take it the rest of the way. I see young parents today wearing themselves out trying to entertain their children and keep them from ever being bored. Don't do that. Let your child be bored. If he gets bored enough, he will think up something creative and wonderful to do.

Your child does want to be with you, but that doesn't mean he has to have your undivided attention all of the time. Toddlers have a pattern of ranging out and coming back, showing you what they are up to, and then going off to play again. In fact, studies show that toddlers check back in an average of 10 times an hour, for an average contact time of 30 seconds to a minute. Admire whatever your toddler wants to show you, call it by name, demonstrate something new about it, and send him on his way. Preschoolers are capable of independent play for more sustained periods of time, but your preschooler will still want to be where you are. Keeping his toys close to where you are working, taking a moment to watch (but not interrupt) while he plays, and letting him join in with your activities are all ways of sharing enjoyable time with your child without your having to be an entertainment committee.

Do plan for some uninterrupted playtime with your child, on a daily basis if you can manage it. Twenty minutes is enough, but make the time reliable and uninterrupted. With playing, as with eating, children like to take the lead, and they enjoy your supportive presence. You don't have to pile up blocks for your child to knock down or make elaborate houses or teach about the laws of shapes and sizes and proportions. All you have to do is be there, pay attention, ask about what your child is doing, and make little comments, like "That's a big wall." You can even do all this in a prone position, as long as you truly pay attention and take an interest. Of course, you can add your own ideas about building corrals for the animals out of blocks or playing house with the little people. You can lose at Candyland for the hundredth time, and your child will think it as fresh and exciting as the first time. Don't take over. This is your child's time, and you are there to take an interest.

Once again, playing together doesn't have to go on forever for you and your child to connect. Set a timer. Knowing there is a set limit will free you to take this time. If you have more time to play after it rings, you can go on playing, but when you want to quit, don't hesitate to say so.

SOME CHILDREN ACT LIKE THEY CAN'T REGULATE

For some children it is particularly hard to be trusting with feeding. In the section "Vulnerable Children" in chapter 6 (pages 212-215) we'll talk in detail about such children. In general, it is harder to be trusting and accepting when feeding children who are unusual, whose health, temperament, ways of communicating, size and shape, or eating behaviors are outside the norm. Parents intuitively take evasive action with such children and try to moderate and control their behaviors. That is where they get into problems, because the control leads to struggles, which in turn interfere with the child's eating capability. Here's the hard part: The approach for the cautious, vulnerable child is the same as for the sturdy, communicative, adventurous child. Hang in there with the structure and limits, be friendly and supportive, and give your child the opportunity to learn to manage his own caution, aggression, or upset. To help you with that, here are some stories about children who were vulnerable in one way or another and how their vulnerability affected their eating.

Bridget Was Passionate about Eating. Ten-month-old Bridget loved eating so much that her eyes would light up and she would sit rigid in her chair, eyes fixed on the bowl, eagerly anticipating the first bite. When she finally got the food in her mouth, Bridget would *moan* with pleasure. Bridget loved feeding herself with her hands, folding her fingers over to capture the food, gleefully pressing it into her mouth, moaning and giggling. Bridget's mother was humiliated by Bridget's exuberance. She thought that Bridget's passion for food was downright indecent, and she feared that Bridget's enjoyment of eating would make her too fat. It particularly embarrassed Bridget's mother that her friends and family so loved watching Bridget eat that they gathered around to watch, laughing and exclaiming.

The mother's fears were being confirmed. Between the ages 7 and 18 months, since she had started on solid food and then table food, Bridget's weight had crossed from her usual 50th percentile to well above the 95th percentile. Bridget's parents had tried to carry out the doctor's advice to stop letting Bridget eat so much, but then Bridget's constant refrain became, "I'm hungry, I'm hungry." What should she do, wondered the mother. Whenever she tried to restrict the amounts her daughter ate, not only would Bridget put up a fuss but Bridget's father would give in to her fussing. "Oh, let her have a little more," he would urge. "It can't hurt."

My question was quite different from the mother's. Rather than trying to figure out how to get Bridget to eat *less*, I wondered why she was eating more than she seemed to need. From her growth records up to age 7 months, Bridget had demonstrated that she was capable of regulating her food intake and growing in a predictable fashion. Of course, it is always hard to reconstruct these scenarios, but from the videotape of the family meal, I thought I had my answer. Bridget was a performer, and she performed with her eating. She had gotten so much attention for the way she ate that she had learned to eat for her audience rather than paying attention to how hungry and how full she was. Before I planned the treatment, I did have a question for the mother. Why did she let her friends and family make such a fuss about Bridget's eating? She answered that it was hard for her to stand up to them, but she *could* do it with other issues. In this case, she felt that something was the matter with her own response, and because of that she didn't trust herself to do anything.

What was the solution? Get Bridget out of the spotlight. Get her up to the table with the rest of the family, ignore the way she eats, be matter-of-fact about feeding her, and include her in the family—but stop making her the star. They were to give her the same attention as everyone else—pay attention and talk to her some, expect her to listen quietly when other family members talked, respond to her overtures that had to do with talking and babbling, but ignore her eating. Ignoring what we didn't want her to do—showing off with her eating—was the key. It helped. Having lost her audience, Bridget went through a brief period of exaggerating her behavior to recapture the lost attention, but the family steadfastly ignored her eating and made an effort to give her extra attention in other ways, outside the meal. Then she went through a week or two when she didn't take much interest in eating, and then she began acting like a normal toddler. She ate a lot sometimes, not so much others, was enthusiastic about a food one time and wanted a lot of it, and then wasn't at all interested another time. Her refrain of "I'm hungry, I'm hungry" went away, and she seemed to forget about food except when it was time to eat. Her weight leveled off, which seemed to me to be a very positive outcome. The doctor wanted them to restrict her eating to get her weight to go back down to the 50th percentile, but Bridget's parents decided not to do that. They knew that if they restricted her eating they could initiate a whole set of eating problems.

Even though she *loved* to eat, Bridget had always known how much to eat. It was all the interference from the outside that had confused her. When that interference was set aside, she was able to go back to paying attention to her hunger and fullness to tell her how much to eat.

Michael Would Eat Only for Applause. Michael kept himself the center of attention with his eating as well, but for quite a different reason. He had been born prematurely, and during his early weeks he had been fed only through a tube threaded through his nose and into his stomach. Like a lot of prematurely born children who are cared for in the newborn intensive care nursery, Michael had had a lot of unpleasant procedures done to his mouth. As a consequence, not only did Michael not know what eating was, he had learned that anything that happened to his mouth would be negative and uncomfortable. Since feeding was something that just happened to him, Michael hadn't made the connection between being hungry, eating, and getting relief from hunger. Little wonder that he became extremely cautious about learning to eat. To read more about children like Michael, see the section "How to Make Solids-Feeding Fun" (pages 255-258) in chapter 7.

Two-year-old Michael's parents and his occupational therapist had been successful in teaching Michael to take his bottle, and they had gotten him to the point that he could swallow semisolids and even chew and swallow some solid food. The problem was that Michael would eat only with considerable urging from others, and his parents were tired of working so hard to get food into him. He was still being fed through a tube that went through his abdominal wall into his stomach, and they wanted to get rid of that as well. Videotapes of the family's mealtimes demonstrated what the parents were saying. Michael's mother was on her knees in front of his high chair tray, urging Michael to eat. Michael was busily stirring and stirring his food. "Now take a bite," his mother urged over and over. After she had urged long enough and Michael had stirred long enough, he took a tiny bite. Sometimes he let her fill the spoon and put the food in his mouth, but then he would not quite open his mouth for it. Sometimes he put the spoon in his mouth himself, but when he did he was careful to only dip the spoon in the food and not really *fill* it. The meal went on for 25 minutes. I was tired of watching it, so I can imagine what it felt like to take *part* in it. A similar routine took place at school—after Michael ate a certain prescribed number of bites, he would be allowed to play with his car for a few seconds, then the car was taken away and more bites were required for Michael to earn another round of playing.

I advised the parents to start feeding Michael as if he were the usual toddler—get him up to the table with them, offer him soft table food, then turn his eating over to him. They were to tube feed him away from mealtimes so he could be hungry at meals, but other than that they were to let him take over. At first, he stopped eating even the tiny quarter spoonfuls that they had been managing to get down him. But as they got better at ignoring his eating and expecting him to simply behave nicely at the table, he started taking an interest in his food. Ever so gradually he ate more and more, until he got to the point that he was eating fairly respectable toddler-type meals. He ate best, however, at child care, where he enthusiastically participated in meals and snacks and quite matter-of-factly ate as much as the other children did. That told me that his parents were still hovering a bit with his eating—prompting and interfering and making it seem as though eating was still their project and not his. They had been through a lot with him, and they just couldn't quite bring themselves to take the risk of letting him regulate his own food intake. Because of that, they had to continue the nighttime tube feeding for a year longer.

Even with this difficult history, somewhere inside of him Michael wanted to grow up and wanted to take responsibility for his eating. When his parents stopped putting so much pressure on him to eat, he began taking some initiative. He pushed himself along to learn how to eat. It appeared that he started to notice his hunger and to be aware that eating made his hunger go away.

Alice *Knew* How Much She Needed to Eat. Alice was 6 months old, a beautiful, alert little child. However, she had gained only just over 3 pounds and grown 5 inches since birth. Alice's parents had taken her for a chromosomal examination and for endocrine tests to find out whether anything was wrong. But no one could really say. Actually, other than her size, nothing really *was* wrong with Alice. She was just tiny.

The parents, of course, were concerned. They wanted to be sure that they were doing everything they could to encourage Alice to grow. But they said that she was very emphatic about how much she wanted to eat, and she cried and fussed when they tried to encourage her to take more than she wanted. We decided we would try concentrating her formula. We knew we would have to be careful in doing this. For one thing, we knew that giving her more nutrients and less water per unit volume of formula could dehydrate her. The doctor was alert to this possibility and saw her frequently to watch for any signs of dehydration. We also knew that we might just make Alice fat with our extra calories, so the nurse weighed and measured and plotted her carefully to make sure that if she accelerated her growth rate that it would occur in both height and weight. Alice was perfectly proportioned, and we didn't want to spoil that.

Then we set about modifying the formula. Since she was taking a formula that had more protein than she really needed, the first thing we did was add a little syrup, increasing her calories by about 7 percent. Alice responded by decreasing her volume of intake by 7 percent. Since that hadn't worked, we put her back on the regular formula while we reevaluated, and she immediately increased her volume to its previous level. We then speculated that Alice may not have liked the increased sweetness of the syrup, so this time we tried adding oil, figuring that would change the flavor less. We again increased the calories by 7 percent, and once again, Alice was ahead of us. She cut her intake by 7 percent. Back on the normal feed went Alice, and back to the previous volume went the intake.

Our last try was to simply concentrate the regular formula. We carefully took out some of the water to concentrate it by 7 percent; and Alice again decreased her intake. At that point, we gave up. Our only other option would have been to tube-feed Alice, and that didn't seem right. Alice was eating enough for her, and tube-feeding would have meant overfeeding. Knowing Alice, she probably would have compensated for the tube-feeding by taking less formula! The parents decided that they had done all they could and that they simply had to support the growth pattern that was normal for Alice. They moved away, and the last time I saw Alice she was 9 months old and weighed 9 pounds. She was feeding herself tiny amounts of food from the table. She was pulling herself up and walking around things

and startling everyone because she looked like a newborn.
When Alice was 12 years old, I tracked her mother down and
talked with her on the telephone. She said that Alice had stayed
very small, but that she was an alert, together child who did
well in school and did well with her friends. She had continued
to be a good regulator, firmly eating the amount of food that
she needed—no more and no less. I was so impressed at those
parents' ability to behave in such a moderate and accepting way
with Alice. They did what they could, and then they left it up to
Alice. It was clear that Alice knew how to eat and grow, but her
unusual growth pattern made it hard to see that and be accepting of it.

Bethany Didn't Eat Enough. Like Alice, 15-month-old Bethany
was tiny. However, unlike Alice, Bethany was falling off her
growth curve and seemed absolutely unwilling to eat.
Bethany's parents were convinced that she'd starve if they
didn't take charge. Her father held her head and tried to force
food between her lips. She fought back and screamed so loudly
that they worried that the neighbors would think they were
abusing her. Actually, they were. Being forced to eat is miserable, and they were being profoundly disrespectful of Bethany
by forcing her to do what she so clearly didn't want to do.
However, Bethany's parents were more afraid than abusive.
From the beginning, Bethany had been tiny. Her weight was
below the 5th percentile when she was born. She grew at that
level for two months and then her weight started to drop off. It
dropped lower and lower, until, by the time I saw her, it was far
below the 5th percentile.

The problem was that Bethany had ear infections. When she
had an infection, it seemed to make her too miserable to eat,
and taking the antibiotics decreased her appetite further. After
she recovered, her appetite would come back, but before long
she would get sick again, and the whole cycle would repeat
itself. Her parents had been made aware of her decreasing
growth rate and had become more and more forceful about
feeding her. Rather than eating, Bethany had become increasingly forceful about refusing.

The solution was for them to back off and establish a
division of responsibility in feeding. Like other toddlers,
Bethany had gotten so caught up in the battle with her parents

that she hadn't been able to tune in on her own hunger and interest in food. When they stopped fighting with her, she began to eat. It didn't happen right away. For a couple of weeks she ate little if anything. But they made sure to have one or two of the foods that she seemed to like at least some of the time, and gradually she began taking an interest in eating. Even after she started eating better, Bethany ate amounts that seemed too small to her parents. However, the amounts were right for her, because her growth leveled off and ever-so-gradually started to creep back up again. Elated by their success, the parents were tempted to push food a bit, but when they tried Bethany let them know promptly that they were *not* to mess with her eating. Eventually the parents even learned to relax a bit when Bethany was ill or went off her feed for other reasons. Like a lot of children with a less-than-optimum early history with eating, Bethany tended to lose interest in eating when she was going through developmental changes or busy and excited about other things. However, if her parents held steady, she started eating again and then made up for lost time. Even with her intermittent illnesses and poor eating, Bethany would likely have caught up between times if her parents hadn't gotten so scared and so pushy.

Children are remarkable regulators, and they can compensate for the ups and downs in their food intake. A child who grows slowly early on is not necessarily going to keep on growing slowly. Children do catch-up growing. When they get through a period of illness or have a slow start for any reason, they often grow faster for a while. I haven't included any stories here about the child who seems to eat "too much" because I told those stories earlier—about Mary and about Todd. The point with these children, and all the others I talk about in *Child of Mine,* is that you can trust them. Relax and enjoy your child; don't feel you have to hover or manage. Eating with your child, observing his delight and accomplishment with eating, and watching him grow and develop can all be endlessly joyful and rewarding for you. Don't spoil it by feeling you have to manage it. Do your job with feeding, and let your child do the rest. Your child knows how to eat and grow.

CHAPTER 3

YOUR FEEDING DECISION: BREASTFEEDING OR FORMULA-FEEDING

YOUR FIRST TASK IN FEEDING your infant is to decide which kind of milk feeding you will use. I will be talking about breastfeeding and infant formula–feeding in detail in chapters 5 and 6, and I encourage you to read those chapters as part of your process of deciding. For now it is enough to say that the only food that your baby needs for the first 5 to 6 months of life is either breastmilk or a formula that you buy especially for her.

I will tell you right away that I think breastmilk is best. If you can, I would like to have you breastfeed your baby. However, your relationship with your baby is far more impor-tant than your manner of feeding. Breastfeeding can help you be warm, close, tuned in, and responsive to your baby. If you don't like breastfeeding, it can also get in the way. Think about it ahead of time and keep on thinking. Don't just automatically rule breastfeeding out and forget about it. Get past your nega-tive feelings if you can. If you are undecided, start out breast-feeding your baby; you might like it. On the other hand, you might find you dislike it so much that it interferes with your being a good parent. Then it's better to bottle-feed. If you do it right, formula-feeding is fine. Babies fed both ways can be appropriately fed—or overfed—or underfed.

Most important, in my view, is the help breastfeeding gives

you with the feeding relationship. During your baby's first year, you will spend most of your time together feeding. That makes feeding of primary importance to your baby not only nutritionally but also in terms of the love you convey and in terms of her growth and development. Breastfeeding reminds you that you are important to your baby and supports the feeding relationship. It teaches you to follow your baby's lead with feeding and programs in positive ways of being with your baby and being a parent. You can parent in all the same positive and responsive ways with formula-feeding, but it isn't automatic. It's easier to impose amounts and schedules on the bottle-fed baby. It's also easier to get the idea that you are interchangeable with anyone who can hold a baby and give a bottle. Not true. Your baby knows you and you know her. Other people can hold your baby, diaper her, or even walk the floor with her. For feeding, she needs you.

Breastfeeding is important for nutritional and medical reasons as well. Breastfeeding is nutritionally superior, protects your baby against infection, is economical, and error-free. Breastmilk is convenient and clean; fed straight from the breast, it is not subject to contamination. Breastfeeding helps babies to stay well—it helps protect against infections.

ENCOURAGEMENT HELPS; PRESSURE DOESN'T

I am not going to try to force or guilt-trip you to get you to breastfeed. I will try to *expose you to the possibilities.* I do hope you will expose yourself to the possibilities as well—that you will think about breastfeeding carefully before you rule it out, give yourself plenty of time to get comfortable with the idea of breastfeeding, and seek out someone you know who has successfully breastfed. Check out the people who provide support and advice to find out whether you will be comfortable working with them. Even after you have done all that, however, the final decision is yours, so don't force yourself, and do give yourself an out. Parents who feel guilty about not breastfeeding are those who haven't thought about it carefully.

There could be good reasons for you to bottle-feed. There are negatives and disadvantages to breastfeeding, and I will talk about them. The early learning time with a first baby is demanding regardless of whether you breastfeed or bottle-feed.

In some ways, breastfeeding is more complicated, and you may as well take that into account. I assume that you know far better than I do about your own life, feelings, preferences, and circumstances. You are likely to be able to anticipate which method will work best for you (as long as you remember that you can't *really* know until you get there). I think formula-feeding provides an adequate substitute for breastmilk. It is adequate, that is, if you go by what your baby tells you in feeding, make feedings important enough to do most of them yourself, pay careful attention to sanitation, and use excellent preparation technique.

Some of my readers and reviewers have been after me to come down harder on the side of breastfeeding. I am not about to put pressure on you to do it. Ongoing campaigns by the American Academy of Pediatrics, the Bureau of Maternal and Child Health, and the WIC program (Special Supplemental Nutrition Program for Women, Infants, and Children) have been successful in increasing the incidence of breastfeeding. Across the United States, about 60 percent of babies are being released from the hospital fully breastfed, and by 6 months of age about 20 percent of infants are still breastfed.[1] I fervently hope the campaigns succeed by virtue of informing and supporting parents in making their feeding decision, not by putting pressure on them to breastfeed. It is such a personal decision. As one woman said after she started out breastfeeding her child and found she just didn't feel right about it, "I can't do it—I wish I could, but I can't."

Breastfeeding campaigns essentially compete for your attention against the advertising campaigns of the infant formula companies. Formula marketing is formidable and versatile, with efforts ranging from professional journal, popular magazine, and television advertising to formula giveaways in hospitals and medical clinics. The formula companies say that "breast is best" and even put out breastfeeding booklets. Once they get your attention, however, they go on to say, "but if you can't breastfeed, our formula is best." Is that encouraging or undermining breastfeeding? You decide. I do know that it doesn't make a lot of sense to make breastfeeding a national health priority and then allow formula companies to continue to give formula and other gifts to health workers who are in a position to pass along their product to young parents. It seems to me that that is giving the strongest of mixed messages.

The problem is that the competition for your attention can get a bit zealous at times and make you feel guilty if you don't want to breastfeed and undermine you if you do! It's not helpful for you if you end up feeling bad or somehow inadequate if you can't or don't want to breastfeed. Those feelings can be serious. Jennifer, for instance, was herself doing breastfeeding promotion. During her pregnancy, her colleagues gave her an enormous amount of approval, encouragement, and information, and she looked forward eagerly to breastfeeding her baby. She couldn't do it. She did all the right things, but she was one of those 5 percent of women who simply cannot breastfeed. She was devastated, and her disappointment made her unhappy and miserable during the first several weeks of her baby's life. There had been so much breastfeeding fervor in her agency that she felt downright humiliated and inadequate.

Encouragement is good. Exposing you to the possibilities is good. Not taking an automatic "no" for an answer is good. Pressure is not good. If someone takes it upon him- or herself to make choices for you, turn a deaf ear. Pressure and strong-arm tactics never truly helped anybody succeed. Pressure backfires with children and their eating, and the same holds true for you and your breastfeeding. To do well with breastfeeding, you need an out. In fact, if you have an out, like your children, you will do more and dare more than you would otherwise. If you are being told you *have* to breastfeed—or bottle-feed—for the good of your baby, don't listen. You don't have to. Your baby will be fine. Keep the topic open for yourself; don't just rule it out. Give breastfeeding a try if you are willing. Whatever you decide to do, stow the guilt. You will have plenty of opportunities to feel guilty as a parent without feeling guilty about *that,* too. However you decide to feed your baby, give yourself credit for having reached a carefully considered decision that is best for you and your family. You can feed your infant well either way. You can have a warm, close feeding relationship either way.

My task, then, becomes one of helping you make a decision, based on your knowledge of the needs of your family.

PERSONAL PREFERENCE

Some women get a real emotional and physical high from

breastfeeding. Others see it as all in a day's work. Some men are moved and inspired by watching their child being breastfed. Some fathers* are fine with it but not particularly touched. Some mothers and fathers are turned off by it and can't imagine doing it. It's important for both of you to consider and respect your own feelings in making your choice. A good feeding relationship with your infant is all-important, and if you are not comfortable with your feeding method, you won't be able to hide it from yourself, each other, or your baby. Even the sophisticated components of breastmilk can't make up for feeding in a way you find unpleasant. You may be the main parent or a stay-at-home dad, and bottle-feeding may fit that lifestyle better. Keep in mind, however, that many working moms and stay-at-home dads work breastfeeding into their routine.

Particularly if this is your first child, you can't really anticipate how you and your mate will react to your baby until you have her. You might get so besotted and involved that you can't stand to leave her. On the other hand, you may feel hemmed in and really feel you need some time to get out. Your baby will have a lot to do with your feelings about needing to get away, as well as your feelings about the feeding relationship. Your baby may be so placid, easy to satisfy, and predictable that you can even take her to the movies with you, and you may feel so relaxed around her that you don't feel tied down. On the other hand she might be an unsettled, disorganized baby who is hard to read and hard to satisfy. Having a breather from a high-maintenance child can be wonderful. Getting a night off when you are breastfeeding is not impossible, but it is more complicated. Here's a hasty word of encouragement: children change. Also keep in mind that those first few months are fleeting, and taken in the context of your life with your child, they will seem like they lasted all too short a time.

---

*In these days of political correctness, almost any terminology I use is likely to offend someone. When I say "mother," I mean "the mothering one," or the one who takes primary responsibility for the infant and is likely to be closest and most bonded with the infant. When I say "father," I mean "the fathering one," the one who is almost as close to the infant but whose primary role is to support the mother. I leave it to you to interpret that language and those roles in your personal partnership—and parenting—arrangement.

Feelings change, too. The feelings we are talking about, of course, are negative feelings: distaste, anxiety, jealousy, entrapment. Having those feelings doesn't mean that you can't choose to breastfeed. It does mean that you have to deal with your feelings and wait to decide until after you have done that. In my experience, negative feelings have a chance to change, to lessen, provided they are expressed. As a young father observed as he grappled with his own emotions, "the way I understand it, feelings are like an engine deep inside of you. If you don't know what you're feeling, that engine can run you." Well said. Particularly when it has to do with their baby, many people feel bad about their negative feelings and don't want to express or even experience them. It's too bad, because that means the feelings will get stuck. Bringing the feelings to the light of day takes away their sting and lets people change. Acknowledging them, experiencing them, sharing them with others, and having them be accepted all help.

KNOWING HOW IMPORTANT YOU ARE

You are your baby's parents, and you will be the most important people in the world to her. She will be born knowing you. From birth, she will recognize your voice and brighten up and look toward you when you talk with her. She will eat best, and feel most nurtured with her feeding, if she is fed by the people she feels most tuned in with and attached to—her parents. You wouldn't feel comfortable eating with just any old body who came along, and she doesn't either. Breastfeeding lets you keep her all to yourself for feeding. If you are breastfeeding, relatives, neighbors, and friends won't be able to press you to let them feed your baby. There will be other times to share your baby, but feeding need not be one of those times. If you are formula-feeding, find other ways of kindly saying "no, this is my job."

Breastfeeding is more likely than formula-feeding to call out support in other people. Whether you breast- or bottle-feed, you need support. Having a new baby is an earthshaking experience. Try to get help, and give your help some guidance about what they can do: take care of you and let you take care of your baby. Ask them to cook, clean, do laundry, provide moral support, give encouragement, provide another set of eyes and ears as you try to understand what your baby is telling you, and most important of all, be a calming presence while you get used to being parents. I had the very great privilege of being new-baby helper for two or three weeks when all three of my granddaughters were born. It was wonderful for all of us. After the birth of their first baby, Emma, my daughter, Kjerstin, told me that she was in a daze and said her husband, Glenn, was "walking into walls." I think she meant he was in a daze as well, because I never caught him stuck up against a wall! They were both in that mild state of shock that many of us experience when we realize just how vulnerable and dependant a newborn baby really is. In spite of their shock, I felt they both functioned amazingly well. When the twins, Adele and Marin, were born, it took all three of us to observe and understand their feeding behaviors so Kjerstin and Glenn could do what the babies needed. We had a running joke that started, "I have a theory. . . ." That meant that we had been observing the action and thought we could explain and supply a solution for the dilemma of the moment.

Kjerstin and Glenn benefited from my support so they could learn to be parents. My being there made them feel they had someone to fall back on. I certainly didn't know all the answers, but I did help them to settle down so they could do their own thinking. All young families need that support, even though there is precious little of it around these days. Parents are released from maternity wards 24 or 48 hours after the birth of their baby, which is before breastmilk even comes in for most women and certainly too soon to know how the baby will behave. Grandparents live far away and have their own lives, which is as it needs to be. New-baby help is expensive and hard to come by. But Mother Nature never intended raising children to be a solo job. Tell your parents I said if they can squeeze out the time to be backup and support for you for a week or two, they will find it wonderfully rewarding and even healing. There is nothing quite like the satisfaction of helping a new young family get off on the right foot, and being with a newborn one step removed from your own babies is a wonderful way of putting your own parenting in context and forgiving yourself for your mistakes. It is also a good way of beginning to learn to be a grandparent: your backup and support is important, but you do need to provide it secondhand.

Kjerstin was breastfeeding, so she had to be calm and rested enough to learn how that process worked: how to help Emma take the nipple properly, how to tell whether she was getting enough to eat. But a lot of the challenge with Emma had to do with Emma: reading her, understanding what she needed and how to help her to be happy and comfortable. You can breast-feed successfully without emotional and situational support, but it is not easy. It's perhaps a bit easier with formula-feeding, because you don't have your own physiology to take into account. But either way, you have to get to know your baby so you can help her be settled and comfortable. An unsettled, irritable baby will be unsettled on either breastmilk or formula.

Not least in knowing how important you are, breastfeeding can help you feel good about your body and about yourself for being able to provide for your baby.

CONNECTING WITH YOUR BABY

To be honest, I couldn't help but feel a little twinge of dismay when I heard that my young friend and his partner were for-mula-feeding their baby. But then I listened to him talk and realized that he was absolutely nuts about his daughter, that he would be doing most of the parenting, and that he was likely to be a very tuned-in father. In being disappointed about the bot-tle-feeding, I was making assumptions about the *quality* of the feeding. The bottom line? It is the relationship that is most important, the method of feeding comes after.

You get attached to your baby by getting to know her, by taking care of her, and by being with her on a day-to-day basis. A very good time to start getting to know your baby is right after delivery. Babies are wide awake for an hour or two, parents are excited, and it is a rewarding time for parents before fatigue overtakes everyone. Studies say that the formation of intense attachment between parents and infant occurs readily during a sensitive period in the first 24 hours of life. Hospital staff can be especially helpful if they give you access to your baby in the delivery room and right after. The delivery-room breastfeeding is particularly important to give the infant a chance to latch on instinctively, whereas she may have to be taught later on. The hospital staff can also be helpful by showing you how to read your baby's cues that tell you what she wants and needs.

Parenting goes best when you realize that your baby is a little person who is capable of communicating with you. Bonding can take place any time in the first several weeks, but particularly for parents who are coping with difficult life circumstances, having that early, very close time can have a long-term impact on the relationship between parent and child.

The American Academy of Pediatrics recommends that all newborn breastfed babies discharged less than 48 hours after delivery be seen 2 to 4 days after discharge from the hospital, and then that they be seen again either 2 weeks or 1 month later.* The right-after-discharge visit is important to make sure that your baby's mouth is correctly positioned on your breast for nursing (what is called "latch-on") and that you are holding her properly and that she is awake and alert and feeding. With the early discharge, few infants have successfully fed by the time they leave the hospital. Formula-fed babies are routinely first seen at 1 month. However you are feeding, if you feel you need it, don't be shy about asking for a follow-up visit before the prescribed period, or at least making a phone call to share your concerns. Hospitals as well as clinics will do these checks, as well as check your baby's suck and latch-on and answer your questions.

Whether you choose to breast- or bottle-feed, find out your OB ward's policies about keeping babies with parents right after they are born and about having your baby in your hospital room (what is called "rooming in"). Unless your pediatrician thinks there is a good reason for keeping your baby in the nursery, ask for contact with your baby right away and keep her close. Furthermore, ask for the 1- or 2-week weight check as well. Many doctors offices don't charge for weight checks.

GETTING ADVICE AND HELP

As I said earlier, you need support. You will do best with feeding your baby if you have other people to back you up. For either breast- or bottle-feeding parents, support systems are not well developed, so you will most likely have to be willing to go

---

*I prefer 2 weeks. Since the Academy of Pediatrics gives contradictory statements about the 2-week follow-up, you may have to ask for it specifically.

after help and be insistent about lining it up. See the section "Support and Teaching" in chapter 5 (pages 183-192). In some settings, given today's emphasis on breastfeeding, you may have more access to encouragement, help, and information if you are breastfeeding than if you are formula-feeding. If your hospital is tuned in to breastfeeding, and some are, there will be an on-staff lactation consultant who will visit during your brief hospital stay. The consultant will help you to observe, understand, and interpret your baby and will help you get breastfeeding off to a good start.

Some pediatric clinics at least have on call a lactation consultant who can answer your questions or speak to your concerns about breastfeeding. Lactation consultants are well trained, certified, and experienced people who can help you with breastfeeding. They will help you solve problems and will not insist that you keep breastfeeding no matter what. They will keep you from going on guilt trips, encourage you to use an occasional relief bottle if they think it is called for, and help you keep in perspective that you are really doing very well even when it seems as if you aren't. Find a consultant you like and respect who can give you advice in a way that you find helpful and supportive.

My only trouble with lactation consultants is that they confine their work to breastfeeding parents! I have found formula-feeding parents to be equally in need of help in learning about their babies, about technique, and about getting feeding and parenting off on the right foot. Emma was breastfed, but her new-baby challenges could have affected formula-feeding as much as they did breastfeeding. At Emma's first breastfeedings, she wasn't latching on properly when she nursed. The lactation consultant identified that her suck was poor, particularly when she was held on her left side. The consultant showed Kjerstin and Glenn how to use a finger to massage the roof of Emma's mouth to get her suck going, then transfer to the breast to keep it going. If Emma had been formula-feeding, I wonder if such help would have been forthcoming. The attitude toward bottle-feeding seems to be that there is nothing to it: you screw the nipple into the baby's mouth and that's the end of it. Not true. Formula-feeding parents need help and support, too. Not only do they have to get to know their baby, but they have to master the mechanics of preparing and giving bottles as well.

EATING WHILE BREASTFEEDING

Whether you are breast- or formula-feeding, you will have to eat. You don't have to eat boring food, but you do have to eat. This goes for fathers as well as mothers. You will need your strength, endurance, and emotional steadiness in order to be a good parent, and when you are hungry or going without food, you will be worn out, cranky, and discouraged.

In order to encourage them to breastfeed, many consultants make a point of reassuring pregnant women they don't have to do anything special with regard to their eating. I am not sure of the logic behind such a statement, but I hope it is the assumption that everybody eats and eats as much as they are hungry for. It is true that you can trust your hunger and appetite to tell you how much to eat. What is faulty is the assumption that most people do a decent job of taking care of themselves with food. To do well with eating, you need regular and reliable meals made up of enjoyable, satisfying, and filling food. In my experience, people in general and young people in particular do a poor job of providing for themselves with food. You are now—definitely—a family. I said in *Secrets of Feeding a Healthy Family* that you are a family when you begin taking care of yourself. If you haven't already been treating yourself like a family and taking care of yourself, it's time to start. Feeding yourself is part of becoming a family. It's all right to eat out— even if you go to fast-food places—but it's hard to do that all the time. To feed yourself three times a day, day in and day out, you have to cook. When your child is ready to join the family table, it makes all the difference if you are in the routine of having family meals. If you don't have family meals, her eating won't turn out well. Read *Secrets of Feeding a Healthy Family* if you need help learning how to cook well in a hurry and learning that feeding yourself well doesn't mean that what you cook and eat has to be difficult, time-consuming, tedious, or expensive.

I said earlier that breastfeeding attracts support, and it is particularly true with food. Others are more likely to feed you while you are breastfeeding than when you are formula-feeding. That's good, because breastfeeding requires, most of all, calories, particularly after the first month, and particularly if you haven't gained much weight during pregnancy. Quality of your diet comes after quantity, because with the exception of the water-soluble vitamins like the B vitamins and vitamin C, your body will sacrifice nutrients from itself in order to provide the nutrients in your breastmilk. Eating an overall well balanced diet is most important for you—to keep yourself from being nutritionally depleted.

You will provide enough breastmilk for your baby if you eat as much as you are hungry for. The only time you will have to go beyond your hunger is if you find your appetite isn't very good, when you are overtired, very nervous, or heat-stressed. If, however, your appetite is generally poor or if you have a long list of foods you avoid or if you are in the habit of ignoring your feelings of hunger and appetite for food for whatever reason, you may have trouble producing enough breastmilk. You can limp by on too few calories and you may even get away with it, but if your food intake drops too low it may decrease your breastmilk supply.

MAKING ENOUGH BREASTMILK

Beyond the demands of you and your own diet, a common reason women give for deciding to bottle-feed is that they think it is difficult to provide enough milk for the baby, and they don't know whether they can do it. They worry that they won't know whether their baby is getting enough. Often they have heard stories of someone whose milk supply was inadequate, or who simply "dried up" and was forced to wean her infant from breast to bottle. From time to time we hear stories about dehydrated and poorly growing breastfeeding infants whose parents did not realize that their babies were having trouble.

Babies can get in trouble if breastfeeding parents don't know what they are doing. Breastfeeding is not entirely instinctive. Even our closest relatives—chimpanzees, gorillas, monkeys, and other primates—learn how to breastfeed by observing the process in others. We are starting to rebuild our breastfeeding tradition, but most women my age, today's grandmothers, didn't breastfeed. When women in my generation were having babies, formula-feeding was popular and breastfeeding was considered somewhat eccentric and a bit of a nuisance by the medical community. Support and advice were hard to come by. If we did try to breastfeed, failure rate was high, partly because it was just too easy to supplement with a bottle. We had seen our brothers, sisters, and cousins being bottle-fed, so that seemed more natural. The situation is better now, but not entirely rosy. Although you get encouragement and even pressure to breastfeed, you may or may not be exposed to breastfeeding, and you may or may not be offered the information and support you need to be successful.* It's available, but you may have to seek it out.

Production. Breastmilk is produced according to a law of supply and demand. The more often and more completely your baby empties your breasts, the more breastmilk you are stimulated to produce. As your baby gets bigger and more active, she will have days when she is hungrier, eats more frequently, and stimulates you to make more breastmilk. After a day or two of frequent nursing, your production will increase and she'll eat less often. Don't plan on a feeding schedule for either your breastfed or bottle-fed baby. Breastfed babies need to be able to nurse more frequently at times to get you to increase your breastmilk production. Bottle-fed babies need to have you pay attention to them and feed at a time that is right for them, not at a regimented feeding time.

Your ability to produce breastmilk has nothing to do with the apparent size of your breasts. You can be flat-chested and still have all the alveoli (milk-producing cells) you need to make breastmilk. Larger breasts contain more fat and fibrous tissue than smaller breasts, but not necessarily any more milk-producing anatomy and physiology. Breast surgery, however, can adversely affect your ability to make and deliver milk to your baby. Breast implants may interfere because they mechanically rearrange the milk-delivery apparatus in the breasts, but there is still a chance that the breast tissue will be intact enough to allow you to breastfeed. Breast-reduction surgery, however, since it usually involves removal and reattachment of the nipples, is more likely to disrupt breastfeeding. The ducts, sinuses,

---

*If your mother bottle-fed, she may be intimidated by your breastfeeding, because she feels she can't help or advise you. Not true. She can support you and help you understand your baby; that's 90 percent of the task. Even if your mother breastfed you (as I did my children), you may still need advice from a lactation consultant, because your baby may offer you challenges your mother didn't encounter.

and nerve endings may have been severed and therefore may no longer be functional.

Statistics show that most women can breastfeed their infants. As I said earlier, only 5 percent of women have physical barriers to breastfeeding. Most cases of breastfeeding failure come from anxiety or lack of understanding of the breastfeeding process. Some of our best statistics on this came from developing countries, where 40 years ago almost all mothers were successful at breastfeeding their infants, even when they were poor and not eating well. I say *were* successful, because with the advent of Western ideas and customs, ready availability of infant formula, and planting of the seed of doubt, breastfeeding "failure" is on the increase, as is bottle-feeding. There are contributing factors, such as movement away from family support, mothers working away from their babies, and imitation of Western patterns of infant feeding (i.e., relying routinely on bottle-feeding). However, the basic fact remains that before these intrusions, a very high percentage of women breastfed successfully. Now that women are receiving support and information from each other, from well-informed health professionals, and from well-written books, the success rate in this country is again going up. If you want to breastfeed, chances are excellent that you will be able to do it.

Letdown. Letdown is the process that gets the milk from the manufacturing site (alveoli high in the breast) through the ducts into the lactiferous sinuses, which are enlarged areas of the ducts about ³/₄ to 1 ¹/₂ inch back from the nipple pore. (Look at Figure 5.2, page 147, for an illustration of breast anatomy.) Once the milk gets into the sinuses, the job of letdown is done, because at that point your baby squeezes the milk out through the pores of the nipple with pressure from her jaws and stroking with her tongue. When your baby starts to suckle— or, eventually, when you hear her cry or even think about her— you release the hormone oxytocin, which makes the muscles around the alveoli contract and squeeze the milk down the ducts. With a new mother who hasn't breastfed before, it takes a few days to get the letdown process working well. If that mother is extraordinarily anxious, her anxiety can interfere with letdown. The milk is there, at least initially, but anxiety, awkwardness, and misgiving can make the mother tense and impair delivery of milk to the infant. The milk stays in the alveoli, the biological message is relayed to the mammary tissue to make less, not more, milk, and milk supply does, indeed, decrease. However, keep in mind that all new mothers are anxious, and most get past those feelings. Encouragement, moral support, and time generally get the system working just fine.

KNOWING YOUR BABY IS GETTING ENOUGH

You may decide to bottle-feed because you want to know how much your baby is eating. Although that is a legitimate concern, that's not as important as knowing that your baby is getting *enough*. Babies vary a great deal in how much they need to eat. Even if your baby is bottle-fed, you can only go by her hunger and fullness signals to feed her as much as she wants. Even newborns know when they are hungry and full, and you can generally trust those signals. When you go to your health care provider and have your baby weighed, you will have more evidence that she is eating the right amount, because she will have grown well. Some babies are at or above their birth weight by the time they are a week old (babies lose weight right after they are born), and some breastfed babies take 3 weeks before they get to that point. It varies. Your breastfed baby might eat a little or a lot, and she might grow a little or a lot. The same holds true for the bottle-fed baby.

With the bottle-fed baby you can, of course, actually see that something is going in. With the breastfed baby, you can tell that something is going in, but your evidence is indirect. You go by what is coming *out* and by your baby's behavior. At first, your baby's stools will be a very dark, tarry meconium. About 3 to 5 days after delivery your milk will come in. Two to three days after that, your baby will be getting enough to eat when she is breastfeeding 8 or more times in 24 hours, has six to eight wet diapers a day, and has three or four or more stools. If you don't see that, call your health provider.

NUTRITIONAL DESIRABILITY

Nutritionally, breastfeeding is and probably always will be

more nutritionally sophisticated than formula-feeding. Simply because a formula manufacturer says its product is "like breast-milk" doesn't mean it is the *same* as breastmilk. In this country, as in other technologically advantaged countries, we have access to refrigeration and are generally able to maintain adequate standards of sanitation. Most people can read and follow directions and are able to afford enough formula for their babies.* All of these factors have allowed successful formula-feeding. The health advantages of breastfeeding to the baby are modest but real. Breastfeeding is not the life-or-death matter it is in some developing countries, but even in this country, the more limited the life circumstances of parents, the greater the advantages. Compared with formula, breastfeeding offers some protection against ear infections and lower respiratory infections like wheezing and coughing. Fully breastfed babies may spit up less often and have fewer allergic reactions even when they are preschoolers.[2]

Some breastfeeding enthusiasts go beyond these modest but important distinctions and claim immunity from obesity, diabetes, and cancer, greater intelligence, and virtually complete protection from allergies. Research supporting these claims is scanty and contradictory. Although breastfed babies grow a bit more slowly than formula-fed babies from age 3 to 12 months, breastfed babies are no less likely to be fat as adults. Children who have been breastfed as babies appear to score about 2.5 points higher on IQ tests than formula fed babies; prematurely born breastfed babies score 5 points higher. These are differences that have been adjusted for the economic and social circumstances of the family. In studies concerning nutrition and intelligence in children, a rich and stimulating environment can make up for nutritional limitations.[3] Breastfeeding helps prevent allergies, but it may not solve all your baby's allergy problems. A very small group of extremely allergic breastfed babies react to even minute amounts of food substances in their mother's milk and have to be put on a special allergen-free formula. To continue breastfeeding, mothers of those highly allergic

---

*For families who are economically limited and at nutritional risk, the WIC program (Special Supplemental Nutrition Program for Women, Infants, and Children) provides food for breastfeeding women or formula for infants.

infants have to eliminate so much from their diets that their food becomes very incomplete nutritionally.[4]

We are sophisticated enough to admit that we don't know all there is to know about nutrition. Attempts of nutritionists and formula manufacturers to duplicate nature, that is, trying to duplicate breastmilk with formula, are constantly improving, but all must still acknowledge that there is more to be known. Given our obsession with avoiding heart disease, a major difference between formula and breastmilk that isn't mentioned much is that breastmilk is high in cholesterol, which is a major building block for brain and nervous tissue for the still-developing newborn. Formula has none. Although babies and other people can make cholesterol if they don't eat it, providing it ready to go is still a better idea for the newborn who has other biochemical work to do.

Other differences between formula and breastmilk aren't so straightforward, but they are just as important. Research on breastmilk components continues to turn up remarkably sophisticated and intricate interactions between infant need and nutritional provision. For example, colostrum (the yellowish fluid produced before breastmilk) and early breastmilk are relatively high in zinc. This high level is provided at a time when the "still-unfinished" newborn has special needs for zinc as a building block for zinc-containing enzymes. Nutritionists are still debating the right levels of zinc to put in formulas. In addition, colostrum and early breastmilk contain proteins that give the baby immunity, at a particularly vulnerable time, from organisms that enter through the intestine. As a matter of fact, factors in breastmilk that appear to confer immunity from viruses and bacteria are amazingly diverse. One that is particularly interesting is the form of fat in the breastmilk—monoglycerides and free fatty acids of a particular chain length—which appears to destroy certain viruses and bacteria by dissolving the fatty sheath around them.[2]

Breastfed infants get enough iron for their needs, but not too much. That balance is important to preserve the unique diarrhea-combating bacteria in their large intestines, *Lactobacillus bifidus*. Breastmilk contains a relatively small amount of iron, which the infant almost totally absorbs. Furthermore, that iron is carried on a protein called *lactoferrin*, which keeps the iron for the exclusive use of the baby. In contrast, only about 10 percent of the iron in formula is absorbed. Unabsorbed iron nourishes less desirable bacteria in the colon, such as *Escherichia coli,* a bacterium that can grow too much and thereby cause diarrhea.

Breastmilk is living. That may conjure up in your mind visions of little creatures swimming busily around, and it may gross you out. What I mean is that, for instance, the immunity-conferring substances (immunoglobulins) are in a form that can be destroyed by heating. The same substances are in cow's milk, in a form that is of benefit to the calf. But you must never, I repeat *never* give your baby or child unpasteurized cow's milk, because it might be contaminated. Since it is living, breastmilk can contain active substances that even help it digest itself. For instance, it contains lipase, an enzyme that helps the infant's immature intestine to digest fat. Taking breastmilk unpasteurized, directly from the breast, is a benefit formula can't duplicate.

Breastmilk is constantly changing. In some ways breastmilk for the newborn is different from that for the child a few months old; a specific example would be the variation in zinc levels. Also, within each breastfeeding, the first milk is quite low in fat and looks thin and bluish. Then as the feeding progresses it contains more and more fat, until most of the fat is produced in the last minute of nursing. The infant then stops nursing and will resume only with the lower-fat milk from the other breast. This may have something to do with signaling the infant to stop nursing. Breastmilk is nutritionally very nearly complete for the early months, with the exception of iron and vitamin D *for some babies.*

Commercial infant formulas are good imitations of breastmilk. They are digestible, we can generally keep them sanitary, and we are able to give them to our infants in adequate amounts to allow appropriate growth. Their nutritional adequacy is demonstrated by the healthy and robust babies they produce. Commercial formulas are complete to the limits of present knowledge—no supplements are necessary. Formula manufacturers respond to research on breastmilk by duplicating breastmilk components as much as they can. However, when manufacturers boast in their advertising of some new breakthrough in formulation and claim that their formula is "more like mother's milk," that does not mean that the nutritional gap between breastmilk and formula has closed. Such formulas may have the protein, the fat, and/or other ingredients in a form similar to that in breastmilk. Recently, for instance, formula manufacturers have been experimenting with nucleotides to try to duplicate the immunity-conferring properties of breastmilk. The nucleotides have helped a little, but babies on formula still don't show patterns of immunity as good as those of even partially breastfed babies.

ECONOMY AND CONVENIENCE

According to the American Academy of Pediatrics, breastfeeding is about half as expensive as the most commonly used formula (the liquid, concentrated formula that you mix with an equal amount of water). The academy estimated that the cost of extra food to support breastfeeding would be about $450 per year, compared with about $900 for formula.[2]

Giving your baby formula raises the issue of sanitation. For the newborn bottle-fed baby, you need uncontaminated, boiled water and nipples and very clean bottles—you'll learn more about this in chapter 6, "Formula-Feeding Your Baby." With breastfeeding, you can be safe, secure, and self-reliant about feeding your baby. You don't have to worry about the safety of the water supply or keeping enough formula in the house or having clean nipples or bottles. Breastmilk is clean, ready to feed, and just right for your baby's needs. My 4-year-old niece, Shelly, had her first exposure to breastfeeding when she watched me feed my then-infant son Lucas. Shelly got the idea right away. Including her mother in her later being-a-mommy play-acting, she lifted her shirt and plastered her doll to her flat little chest. "Yes, this is how I do it," she chatted. "All I do is hook him on right here. Isn't that just the handiest thing?" Breastfeeding *is* handy.

However, there is also the consideration of *where* you can breastfeed your baby. Social custom allows you to bottle-feed a baby in a restaurant, a waiting room, or any public place. It is ironic that social custom is not as free in defining acceptable locations for breastfeeding. You may be adroit enough or uninhibited enough to feel comfortable about feeding your infant almost anywhere, and I say "Good for you!" But the fact remains that at some times and in some places, some people will frown at your breastfeeding your infant. And *that* has something to do with convenience. On the other hand, keep in mind that it isn't always bad to have to retire and retreat to feed your baby. You are likely to welcome getting away from a crowd of people to have a quiet personal time for just the two of you. Some babies, in fact, need such a quiet place to eat well that you may find yourself retreating whether you are breast- or formula-feeding.

Is it more difficult to prepare bottles or to learn how to breastfeed? It seems to me to be a matter of individual judgment and preference, and I can argue on one side or the other equally well. It saves a lot of preplanning and packing to take the breastfed baby and disposable diaper and be all set for an outing. For long trips it's even better. On the other hand, you'll need to pamper yourself a bit more to help establish and maintain a breastfeeding relationship. Formula-feeding has the advantage of giving you more flexibility for coming and going. On the other hand, how much do you want to go when you are besotted with your new baby?

Which is easier? Again, it's a matter of your perspective. In chapter 5, "Breastfeeding Your Baby," you will learn a lot about mastering breastfeeding. In chapter 6, "Formula-Feeding Your Baby," you will learn a lot about mastering equipment and choosing formulas. Either feeding method will give you much to learn and will require your intelligence, sensitivity, time, and effort.

WORKING

Working outside the home will have a major impact on your decision whether to breast- or formula-feed. Many women are able to breastfeed even if they are working full time. It takes a cooperative baby, however, and sometimes babies wean themselves abruptly to the bottle. It appears to be most successful if Mom can have a pregnancy leave of at least a month to 6 weeks when she breastfeeds totally, to get her breastmilk supply well established. Then when she goes back to work her supply has a better chance of maintaining itself with nursing during the times she's at home. Appendix D, "Breastfeeding While Working," contains a more detailed discussion of the issues involved. It also helps to have a supportive work environment where Mom can pump and refrigerate breastmilk, or better still, get to her baby during working hours so she can breastfeed.

Bottle-feeding working mothers feel bottles are more desirable because their baby won't have to make a transition in feeding. They think they would end up formula-feeding anyway and don't think it's worth the trouble to get their breastmilk established. Bottle-fed babies don't have to make an adjustment from breastfeeding to formula-feeding. However, bottle-fed babies do have to make other adjustments in feeding when they go to child care. Everyone feeds differently, and the child care provider has to learn to read your baby's signals. Your baby will adjust. In the meantime, you don't need to deprive yourself of breastfeeding. Even if it is for only a couple of weeks, both you and your baby will benefit. However, whatever the reason for formula-feeding, both groups include parents who are concerned about their babies and have come to thoughtful and considered decisions about the feeding style that is best for their family.

SEXUALITY

Most of the change in your sex life and your personal relationship will come about because you have a baby, not because you choose to breastfeed. Whether you breastfeed or bottle-feed, babies take time and energy, invade your privacy, and change your sex life. With breastfeeding, there are additional factors that the two of you need to discuss. Whether you breast- or bottle-feed, you both will give your baby time, attention, and emotional involvement that previously would have been reserved for each other. With breastfeeding, it may seem that the mother-baby relationship is somewhat exclusive. It's important to talk about how you react to this. There may be little that can be done about changing the situation, but talking and sharing feelings can help a great deal to relieve anxiety and help keep you close.

Both men and women fear that breastfeeding will be an intrusion on their sexual relationship and worry that breastfeeding will lead to a loss of interest in sex. At times it is disturbing to men to see their mate's breasts, which they consider to be a sexual organ reserved for their erotic pleasure, used in a fashion that seems to be divorced from sexuality. The truth of the matter is that breastfeeding is *not* divorced from sexuality, either emotionally or physiologically. Masters and Johnson found that postpartum women who breastfed returned more rapidly to nonpregnant levels of sexual interest. Some women said they were more interested in sex when they were breastfeeding than they had been before they became pregnant.

This sexual association with breastfeeding can be a cause for concern. Some women experience sexual arousal from nursing; some don't. Those who do may worry that they are somehow abnormal. They aren't. All women, with the initiation of suckling, release prolactin from the pituitary gland, which causes uterine contractions during the feeding and for about 20 minutes after the feeding. This is one of the advantages of breastfeeding, as it enhances the return of the uterus to a more nearly pre-pregnant size. Some women experience sensations from the contractions as sexual; some do not. Others are not even aware that there are contractions. All are normal perceptions.

The sexual association with breastfeeding can go the other way as well. Sexual arousal and orgasm frequently are accompanied by milk dripping from the breasts. That is because breastfeeding and sexual arousal use the same nerve pathways and hormones. The hormones prolactin and oxytocin are secreted in response to suckling and allow milk secretion and milk letdown by the breast. The same hormones are released in response to sexual arousal.

The possibility that nursing will stimulate you erotically may be perfectly logical and acceptable to you. On the other hand, it may be alarming and disagreeable. Having milk drip from your breasts while you are making love may be a real turn-on for you—or a real turn-off. It's hard to know how you will react. It may be better just to take a wait-and-see attitude: try out breastfeeding, let yourselves feel what you feel, and then discuss it.

APPEARANCE

Most women are concerned about their figures. They are eager to return as quickly as possible to their pre-pregnant weight and shape, and they wonder how breastfeeding will affect that. Some have heard that they have to gain weight to breastfeed.

Most expect to lose weight when they breastfeed and are disappointed when they do not. Breastfeeding helps you lose your pregnancy fat. It might or might not help you lose weight.

Breastfeeding uses calories from your body as well as from your diet, drawing on the fat you stored during pregnancy. One of the ways your body prepares for lactation is by fat deposition during pregnancy. About a third of your weight gain during pregnancy is fat, which represents an immense calorie store— on the average about 28,000 calories. Breastfeeding allows you to utilize this calorie store in providing some of the calorie demands of lactation, which for the newborn usually start out at around 400 calories per day. As you draw on this calorie store you will lose that fat gradually. If you don't gain much weight during pregnancy, you will have to be particularly careful during early breastfeeding to eat enough.

Breastfeeding also forces you to be patient in your attempts to regain your figure because many women find that even if they lose weight while breastfeeding, their bodies go back to pre-pregnant size and shape only when they are no longer lactating. Dieting, especially strict dieting, to try to lose weight can impair your breastmilk supply. Generally, a weight loss of no more than a half pound per week is safe, but the best indicator is how you feel and how your body performs. To maintain your spirits, your energy level, and your breastmilk supply, you do need to eat enough.

My recommendation is that you feed yourself well and reliably, be active, and then see what your body does. I am opposed to weight-reduction dieting in general because I don't think it is good for you and in the long run can make you fatter rather than thinner. However, I am realistic enough to know that some people value dieting, are capable of it,* and are willing to put up with the discomforts of food deficiency in order to keep themselves stylishly thin. As far as milk production is concerned, you don't have to be as patient about waiting to diet when you are formula-feeding. But I still have my reservations about your dieting right after delivery. In my judgment it isn't physically or emotionally wise to cut down on food intake

---

*If you undereat and then overeat, however, you are not capable of dieting. In the long run your failed attempts at dieting will make you fatter, not thinner, and the quality of your diet will suffer.

when you have so many new demands on you. But in any event, dieting while formula-feeding won't impair the baby's milk supply.

SAFETY

A certain very small and variable percentage of every drug you take will show up in your breastmilk. To breastfeed, it is important to be as careful with alcohol and caffeine as you were during pregnancy. Smoking does not rule out breastfeeding but, as for formula-feeding, it is best to stop if you can. When you smoke, go away from your baby. Be very careful about your medicine selection and consumption while you're breastfeeding. Certain antacids, anticoagulants, hormones, anticonvulsants, laxatives, and all illegal drugs are absolutely contraindicated for use while breastfeeding. Chemotherapy drugs for cancer and drugs for control of AIDS are also out. In developed countries, women with AIDS are discouraged from breastfeeding because the breastmilk can pass the virus along to the baby. Women with active tuberculosis could give their baby the disease with the close contact of either breast- or formula-feeding. However, after the mother has been treated for 2 or more weeks, breastfeeding is okay. To find out whether the medications you take or the drugs you use will rule out breastfeeding, check with your physician and your pharmacist. The American Academy of Pediatrics regularly publishes updates on drugs and breastfeeding, and your consultants will have access to that information.

You also need to think about environmental contaminants when you are breastfeeding. Certain chemical pollutants in the food chain are excreted in the fat of breastmilk. The insecticide DDT was banned from general use years ago but is still present in breastmilk. It appears, however, that the maximum your baby is likely to get in breastmilk is several hundred times less than that known to cause acute intoxication in humans. In addition, it is somewhat cold comfort to know that the newborn already has more insecticide stored in body fat from exposure before birth than she is likely to get from being breastfed. In other words, the exposure is unavoidable, and it is unlikely that you will exacerbate the problem by breastfeeding.

More recent has been the concern about polychlorinated

biphenyls (PCBs) and polybrominated biphenyls (PBBs). The first is a heat-transfer agent, the latter a fire retardant. They are present in the food supply purely by accident, sometimes as a waste discharged into water from factories. These, too, are carried in body fat and are transferred to the fetus and to breast-milk. Currently most health authorities, on the basis of the absence of evidence of harm to infants from present levels of PCBs and PBBs in breastmilk, are recommending no change in current nursing practice. However, they are recommending that young women, especially if they are pregnant or lactating, limit their consumption of game fish from PCB-containing waters. Further, they are recommending that, if a woman has been exposed to known contaminants, she get her breastmilk ana-lyzed and decide on an individual basis whether to continue breastfeeding. If you fish, you can get up-to-date recommenda-tions on fish to eat and not eat from the back of your fishing license and your state health department.

Cows' milk contaminated with PCB is simply not allowed on the market. Further, these substances are stored in fat, and milk fat is replaced with vegetable fat in formulas, eliminating a substantial source of these contaminants. Commercial formulas, however, are not without their dangers. Unless handled proper-ly, they can be contaminated bacterially. Also, they have to be mixed absolutely accurately and properly. If formula is diluted too much it can make the baby grow too slowly. At the other extreme, if it is diluted too little it can make the baby dehydrat-ed. There have been mistakes over the years in formula produc-tion, and certain essential nutrients have been too high or too low. Those errors have been tracked down and corrected, but in the meantime babies have not done well.

SUMMARY

They say in the real estate world that the three important con-siderations in buying a house are *location, location,* and *location.* Beyond the situations that may force you to bottle-feed—the rare condition of being physically unable, a severely allergic baby, certain illnesses, or your having to take a medication that isn't good for your baby—the three important factors in your feeding decision are *feelings, feelings,* and *feelings.*

All your logic may tell you that breastfeeding is the most desirable alternative. But your feelings may say you don't *want* to. Don't let anyone—not even yourself—tell you you shouldn't be feeling that way. They are your feelings and they are valid. If you would like to change your feelings, that's another matter. Think about how you feel, and talk about it with your mate. Explore your feelings and see if you can find out where they come from. Step back and try to get a broader perspective on the matter. Your feelings may have something to do with the way you see yourself in relation to each other or in relation to the world in general. Your negative feelings about breastfeeding do *not* mean that you don't love your baby.

Find out how your partner is feeling. Keep in mind as you listen that there is room for each of you to have *different* feelings. You can only acknowledge and accept. You can't persuade or argue someone out of his or her feelings. Nor do you need somehow to change things to make the feelings go away. Sometimes that's possible, but often it's not. Consider getting some professional help if you have difficulty talking with one another, are very upset about making the decision, reacting in a way that puzzles or distresses you, or suspect that you have been traumatized in a way that impacts your decision. The more comfortable you can be with yourself and with each other, the more you will have to offer your baby. Not only that, but it will help you to have a joyful experience of parenting, no matter how you decide to feed your baby.

Spending some time exploring in this fashion *before* the baby comes, as you both decide on a milk feeding, is good preparation for *after* the baby comes. Then you may have ambivalence about many things, and you certainly will have feelings and reactions to being new parents. For that to be a joyful time that makes you closer, you must keep talking to one another. A major key in caring for your child is caring for your relationship. You will be steadier and have more to offer your baby if you support each other.

CHAPTER 4

UNDERSTANDING YOUR NEWBORN

CONSIDER THIS BRIEF CHAPTER an essential part of your reading whether you are breastfeeding or formula-feeding. Infant sleeping and eating behavior, developmental tasks, and temperament are all closely tied up with eating. The more you understand about your child the more you will be able to help and the more rewarding parenting your newborn will be for you.

FEED TO HELP YOUR NEWBORN WITH DEVELOPMENTAL TASKS

Feeding is so much a part of your child's early years that feeding and development are inseparable. At each age and stage, your child matures in certain ways and accomplishes certain behaviors so she can move smoothly on to the next maturational level and set of accomplishments. The first stage of development is *homeostasis*. Homeostasis is maintaining a relatively stable state of equilibrium—being calm in spite of outside stimulation and not too rattled to attend to the task at hand. A baby who has achieved homeostasis is organized: she can wake up, stay quiet and alert when she is awake, remain comfortably asleep when she is asleep, and make the shift from one state to the other with little commotion. A baby who has achieved homeostasis is easy to be around. She is not easily upset, and when she *is* upset she is relatively easy to read and calm down. You can figure out what the problem is and successfully apply the solution. Although she sleeps well, the baby who has achieved homeostasis doesn't sleep *too* much. She is able to wake herself up periodically and ask to be fed and stay awake long enough to eat as much as she needs. Hand in hand with a child's achieving a state of equilibrium is her ability to take an interest in what goes on around her. Each helps the other. An infant is calmed and relaxed by taking an interest in the world; her being calm and relaxed helps her to take an interest.

Achieving homeostasis takes time. At first your baby may be calm and alert only infrequently and for short periods. But as she matures, those periods increase in length and resilience. She will increasingly be able to deal with stress and unsettling experiences without getting flustered, calm herself down, and deal with the situation at hand or tune it out and avoid it. Keep in mind that those unsettling experiences can be both positive and negative. The excitement of talking with you can be just as unsettling as the aggravation of wet pants. You will see your baby engaging and then disengaging with you. She will look and seem interested for a time, and then turn her eyes away. She looks away to calm herself down and keep from being overwhelmed. If you wait and neither lose interest nor try to get her attention back, she will turn her attention back to you again, and the two of you can go back to looking or talking.

Once your baby is fairly good at maintaining her equilibrium, she will be ready to start working on attachment. That's the falling-in-love stage that begins at around two months of age, where your baby starts to smile and show delight in your presence. Attachment builds on homeostasis. For your baby to take pleasure in the outside world, some of the commotion within has to have subsided. An attached baby smiles and you smile back; she reaches out and you reach back. It's natural to respond, and essential as well. If attachment goes well, the infant emerges with such a sense of trust and confidence in herself and you that she can move into the next stage of development: the separation and individuation of the toddler phase. Your toddler develops a sense of her own autonomy by struggling to do things for herself, by exploring, roaming out, and even defying you. To take chances with you, she has to feel firmly attached. She has to love you and trust that you love her in return. On the other hand, the firmly attached toddler is less oppositional and more obedient than one who has been parented in a less supportive and responsive way. Child development studies show that toddlers are more likely to be compliant with direction and limits if parents have sensitively responded to them when they were infants.[1]

The stages and developmental tasks blend into each other, and a child doesn't stop working on one task when she picks up another. For instance, infants in general and the disorganized baby in particular continue to work on homeostasis—on being steady and calm—throughout the first year and even longer. For another example, babies start to work on autonomy as newborns through your respecting and responding to their cues in guiding the feeding process. However, autonomy doesn't become the *main* issue until toward the end of the first year. We'll look more at the beginnings of autonomy in chapter 7, "Feeding Your Older Baby," and we'll examine the continuation of the separation and individuation process in the chapter 8, "Feeding Your Toddler."

You certainly don't have to be the perfect parent, but you do need to do well enough during the first 6 months to allow your baby to make a good start toward achieving homeostasis and attachment. Your child's characteristics as well as your own can complicate the process. If, for instance, your newborn is particularly disorganized and irritable or sleepy, you may need help understanding and being successful with her before you can move to the attachment stage. Your life circumstances, attitudes, and feelings come into play as well. If you are preoccupied, overstressed, depressed, or afraid of spoiling your baby, you might not be as responsive as she needs you to be. If parents are unable or unwilling to respond, babies give up and stop being so engaging. To deal with negative patterns of parenting, you may need to seek outside help or examine your priorities. Keep in mind that early help is generally short term and can help you reap major rewards in your relationship with your baby. When parents change, infants change rapidly. Needing help is not a problem; needing help and not seeking it *is*.

Homeostasis and Feeding. A child is born unfinished. Her nervous system and gastrointestinal tract are still maturing and her brain is rapidly growing. All continue to mature over the first several months and throughout her second year. In fact, the period of rapid brain growth extends over the first two years of your baby's life. After they are born, some babies have more mellowing to do than others. One child will be born with such a touchy nervous system that she is erratic, hard to read, and difficult to settle; another will be steady and predictable.

Tuning In to Your Baby's Rhythms. Your baby's ability—or inability—to keep herself calm and alert will have an impact on feeding. Many newborns have trouble staying awake long enough to eat without getting jittery and fussy. Then it may be hard for them to make any sort of dignified shift from being awake to being asleep; they may fuss and scream and have a dreadful time settling down. Waking up again, they may be upset right off the bat, or they may have trouble waking up enough to eat. Having your baby get to the point that she can be quiet and alert when she's awake, reasonably composed about going to sleep, sleep for longer periods, and wake up again and be reasonably serene is part of the maturation process that takes place over the early weeks and months. Your baby may be born organized and able to comfortably manage her sleeping and waking cycles, or she may require considerable help over an extended time.

Feeding will go best when your baby is quiet and alert. Familiarize yourself with her sleep cycles, and do your best to wait to pick her up until she is *truly* waking up. During sleep, she will at times sleep deeply and quietly; at other times she will sleep lightly and move around, make noises, and even sound like she is waking up. Wait. She could just be going through a light sleep phase, and if you leave her alone, she could go back to sleep again. Most babies go through more than one sleep cycle before they are ready to wake up. Once your baby appears to be truly waking up, pick her up, change her diapers, talk with her, and wait until she gives you signs that she is fully awake and ready to eat before you try to feed her. If she wakes up fussing and crying, help her to calm down before you try to feed her. When she is ready to eat, she will look at you bright-eyed, curl up, and mouth and root for the nipple. When she is finished eating, she will uncurl and relax her arms and legs; she may come off the nipple, and she might even push away with her hand. She will get to the point that she will be awake for a while after she eats. Read her cues and put her down when she is drowsy but still awake, before she gets fussy and overstimulated. She may frown, yawn, squirm, hiccup, look away, or lose her bright-eyed look. Figure 4.2, "What Is Your Baby Telling You?" on page 122, lists baby cues and their possible meaning.

Giving your baby something to look at and be interested in helps her stay calm as well. Feeding her, talking with her, hanging a mobile over her crib, or carrying her around and letting her sit in her infant seat while you go about the house doing your tasks will all help with homeostasis. Notice that when you talk with your baby, she looks and talks for a while, and then she looks away. Looking away is her way of settling herself down from the all the excitement of the conversation, and the more excited she gets, the longer she takes to quiet down. Wait. Don't try to get her attention back, and don't wander off. She will return her attention to you. If you neither chase her nor wander off, her interruptions will get shorter.

Share Control with Your Baby. Your baby will calm herself down best and eat best when she feels you'll do what she wants. She is a fully social being, even at birth. She was born with a hunger to be understood and, like all the rest of us, will be most captivated and engaged—and therefore calm and organized—when she feels others are on the same wavelength with her. She will feel understood when you sort out her cues and properly decipher her messages about what she wants and needs. In Figure 4.1, "Control of Feeding," I have differentiated between approaches in which you and your baby share control and approaches in which you put yourself in control. The control-sharing approaches support homeostasis and the attachment that follows. The taking-control approaches undermine both. You share control in feeding when you keep your baby an active part of the feeding process. From birth, babies know how much they need to eat. You help your baby to be calm and organized *and* help her to eat and grow best when you depend on her feeding cues to dictate amounts. You support homeostasis when you work to calm and organize your baby, feed in a smooth and continuous fashion, and pay attention to what she tells you to guide the feeding process.

FIGURE 4.1 CONTROL OF FEEDING

You and your baby need to share control of feeding. You help her wake up and stay calm. Then you pay attention to what she indicates about how she wants to be fed and how much she wants to eat. Babies eat best when they feel you'll do what they want. Check yourself. Do you and your baby share control of feeding?

Parent and Baby Share Control	Parent Doesn't Share Control
• Pay attention to what your baby tells you	• Go by how you want to feed your baby
• Let your baby eat as much or as little as she wants	• Make your baby eat a certain amount
• Feed on demand	• Stop feeding before she is full
• Sit still when you breastfeed or hold the bottle still	• Make your baby go by a schedule
• Touch your baby's lips to let her "open up" for the nipple	• Move around during feeding
• Feed smoothly; don't interrupt	• Jiggle the bottle
• Try to solve problems	• Push the nipple into your baby's mouth
• Let your baby slow down or stop sucking	• Stop the feeding to check how much your baby eats
• Let your baby go back to eating after she pauses	• Jump to conclusions about why your baby does what she does
• Help your baby settle down if she gets fussy, and then offer more	• Keep on feeding when your baby turns away or shuts her mouth
• Take "no" for an answer	• Stop feeding when she slows down or stops sucking
	• Stop feeding when she fusses

To understand more clearly why the behaviors that share control *support* homeostasis, consider how the behaviors that *don't* share control *undermine* homeostasis. When you impose a feeding schedule, your baby will likely have to cry for a while before you feed her, or you may attempt to feed her before she is alert and hungry. Forcing her to eat when she doesn't want to will upset her and make it hard for her to settle down and eat well. Waiting to eat will also upset her, and she may get so tired from crying that she goes to sleep before she eats enough. If you feed her past the point that she indicates she has had enough in order to get her to sleep longer or to satisfy some outside prescription or agenda about feeding amounts, she will fight and resist, and feeding will end on a sour note. Afterward she will be upset, and that will affect her sleep. If feeding is unpleasant enough, often enough, she will develop lasting negative feelings and attitudes about feeding. She will carry her anxiety and upset *into* the feeding. She will learn that when she gets hungry, something bad is about to happen to her. Rather than relaxing and enjoying feeding, she will tense up and be upset before, during, and after feeding. If such early negativity persists, it can have a profound impact on her eating attitudes and behaviors, as well as on the way she feels about herself. On the other hand, newborns are flexible, and if you change your attitude and behavior, their feelings and behaviors change rapidly in response.

Be alert to your agendas in feeding, and set them aside. Your agenda in feeding may come from the way you treat yourself, your own dreams and hopes for your child, or from somebody's overreacting to your child's particular characteristics. Read the section "Vulnerable Children" (pages 212-215) in chapter 6. Keep in mind that if you become controlling with feeding, you are likely to create the opposite of what you intend. Parents often use taking-control methods to get a child on a feeding schedule, but such tactics actually make children less regular and predictable by undermining feeding. Control-sharing tactics help children to be the most organized, fully awake, and comfortable and allow them to eat best and last longest between feedings. Sometimes parents use taking-control methods to get their child to eat less or more. They don't work for that either. Children who are made to stop eating before they are satisfied become preoccupied with food and prone to overeat when they get the chance. Children who are made to eat more than they want become revolted by food, upset about feeding, and prone to undereat when they get the chance. The best indicator of whether you have an agenda that causes you to take control is whether or not you're having fun when you feed your baby. If you're not having fun, then chances are good that your agenda is getting in the way, and it's likely that your baby isn't having any fun either.

HELP YOUR BABY DO A GOOD JOB WITH EATING

In order for your baby to do as good a job as possible with her eating, it is important to time the feeding for when she's hungry, calm, and awake, but not overstimulated or exhausted from crying. Then work with her to help her stay calm and awake, feeding in a smooth and continuous fashion until she indicates that she has had enough to eat. Interrupt the feeding only to change breasts or to burp her if she seems like she is full of air. If she stops and seems comfortable, let her rest and look at you or talk a bit. Chances are that she is just taking a breather or wants to socialize. In fact, the pauses in feeding are generally social times for babies. If you hold off and don't get too active, the pause can give you a sweet little moment for you to enjoy each other before she goes back to the business of eating.

We can't think ourselves into your baby's skin, but let's try to understand what it might be like for her to have trouble waking up and staying awake to eat. Imagine yourself in a lecture right after lunch, fighting to stay awake. How tuned in and effective are you going to be? To get a feeling for what it must be like for your baby to be overstimulated, imagine yourself having had too much caffeine or feeling so overstressed that your nerves jangle. Like your baby, it will be hard for you to get organized and stay organized so you can do a good job with the task at hand. Now imagine yourself in that wonderful state of *flow*, where you are calm, awake, tuned in, and able to attend to the task at hand. Feeling that way is wonderful for you, and it is wonderful for your baby as well. She feels best, is the most sociable, and is able to do the best job with eating when she is calm and awake.

Help Your Baby Be Calm. Experiment with what allows your baby to stay calm and awake during the feeding. She may be able to manage it all by herself, or she may need particular help from you. Hold her about a foot from your face while you feed, and look at her. She will periodically look back but seem to be looking at your ear or over your shoulder. Initially babies' peripheral vision is most developed—they see best out of the corners of their eyes or to the sides. Babies are most interested in your face and eyes and will gaze longest toward faces or patterns of light and dark that resemble faces. Talk with her—she knows and recognizes *your* voice and will be interested. Experiment with your tone and tempo of speaking to see what your baby responds to best. You might find a sweet, soft voice works well, or a high-pitched talking-with-baby voice. Also experiment with making conversation. You might find that your regular talking voice is most interesting to your baby. At the same time as you experiment with what perks up and interests your baby, also be alert to what overstimulates her. That high-pitched baby voice may make her feel like she wants to get away.

Experiment with movement as well. Is her sucking more sustained and regular when you rock or when you stop rocking? Experiment with how snugly or loosely you hold her, how upright or flat. Do be sure to hold her firmly enough so she doesn't feel like she will fall, but loosely enough so she has a little room to maneuver. She will be most relaxed and organized if her feeding position is good—line up her ear, shoulder, and hip; have her head straight or her chin tipped up slightly. Be mindful of how you touch her, and do it slowly, smoothly, and gently but firmly. Does she become more calm and alert when you stroke her arms, hand, legs, back, or tummy, or when you hold your hand still? Touch her in a way that *you* enjoy being touched. Generations of parents have been taught to tickle their babies to wake them up—under the arms, under the chin, or on the bottoms of the feet. Think about it. How do *you* like to be tickled? Your baby might not mind or she might even *like* it, but if she seems irritated and shows signs of tuning out, the way you are touching her may be upsetting for her. Your baby will let you know she is overstimulated by looking away, breathing fast, yawning, frowning, or losing her bright-eyed look. Keep in mind that it isn't *you* she is reacting against but only what you are doing. You are tremendously important to your baby, and your being positive with her will allow her to enjoy being with you even more.

Avoid using irregular, jerky movements, because they irritate and disorganize babies and make it hard for them to do a good job with eating. Studies have shown that a baby will eat and grow less well when the feeder jiggles her, jiggles the bottle, pulls the nipple out of her mouth and puts it back in again, burps her frequently, repeatedly checks the level of milk in the bottle, frequently rearranges the blankets, and tickles the bottoms of the baby's feet.[2] These methods for waking babies up and getting them to eat are such a part of the tradition of parenting that you may even be taught them. Tradition is wrong on this one—the methods *absolutely* do not work. Babies enjoy eating and interacting *less* when they are tormented, and the sensitive, tuned-in feeder certainly does not enjoy tormenting an infant.

YOUR BABY'S SLEEP AND AWAKE STATES

The understanding of infant sleep states is primarily the result of the observations of pediatrician and author T. Berry Brazelton.[3] His work was applied and demonstrated in further detail by University of Washington nursing professor Kathryn Barnard.[4] Their work forms the basis of this discussion. Like adults and older children, babies cycle in their sleep and awake states as follows:

• Quiet sleep (no rapid eye movements, or REM)
• Active sleep (REM)
• Drowsy
• Quiet alert
• Active alert
• Crying

During sleep, babies cycle from quiet to active sleep and perhaps back again. A drowsy infant will first go into a period of active sleep, then quiet sleep, then active again. She might begin to wake up at that point and enter an even more alert, drowsy state, or she might cycle back through active sleep into another quiet sleep stage before she returns to active sleep and wakes up further to the point that she is drowsy. At that point, she will benefit from your waking her up further to the quiet alert state in which she will do her best job with eating. Observational research in newborns shows the sleep cycle to last about 60 minutes with a range of 60 to 90 minutes. Quiet sleep occurs for 15 to 20 minutes of the 60 minutes, and active sleep takes from 35 to 60 minutes during that time.[5] At the end of the sleep cycle, the baby comes out of active sleep and moves into a drowsy state before beginning to wake up more fully and progressing to the quiet alert state.

Your task is to time your care and socializing for when your baby is finished sleeping and is ready to become quiet and alert.

Let her be when she is sleeping quietly. The quiet sleep state is relatively easy to identify because she will lie quietly, not move, breathe regularly, and be generally unresponsive. It won't work to try to wake her up when she is sleeping quietly, and it is possible that any amount of commotion can go on around her and it won't disturb her sleep. However, until you know your baby well, it's harder to distinguish between the active sleep state, in which she will cycle back to sleeping quietly again, and the drowsy state, in which she is preparing to wake up. Only trial and error will allow you to make the distinction. The more you are able to tell, the better feeding will go. A not-ready-to-wake-up baby won't wake up thoroughly and won't be as alert and organized as she needs to be to do well with feeding.

In both the drowsy and active sleep states, your baby may move around more; she may flail about with her arms and legs, make noises, and breathe irregularly. The actively sleeping baby may move her face and even smile, and her eyes may move under her closed eyelids. The drowsy baby will open and close her eyes and have the kind of glazed, heavy-eyed look that you and I get when we stumble out of bed in the morning. If you're not sure what you're seeing, leave your baby alone. She may go back to sleep, or she may wake herself up.

The trick is adjusting and timing your caretaking so your baby doesn't get flustered and fussy. If she gets overstimulated or too hungry, she will move out of the quiet alert state, become more agitated, and move into an *active* alert state, in which she will move her body more, lose her bright-eyed look, develop a dull-looking face, and start to fuss. If she gets more agitated and upset still, the next step, of course is crying. Crying is a late hunger cue and an unnecessary one. It is best to catch your baby in the quiet alert state and feed her them. See Figure 4.2, "What Is Your Baby Telling You?" for more description and explanation of infant cues.

Beyond the basics, the variations are endless. One baby will bring herself all the way up to a quiet alert state without any help, and another baby will start to fuss the minute she starts to wake up. Still another may sleep so long that she needs you to intercept her drowsy periods to help her wake up to eat. For that baby, catching her during either active sleep or her drowsy time will allow you to help her to wake up fully.

FIGURE 4.2 WHAT IS YOUR BABY TELLING YOU?

Here are some clues to the sign language your baby might use to let you know how she is feeling and what she needs. Keep in mind that to really understand your baby, you need to know what is going on around her–what has happened before, when she has eaten, when she has slept. Also keep in mind that you will see a variety of cues–the idea is to look for the predominant ones. Finally, keep in mind that these cues are just places to start in understanding what your baby is telling you. It won't be long until you know her best of all; then you will be able to understand far more clearly than anyone else what message her behavior carries.

I'm hungry or I want to talk
Looking at your face
Moving her hands and arms
  toward you
Turning her head toward you
Smiling
Smooth movements of her
  arms and legs
Raising her head
Eyes wide and bright
Face bright

I'm *really* hungry
Making loud feeding sounds
Fussing

I'm full
Stops nursing
Relaxes

Arms and legs extended
Fingers extended

I'm *really* full
Pushing away
Crying or fussing

I need a break
Looking away
Breathing fast
Yawning
Forehead wrinkled
Dull-looking face and eyes
Frowning

I *really* need a break
Back arching
Pushing hand toward you
Crying, fussing
Falling asleep

Getting Ready to Eat. Like our early-morning selves, your drowsy baby needs help waking up more fully before you feed her. You quite naturally do this by picking her up, talking with her, and turning on the light so you can see to change her diapers. Even newborns perk up when they have something to look at or listen to that interests them, like something shiny or colorful hanging over the changing area. Soon your baby moves into the quiet alert state in which she will realize she is hungry and announce that fact to you. Her announcement may take many forms: she may look at your face, move her head, arms, and legs and even her whole body toward you, and her movements will be smooth. Her eyes may be wide and bright, and in fact her face will look bright. She won't show you all of these signs, and she may show you some I haven't mentioned. You soon will know she is ready to eat by her own distinctive messages, and you will also note that she won't eat well until she is ready.

As is apparent from our discussion, newborns not only have trouble waking up enough to eat and socialize but also are vulnerable to becoming overstimulated. Keep in mind that your infant comes from the dark, unvarying, relatively quiet place of the womb into a light, noisy place full of sights, varying light and dark, smells, and sounds. For her, it must be like it would be for you or me to move onto the midway of the county fair! Most babies are born prepared for the excitement, and they have ways of internally screening too much stimulation. Their ability to sleep deeply and remain in that state despite considerable efforts to wake them up is an example of the ability to screen out stimulation. In addition, when they are in other states of alertness they can soothe themselves by closing their eyes or sucking on their hands or a pacifier. You soothe your baby by wrapping and holding her gently but firmly and moving in a slow, repetitive, rhythmic way. Some babies have a very low tolerance for stimulation, are easily set off into upset screaming, and quiet down only with difficulty. Others are steady and appear to be relatively impervious to stimulation coming from the outside, or they can help themselves to settle down by sucking or by going to sleep to get away from commotion. For babies who have immature digestive systems, the stimulation appears to come from the inside as well, in the form of stomachaches or gas pains. Such babies not only can't screen out the commotion of the midway, they must feel like they have eaten too much cotton candy!

Be Consistent with Your Unsettled Baby. Prematurely born babies or the temperamentally irritable babies we'll talk about later in this chapter are harder to read and harder to tune in on. It's a real trick getting on the same wavelength with them. They have difficulty waking up, and when you try to help them wake up to the quiet alert state so they can eat, they can easily get flustered and start fussing and crying. Then it is hard to settle them down so they can do a good job with eating. The understandable error that parents of such unsettled babies often make is casting about, trying first one solution and then another, like changing formulas, changing nipples, and changing soothing methods. All of that changing just stimulates the baby all the more. Only time fixes it, and in the meantime you have to maintain within yourself your conviction that you truly are a good parent. Do look for outside encouragement, support, and problem-solving help, and do avoid so-called helpers who are critical and blame you for your baby's problems.

If you have such a baby, keep trying and doing what you know to be the right thing, even though your baby can't consistently respond to it. Your baby's maturation and your tuned-in caretaking will pay off eventually. Such babies are especially hard because, *even if you are doing the right things,* for the first few months little helps. As a consequence, there is no way to learn what is effective or ineffective and refine your methods. Such babies don't give you much help with parenting because they can't help *themselves.* Most often, with newborns, we learn our methods of comforting, soothing, and organizing from our babies: If it works, we keep on doing it. If it doesn't work, we discard it. Many times, our trial and error sorting isn't even a conscious process. Parents who start out jiggling bottles, for instance, stop doing it within a couple of weeks because they unconsciously note that their baby starts sucking again only when they stop jiggling.

Sleep Cycles Become More Defined. Right after she is born, your baby may sleep for long stretches and her sleep cycles may be somewhat mushy and ill-defined. After the first few days she may sleep for only short periods and then be awake for short periods. She will eat often and irregularly and is likely to show patterns of cluster feeding, in which she wakes up and wants to eat every hour or so for 2 or 3 times in a row, then sleeps longer before asking to be fed again. As your baby gets older, she will sleep longer, show more clearly defined sleep cycles, and stay awake longer. Most babies know the difference between night and day and will sleep longer at night. Keeping the night feedings dimly lighted, calm, uneventful, and as brief as possible helps to make the distinction. During the first few weeks your baby may stay awake a couple of hours at a stretch, and by three months she may increase her awake time to 3 hours.

Put your baby back down to sleep when she is drowsy but still awake. She will tell you she is getting tired by looking away, breathing fast, yawning, wrinkling her forehead, frowning, and acquiring a dull look. If you can catch those early "I need a break" messages, she will be able to settle herself down to go to sleep more easily. She might fuss a bit, but it will be a singing-to-sleep kind of fussing. If you miss the early messages that she needs a nap, she will get more upset and stimulated and give you the message "I *really* need a break." Then she will arch her back, push her hand toward you, fuss, and cry. At that point, she may find it harder to settle herself down to go to sleep, and she may need some help from you. Sing to her or talk with her in a slow, steady, soft voice; swaddle her, rock her, or walk the floor a bit and let her suck on her hands or a pacifier. You will find additional suggestions on page 131. Whatever method you choose, do it slowly and over and over again to give it time to work. Once she is calm and drowsy, put her to bed. Even if she fusses a bit to go to sleep, you will have helped her to settle down so she is no longer so upset she *can't* go to sleep.

That all adds up to quite a tall order. You need to read your baby's sleep states and catch her when she's awake but not *too* awake. Then your task is to help her stay awake while she eats without having her get upset. Enjoy her while she wants to be enjoyed, and then put her down when she has had enough— when she is drowsy but not overstimulated. It isn't easy, and it is a process of trial and error that you will continue during her early months. Celebrate the moments when you and your baby are on the same wavelength, and chalk the other moments up to experience. Your baby helps by getting more predictable and more settled. Eventually, despite all this complexity, you will become an expert at reading your baby and doing what she needs.

UNDERSTAND YOUR BABY'S TEMPERAMENT

Your baby was born with certain personality characteristics, including activity level and regularity. As she grows, these characteristics will both persist *and* be modified by life experience. The most famous and far-reaching study of temperament was

FIGURE 4.3 PERSONALITY CHARACTERISTICS OF INFANTS AND YOUNG CHILDREN

The most famous and extensive study of temperament is called the New York Longitudinal Study and was done by psychiatrists Alexander Thomas, Stella Chess, and Herbert Birch. According to their findings, babies in their first days and months of life differ in the nine personality traits listed here. The descriptions and examples in each category are mine. I am sure as you read through this list you will be aware that both negative and positive qualities have their appeal. A baby who moans and wiggles with delight when she is fed may also be the one who is mightily offended if you happen to do something not to her liking. You can't have the one without the other.

Activity level. An active baby might kick a lot in the uterus and move around a great deal in the bassinet and ever after. She will squirm when she is fed and changed and probably won't be very cuddly. A less active baby will sit quietly in your arms or lie quietly in her bed.

Approach-withdrawal. One baby will delight in anything new, whereas another will be more wary and shut down or get upset. The first bath will make one baby laugh and another cry. One baby will enthusiastically devour the first spoonful of cereal, and another be outraged by the offer.

Rhythmicity. One baby might be absolutely predictable and sleep, eat, and even have her bowel movements at predictable times. Another baby will rarely show the same pattern twice and then only by chance.

Adaptability. Most babies don't accept change immediately, but the more accommodating one gets used to new circumstances far more quickly. A flexible baby will easily fall asleep in a new bed after a night or two; a less adaptable baby may take

(continued next page)

conducted by psychiatrists Alexander Thomas, Stella Chess, and Herbert Birch. According to their findings, babies in the first days and months of their lives differ in the nine personality characteristics outlined in Figure 4.3, "Personality Characteristics of Infants and Young Children." In terms of combinations of personality traits, these researchers pointed out that most young infants can be described as one of three types. They described about 40 percent of infants as *easy*, 15 percent as *slow-to-warm-up*, and 10

FIGURE 4.3 PERSONALITY CHARACTERISTICS OF INFANTS
AND YOUNG CHILDREN (CONTINUED)

weeks to become fully comfortable with the new environment.

Intensity of reaction. One baby will moan and wiggle with delight when she is fed and act mightily offended if she gets done eating and you fail to immediately stop feeding. Another will be more neutral. She will be tuned in and give feeding cues, but her expressions won't be so emphatic or revealing.

Degree of responsiveness. One baby will seem to sense every sight, sound, and touch, another will tune out the loudest noises and the brightest lights. One baby may eat well only in an environment with few distractions; the other will not be deterred from eating even by the greatest amount of commotion.

Quality of mood. One baby will show mostly a positive, joyful, and friendly attitude; another

will be less friendly, perhaps more sober, sad, or more easily offended. Most babies are somewhere in between the extremes.

Distractibility. All babies show hunger cues when they want to eat, but some will stop asking for a few minutes if you give a pacifier or sing a song. Others are absolutely single-minded and will not be deterred from being fed.

Persistence and attention span. These two attributes are in the same category and are generally related. A persistent child will continue to pursue an activity in the face of obstacles, and the child with a long attention span will pursue an activity for an extended time. One baby will struggle to get her fingers to work so she can pick up food from a high chair tray. Another baby will give it a few tries and then wait to be fed.

Thomas A, Chess S, Birch H. *Behavioral Individuality in Early Childhood.* New York: New York University Press, 1963.

percent as *difficult*. Notice that 35 percent of normal infants don't fit into any of these categories. Despite my considerable respect for the insights this work has given us, I must tell you that I am not comfortable with the terms *easy* and *difficult*. They tell more about agendas for children than they do about the children themselves. In *Child of Mine*, rather than using those value-laden terms, I will use more descriptive terms and may call "easy" children relaxed, calm, or organized and "difficult" children tense, disorganized, irritable, or unsettled.

And that is, indeed, what the terms mean as they are used by these experts on temperament. Thomas, Chess, and Birch describe the "easy" baby as having regular sleeping and eating patterns, a positive approach to new situations, easy adaptability to change, and an overall mild or moderate mood. It is easier to be successful with such babies. Their regular patterns and moderate responses make them easy to read, understand, and satisfy. Fortunately, 40 percent of babies fit into this category, and in the best of all possible worlds all first babies would be relaxed babies! The babies researchers described as "difficult," through no fault of their own or anybody else's, are uptight, negative, erratic, unpredictable, and difficult to read. When these pessimistic and disorganized babies get upset, parents tend to feel somewhat anxious because the babies are difficult to console. The babies sleep and eat irregularly and are likely to react negatively—and emphatically—and withdraw when they are presented with new situations or new people. It takes irritable, disorganized babies a long time to get used to anything new, including new food. I feel moved to observe as I have elsewhere, however, that bewitched parents of even the most challenging child tend to remain unswayed in their conviction that they have the *perfect* child.

Like the negative child, the slow-to-warm-up child is wary of new situations and new people, but she is more *skeptical* than downright rejecting. She adapts slowly, and her patterns of sleeping and eating are somewhere between the two extremes: not as organized as some, but not as disorganized as others. This child tends to be wary of new food experiences rather than offended by them. The babies that don't fit in these three categories show other combinations of attributes. To read more about infant and child temperament, see the book *Know Your Child: An Authoritative Guide for Today's Parents* by Chess and Thomas.[6]

To help yourself with negative extremes in your baby's temperament, keep a few points in mind. First, you didn't cause it. For whatever reason, your baby *came* that way. Second, you absolutely have to stow your agenda. The unsettled, aggressive baby is full of surprises, and you might as well relax and enjoy them rather than trying to change her. Third, while your task early on is to help your baby be as calm and organized as she can be, in the long run she will need to learn to manage *herself*. Eventually, the strongly reacting child can learn to calm herself down and deal with her own extreme reactions rather than simply imposing them on other people.

Much of that learning comes from the way you interact with her. The irritable and negative child can become more moderate in her responses. You can help, for instance, by reading her cues and stopping feeding when she *says* she wants to stop rather than making her *insist* that you stop. The cautious child can learn to manage her own anxiety and move ahead *at her own speed* into the situation that makes her anxious. Being careful not to overwhelm her will help. If you brush her lips with the nipple and wait for her to open up before you try to feed her, she will get early experience with getting *herself* to do what needs to be done. These interactions repeat themselves over and over as your child gets older. Both the reactive child and the cautious child will push along to learn and grow *as long as we don't force them or rescue them*. If we do force or rescue them, their negative tendencies will only be exacerbated.

HELP YOUR BABY TO QUIET HERSELF

After your baby gets through the first few weeks of the newborn period, it will be helpful to begin gradually teaching her to settle herself down. You will, of course, continue to help your baby settle down, and certainly it is always okay to pick her up and provide help, comfort, and support. Babies who are held lots don't get spoiled. They actually cry less than babies who aren't held as much, and as I pointed out earlier, they are more compliant as toddlers.[1] However, it doesn't have to be one or the other, and both you and your baby will benefit from her learning to settle *herself* down. A baby who can't calm herself down can keep you too busy and worn out trying to do it for her and can lead you to expect less of her later on—and she of herself. You won't always be able to take care of stresses for her and make her way smooth, so eventually she has to learn to remain calm in the face of upset or to tune out stimulation that is too much for her. Furthermore, there is the matter of sleeping through the night. While she will be too young to do that during her early months, her learning to calm herself now will hasten her being able to sleep the night through. Let me tell you why.

Based on parent surveys, Michigan psychologist and infant sleep researcher C. Merie Johnson observed that parents will try just about anything to get their children to sleep at night.[7] They nursed them to sleep, eliminated naps, let them sleep in the same bed as parents, and actually placed puppies in the crib. In my own observation, many times feeding problems start in the name of sleeping. Parents may prematurely start solid foods or put cereal in the bottle in the erroneous belief that solid foods will get their child to sleep through the night. Some parents force food on their children in the evening in hopes that eating more will make children sleep all night. None of these tactics work, because they don't deal with the heart of the problem.

As Johnson reported, sleeping through the night isn't actually sleeping without stopping all night long. Adults as well as children wake up at night. For adults as well as for infants, the trick is to be able to stay relaxed and go back to sleep. Older infants and toddlers who don't regularly sleep through the night haven't learned to soothe themselves to sleep and have instead come to rely on "signaling" their parents to help them back to sleep. Conversely, a child who is able to settle herself down will be able to soothe herself back to sleep when she wakes up at night. That way, when she gets to the point that she is no longer hungry at night, she will simply put herself back to sleep. Formula-fed babies get over their night hunger sooner than breastfed infants. In fact, many breastfed infants continued asking to be fed at night until they were weaned. Infants who slept in the same bed with their parents were two to three times more likely to wake at night than those who slept alone. In the month preceding the survey 70 percent of children with sleep problems had slept in the parents' bed all or part of some night, compared with 23 percent of the group without sleep problems.[7] Sleeping with parents can also be dangerous for babies, as indicated by recent reports of infants who smothered or were injured falling out of bed when they were sleeping with their parents.

Johnson's research makes the sleeping—and parenting— issue pretty clear. Your baby will do what you have taught her to do. Although it is fun and rewarding to feed or rock a newborn to sleep and easier at first to keep a baby in bed with you, that fun and reward won't go on forever. Keep in mind that by the time your child is 7 or 8 months old, you will get tired of getting up at night to feed or rock her back to sleep. At that point, remember that she isn't being a bad and uncooperative child. She is actually being very cooperative and indeed doing exactly what you have led her to believe you want! Rather than waiting for yourself to get fed up with the night routine, begin preparing her during her early months for sleeping through the night by helping her learn to calm herself when she wakes up. During the day, if she wakes up fussing and crying after naps, go through the little calming-down routine that follows. You don't have to use all the methods, but do go through a progression of less to more, using one approach after another until your baby settles down. Give each approach about 20 seconds, and then if she is still crying, add another.

- Leave her alone to see if she can quiet herself.
- Show her your face. Lean over and look at her so your face is about 10 inches from her face and remain quietly in that position.
- Still looking, talk with her in a normal voice or whatever voice she prefers.
- Still leaning over and talking, put your hand gently on her tummy and hold it there.
- Still leaning over and talking, restrain one or both of her hands gently against her chest.
- Wrap her snugly in a blanket, still looking and talking.
- Pick her up and hold her snugly against your chest, still looking and talking.
- Add on rocking back and forth, still looking and talking.
- Put your finger or a pacifier in her mouth, still rocking, looking, and talking.

This is a method that was described by Kathryn Barnard based on her observational work with newborns.[4] As your baby matures, you will need to go through fewer and fewer of these steps, until she is able to be quiet and entertain herself for a few minutes after she wakes up. Of course, as she becomes more aware of what goes on around her and more physically capable, much of her quieting will come from her being able to look around and entertain herself by cuddling her blanket, feeling her toys, or looking at something suspended over her crib.

Knowing that your baby would put herself back to sleep if she could will help you later on. When she gets to be 8 months old and you want her to sleep through the night, you won't have to lie in bed listening to her cry and guessing whether or not she is hungry. If she calls out for you, it is likely to mean that she really *needs* you. Breastfed babies take longer to get over getting hungry at night than formula-fed babies. As I pointed out earlier, most breastfed babies don't sleep through the night until they are weaned. Be as matter-of-fact as you can about the night feedings, and don't assume you are doing something wrong. Getting up at night with a baby isn't nearly as tiring or upsetting if you don't start questioning either yourself or your baby.

It should be obvious from this discussion that I am *not* in favor of making young infants cry it out as a way of getting them to sleep through the night. In fact, I am strongly opposed to letting newborns cry it out to get them to sleep through the night. The vast proportion of newborns are in no way nutritionally, emotionally, or developmentally ready to make it through the night without care and feeding.

HELP YOUR BABY WITH ATTACHMENT

If all has gone well with homeostasis, at about age 2 to 3 months your baby will begin to work on the falling-in-love of attachment. As I said earlier, to effectively move on to the next stage in development—from homeostasis to attachment—she has to have more-or-less achieved the one at hand. To be able to take an interest in you, to tune in, reach out, talk back and forth, smile and laugh, she has to have gotten her nervous system pretty much under control. Think of your jittery and overstimulated self. How sociable are you? Think of your tired and sleepy self. How much do you want to hang out and have a good time with other people? I rest my case.

Around the age of 2 to 3 months, your baby begins learning to love you and learning that you love her in return. The same control-sharing approaches that you used to help her with homeostasis now become important in helping her with attachment. She will feel loved—and loving—when she feels understood. By feeding your baby the way she wants to be fed, you're sending her a powerful message: You see her and hear her, you care about her, and want to give her what she needs.

During this stage, your baby will learn to delight in socializing with you. When she smiles and babbles to you, reaches out to you, listens to you, and watches you, she's trying herself—and you—out. Your taking an interest, responding a lot of the time, and initiating the smiling, laughing, reaching out, and affection some of the time will make her feel secure and loved. You give and receive love in the whole give-and-take that goes on in feeding as well. She shows signs that she is ready to eat, and you show your love and respect by feeding promptly. She lets you know whether she wants to eat fast or slowly and whether she wants to eat continuously or take breaks to socialize. Your willingness to go along with her makes her feel warm and loving toward you and good about herself. She is able to think, on whatever level babies think, "I must be pretty special to be treated this way." Whether your baby eats well or poorly depends on her feeling connected with you. She wants to eat, but just as important, she is interested in *you*. She watches, smiles, babbles, and reaches out to you to get your attention and keep you close. When you follow her lead in feeding and watch, smile, babble and reach back, you help her feel connected with you, which in turn helps her feel calm and tuned in to her own feelings of hunger and fullness. Take time to talk and smile gently, but don't be overstimulating or entertaining. Since babies and young children are easy to overwhelm, respond quietly with less energy than she put into it. Let her keep the lead. By this time, she will be better at giving you clear signs, and you will be better at knowing what her signs mean. You will be more able to feed her promptly, when she is calm, alert, ready to eat, and neither too sleepy nor overstimulated.

Play Games with Your Baby. Outside of feeding time, to help you get on the same wavelength with your baby, try this: Put her in an infant seat and sit directly in front of her. Have a pleasant expression on your face, but don't smile or laugh. Sit quietly and look at your baby, and let your baby look at you. When she makes a sound or a gesture, imitate her. Do your imitating gently so you don't overwhelm her. Let her be in charge of the interaction. When she looks away, sit quietly and wait. When she looks back, be prepared to imitate her again. You'll notice that your baby brightens up and takes an increased interest in you. She is getting the message that you see her and hear her, but that you're not going to try to take over. It makes her feel good that you take an interest in her.

Not only are you connecting with your baby, but she is getting her first taste of taking turns, which becomes more apparent as she gets on toward 6 months. Of course, you have been taking turns all along in your feeding interactions. Now it becomes a more conscious process for your baby, and one that she delights in. Taking turns is the first step in learning the social art of conversation and arriving at an intellectual understanding of cause and effect. Your baby at this stage will love having you do everyday tasks in repetitive ways. If you brightly say "up you come" before you pick her up, eventually you will see her moving her arms and legs toward you as she anticipates being picked up. Give her time to respond before you pick her up. Just as we do in our conversations with other people, she will prefer "telling" you and having you respond rather than having you run the conversation. Singing a little song, "here we go to get some food" will let her have the pleasant anticipation of being fed, and she will eventually wait more patiently if feeding is a bit delayed. The good spoon feeding that we talk about in chapter 7 is another example of taking turns. You offer the spoon and wait for your baby's response. She opens her mouth and leans forward to take the food in her mouth and close her lips. You take the spoon out, fill it, and offer it again. Both you and your baby are honored by such turn-taking. Your baby gets the reward of your respectful attention as well as enjoying eating and satisfying her hunger. You get the reward of observing and responding to your baby's initiative as well as interacting smoothly with her.

Babies love repetitive games that go with predictable gestures and words, and eating is the best repetitive game of all. They love being able to anticipate what happens next and participate in the action. Patty-cake and peek-a-boo can be played as short repetitive games. But the games that are most fun are the ones that you will happen upon and make up as you go along. "Up you come" can be a repetitive game, as you say the words and lift your baby from a lying down to a sitting position, over and over again. You will find your baby tensing up and lifting off a bit to participate in going up. "Kiss your ear" can be a perfectly inspiring game. After a few times of your tipping her back to say "kiss your ear," then forward to kiss her, she'll start to take an active part. She will be slow on the uptake, so be sure to give her time to play her part. She will tip her head forward and lean toward you, then back again as you hold her away. It's all just too captivating for words, and the fact that you are doing it makes it simply the best. However, keep in mind that such thrilling play can also overwhelm your baby, so periodically she will have to stop, look away, relax, and give herself time to settle down. If you wait, she will return her attention to you and be ready to play more. Don't chase when she gives herself one of these little time-outs, and don't wander off. The more able you are to wait her out, the more ready she will be to return to the game.

Baby games and the early relationship you establish with your child form the basis for everything that comes after. One stage flows into the other. The infant becomes the toddler and then grows into the child. It's so good to be a part of all of this!

CHAPTER 5

BREASTFEEDING
YOUR BABY

IF YOU FEEL AWKWARD and somewhat intimidated the first time you breastfeed, you are not alone. It is all new and strange, and you may not even have had the chance to watch someone else breastfeed before. You are even less likely to have had enough instruction to have a working knowledge of the process. Breastfeeding has traditionally been solely a woman's activity, and new mothers would have an experienced woman teach them how to breastfeed. If you have someone in your life who can do that for you, you are the lucky exception. Make sure, though, that she teaches both you and your partner. He is an important part of the process, and he will need to know the principles for when it's just the two of you figuring things out. If you don't have a partner, recruit someone to be your support person.

In our culture, breastfeeding and getting to know a new baby is now more of a couple issue, with new and equally inexperienced fathers being the primary support people. This chapter is written for you, Dad, as much as for you, Mom. In her surveys of graduates of infant intensive-care nurseries and

For her help in reviewing this chapter and giving advice about current practices in breastfeeding, thanks to Certified Lactation Consultant Susan Clark, MS, RD, Lactation Management Services, Midland, Michigan.

their parents, Karen Pridham, a professor of nursing at the University of Wisconsin, has found that young mothers most often identify their baby's father as being their primary source of support for issues like amounts, spacing, and timing of feedings.[1] This is a team effort. Although babies are tough little creatures who are adapted to making up for inexperience in their parents, it is nonetheless frightening to have responsibility for such a precious little life. You simply need to help each other and share the responsibility for the decisions you make as you combine your mutual observations and ingenuity to understand your baby and do what is right for him. Neither of you has to be an expert. Baxter Black says, "you miss more by not *looking* than by not *knowing*." I especially like that quote because, after all, Baxter Black is a cowboy veterinarian, and he was talking about *sick horses*. What could be more manly than that?

You also have a lot to get accustomed to. Breastfeeding isn't terribly hard, but it may seem so during the first 3 or 4 weeks. Think about the last time you learned to do something that required both development and skill, as well as a close collaboration with another person, like dancing, singing, sharing a task, or occupying the same physical space. How long did it take until you worked smoothly together and got most of the bugs out of the process? Like those processes, breastfeeding depends on a sophisticated relationship between two people and the functioning of body parts in a way that they haven't had much opportunity to function before. It takes time to get everything working and to get on the same wavelength.

My goal in this chapter is to give you the basic information as concisely as possible. There is a better supply of good people and good information than there was 20 years ago when I first wrote *Child of Mine*. Health professionals are more positive about breastfeeding, and the certified lactation consultant has become a mainstream professional. Almost any community has a lactation consultant who can advise you, and you can expect your hospital or clinic to help you get hooked up with one. There are also good books, and I'll give you some recommendations at the end of this chapter. But even with the availability of this good information and support, I have been surprised and gratified at the number of people who tell me, "I read your breastfeeding chapter over and over when I was breastfeeding, and it helped me so much." As a consequence, beyond some rearranging and taking some liberties with my stories to reflect our times, this chapter has not changed much from the first edition.

A COURSE ON BREASTFEEDING IN TWO SHORT PRINCIPLES

Thriving while breastfeeding depends on the mother's ability to produce breastmilk and make it available to her baby; it also depends on the baby's ability to stimulate the breasts and nurse, digest, and tolerate the breastmilk. For a summary of the issues, see Figure 5.1, "Checklist for Successful Breastfeeding," on the next page. Most babies and most mothers have the necessary health and physical attributes to breastfeed. A very few do not. Assuming that you do, we will turn our attention to the two main issues in learning how to breastfeed.

- You need to understand the principles of breastfeeding, master the mechanics, and provide yourself with support.
- You need to read and evaluate your baby so you know that breastfeeding is going well.

Let's take a look at two sets of new parents as they began learning these principles.

A TALE OF TWO BABIES

Janet and David, Martha and Robert were all first-time parents. Both mothers had good pregnancies, carried their babies to term, and had normal deliveries. Both delivered in a hospital with a supportive nursing staff who helped them with the details of getting started breastfeeding. The nurses were understanding and didn't seem to be at all surprised that Martha didn't even know how to hold Zachary and that Janet had a rather difficult time knowing how to position herself comfortably while keeping Emily's back and neck straight so she could suck and swallow well. Emily was so pliable that it seemed like trying to straighten out a noodle! Finally, one nurse said, "tummy to tummy," and that made both of their positions fall into place.

FIGURE 5.1 CHECKLIST FOR SUCCESSFUL BREASTFEEDING

Any amount of breastmilk is good—the more the better. Most of the problems in breastfeeding grow out of lack of support by our culture, lack of education, and lack of skilled guidance by health practitioners. As you review this list of your contributions and those of others to breastfeeding, I think you will be surprised at how many people it takes to breastfeed a child. That is positive for everyone. We all benefit when we are allowed to support young families and participate in raising children.

Mother's contributions
☐ Good health
☐ Eats well enough to feel good, be steady, relaxed, and positive
☐ Gets pretty good rest
☐ Has a relaxed, positive attitude
☐ Follows baby's cues in feeding
☐ Understands supply and demand
☐ Has moral and situational support
☐ Avoids street drugs and minimizes alcohol and smoking
☐ Asks for help when she needs it

Baby's contributions
☐ Can wake up and stay awake to nurse
☐ Eats often enough
☐ Has a good suck and suck-swallow pattern
☐ Mouth and throat are normally formed
☐ Mouth is large enough to fit on mother's breast
☐ Has the energy to breastfeed
☐ Stomach and intestines work properly
☐ Has enough pees and poops

Family's contributions
☐ Gives emotional support, like listening and encouragement
☐ Gives situational support, like accepting and encouraging breastfeeding, doing housekeeping, and running errands
☐ Gives parenting support, like observing the baby and feedings
☐ Provides a calming presence

Health care provider's contributions
Before the baby comes
☐ Discusses particular concerns about breastfeeding
☐ Discusses benefits of breastfeeding
☐ Physically assesses breast and nipple
☐ Teaches about infant feeding and care
At the hospital or birthing center
☐ Appropriate management of anesthesia during labor
☐ Breastfeeding-friendly policies and procedures
☐ Knowledgeable and skillful staff
Following discharge
☐ Recommends follow-up visit early after discharge
☐ Problem-solving and guidance

Work place contributions
☐ Allows sufficient leave time
☐ Gives breaks to go to the child care site or to express breastmilk
☐ Provides a private place for expressing breastmilk and a cold storage place
☐ Provides close-in parking places for new parents (oh, fabulous day!)

Child care center contributions
☐ Offers flexible feeding procedures that support breastfeeding

Each mother needed the nurse's encouragement to go through the process of getting well settled in a comfortable chair, putting a pillow on her lap, and settling her baby in the crook of her arm to nurse. Janet appreciated being helped to nurse while lying down, but Martha preferred sitting up. Both had read about positions and preparations in books, but they were surprised at how awkward and self-conscious they felt as they actually went through the motions. At each feeding the nurses were careful to start the babies on alternate breasts, and they even suggested keeping track with a safety pin on the bra cup. While that seemed to be a silly suggestion at first, both mothers found they had so much coming at them that they had difficulty remembering.

All the parents were surprised to see their babies behaving in such predictable ways. The nurse showed them how stroking the baby's cheek nearest the nipple made the baby turn toward the nipple, and right on cue, each did, mouth open, searching for the nipple. Martha was particularly startled when Zachary latched on to her breast. It was remarkable to see so much of her nipple and areola disappear into that tiny mouth. He put so much pressure on her breast with his jaws that it almost hurt—in fact, it *did* hurt a little when he first latched on! Zachary seemed to know all about getting properly attached and nursing.

Emily was not as quick getting going. She seemed to be satisfied to take just the very end of the nipple in her mouth, and when she clamped down it hurt a lot! The nurse showed Janet how to give Emily some help latching on by flattening her nipple and areola between her thumb and forefinger* and pressing in toward her chest wall, then placing it into Emily's mouth. It also seemed to help if she extended Emily's neck and tipped her head back a bit, because Emily's mouth came open further and she could latch on better. But even when Janet managed to do all that—and it seemed like a lot—Emily seemed to do better on the right breast than the left. When the lactation consultant stopped by, Janet hesitated to even mention that because she wondered if it was just her own awkwardness that created the problem. To her surprise, the consultant picked right up on her

---

*Using your thumb and forefinger to compress your nipple is called the *C hold.* If that seems awkward or like your fingers get in the way, try the *V hold,* where you compress your breast using your forefinger and second finger.

observation and wondered out loud whether Emily was having trouble getting her suck going. She put her finger in the baby's mouth, fingernail down, gently rubbing the roof of Emily's mouth until she actively started to suck. After the consultant showed Janet and her husband how to do the same thing, she quickly placed Emily on Janet's breast and Emily did fine: she took the nipple and areola and sucked well.

Each couple was surprised at their baby's willingness to nurse just to get the small amount of clear to yellowish colostrum that was available early on. But it was worrisome to all of them to be discharged from the hospital before the breastmilk came in, and the sample formula kits looked pretty appealing. However, the dietitian who visited reassured them that the milk would come in soon enough. In the meantime, colostrum seemed to be satisfying for the babies, and it conferred such important immunity factors that it was wise just to let the baby have the colostrum. It could be that the baby gets only about 50 to 100 calories a day from colostrum, but since it takes babies a few days before they really work up an appetite after being born, the colostrum seems to do the trick until the milk comes in.

Both babies had alert pediatricians who asked their parents to return for a clinic visit about 5 days after they were released from the hospital. By that time, both mothers' breastmilk had come in, and all were interested to see that it was, indeed, thin and bluish-looking and that the milk toward the end of the feed was creamier and more opaque looking. That confirmed what they had read about the variation in fat content between the "fore," or early milk in the feed, and the "hind," or later milk. Janet said her breasts were full, and she was very aware of let-down—she could feel a tingling and prickling in her breasts. Martha said her breasts were softer and she couldn't feel any letdown, although she could tell by Zachary's slower, longer sucks when he started getting milk.

Despite all the commotion of getting everything pulled together for the very first outing, David was alert enough to ask the pediatrician what she was checking Emily for on that early visit. "Jaundice (yellowing caused by normal breakdown of the newborn's extra red blood cells),* dehydration, and general

---

*For a discussion of jaundice, see pages 194-195.

signs that your baby is healthy," she answered. "We also check on breastfeeding—whether the milk has come in and how the feedings are going. By now we like to see about 6 or 8 wet diapers a day, and many of those diapers should have at least a little poopy yellow stain." Both sets of parents and both babies passed muster, both babies had gained some weight since hospital discharge, and Emily had gained back to her birth weight. Both sets of parents were advised to schedule a second visit in a month's time. Robert wasn't comfortable with that idea, especially since Zachary hadn't gained back to his birth weight, so he asked whether they could come back sooner. The pediatrician reassured him that all was well, but Robert persisted, and they scheduled a visit 2 weeks later.

After that visit, our stories diverge. Janet and David's baby became increasingly active, demanding, and dissatisfied. Emily slept irregularly and woke up yelling and seemingly starved. She wanted to nurse at least every 2 hours all day, although there was really no pattern to it, and she woke up at least twice nightly to eat. She was an eager nurser and had a powerful suck. She had no patience with an empty breast, would come off yelling, and stopped fussing only when her mother switched her to the other breast. Then she also rapidly emptied it and looked around for more. It was hard to know what she really wanted and hard to help her to be settled and content. She took short naps and was soon up again, demanding to be held and comforted and entertained, and she soon nursed again.

David helped all he could by getting Emily up and bringing her to Janet for the night feedings, and by diapering, soothing and dressing her during the day, but Janet was getting pretty worn out. David worried out loud that Emily's eating so often and seeming so unsatisfied meant that she wasn't getting enough to eat. Then in the same breath he would announce to himself that he surely was changing a lot of wet, poopy diapers, and that was supposed to mean things were fine. They kept track of Emily's pees and poops for a few days, making hatch marks on a piece of paper, feeling embarrassed the whole time for being so anal. But it turned out to be reassuring, because her output was just what they had been told it should be. It didn't help, though, when a visiting acquaintance was critical of how often Emily ate and even suggested that Janet's milk disagreed with her and that Janet should give her a bottle so she could get

Emily on a schedule. Janet and David knew they'd been hit with a couple of those wrong ideas about breastfeeding that made people grab a bottle whenever the going got tough, but the whole episode upset Janet anyway. She was feeling so insecure that she couldn't take much at that point. David told the friend politely but firmly that Emily was doing just fine and they wouldn't be using any bottles any time soon. Janet put in a call to the breastfeeding consultant they had liked in the hospital. After asking a few questions about—what else, pees and poops, and how Janet was feeling—the consultant reassured them that they were doing very well. That helped a lot, but between the two of them they still worried and had to reassure each other all over again that they were on the right track.

Martha and Robert seemed to be having an easier time of it. For one thing, Martha's mother had come to stay with them for a couple of weeks, and that helped them feel calmer about taking care of Zachary. They were still nervous, even if Zachary was such an easy baby. He slept for 3 to 4 hours at a time; then when he woke up he was still sleepy. During nursing he did a lot of starting and stopping and often drifted off before he had made much headway on the second breast. Martha's mother kept an eye on things and wondered if that was all right, but she didn't say much about her concern for the first day after the clinic visit. But the next day, after she went to change Zachary's diaper and found it dry for the second time, she announced that she was afraid Zachary was too sleepy for his own good and needed some help in staying awake to eat.

Martha's mother wasn't entirely sure how to do that, especially since she had read *How to Get Your Kid to Eat . . . But Not Too Much* and realized the tactics that the nurses had shown them in the hospital were all the ones that Ellyn Satter said were just irritating and made babies eat less, not more: jiggling, tickling the bottoms of the feet, stopping the feeding often to burp the baby. They did unwrap Zachary and sit him up, but he still seemed very sleepy. Finally, in desperation, Martha's mother suggested talking with him. Martha started by talking in a gentle, soothing, commenting sort of voice, but her mother said, "try experimenting with your voice, and seeing what makes him take an interest." He seemed to prefer it when his mother made conversation with him, so Martha chatted away while she fed him, telling him all about how beautiful he was and about his trip home from the hospital and anything else she could think of. Zachary brightened right up, his eyes came wide open, and he ate steadily. Throughout the feeding he looked intently at a spot right above Janet's right ear. Between feedings, Robert held him close to his face and talked to him as well. That seemed to perk Zachary up for a while longer before he started to squirm and lose interest, when they would put him down for another nap. Within a day of more-frequent waking, Zachary started to wake himself up more often and more thoroughly to be fed, and after another day or two his increased output of pees and poops made them feel they could trust him again to do his part of the job.

Martha and Robert still weren't sure about how Zachary was doing, however, until they went in for the 2-week check Robert had asked for. It turned out well—Zachary had gained back to his birth weight and seemed to be doing just fine. They told the nurse practitioner about Zachary's being so sleepy, and she asked them a lot of questions about it. She told them they had done the right thing. However, she went on to say that from now on they should wake him up every two hours to eat. She gave them more advice about how to help Zachary wake up and stay awake: unwrap him, sit him up, move him around, and talk with him briskly. They told her that similar tactics hadn't helped to wake him up, and she pointed out that they had to work with him for 10 or 15 minutes before he would wake up well.

They tried putting Zachary on the 2-hour schedule, but it didn't work very well. They didn't feel comfortable doing all those waking-up things to him when he seemed so tired. Furthermore, he didn't eat as well when they woke him up rather than letting him start to wake himself up. So they went back to following his lead with sleeping and eating, while at the same time they kept a close eye on his nursing behavior and on his pees and poops. He did fine. He kept himself for the most part on an irregular 2- to 3-hour schedule. Once in a while he would wake up after an hour or so and want to be fed and might even want three feedings close together. He slept about 4 hours at a stretch at night, but since his output continued and since he stayed awake during feedings, they decided they could again go by what he told them. Surprisingly, he seemed for the most part to prefer the widely spaced feedings, especially in the early afternoon and at night, sleeping easily three hours at a stretch. But when he woke up, he woke up thoroughly, ate well, and even stayed awake for 20 or 30 minutes around eating time. And of course, they had gotten in the habit of keeping an eye on his pees and poops, and his output was fine. When they went back for their 1-month checkup, they found he had continued to do well.

In contrast to Martha and Robert, it was an exhausted, harassed, and insecure Janet and David who presented Emily for her 1-month checkup. To her parents' astonishment, Emily had gained almost 3 pounds in that short time. They protested that there must be a mistake, pointing out how unsatisfied she seemed to be and how frequently she wanted to nurse. The physician's assistant reassured them that Emily's demanding to be fed often and eating thoroughly each time was exactly what she needed to do to get breastfeeding off to a good start. Emily's eating schedule, although it seemed hectic and pressured, was just right for her and was apparently helping her to thrive. Knowing that, her parents were able to relax and quit feeling like they were doing something wrong. As a result, Emily's eating schedule, even though it didn't get any less frequent for another month or so, wasn't as wearing on them.

THE PARENTS' PART OF BREASTFEEDING

The experiences of these new parents represent more or less the normal extremes of newborn nursing behavior and give some idea of what you might expect. Emily and Zachary challenged their parents in different ways, and both sets of parents did well in reading the signs and evaluating what was going on with breastfeeding. That is not to say that it was easy. They were anxious and unsure of themselves and felt more comfortable only after the breastfeeding and parenting began to feel more familiar to them. It helped even more when they got some outside confirmation that their infants truly were getting enough to eat.

Anatomy, Production, and Letdown of Breastmilk. Both Janet and Martha had done their reading, but their bodies still taught them some early lessons about the anatomy, production, and letdown of breastmilk. Let's discuss those issues in more detail.

By the time we finish, I think you will be able to see why it takes a while for a newly lactating body to get the whole process going!

Anatomy and Proper Latching On. Janet and Martha both had good instruction in getting their babies properly latched on the breast so that not only the nipple area but a significant amount of the areola, the colored area surrounding the nipple, was in the baby's mouth. To understand why that's important, we have to know something about the structure of the breast. Take a look at Figure 5.1, which shows a cross-section of a lactating breast. As you can see, the milk-producing parts of breasts look like bunches of grapes. The "grape" is the alveolus, which is made up of the cells that are the milk factories of the breast.

FIGURE 5.2 CROSS-SECTION OF A LACTATING BREAST

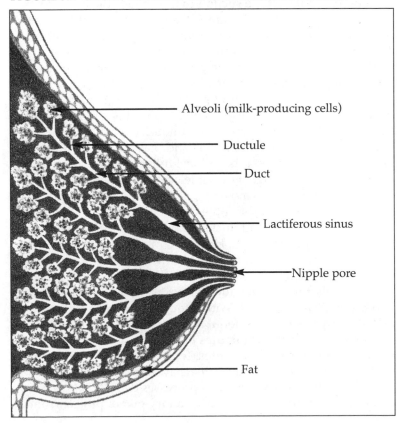

Alveoli (milk-producing cells)

Ductule

Duct

Lactiferous sinus

Nipple pore

Fat

The stems leading from the clusters of alveoli are the ductules that carry the milk to a series of increasingly large ducts until the milk is fed into one of the 15 to 25 lactiferous sinuses, which will be described in more detail below. From there, each of the ducts carries milk to a pore, or opening in the nipple. In case you haven't made the connection, there are 15 to 25 pores, as well, which spray the milk into the baby's mouth in a fine mist.

The lactiferous sinus, an enlarged part of each lactiferous duct, is under the areola and/or the margin of breast with the areola around $3/4$ to $1 1/2$ inch back from the nipple pore. Noting this bulging area in the duct will help you understand the principle of proper latching on. To get milk from your breast, your baby's jaws and lips have to be far enough back to squeeze the lactiferous sinuses and express the breastmilk through the pores in your nipple. He uses suction to keep the nipple and areola in his mouth, but it isn't the suction that provides the milk, it is the squeezing action on the sinus. It's the principle of the water pistol. Your baby's jaw is the piston; the sinus is the chamber.

However, as with the water pistol, the sinus has to be loaded in order to get anything out of it, which brings us to making the distinction between *production* and *letdown*. Within 3 to 5 days after you have your baby, you will begin to produce breastmilk in the alveoli of your breasts. That is a more-or-less automatic process for all but a tiny minority of women. You will know that the milk is "coming in" and that the alveoli are producing because your breasts will feel fuller and heavier and you may have some leaking. Only some of that fullness and heaviness is milk production; most of it is increased blood and lymph circulation to your breasts. Some of that breastmilk will find its way into the ductules and ducts, and when your baby starts to nurse he will get some milk. However, most of the milk is made on the spot and delivered to your baby by the letdown process. During letdown, tiny muscles around the alveoli contract and force the milk through the duct system we just talked about and into the lactiferous sinuses. With letdown, you get a flow of milk that rapidly delivers about 50 percent of the milk to the sinuses within the first 2 minutes of nursing, about 80 to 90 percent within the first 4 minutes. It takes longer than that for the baby to get it out, but the milk is available.

The production and letdown processes depend on the secretion of two hormones from your pituitary gland, prolactin and oxytocin. Prolactin stimulates milk production; oxytocin stimulates letdown. Like an assembly line, you simultaneously make milk and deliver it to your baby during the nursing process.

Production of Breastmilk. During pregnancy, the milk-producing anatomy of your breasts grows and develops, and by somewhere in the second trimester you become capable of milk production. The alveoli multiply in numbers and mature to the point that they can produce milk, and the transportation system forms and matures (the ductules, ducts, and sinuses). However, while much of the *capability* is there, you don't actually *make* milk until your baby suckles. Right after he starts suckling and all the while he suckles you release a hormone, *prolactin*, from your pituitary gland. Prolactin not only stimulates the alveoli to continually make milk and release it to the ductules, but also more-or-less continually stimulates the alveoli and ducts to increase in numbers. When your breasts "empty" at any nursing it is because the immediate supply of ingredients—components for making breastmilk—decreases. That supply is rapidly built up, after which time you again are ready to produce. Between nursings you make some breastmilk and your breasts may seem to fill up, but for the most part you are restocking the biological shelves to produce more breastmilk for when your baby nurses again.

When your baby has hungry days and eats often, you make more prolactin, which in turn stimulates breastmilk production *and* growth of more alveoli and other breast tissue. Your baby is hungry, not because your breasts are empty but because his needs for breastmilk have exceeded your ability to produce enough at any one time. As you nurse longer and more frequently, you release more prolactin, grow more milk making and delivery structures, and are able to produce more breastmilk.[2]

The shorthand method is to speak of this process as "filling" and "emptying" the breasts. That's fine, but understanding the *actual* process is important in guiding your tactics and preserving your peace of mind during those unavoidable hungry days. One young mother was told by her doctor that nursing any more often than every 45 minutes didn't help increase milk production because it took the breasts that long to fill up again. Others say they hear over and over again that it takes 2 hours. The upshot of that bit of misinformation, of course, is that nursing mothers become preoccupied with waiting for breasts to fill up, which hardly ever happens during a baby's hungry days. If the baby wants to nurse after half an hour, such advice makes it seem hopeless to feed him. As a consequence, hungry days go on for longer and mothers are more anxious than they need to be. The take-home message? If your baby wants to eat after half an hour, feed him. You will be able to make milk again because most of the milk is made when your baby asks for it.

Letdown of Breastmilk. While breastmilk is produced and released by the cells of the alveoli, the letdown process squeezes it from the breast alveoli into the ductwork. Oxytocin, another pituitary hormone, is responsible for activating this letdown process. Oxytocin, like prolactin, is continuously manufactured and stimulates letdown while your baby nurses. In the early feedings after birth, it may take 3 minutes or more of nursing before you begin letdown. After a few days, your hormone production will pick up and you will generally begin to let down within 30 seconds after you start nursing, or even when you hear your baby cry—or even when someone else's baby cries. You may find yourself letting down at odd times and not even be aware of why you're doing it—maybe a subtle smell or sound. That is the letdown of the relatively small amount of breastmilk that you make between feedings.

Some women feel a tingling sensation, a feeling of pins and needles, beginning right after they start nursing and then going away gradually; others feel nothing at all. The letdown hormones cause contractions of the uterus as well, and sometimes women can feel those contractions, ranging from mild to painful. Other women get a sensation of intense thirst. With letdown you will probably get dripping or even spurting of milk from the breast your baby isn't nursing from. Even if you don't feel or see anything, you will be able to tell you are letting down because your baby's nursing pattern will change. His suckling will slow down, and he will take deeper swallows.

Without the letdown reflex of those tiny muscles, the infant could get only the small amount of milk that is stored in the duct system, the milk would not be removed from the ductules, and the milk-producing cells would get the message to make less milk. Although we hear a lot about letdown problems, your frequent nursing will get your letdown working well during the first week. However, in case you worry about it, as a lot of people do, and since anxiety and tension can interfere with the letdown process (and what new parent isn't anxious and tense), you may also benefit from having some tactics to help yourself with letdown. You'll find such tactics in appendix C, "Helping Yourself with Letdown."

Get Ready to Breastfeed. Wash your hands thoroughly before you feed your baby, especially if you have just finished changing his diapers. Be particularly careful to wash your hands if you have been working with raw produce or meat. For more about sanitation, see pages 239-241 in chapter 6 and also see appendix R, "Food Safety." The bacteria that are on your breasts are all familiar to your baby, so you don't have to do a lot of nipple washing or sanitizing or clothing sterilization. Your regular showers will do.

Get yourself something to drink and a snack if you are hungry. Turn on the telephone answering machine. Put a "no soliciting" sign on the door. Make a mental note of which breast you are starting on so you can start with the other one at the next feeding, or use a safety pin on your bra cup to help you remember.

Get Comfortable to Breastfeed. In the early months, most of the time you will spend with your baby will be when you are feeding him, so it is important for you to get as physically comfortable as possible. If you aren't properly positioned, breastfeeding (or formula-feeding, for that matter) can be a real backbreaker.

First, get a good chair that supports your back and arms and fits your body. Support your feet well on the floor, or get a stool that props your feet up at a proper height so that sitting doesn't put a strain on your back. You can get a breastfeeding stool that raises your feet and supports them at an angle so you can relax your leg and back muscles. I think such a stool makes a good investment. Also consider getting a breastfeeding pillow—tell your support system that either makes a wonderful gift. Go to your favorite baby store and check out the models available. The best pillows are shaped so they curve around your stomach and give your baby space to lie flat and comfortably on his side across your stomach. The pillow needs to be wider under your elbow to give support while you hold your arm under your baby's neck and head. The pillow has to be the proper height to allow you to relax the muscles in your arm and back as you hold your baby to your breast.

Most mothers find that they nurse sitting up most of the time, but other positions may be helpful to you as well. While she was still in the hospital, Janet appreciated being able to nurse while lying down, and Emily seemed to like it too. Janet did a lot of her night feedings that way, and she felt that it helped keep her from being so tired out with Emily's frequent needs for feeding. Most times, Janet didn't really go back to sleep while she fed Emily, but she would doze and rest, and David stayed awake so he could put Emily back into her own bed when she finished eating. They worried about leaving her in bed with them the rest of the night for fear they would roll over on her.

Some mothers like using the football hold to nurse their babies. That's where you hold your baby on his back under your arm, with his head forward, as if he were a football. That works best if you are sitting up in bed with pillows propping up your back and the nursing pillow with the wider end forward. Both the football hold and lying down to nurse are helpful early on for changing the pressure points on your areola to avoid getting so sore in any one spot. You may get sore and tender and be aware of some discomfort each time your baby starts nursing, but if everything is going well, the discomfort will decrease. If you get sharp pains in your nipple area, check right away to see that your baby is latched on properly. If he is and the pains don't go away after a couple minutes of nursing, do some problem solving or get in touch with your breastfeeding consultant. Also see the section on evaluating your baby's suck on pages 170-171.

Understand How to Produce Enough Breastmilk. Breastfeeding works by a law of supply and demand, so your breastmilk supply will match your baby's needs. Emily was a hungry baby who continually pushed her mother to make plenty of breastmilk. Zachary, however, was not so hungry, at least at first, so he wasn't as helpful to his mother in getting and keeping up her breastmilk supply. His grandmother's detecting his too-sleepy patterns early was important, because if Martha's breasts had been understimulated much longer, she could have decreased her production quite a lot and not been able to keep up with Zachary's hunger for a while once he woke up and got started eating better.* Getting too far behind can be a problem. If they had waited until the 2-week check to catch Zachary's sleepiness, Martha would have had to work to build up her breastmilk supply (see the discussion on pages 162-164 about hungry days), but she probably could have done it. If they had let that pattern persist until he was a month old, Zachary could have been dehydrated and may have needed to be formula-fed for a while, and he may also have needed medical intervention such as intravenous feedings to get him back on track. The formula *is* necessary because a baby must be getting adequate calories to be a vigorous feeder. Oral rehydration fluids, glucose water or sterile water, are not good substitutes for formula because they don't give enough calories.

As your baby gets bigger and hungrier and needs more breastmilk, at times you won't make enough. This is not the beginning of the end, but only a normal part of the process. Your baby will be less satisfied at feedings and will want to eat more frequently. The solution to is to nurse more often. Stimulate your breasts more often to produce, and your breasts will respond by generating more milk-making anatomy and producing more breastmilk. Getting your production capacity shifted up to a higher level may take a couple of days during which your baby will be demanding and restless. But you'll catch up again, and you and your baby will be in balance for a while. Those catch-up days are hard and may make parents wonder whether breastfeeding is worth the effort. Keep in mind that it is nature's way, that being moderately hungry for a couple of days before getting enough to eat is a necessary and not-overwhelming frustration and that nobody's life is free of aggravation. Letting your baby cope with his own hindrances is important learning for you, as well, because it makes the point that you can't really make his way entirely smooth, even at this young age. You might also notice that, like all adversity, having

---

*Sometimes, if the mother gets too worn out or far behind the baby's needs, it's necessary to give a relief bottle or two while the baby builds up his supply. It's a balance—your baby needs to be hungry to nurse well, but if he gets too hungry he may be more sleepy and won't be as energetic about nursing as he could be. The idea with relief bottles is to phase them out once you get caught up again.

to put up with being hungry for a day or two teaches him something. After a couple of restless and wakeful days you will likely find that your baby is more alert and tuned in to what is going on around him.

Feed Often Enough, but Don't Give Snacks. Your breastfed baby is likely to eat often—every 2 hours or less—and at irregular intervals. Your baby's temperament has a lot to do with his feeding pattern. Some babies like Zachary are just naturally regular in their habits—with a baby like Zachary, you both fall into a fairly predictable feeding and sleeping pattern. Zachary seemed to get caught up in the mornings from his long night stretches by cluster feeding—he would eat twice in as many hours, or even three times; then he seemed to be comfortable enough to go a longer stretch in the afternoon. This pattern of cluster nursing is typical, especially for babies who sleep relatively long stretches. Emily's pattern was also typical, even if it was harder to live with. She was irregular, demanding, and dissatisfied. She rarely did the same thing twice. Babies like Emily tend to be more easily agitated and have more trouble getting organized. Only time takes care of the problem—trying to force a schedule does not. In fact, it makes the situation worse and it can also destroy your attempts to breastfeed. Your breastfeeding baby may have to nurse 8 to 12 times per day in the early weeks. That is tiring, especially when combined with all the other care required by a new baby. I once figured out that, on the smoother days, the feeding, changing, washing, cleaning, caring, and adoring of a new baby takes about 6 hours.

Although frequent feeding is the norm, you may not be so happy if your baby gets into a snacking pattern in which he nurses for brief periods even more often than usual. You can make the distinction by the quality of his nursing. Snacking is when he seemingly asks to nurse, takes just a few swallows, and then falls asleep or loses interest. Like any little snack, it is only briefly satisfying, and he'll be hungry again soon and do it all over again. While you don't want to force down the number of feedings, that snacking pattern isn't the best for your baby or the breastfeeding. Nursing so briefly, he may get only the low-fat fore milk and not the higher-fat hind milk he also needs. On the other hand, in cultures where women keep their babies with them constantly and use a very frequent feeding pattern with shorter intervals between feedings, it appears that feedings have consistently higher fat concentrations.[3] Lacking any definitive answer on this issue, I would suggest you look at your milk. If it's blue, it's low in fat. If it looks creamy, it is higher in fat.

The solution to snacking is not trying to stave your baby off or forcing him to eat, but rather helping him to regulate his sleep cycles. Staving him off could make him frantic and upset so he won't be able to do a good job with feeding. Trying to get him to eat more at a feeding so he'll last longer in between makes feeding unpleasant for both of you and may take away his ability to know when he's hungry and when he's full. As I point out in appendix J, "Children and Food Regulation: The Research," studies show that babies actually eat less and grow less well when parents try to get them to eat more than they want. So how do sleep cycles come into it? To eat well, your baby needs to be fully awake and focused during the feeding. He needs to be alert but calm, not so stimulated that he is agitated and upset. Martha and Robert's tactics with Zachary are a good example of how you can help your baby be both calm and wide awake for a feeding. They waited to get him up until he was really starting to wake up; then they talked with him to help him stay awake. For a more thorough discussion of sleep patterns and for suggestions about how you can help your baby learn to be a good sleeper, refer back to chapter 4 and also see the section "Do What Your Baby Needs So She Can Eat Well" on pages 205-211 of chapter 6.

Keep Feedings Moderate in Length. Feeding a newborn can take an hour by the time you feed, burp, change, and play. Most of that has to do with your inexperience and need for contact rather than with your baby's need for nursing. A hungry, vigorously sucking baby can get much of what the breast has to offer at any one time in 4 to 5 minutes, most of it in 7 to 10. After that, it's just a trickle. If you let him nurse for 15 minutes on each side, that is more than long enough, provided he is actively nursing. There is really no need for you to make the feeding more than 20 to 30 minutes in length, although if you like letting your baby continue to suckle longer it's fine. If you don't enjoy that prolonged suckling, and if your baby continues to have a strong sucking need, it is okay to use a pacifier. Wait until your baby is about 6 weeks old, when you get breastfeeding well established. Then *offer* the pacifier, but don't insist on it. Don't put honey on the pacifier because it could give your baby botulism, a type of food poisoning. Studies in Brazil, where the pacifier is a standard part of every baby's equipment, show that pacifier use only interferes with breastfeeding when a baby is pressured strongly to take it.[4] It can lighten your load a good bit to know that your baby doesn't have to nurse so long at any one time to get enough. Some mothers think they should nurse 45 minutes or more, and if their baby wants to be fed every 2 hours or so, they spend most of their time nursing.

To hold down on feeding times, don't overdo the ritual that goes along with feeding. Elaborate hand and nipple washing may just be wearing you out. At night you might consider using heavier diapers to cut down on the amount of fussing that goes along with feeding time. The more quiet and the less commotion you have for the night feedings, the more likely it is that your baby will go sweetly right back to sleep—and you will as well.

When your baby gets a little older—around 4 to 6 months—you are likely to see the length of feedings decreasing a good bit. Older babies nurse fast and get on with what they were doing. They often come off the breast to investigate any distraction, or worse yet, try to look around without letting go! Because babies this age can often empty a breast in 5 minutes or less, their mothers worry that they are not getting enough to eat. Their mothers also miss the long, quiet, intimate feedings. But those older babies seem to be able to maintain and even increase milk supply on fewer feedings and still benefit from even the brief intimacy. Do keep an eye on growth rate in these middle-aged babies, and if your baby doesn't seem to be growing as fast as he needs to, go back to your strategies for increasing breastmilk production. Review the discussion of what is normal growth on pages 34-38 of chapter 2. Rest more, nurse more often, and cut down on distractions while you nurse. Since most babies can do very well on breastmilk alone for the first 6 months, these nursing and growth patterns are not a sign that they need to be started on solid foods. As I point out in chapter 7, there are other signs that are better guides. Your baby will be ready for solid foods when he can sit up and open his mouth; when he sees the spoon coming he will close his lips over it and voluntarily swallow semisolid food.

Mother's Fluid Intake. Although it's important to drink enough liquids to quench your thirst, you do not have to force yourself to drink more than that. One of the myths about breastfeeding that has been passed on in the best circles for years and years is the idea that if the mother markedly increases her fluid intake, it will increase the amount of milk she makes. When that theory has been put to the test, it turns out that drinking water or other fluids beyond thirst actually impairs breastmilk production. Beer has an especially good reputation for increasing breastmilk production, but sadly enough it doesn't seem to have any magical properties. In fact, drinking more than a single can of beer or its equivalent can hinder letdown because the alcohol inhibits oxytocin release.[5]

On the other hand, if you are clearly dehydrated, your milk supply will go down. Of course, if you find it easier to drink your extra calories rather than eat them, fluid intake can have quite an effect on your milk production. But simply forcing fluids in an attempt to increase lactation is apparently a tactic that backfires.

Eating Well While Breastfeeding. My best advice is what I gave you in chapter 3. Whether you are breast- or formula-feeding, you will have to eat. You don't have to eat *boring*, but you do have to eat. This goes for fathers as well as mothers. You will need your strength, endurance, and emotional steadiness in order to be good parents. When you are hungry or going without food, you will be worn out, cranky, and discouraged.

Research is contradictory about how much you need to eat in order to provide breastmilk[2]. Women in limited financial and nutritional circumstances do provide for their infants pretty well during the first 6 months. Concrete evidence of how little food is too little comes from studies of lactating baboons, whose volume of breastmilk was impaired only when their dietary intake was cut to 60 percent of their usual needs. There is some evidence that women who eat too few calories and have low body fat stores produce breastmilk that is too low in fat and therefore too low in calories. There is equally good evidence that indicates the opposite. Since breastmilk composition varies so much from one woman to the next and from feeding to feeding, it is hard to know whether and how much diet affects breastmilk composition. Not knowing, my best advice is to eat

enough and eat a varied diet with a good distribution of protein, carbohydrate, and fat. Don't skimp on the fat. You need it
for calories and for making your food taste good. Furthermore,
the fat in your breastmilk will reflect the fat in your diet.
Maintaining a good variety of fats in your diet—including
monounsaturated, polyunsaturated, and saturated—will ensure
that your breastmilk gives your baby the essential fatty acids he
needs for his brain and nervous system development.

My conviction is that you have to feed yourself if you are
going to feed *and nurture* your child. If you are good at tuning in
on how hungry and how full you are, and if you are eating regular and satisfying meals, you can eat as much as you are hungry
for. Keep an eye on your weight. If you are losing no more than a
half pound per week, *provided you have it to lose,* you are probably
eating enough. If you gained less than the average of 25 pounds
during pregnancy, particularly if you were slim to start with, it is
wise to eat enough so you don't lose weight at all.

Again, I encourage you to go by your internal cues. Have
regular and appealing meals that include fat for both nutritional
value *and* pleasure, go to the table hungry, eat until you are
fully satisfied, and then stop. You will be able to stop because
you know another meal is coming and you will be able to do it
again. Since we are so obsessed with food avoidance, fat avoidance, and slimness in our culture, I will belabor the point. A
number of studies of lactation failure have identified part of the
problem as extremely poor food intake by the mother. Check
yourself. Do any of these patterns describe yours?

• Low weight gain during pregnancy for whatever reason.
• Dieting to lose weight, both during pregnancy and lactation.
• Poor eating habits in general.
• Very tired and seemingly experiencing some loss of appetite
  due to fatigue.
• Too busy to eat.
• Careful to avoid eating fat.
• Have a long list of foods to avoid.
• Don't have enough money to buy food.
• Go hungry in order to feed your children.

If you see your food behavior on the list, take particular care to
feed yourself well. If your appetite is poor, you may have to eat

beyond your hunger for a week or so. Be sure you are eating enough fat—it makes food more appealing and gives you more calories with less volume. If you are reading this before you deliver, now is the time to start cooking for yourselves and to get in the habit of eating meals. Get a copy of my book *Secrets of Feeding a Healthy Family* to find out how and to quiet your nerves about eating fat. Finally, if you are struggling with food insufficiency, seek financial help for buying food from the WIC program, food stamps, or other sources of public support.

To eat well, you must have three reliable meals a day. Snack between times as well if you are hungry. Given reliable access to good-tasting food, you may not even be aware of eating more than usual, but your hunger and appetite give you the best guide. Energy requirement has so many variables—your need, your baby's need, how much weight you gained during pregnancy—that it is hard to say just how much extra you need to eat for breastfeeding. A ballpark estimate would be that the newborn baby needs about 400 calories, and since (another guess) 100 calories of your calories convert into 90 calories in breastmilk, you probably begin by using about 450 calories a day to make breastmilk and about 1,000 calories toward the end of 12 months of breastfeeding. Probably. The only sure guides are your hunger and appetite and your baby's growth. Babies vary from one another in their calorie requirements by as much as 50 percent, and furthermore they frequently eat twice as much one day as another.

If necessary, protein for breastmilk production will be taken from your own body's muscles and organs—your heart and lungs, for instance. However, to get enough protein in your diet to provide for yourself as well as your baby, you need only 12 to 15 grams more of protein a day. Since a 1-ounce serving from the meat group gives 7 grams of protein, and 8 ounces of milk gives 8, an extra egg and an extra glass of milk will provide for your additional protein needs.

What to Eat While You Are Breastfeeding. Listed below is the minimum to eat while you are breastfeeding to get the protein, vitamins, and minerals you need. These minimums, however, may give you only about half the calories you need for yourself and for breastmilk production. See appendix O for more detailed information about what's included in each food category and what constitutes a serving. You need to have

meals to be able to do a good job with eating during lactation—
and during any other part of life. Ignore the current "wisdom"
about nutrition, and use enough salt and fat to make cooking
and eating meals rewarding. For more guidance about meal
planning and cooking in general and realistic use of fats and
sugars in particular, see *Secrets of Feeding a Healthy Family.*
Remember, the following list gives your *minimum* requirements
for protein, vitamins, and minerals, but *not* for calories.

Bread, cereal, rice, and pasta group: 6 servings
Fruit group: 2 servings
Vegetable group: 3 servings
    Fruit and vegetable groups combined: 5 servings
Meat, poultry, fish, dry beans, eggs, and nuts group: 3 servings
Milk, yogurt, and cheese group: 3 servings

    Vitamins and Minerals. "A tooth for every child," the
grandmothers used to say. Well, true—but not true. If need be,
calcium will be taken from your bones for breastmilk production. You can protect your bones by drinking milk, but not
completely. Women who breastfeed past 6 months do break
down bone tissue even if they are well nourished. However,
after weaning, that bony tissue is built right back up again,
so the breakdown becomes a problem only when another
pregnancy follows right after weaning.[2]
    Your intake of some vitamins and minerals is reflected in
your breastmilk; intake of others appears not to be. Breastmilk
nutrients that can be affected by what you take in are manganese, iodine, vitamin A, vitamin C, and the B vitamins, with
the exception of folic acid. Manganese is found in whole grains
and nuts. Iodine is in iodized salt and is also present in ample
quantities as a byproduct of the production of milk and com-
mercially baked bread. Vitamin A comes from whole and fortified milk and from dark green and deep yellow fruits and
vegetables. The only B vitamins that are likely to present a
problem, and then only if you are vegan (eat no animal protein),
are B6 and B12, so talk with your doctor about a supplement.
In fact, consult with a dietitian, because eating successfully
as a vegan is complicated, especially during pregnancy and
lactation. Although vitamin D nutrition is an issue for your
baby after he is 6 months old, breastmilk is not a good source

of vitamin D, so I will not recommend supplementing your diet to provide it. You will get vitamin D for your own needs from egg yolks and fortified milk.

The bottom line is that you can get what you need from a respectable mixed diet. If you want to supplement to be sure you get the vitamins and minerals you need, take a broad spectrum (lots of different) vitamin-mineral supplement with generally no more than 100 percent of the daily value (DV) of any nutrient. Don't try to piece together a supplement package by taking a little of this and a little of that—or worse, a lot of this or that. Taking too much of any one nutrient can cause imbalances that can rob you of another nutrient. You don't need a prenatal vitamin when you are breastfeeding—those are only for when you are pregnant.

Foods to Avoid While Breastfeeding. Traces of anything you eat can show up in your breastmilk. If you eat lots of onion or garlic, chances are your breastmilk will taste like onion or garlic. Most babies do not seem to mind. In fact, breastfed babies appear to be more willing to accept solid foods when the time comes to introduce them, presumably because they already know the taste. Some babies, however, seem to get fussy or have symptoms of food sensitivity or even allergy when their mothers eat certain foods.

It is probably the unusual child who reacts to his mother's diet. Further, it is hard to sort out whether infant behavior is a true reaction to food or simply a coincidence, since all babies are fussy, become congested, or appear colicky at times. Colic is "unexplained fussiness" that afflicts about 10 to 20 percent of babies under age 3 months. Generally, time is the only cure, but if you have a markedly fussy or colicky baby, it is worth a try to see if your food could be causing it. Your baby could have an immature or a particularly sensitive gastrointestinal tract, and he might do better if you kept your diet a little less challenging. Try removing the suspected food from your diet for a few days, see if his symptoms disappear, and then reintroduce it and see if they come back.* The foods that are most often suspected of causing colic and stomach and intestinal upsets are cow's milk;

---

*However, whenever you challenge with something your baby has reacted to in the past, be careful. If he reacted strongly, reintroduce the food only under a doctor's supervision.

eggs; sulfur-containing vegetables like onions, garlic, and dried beans; and cruciferous vegetables like cabbage, cauliflower, and broccoli.

The Severely Food-Allergic Infant. For babies with strong family histories of allergy, breastfeeding is highly recommended, and exclusive breastfeeding for the first 6 months is generally helpful in decreasing babies' allergic reactions. However, a small percentage of exclusively breastfed infants appear to become allergic to the minute quantities of substances from their mother's diets that pass into the breastmilk. Those very unusual babies are challenging because they react so strongly that they eat poorly, develop eczema, and often have stomach and intestinal symptoms like vomiting, loose stools, and diarrhea. Not surprisingly, these infants sleep poorly (you would too if you were hungry, itched, and had a stomachache) and grow more slowly. To continue breastfeeding, mothers of these highly allergic infants have to follow such restricted diets that it is difficult for them to maintain their own nutritional well-being as well as the amount and quality of their breastmilk. These highly sensitive babies even react to the standard protein-predigested formulas like Alimentum, Nutramigen, and Pregestimil and need an even more predigested formula like Neonate before their symptoms disappear. Whether it is necessary to wean such an unusual and highly allergic infant from the breast depends on whether it is feasible for the mother to restrict her diet to the point that the baby's allergic symptoms can be controlled.[6] Discuss special formulas with your pediatrician and pediatric dietitian.

Hungry Days. During the weeks and months of nursing, the times when you are in balance with your baby's needs will alternate with times when his needs increase and you fall behind in breastmilk production. His growth spurts, and hungry days, may take place at fairly predictable times, such as at 7 to 10 days of age, 5 to 6 weeks, and at 3 months. Other growth spurts, however, are not so predictable. Some babies appear to have one hungry day a week, whereas others seem to be pressing all the time. It may be that Emily was one of those pressing-all-the-time babies. Emily grew fast, so she may have needed more to eat than the average baby. If you look at Figure 2.2 on page 52, you will see that a newborn who is eating a lot can take in as much as 450 calories per day. Since breastmilk (or formula) has 20 calories per ounce, that 450 calories comes to about 23 ounces of breastmilk. That's a lot when you're just getting started nursing. When they get on toward 6 months, some fully breastfed babies can eat 45 ounces or more.

Generally, your milk supply will increase after you nurse often for about 48 hours. Hungry days are tough, tiring days. Your baby will be wakeful, hungry, and dissatisfied, and you seemingly will do nothing but nurse. You may even ask yourself why you don't just give a bottle and put you both out of your misery! While a relief bottle can be helpful at times, for the routine hungry days giving a bottle isn't the answer. Hang in there and reassure yourself that those hungry days have a developmental as well as a nutritional function. Being hungry and dissatisfied for a time may wake your baby up and stimulate his interest in the world around him. Often after hungry days parents say their babies have increased their quiet alert times. To help you both get through those days, try carrying him around in a back- or front-pack while you do your chores. Give your body some help as well. You can't make milk out of thin air. Get some outside help for the chores, or pretend you are snowed in and have to cancel your appointments and let everything go. Eat well and drink enough. Whatever your approach, make nursing, eating, and resting your main focus for a couple of days.

These hungry days do not mean that your breastmilk supply is drying up. Do not reach for a bottle. Remember the law of supply and demand: the more you stimulate your breasts, the more you make. If you don't stimulate your breasts more, you won't make any more. If you give a bottle your baby will be satisfied and won't stimulate your breasts, your milk supply will fall behind his needs, and you will be stuck with giving a bottle. The next time he has hungry days, you will do it again, and you will be stuck with more bottles. This is a miserable pattern to get into, because you feed and doubt, feed and doubt—and run for the bottle. If the pattern goes on too long, a baby can start preferring the bottle and breastfeeding will be over. It doesn't have to happen that way, but you do have to know what you're doing and hang in there on those hungry days.

Life—and nursing—will get easier. As your baby gets older

he'll take less time to eat and go longer between feedings. But even for an older baby, there is no predicting the pattern of nursing. You may need more or less breast stimulation than another woman, and your baby may be more or less hungry than another baby. Feeding frequency is a highly individual matter that can be determined only by mother and baby.

Activity during Breastfeeding. Studies have shown that mothers who are very active do just as well with breastmilk production as mothers who are not. Women who exercise need more calories; they eat more and produce the same amount of breastmilk as they do when they aren't exercising. Although generally active women who breastfeed have lower body fat than generally sedentary women, it appears that increasing activity during breastfeeding doesn't decrease body fat. It does, however, increase fitness. As long as you do the activity for enjoyment and to take care of yourself, it undoubtedly also has the same emotional and social benefits that you get from such activity any time. However, exercising for the primary purpose of losing weight is demoralizing. Trust your body to tell you when to start exercising again.

KNOW AND UNDERSTAND YOUR BABY

Your baby will eat best if you follow his lead in feeding and do what he wants you to do. Babies show huge differences in their temperament and ability to organize their sleep and awake states. I discussed these issues in chapter 4 and I encourage you to review those sections right now. In the section "Do What Your Baby Needs So She Can Eat Well" on pages 205-211 of chapter 6, you will also learn about following cues, about how babies "talk," and about keeping the baby in control of feeding. Do read that part. Why did I cover it there and not here? Well, to be truthful, it's because I ran out of space in this chapter! But it's also because breastfeeding more or less automatically takes care of some of the issues for you. You have to be a better observer if you are breastfeeding. However, to keep on with your admirable tactics, you will benefit from consciously knowing what you are doing. In addition, if you are controlling and don't follow your baby's lead with feeding, chances are you won't be breastfeeding for long.

Help Your Baby with Self-Regulation. The newborn's task is to get to the point that he can regulate his sleep states and keep himself calm when he is awake. That means he can be asleep when he is asleep, awake and composed when he is awake, and can make the shift from one state to the other with a minimum of fuss. Some babies have their work cut out for them. Janet and David, like most besotted parents, thought they had the perfect child, but their Emily was a temperamentally active and intense infant, and she was disorganized besides. She reacted negatively to change and was challenging to understand and comfort. Her sleep states were irregular, and she had difficulty being awake without getting upset. On the other hand, Zachary was probably a relaxed and flexible child, and that made it far easier for his parents to be successful with him. Although when you remember the trouble they almost got into with his sleeping too much and eating too little, it may be that in some ways it could have been harder to be successful with him. Zachary didn't bother them when they needed to be bothered. A hungry, awake child like Emily keeps after her parents until they give her what she needs.

Whatever your child's temperament and level of organization, you will help him to become and remain organized and learn to cope with his particular temperament if you feed in a way that is tuned in and responsive to his signals. Follow his lead with feeding and do what he wants you to do. Feed him when he's hungry, calm, and awake—don't try to wake him up before he is ready (unless he has an early too-sleepy period like Zachary did), and don't make him wait to eat until he's all worked up or exhausted from crying. If he's upset, help him calm down. Wait to get him out of bed until it's clear he's really waking up. If he's still drowsy, wait for him to wake himself up before you try to feed him. Talk with him while you feed to help him stay awake and alert. Feed in a smooth and continuous fashion, being careful not to get him stirred up with unnecessary moving around, burping, or wiping. Burp only if he squirms or has a preoccupied look on his face that makes him look like he is full of air. Let him pause in eating if he wants to, but again, don't stir him up. This is your social time. Be interesting, not exciting or overstimulating.

Read Your Baby's Signs. Your baby will be ready to eat when his eyes are open wider than usual and his face looks bright. He may curl his arms and legs up, and when you touch his mouth, cheek, or chin, he will turn toward the touch to root and make sucking motions. He may tuck his hands under his chin or suck on them. Eventually, he will fuss, but fussing is a late hunger cue, so work toward catching his earlier signals. Prolonged fussing will work him up, and he won't eat as well. Observe his habits: Does he want to eat right after he gets up, or does he want to socialize a bit first?

When he's full, his sucking will slow down, he will let go of the nipple, he will even turn away, and his rooting reflex will go away. If you miss the earlier "I'm done" signals, he will become more definite: He will kick and squirm, arch his back, or get fussy. Let him rest during the feeding if he wants to; then offer the nipple again. Many times babies pause to rest and socialize, so sit still, talk a bit, pay attention, and see what happens. Then offer the nipple again, but don't get pushy—you are only check-ing to be sure he has had enough to eat. Some babies get full abruptly and won't take another swallow. Other babies drift into being full, gradually slowing down and losing interest in sucking. Respect your baby's cues. Don't try to get him to eat more when he's full. Often newborns will go off to sleep when they are full, but it is better if your baby is still awake at the end of the feeding. That way you know he has had enough to eat. Furthermore, being put to bed sleepy but awake teaches your baby to put himself to sleep and heads off developing sleep problems later.

As with hunger and fullness, your baby will move through a cycle of being alert and sociable on the one hand and wanting to be left alone and get some sleep on the other. Recognizing those cues improves feeding, because the quality of your baby's sleep will influence the quality of his wakefulness and his abili-ty to eat well. Your baby will tell you he wants to interact when his eyes and face are bright, when he smiles and looks at you, and when he moves his arms and legs smoothly toward you. When he is saying "I need a break," he will look away, kick and squirm, push toward you with his hand, pull away, arch his back, and fuss or cry. If you can catch his early signs of needing a break, it will be easier for him to settle down and go to sleep.

For a listing of your baby's engagement and disengagement cues, see Figure 4.2, "What Is Your Baby Telling You?" on page 122.

Allow for Individual Differences. Along with differences in temperament, babies vary in the way they eat, sleep, and react to life in general. Zachary and Emily have already introduced us to some of those differences. Let's look at a few others.

The I-Want-to-Eat-All-the Time Baby. It may worry you if your baby seems hard to satisfy—if he is hungry and demands to be fed often. However, it is likely he will be waking himself up appropriately and finding out he is hungry. His asking to be fed often will stimulate you to make more breastmilk, and you will be able to keep up with his needs. Often, when those babies go in for their early checks, it turns out that they have gained well. If you have a fussy, irregular baby, it may be hard to sort out what his signals mean. Does he want to eat? Does he just want to be held and comforted? Does he want to go back to bed? It doesn't hurt to feed a baby if you are not sure, because he will let you know soon enough if he's not interested. However, you might want to get in the habit of sorting out what he wants, rather than feeding him first thing. Part of the problem with fussy, irregular babies is that they haven't learned yet to maintain a quiet alert state. They work themselves up and benefit from some help getting calmed down and staying calm. Review the soothing techniques discussed on page 131 of chapter 4, and go through the routine with him. Keep in mind that you are not trying to stave him off and get him to eat less often. You are only going through a process of trial and error to figure out what he *does* want.

If, however, you go through the routine and he seems to be hungry, go ahead and feed him. You are not trying to deprive him of food with these tactics; you are simply giving him a chance to settle down. Rather than depending only on feeding to calm him down, he will calm down first and arrive at feeding able to do a better job of eating. If he eats better, he won't be as likely to ask to be fed again right away. But get it straight what you are trying to accomplish: you are not trying to get him to eat less; you are helping him to sort out whether or not he's hungry.

The Too-Sleepy Baby. Sleepy babies can fool parents, because they act happy and content and they seem like they are getting enough to eat. Observing your baby's sleep patterns will tell you whether your baby can wake himself up to ask to be fed. Once in a while there will be a newborn who sleeps in stretches that are too long, and when he does wake up and ask to be fed, he remains too sleepy to do a good job with eating. If you're not seeing enough pees and poops and if your baby is sleeping more than 2 hours at a stretch, it could be that you need to start waking him up for feedings. Pay attention to the sleep cycles discussed in chapter 4 (pages 120-121) and catch him when he is sleeping actively or is drowsy. It will be far too hard to awaken him thoroughly when he is sleeping quietly. The cure is easy and no harm will be done if you catch the sleepy baby right away, and you will if you know what to look for. After a day or two of waking your baby more often and more thoroughly, he'll perk up and you can go back to trusting him again to tell you when he's hungry—but still keep an eye on the pees and poops. This is an easy catch and cure but an important one. If his sleepiness and poor eating go on too long, he could get into trouble with undereating and dehydration.

Not all babies who sleep a lot are too-sleepy babies. Relaxed babies with regular habits may sleep for 3 hours or more at a stretch. In contrast, a too-sleepy baby has trouble waking himself up to be fed and staying awake so he can eat well. Surprisingly, the tactics just discussed for helping always-hungry babies, as well as those we'll discuss for helping colicky babies maintain a quiet alert state are also helpful for the too-sleepy baby. To help your drowsy baby wake up, talk, touch, and move in a way that is more active, interesting, and unpre-dictable. Vary your tone of voice and your speed of talking, give him something to grasp or suck, sit him up, unwrap or undress him. However, don't be irritating. You are trying to help your baby take an interest, not make him go to sleep to get away from all the commotion.

After feedings, increase your contact with your too-sleepy baby, and keep him with you in an infant seat as you move around the house. Give him something interesting to look at. Feed him promptly when he asks for it and is fully awake. Keep talking with him until he can get through a feeding without going to sleep. If he starts to drift off, stroke him under the chin, from throat to mouth, while he nurses. Interrupt the nursing by changing his diaper if you have to, or give him a bath before he eats to perk him up a bit.

The Colicky Baby. Although everyone fears and dreads colic, nobody is able to define it. Colic is the newborn pattern of crying, fussing, and appearing to be in pain for part or in some cases almost all of waking time. Colicky babies apparently have nothing medically wrong with them, but they are not to be comforted, seemingly no matter what you do. The best guess is that colic is the result of an immature nervous or digestive system, and most babies outgrow the pattern by the time they are 3 to 4 months old.

With your fussy and irritable baby, go through the same self-quieting routine that I described on page 131 of chapter 4. Take it slow and easy, giving each step at least 20 seconds before you move on. Keep in mind that the overstimulated infant can act just like a colicky baby, so be careful not to be so active that you contribute to his problem. Your soothing probably won't help at first. In fact, it may not help for a long time. However, you are doing the right thing even if your baby can't respond right away. Over the first 6 months, he will settle down and start to get a grip on himself. Again, that's important learning for when he gets older.

Babies with Special Needs. Good health is an indispensable part of thriving while breastfeeding. Sometimes you can do everything right and breastfeeding simply will not work, for reasons that are outside of your control. If you are very sick, or your baby is very sick, it may make it impossible to breastfeed. Babies with heart defects sometimes don't have enough energy to take on the extra work of breastfeeding. Babies born with structural abnormalities, like cleft palate, have a harder time breastfeeding. If the cleft is severe and extensive, breastfeeding may even be impossible.* Some babies are born with insufficient neurological or muscular control to be able to breastfeed, like some babies with low muscle tone. And some babies have galactosemia, an inborn error of metabolism that demands highly specialized diets.

Parents who feel strongly about breastfeeding will often express breastmilk and arrange to have it fed to their babies with a bottle or stomach tube until they are able to nurse. More and more parents of babies with cleft palate or neuromuscular limitations give their baby expressed breastmilk. While they are in the hospital, many prematurely born babies are often given

---

*It may be possible for you to express breastmilk and give it to your baby with a nipple especially designed for a cleft palate.

breastmilk with additional human milk fortifiers to provide the extra nutrients infants need to support their early make-up growth and development. It is quite a commitment to provide pumped breastmilk for a premature infant or a sick baby, particularly when you factor in the stress of having a ill baby. It can be done, but take a feeling-your-way, wait-and-see approach. You will be feel more successful and put less pressure on yourself if you think in terms of providing your baby with part of his nutritional needs and preserving your breastmilk production for when your baby gets home from the hospital. Then he can nurse to help you get caught up with his needs. Do be sure to provide yourself with lots of emotional and situational support and plenty of rest.

Babies may have trouble with the functioning of the stomach and intestine. Babies who have pyloric stenosis (narrowing of the passageway between the stomach and intestine), or who spit up excessively, may grow less rapidly than other babies, at least for a time. Often you will see catch-up growth once the problem is resolved. Babies with infections, lung problems, or conditions requiring surgery will not thrive in the same way as babies who do not have to struggle against such problems. These babies will likely do as well with breastfeeding as with formula-feeding. However, you must carefully follow your baby's growth and health with the aid of your physician.

Evaluate Your Baby's Suck. If your baby is properly placed on your nipple you will feel an almost (or downright) painful pressure when he first starts nursing. If he is improperly placed and clamps down on your nipple, it will hurt sharply and unpleasantly. Of course, once the milk lets down, his sucking pattern will change to the longer, slower rhythm we talked about earlier. Before then, you need other evidence. Some mothers report that the baby's ears wiggle when he is nursing appropriately. This is probably a good sign, as it lets you know he is using his jaw in an appropriate up and down motion. The temples near his upper jaw will also move in and out. Here are some additional signs that your baby is suckling properly.

- Is his lower lip out and not tucked in?
- Are his cheeks rounded and firm? If they are drawn in too much or dimpled, he may not be maintaining enough suction.

- Is his tongue visible when you draw his lips aside? If not, it may be curled backward instead of being placed properly beneath the nipple.
- Is it difficult to get him off the breast? If he is properly attached you will have to break the suction to remove him comfortably. Put a finger in the corner of his mouth.
- Once the milk lets down, can you hear a noisy "drawing" sound as milk is removed from the breast? If he is improperly positioned, you will hear a soft, clicking sound.
- Can you hear him swallow?

To correct faulty suck, use your finger to get your baby's suck going before you offer the nipple. Put your finger on his tongue, fingernail down, and let him press it against the roof of his mouth as he sucks. Notice the strength of his suck. Tilt his head back a little so he can move his jaw and swallow well and so he's in a good position to get the nipple well up against the roof of his mouth. Take your finger out of his mouth and quickly offer your breast, flattening out your nipple between your thumb and forefinger (or your first and second finger if you prefer the V hold to the C hold) and pressing it against your chest wall. You might even squirt a little milk into his mouth to get him to open up more.

Can your baby put his tongue over the lower gum line? Some babies are "tongue tied." That is, the *frenulum*, the attachment of the tongue to the floor of the mouth, is too short to allow the tongue to move freely and may interfere with nursing. I say "may" because the advisability of clipping the frenulum to free the tongue is hotly debated in breastfeeding and medical circles. Suffice it to say that if your baby is having trouble nursing you need to seek experienced medical help and not just settle for someone's offhand opinion.

Evaluate Your Baby's Position. The way you position your baby's body when you feed him will help him suck and swallow well as well as be calm and alert while he eats. If he feels comfortable and well supported, he will feel more relaxed and able to apply himself to the job at hand. On the other hand, it will agitate and upset him if he is in a cramped and uncomfortable position. His head, neck, and body need to be lined up properly for him to be comfortable and to eat well. Here are some signs that your baby's position is good.

- He is lying on his side with his stomach touching yours.
- His head is facing straight ahead, not twisted.
- His shoulders and hips are straight, not twisted.
- His ear, shoulder, and hip are in a straight line.
- His head is supported.
- His head is slightly higher than the rest of him.
- His chin is tucked in and down slightly, not tipped back.
- You hold him firmly so he doesn't fall, but not so tight he can't wiggle.

Try Out Proper Positioning and Sucking. Ohio Certified Lactation Consultant Martha Grodrian Brower makes parents aware of the importance of positioning by coaching them in practical exercises. Let's follow your baby's lead to help you get a feeling for properly aligning him so he can eat well. First, turn your head so you are looking over your shoulder and up toward the ceiling. Attempt to swallow. Now face directly forward with your head and neck straight and balanced on your shoulders, and notice how your swallowing changes. The first position is the one your baby will be in if you feed him lying on his back so he has to twist his neck to nurse, the second if he is lying on his side, properly aligned. I think you will agree that facing forward makes it much more comfortable and easier to swallow. Your baby will be in proper position when his stomach is touching yours and his ear, shoulder, and hip are in a straight line.

Now experiment with proper latch-on by putting your thumb into your mouth. First insert only the tip, resting it behind your front teeth. Suck, and notice what your tongue does. Now insert your thumb further, resting the tip against the roof of your mouth, again suck and notice what your tongue does. The first mimics incorrect latch-on; the second mimics correct.

Rather than *sucking*, the process of breastfeeding is more accurately called suckling, because it is a three-fold action of suction, compression, and stroking by the lips, jaws, and tongue. When your baby is properly placed on your breast, he will use suction to draw your nipple and much of your areola into his mouth far enough that his jaws are over the lactiferous sinuses. That suction and pressure makes your nipple get longer and keeps it in place against the roof of his mouth. With the aid of his jaw for support and force, he uses his tongue to stroke the bottom of the nipple and squeeze the milk from the lactiferous sinuses and out through the nipple pores. Suction is important, not to remove milk from the breast but to hold the nipple in place in the baby's mouth. That's why the baby with severe cleft palate can't breastfeed: the opening in the palate interferes with suction. Your baby's tongue will be fully extended along the nipple, stroking the bottom of it and moving backward and forward in a swallowing action that alternates with the suckling. A baby who is poorly placed will take only the end of the nipple in his mouth, and his tongue will push against the nipple rather than stroking the nipple and areola. His mouth won't be far enough back on the areola to compress the lactiferous sinuses, he won't be able to get any milk for his efforts, and it will be painful for you.

Evaluate Your Nipple Shape. To allow proper latch-on, the nipple has to protrude when the baby sucks on it. To find out if your nipples protrude, squeeze just behind your nipple with your thumb and forefinger. Does it stick out, stay flat, or dimple back in toward your chest wall? When they are stimulated or cold, do your nipples become erect? The nipple that remains flat or moves inward has tiny adhesions to the inner breast tissue that make it pull in rather than sticking out. If the nipple remains flat or shrinks in when it is stimulated, you may have inverted nipples. Have your health professional check your nipples. One nipple may be flat or inverted, the other not.

Many times inverted nipples become protractile during pregnancy. Even if your nipples aren't nicely protractile by the time you deliver, it won't rule out breastfeeding. Many times a baby with a good healthy suck can bring out flat or inverted nipples, especially if he is allowed to nurse within a couple of hours after he is born. Here are some additional strategies to help you with flat or inverted nipples.

- Get help and support from an experienced person.
- Flatten your areola between your thumb and forefinger, pressing in against your chest wall to help your nipple protrude.
- Hand-express a little milk just before you start to nurse to soften your breasts and make it easier for your baby to latch on.

- Use a breast pump just before you nurse—the suction will pull out your nipples and soften your breasts so your baby can latch on.
- If your baby hasn't latched on by the time your milk comes in, begin bottle-feeding using expressed milk.
- Continue to offer your baby the breast when he is calm and your breasts are soft.

Being persistent with this process over several days can be frustrating, time-consuming, and difficult, so it is extremely important to seek help and advice. One day your baby may suddenly latch on, and your efforts will be rewarded.

Interpret the All-Important Pees and Poops. Remaining properly hydrated is particularly important for a newborn. Your breastmilk is concentrated exactly right for your baby—it has only as much protein, sodium, and potassium as he needs. As a consequence, your breastfed baby's urine won't be very concentrated—it won't be very yellow. After your milk comes in, the major sign that your baby is getting enough to eat is a lot of urine—as I have said before, 6 to 8 or more wet diapers a day. However, getting to that point may take several days and even up to a week. For the first 24 hours your newborn is likely to be wide awake, but the next 1 or 2 days he may be sleepy and not too interested in eating. He will wake up to eat, get a small volume of the all-important colostrum, and go right back to sleep. During that time, he won't generate much urine. However, once your breastmilk comes in, he will start to wake himself up more often to nurse and his volume of urine output will increase.

Early poops are the dark brown or greenish-black, sticky meconium that was in your baby's intestine before he was born. Colostrum appears to have a laxative effect that helps his intestine start to work so he can pass the meconium. Once your breastmilk comes in and he is nursing well, his stools will turn yellow and be soft and curdled or seedy, like yellow cottage cheese. It's not unusual for stools to be so liquid that they leave only a yellow stain in the diaper. When I said earlier that a newly breastfed baby will likely have a bowel movement in almost every diaper, I was counting this small amount of yellow stain as a bowel movement. At times stools are an alarming green color, and that is of no consequence. Yellow or green, your baby's stools will actually smell quite pleasant—certainly not unpleasant like adult bowel movements—and will have a sweet or cheesy odor.

Your baby may pass his stools with no apparent effort, or he may become preoccupied, stiffen, and turn red in the face. That "stool passing" posture and facial expression is so typical that it may amuse you. Your baby may stop a feeding to fuss and grunt and not be able to continue eating until he gets the job done—or even until he gets his pants changed.

Some babies don't like messy pants and will fuss and seem uncomfortable; some don't seem to notice. Generally, breastfed babies don't get sore in the diaper area, but they may, especially when they are very new and their bottoms are very tender. Wash and dry your baby's bottom thoroughly after each diaper change. Cover the sore area with an ointment containing zinc oxide, which is white and sticky and stays on to offer protection. Expose his bottom to the open air to help it heal—lay him on top of his diaper on the floor for a few minutes rather than putting it on. Given that we are talking about a "he" in this chapter, and given that you might not enjoy having your floor sprayed, you might want to lay him on his side or save the open-air tactic for his awake times when you can put him on his stomach and keep an eye on him. You doubtless have already been warned many times to put your baby to bed on his back or side to decrease the risk of sudden infant death syndrome (SIDS).

Understand Patterns of Growth. Your baby's growth and weight gain are your most concrete ways of assessing your breastfeeding regimen. This is not, however, to say that your breastfeeding is unsuccessful if you have not provided fully for your baby's nutritional needs. You will learn about situations in which you may not be able to fully breastfeed in our discussion of special issues in breastfeeding.

If Zachary had continued with his early sleeping and breast-feeding pattern, he would likely have gained weight poorly or even lost weight without acting like he was underfed—being fussy or acting hungry. Like Zachary, some babies have trouble waking up to ask to be fed, and they have trouble staying awake while they eat. They undereat, and if they are allowed to continue in the undereating pattern, it appears to make them even sleepier. They eat even less, and a downward spiral develops. Leaving inexperienced parents more or less on their own to catch this pattern is not good. In my view, early hospital discharge does not go well with energetic promotion of breastfeeding. As a matter of fact, it doesn't go with feeding babies at all. The pattern can develop with formula-feeding as well as with breastfeeding. Parents feeding either way can make mistakes in feeding that can bring them to their first checkup with an infant who shows abnormally slow growth and even dehydration.*

Right from the first, your baby will be weighed and measured and the data will be plotted on standard growth curves. (There's more discussion about growth curves on pages 34-38 in chapter 2 and in appendix A, "What Is Normal Growth?") However, in the first few weeks, until he makes up for his after-delivery weight loss and starts to develop a pattern of growth, it is hard to tell just what your baby's growth rate is going to be. Generally, full-term babies lose about 5 to 8 percent of their body weight in the first week after birth and generally are expected to regain their birth weight by 10 days of age. Then they gain about 5 to 7 ounces per week during their first month or two. However, not all babies show this pattern. In a study done in Iowa, at least 10 percent of 149 normal breastfed infants had not regained their birth weight by age 14 days.[7] After age 3 months, breastfed babies grow somewhat more slowly than formula-fed babies do, gradually dropping down by as much as one percentile grid line between 3 and 12 months. This is perfectly normal growth and only a different pattern.[8]

Distinguish Slow Growth from Poor Growth. The best way to decide whether slow growth is normal growth is to evaluate the feeding relationship. Look again at Figure 5.1, "Checklist for Successful Breastfeeding," on page 140. If the mother factors and the baby factors check out and the baby looks healthy and is in good shape, the baby is probably growing in a way that is right for him. Here is what it looks like if your baby is truly doing poorly:

• There are fewer pees and poops.
• There are few feedings.

---

*I am making the distinction between abnormally slow and clearly inadequate growth, as distinguished from the normally slow-growing baby we will discuss later.

- The number of feedings is decreasing.
- Your baby is overly sleepy.
- He has a weak suck.
- Your baby doesn't show much interest in feeding.

If you have any doubt at all about whether your baby is doing well, *immediately* call your health care provider.

With a baby who gains weight slowly, it helps to keep a daily record of feedings and wet and dirty diapers. Your baby is likely to be doing all right if he is eating 8 or more times in 24 hours, has 6 to 8 wet diapers, and 3 or 4 diapers per day having at least a small amount of yellow or green poopy stain. It also helps to ask an experienced person to observe a breastfeeding, looking for things like infant alertness, sucking pattern, and signs of milk flow. Your observer can note your awareness of milk letdown and how involved and relaxed you are with your baby. The chapter summary on pages 199-200 will give your observer a good guide of what to look for.

Just as Zachary was growing relatively slowly and was normal, Emily was growing relatively rapidly and was equally normal. Babies who eat and grow at the extremes are perfectly normal, but their parents do tend to get worried. They will try to get the big baby to eat less and the small baby to eat more, often without being aware of it. The irony is that such tactics tend to backfire. An infant who is encouraged to eat more than he wants will eat less and will grow more slowly; an infant who is restricted puts more pressure on feeding and may overeat and grow too fast. An advantage of breastfeeding is that it is harder to be so controlling, even though it can be done.

Parents of large, actively growing babies are particularly vulnerable. Even some health professionals get concerned about normal fatness in babies. Just the other day a lactation consultant told me about a physician who advised the mother of a healthy and robustly growing breastfed baby to cut back on the number of feedings because her baby was too fat. Sadly, she followed his advice and soon thereafter she stopped breastfeeding. Even people on the street are likely to make rude comments like "what are you feeding that baby?" The fat baby is no more likely to grow up fat than the average or slender baby.

Whether your baby is relatively large, relatively small, or somewhere in between, it is far better to concentrate on establishing a positive feeding relationship and let amounts and growth take care of themselves. At this early age—or at any age, come to think about it—how much your child eats is *his* business. Letting go of what you can't control will be good training for when your child becomes a toddler.

Take It Slowly with Teaching the Bottle. Most breastfeeding parents feel more comfortable if their baby knows how to take a bottle. By the time your baby is a 4 to 6 weeks old it is safe enough to teach him how. Breastmilk supply and letdown will be well established, and your baby will be good at suckling. It's you, Dad, who is likely to be most successful with encouraging your baby to take a bottle. You know each other, and unlike the majority of his interactions with his mother, his early experience with you has not led him to expect you to breastfeed him. Consequently, I will direct this section to you.

It's not so much that your baby doesn't like the bottle, it is just that the nipple and the method of getting food out of it is totally unfamiliar and he doesn't know how to do it. If there is formula in the bottle, it will taste different, which is pretty alarming to the newborn whose whole world is negotiated through his mouth. Take it slowly and gently. Most people who try to teach babies to take a bottle expect too much too quickly and don't give them time to learn. Babies feel the pressure and they are less, not more, able to take the bottle. Plan that it will take at least 10 practice sessions before your baby takes much more than an ounce from the bottle. He has to get accustomed to the feeling of the rubber nipple in his mouth, catch on to the fact that the stuff coming out of the nipple is food, and gradually learn how to suck and swallow in a whole different way.

Plan to do your practicing when your baby is a little hungry but not famished. If he is too hungry he will be desperate to eat and will be unwilling to experiment. For the first lesson, it is enough to put the nipple in your baby's mouth to see what he does with it. Put a little drop of formula on the tip, and he will probably take the nipple willingly enough. However, he will likely soon spit it out and will be unwilling to take it again until the next session. Each time you offer it to him you will get a little further—he will leave it in his mouth longer and will experiment more with getting the food out of it. Take your time on this process, or it will go slower, not faster. Some babies get so upset by being made to take a bottle when they don't want to that they throw up. You don't have to force—eventually he will get so he can take a bottle, even if he doesn't like it as well as taking the breast.

Hold him while you offer him the bottle. You don't necessarily have to hold in the breastfeeding position, but do hold him. In fact, holding him in a different position might make bottle-feeding less confusing for him, because he will get the message right away that this is quite different from breastfeeding. You might feel more comfortable propping him up in the little seat you make for him by crossing your ankle across your thigh. Do the feeding yourself. Except for the rare occasion, don't pass your newborn around to a lot of other people to be bottle-fed. He is most comfortable with you; you know him the best and you can read his signals.

Some people swear by one brand of nipple, others another. Most often I hear the Nuk nipple recommended. I think it is most important to pick out a nipple and stick with it. Every time you change nipples your baby has new learning to do and he has to get accustomed to a new feeling in his mouth.

If you plan to give your baby the bottle for only the occasional relief feeding, and if your baby is very reluctant to take the bottle, consider using a cup or a spoon to give a small amount of breastmilk or formula. Although your baby's mouth won't really be ready for cup drinking until he gets toward the end of the first year, he will suck on the rim of the cup and the surface of the liquid and get in enough to tide him over to the next feeding.

Expressing Breastmilk. We move now from the topic of teaching your baby to take a bottle to the related question of what to put *in* the bottle, which brings us to the subject of manual expression of breastmilk. Many parents who want to use a bottle only for the occasional night off would prefer to give their baby breastmilk rather than introduce a formula. If it can be done without a lot of upset and frustration, I think it is a good idea. Formulas are also just fine for relief bottles—read up on them in chapter 6 to choose one that is right for your baby.

Most women who express breastmilk on a regular basis rent the heavy-duty pumps from a hospital, clinic, breastfeeding support group, or supply store and then purchase their own fittings (the hoses and valves, flanges that go on the breasts, and bottles for catching the milk). For a more occasional use, you can experiment with a smaller mechanical breast pump; try the hand-operated piston, or you can remove milk from your breasts by hand expression. For any method, start with breast massage and plan to express for 3 to 5 minutes on each breast at first. Later on, you can work up to 10 to 15 minutes. Your milk will first come out in small spurts and then will flow freely. But don't worry if nothing comes out the first few times you try— you'll soon get the knack of it. As you express, you may find that repeating the massage briefly helps to work the milk down. You may also find it helpful to switch from one breast to another, because the second breast will let down milk in response to stimulus to the first. Wash your hands, then stroke from the outside edge of the breast toward the nipple, applying gentle but firm pressure with the palms of your hands. Alternate your hands as you work around your breast, stroking from the shoulder down, the side in, the waist up, and the breastbone in. Massage around each breast several times before you make any attempt to manually express milk.

Then place the funnel-shaped flange of the breast pump over your breast. Moisten the flange with water or the first few drops of milk to lubricate it. Let your nipple slide along the inside of the top part of the flange until it is lined up with the opening in the center of the flange. The sliding helps stimulate the letdown reflex, and the moistening lets the flange make a better seal with your breast. Hold the flange just tightly enough against your breast to make a good seal, but not so tightly that you dig it into your breast and pinch off the milk flow. The milk will be removed from your breast by suction. Stop pumping one minute after the milk has slowed, and break the seal by pressing your finger against your breast where it contacts the flange. Repeat the massage on the other breast before you begin to express from that side. After each use, make sure that you thoroughly wash all parts of the collecting apparatus that come in contact with the milk. Rinse them thoroughly, and allow them to air dry.

To hand express, lean over a sterile container for catching the milk, place your thumb and index finger on your areola about an inch back from your nipple (this will be right over the lactiferous sinuses). As you press gently inward toward your chest wall, squeeze your thumb and forefinger gently together gently. The repeated motion is to push back and squeeze, push back and squeeze. Keep your thumb and finger in the same position until no more milk comes out; then rotate to another position and repeat.

Storing Breastmilk. Breastmilk spoils very easily—it must be properly handled and stored to keep it safe and nutritious for your baby. Store the milk in disposable plastic baby bottle liners. In September 1999 I asked Robert Bradley, Ph.D., for recommendations on safe milk handling. Bradley and his colleagues at the University of Wisconsin food science department have done considerable research on freezing milks of all kinds. He recommends keeping unfrozen breastmilk in the refrigerator for no more than 24 hours and frozen breastmilk at 0 degrees Fahrenheit or lower for no longer than 45 days. If you are planning to freeze breastmilk, do so right after you collect it. Unlike the homogenized and pasteurized milk you are accustomed to, breastmilk can change in flavor and texture with time. The fat may separate out and may even cling to the side of the container, but when the milk is warmed up it will let go. Breastmilk is raw milk and contains many active enzymes that function even at freezer temperatures. Protein will clump as the result of freezing and may plug the nipple, although the breastmilk is as nutritious as ever for your baby.

I recommend baby-bottle liners for storing breastmilk because the plastic in these bags is formulated to keep plasticizers from leeching into the milk. Protect the bags from being banged around and broken in the freezer by wrapping them or putting them in a rigid container. Glass or plastic bottles are also fine, but do be scrupulous about cleaning and sterilizing. Start by freezing your breastmilk in 4-ounce batches so your child care provider can thaw it in the amount she is likely to need. Label each bottle with the date and perhaps the amount. Most babies take somewhere around this amount at first, and you don't want to waste the precious stuff. Breastmilk stored in such small amounts in plastic bags freezes quickly and can be thawed quickly under cold running water. Use the bottle intended for the disposable liner you used for storage, or you may pour the breastmilk into a regular bottle to feed it. Warm it for feeding by immersing the container in warm water. Don't microwave it or get it too hot because that will destroy the enzymes and the anti-immunity factors. Discard any unused breastmilk after the feeding. Rotate your supply of breastmilk in the freezer, using the containers with the oldest dates first.

Some women can get 8 ounces of breastmilk at a time when they hand express. Most express only a couple of ounces at a time and accumulate breastmilk stores gradually. Bradley says you can freeze small amounts as you go along and combine them in the same container, as long as the quantity you add (the just-collected, liquid milk) isn't greater than the amount that is already frozen. Putting too much liquid milk in with the frozen milk will thaw it, impair the quality, and may even allow bacteria to grow.

Be Wise about Vitamin and Mineral Supplements. Breastmilk is nutritionally complete. However, common practice raises concern about some nutrients, so we will discuss them specifically. If you eat well your breastmilk will have an ample supply of vitamins A, B, and C, and if your baby is at all exposed to sunshine—unless he is always well slathered with sun screen—he will make enough vitamin D with his skin. Even the Academy of Pediatrics recommends vitamin D supplements only for dark-skinned, covered up babies living where they don't get much sunshine. In contrast, Health Canada, making recommendations for a farther-north country with greater seasonal variations in sunshine and less direct sunshine overall, recommends routine vitamin D supplements for breastfed babies from birth. If I lived in Alaska or even cloudy northern Washington State, or if I had any doubt at all about a baby's vitamin D nutrition, I would go by Canadian recommendations. A safe and adequate dose of vitamin D is 200 international units (IU) per day. Unless you overdose with vitamin D, it can't hurt and can even head off problems. Every year we read reports of a few babies with vitamin D deficiency rickets, a serious bone disorder. They are babies who get very limited exposure to sun.

Iron is another of those often-debated supplemental nutrients. Regardless of maternal iron status, term infants are born with a good supply of iron. The newborn has need for, and utilizes, very little dietary iron before the age of 4 to 6 months. Prematurely born babies don't have the iron stores and need to have them supplemented from age 2 months. Newborns get their iron from breaking down the extra red blood cells they were born with and from breastmilk iron. Although it is in low concentrations, about 50 percent of breastmilk iron is absorbed (a relatively high absorption rate) and provides protection against iron-deficiency anemia. Furthermore, breastmilk iron is carried in a form, *lactoferrin*, that prevents its use as a nutrient by undesirable intestinal bacteria and protects against infestation by those bacteria. Supplemental iron, on the other hand, nourishes intestinal bacteria as well as the child and also changes the type of bacteria. Breastfed babies owe their sweet-smelling stools to an intestinal predominance of *Lactobacillus bifidus* and may owe their resistance to intestinal upsets to the same organism. With greater access to iron, the *Escherichia coli* in the intestine grow more, your baby is somewhat more vulnerable to intestinal infections, and stools get smelly.

To preserve that intestinal immunity as long as possible, for the occasional relief bottle (no more than one a day), use a formula that is not fortified with iron, if you have a choice. If you don't have a choice, go ahead and use the iron-fortified variety. However, when your baby starts taking more than one bottle of formula a day, do be sure to switch to the iron-fortified version. By then, the intestinal bacteria will have changed anyway, and your child will need the iron nutrition.

Although fluoride is important to tooth health, and although breastmilk is not a particularly impressive source of fluoride, beginning fluoride supplements is delayed for all infants until after 6 months of age. The problem is that it is hard to predict how much fluoride your baby will get, and too much can cause fluorosis, or white mottling of the tooth enamel—or even colored mottling in extreme cases. This mottling can take place even before teeth erupt. Because the incidence of fluorosis had increased in the last 20 years, in 1995 the American Academy of Pediatrics and American Academy of Dentistry stopped recommending fluoride supplements for breastfed infants at birth and instead recommended fluoride supplements for infants starting at age 6 months. We will discuss that recommendation further in chapter 7, "Feeding Your Older Baby." The schedule of fluoride supplements is given in appendix P, "Vitamins and Minerals for Children."

SUPPORT AND TEACHING

Breastfeeding may be getting easier in our culture, but you still can't say it is easy. Many obstacles to breastfeeding have to do with lack of support for *parenting*. Hindrances cited by the American Academy of Pediatrics in their 1997 statement on breastfeeding and the use of human milk include physician indifference and faulty information; not enough breastfeeding education before delivery; hospital policies and practices that undermine breastfeeding; interrupting breastfeeding for no good reason; early hospital discharge; lack of timely, routine follow-up care; mothers returning to work (especially when there are no facilities or support for breastfeeding); lack of broad societal support; advertising and other media that promote and show mostly bottle-feeding; and formula company giveaways.[9] Not named directly, but embedded throughout the list, is lack of support. As was apparent in our breastfeeding stories, there is an important role to be played in breastfeeding relationships—that of support and teaching. Since nobody is going to come along and give you much help in combating all that breastfeeding negativity, you will have to combat it for yourselves, starting before your baby is born.

Parenting the New Family. Cultures in which breastfeeding is common and successful have a special system of support to help the young woman learn to mother. Dana Raphael, an anthropologist who has made a detailed study of lactation in primitive societies, calls this supportive function the *doula* role. The term *doula* has now been appropriated by people who help the mother through labor and delivery, but for our purposes we will keep Dr. Raphael's original meaning. The doula is the supplier of information, the giver of physical and emotional support, and the one who instills confidence.

Since we no longer have these sophisticated support people around, you will have to cobble together this doula role for yourself. You may be fortunate enough to have a knowledgeable helper: your mother, a special friend, or a new-baby nurse who can help you for the first weeks after your baby is born. Most new parents, however, will have to draw on several resources to put together a well-functioning system for themselves. To build that system, begin talking with your friends to start collecting names of institutions, professionals, and other people who are committed to and comfortable with breastfeeding and who are well informed and truly helpful. You'll benefit from a knowledgeable and supportive obstetrician and pediatrician (or other health professionals who take care of your pregnancy and infant), a hospital with breastfeeding-supportive routines, an experienced lactation consultant, and a person or people who can provide ongoing situational and moral support.

Supportive Obstetrical Care. Because the whole birthing experience is such an intense one, the obstetrician, midwife, nurses, and nutritionists with whom you work before delivery become very important people in your life. Keep in mind that during labor and delivery you are likely to be very sensitive. Even a casual comment may seem to you to be serious criticism; or a simple gesture of praise may be reassuring out of proportion. You are justified in looking for an obstetrician who is supportive and sensitive to your emotional as well as physical needs. People who care for you during your pregnancy can help you start to learn what to expect and to identify any conditions that need to be attended to ahead of time.

Discuss the delivery routine. Breastfeeding goes better if you hold down on sedation and anesthesia and if you have access to your baby early and often. Ask about sedation and make sure your baby can be with you in the delivery and recovery room.

The Hospital Setting. Find out from your obstetrician about hospital routines, and double-check what you are told. Talk to other parents who have delivered at the hospital, ask your pediatrician, and ask when you go on tour. Specifically, find out

- Whether the hospital system and staff encourage parents and babies to be together in the delivery room and right afterward
- Whether they support rooming in (i.e., having the baby with you in your room rather than having him taken back to the nursery between feedings)
- Whether they have a positive attitude about breastfeeding and give good instruction
- Whether they have a certified lactation consultant
- Whether they refrain from giving formula to breastfed babies

The most helpful hospital routines are the ones that encourage you to nurse according to your baby's needs, both while you

are in the hospital and when you return home. Until about 15
years ago, however, hospitals whisked the baby away immediately after birth, bathed him, and then popped him into a little
warming oven to make sure his temperature was stabilized
before he was returned to his parents. Routines for the most
part have changed, and you are likely to find that your hospital
will encourage you to have access to your baby during that
important, exciting, and extremely receptive time right after
birth. But don't take it for granted. I was surprised when my
youngest granddaughters got the warming oven routine, apparently because they were "small." Actually, they each weighed
about 6 pounds and were in good shape, but their being twins
and their small-but-normal size still set off the hospital routine.
Not being able to get their hands on those babies was intensely
frustrating for their parents.

Rooming in, as I've already mentioned, is having the baby
in your room with you at the hospital rather than him being
taken to the nursery between feedings. While rooming in may
be an alarming concept that you would just as soon avoid, it is
better for you to get some comfort with your baby while you
have the backup and support of the hospital personnel. The
best obstetrical nurses will show you how to read your baby's
signals, soothe and comfort him, and take care of his physical
needs. If he is your first baby, you probably won't know the
simplest tasks like diapering, holding, and burping. Almost
every hospital has a lactation consultant, but most of the breastfeeding instruction is still done by the obstetrical nurses. You
will likely find one or two nurses who fit well with your needs.
You can ask for them using those very words.

Beyond helping and supporting you and your baby and
keeping an eye out to make sure you are both physically well,
there really isn't a lot to be done medically in an obstetrical
ward. New parents and babies aren't sick, they are just getting
accustomed to each other and getting their systems going. Some
hospital routines may have more to do with the hospital's trying to earn its money than with what you and your baby really
need. The idea of unnecessarily taking new babies away from
their parents and putting them in a warming oven is one example. Waking babies up every 2 to 3 hours to feed them when
everyone is exhausted from the birth process is another. Giving
babies glucose water is still another. Ask about these routines

ahead of time—once you get there, you will be stuck with them if they are indeed part of the system.

Glucose water has so many negative effects attached to it that it is surprising that it is still used so routinely as part of hospital practice. Practically, the biggest problem with giving nursing babies *small amounts* of sugar (glucose) water is nipple confusion. The rubber nipple on the bottle calls for a completely different nursing pattern than the breast. Nutritionally, the problem is that giving glucose water may interfere with the early establishment of breastfeeding. Medically, the short-term problem that grows out of *that* is that your baby may develop jaundice (see the section on jaundice later in this chapter, pages 194-195).

The Pediatric Staff. The physician or other health provider caring for your baby will be most involved with your breastfeeding. Check the local breastfeeding grapevine to find a physician who is knowledgeable and supportive. Not all are equally capable. Despite the American Academy of Pediatrics' official position that breastfeeding is best, a 1997 survey reported in the professional journal *Pediatrics* that only 65 percent of responding pediatricians recommended exclusive breastfeeding the first month after birth and only 37 percent recommended continuing breastfeeding for 1 year. Most pediatricians agreed with or were neutral about the statement that formula-feeding and breastfeeding are equally acceptable methods for feeding infants. Many pediatricians indicated that they would recommend—erroneously—against breastfeeding for certain medical conditions such as mastitis (23 percent), nipple problems (20 percent), seemingly inadequate milk supply (19 percent), slow weight gain on the part of the infant (17 percent), poor health of baby (13 percent), and jaundiced infant (8 percent). In fact, breastfeeding is appropriate for all of these conditions. The pediatricians who appear to be most knowledgeable and supportive of breastfeeding are those whose own child has been breastfed.[10]

In my experience, pediatricians and other health workers may or may not be helpful with feeding in general and breastfeeding in particular. Child health workers love kids and want the best for you and your child, but they are medical people and their primary concern is your child's medical well-being. Any training with breastfeeding, or with feeding at all, is likely to be brief and superficial. Your health care worker might be experienced and tuned in enough to say, "follow your baby's cues and trust what he tells you," and she may even give you some help in figuring out what those cues are. However, the health care worker who is stuck in the medical model of taking control might say, "here's how much your baby should eat," or worst of all, "you shouldn't feed him so often." This is destructive advice no matter who gives it. However, keep in mind that controlling advice is so much a part of feeding lore that they may not *know* how destructive it is. Inform your care provider as tactfully as you can. She is likely to be receptive, because we all learn from our patients. You will be doing yourself the favor of recruiting support, and you'll be doing other parents the favor of seeing to it that they get better advice as well. Consider telling your health care provider about *Child of Mine* and encouraging her to read it.

It's now standard practice for health care providers to offer parents a pre-delivery visit, although a minority of parents accept the offer. Do have your visit. It will increase your comfort and confidence after you have your baby. When you visit, find out precisely *who* will be giving you the care at your doctor's office. You may spend more office and telephone time with a nurse, nurse practitioner, or physician's assistant than you will with the doctor, so you need to be comfortable with them as well. Don't hesitate to ask to speak and work with the person you want—not everyone will be a good fit for you. Get your own personal impression of your providers' ideas and attitudes about breastfeeding. Find out the frequency and scheduling of follow-up visits and how flexible they are about scheduling extra visits. Does someone in the office follow up on breastfeeding couples, and do they call you or wait until you call them? Keep in mind that after you deliver you won't have much emotional or physical energy for seeking out help, so it is better if they call you.

Regular and Frequent Office Visits. Recommendations on the timing of new baby office visits are inconsistent. The American Academy of Pediatrics recommends that breastfed babies who are released from the hospital 24 to 48 hours after delivery be brought for an office visit 4 to 5 days after hospital discharge. (In an increasing number of states, visiting nurse services are organized to do the 4- to 5-day follow-up care at a home visit and report back to the pediatrician.) Recommendations on the timing of the next visit are contradictory. In their 1998 Pediatric Nutrition Handbook, the academy recommends a 2-week interval. In their statement on breastfeeding and the use of human milk, the academy recommends a 1-month interval.[9] I would feel a lot more comfortable if you were having the 2-week visit. As we discovered with Zachary and his parents, that is long enough to wait if you happen to have an infant who gets a slow start. Even Janet and David with their sturdy Emily could have been helped greatly in getting through those difficult early weeks if they had come in 2 weeks earlier. In case this makes you doubt your breastfeeding, keep in mind that the same thing can happen if you formula-feed. Formula-fed babies too can be too sleepy and fail to ask to be fed. Formula-feeding parents may pick up on misguided scheduling information and feed their baby on a too-infrequent schedule that doesn't give him enough to eat.

It is wise to get monthly follow-ups until age 6 months. As I said earlier, the 3-month-old baby occasionally falls off on weight gain. Further, the 4- to 6-month-old baby often changes his feeding patterns so dramatically that you will appreciate the reassurance of knowing things are going well.

An Experienced Teacher and Support Person. You can do a good job of studying and doing your homework about breastfeeding, but once you are actually doing it, you will still benefit from having someone remind you of what you already know. Keep in touch with someone you trust, by telephone or in person. Have her start when your baby is about a week old, when you are likely to be feeling isolated after leaving the hospital. Then she can reassure you that it is normal for new babies to eat frequently and that the decrease in the size of your breasts is not loss of milk but only loss of the engorgement that goes along with early lactation. Or, better yet, she can listen to your concerns and allow you to figure all of that out for yourself. It would be great if she would show up or get in touch again at 2 to 3 weeks to find out about the weight check and help you deal with, or celebrate, your appointment with the doctor. Your baby is likely to be getting more alert and demanding about that time, and also you may be starting to put more demands on yourself, assuming that you are through the early new-baby period. These developments can combine to make a fussy baby and may cause you to question whether breastfeeding is really worthwhile. Then it's important to have a gentle reminder to take care of yourself and to remember that it really takes at least a good 6 weeks to get through that intensive new-baby learning experience.

It is also helpful to be reminded that the new-baby adjustment period is, even under the best of conditions, a challenging time. One woman observed that for her getting through that newborn time was no easier with her fifth baby than it had been with her first. At 6 weeks postpartum, it can be helpful for you to be reminded that you are likely to encounter some hungry days and to be counseled about how best to respond to them. You may see your breast size continue to dwindle and appreciate the affirmation that mammary tissue is still there and functioning as it should be.

Your support person may be a good friend, a relative, a lactation consultant, a nurse or dietitian in the doctor's office, a community health nurse or nutritionist, or a member of a breastfeeding support group. You may in fact find that going to support group meetings is a good way of getting the contact and reassurance you need. If you choose the support-group approach, it is best to get started going to meetings before your baby is born. You might find that the support group will provide you with a friend who will seek you out during that early new-baby time. Watch out, however, for advice and "support" from people who are skeptical of breastfeeding or who have had an unsuccessful breastfeeding experience. They could be unintentionally but ever-so-subtly undermining your efforts. Feel no pressure to accept any advice you don't agree with—whether the advisor is experienced with breastfeeding or not.

Situational and Moral Support (Especially for Fathers). A new mother is emotionally and physically dependent and needs to be mothered. This role is often played by the father, but if you are a new father, you know that you could use some mothering yourself. You are doing your own adjusting. Your responsibilities have increased tremendously, your life and schedule have been immeasurably complicated, and if you are like most new fathers you don't know what to expect or how to cope with a new baby. Many new fathers find babies only start to get really interesting at around 2 to 3 months, when they start to smile and are more responsive. At the same time, you may find that your partner is exceptionally preoccupied with the baby, up and down, touchy, demoralized, and even depressed. Get help. Get good help. Mother Nature never intended raising children to be a solo job.

You need the help and people in my generation need to help you. It's part of the cycle of life. Tell your parents, or whoever parents you, that I said if they can squeeze out the time to be backup and support for you for a week or two, they will find it wonderfully rewarding and even healing. There is nothing quite like the satisfaction of helping a young family get off on the right foot. Not only that, but they will likely find as I did that being with a newborn one step removed from your own babies is a wonderful way of putting your own parenting in perspective. Your helper doesn't have to be an expert—you have plenty of experts to back you up. Your new-baby helper can cook, clean, do laundry, provide moral support, give encouragement, add another set of eyes and ears as you try to understand what your baby is telling you, and most important of all, be a calming presence while you get used to being parents. One of my colleagues wrote lovingly and fondly of her mother's help with new babies. One evening her mother prepared a lovely dinner, lit the candles, and left her and her husband alone for a special and undisturbed time to themselves. What a wonderful gesture! The mother's giving her blessings to them as a couple was a powerful way of providing support to that young family!

To understand the principle of the calming presence, let us briefly consider the early days of horse racing. Since successful thoroughbred racehorses are often jittery, especially in all the commotion before a race, trainers would put a goat in the stable with them. The placid, cud-chewing, unflappable goat would help calm the excitable racehorse. The saying "get your goat" is said to come from the underhanded tactic of stealing the goat, whereupon the horse would apparently be too upset to run well in the race. Of course, the days of calming a horse in this way are long gone, but the principle remains. Many parents take turns being the goat. When you are new parents, you both need a goat. Even an inexperienced helper can help settle you down, if he or she is able to be a good goat.

When you can't get good help, at least cut yourself some slack. You don't have to know the answers. You do, however, have to share responsibility for making the decisions about your baby—not just saying "anything you want dear." Being informed, thinking through the issues, and talking them over thoughtfully, as Emily's and Zachary's parents did, are all tremendously important. Even when you have to go off to work, taking that responsibility will keep you an active participant in your baby's life.

SPECIAL ISSUES IN BREASTFEEDING

Here is a collection of issues you may encounter with your breastfeeding. On the other hand, chances are good that you will not have any of them. Knowing how to catch complications early, however, can keep them from being problems. For instance, catching a plugged duct and taking remedial action can prevent its developing into a breast infection. There is no reason to get all upset about these problems. Try to remain philosophical as you read about and experience them. Remember that breastfeeding is an association between two people that, like any other intimate relationship, takes negotiating and managing to have it work out well for all concerned. Any problems that crop up are not a sign that breastfeeding is going poorly, but rather a common part of the process that you can hope to more-or-less take in stride as you work out your system.

Cesarean Section. Lactation is stimulated when the placenta is removed from the uterus, when the high levels of pregnancy hormones (estrogen and progesterone) drop, allowing prolactin levels to increase. Having the baby move through the birth canal isn't necessary. Breastfeeding after surgical birth is the same as breastfeeding after vaginal birth except that you are sore in a different place and for a longer time. Your stomach may be so tender when you hold your baby that you want to nurse lying on your side or use the football hold for a time. Otherwise, breastfeeding is the same.

Engorgement. A condition of the breasts that generally takes place on the first full day of lactation, engorgement means that the breasts are hot, heavy, hard, and painful. It lasts about a day.

While your breasts will get larger and fuller and may even feel firmer when your milk comes in, engorgement goes beyond that. Since the swelling can get to the point that milk release is slowed, it is difficult to relieve. The engorgement comes only partly from milk but is more due to the increased circulation of blood and lymph that accompanies the beginning of lactation. Only a minority of women become engorged, and you can increase your chances of preventing it by nursing early and often—8 to 12 times a day. Let your baby nurse 20 minutes or more on the first breast, finishing off the second with a breast pump if you are uncomfortable. Remember, this is only for the first 2 to 3 days after your milk comes in. Be sure to nurse at night even if the nursing staff offers to let you sleep, and keep track of which breast you start on and alternate breasts. Don't use a pacifier.

To deal with engorgement, use cold packs or cloths on your breasts between feedings, and if you take a hot shower, keep the hot water off your breasts. Since your nipples will be stretched flat by the swelling, help your baby attach to the nipple by hand-expressing some milk to soften your breast just before you feed. Then compress the areola between your thumb and forefinger as he latches on.

Some people swear by putting cabbage leaves in the bra, an ancient remedy for reducing engorgement. I got this method from Jan Bargar, a Chicago lactation consultant, but the method is well known in the profession. We are crossing into the realm of folk medicine, but if you are engorged you will be happy to have something to try. Get a large head of cabbage, discard the dry, roughed-up outer leaves, and remove two large inner leaves. Wash, pat dry, remove the center vein (for comfort) and crush slightly. Put a leaf inside each bra cup covering each of your breasts. Reportedly, you will feel immediate relief. Keep changing the leaves every hour or so when they become limp and wilted. As soon as your breast softens and your milk begins to drip, breastfeed or use a pump. Although your breasts may still feel full, if your milk is flowing and your baby can latch on, you will be cured. Stop the cabbage as soon as the engorgement has subsided—prolonged use of cabbage leaves is another folk remedy, this one for drying up the breasts.

If the measures I have described don't give you relief in 24 hours, get in touch with a lactation consultant.

Jaundice. If your baby is jaundiced, his skin and perhaps the whites of his eyes will be yellow, and blood tests will show that he has a high level of *bilirubin* in his blood. Jaundice is more frequent with breastfed babies, not because there is anything in breastmilk that *causes* it but because breastfeeding that gets off to an unusually slow start can slow bowel function. Formula-fed babies that are underfed or infrequently fed can become jaundiced as well. The normal full-term newborn has a very high red blood cell count. Those red blood cells helped him to make good use of the low amount of oxygen that was delivered to him across the placenta. After birth he has access to a higher level of oxygen, so his system begins breaking down the extra red blood cells that he no longer needs. The eventual product of that breakdown is bilirubin. The liver removes bilirubin from the blood by binding it chemically to particular protein fractions (albumin and glucuronic acid, for the biochemically inclined) and secreting it as part of bile into the large intestine and from the body as part of the stools.

If any part of that process is slowed or breaks down, the infant can accumulate bilirubin in his blood and show the characteristic yellow coloring of jaundice. An excess of bilirubin can cause cell damage, so doctors are appropriately attentive to jaundice and high bilirubin levels. Premature babies are especially susceptible to jaundice because they don't have the protein stores of term babies for binding the bilirubin. In addition, illness from other causes can make them more susceptible to lower levels of bilirubin. Term babies most often have trouble with jaundice when feeding is delayed or infrequent. That's because stools may be delayed or slow in passing through the colon. In the course of that slow passage, bacteria in the colon have time to break the protein-bilirubin bonds, and then the bilirubin can be reabsorbed into the bloodstream. Meconium contains quite a bit of bilirubin, and if your baby is slow about getting rid of his meconium he may reabsorb part of that bilirubin.

According to physician and breastfeeding expert Ruth Lawrence, the procedure for avoiding jaundice in the term baby is, simply, the same good breastfeeding technique that we have been discussing throughout this chapter: Nurse early and often. Avoid water and glucose water. To avoid reabsorption of bilirubin, Lawrence recommends to physicians that they stimulate the first stooling if it hasn't happened in 24 hours. As time goes by, continue feeding frequently and stimulating breastmilk production and carefully monitoring pees and poops. Lawrence notes that formula supplements are to be avoided during the first few days as long as breastfeeding is going well.

If bilirubin levels are particularly high or those high levels persist for several days, Lawrence recommends supplementing breastfeeding with formula while continuing to stimulate breastmilk production.[11] Your doctor may also recommend treatment with ultraviolet light (phototherapy). Do what your doctor says about supplementing breastfeeding and using phototherapy. Excessive and prolonged jaundice is not good for your baby, and you can continue to work on establishing and maintaining your breastmilk supply.

Leaking. Some women leak more than others, and some are more annoyed and embarrassed by leakage than others. To stop your breasts from leaking, put firm pressure against your nipples.* Fold your arms across your breasts and press them firmly toward the chest wall or press with your thumbs and forefingers directly on the nipple. To protect your clothing you can use absorbent pads or plastic liner pads. The absorbent pads are better because they'll keep your breast drier, but either can hold moisture on your skin and cause irritation.

Sore Nipples. The parts of your nipple that are most stressed during nursing are the points at the corners of your baby's mouth that are compressed by nursing and the part of the nipple and areola that your baby strokes with his tongue. Be sure your baby is properly attached whenever he nurses. Then shift the stress points around by changing your nursing position— sit, lie down, and use the football hold.

Chafed or cracked nipples can be especially tender and painful. Put cool compresses on your nipples after you nurse, and then leave your bra and shirt open so they are exposed to the air. You may also find that letting them dry and applying lanolin helps. If your sore nipples do not improve in a few days, have a knowledgeable person watch your breastfeeding to see whether your baby is latching on properly.

---

*This may not be such a good tactic if you are prone to plugged ducts.

Plugged Duct. A red and tender area on your breast just behind the areola may be caused by a plug of coagulated milk in the lactiferous duct. To move the plug out, take a hot shower, and while the hot water flows over your breast, massage your breast from well behind the plugged area toward the nipple. Nurse your baby right after, again massaging the affected area, and the nursing will probably dislodge the plug. Pumping will also help. Of course, hot compresses with massage helps as well.

Breast Infection. A breast infection, or mastitis, can start out looking like a plugged duct. It will be an infection if you feel like you have the flu: elevating temperature, aching all over, and feeling worn out. If you ache and feel tired out, take your temperature. If it is elevated, assume that you have a breast infection until you have seen your gynecologist. He or she is likely to prescribe antibiotics, but you don't have to wean. Your baby will get such a small amount of antibiotic that it is unlikely to affect him, but ask your doctor and your baby's doctor to okay the medication. It is fine to take acetaminophen or ibuprofen, but not aspirin (babies and young children are sensitive to aspirin). Lie down and rest as much as you can—your body needs help to fight off the infection.

Again, don't wean your baby just because of a breast infection. The infection will go away fastest, and you will be most likely to avoid developing a breast abscess, if you keep the milk moving and keep emptying your breast. In fact, some people even avoid antibiotics and use the same strategy for breast infection as for a plugged duct. If you choose this approach, keep in touch with your doctor and expect to be better within 24 hours. If you aren't any better by then, it's wise to start on antibiotics while you continue with your other tactics.

Breast infections are not that common—the data indicates that only about 3 percent of women get an infection during the first 6 weeks of nursing. Failure to empty the breasts regularly, clothing that is too tight, and too much fatigue and stress seem to be the usual causes. I once got a breast infection when I got mixed up and nursed first on the same breast twice in a row. It probably started with a plugged duct, but since I was new to breastfeeding I hadn't noticed it. At that time, my doctor wanted me to take my baby off the breast while I was on antibiotics, but I resisted his advice and kept on nursing. I had read other advice in nursing books (I have already mentioned that I didn't have very good advisors 30 years ago), and it seemed so hard to do it the other way when I was already feeling rotten. It wasn't easy to go my own way on that issue because I worried that I would somehow be hurting my baby, but I'm glad I did.

Breast Abscess. An untreated breast infection, especially if the breast isn't being emptied, may turn into a breast abscess. This is an infrequent but very serious condition—it is a pronounced infection in a local area of the breast, accompanied by flu-like symptoms and a clearly defined, red, hot, painful area. It requires surgical drainage (like opening a boil), and you probably won't be able to nurse from an abscessed breast until it is completely healed.

Breastfeeding While Working. It may be possible to breastfeed your baby when you go back to work, or it may not. It's worth making the effort. At the very least, you will be able to postpone the time when you will have to wean your baby totally from the breast. At the very most, you will be able to work full time and provide your baby with enough breastmilk to fill all (or most) of his nutritional needs. Most likely your experience will turn out being somewhere between the extremes—you may be able to breastfeed totally, if you work less than full time, or you may be able to provide only some of your baby's nutritional needs if you work full time. For a more detailed discussion of breastfeeding while working, see appendix D.

Relactation and Induced Lactation. Sometimes, due to illness or absence, women have to stop breastfeeding for a time and then want to resume. Women who adopt babies sometimes want to breastfeed them. Women who have attempted relactation and induced lactation have met with varying degrees of success. However, most women who went through the process felt positive about it, and their good feelings had very little to do with either the length of time they nursed their baby or their baby's need for supplementary formula. See appendix E, "Relactation and Induced Lactation," for more discussion of the considerations and techniques involved.

Health Conditions, Medications, and Drugs. If you have diabetes or cystic fibrosis you can breastfeed. Both take the same
careful management as when you are not breastfeeding. In both
cases, your breastmilk will be the same.

It is best to use prescription and over-the-counter medications as little as possible during nursing and not to use street
drugs at all. Certain of the antacids, anticoagulants, hormones,
anticonvulsants, laxatives, and all illegal drugs are not recommended for use while breastfeeding. Chemotherapy drugs for
cancer and drugs for control of AIDS are also out. Women in
developed countries who have AIDS or active tuberculosis are
discouraged from breastfeeding, those with AIDS because the
breastmilk can pass the virus along to the baby, and those with
TB because close contact with the baby could infect him.
However, after tuberculosis has been treated for 2 or more
weeks, breastfeeding is okay. Some medications and all street
drugs present a significant risk to a breastfed baby. The
American Academy of Pediatrics' latest summary of drugs and
other chemicals in human milk was published in November
1989. Be sure your advisor has a copy of that publication or an
updated version of it. The list is long and complex, so rather
than trying to summarize it, I encourage you to refer to the list
itself. About 1 percent of all drugs pass through to the baby, so
take any drugs you must take right after you nurse so there'll
be time to clear them from your system before the next breastfeeding. When choosing necessary medication, avoid the long-
acting dose (your baby has trouble detoxifying it); instead, take
medication right after you breastfeed, and watch your baby for
unusual signs or symptoms such as changes in feeding or sleeping or increased fussiness or rash.

Low doses of common drugs, such as caffeine, alcohol, and
oral contraceptives, deserve special consideration. Caffeine may
interfere with relaxation, for both you and the baby. Alcohol in
doses as small as two drinks cuts down on oxytocin release and
interferes with milk letdown. Smoking cuts down on prolactin
release, and smoking a significant amount can reduce your production. To avoid exposing your baby to second-hand smoke,
don't smoke in the car or the same room with your baby. Birth
control pills, especially the higher-dosage ones, have been
accused of (and defended against) decreasing breastmilk supply. Since the estrogen and progesterone in the pills were the

hormones that decreased at the time of delivery and allowed the increased prolactin levels that set off milk production, it seems the pill would interfere. In my opinion, it is best to avoid oral contraceptives and to be conservative about alcohol and caffeine use. Do talk with your physician if you want to use oral contraceptives.

To conclude, here is a summary of the basic points of this chapter.

- Enjoy your baby.
- Feed your baby on his schedule, when he is hungry and fully awake.
- Sit with your back and shoulders straight and your feet supported in a comfortable chair so you can hold still while your baby nurses.
- Put your baby on a pillow to keep the strain off your back and shoulders.
- Cuddle your baby while you feed him. Give him a little room for wiggling, but hold him tightly enough that he doesn't feel like he might fall.
- Have your baby lie on his side with his stomach on yours, with his head, shoulders, and hips straight.
- Tilt his head back a little so he can move his jaw and swallow well. Point your nipple straight out or up, not down.
- Support your baby's head, making sure it's higher than the rest of his body. If he's lying too flat, the milk could get into his ears and cause an earache.
- Check to see that he is latched on properly. Much of the nipple and areola will be in his mouth.
- Relax and enjoy watching your baby while your milk lets down.
- Notice that after letdown, your baby takes longer, slower suck-swallow motions.
- Listen for a drawing sound that lets you know he is getting milk.
- Let him eat as fast or as slowly as he wants to. If your breastmilk is flowing too quickly and your baby seems to be gagging, hand express a little breastmilk to slow things down.
- Talk with your baby in a way that he seems to enjoy, but don't be so active that he gets distracted from eating.
- Hold him quietly while he pauses and rests. He may just

want to look at you and make noises with you a bit before he goes back to eating.

- Burp him only if he seems like he's full of air. He'll stop eating and may seem uncomfortable.
- If he stops to fuss, soothe him and again offer the breast. Don't force—you are just checking to see whether he has had enough.
- Keep the feeding smooth and steady. Don't stop to do other things like wipe his chin or arrange his clothes and blankets.
- Work toward having him stay awake through the whole feeding. Start feeding when he is fully awake, and help him to stay awake by looking at him and talking to him while he eats.
- Take care of yourself: eat well, drink enough, rest enough, and avoid getting physically overstressed.
- Enjoy your baby.

Adapted with permission from *ELLYN SATTER'S NUTRITION AND FEEDING FOR INFANTS AND CHILDREN: Handout Masters.* Ellyn Satter Associates, Madison, Wis., 1997. For information about Ellyn Satter's books and teaching materials, see **www.ellynsatter.com** or call 800-808-7976.

Books to Read. This has been a breastfeeding primer in a few pages. I hope it gives you an accessible reference to the main issues that, like my earlier readers, you can return to again and again. For more detail or to review issues I haven't covered, books I recommend include the following:

Eiger MS, Olds SW. *The Complete Book of Breastfeeding.* New York: Bantam Books, 1999.

Huggins K. *The Nursing Mother's Companion.* Boston: Harvard Common Press, 1999.

Neifert M. *Dr. Mom's Guide to Breastfeeding.* New York: Plume, 1998.

CHAPTER 6

FORMULA-FEEDING YOUR BABY

IN OUR DISCUSSION of formula-feeding, we will be dealing with three main topics:

1. How to understand what your baby wants so you can do a good job of feeding
2. What to put in the bottle
3. Techniques for keeping clean and getting the equipment to work right

The *way* you feed your newborn is as important as *what* you feed her. Tuning in on what your baby tells you—and understanding it—is an essential part of allowing your baby to eat and grow well and letting her grow up feeling good about herself and about the world. Beyond that relationship, you must use infant formula if you formula-feed your baby. Infants are nutritionally vulnerable, and what they eat has to be uncompromisingly appropriate. Infant formula must be easy to digest, it must be absolutely appropriate for your baby's nutritional needs, and it must not disrupt her fragile body chemistry.

For her technical review of the formula information and advice about current practice in formula use, I thank JoAnn Tatum Hattner, MPH, RD, Certified Specialist in Pediatric Nutrition, Palo Alto, California.

201

Breastmilk and commercial formulas adequately fill these specifications. Other formulas, such as the partially predigested formulas and the premature infant formulas, are more highly specialized to provide for infants with special needs.

Although modern formula-feeding is convenient and safe, it is important not to become casual about the mechanics of preparation. The water supply must be clean and safe, the nursing equipment must be sanitary and comfortable (for both feeder and child), and the formula must be prepared precisely according to directions.

Before you can meet your baby's needs, you have to get your own needs met. In chapter 5, in the section titled "Support and Teaching" (pages 183-192), I made quite an issue of encouraging parents to provide for themselves. Please read that section if you haven't already, or reread it if you need to, and think about the support *you* need in learning to be a parent. Keep in mind that most of the issues I discuss have to do with being a *parent*, not just being a *breastfeeding* parent. You need regular and frequent office visits, you need an experienced teacher and support person, and you need situational and moral support. You will be making a great many emotional and physical adjustments. You will have much to learn, and you will feel overwhelmed and befuddled at times. Learning the lessons ahead of time and actually applying them when the time comes are two different things. You will be anxious, and that's all right—we all learn better when we are a little anxious. But if you are *too* anxious it makes it hard to learn. Do seek help, and accept help and support when it is offered. It will make parenting much more joyful and relaxed for you.

THE FEEDING RELATIONSHIP

Feeding is about loving and respecting, about knowing your child and doing what is right for her, and about being successful with her. Whether you and your child come out of her infancy feeling good about yourselves and the relationship and whether your baby grows well or poorly are determined to a large extent by what happens in feeding. Feeding provides you with your best opportunity during the early months to get to know your baby. Feeding can provide your baby with a powerful message that you see her as a valuable person, that you respect her and are willing to go to some trouble to work things out with her. Feeding well satisfies your needs as well. It is important for you to know that you can give your baby what she needs to make her happy.

In infancy, establishing a positive feeding relationship with your child depends on a division of responsibility:

- You are responsible for *what* your child is offered to eat.
- She is responsible for *how much* she eats.

Your job in managing bottle-feeding is straightforward: you get to choose the formula that goes in the bottle, although, as I will point out later, to do that you will have to keep your baby's needs in mind. After you make the formula-feeding decision, you follow your baby's lead. She knows not only how much she needs to eat but also how often, at what level of skill, how long, and how fast. Early on, your task as parent is to understand what she tells you. Feed her promptly when she asks for it—after she is wide awake but not overstimulated—and feed in a smooth and continuous fashion, paying attention to information coming from her about the timing, tempo, and duration of the feeding. In brief, your job is to do whatever you can to make her happy.

GET COMFORTABLE TO FEED

You can safely enjoy your newborn and dote on her all you want. You won't spoil her; spoiling comes later. Part of your comfort in feeding is attitude adjustment—being clear about what is realistic to expect from your newborn and what is not realistic. Part of your comfort is actual *physical* comfort. You will be spending a lot of time feeding, so you need to give some thought to setting up your environment so you can be physically relaxed.

An Infant Is Not a Toddler. In telling you that your job is to make your baby happy, keep in mind that I am talking about the way you feed your *infant*, not the way you feed your *child*. To make this point, allow me to restate what I said in chapter 4: The toddler has a whole different set of developmental tasks than the infant does. The infant's task is to achieve homeostasis and attachment. Homeostasis is the ability to maintain a relatively stable state of equilibrium—being calm in spite of outside stimulation and not being too rattled to attend to the task at hand. Attachment is learning to love and be loved. The toddler works on separation and individuation, that is, learning that she is separate from you. It is only when she goes into that stage that she needs structure and limits.

Your child works on homeostasis as she learns to manage her sleep states so she can stay calm and organized while she eats. She works on attachment by learning to connect emotionally with you, then learning to communicate deliberately with you. Following your baby's lead and feeding in the way she wants to be fed is the best thing you can do to help your baby achieve homeostasis and attachment. Toward the end of the first year and into her second year, her task becomes the separation and individuation of the toddler. At that point her need will be to find out that she is her own person, separate from her parents and from the other people in her life. If at that stage you cater to her every wish and try to make her happy no matter what, you will be parenting poorly. She has to say *no* to you in order to prove to herself that she is a separate person. And you need to say *no* to her not only to keep her safe and to provide her with opportunities to learn but also to provide her and yourself with the structure you both need to feel comfortable.

I am reminding you of this fundamental difference between infants and toddlers because some parents become alarmed when I talk about trusting babies and catering to them and trying to make them happy. They fear that this kind of parenting will produce a child who is a tyrant and that to prevent that they have to take control right from the beginning. That kind of thinking often leads to imposing feeding schedules early on and forcing young infants to sleep through the night before they are ready. I agree that if you cater to your *toddler* you run the risk of producing a tyrant. I do not agree that there is danger in catering to your *baby*. In fact, parents who are more sensitive to infant signals raise toddlers who are more likely to be obedient and compliant, not less so. Toddlers who have been parented in an accepting way when they were infants are more cooperative and willing to accept structure and limits when they become toddlers.[1] Responding to your baby's cues now makes her feel good about herself and frees her to want to please you later on. Raising children, you will often deal with issues of control. In going by this early division of responsibility, you will be acknowledging that it isn't appropriate to try to control your infant's feeding schedule.

Take Care of Yourself. In chapter 3 I urged you to do most of the feeding yourself. You know your baby and can read her feeding cues. She knows you and is most secure with you. For most of the time you spend with your baby in the next few months you will be feeding her, so it is important that you get as physically comfortable as possible. If you aren't properly positioned, feeding can be a real backbreaker.

First, get a good chair that supports your back and arms and fits your body. Support your feet well on the floor, or get a stool that holds your feet up at a proper height so sitting doesn't put a strain on your back. You can get a feeding stool that raises your feet and supports them at an angle so you can relax your leg and back muscles. I think such a stool makes a good investment. Also consider getting a breastfeeding pillow (tell the folks in your support system that either would make a wonderful gift). Although they are called "breastfeeding pillows," they work very well for bottle-feeding as well. Go to your favorite baby store and check out the models available. The best ones are shaped like a strange looking figure 8 so they curve around your stomach and give your baby space to lie flat and comfortably. She can lie on her back or on her side, as long as you are careful to present the bottle from straight on. The pillow that is nicely shaped for bottle-feeding sticks up higher at the head end and is lower at the foot; this arrangement helps you to hold your baby's head higher than the rest of her body. The pillow will hold your baby up at a good height so she can clearly see your face. Newborns gaze and are interested longest when they are looking at faces, and they can focus only on objects that are a foot away or less. Your baby will look at your face and then look away. She will, however, look longer and more often if you keep looking (but don't try to entice her back), so when she is ready and looks back again you will be there waiting to look at her and talk to her.

DO WHAT YOUR BABY NEEDS SO SHE CAN EAT WELL

Your baby will eat best when you follow her lead in feeding. To help her eat well you need to help her be calm and awake, to connect with her emotionally, to understand her feeding and sleeping cues, her temperament, and her eating style. For some background about your baby's social and emotional development, review chapter 4, "Understanding Your Newborn."

Help Her Be Calm and Alert. Feed your baby when she's hungry, calm, and awake but not overstimulated or exhausted from crying. If she's upset, help her calm down. If she's sleepy, wait for her to wake herself up before you try to feed her. Cuddle your baby while you feed her. Hold her firmly so she doesn't feel like she might fall, but not so tightly that she has no room for wiggling. Keeping her comfortable and in control helps her eat well. Help her swallow well by lining up her head, shoulders, and hips and tipping her head back just a bit, holding her head up higher than her body so the formula doesn't get into her inner ear when she swallows. Offer her the nipple by brushing it against her cheek or lips. If she is hungry, she will turn toward the nipple and open her mouth so you can put it in—you won't have to pry her lips apart or force it in. Once you start feeding follow her lead and keep the feeding smooth and continuous. Hold the bottle—and your baby—*still,* get the bottle to flow smoothly and the nipple to feed at a comfortable rate. Don't do a lot of interrupting to check the formula level in the bottle, wipe her off, straighten her clothes or burp her unnecessarily. Burp her only if she seems like she is full of air—she'll stop eating and may seem uncomfortable. Every time you interrupt the feeding, it upsets her a little. If she gets upset enough she may stop eating, even if she hasn't had enough.

Talk with her in a quiet and encouraging manner while she eats, but don't be so entertaining that she forgets what she is doing. Experiment with your voice to see what tone and tempo of speaking helps her to stay awake and remain quiet and alert. Hold your face close to hers—she is likely to find it fascinating, and at first she can't see very far. Experiment with touching her, and notice what keeps her calm and alert and what makes her jittery or makes her close her eyes.

Read Her Signs. When your baby is ready to eat, her eyes may be open wider than usual and her face will look bright; she will curl her arms and legs over her tummy, and when you touch her mouth, cheek, or chin she will turn toward the touch to root and mouth. She may bring her hands up under her chin or suck on her hands. Eventually, she will fuss. Fussing is a late hunger cue, so as you become more accustomed to reading the earlier signs, she won't have to fuss to tell you she's hungry. If she fusses for long, she'll get herself so worked up that she won't eat well. Babies vary in the way they get ready to eat. Does she want to eat so soon after she wakes up that she doesn't even have patience for a diaper change? Or does she need to rest or talk a bit before she gets ready to eat?

Let her eat as much or as little as she wants, and stop feeding her when she shows that she is full. She will slow down her sucking, let go of the nipple, and turn away to indicate that she has had enough to eat. Her rooting reflex will go away when she is no longer hungry. If you don't pick up on the earlier "I'm done" signals, she may become more firm to give you the message: she will kick and squirm, arch her back, or get fussy. If she wants to rest during the feeding, let her, and then offer her the nipple again. Many times your baby will pause to look at you and socialize, so sit still, talk a bit, pay attention, and see what happens. When you offer her the nipple again, don't get pushy—you are only checking to be sure that she has had enough to eat. Some babies get full abruptly and won't take another swallow. Other babies drift into being full, gradually slowing down and losing interest in sucking. Respect your baby's cues; don't try to get her to finish a bottle when she's full. Often newborns will go off to sleep when they are full, but it is better if your baby is still awake at the end of the feeding. That way you know she has had enough to eat. Furthermore, being put to bed sleepy but awake teaches your baby to put herself to sleep and heads off sleep problems later.

As with hunger and fullness, your baby will move through a cycle of being alert and sociable on the one hand and wanting to be left alone and get some sleep on the other. Your being able to recognize those cues has an impact on feeding because the quality of your baby's sleep will influence the quality of her wakefulness. Your baby will tell you she wants to interact when her eyes and face are bright, when she smiles and looks at you, and when she moves her arms and legs smoothly toward you. When she needs a break, she will look away, kick and squirm, push toward you with her hand, pull away, or arch her back and fuss or cry. If you can put her to bed when you catch her early signs of being tired and needing a nap, it will be easier for her to settle down and go to sleep. For a list of your baby's sleep states, see the section in chapter 4 titled "Your Baby's Sleep and Awake States" (pages 120-125); for a list of some of the most common engagement and disengagement cues, see Figure 4.2, "What Is Your Baby Telling You?" on page 122.

You Don't Have to Be an Expert. Fortunately, your sorting and identifying don't have to be perfect, because at first the cues can be subtle and confusing and the process more one of trial and error than your getting right to the issue at hand. However, you will get better and better at knowing what she wants and her messages will become more and more clear. Gail Price, a graduate student in clinical psychology, demonstrated in her research that mothers could easily learn how babies "talk." Price videotaped 40 sets of first-time mothers and their babies and divided them into two groups. One group got to see the tapes of their feeding sessions and one group didn't. Soon after hospital discharge, Price watched the tapes with the first group of mothers and asked one question: "What is your baby saying to you?" She didn't *teach* anything; she only sat with them while they did the observing. The mothers caught on quickly to the idea that their babies were communicating with them and were open about critiquing themselves. Most times they could see that they had done something that helped their baby calm down or better attend to her eating. At other times the mothers were uncomfortable with the interaction, feeling they had done something their baby didn't like. For instance, one mother commented, "I'm burping him so hard I look like I am killing him. Oh, you poor baby. Why didn't you tell me?" While the mothers didn't like their mistakes, they didn't get too upset about them as long as they knew they could find a better way. For instance, the mother who felt she burped too hard observed that her sleepy baby opened his eyes and sucked when she talked with him or touched his fingers, but not when she jiggled him. In that area, she had been unconsciously using a more helpful approach.

When all the babies and mothers were again evaluated after 4 to 6 weeks, Price found that the mothers who had gone through the exercise of looking for communication signals from their babies were more skillful at feeding their babies than the mothers who hadn't had that kind of information and encour-

agement. The mothers who had learned to look for communication felt they could figure out what their babies wanted and
respond accordingly. The other mothers tended to see their
babies as set in their ways and didn't think that their own
behavior affected their babies one way or the other. The point?
That nobody was an expert but that the mothers who had it
pointed out to them that babies communicated could learn to
read the signs. When she did this research, Price was a graduate
student who didn't know the first thing about babies, and the
mothers were first-time mothers.[2]

Check Your Baby's Suck and Swallow. If all goes well, your
baby will feel relaxed in your arms, move her arms and legs
easily, and be able to eat from the bottle smoothly and steadily,
comfortably sucking and swallowing. She will not be snorting,
coughing, and gagging, coming off the bottle to cry, arching her
back, or kicking and squirming. If you see any of those behaviors, something is wrong. It might simply be that the bottle or
nipple isn't working right—feeding too fast or too slowly—and
you need to adjust it. (You'll learn more about managing the
equipment in the section titled "Bottle-Feeding Equipment and
Technique" later in this chapter.) However, it could be that your
baby is having some difficulty sucking or coordinating her suck
and swallow. Talk with your health care consultant about your
concerns, and keep asking until you get a satisfactory answer
and some help. If you see this behavior in the hospital, ask to
speak with a lactation consultant. Lactation consultants are
accustomed to evaluating infants' suck and swallow patterns,
so even though you're not breastfeeding, ask. (In chapter 5, I
relate the story of Emily, who had some trouble getting her suck
going.) Occupational therapists and speech therapists also are
expert at evaluating oral-motor patterns and can help you to get
your baby's suck corrected. If at first you don't succeed in getting it straightened out, don't give up. If you feel your baby has
a deficient sucking/swallowing pattern, keep looking until you
get help. A poor suck can make feeding a struggle, and feeding
problems that get started early can persist and make feeding
miserable for a long time.

Don't Prop the Bottle. Don't put your baby down to sleep with
a bottle. Don't put her in her infant seat to eat, either, even if

you hold the bottle for her. To eat well and to know that you love her, she needs you to cuddle her while she eats. Leaving her to feed herself will make her feel lonely and make it hard for her to eat the amount she needs. If babies don't get their emotional needs met, they are more likely to eat too much or too little. Putting your baby down with a bottle could also give her an earache, make her choke, or give her *nursing-bottle tooth decay*. This is tooth decay that an older baby gets when she goes to sleep with formula (or any other liquid besides water) in her mouth. If your baby falls asleep during a feeding, move her around a little so that she swallows the milk left in her mouth.

Share Control with Your Baby. Because bottle-feeding lends itself to certain controlling maneuvers, you must take care to avoid common pitfalls. All of the approaches to feeding I have covered so far are approaches that allow the two of you to share control of feeding. Feeding your baby on demand is absolutely essential. For your baby to eat and grow in the way nature intended, you must share control with feeding. (To examine the research about the topic, see appendix J, "Children and Food Regulation: The Research.") Sharing control with your baby will help her more than anything else you can do to quiet herself, eat well, and learn to manage her sleep and awake states. Even though she is at such a young and tender age—or perhaps because she learns it so early it becomes instinctive—her self-quieting capability can remain with her for life and provide her with the ability to keep a grip on herself in the midst of life's inevitable frustrations.

On the other hand, you will be overly controlling and will absolutely interfere with your baby's ability to quiet herself if you go by what you want rather than by what your baby wants in feeding. You are being controlling if you

- Pick out the schedule
- Make your baby eat a certain amount
- Stop the feeding before she is full
- Jiggle her or the bottle to get the feeding to go a certain way or at a certain pace
- Try to get her to hurry up to finish the bottle
- Try to get her to eat more than or less than she wants
- Try to get her to last longer between feedings

• Make her wait to eat when she is hungry
• Feed past her "I'm full" signals

Such tactics will make your small child eat worse, not better, and can make your large child eat more. They can actually *interfere* with arriving at a schedule because staving your baby off when she is crying and asking to be fed can get her so worn out that it is hard for her to stay awake long enough to eat well. Look again at Figure 4.1, "Control of Feeding," on page 116 for a comparison of feeding practices that share control between baby and parent with those that do not.

Controlling tactics are not at all helpful with any newborn, and they are particularly negative for irritable, disorganized, and colicky babies. Those babies, through no fault of their own or anybody else, are born irregular, easy to upset, and hard to understand. Trying to control such a child won't work. On the other hand, if you happen to have a compliant, placid child, you may be able to control feedings and get away with it—at least for a time. However, if you keep on with your controlling tactics, sooner or later your child will become resentful of being ignored and overruled, and you will have trouble. If it doesn't happen for the first few years, I promise you it will when she is a teenager.

If by now you are looking over your shoulder and wondering who in the world I am talking to, for surely you would never treat your darling child that way, you have good cause. If you are reading this book, I am sure that you are too tuned in to be controlling and disrespectful of your child. However, from time to time you will hear some persuasive arguments for being controlling. Parenting by the clock is a regrettable trend that is becoming accepted in an ever-widening circle of parents. To keep you on the right track, it may help you to know why such parenting is unwise and destructive. Your relatives and friends who believe strongly in parenting by the clock won't necessarily be able to hear your point of view, but you need to know what is wrong with such rigid style of parenting.

BABIES VARY

Ask any parent of two or more children raised in the same household in seemingly the same way and you will be told that no two babies are alike. Babies vary in size, shape, temperament, activity level, ability to get organized and stay that way, physical sturdiness, sucking and swallowing ability. . . . I could go on. Each baby offers particular challenges and rewards. Parents are tested more by some babies than by others. It will be sheer luck if you get a comfortable fit between your temperament and your baby's characteristics. If you are a laid-back, mild-mannered person, an aggressive, active baby may challenge you considerably. Help her, but don't try to change her. It is vital for you to see your baby as she really is. To learn to appreciate and enjoy her, you may have to examine your dreams and agendas and set them aside.

Vulnerable Children. I see many children in my clinical office who are eating and growing poorly, are very finicky, or are perceived as—or actually are—too small or too thin. I hear about these children from my professional network as well, and from their parents when I am on the road speaking. I have had enough opportunity to do detailed evaluations of my clinical children to know the consequences and read the signs. Almost without exception feeding is distorted. Parents love their babies and want the best for them. Parents would not knowingly behave toward an infant in a hurtful or disrespectful way. But time after time I see parents foisting a bottle on a baby when she doesn't want it, refusing to take no for an answer—even when the child is crying, struggling, shutting her mouth, turning her head away, and arching her back. I hear stories of parents tricking children to eat—making them laugh and then putting in the nipple, or feeding children while they are asleep.

Parents know these feeding methods are hurtful, but they use them anyway. Why? Sometimes it is because they have an agenda—they want their child to sleep or eat in a particular way or to be a certain size or shape. More often it's because they are scared. If a baby is ill or prematurely born, or even if a child is exceptionally small, the risk of becoming controlling with feeding is high (see appendix H, "Feeding Your Premature Baby"). Sometimes it is only a label that scares parents. For instance, babies are made eligible for the WIC program (Special Supplemental Nutrition Program for Women, Infants, and Children) on the basis of nutritional vulnerability—they are certified as being at nutritional risk.* Some children are classified as being medically at risk—they have physical, nervous system, muscular, or behavioral characteristics that health workers consider to make them particularly vulnerable. Although these designations have their purposes, the consequences to feeding are so grave that a child should *not* be labeled as being at risk, or at nutritional risk, unless parents are given excellent and accurate feeding guidance at the same time.

Too often, the feeding guidance parents are given is destructive. It comes in the form of "get him to eat, I don't care how you do it," or "get so-and-so ounces of formula in every day" or "wake her up to feed every 2 (or 1 or 3) hours." At times the advice comes with a demonstration on how to jiggle the baby or jiggle the bottle or run your fingernail across the bottom of her feet to get her to wake up and eat. As I pointed out earlier when I was warning against being controlling, such tactics either make babies too upset to eat or wear them out so they go back to sleep to get away from all the commotion.

Even without such counterproductive teaching, parents of apparently vulnerable children try to help out—they try to get the baby to eat more so she can get well or get big or even survive. Studies of newborn formula-fed infants who were not ill but only small showed that parents, almost without exception, became more controlling in feeding: they jiggled the baby, they jiggled the bottle, and they tried to get the baby to eat more when she really wanted to stop. (For background on this and other research studies, read appendix J, "Children and Food Regulation.") It is understandable—if the baby seems to need help, parents try to give it. The problem is that those pressing, forcing tactics consistently backfire. From birth, the more controlling parents get with feeding, the less children eat and the more poorly they grow. As with helping your child become

---

*Children are identified as being at nutritional risk if they are relatively small, relatively large, have low iron stores or anemia, were products of a high-risk pregnancy, or have had a significant medical condition. Children can also be eligible for WIC if it appears that their food intake is nutritionally marginal. Recently WIC began making children eligible if WIC certifying professionals uncover inappropriate feeding practices such as forcing, ignoring, restricting, or developmentally inappropriate feeding.

organized, the way to help a small or ill child eat as much as possible is to share control in feeding—to follow her lead. Even healthy premature babies as small as 3½ pounds are capable of signaling their need for food. In my view, a premature infant is not ready to go home from the hospital until she is eating on demand and until her parents can understand and interpret her feeding cues. If that child—or any child—is not capable of eating enough, she must be given tube-feedings to supplement. (You'll learn more about tube-feedings in chapter 9, pages 416-420.) *That child—or any child—must not be force fed.* Forcing your child to eat more than she wants doesn't help. It makes matters worse. It spoils the feeding relationship and that undermines your child's ability to eat and grow in a way that is right for her.

The occurrence of the following characteristics in your child may elicit forcing or controlling behaviors on your part. You may be especially tempted to be controlling under the following circumstances:

• Your child is disorganized and has an irritable temperament.
• Your child is hard to read and exhibits confusing hunger and satiety cues.
• Your child has been labeled "at risk" or "at nutritional risk."
• Your child is relatively small or large.
• Your child eats very large or small amounts.
• Your child has been ill.
• Your child was prematurely born.
• Your child has neuromuscular or cognitive limitations.
• Your child requires a modified diet.

These characteristics may also elicit forcing and controlling tendencies in your *advisors,* and as a consequence the advice you get may be negative. My healthy twin granddaughters each weighed about 6 pounds when they were born, a perfectly respectable and even admirable birth weight. However, the nursing staff labeled them as being too small and therefore considered them untrustworthy and in need of vigilant supervision to see that they ate enough. The nursing staff instructed their parents to wake them up every 2 hours to feed them and demonstrated the very same agitating and upsetting tactics I have just criticized. I am happy to say that when their parents got them home, they stowed the controlling tactics and followed the babies' lead in feeding. If any of the attributes described in the above list fit your child, be particularly careful to avoid your controlling impulses, ignore the controlling advice you get from others, and share control of feeding with your baby. If feeding feels continually unsatisfying to you, get help. Problems you solve or prevent now won't come back to haunt you when your child is older.

Relatively Large and Small Babies. Babies who are relatively small or large, or who eat relatively small or large amounts, are highly likely to be perfectly normal. The problem, as I have just pointed out, is that parents—and even health care workers—do tend to get worried and try to moderate the babies' seeming extremes of size or eating. Alarmed adults try to get the big baby to eat less and the small baby to eat more, often without even being aware of it. As I have said before, the irony is that such tactics tend to backfire. An infant who is encouraged to eat more than she wants eats less and grows more slowly; an infant whose food intake is restricted puts more pressure on feeding and is more likely to overeat and grow too fast.

Parents of large, actively growing babies are particularly vulnerable. Even some health professionals become concerned about normal fatness in babies, and people on the street make rude comments like "what are you feeding that baby?" or "she doesn't look like it would hurt her to miss a meal." Don't pay attention. The fat baby has no more likelihood of growing up to be fat than the average or slender baby. For more information about the topic of children and weight, see appendix J, "Children and Food Regulation: The Research."

Whether your baby is relatively large, relatively small, or somewhere in between, it is far better to concentrate on establishing a positive feeding relationship and let amounts and growth take care of themselves. At this early age—or at any age, come to think of it—the amount your child eats is her business. You can't—and mustn't—control it. Letting go of what you can't control will be good training for when she becomes a toddler.

The I-Want-to-Eat-All-the-Time Baby. With a fussy, irregular baby it is hard to sort out what signals mean. Does she want to eat? Does she just want to be held and comforted? Does she want to go back to bed? It doesn't hurt to feed a baby if you are not sure, because she will let you know soon enough if she's not interested. However, you might want to get in the habit of sorting out what she wants rather than making feeding the first solution you try. Your fussy, irregular baby works herself up and will benefit from some help getting calmed down and staying calm. Check the soothing techniques covered earlier in chapter 4, in the section called "Helping Your Baby Quiet Herself" (pages 129-132), and go through the routine with her: leave her alone, look at her, talk to her, wrap her in a blanket, and pick her up. Keep in mind that you are not trying to hold her off to get her to eat less often. You are only going through a process of trial and error to figure out what she *does* want and to help her learn to settle herself down.

If, however, you go through the routine and she seems to be hungry, do feed her. You are not trying to deprive her of food with these tactics; you are simply giving her the opportunity to settle down. Rather than depending only on the feeding to calm her, you are helping her to calm down first and arrive at feeding able to do a better job of eating. If she eats better, she won't be as likely to ask to be fed again right away. But *be clear* what you are trying to accomplish—you are not trying to get her to eat less; you are helping her to sort out whether or not she's hungry.

The Colicky Baby. Although everyone fears and dreads colic, nobody is able to define it. Colic is the newborn pattern of crying, fussing, and appearing to be in pain for part or in some cases almost all of waking time. Colicky babies apparently have nothing medically wrong with them, but they seem inconsolable no matter what you do. The best guess is that colic is the result of an immature nervous or digestive system, and most babies outgrow the pattern by the time they are 3 to 4 months old. Babies are, after all, born with nervous systems, muscles, and digestive systems that still have some growing and developing to do.

With your fussy and irritable baby, go through the same self-quieting routine that we just reviewed (presented in chapter 4, page 131). Take it slow and easy, giving each step at least 20 seconds before you move on. Keep in mind that the overstimulated infant can act just like a colicky baby, so be careful not to be so active that you contribute to her problem. Your soothing probably won't help at first, and it won't help for a long time. However, you are doing the right thing even if your baby can't respond right away. Over the first 6 months, she will settle down and start to become more predictable and responsive.

Many times parents of seemingly colicky babies get into a pattern of switching formulas. It's an understandable solution, because colicky babies frequently curl over their stomachs and seem to be in pain. Trying out first one nipple and then another is also common, probably because colicky babies seem hungry but then spit out the nipple. Often neither solution will be helpful, and the changes can even contribute to the problem. A newborn's main connection with the world is through her mouth. Although her formula tastes vile to us, it tastes wonderful to her. The alarmingly different taste of a new formula can upset and contribute to her difficulty. The same holds true for seemingly minor differences in nipples. A Canadian study of almost 800 healthy infants found that roughly 60 percent of parents reported that their infants had colic. Although the infants were kept on the same formula, in most cases by the time they were 4 months old the symptoms decreased, probably because of the baby's normal growth and development.[3]

The Too-Sleepy Baby. Not all babies who sleep a lot are too-sleepy babies. Relaxed babies with regular habits may sleep for 3 hours or more at a stretch. In contrast, a too-sleepy baby has trouble waking herself up to be fed, and she has trouble staying awake so she can eat well. Your baby will be eating enough if during the first 2 to 3 weeks she eats 8 or more times a day and has 6 to 8 wet diapers a day. Your baby may have one to three diapers a day with stools in them as well. Your baby's stools are likely to be soft to formed and may have some water in them and be yellow to yellowish-green in color.

Surprisingly, the tactics for helping always-hungry and colicky babies maintain a quiet alert state can also be helpful for the too-sleepy baby. No matter their age or their temperament, any time you treat children with respect it helps them perk up and encourages them to take an interest! Help wake up your drowsy baby by looking, talking, touching, and moving in a way that is more active, interesting, and unpredictable. Vary

your tone of voice and your speed of talking, give her something to grasp or suck, sit her up, and unwrap or undress her.
Experiment with moving her and rubbing different parts of her
body using different amounts of gentle pressure and notice
what makes her open her eyes and brighten up. Time her diaper change to take advantage of immediate alertness as well as
wake her up partway through the feeding. However, be careful
not to be irritating. Look again at Figure 4.2, "What Is Your
Baby Telling You?" on page 122, and carefully tune in on and
respond to her cues. You are trying to help your baby take an
interest, not to force her to go to sleep to get away from all the
disturbance.

Between feedings, maintain your contact with your too-
sleepy baby to gradually increase her calm and awake time.
Play with her gently awhile, in the way you have discovered
that she likes. Put her in an infant seat and move her with you
around the house. Give her something to look at. But keep an
eye on her, and be alert to her messages that say "I need a
break." She may frown, hiccup, look away, or lose her bright-
eyed look. Then it is time to put her down for a nap.

If you catch this too-sleepy pattern early, a few days of
remedial action will help your baby change her too-sleepy patterns and you will be able to go back to trusting her again.
However, keep an eye on her wet pants to be sure she is eating
and wetting enough.

LET YOUR BABY DECIDE HOW MUCH TO EAT

Your baby is born wanting to eat and knowing how much she
needs to eat. The only way you can tell how much formula your
baby *should* eat is to pay attention to *how much* she is eating. At
any one feeding, and in any one day, the amount of formula
that your baby takes will be an individual matter, depending on
her age, growth rate, activity level, and efficiency of metabolism. She may start out by eating 2 to 3 ounces at a feeding;
then she may move up to 4, then 6, then 8 or more. At any one
feeding, keep offering your baby formula until she indicates
that she has had enough. Sometimes she will eat a little; sometimes a lot. Offer a second bottle if you have to. You can trust
her to regulate her food intake with her own cues of hunger

and satiety. Your role is to learn to detect those cues and to respond to them.

For your own interest and reassurance I am going to give you some figures on typical daily formula intakes, ranging from the baby whose eating is at the relatively low end of the spectrum, on the average, to the baby whose eating is on the relatively high end. Keep in mind that when your baby starts eating solid food she will take less formula.

0 to 1 month	14 to 28 ounces
1 to 2 months	23 to 34 ounces
2 to 3 months	25 to 40 ounces
3 to 4 months	27 to 39 ounces
4 to 5 months	29 to 46 ounces
5 to 6 months	32 to 48 ounces

As you can see, there is a huge difference among babies. Keep in mind that the baby who eats the most may not be the baby who is the fattest or even the biggest. Some babies who eat a lot are lean and active. Some babies who don't eat much are chubby and not as active. Whether your baby is lean or chubby, eats a lot or a little, assume that it is right for her. As long as she is growing consistently, don't be alarmed even if the amount your baby eats falls outside the ranges listed above. Many days she is likely to take more than the highest amount or less than the lowest amount. As I will cover in detail in chapter 7, if your baby eats a lot of formula, it is *not* a sign that she needs to be put on solid foods. A bit of wrong advice that simply will not go away is that babies need to be put on solid foods when they take more than 32 ounces of formula. Again, *wrong!* Using that uniquely misguided logic and reading the list above, some infants who are 2 months old would need solid foods. They don't. They need more formula.

Your baby will vary a great deal in her day-to-day formula intake. In chapter 2 you learned about Baby "J" and how his food intake varied even through he grew consistently (pages 54-55). A Texas anthropologist who kept a daily record of a little boy's food intake from age 1 week to 9 months found that intake from one day to the next fluctuated considerably. For instance, when he was 2 months old, his formula intake ranged from 19 to 35 ounces a day. Despite his fluctuations in food intake, his growth was smooth and consistent. Furthermore, the little boy had a low need for food. His growth was right in the middle—neither big nor small—but his average food intake was near the lower end of the range.[4]

During the early months your baby will gradually increase the amount of formula she consumes at each feeding, the time between feedings, and the total amount of formula she takes.

LET YOUR BABY DECIDE HOW OFTEN TO EAT

As with quantity, you must give your child a say in determining the frequency with which she is fed. Physicians will often ask about the number of times a child is fed in a day. Some even have the audacity to *dictate* the number of feedings. Parents often appear startled by the inquiry and will respond with something like "well, let me see, she wakes up in the morning and wants to be fed, that's one time, and then sometimes she wants to be fed again about nine o'clock, but sometimes she doesn't, and then. . . ." Unless they are put to the test, they simply don't know. If you regularly wash a batch of nipples and bottles, you will have a general idea of the number, but beyond that you may not know. It is as it needs to be.

Your baby will eat as often as she needs to. As she gets bigger and her stomach holds more and her digestive process accommodates more, she will eat less frequently. By the time she is 12 to 15 months old, she will probably be eating about six times a day: three meals and three snacks.

Your newborn baby wakes up at night to eat because she is hungry and needs to be fed. Accept it. If you don't fight it, it will be easier to get up. Furthermore, the more accepting and responsive you can be with your baby, the more rapidly she will mature and the sooner she will get to the point when she can sleep through the night. Babies first manage to make it without their night feeding and *start* to sleep through the night when they are about 16 weeks old.[5] Although it is exhausting to get up to feed a baby at night, it must be done. Don't give cereal to hasten sleeping through the night—it doesn't help. You can be most helpful to your baby with sleep issues by paying attention from the first to her sleep cycles and cues and putting her to bed when she is drowsy but not asleep. Waiting until she is overtired and overstimulated can make it hard for her to go to sleep. While it is tempting and so rewarding to rock or feed your baby to sleep, you will also be teaching her that she can't go to sleep without it. If she learns early on to put herself to sleep, it will prevent sleep problems later.

YOU MUST USE INFANT FORMULA

Every so often I read or hear about babies being fed nondairy coffee creamer instead of formula. Although most people know better than to do something so nutritionally horrifying, I have again started to hear about chubby 3- to 4-month-olds being put on 2 percent milk, presumably to slim them down, which is also horrifying. Babies don't get the nutrients they need from such formula substitutes; they can't digest them properly and they have grave difficulty maintaining their body chemistry when they are given anything but infant formula.

Giving your baby infant formula is essential until after she is very well established on table food, which will happen toward the end of her first year. Your newborn requires very special nutritional care. She has a limited ability to digest food and to maintain her proper body hydration and chemistry, and her milk feeding has to be especially concocted to help her. Furthermore, since she can only cuddle, root, and suck, she must be held and fed by nipple. If you have objections to infant formulas and aren't going to breastfeed, it is better to swallow those objections and purchase the formula. One such objection, growing out of a general suspicion of mainstream food companies, was displayed by a young woman who called me looking for a recipe to make her own infant formula. I advised her to purchase infant formula and informed her that it wasn't wise to try to match at home the sophistication of infant formulas. Generally people who are so skeptical of the food supply choose to breastfeed, but for some reason she could not. Possibly soy formula use has increased so quickly—way beyond any medical or nutritional indication for use—because of today's unfounded suspicion of animal foods and equally unfounded glorification of the soybean.

One reason parents object to commercial infant formulas is expense. This is a reasonable objection, because formula is expensive, especially if your baby has a big appetite. Concentrated liquid formula and powder tend to be the cheapest, and the ready-to-feed variety is the most expensive. Do your own pricing to find out which is most economical in your area. Read labels to see how much formula the powder or concentrate makes, and figure out the cost per ounce. Sometimes parents give their baby pasteurized whole milk as a last resort to cut costs, but that is not a good choice. Pasteurized milk sets up such a tough, cheeselike curd in the stomach that it is hard to digest. It is not balanced nutritionally. Furthermore, it could give your baby an upset stomach, and it could cause an imbalance in your baby's body chemistry. Formula has been treated to make it set up a soft custardlike curd that is easy to digest when it is mixed with the acid in the baby's stomach. If your income is so low that you can't manage to purchase formula for your baby, consider applying for the WIC program (Special Supplemental Nutrition Program for Women, Infants, and Children) to get financial help. The WIC program will help you purchase formula and other foods for your child as well as give you nutrition and feeding guidance and support. The people in the program will also direct you to other sources of financial help. Don't hesitate to go for help if you need it—many families need a hand along the way when their children are small and they are just getting started. The WIC program is a wonderful program whose staff members will treat you with respect.

Some parents start infants early on solid foods as a way of cutting down on formula costs, but that isn't a good idea either. It doesn't save much money, and starting solids too early can cause problems for baby *and* parent. Your baby will be ready to start learning to eat solid foods when she can sit up, open her mouth when she sees the spoon coming, closes her lips over the spoon, and can transfer food from the front of her mouth to the back. About that time she will be able to digest and absorb the nutrients in solids, but right now she is several months away from that.

If you want to know what formulas I recommend, read on. If you need to be further convinced that formula is really necessary, see appendix F, "Nutritional Principles for Baby Formula."

Choosing Formulas. Infant formulas are not perfect, but they are good. Your baby will grow and do well on them. Chances are you will start your baby on whatever formula your hospital uses and continue to use that brand as long as you need formula. That's fine. Even though your hospital chooses formula based more on economics than nutrition, all the major formulas are good. A formula company gives a hospital an economic incentive to use their formula for that very reason: parents tend to continue with the formula they started on in the hospital. Some hospitals use competitive bids to choose their formula; others switch off from one formula to the other to even out the favors. Most WIC programs put their formulas out on competitive bids, so you may find your baby's formula being switched depending on where you are in the bidding cycle.

For most babies, any of the standard formulas work just fine. However, if your baby will inherit a tendency to allergy, you might want to be more proactive and ask or make arrangements before you deliver to be sure a particular formula is available. To head off an allergy, it may be wise to start her on Good Start in the hospital. Good Start is made from predigested whey, and studies show that babies are somewhat less likely to develop allergies on it.[6] If your baby was born prematurely, when you take her home from the hospital you may be advised to give her one of the premature transitional formulas that have 22 calories per ounce and more nutrients to support her continued rapid growth.

Once you start on a formula, keep using the same one if you possibly can. If you have to change—if the WIC program changes vendors, for instance—do it gradually, mixing the old gradually with the new until you make the shift. Keep in mind that if your baby fusses during or after feeding, spits up, pulls off the nipple, or doesn't seem to want to eat, the problem is not likely to be the formula.

The problem might be the baby's physical, nervous, or digestive system immaturity or the way the two of you interact during feeding. Most babies settle down with time. Use trial and error to figure out why she's having trouble. If feeding is stressful and you can't get it to go right, get professional help.

Cow Milk–Based Formulas. Enfamil (Enfalac in Canada), Similac, and Good Start are some of the commonly available cow milk–based formulas. SMA, a formula available in years past from Wyeth, has pretty much disappeared from the U.S.

market but has recently been making a comeback under the label of Babymil and generic store-brand formulas. In general, babies grow and thrive on all of them, and mostly the differences are minimal. There are, however, some differences in formulation that may be helpful for your baby. Some formulas are casein-based, some are whey-based, and some use a combination of protein. One of them—Good Start—is based on partially predigested whey, which makes it less allergenic. The protein in high-whey formulas more closely mimic human milk, and while premature babies may do somewhat better on them, term babies appear to do equally well on high-casein or high-whey formulas. Some manufacturers say their formula is "humanized" or "closer to breastmilk," but those are just words intended to give the impression that the unique characteristics of breastmilk can be duplicated. Those formulas are unlikely to be any better for your baby than those that don't use the buzzwords.

Soy-Based Formulas. Isomil, ProSobee, Alsoy, and other soy-based formulas now make up 25 percent of the formula market in the United States. Wyeth's Babysoy and generic store-brand soy formula are also available. These formulas are made of soy protein isolate that has been pressed, ground, and precipitated from the whole soybean and then fortified with methionine. Since soy formulas are free of lactose (milk sugar), the most common reason parents choose a soy formula is that their child is lactose-intolerant, meaning that she can't digest the lactose in cow milk–based formulas. However, you can now get lactose-free cow milk–based formula. The label will say something like *Lactofree*, which can either be a brand name or a generic description.

Lactose intolerance in infancy is most likely a temporary condition. If your baby has had severe diarrhea, and if that diarrhea persists after she goes back on her regular formula, it is likely that her ability to digest milk sugar has been temporarily impaired. Then your baby may be put on soy formula for a week or two to keep her from developing an allergy to cow milk protein and to avoid the abdominal discomfort, diarrhea, and gas caused by poor lactose digestion. Then she will go back to her regular cow's milk formula. Babies with a rare inborn error of metabolism, *galactosemia,* can't tolerate galactose, one of the breakdown products of lactose. Those babies, as well as those with hereditary lactase deficiency, must be given only soy formula. But those conditions all put together probably account for less than a quarter of the babies who are on soy formula.

So why are so many babies on soy formula? Is it because soy is one of those currently favored foods, assumed to be somehow magically good for us? If that's the case, it's the wrong reason. While soy can certainly make a contribution to a healthful diet, there is nothing magical about it. In fact, soy formulas for infants may have some shortcomings, depending on how you read and interpret the literature. The infant's potential intake of phytoestrogen (a form of the female hormone estrogen) from soy protein formula is higher than that demonstrated to influence the menstrual cycle of humans.[7] The aluminum content of soy milk is 10 to 300 times higher than in human milk, and for that reason, premature babies must definitely *not* be put on soy formula. While the American Academy of Pediatrics says there is no cause for concern for term infants, and while aluminum has not been demonstrated to be toxic for humans, my own point of view is, why risk it if you don't have to? Soy formula is not superior to cow's milk formula. It is just as likely to cause stomach and intestinal problems and allergies.[8]

Sometimes babies have trouble digesting not only lactose but sucrose as well. Sucrose is common table sugar. To avoid sucrose as well as lactose, read the ingredients list on the formula label and select a soy formula that contains corn syrup solids and/or another carbohydrate source such as modified tapioca starch rather than sucrose. You will find a list of the carbohydrate ingredients in formula in Figure 6.1, "Protein and Carbohydrate in Formula" on page 227. You will, of course, need the help of a pediatrician or pediatric dietitian if you get into formula-selection issues that are this technical in feeding your baby.

A last note about soy: soy milk is not a substitute for soy formula. Nutrient density as well as proportions of protein, fat, and carbohydrate are inappropriate when soy milk is used as the sole food of a young infant.

Unusual Formulas for Allergies or Special Health Care Needs.
Babies rarely have allergic reactions to formula, nor do they

usually have any trouble digesting formula. However, some do, and because there is so much confusion about the issue, appendix G, "Formulas Off the Beaten Path," takes a closer look at some of the more unusual formulas. Look there for more information about formulas for premature infants, for babies who have trouble eating enough to satisfy their nutritional needs, or formulas for infants who have a particular health condition that can be managed only by careful nutritional manipulation of their diets. As with all infants, to use these formulas you need careful advice and support from your health care provider. The material in appendix G is intended as background information to help you be more clear about why you are using a particular formula and what you are trying to accomplish.

Store-Brand Formulas. If all goes well, what I've just told you is all you'll need to know about formulas. Furthermore, now that store-brand infant formulas are coming on the market, knowledgeably reading labels is your only way of knowing what you are getting. At the current time, the milk-based store brands are being made by Wyeth, which means that the protein will be in the form of whey and nonfat milk. However, if and when other manufacturers identify store-brand formula manufacturing as a profitable venture, that could change. To determine whether a store-brand formula is similar to the one your baby is currently taking, read the label. Pay particular attention to the protein ingredients, since if your baby is at all sensitive, she will be most sensitive to the protein. Figure 6.1, "Protein and Carbohydrate in Formula," tells you what to look for.

Changing Formulas. Don't be too ready to switch formulas. Babies rarely have allergic reactions or trouble digesting formula. Few upsets are of the sort that require special feeding. It appears that, regardless of feeding, about 40 percent of babies have colic, or inconsolable crying after feeding, and about 40 percent vomit from time to time after they are fed. Studies show that by age one year 14 percent of babies have had at least one episode of marked vomiting and diarrhea and 16 percent are still waking up at night.[9] In most cases these problems would have persisted despite a change in feeding. Symptoms of food sensitivity or allergy that you and your health care provider can identify include frequent stomachaches or vomiting (not just spitting

FIGURE 6.1 PROTEIN AND CARBOHYDRATE IN FORMULA

Cow's milk has its protein in two forms: casein and whey, or curds and whey if you are a fan of Miss Muffet who sat on the tuffet. Cow's milk whey more closely resembles the lactalbumin (milk protein) of human milk. As a consequence, many formula companies have emphasized whey rather than casein in their formulas. To find out whether you have a casein-based, whey-based, or predigested formula, look for the following ingredients on the label.

Type of protein	Look for these ingredients:
Mostly casein	Nonfat milk
	Nonfat milk and whey (the first listed ingredient predominates)
	Caseinate, sodium caseinate, calcium caseinate
	Isolated casein
Mostly whey	Whey and sodium caseinate
	Whey and nonfat milk
Predigested whey	Enzymatically hydrolyzed reduced-minerals whey
Predigested casein	Casein hydrolysate with added amino acids

The form of carbohydrate is less critical than the form of protein, unless you need to keep your baby off lactose for a time. As I pointed out earlier, your lactose-intolerant baby may also be intolerant of sucrose, common table sugar, so you may as well look for a formula that avoids both. Possibilities of other forms of carbohydrate that don't contain lactose or sucrose include the following:
• Corn syrup solids
• Maltodextrin
• Modified tapioca starch
• Modified corn starch

up), cough, runny nose and wheezing, skin itching, and rash.

If you decide to change your baby's formula, consult with your health care provider, and keep in mind that it's the protein that is the issue and not the fat or carbohydrate. Do as little as you can to get the results you want. You might try Good Start if you have been using a cow milk–based formula, either casein or whey. You could also experiment with soy, but keep in mind that about 15 percent of infants who react strongly to cow's milk are likely to react as strongly to soy.[10] Furthermore, children who have had viral enteritis are likely to react negatively to both cow's milk and soy formula.

If nothing else helps, you and your health care provider may decide that your baby needs a more fully predigested formula like Nutramigen, Alimentum, or Pregestimil or, for the baby who is super-allergic, Neocate.

Feeding Your Older Baby. Wait to feed your baby whole pasteurized milk until she is at least 1 year old. As long as you give her formula from the cup, in fact, there is no need to be in a hurry about getting off the formula. Be sure to leave your prematurely born baby on formula until 12 months corrected age and even beyond. Many premies are slow and cautious about starting on solid foods, so both parent and baby benefit from the nutritional security of formula for a while longer. If you have a prematurely born baby, the last thing you need is feeling you have to hurry up and get her on solid food so she will be all right nutritionally. She'll get there. In fact, she'll get there faster if you don't feel you have to hurry her up.

In addition to the standard formulas, there are some other, special formulas that are marketed to children age 12 months and older and some that are intended for children with special health care needs. You can read about them in appendix G, "Formulas Off the Beaten Path."

Vitamin/Mineral Supplements. Commercial infant formulas are nutritionally complete and don't need to be supplemented with any vitamins or minerals. However, even though neither formula-fed nor breastfed babies need them, and even though supplementing them gives babies way more than they need, vitamins A, B, D, and sometimes C are routinely prescribed in some health care offices. Giving these nutrients as drops, in addition to formula, results in overdosing, and there is nothing to be gained by overdosing with any of the nutrients. Too much of any nutrient can give undesirable side effects and impair the utilization of other nutrients. I think you are safe for the time being from being urged to give your baby extra vitamin C "to prevent colds," but vitamin C dosing is increasingly the practice on the grounds that "it won't hurt and it might help." There is no good evidence that it helps, and it can hurt. In case you need some help warding off nutrient overdosing, you will find further information on the topic of nutritional supplementation in appendix P, "Vitamins and Minerals for Children."

Fluoride. Although fluoride is important to tooth health, and although the water you use for diluting your baby's formula may or may not be a particularly impressive source of fluoride, beginning fluoride supplements is delayed for all infants until after 6 months of age. You can learn more about fluoride in chapter 7, "Feeding Your Older Baby," and in appendix P, "Vitamins and Minerals for Children."

Iron. Iron in red blood cells carries oxygen to all parts of the body. When children don't get enough iron, they may look pale, act cranky, and not have much energy. The ease with which anemia can be prevented, coupled with the grave consequences of iron deficiency, makes iron a hotly debated nutrient in infant nutrition. For the term infant, the issue is *prevention* of the iron anemia that can appear after age 6 months and more often after 1 year of age.

Regardless of the mother's iron status, term infants are born with a good supply of iron. The newborn has need for, and utilizes, very little dietary iron before age 4 to 6 months. Prematurely born babies don't have the iron stores and need to be supplemented after age 2 months. After age 6 months, however, babies' iron stores begin to be depleted, and unless they get a good source of iron in their diets they can develop iron-deficiency anemia. The principle behind iron-fortified infant formula is preventing the iron depletion. As with children suffering from any other nutritional deficiency—indeed, from not enough food altogether—anemic children are tired, listless, and unable to explore and learn. Presumably, once they are better nourished they make up for lost time. Some studies raise doubts about whether children fully recover from the intellectual impairment of iron-deficiency anemia. On the other hand, iron-deficient infants tend to have iron-deficient mothers who haven't the energy or resources to provide a rich environment. The studied babies may not have done as well intellectually because they were understimulated as well as undernourished. Being on the safe side, the American Academy of Pediatrics feels so strongly about the iron issue that they have recommended that non-iron-fortified formulas be removed from the market. Although the issues may be grave, you need not panic. You can easily prevent anemia by giving your baby iron-fortified formula. Take the iron issue seriously enough to give your

baby iron-fortified formula, but do not overdose your child
with iron.* Iron-deficiency anemia is absolutely and easily
preventable.

. Why would you *not* use iron fortified formula? Because
many mothers are absolutely convinced that iron-fortified formulas are constipating and that they upset baby's stomachs.
They are not and they do not. Double-blind studies—in which
neither researchers nor mothers knew whether their babies
were taking iron-fortified formulas—found that babies on both
formulas had the same numbers of stomach and intestinal
upsets and the same amount of constipation and diarrhea. The
Canadian study I mentioned on page 217 that found 60 percent
of infants had colic used non-iron-fortified formula. If you are
still unconvinced and you still want to use the non-iron formula, you must give your baby iron drops. See your health care
provider about a recommendation for iron drops and about
instructions for proper dosage. Also read appendix L, "Iron in
Your Child's Diet."

THE WATER SUPPLY

Before we discuss equipment and technique, we must digress a
bit to talk about water, a vital ingredient as well as the medium
for sanitation. To successfully formula-feed, much depends on
water. The ideal water for the young infant is clean water that is
low in lead, nitrate, sodium, and pesticides and is fluoridated.
Most of our city water supplies are acceptably sanitary and safe,
although with increased population densities and ever-decreas-
ing city budgets for maintaining high water quality standards,
there are occasional breakdowns in water treatment procedures.
As a consequence, it is wisest to boil water for your baby's first
6 months. If you have your own well, have your water tested at
least once a year for cleanliness, nitrate, arsenic, and pesticide
levels by the state laboratory of hygiene. If you have any doubt

---

*In fact, giving iron-fortified formula already involves a certain amount
of inevitable overdosing. Iron-fortified formula provides 12.8 milligrams of iron per liter, and babies appear to do well on only 6 or 7
milligrams iron per liter. Too much iron in the diet can impair zinc and
perhaps copper absorption.

concerning the safety of your well water, purchase bottled water for your baby. Levels of contaminants too low to harm you can be harmful to your baby's immature system. If you have other questions about water quality, call the Environmental Protection Agency's Safe Drinking hotline at 800-426-4791 or see their Web site: **www.epa.gov/safewater**

Boil Water at First. For the first 6 months, boil your baby's water for three minutes—this includes water for drinking or for mixing formula. Many water bottlers take water from the ground and run it through a filter to take out sediment, and that is the total extent of their treatment. Since that makes bottled water—including purified and distilled water— essentially the same as tap water, it's wisest to boil that too. The only water that doesn't have to be boiled is labeled as meeting U.S. Environmental Protection Agency purified water standards. Consult with your health care provider about whether your water should be boiled after your baby is 6 months of age.

City water supplies as well as bottled waters are required, by law, to be periodically tested to be safe, and the quality of water for the vast majority of Americans is safe. The problem for both lies in what happens between the tests, when contaminants can creep in and make water temporarily unsafe for drinking. Furthermore, few water utilities perform the expensive extremely fine mesh filtering needed to remove the parasites *Giardia* and *Cryptosporidium*. Contamination from these parasites comes from surface water that seeps even into city water supplies. Both cause severe cramping and diarrhea, which can lead to dangerous dehydration, especially for infants. Boiling destroys both parasites, and since they are so dangerous for infants, it is better to take no chances. When your baby gets older, her greater size and more resilient system will help her withstand mild dehydration. Then she can drink unboiled water like you do.

People who get their water from a private well or from the small water systems that serve only a few thousand people have to be particularly careful about the quality of drinking water. Water from these sources needs to be tested periodically, and if there is any risk at all of nitrate contamination, infants under age 1 year must be given nitrate-free bottled water.

Lead. Lead is a problem for those of us who live in older houses. In years past, lead-containing solder was used in the joints of water pipes, and a certain amount of that solder leeches into drinking water that stands for any length of time in pipes. Generally, city pipes don't have lead in them—only the pipes that lead from the street into your home and the plumbing inside your home. Newer construction uses plastic pipes, so lead is no longer a problem. To take care of the lead problem, before you draw off water for your baby—or for you—run the cold tap for 2 or 3 minutes, or until it feels cold. That gets rid of water standing in the pipes that contains higher levels of lead or other trace elements. (In large apartment buildings this might not work because of the length of the pipes.) Boiling doesn't get rid of lead or trace elements and in fact only concentrates them so you get more trace elements per unit volume. Avoid using hot tap water to mix formula because the hot water dissolves more lead. If your hot water is softened it will also contain higher levels of sodium than hard water.

Nitrate. If you have your own well, be particularly careful that the nitrate level in your water is less than 10 parts per million (ppm). With growing population density and with more and more people moving into agricultural areas, nitrate in well water is becoming an increasing problem. Be particularly careful to test your well after heavy rains, flooding, irrigation, or fertilizer application near your well. Nitrate contamination of water is a problem for the infant under age 6 months because her body chemically changes nitrate to *nitrite,* which displaces oxygen in red blood cells. This condition, *methemoglobinemia,* or *blue baby,* interferes with the oxygen-carrying capacity of the blood and can make infants very ill and can even cause death. Boiling the water doesn't help; it only concentrates the nitrates. If the nitrate level is 10 milligrams per liter or more, you will need some other source of water until your baby is on a mixed diet. If in doubt about the nitrate content of your drinking water, use bottled water.

Sodium. The concern with sodium in drinking water relates to possible long-term effects of excessive sodium intake, such as increased blood pressure. Sodium in water may occur naturally or it may be added by the water softening process. Have your water tested if you suspect it is salty. Use only unsoftened water to dilute formula or juice.

Home Water Purification Units. Carafe filters and countertop units remove bad tastes, odors, chlorine, and organic chemicals, but they do not remove lead, nitrate, sodium, or pathogens. Some specialized filters remove only sediment. Only filters that have been rated as 1 micron *absolute* or smaller will get rid of *Giardia* and *Cryptosporidium*. If a cartridge is labeled only as 1 micron, or 1 micron nominal, it won't do the job, because it will have some larger mesh, as well as the smaller mesh. Home water purification systems that use a process called reverse osmosis remove *Giardia* and *Cryptosporidium*, but the down side is that the process removes fluoride as well. If you have a reverse osmosis unit, you will know it. The units are expensive, require a large storage tank, and have a separate faucet. Check with the manufacturer to find out what is removed by your water purification unit.

BOTTLE-FEEDING EQUIPMENT AND TECHNIQUE

As with your choices of formula, get your planning, decisions, and purchasing done as much as you can ahead of time. After your baby comes, you won't have time for this!

Nipples and Bottles. Along with boiling water for 6 months, I recommend boiling nipples, rings, and bottles for the first 3 months. If you use the bottles with the disposable plastic liners, you don't have to boil the bottles.

You need equipment that works well and that you and your baby can manage well. A nipple that is comfortable in your baby's mouth and that feeds the formula at a manageable rate has everything to do with establishing smooth and comfortable feeding. If your baby is working too hard to get the formula or is getting overwhelmed by a flow that is too fast, she will repeatedly pull off the nipple and fuss. That will frustrate you both. Usually babies are flexible about accepting the nipple you offer, but occasionally an infant likes a particular one best. There are three main types of nipples: the traditional Evenflo, the Playtex nurser, and the Gerber Nuk. The Nuk nipple is "orthodontically" shaped, and it looks like it has been left too close to the stove.

Nipple openings are either holes or cross-cut. It doesn't matter which you use as long as the nipple flows well. Often the cheap nipples on the prepackaged bottle-plus-formula kits you get from the hospital flow too fast or too slowly, so be prepared with your own supply. When you hold the bottle upside down but don't squeeze it, the formula needs to come out in steady drops that follow each other closely but not in a constant flow. A flow that's too slow can frustrate and wear out your baby; a flow that's too fast can gag and frighten her.

Bottles can be the traditional rigid glass or plastic types, or the sort that have a throw-away plastic liner. I prefer the bottles with disposable plastic liners because they are sterile and you'll need to boil only the nipples and rings. If you want rigid-sided bottles, the choice between plastic and glass is up to you. Glass is easy to clean, dries fast, and holds temperature better than plastic. Because glass keeps its shape, it makes a reliable measuring tool. On the other hand, plastic won't break, although it really takes quite a bit to break a glass bottle. Since glass holds the temperature better, a feeding stays warm longer, and a cold bottle in a diaper bag stays cold longer. Fancy bottle design may please adults, but it doesn't do anything for babies. By the time she is old enough to notice, it will be time for your baby to be weaned from the bottle. Bottles shaped like animals, with all their little wrinkles and gizmos, are hard to clean. So are bottles shaped to look like a big oval or those that have handles to make them easier for babies to hold. Your baby needs to have you hold her when she has a bottle. If she is too old to hold while you feed her, she is too old to have a bottle. Baby bottles that look like soda bottles give the message that soda is all right for babies. It is absolutely *not*.

Get the Bottle to Feed Smoothly. I have already mentioned the importance of feeding smoothly, and well-functioning equipment is essential to maintaining a smooth and continuous feeding. If your equipment doesn't work well, feedings will frequently be interrupted, your baby will get upset and frustrated, and she will have a difficult time maintaining her composure and her willingness to eat.

Throughout the feeding, keep the bottle properly tilted so the nipple is well filled with formula. Otherwise your baby will suck in air, certainly become frustrated, and possibly get a stomachache. You don't have the air problem in the bottles with the plastic liners; the liners simply collapse as they empty. Before you start the feeding, push on the bottom of the bag to force out the excess air. Keep pushing until you get a little squirt of formula, and then feed. Your baby can suck right down to the last drop without getting excess air. Loosen the nipple ring on the rigid-sided bottle just a bit so air can get into the bottle as your baby eats. If air doesn't flow into the bottle during the feeding, your baby will create a vacuum as she sucks and the formula won't feed down right. The nipple will collapse, and your baby will be forced to pull away before she wants to. She will learn to accommodate by coming off the bottle momentarily, but why frustrate her if you don't have to? When you get the nipple ring properly adjusted, as your baby sucks you will be able to hear the air feeding into the bottle and see the air bubbles coming into the formula.

Dilute Formula Exactly Right. Follow instructions exactly when you prepare formula. Measure liquids with standard clear measuring cups with the volume marked off on the sides. Measure water after you boil it, not before, because the evaporation from boiling will change the measurement. Get your eye down even with the level of water on the side of the cup to make sure you are measuring liquid accurately. If you are using rigid-sided bottles, check the measurement markings with a standard measuring cup to be sure the markings are accurate. Don't measure in the baby bottles that have disposable plastic inner liners—you can't get an accurate measurement. If you don't believe me, run your own experiment with a standard measuring cup.

The ready-to-feed formula will say "ready to feed." It generally comes in a large can—about a quart. You can pour that directly into the bottle and feed it. The concentrated formulas generally come in 13- or 14-ounce cans and you dilute the formula with an equal amount of water. I think it is best to make up a whole can of formula at a time, using the can to measure the water for diluting. You can then keep the diluted formula in the refrigerator and fill your baby's bottles as you need them. If you make up one bottle at a time, be very sure your measuring equipment is accurate. If you are using powdered formula, it will come with a little scoop for measuring and directions for how many ounces of water to use per scoop. Use the scoop, and use it the way the directions on the container tell you to. The scoop's diameter and depth are carefully configured to allow you to measure as accurately as possible. The directions will even tell you how to *fill* the scoop and how to level it off. Follow them. Often the package will tell you to scrape the scoop along the side of the can to even it off. Do what the package says, don't shake or tap it. That changes the way the formula packs and makes for inaccurate measurement. If you change to another brand of formula, use the scoop that comes with the new brand, and again read the package directions. Don't assume the procedure is the same for all brands. For instance, in the United States we use one scoop per 2 ounces of water; in some other countries, the scoops are smaller and you are supposed to use one scoop per ounce of water.

Even small errors in measurement can make a difference in the eventual concentration of the formula, and that can have serious consequences for your baby. If formula is too concentrated (made up with too little water), it can stress your baby's kidneys and digestive system and she may become dehydrated. If formula is too dilute (made up with too much water), it can make her grow poorly because it won't contain enough calories and nutrients.* Certain susceptible children fed too-dilute formula or too much supplemental water can develop water intoxication, or overloading with water. Water intoxication puts a burden on the baby's circulatory system and dilutes out the bloodstream minerals that the body needs to function normally.

Modern formula preparation is deceptively simple—so simple, in fact, that it is easy to become lax and inattentive and to make some serious errors. Not only do people make mistakes, but sometimes they vary the concentration of infant formula on purpose. A 1999 survey of infant practices showed that 10 percent of mothers deliberately diluted their formula and 2 percent concentrated it.[11] Reasons given for both practices were based on erroneous beliefs like attempting to control constipation or diarrhea, controlling the baby's weight, and package sizes that

---

*Babies over 6 weeks of age will tend to increase their formula intake and make up for the too-great dilution, but babies under that age will have trouble eating enough to get the calories they need.

did not come out even with the baby's bottle. Occasionally someone will feed concentrated infant formula full strength (the liquid that you are supposed to dilute one-to-one with water), by accident or otherwise. The results can be tragic. Sometimes people dilute formula more than they are supposed to in order to save money or to get their baby's growth to slow down. The take-home message: When you are making up baby formula, don't get it *close*—get it *right*!

Warm—or Don't Warm—the Bottle. Babies don't seem to mind whether their bottle is warmed or straight out of the refrigerator, as long as it is a consistent temperature from one feeding to the next. I like the idea of giving a baby warmed formula, but considering the practicalities of feeding, I come down on the side of the cold bottle. If you feed the formula cold, you won't have to wait to warm it up before you feed. If your baby takes more than one bottle, you won't have to make her wait as long while you get the second bottle ready. Keep in mind that when you take bottles with you to go out that you need to keep them cold until you feed them, so if you plan to feed your baby on the run a lot, you might want to get her accustomed to taking cold formula.

If you warm your baby's bottle, do it immediately prior to feeding. Don't let bottles stand out of the refrigerator to come to room temperature between feedings. To warm your baby's bottle just before you feed it, set it down in a container of hot tap water or hold it under hot running tap water. Test a few drops on the inside of your wrist. If it's the right temperature you won't be able to feel either warm or cold because it will be the same as your body temperature.

While microwaving is generally not recommended for warming baby bottles, half of mothers report that they heated bottles in a microwave oven.[11] It's a dangerous practice because a microwaved bottle that feels lukewarm on the outside may have pockets of scalding liquid deeper inside. Some babies have been so badly burned by microwaved infant bottles that they have had to be hospitalized. On the assumption that parents will use the microwave anyway, the following protocol has been developed. To ensure your baby's safety, it is absolutely essential that you take the following precautions if you microwave formula:

- Microwave the bottle *without a nipple or cap* (so it doesn't explode).
- Heat 4-ounce bottles no more than 30 seconds; 8-ounce bottles no more than 45 seconds (on full power).
- After microwaving, replace the nipple assembly and mix the contents of the bottle by turning it upside down, then right side up, 10 or more times.
- Check the temperature by placing a few drops of liquid on your wrist.
- If it's too hot, wait. If too cold, take the cap off and start over.

After all that activity, it seems to me that setting a bottle down to warm in a deep container of hot tap water is faster and easier! However, it is good to know the method for the occasional time when you are out and have access to a microwave.

Keep Formula Fresh and Cool between Feedings. An opened can of liquid formula or formula reconstituted from powder can be kept tightly covered in the refrigerator for up to 48 hours. Refrigerate it immediately after it is opened or reconstituted. Store the cans of powdered formula in a cool, dry place and use within a month after you open it. Because even carefully handled powdered formula contains a small number of undesirable bacteria, it wouldn't hurt to store the container in the refrigerator after you open it, especially if you will be keeping it for longer than a month.

Check your refrigerator temperature to see that it is somewhere between 35 and 40 degrees Fahrenheit. Food keeps best when it is kept as cool as possible without freezing. Generally a food held between 40 and 140 degrees (optimum temperatures for bacterial growth) for 2 hours or more is considered to be contaminated and should be discarded. Once you start feeding from a bottle, an hour is the limit. Discard any formula left standing in a bottle an hour after the feeding starts. Bacteria from your baby's mouth get in the bottle when she nurses, so once you have fed from a bottle, throw the formula away. Don't refrigerate it and reheat it because the bacteria can multiply rapidly.

Keep time and temperature in mind when you carry bottles in a diaper bag. Have the formula very cold when you pack it, and tuck in a refreezable ice pack. If you are going to be away from refrigeration for a particularly long time, you might consider getting a bottle-carting bag with an ice pack or buying the single-feeding bottles or cans of formula.

Develop and Maintain High Standards of Sanitation. There is no way of knowing how often babies get sick from contaminated or over-concentrated formula. Be scrupulous about cleanliness when you handle your baby's formula, bottles, and nipples. Babies have low immunity to bacteria in the digestive tract and are more sensitive to irritating substances than older children or adults. The baby who has diarrhea or is vomiting from a food infection risks dehydration. In our clean environments there is no excuse for food infections.

First, your hands must be clean. Wash your hands before you feed your baby, after you go to the bathroom or change diapers, before you handle food, and after you handle any meat or fresh produce. To wash your hands thoroughly, the International Food Safety Council says to wet your hands, soap them thoroughly, and rub them together, fronts, backs and forearms, for 20 seconds before you rinse. This is long enough to sing "Happy Birthday" twice. Lace your fingers together and rub them up and down to wash between them. Curl your fingers and hook your hands together to soap the fingertips. Rinse your hands thoroughly and dry them on a clean dry towel. Change your towel daily or more often than that if it gets so much use that it is always damp. Use regular hand soap. Anti-bacterial cleaners contain antibiotics, and routine use of antibiotics tends to produce antibiotic-resistant bacteria. The problem with antibiotic cleaners is the same as with antibiotic medicines. Using antibiotics when you don't really need them can build up resistance in the bacteria and make the antibiotics useless when you really do need them. Using soap is enough to clean thoroughly, and for really tough disinfecting jobs, chlorine-type bleach is a good choice.

Keep your work area clean and dry. Bacteria require three conditions to multiply: nutrients, heat, and moisture. That is, they need smears or quantities of food, they need moisture (dried smears don't culture germs), and they need the proper temperature to grow. Bacteria are always with us. Your task is to deprive them of any or all of their requirements for growing and thriving. You do that by keeping your tools and work surfaces clean and dry and by refrigerating foods promptly.

Once you get your hands and sink clean and rinsed, clean the exposed top of the formula can, the bottles, nipples, measuring cups and spoons and stirring spoons, the can opener, and other equipment you use in formula preparation. Use a clean dishcloth. If you use a bottle brush, wash and rinse it carefully after each use and put it where it can quickly dry and stay dry. Remember, any time you leave things wet you provide a good medium for bacterial growth.

After 3 months, you can stop sterilizing your equipment, but keep boiling the baby's water for another 3 months. Sterilize by boiling everything for 3 minutes before you make up the bottles: the water used in formula preparation, the bottles, the nipples and nipple covers, and the measuring and mixing equipment. Your dishwasher won't get the temperature high enough to sterilize unless it has a heat booster with a special sanitizing cycle. That gets the temperature up to 180 degrees so it kills bacteria. If you don't know for sure that your dishwasher has a sanitizing cycle, chances are it doesn't, because you have to pay extra to get it and the control panel would give you the option of turning it on or off. A water temperature booster gets the temperature up only to 140 degrees, and the drying cycle, even though it feels hot, doesn't sanitize. Boiling is better for sterilizing, and sterilizing for the first 3 months will get your infant through the time of highest incidence of gastrointestinal upsets and allow her to develop some tolerance for bacteria. After 3 months, your baby can handle more bacteria, but cleanliness is still essential. Even after you stop sterilizing the other equipment, I would encourage you to boil the nipples, let them air dry, and store them in a clean, dry place.

After your baby is 3 months old, it's okay to depend on your dishwasher for washing bottles and rings as long as water gets up to 140 degrees and the rinse cycle gets rid of the caustic dishwasher detergent. Check the instruction booklet on the dishwasher to be sure that you are using the correct amount of detergent, and carefully measure that amount into the machine. Rinse the bottles and nipples beforehand to get the milk film out and force water through the holes of the nipple. Consider getting one of those little baskets to contain the small pieces and keep them from floating around in the pressurized water.

To hand wash, carefully scrub the bottles and nipples in

hot, soapy water, force water through the holes of the nipple, and then rinse in water as hot as your hands can stand. Be sure that you get all the suds off, as dried soap scum contains food particles and, again, provides a good medium for bacterial growth. Invert the bottles in a drying rack, put the nipples in a clean strainer, and let them air dry.

Your health care worker may or may not agree with my recommendations about sterilization, and he may even reassure you that shortcuts are all right. Proceed at your own risk—and your baby's risk. I have observed that people can be woefully casual about sanitation and food-handling. Unless they are taught, many don't think to wash their hands before they start working with food, they don't know about proper dish-washing techniques, and they leave food standing out at room temperature.

I am not encouraging you to become a fanatic about cleanliness. It would be going too far to imitate a fabled professor of mine who washed his doorknobs with alcohol. It certainly would be going too far to yell at big brother or sister about touching the baby's hands with grubby little paws or sharing toys with her. Your baby will get bigger, and her size will give her more resilience in maintaining her body hydration and chemical balance. She will naturally and gradually be exposed to germs in her environment, and she will develop resistance to them. As she becomes exposed, her intestine will become less sensitive and react less. With careful handling of formula, you keep the bacterial level down and give her a chance to develop her ability to live with the necessary germs in her environment. For a general discussion of keeping your food and kitchen clean and avoiding unnecessary and harmful contamination, see appendix R, "Food Safety."

TWO IMPORTANT CONSIDERATIONS

Honey. I can't believe I have gotten this far without mentioning diarrhea or honey. Honey is easy. Don't give your baby honey until she is 1 year old, because it could cause botulism, a type of food poisoning. Don't put honey on the pacifier, and don't give her anything that is baked with honey, because baking doesn't kill the botulinum spores that cause the poisoning.

Diarrhea. Diarrhea is not quite so easy, but I will make it as quick and painless as I can. Diarrhea caused by an illness can be serious; diarrhea caused by teething or a change in diet or who knows what else is simply a nuisance. Disposable diapers help to sop up the mess, but often good diapers and time are the only solutions. In chapter 9, "Feeding Your Preschooler," you will learn about dietary factors related to the nuisance kind of diarrhea. In appendix S, "Diarrhea and Dehydration," you can learn more about the serious kind of diarrhea and find some guidance about detecting dehydration.

With diarrhea caused by viral infection, the primary concern is dehydration. The diarrhea of a child who is truly ill, especially if she is also vomiting, has fever, or both, can take a considerable amount of water out of her body. An infant cannot let her adults know she is thirsty and can actually sleep herself into dehydration. If the dehydration goes too far, the child may have to be hospitalized and put on intravenous fluids. While this is serious, it is unusual for dehydration to get to the point of being a medical emergency.

Diarrhea will have an impact on feeding only if it is mismanaged. Gastroenteritis can spoil the appetite, but after eating poorly for a few days, infants recover and make up for lost time. If you can keep calm and do not push food on your baby, her appetite will recover nicely. The main problem arises when parents and health care workers overreact to diarrhea—both the serious and the nuisance kind—by putting children on various kinds of dietary restrictions. Sometimes the dietary restrictions are so drastic, or are applied so frequently, that children do not grow well. In most cases it is the diet rather than the diarrhea itself that causes the growth impairment.

To take care of the child with gastroenteritis, offer a commercial oral rehydration therapy fluid (ORT) and feed as usual to the extent of your child's hunger and appetite. ORT brand names include Pedialyte, Infalyte, Nutramax, and Rehydralyte. ORT will give your baby the glucose and electrolytes she needs to maintain her blood chemistry and fluid balance. Offer the ORT often and in small quantities, offer her breastmilk or formula as usual, and let her eat as much or as little as she wants. You will have to change her formula only if the diarrhea persists for several weeks after she is better—consult with your health care provider. It is no longer recommended that you stop feeding while your child is ill or that you substitute some other dietary concoction like the traditional BRAT diet (bananas, rice, applesauce, and toast). If the BRAT diet is new to you, forget you ever heard it. It doesn't work and is inferior nutritionally to your baby's usual feeding

Don't substitute juice, Jell-O, soda, or any other liquid for the ORT or the formula. Any of them can worsen the diarrhea by allowing undigested sugar into the child's colon, which in turn attracts water and nourishes undesirable bacteria. The commonly used apple juice is particularly undesirable because it contains fructose, which is poorly digested, and *sorbitol*, which isn't digested at all. Both attract fluids into the intestine and make stools more liquid. There, that wasn't so bad, was it?

This has been a chapter with a shifting focus and lots of detail. To conclude, here is a summary of the basic points.

- Enjoy your baby.
- Cuddle your baby while you feed her. Give her a little room for wiggling, but hold her firmly enough so she doesn't feel like she might fall.
- Hold your baby so she can look into your face while she eats.
- Put your arm under your baby's neck to support her head, making sure that it's a little higher than the rest of her body. If she's lying too flat, the milk could get into her ears and give her an earache.
- Loosen the ring on the bottle slightly to let some air in. Otherwise, the nipple will flatten out and your baby won't get any formula. Squeeze extra air out of the plastic liners.
- Wait for your baby to open her mouth for the bottle. Touch her cheek or lips with it; or when she's older, show it to her.
- Hold the bottle *still*, tipping it so that the nipple is filled with formula.
- Let her eat as fast or as slowly as she wants. Get the nipple to flow at the right speed so she can handle it.
- Talk to her in a quiet and encouraging manner while she eats, but don't give her so much attention that she gets distracted.
- Hold her still while she pauses and rests. She may want to look at you and make noises with you before she goes back to eating.
- Burp your baby only if she seems to be full of air. She'll stop

eating and may seem uncomfortable.

- If she stops to fuss, soothe her and again offer the bottle. Don't force more food—you're just checking to see if she has had enough.
- Keep the feeding smooth and steady. Don't stop to do other things like wipe her chin, arrange her clothes and blankets, or check how much formula is left.
- Work toward having her stay awake through the whole feeding. Feed her when she is fully awake but not exhausted from crying. Look at her while she eats and talk to her softly. Treat her in a way that helps her remain awake and calm.
- Choose a baby formula and stay with it if you can. Don't keep switching around.
- Mix formula just right. Be meticulous about measuring.
- Be equally meticulous about sanitation. Sterilize equipment for the first 3 months, boil water for the first 6 months.
- After that, make sure your water supply is clean and safe.
- Enjoy your baby.

Adapted with permission from *ELLYN SATTER'S NUTRITION AND FEEDING FOR INFANTS AND CHILDREN: Handout Masters.* Ellyn Satter Associates, Madison, Wis., 1997. For information about Ellyn Satter's books and teaching materials, see **www.ellynsatter.com** or call 800-808-7976.

CHAPTER 7

FEEDING
YOUR OLDER BABY
6 TO 12 MONTHS

IF YOU ARE LIKE MOST PARENTS approaching the question of starting solid foods, you want to know when to start, what to start, and how to go about it, and you want to know it right now. We'd best get that laid out for you so you can rest your mind. Later we will get into the fine points and the whys, but like your hungry infant you will have little patience with messing about until you deal with the issue at hand.

WHAT YOU NEED TO KNOW TO GET STARTED

Teaching your baby to eat solid foods is like taking a trip, and like any trip it has a destination. Here's where we're going: by the end of this first year, your baby is likely to be sitting up at your family table finger-feeding himself pieces of soft table food and drinking from a cup. From the beginning of the trip to the end you will be in constant transition. If you get too settled with any one approach to feeding, you are likely missing something. If you get into trouble during this time, it is likely because you are looking for a predictable timetable to guide you through the many transitions. No such timetable exists—your baby is the only one who knows.

You can get through this time of rapid transition with a

minimum of hassle if you start late with infant cereal, putter along with that until you get the spoon-feeding down pat, and then over the next 2 to 3 months progress through lumps and soft pieces to table food. It is only when you start before your baby is developmentally ready that you have to spend a lot of time puréeing food or feeding little jars of baby food.

When to Start Solid Food. Start when your baby is ready. Go by what your baby can *do*, not by how old he is. Your baby will give you signs to let you know when he's ready for solid foods, signs that for most babies appear somewhere in the age range of 5 to 7 months. How does your baby tell you he's ready to start solids? You'll know the time is right when your baby can play an active part in feeding. He'll be able to do that when he can

- Sit up, alone or with support
- Use the muscles in his neck to hold his head up straight
- Mouth his fingers and his toys
- Open his mouth when he sees something coming
- Turn his head away if he doesn't want it
- Stay opened up if he *does* want it
- Keep his tongue flat and low so you can put in the spoon
- Close his lips over the spoon
- Scrape food from the spoon with his lips
- Keep the food in his mouth rather than squeezing it back out onto his chin

Don't start solid foods too early. Your baby will be far more interested in solid foods and you will both enjoy the process lots more if you wait until he can be an active participant. In fact, the difference between feeding solids to the ready baby and to the too-immature baby is night and day. Again, go by what your baby can *do*, not by how old he is. Some babies, like prematurely born babies, may take longer to get ready than others, even when you go by corrected age. Wait. Your baby will be ready when he's ready. You can't rush him along by starting solids. After he is sitting up, you can check with the spoon every few days to find out what his mouth is doing, but otherwise take your time. Before you take the big step to starting solid food, it is all-important that you and your baby feel successful with the breastfeeding or formula-feeding that comes

before. With children who have medical or oral-motor challenges, it can take the whole first year or even longer to get that
nipple-feeding step to go smoothly. It seems to me that you
both need time to enjoy those cozy cuddles and the rewards of
successful nipple-feeding before you move on to the next step.
You will know when to move on because your baby will show
the developmental readiness signs.

Just as it doesn't work to start solid foods too early, it's not
a good idea to wait too long to start them either. Missing a
child's period of developmental readiness for learning to eat
from the spoon makes it harder for him learn to eat solid food.
The fully breastfed baby starts to run out of iron stores in the
second 6 months and could develop anemia. The infant on iron-
fortified formula could get by nutritionally by taking more and
more formula, but developmentally he wouldn't learn what he
needs to about eating a variety of food.

What to Start With. Start out with iron-fortified baby rice or
barley cereal, mixed with formula or breastmilk. Your breastfed
baby will like the cereal better if you warm the formula to bring
it up to lukewarm—breastmilk is warm already. Don't put the
cereal in your baby's bottle. Start with thin cereal, and thicken it
up as your baby gets better at eating it. Experiment with the
consistency that works the best. Keep feeding cereal alone until
your baby is good at eating from a spoon and eats at least a
couple of tablespoons of cereal (dry measure), twice a day. Then
thicken it up and even leave in a few lumps to encourage your
baby's developing mouth skills. There's no hurry to add anything more—this step works best if it takes a month or more.
Your baby doesn't crave variety—keep in mind that he has been
eating the same thing for his whole life!

Once he has mastered eating thick cereal from a spoon, he's
ready to start learning to eat fruits and vegetables that are
mashed with a fork or put through a baby-food mill or grinder.
Puréed food or commercial baby foods are all right but not really necessary unless your baby has a particular need for the very
smooth texture of puréed food. Add a tablespoon or two of
fork-mashed, milled, or puréed fruit or vegetable along with the
cereal meal, but don't mix them together. He needs to learn
about the new taste separate from the cereal taste. Take your
time adding each new food, giving him time to adapt to the

new taste and texture and checking for negative reactions. Work up until he is having two or three cereal and fruit or vegetable "meals" a day. That will get you started—we will finish the trip to table food below. These steps and the ones that follow are outlined below and in Figure 7.1 on pages 250-251, "What Your Baby Can Do and How and What to Feed Him."

How to Spoon-Feed. As with nipple-feeding, it's important to share control with your baby when you feed him solid foods. You do that by offering him the spoon and then waiting for him to clearly tell you he's ready before you try to feed him. Hold the spoon about a foot away from his mouth and wait for him to look at it—or at you—and look interested before you give it to him. At first, put just a little on his lips so he can taste it. He will lick his lips. Offer him the spoon again, and do what he tells you. If he just parts his lips, give him a little more on his lips. If he turns his head away, quit. Put the spoon in his mouth only if he opens up. Don't get pushy, and don't do the whole job for him—give him the food only if he does his part by look-ing at you and opening his mouth.

- Put him in the high chair, perhaps propped up with a couple of pillows.
- Have him sit up straight and face you; that way he'll swallow better and be less likely to choke.
- Sit directly in front of him.
- Use a small, shallow-bowled, long-handled baby spoon.
- Hold the spoonful of food so he can see it—about 12 inches away from his mouth.
- Wait for him to pay attention before you try to feed it to him.
- At first, put some on his lips.
- Offer another spoonful, and do what he tells you.
- Put food in his mouth only if he opens up.
- Feed as slowly or as fast as he wants to eat, but wait for him to show you he's ready before you offer the next spoonful.
- Let him touch his food when he wants to. This gets messy, but that's okay.
- Talk to him and keep him company, but don't be exciting or entertaining.
- Stop feeding as soon as he shows you he's done.

When your baby has finished eating, he may lean back, press his lips together, turn his head away, shake his head, clamp his lips shut, or act bored. When you offer the spoon and try to get his attention to feed him, he won't give it to you. Stop when he lets you know he wants to stop, even if he eats only a bite or two. Don't make him fuss to get you to pay attention. If you take his word for it, he'll learn faster, not slower. Babies—and all the rest of us—eat better when they feel like they have control over the situation.

What to Do about Breastfeeding or Formula. When you first start solids, offer the nipple-feeding first and the solid foods afterward. Before he finds out that solid foods are *something to eat*, your hungry baby will have little patience with messing about with a spoon. After he gets comfortable with eating cereal, you can offer him the solids partway through the nipple-feeding—after one breast or when he takes a breather from his bottle—then finish by offering the rest of the breast- or formula-feeding. That will get you through the first couple of months. Wait to offer the solids first until he is ready to start drinking from a cup—we'll talk about that in the section on oral-motor development (pages 267-273).

What to Do about Nutritional Supplements. Your baby does not need a multivitamin or mineral preparation. Formula and breastmilk, with the exception of vitamin D and fluoride for some children, are adequate for your baby's needs. The amount of breastmilk or formula your baby takes will drop when he starts eating more and more solid foods, but if you choose the solid foods well he will still get what he needs. However, if you won't feel comfortable unless you give your child a "vitamin," read appendix P, "Vitamins and Minerals for Children," so you can do a good job of choosing.

Vitamin D. Formula has plenty of vitamin D, but breastmilk is not a good source. Pasteurized milk is fortified with vitamin D, so at the end of this first year when your baby starts drinking whole pasteurized milk, he will be well covered. Until then, you have to depend on either the sunshine or supplements. If your baby is at all exposed to sunshine—unless he is always well slathered with sunscreen—his skin will make enough vitamin

FIGURE 7.1 WHAT YOUR BABY CAN DO AND HOW AND WHAT TO FEED HIM

In making feeding decisions for your baby, go by what he can do, not by how old he is. The ages in this figure are given in ranges, and even then

Age	Feeding capabilities
Birth to 6 months	Cuddles Roots for nipple Sucks Swallows liquids
5 to 7 months	Sits supported or alone Keeps head straight when sitting Follows food with eyes Opens for spoon Closes lips over spoon Moves semisolid food to back of tongue Swallows semisolids
6 to 8 months	Sits alone Keeps food in mouth to munch Pushes food to jaws with tongue Munches, mashes food with up-and-down movement Palms food (palmar grasp) Scrapes food from hand into mouth Drinks from a cup but loses a lot
7 to 10 months	Sits alone easily Bites off food Chews with rotary motion Moves food side-to-side in mouth, pausing with food on the center of the tongue Begins curving lip around cup Palmar changing to pincer grasp (thumb and forefinger)
9 to 12 months	Getting better at picking up small pieces of food (pincer grasp) Curves lip around cup Getting better at controlling food in mouth Getting better at chewing
12 months and beyond	Becomes more skillful with hands Finger-feeds Improves chewing Improves cup-drinking Is interested in food Becomes a part of the family with respect to eating

Adapted with permission from EM Satter and PB Sharkey. Montana Feeding Relationship Training Package. Madison, Wis.: Ellyn Satter Associates, 1997.

they are ball-park estimates. Your baby is the only one who can really say when he's ready!

Manner of feeding	Suggested foods
Cuddling and nipple-feeding from breast or bottle	Breastmilk and/or iron-fortified infant formula
Spoon-feeding of smooth semisolid food Cuddling and nipple-feeding from breast or bottle	Iron-fortified rice or barley cereal mixed with breastmilk or iron-fortified formula Breastmilk and/or iron-fortified formula
Spoon-feeding of thicker and lumpier food Finger-feeding of thicker, lumpier food: "If it hangs together, it's a finger food." Cup drinking Cuddling and nipple-feeding from breast or bottle	Well-cooked, mashed, or milled vegetables and fruits Mashed potatoes Sticky rice Wheat-free dry cereal like Cheerios or Corn Chex Breastmilk and/or iron-fortified formula
Finger-feeding of lumpy food and pieces of soft food Cup drinking Cuddling and nipple-feeding from breast or bottle	Chopped cooked vegetables Chopped canned or cooked fruits Cheese Mashed cooked dried beans Strips of bread, toast, tortilla Crackers and dry cereals containing wheat Breastmilk and/or iron-fortified formula
Finger-feeding of soft table foods Drinking by himself from a covered toddler cup Cuddling and nipple-feeding, away from mealtime	Cut-up soft cooked foods Cut-up soft raw food (like bananas or peaches) Tender chopped meats Casseroles with noodles cut up Dry cereal Toast and crackers Eggs and cheese Breastmilk and/or iron-fortified formula
Finger-feeding soft table foods Cup-drinking by himself Nipple-feeding only at snack time, not at mealtime Begins to use spoon	Everything from the family table that is soft Avoid smooth pieces that can choke: whole grapes, hot dog rounds Cut up meat finely All right to change to whole pasteurized milk

For more information about Ellyn Satter's other books and teaching materials, see **www.ellynsatter.com** or call 800-808-7976.

D. In chapter 5 you learned about vitamin D supplements (pages 182-183). My recommendation: if in doubt, give your baby a supplement, but give *no more* than 200 IU (international units) of vitamin D per day. Too much vitamin D, as well as too little, can weaken your baby's bones.

Fluoride. Fluoride, of course, is important for strong teeth, but it's easy to get too much, so read on before you consider supplementing your baby's diet with fluoride. Children who get recommended amounts of fluoride from birth have an average of 60 to 65 percent fewer cavities than children who do not get recommended amounts. The problem is that it is hard to predict how much fluoride your baby will get, and too much can cause fluorosis, or white mottling of the tooth enamel or even colored mottling in extreme cases. In the last 20 years, the incidence of fluorosis has increased, apparently because there are so many sources of fluoride. Fluoride in your baby's diet comes from fluoridated drinking water, from formula made with fluoridated water, from foods and drinks that use processing water— both tap and bottled—from fluoridated municipal water supplies, and from fluoridated toothpaste. Properly treated water is fluoridated to a level of somewhere between 0.3 and 1 part per million (ppm). Water is supplemented at a lower level in hot climates where water consumption is higher. Call your city water department to find out the fluoride level in your water, or have it tested. Currently, the American Academy of Pediatrics and American Academy of Dentistry recommend that the child between age 6 months and 3 years who is getting less than 0.3 ppm fluoride in drinking water be supplemented with 0.25 milligrams of fluoride per day. For the complete fluoride dosage schedule, see appendix P, "Vitamins and Minerals for Children."

MORE ABOUT *HOW*

We'll revisit the *what* and *when* topics in more detail, but before we do, let's go to the *how*, and talk about why it is so vitally important to follow your baby's lead in guiding the solids-feeding process. In going by your baby's developmental signs and feeding cues, you will be doing far more than you may realize, not only with getting feeding off on the right foot, but also in supporting your child's emotional, social, and intellectual development. In chapter 6 we discussed the importance of tuning in to your baby and understanding how he "talks" with you and sharing control with him. Then, the paying attention and responding were to help your baby with homeostasis and attachment. Now, the paying attention and responding not only help your baby feel good about himself but also support the process of separation and individuation. He will continue to work on the earlier stages—being engrossed with pleasant feeding helps him to be calm and focused, and being respected in feeding lets him express his love for you and accept your love back. Your participation in the back-and-forth communication of spoon-feeding helps him understand cause and effect and to *know* on a deep level that you pay attention and that he can get what he wants.

Now that he's a more active player, to do well at this stage—to eat well and play well—your baby *has* to be allowed to take an active part. He needs to tell you what he wants and have you listen and respond. In the process, your baby will learn a vitally important fact about himself and others: that he can tell other people what he wants and that others will honor his wishes. He will learn that the world is a friendly place where he will be loved and respected. When you offer your baby a spoonful of food and wait for his response, and he opens his mouth and leans over to let you know that he wants it, you are communicating in both a sophisticated and fundamentally important way. When you further honor his communication and continue the interaction by putting the spoon in his mouth and leaving it there long enough for him to remove the food from the spoon, you show him you are willing to let him take the lead and you encourage him to "talk" with you. You are enacting a communication and relationship pattern that is transformative for him—in his as well as your eyes—and essential to his relationships with other people. Can you see how feeding in this way is like play and how powerfully it supports your baby's cognitive, emotional, and social development?

Solids-Feeding Is Supposed to Be Fun. The sad reality is that this delightful and rewarding interaction is often spoiled for both parents and children by too-early introduction of solid foods and by parents' too-urgent sense that their child must eat. A 1998 survey done by the Beech-Nut baby food company found that spoon-feeding was the least favorite activity of up to 40 percent of surveyed parents, and about the same percentage said they were spending a lot of their time spoon-feeding. Two-thirds of parents said they didn't enjoy bottle-feeding, but they did like breastfeeding, cuddling, and playing with their babies. Since the survey was of parents who had called a help line for information, its design doesn't tell us how parents in general feel about these issues. However, I am still extremely concerned that feeding was so spoiled for so many. In an area as centrally important to the infant and parent as feeding, such negative feelings represent a major loss for parents and children alike.

Why am I so concerned? Because your baby will feel about eating the way you feel about feeding. I am puzzled why those surveyed parents found spoon-feeding so negative. I am captivated by watching babies eat, and when I show videotapes of babies being spoon-fed, my audiences are charmed. My now 6-month-old granddaughters, Marin and Adele, for instance, are a joy to watch eat. Each little girl's eating style reflects her personality. When her mom or dad offers her the spoon, Marin quickly flips her little mouth open wide like a baby bird's. Her attention has a tendency to wander, but if her parents wait, she gets her mind back on what she's doing and goes back to her baby-bird routine. Marin eats enthusiastically, and when she is done, she abruptly stops opening up. Then she becomes fickle and looks at the feeder as if to say, "why would you think I would be interested in *that*?" The whole spoon-feeding process takes maybe 5 minutes, 10 at the most. Adele, on the other hand, is more deliberate about it, but just as willing. She looks at the spoon and at whoever is feeding her and opens her mouth in a more reserved fashion. She sustains her attention to eating and takes somewhat longer than Marin does to eat. But when she is finished, she is just as fickle as Marin: "My dear, whatever can you *mean* by offering me that?"

The parents in my audiences are always captivated when I show 7-month-old Lauren from my *Feeding with Love and Good Sense* videotape. Lauren's daddy is feeding her, and she eats just as enthusiastically and with just as much dispatch as Marin and Adele. Her father is tuned in, follows her signals, and feeds her until she loses interest.

To me, that kind of feeding interaction is just as much fun as play. Parents and infants are working together so smoothly, the infants are showing so clearly that they know how to communicate, and they are taking so much pleasure in being listened to and respected. It doesn't get much better than that, for either parent or baby. In fact, research that compares parents' interactions with their children in feeding and in play say there are some clear similarities. Parents who can follow their child's lead with playing and get pleasure out of the child's initiative and response are parents who enjoy feeding and do a good job with it.

Parents look at Lauren on the feeding videotape and say, "I wish my child were as good an eater as she is." It isn't so much that Lauren—or Adele or Marin—are inherently "good eaters." It is that they are being fed in a way that allows them to do a good job with their eating. In my experience, children want to eat. They want to grow up with respect to their eating. So why can infant spoon-feeding be so negative that almost half of parents in the Beech-Nut study found it unpleasant? Errors in feeding. Now, before you pack your bags to go off on still another of those parent guilt trips, let me hasten to reassure you that if you are tuned in to your baby, you are likely to be doing the right thing intuitively. If not, it's because he hasn't yet reminded you enough times so you can get the point. If you push, the problem is likely to be that you are being given bad advice, and some of that bad advice can overwhelm your intuition and also make you ignore information coming from your baby. We'll talk more about that bad advice later.

Of course, we have to talk about why you would be willing to *accept* bad advice, and that brings us to the topic of your own agenda. An agenda might be something like wanting to be the first in your parenting circle to start your baby on solid foods, as would starting solid foods in order to get your baby to sleep through the night. Either one can make you ignore information coming from your baby. Furthermore, introducing solid foods doesn't help babies to sleep through the night.[1]

How to Make Solids-Feeding Fun. In my experience, every child can be a good eater to the limits of his physical ability if parents know how to go about feeding. The key question is not "why isn't my child a good eater?" but rather "what is going on in feeding that makes it look like my child won't eat?" I have a pretty good idea, and I have it on videotape—many times over. Let me describe one such segment—a short clip also from the *Feeding with Love and Good Sense* videotape. Soon after the sequence with Lauren and her daddy, we see Sarah, a clearly loving mother who is nonetheless absolutely ignoring her 4-month-old daughter Michelle's protests as she rapidly shovels spoon after spoon of solid food into her daughter's mouth. Sarah finally stops, but only after Michelle gets extremely upset and sets up quite a howl. My audiences don't like that one—it makes them squirm in their chairs—because neither the baby nor the mother seem to be having any fun. Why, I asked Sarah after the taping, did she continue to try to feed when her daughter clearly didn't like it? "Because she has to have it," she answered, with real concern. "It's time she starts to take solid food."

Her little girl didn't have to have solid food, because she was taking plenty of formula. The fact that she didn't like solids also indicated she wasn't developmentally ready. But many equally loving parents have the idea that their not-quite-ready child has to have solid foods, that it is some kind of a nutritional emergency, and because of that misconception they barge into solids-feeding, spending hours putting in food, scraping it back off their baby's chin, and putting it in again. All the while, their child couldn't possibly care less, or if he cares, it is because he hates it. If you start solid foods too early, I promise you, feeding will be dead boring at best and wildly frustrating at worst. Your baby won't like it and neither will you.

Here's how you can help your older baby be a good eater and have some fun at feeding times:

- Wait until your child is ready to start solid foods; don't try to start too soon.
- Emphasize the quality of the feeding, not getting food into your baby.
- Look for, wait for, and enjoy his ways of letting you know that he wants food.
- Don't put anything in his mouth without his permission.
- Let him dictate tempo and amounts rather than trying to get him to eat a set amount at a certain rate.
- Go by his developmental readiness and move him along from

semisolid to lumpy food to pieces of soft food and then table food rather than starting too soon or keeping him on puréed food too long.

• Stop feeding when he shows he wants to stop.

Your baby will eat more and will be more willing to experiment with new foods if you follow his lead in feeding. Above all, avoid pressure. Get his permission before you try to put anything in his mouth. Your baby's need to grow up and to master his next step in development will make him open his mouth. He may be anxious or reluctant, but if he is ready and if you give him time and keep the food before him, he will deal with his anxiety and reluctance and open up. Let me give you an example. Marsha Dunn Klein, a licensed occupational therapist in Tucson and author of feeding therapy books, works with children who have oral-motor and behavioral problems with feeding. Klein is committed to keeping the child in control of feeding. She is a perfect wizard at finding ways to keep the child in control with learning prefeeding skills, that is, oral-motor skills that your baby must acquire before he is ready to eat solid food, and then feeding so he doesn't feel overwhelmed at any point. It is Klein's idea to introduce new tastes and textures by putting the food on the baby's *lips* rather than in his mouth. That approach makes all kinds of sense. It is a way of nonverbally saying "this next spoonful is peaches," so he doesn't take a big mouthful of peaches expecting it to be cereal and then get overwhelmed and turned off. Klein is also excellent at presenting difficult concepts in ways that are understandable and accessible to parents.

In *Prefeeding Skills,* the excellent book Klein coauthored with Suzanne Evans Morris, she points out that a child gets ready to eat by doing a lot of mouthing—fingers, toys, the corner of the blanket. In the process, he tones down his gag reflex and makes his mouth less sensitive to taste and texture. If you have ever had your jaws wired, you know that the unused mouth is terrifically sensitive to tastes, textures, and temperatures. Some children don't do much mouthing. For instance, the prematurely born child who has had a lot of unpleasant medical procedures done to his mouth doesn't want anything near his mouth, or the child with neuromuscular limitations can't get things into his mouth. A child who hasn't had much mouth experience needs help desensitizing the inside of his mouth before he can be comfortable eating.

Feeding therapists and parents accomplish that *oral desensitization* by guiding the child to put fingers, toys, or baby toothbrushes into his mouth. That way, the child gets the reward of having the very natural experience of using his mouth to explore. For the child who doesn't like any touch near his face, Klein suggests playing repetitive mouthing games *with the child's clear cooperation.* She may help the child hold the toothbrush, for example, then "walk" it time and time again up his arm up to his shoulder, then to his chin, and finally to his lips. With lots of play and repetition, *provided he is not pushed any further than he wants to go,* eventually the child gives permission to put the toy in his mouth. His permission may come in the form of leaning toward the toy, parting his lips, and maybe even opening his mouth. From then on, it is a gradual working up of time. The child may handle a few seconds of oral touch today and a minute or two by next week. Eventually the child gets a grip on his own anxiety and opens his mouth to let her put in the brush or toy and move it around a bit on his tongue and cheeks. She is careful to watch for his response, and the second he indicates he has had enough, she takes it out.

Klein also talks with parents about *tilt*—the physical positioning of the parent and the child relative to each other. Klein points out that with problem feeding, the tilt is often toward the child. The parent leans forward, encouraging, pushing, even forcing. The child leans back, considering, avoiding, resisting. The goal is for the parent and child to meet in the middle, with the parent holding the food out and the child giving permission by opening his mouth and leaning forward. When the parent stops leaning forward and remains in the middle, the child is freed up to come forward.

Good Feeding Is a Conversation. Good feeding is a sort of nonverbal, nicely flowing conversation. When you talk with someone and they let you know that they take an interest in what you say, that makes you feel good. They can amplify what you were talking about and it is still fine. They can even introduce a new topic of conversation, and if it has something to do with the previous topic or if they've picked out something to talk about that they think you'll be interested in, it is still okay. But if during the course of the conversation, the other person abruptly changes the subject, that response can take your breath away and usually brings the conversation to a screeching halt. Similarly, if you're talking with someone and time after time that person fails to acknowledge what you say or doesn't respond to it, or even worse, does the opposite of what you ask for, that behavior can make you feel extremely upset or discouraged. After a while, you stop seeking that person out, or if you do, you don't expect much.

The same thing happens in a nonverbal way in feeding. If you are feeding a baby and he is excited and wants to eat fast, you feed him fast, and probably even express back to him some of his pleasure and excitement in eating. He opens his mouth and you put food in. He takes a minute to rest and you wait to offer food until he again opens up. The two of you are on the same wavelength, and you are both having a good time. Child development specialists describe this as being in *synchrony* with your child. But if you hold back on the tempo and act displeased or upset at his excitement, you won't be holding up your end of the conversation. If you feed so fast that you keep the spoonfuls coming before he has had a chance to even let you know he wants it, you're doing all the talking. You and your baby will be out of sync—you will miss each other, and both of you will feel disappointed and frustrated.

If your baby is hungry and interested in solid foods and you feed him until he gets full and then you take his word for it when he says he has had enough, you have had a positive interchange. But if he is eating along enthusiastically and you suddenly stop for no apparent reason, you have broken a very basic rule of conversation. You might know you have run out of food, but your baby will not, and he will feel upset. If that sort of thing happens too often, you are not going to be a very favorite conversation partner, and eating is not going to be a very favorite thing for him to do. You'll also be missing each other if you ignore his signals that let you know he has had enough to eat. If you try to get him to eat more than he really wants, you are essentially ignoring everything he says and shouting him down.

Do work on having nice feeding conversations with your baby. It is fundamentally important to your baby's emotional development, to his nutritional well-being, to his eating behavior, to your relationship, and to the way you feel about yourself as a parent. If you can get on the same wavelength with your baby and get so you can talk back and forth successfully, you will be making a fundamental contribution to his nutritional, social, emotional, and intellectual development. It will also be rewarding. You will know your baby better and will feel more relaxed and comfortable with him. And he with you. It is a basic human need to be effective with other people, particularly when that other person is your child. If you are shy about getting to know your baby or fastidious about letting him take the lead and make a mess with feeding, take steps to get over it. If you have an image and a timetable for what you want your baby to be and when you want him to be it, realize how that makes you miss out on the delightful person your baby really is, and do everything you can to set your itinerary aside. If you have a hard time figuring out how your baby communicates—some babies are hard to figure out—or if you have difficulty letting go of control and letting your baby take the lead, get help with it. It's that important.

Separation and Individuation. We are all social beings. From birth, your baby wants to be understood. He will do more and dare more with feeding if you tune in to what he is "saying" and do what he asks. If you take control, he will do less. For a refresher on our earlier discussion of sharing control in feeding, review the section in chapter 6 on sharing control with your baby (pages 210-211), and also look again at Figure 4.1, "Control of Feeding" (page 116). Your child's need to be understood has been there all along, and from birth, feeding goes best if you follow his cues. Somewhere between 6 and 12 months of age, his need to communicate and be understood becomes centrally important for him and soon evolves into a burning need to do it *his way*. Everyone knows about the "terrible twos," when the toddler's drive to explore and be oppositional come to the fore. As we will discuss in more detail in the next chapter, that behavior comes from the toddler's need to *separate and individuate*. In plain terms, the toddler needs to find out that he is a person separate from the people he loves best. He needs to say *no*, to learn and explore, and to do things his own way.

However, not everyone knows that separation and individuation actually begin during the second half of the first year.

Clearly, your baby isn't going to glare and say *no* when you set
a limit, nor will he put himself into dangerous situations or
watch you out of the corner of his eye while he fiddles with the
knobs of the boom box. At this early age, the need to separate
takes the form of your baby's burning need to *do it himself.*
Being a writer and educator, I am constantly struggling to find
ways of understanding and demonstrating these behavioral
complexities in understandable ways. My granddaughters have
been extraordinarily helpful in that regard—more than my own
children were. When my children were small, I was so engulfed
by the process that it was hard for me to see what was happening. But Emma helped me understand what the 8-month-old is
all about.

Emma had moved along very nicely, communicating back
and forth with her parents and learning to eat solid foods. By
age 8 months, she had worked her way up to finger-feeding
herself soft cooked fruits and vegetables, cereals, breads, and
toast. Her favorite was gnawing on strips of toast. Being a bit
rusty on infant feeding, I handed Emma a too-long strip of
toast. She gripped it on the very end, and proceeded to stick it
so far into her mouth that she gagged herself. Whereupon her
mother reached over to adjust Emma's grip so the strip didn't
stick out so far. Instantly, Emma swung her hand back over her
shoulder, moving it as far away from her mother as she could
get it, looking at her mother with a very determined expression
on her face. Words could not have said it more clearly: "I want
to do it *myself.*" Amazing. Perfectly amazing. Eight months!

Your baby's need for autonomy is not a trivial one. Irene
Chatoor, a child psychiatrist specializing in infant feeding problems at Children's Hospital Medical Center in Washington,
D.C., has observed that the age of the highest incidence of
nonorganic failure to thrive is around 9 months, during the first
blooming of the separation and individuation phase of development. Nonorganic failure to thrive is serious growth failure, far
beyond the point of a downward blip on the growth chart.
Babies with nonorganic failure to thrive are so undernourished
that they are thin and short, lack energy to play and explore,
and show behavioral distortions.

I am not going to go into detail about what feeding struggles look like when they are severe enough to affect growth,
because you don't need the trauma. Suffice it to say that parents

push, children resist, parents push harder, and children resist all the more. The child gets so upset about being ignored and over-ruled that he doesn't even know he is hungry. He undereats, not in most cases because there is something the matter with him but because he is so caught up in the struggle that he simply can't help it.

Bad Feeding Advice. Good feeding advice supports you in paying attention to your baby in guiding the feeding process and respects your intuitive need to do what makes your baby happy. Bad feeding advice imposes arbitrary timelines, foods, amounts, and schedules and implies that you should ignore your baby. The worst advice goes further by infusing the arbitrariness with a sense of urgency: do this or your baby will suffer dire nutritional consequences. Sarah, my videotaped mother who was making her baby—and herself—so unhappy with spoon-feeding, had a sense of urgency. She, like a lot of parents, had the feeling that her baby *had* to have that cereal. Where does that feeling come from?

Bad feeding advice comes partly from tradition, from previous generations who have started their children early on solid foods, see nothing wrong with it, and in fact have the conviction that it is essential. In my parenting day, babies were started on solid foods by age 1 month. Now it appears that most parents start infants on solid foods by 3 months of age, which means that tradition is still putting a lot of pressure on you. There was no good reason why we did that. We in earlier generations didn't understand about infant physical and emotional development. We did the best we could, but now you have an opportunity to do it better.

Bad feeding advice comes partly from feeding recommendations that focus too much—or only—on age. As we said earlier, to feed effectively, you have to go by what your baby can *do*, not by how old he is. Any advice is bad advice if it tells you that now that your baby is 4 or 6 or however many months old, he should eat this or that. This advice induces you to ignore your baby and go by the guideline instead.

Bad feeding advice comes from baby food companies with their multimillion-dollar advertising budgets. The major baby food company in the United States encourages starting solid foods when a baby weighs 13 pounds or doubles his birth weight. Both principles represent arbitrary timelines that have nothing to do with your baby's readiness. They don't even make sense with respect to your baby's nutritional needs. Big babies weigh 13 pounds by less than age 2 months. Small babies double their birth weight by age 4 months. At that point, or even by age 6 months—they are still very solidly supported nutritionally by breastmilk or formula.

Weight and growth guidelines plant in your mind the erroneous idea that after a certain early point breastmilk or formula isn't adequate, and they increase your urgency to get your child on solid food. At this writing and for many years, the major baby food company has pushed the 32-ounce rule, which essentially says to start your baby on solid foods when he takes 32 ounces or more of formula. Forget you ever heard it. If you revisit the list in chapter 6 (page 219), you will see that babies can be taking 32 ounces of formula when they are 2 to 3 months old. When they need more food at that point, what they need is more breastmilk or formula. No way are they ready for solid foods. The Committee on Nutrition of the American Academy of Pediatrics has recommended that milk or formula consumption be limited to one quart per day *for the infant over age 6 months*. But even that recommendation is a bit alarming, because the high-consuming 6-month-old will take far more than 32 ounces, and it will be only after eating solids for 2 to 3 months that he will replace much of his formula with solid food. In the meantime, limiting his formula will make him hungry, and his hunger will make his parents frantic, and things will not go well.

"Ah," you may say, "I don't get any advice from the baby food companies." Ah, but you do. Sixty percent of parents say they depend on their doctors to give them advice about when to start solid food and what to feed. The vast majority of doctors recommend starting solid foods at age 4 months. Where is your doctor getting his information? I—and they—would like to think it is from the American Academy of Pediatrics[2] or from some other well-informed nutritionist like yours truly, but the sad reality is that it is more than likely from the baby food companies. The companies with their huge budgets get the word out to physicians—along with free "educational" materials and tear-off sheets with little boxes to be checked to encourage you to feed their brand of bottled baby food. Those are handy little helps in a busy practice, and they do get used. Please keep in mind that in raising this issue, I am not saying that your physician cannot be trusted in all matters nutritional. Question the advice, and tell your physician what you have learned—and where you learned it. You count on your physician to help you to know when you are on the right or wrong track, and you must keep him or her involved in your decision making. If you don't trust your physician, then you must find another one. You must not cut your physician out of the decision-making loop altogether.

Why am I making a point of this? Because there is an alarming child-feeding trend growing out of the popularity of nutraceuticals—the high-dosage, purportedly beneficial "nutritional supplement" market. Parents who are suspicious of both mainstream medicine and nutrition are withdrawing from medical care, failing to feed children properly, and then dosing them with these so-called supplements. Of course, they aren't "supplements" at all but simply naturally derived, virtually untested, and poorly regulated medications. Injudicious neutraceutical use with children, coupled with withdrawal from medical care, can be disastrous. Children can grow extremely poorly and can even show the symptoms of nonorganic failure to thrive.

MORE ABOUT TIMING SOLID FOODS

For most babies, readiness indicators appear around the middle of the first year, and at that point your baby will be an active participant in the feeding process. Once he shows the signs and you begin to offer infant cereal, you have entered the transition period. During this time of rapid change, your baby will first develop the oral-motor capability and learn to transfer semi-solid food from the front of his mouth to the back and send it straight down his throat. Later, rather than sending the food straight down, he will learn to keep it in his mouth long enough to mash it with his jaws before swallowing it. That capability will make it safe for him to eat thicker and lumpier food, like fork-mashed fruits and vegetables, and later he'll move on to the soft pieces of food that come next—chunked fruits and vegetables. With lumps and pieces of soft food, your baby will learn to use his tongue to position the food between his jaws so he can crush and pulp the food before he swallows it. Next he will learn to bite off pieces of cracker or toast and use his jaws and saliva to mush it up.

Meanwhile, he will be sitting up better all the time, leaning over and reaching. His hand coordination will be improving and he will want to use his hands to join in with feeding, touching the spoon and putting his fingers in the bowl as you feed him. Soon after, he will learn that he can get some of that food to stick to his fingers and will be delighted to get some of it in his mouth by himself. Then, if you give him very thick mashed food or if he is ready for soft pieces of food, he will begin using a palmar grasp, capturing food in the palm of his hand by folding over his fingers, then scraping the food into his mouth. Try it yourself—it's quite a trick! Right on the heels of the palmar grasp, so to speak, comes the pincer grasp, in which he uses his finger and thumb independently and in opposition to each other. Many of your baby's changes about this time will not be so apparent—his digestive ability and ability to maintain his hydration and body chemistry become more flexible and not so easily disrupted.

Children Do Better When They Are Ready. Children are far more willing to participate in this learning process if they feel they have control over it. If you wait to start solids until your child is developmentally ready, and if you give your child the opportunity to progress gradually and at his own pace from soft foods to thicker and then more solid foods, he will feel far more in control and will be more cooperative. If you start too early, you will have to put him in an infant seat to support his head, and in that semi-reclining position, he will have very little control. The sitting baby can look at the spoon, feel the food with his fingers, and get his fingers to his mouth, and his response will be something akin to "Hey, this is not a block! This stuff is good!" He can open his mouth and lean forward if he wants to eat; he can close his mouth and turn his head away if doesn't. It's easy to pick up and understand feeding cues from a baby who is sitting up: it's much harder if the baby is in an infant seat.

For your baby, learning to eat from a spoon is a pretty complicated business. Put yourself in his place. First, when you're hungry and want nothing more than a nice, soft nipple, you have to learn to tolerate the spoon—that hard, cold thing with edges. Then you have to figure out that that *stuff* in that strange object is for *eating*. Very puzzling. Then you have to be willing to take a chance on it by closing your lips and taking it into your mouth, after which you have to get your muscles going so you can get it down your throat rather than pushing it back out onto your chin—without gagging. The whole process is littered with pitfalls, especially when you consider that you may have an inexperienced parent who is anxious and maybe a little pushy and who, every time you hesitate, fears you are resisting and increases the pressure.

If you are tempted to push, keep in mind that *children want to grow up*. They have built within them the driving need to get better at everything they do. Eating is no exception. They have enough pressure within themselves to move things along; they don't need any more from us. What they need from us is support, encouragement, and safety as they venture out into strange unknowns. You, on the other hand, may be exerting *too much* pressure to get your child to grow up in a particular way. You may be pushing because of your own needs rather than because of anything that is coming at you from the outside. Check yourself out on this one, because it is so important. Having an agenda for your child can not only cause you to miss out on the fun of feeding now, but later on it can cause you to push to get your child bowel and bladder trained, to excel in school, or to develop skills he isn't ready for. And you won't know you are doing it because your agenda will interfere with your ability to tune in to your child and let him take the lead. You must be honest with yourself about whether you have an agenda, because it is *so* important.

Oral-motor readiness and willingness to learn go hand in hand. To move successfully through the transition period, your baby has to have the oral-motor readiness. A Colorado public health nutritionist studied babies over an entire decade and found that babies under 3 or 4 months old really didn't want much to do with solid foods. In fact, they and their mothers got into some real hassles over the introduction of solid foods, and despite earlier struggles, the babies first cheerfully accepted solid foods at around age 4 months.[3] When your baby is ready, he will eat.

Oral-Motor Development. It's a back-and-forth process. To learn to eat, your baby's nerves and muscles have to have developed to the point that he can master the mechanics of eating. However, he still has to learn to use his nerves and muscles to eat, and he can do that only when you offer the food. When he's ready he can learn, but you have to give him something to learn *with*. Offering solid foods early won't help a child to move along any faster with learning, because he doesn't have the nervous and muscular development as yet. Mostly for the pure joy of understanding more about your baby, but also to be able to evaluate how your child's development is moving along, let's talk in more detail about oral-motor development.

To swallow effectively, a child has to gather the food together with his tongue and propel it down his throat, past the opening of the wind pipe. If he doesn't swallow strongly enough, food remains near the back of his tongue and makes him gag, which pushes the food forward on his tongue. This gagging is a normal part of learning to eat and won't frighten him unless it frightens you or you get pushy and try to get him to be braver with eating than he wants to be at the moment. Until about age 4 months, the gag reflex is very strong. After that, gagging begins to get toned down when your baby mouths—and gags over—toys, fingers, and whatever else he can get in his mouth. I know a little girl who caused her parents great concern because she consistently gagged herself with her fingers and even threw up a little. After a while she became more able to judge how far to put her fingers into her mouth, her gag reflex became less pronounced, and her gagging and throwing up stopped.

To better understand your baby's oral-motor development, let's consider *your* mouth and how it works. The next time you eat something soft like yogurt or ice cream, notice what your tongue and mouth do. As you put the spoon in your mouth, your tongue will get flat and lower in your mouth, your lips will close over the spoon, and you will use your tongue to propel the food from the front of your mouth to the back. When the food gets to a certain point on your tongue, it will activate your swallow reflex and you will send the food on down your throat.

For you, it's automatic, but your baby has to learn to do it all when he learns to eat semisolid food. For nipple-feeding he has used a totally different tongue and lip motion, called an *extrusion reflex*. He has pressed his tongue upward against the nipple, and the nipple has deposited the breastmilk or formula far enough back on his tongue that he has automatically swallowed it. As long as he still uses the extrusion reflex, he can't flatten out his tongue to let in the spoon, he can't move food from the front of his tongue to the back, and he will simply spit semisolid food back out onto his chin. A good way of telling whether your baby is ready to eat solids is by paying attention to the chin—if most of it is coming back out, he isn't ready to start solid foods.

Still eating your semisolid food, notice your swallow when you hold your head in a variety of positions: straight and looking straight ahead; turned to one side or another; with your chin on your chest; looking up. It makes a difference, doesn't it? It is far easier to swallow when your head and neck are straight.

Now try your mouth out on something lumpy—a cooked vegetable, piece of soft fruit or a noodle. Put the piece of food on your tongue and notice what happens next. You won't send it straight down like you did the yogurt, but instead you will use your tongue to move the food to the side, between your jaws, where you will chew it a bit before you swallow it. You may even use your tongue to move the food from one side to the other in your mouth. Your baby gets so he can complete that complex maneuver by first learning to move food to the side of his mouth and mash it between his jaws. Learning is such an effort that you might see him screwing up his whole face and concentrating on getting those little muscles to work. If he doesn't move the lumps to the side by himself, you can help him get his tongue motion and mashing going by putting the lumpy food between his jaws. At first, he won't be able to chew but will only mash the food. He won't transfer food from one side of his jaw to the other until a bit later, and then, right at first, he will pause momentarily with the food in the middle of his tongue before he can get it to finish the trip. That's a risky time, because if he suddenly sucks in his breath, he can pull the food into his windpipe.

Right at first he might try sending the lumpy food straight down, as he did the semisolid food, and have to gag it back out again. Don't worry—his gag reflex will be well developed, and this too-quick swallowing is part of the learning process. Your insurance policy against both situations is to be sure that the pieces of food aren't so big that they can plug up the end of his windpipe. Whole grapes or rounds of hot dogs are about the right size to plug the wind pipe and are also so round and slippery that it is hard for your baby to control their position in his mouth.

Now get a cracker or a piece of food that you have to bite off. You will automatically bite off a piece that is the right size for your mouth—a piece that feels good, that you can chew and swallow easily. Your baby has to learn all that with a process of trial and error. At first he will break off the piece of cracker and then have trouble keeping it in his mouth so he can go to work on it. Depending on whether the piece happens to be the right size, he will be able to get it between his jaws—or won't—so he'll either have fun munching it or have to spit it out again.

Somewhere between the lumps and soft pieces stage you will find yourself offering a cup—we'll talk about what to put in it later. Notice your own cup drinking and how you move your tongue back out of the way and curve your lips so you can drink without spilling down your front. Your baby has to learn to drink from a cup too, and he can learn only when his nerves and muscles get to the point that he can pull his tongue back and curve his lower lip around the rim of the cup. Grappling with all this complexity and struggling to get all those muscles working would be wildly frustrating for an adult. Your baby doesn't seem to mind, or if he does mind, it's the strangeness he minds and not his difficulty getting his parts going. A child's job, after all, is getting everything to work. He will cope and even delight in the process.

Variations on the Oral-Motor Developmental Theme. Now let's talk about all the *other* ways children move along in their progression of learning to eat solid foods. I think, for instance, of Nicholas, whose determination to feed himself far outstripped his capability. At my parent presentations, I show a lovely slide of Nicholas with some bright orange stuff coating his face, with a big ear-to-ear smile. But wait! Is it really a smile, or is it a grimace caused by the spoon he has wedged sideways into his mouth? Soon after he started eating solid foods, Nicolas began absolutely insisting on doing it himself—and he couldn't. He could get his hands into the bowl and cover them with the semisolid food that he could swallow at that point. He could smear the food on his face and get a few grams of it into his mouth. He could grab the spoon and wedge it in his mouth. He thought he was just the smartest baby ever. His parents were frustrated because he wasn't eating much, and he would not allow them to put a spoon near his lips. Time and his parents' ingenuity took care of the problem. They thickened up the baby fruits and vegetables with baby cereal until it turned into a thick, gluey mass like mashed potatoes. Nicholas developed a palmer grasp and was able to begin feeding himself. When making a palmar grasp, a baby folds his fingers into his palm and captures the food.

In contrast to Nicholas, Jonathan at age 5 months took to cereal so enthusiastically at his very first solid-feeding that he set up a terrific howl between bites, complaining because his mother wasn't getting the food there fast enough. As you can imagine, it took a bit of detective work for his mother to decipher what all the fuss was about. Eric at the same age couldn't have been more different from Jonathan. He opened his mouth for the spoon and swallowed, but then he would on no account open up for another bite. His mother got a bit pushy with him because she thought it was, after all, time, but he was firm in his resolve. No spoon. So his mother let it go for a few days, then every 2 to 3 days she made a little batch of baby cereal and offered him a spoonful. Generally one spoonful was all he would take, but after 2 to 3 weeks of her offering and taking no for an answer, he ate the whole batch and complained because she hadn't made enough! One of the truly confusing things about babies and small children is that they don't change gradually. From then on, Eric moved along through the stages of learning to eat solids relatively quickly.

Kent was absolutely uninterested when his mother first offered him the spoon. After weeks of waiting and then trying again, one day his mother let him do it himself. She thickened up his cereal to the point that he could palm it, and Kent ate it all and asked for more. From then on, she became an expert on thick, gluey, and hang-together foods until before too long he was sitting up to the table and experimenting enthusiastically with soft pieces of family food. By the way, instant mashed potato flakes make a good thickener for vegetables.

Elena had her own tempo altogether. She had been born 2 months premature and, like a lot of prematurely born children, developed her signs of readiness more in accordance with her *adjusted* age than her *chronological* age. Elena's signs of readiness began to appear when she was 8 months old, which was actually 6 months adjusted age. At that point, she was willing but cautious. It took her a couple of months to get to the point that she readily ate her rice cereal, and when her mother thickened it up a bit, it took her another week or two to get accustomed to that as well. Suspecting that moving to fork-mashed fruits would be too big of a step for her daughter, the mother next introduced baby food bananas. Sure enough, Elena was skeptical and adapted to the bananas slowly. There is something to be learned even with puréed foods. There are subtle differences in mouth motions to swallow thinner and thicker semisolids. There are differences in the smoothness and slipperiness and taste of cereal versus puréed bananas versus puréed carrots. For Elena, becoming accustomed to changes in the taste and texture of puréed foods was enough—she couldn't contend with lumps at the same time. It took her quite a while longer to make it to and through lumps and finally to table food, but make it she did, thanks to the slow and careful steps her mother took. The progression you learned about earlier would have been too much and too fast for Elena. Her mother was wise to move so slowly, and she was also good at controlling her own anxiety. When children have been prematurely born or are ill, parents often get understandably pushy, hoping on some level for reassurance that their child is really all right.

A special-needs child—a child with Down's syndrome, low muscle tone, or other cognitive or muscular limitations—is likely to need the same late start and slow and deliberate progression. Whenever a child has a condition that complicates getting all the nerves and muscles working smoothly together, it takes sensitivity and restraint to manage. Simply being overprotective and relieving such a child of the need to learn to eat won't help him. He needs to grow up to take his place in the world, and to do that, he needs to eat the food there. Whatever your baby's pattern, he will learn to eat, and he will do it faster and with less struggle if you follow his lead and support him in doing it his way. The more you push, the slower he will go. If you don't offer, he won't learn. There is no nutritional emergency here, and you need not feel desperate about getting your baby to eat from a spoon. In fact, if you *do* feel desperate, it's highly likely that he won't do well—you'll get pushy and he'll get cautious, oppositional, or too compliant. Too compliant in the short term is easy, but in the long term it is hardest of all. You don't get the feedback you need to *cut it out,* and your child will store up his resentment until he gets older and rebels.

With the possible exception of iron for the breastfed baby, breastmilk or formula is adequate nutritionally for the first 6 to 8 months of your baby's life. Granted, if your milk supply is not always keeping up with your breastfed baby, it would be nice if he would accept solids and give you a breather. If he won't, however, rather than getting into struggles about solid foods, it is better to nurse frequently to build up your breastmilk supply or to supplement with formula for a while. If you start feeling desperate or frantic about getting your child to eat solid foods, relax. If you have a problem with your child's eating or growth on formula or breastfeeding, that problem has to be attended to separately. Starting solids will not fix those problems.

Safety. Many parents are concerned about gagging and choking, and with the addition of solid foods, these do become issues to be dealt with. A young baby will gag. Food will go to the back of his tongue before he is ready to swallow it, and his gag reflex shoves the food back out again. Gagging is a normal part of learning to eat and a neurological safety mechanism that helps prevent choking. Your child won't get upset about gagging if you don't, and he will go right on and eat. If you become alarmed and react, however, you can frighten your child and make his gagging worse. Relax if you can, and realize that gagging is absolutely normal. If, however, your child continues to gag a lot and doesn't want anything in his mouth, bring it to the attention of your health care provider.

While gagging is to be expected, *choking* is dangerous. A child chokes when he takes in a breath at the same time food moves past the end of his windpipe. The food plugs up his windpipe and he can't breathe. Excitement that makes a child laugh or catch his breath while he eats can make him choke. Giving a child food that is too difficult before he can manage it can make him choke. Foods that can slip around in his mouth and down his throat, like hot dogs or grapes, are high-risk foods. So are tough foods that can't be gummed up readily, like tough meats. How do you tell the difference between gagging and choking? As long as your child is getting enough air through his throat to cough, he is probably okay. However, if he makes no sound or only a squeaky, whistling, inhaling sound, he may be choking. Always stay with your child while he eats, and talk with your health care provider about first aid for choking.

In gradually building your child's eating skills as you have learned to do in this chapter, you will be taking precautions against choking. Being there while he eats, keeping things calm, and having him sit straight and facing forward are all ways of keeping your child safe. Read more about this topic in the section on gagging and choking in chapter 8 (pages 360-361).

Sleeping through the Night. Parents have heard that solids will make their baby feel *more satisfied*—perhaps meaning that he will sleep longer or maybe be less fussy and demanding—and he may even be able to sleep through the night. I won't argue with your desire to help a demanding infant be a little less demanding, or your longing for a good night's sleep. However, studies don't give much cause for hope that solid foods will rescue you, as feeding infants rice cereal before bedtime does not appear to make much difference in their sleeping through the night.[1] Your baby will sleep or be content for longer periods as he gets older. He will be able to get all the way through the night without eating when his stomach can hold more and his nutritional needs aren't so pressing. Despite those wretched stories by proud parents who boast that their baby slept through the night within a week after he came home from the hospital, most babies don't get to the point that they can sleep 6 or 7 hours at a stretch until 12 to 16 weeks.[4]

As I pointed out in chapter 4, sleep is as much a behavioral as a nutritional issue. Babies, like the rest of us, have periods of light sleep and even wakefulness during the night. Sleeping through the night has more to do with your baby's being able to go back to sleep on his own than actually sleeping through. If you have been putting your baby to bed sleepy but awake and expecting him to finish the job of going to sleep, he will be more likely to be able to put himself back to sleep when he wakes up during the night. If he is hungry, however, he will need to eat before he can go back to sleep. If your baby can soothe himself, you won't have to make the distinction of whether he is hungry or just asking for company—you can trust that he would go back to sleep if he could. Your breastfed baby may not be able to let you sleep through the night until he is fully weaned. Make the feeding as short and as businesslike as you possibly can, and put him right back in bed.

Feeding Frequency. Some guidelines say solid foods should be introduced when the baby regularly eats more often than every 3 hours. I don't think that's right. Some babies, especially breastfed ones, regularly eat every 2 hours. I think, however, that if a baby is eating much more frequently than every 2 hours, or if his growth starts to fall off on *any* feeding frequency, it is wise to seek outside help. Your baby may not be getting enough to eat, he may not be properly utilizing his food, or you may be having trouble getting on the same wavelength with respect to feeding.

What If You Can't Help But Start Solids Too Early? You may have a lot of trouble accepting my advice about starting solid foods late and moving quickly on to table food. Your mother or friends or others in your neighborhood might start solids at 2 to 3 months. I'm sure you will recognize that there is nothing arbitrary about my advice—it's all based on your baby's nutritional and developmental needs. I can still understand your possible discomfort. It's especially hard taking a particular course of action if the people you love aren't backing you up. Their methods have seemingly stood the test of time, and our babies are so dependent on us that it is hard to take chances with doing something new. I remember so clearly when my own first baby was a month old, I did what I was told and started her on solid foods. She did fine and didn't object, being the cooperative child that she was. But it didn't feel right at the time. By the time I had my sons I had read about not starting solid foods so early, and I stepped out of line. I ignored my advisors and waited to start solid foods. It was hard and painful. I knew I was doing the right thing, but it still seemed that I was taking a big chance to do things differently from what had been done by others I cared about.

I would rather you stood up to your mother or your neighbors on behalf of your baby, but you have to do what you have to do. Do, however, pay attention to how your baby reacts to being spoon-fed. If he doesn't like it, if you get into struggles with him to get him to eat, *if it is no fun for you,* it isn't working. Stop trying and wait awhile. Remember those Colorado babies I told you about earlier, who got in such struggles with their

mothers when they were smaller but willingly took solid foods
when they were about 4 months old. If you start your baby on
solids early, here are some guidelines:

- If your baby doesn't like eating from the spoon, don't
  make him.
- If you aren't getting any pleasure out of it, stop.
- To prevent allergies, start with rice or barley cereal, and stay
  away from wheat until your baby is 7 to 9 months old.
- Wait until age 4 months if you possibly can. By that time,
  your baby will be able to manage the spoon better and will
  digest cereal better.
- Use formula or breastmilk to mix up the cereal; don't use
  regular milk or fruit juice.
- Don't put cereal in your baby's bottle. Your baby doesn't
  need it, and if he is too young to eat cereal from a spoon, he
  is too young to eat cereal.

FOOD SELECTION

You choose food for your older baby for both developmental
and nutritional reasons. The developmental part, of course,
is for the purpose of learning to eat: for accomplishing the
oral-motor development you just learned about. The nutritional
part is for the purpose of building up your baby's list of
accepted foods in preparation for the day when he stops
taking breastmilk or formula. Then he will depend on a
variety of food to be well nourished. Once you start feeding
him solids, I recommend moving relatively quickly with
texture but relatively slowly with food selection. However it
plays out with your child, the straight-ahead pattern is the
same: semisolids to thicker and lumpier to soft pieces to finger-
feeding table food.

I recommend moving slowly with food selection because I
am concerned about food allergies, and I think they are far better avoided in the first place than coped with later. Most babies
do not have trouble with allergies, but that is no reason to be
reckless with *your* baby. While I hope your baby gets to the
point that he takes great joy in eating *everything,* that capability
is best built up gradually. To avoid allergies, I recommend that

you wait to start solid foods until your baby's intestine has had time to mature a bit; then add new foods gradually, and check for reactions after each addition. Wait until 7 months at the earliest to add wheat. Wait until 9 months to add eggs. Introduce one new food at a time, trying it out for at least 2 or 3 days, and check for reactions like stomachaches, diarrhea, skin rashes, or wheezing. Then go on to the next new food. If he rejects something, take *no* for an answer for a while, and try it again in a few days. Everything is new to him, and it will take him a while to get used to all the tastes and textures.

Iron-Fortified Baby Cereal. Rice baby cereal, fortified with iron and vitamin C, mixed with breastmilk or iron-fortified formula, is the best solid food to begin with, both developmentally and nutritionally. Rice is the least likely of the grains to cause an allergic reaction. If you get tired of stirring up rice cereal, add barley cereal. Barley is an uncommonly used grain, so if your baby reacts to it, avoiding it won't limit his diet that much. Fortified baby cereal gives the iron your baby needs at this point, and its texture can be varied to fit his mouth skills—some babies do better with it very thin, others manage better if it's thicker. Choosing a brand of cereal that is enriched with vitamin C helps iron nutrition because it improves iron absorption. (Wet-packed infant cereals are also good sources of easily absorbed iron and generally contain vitamin C as well.) As your baby gets better at eating solid foods, you can mix the cereal so that it is thicker and stiffer to give him experience with foods that have more body and texture.

Start out with one cereal feeding per day and work up until your baby is taking 2 to 3 meals per day and eating a daily total of a half cup after it's mixed—more is all right—to give him the 7 milligrams of iron that he needs per day. That will give him enough learning to last for 3 to 4 weeks. Keep in mind that if your baby refuses cereal initially, it is because he is *skeptical,* not because he is rejecting it. Spoon-feeding is so new and such a drastic change for him that it takes a long time, especially for some babies, before they get the hang of it. If your baby is particularly skeptical, be especially slow and cautious about offering the food.

Since at 6 months it's still too early to feed your baby pasteurized milk, mix infant cereal with iron-fortified formula or with breastmilk. For the breastfed baby, using iron-fortified infant formula for mixing up cereal is a good addition at this time. It contains easily absorbed iron and will supplement your baby's iron nutrition. Why not purchase a can of powdered iron-fortified infant formula and mix it up as you need it? If you keep it in the refrigerator, it will stay fresh longer. Read up on your formula choices in chapter 6. If you are concerned about allergies, choose Good Start or one of the protein-predigested formulas discussed in appendix G, "Formulas Off the Beaten Path." Don't use water or juice to mix up baby cereal, especially if you are breastfeeding. Cereal mixed with water or juice is low in protein, and too much low-protein food can dilute the protein in your breastfed baby's diet. Breastmilk has exactly the right amount of protein for your baby. Formula-fed babies get more protein than they need, so mixing cereal with juice isn't as much of a nutritional problem for them, although it is a developmental problem. The mixture will taste like juice, not cereal, and your baby won't learn anything about the taste of cereal. Some baby food companies recommend mixing (their brand of) cereal with (their brand of) juice on the grounds that the vitamin C in the juice will enhance iron absorption. That's true, but choosing vitamin C–fortified cereal is better.

What about Iron Nutrition? The 6-month-old breastfed baby is near the end of his iron stores, so he must get a good source of iron in his diet. If you have been feeding your baby iron-fortified infant formula, he won't need the extra iron, so learning to eat infant cereal is strictly for developmental reasons. If, however, your baby has been getting a non-iron-fortified formula and not getting iron drops, he particularly needs iron, and he needs it *right now*. He will not necessarily be anemic, because his body's iron stores won't yet be exhausted and because unfortified formula does provide a small amount of iron. However, do not delay—get a good source of iron started now.

I realize that some nutritionists recommend meat as a first solid food rather than infant cereal on the grounds that the iron in cereal is not as well absorbed as the iron in meat. While that is true, I have thought about that approach and read about the issue of iron nutrition. I arrived right back where I started: with recommending infant cereal to start. Iron in vitamin C–fortified cereal is reasonably well absorbed; infant cereal mixed with breastmilk or formula gives a good proportion of protein, fat, and carbohydrate. It makes more developmental sense to start with cereal; infant cereal is handy to keep around while an infant pokes along learning to eat solid foods, and infant cereal starts a convenient and logical transition of food additions that arrive eventually at the family table. Look carefully at Figure 7.1, "What Your Baby Can Do and How and What to Feed Him" (pages 250-251). I recommend that most babies start eating meat soon enough—when they arrive at the family table by age 9 to 12 months. If you choose to feed meat first, I won't quibble with you, but I don't think it's necessary.

One jar of meat a day is enough. Meat is high in protein, and commercial baby food meat is high in protein *and* low in fat. As a consequence, meat as a first addition can cause an imbalance in your baby's diet. As we discussed in chapter 6, your baby needs protein but not so much that he overloads his kidneys; he needs fat for staying power and carbohydrate for energy.

Keep in mind that maintaining your baby's iron nutrition is an ongoing nutritional task that is best accomplished by having regular meals and offering a variety of wholesome foods. For more on iron nutrition, see appendix L, "Iron in Your Child's Diet."

Why I Don't Recommend Other Solid Foods First. I have already told you my objections to meat as a first solid food. Other first solid foods have other shortcomings. Some that are fine developmentally, like yogurt, cottage cheese, puréed meat, egg yolks, and puréed fruits and vegetables aren't as nutritionally helpful. Yogurt and cottage cheese are low in iron and simply give more of the same milk nutrients that the baby has been getting all along. Egg yolk gives way too much fat, and the iron isn't absorbed well. Vegetables and fruits offer most of their calories as carbohydrate and can push dietary carbohydrate up too high. While they give a little iron, it really isn't enough. Depending on how they are grown, some vegetables like spinach, beets, and carrots may be high in nitrate, and as we said in chapter 6, if your baby gets too much nitrate he can become dangerously ill from *methemoglobinemia*. When you start him on vegetables, keep the serving sizes down to around 2 to 3 tablespoons at a time.

"Adult" cereals that recommend themselves as good

sources of iron for babies, Cream of Rice, Maltomeal, and Cream of Wheat, have only 2 to 3 milligrams of iron per 3-ounce serving. Furthermore, it is in the form of *iron phosphate,* which is poorly absorbed. In reality, that iron is there more for the label than for nutrition. However, if you hate the idea of infant cereals and if your baby is on iron-fortified infant formula, you have some flexibility: you could start him out on Cream of Rice. Wheat can be allergenic, so avoid the Cream of Wheat and Maltomeal as well as multigrain cereals.

Don't sweeten your baby's cereal, and particularly avoid honey until your baby is 1 year old. He may accept it more quickly if it is sweet, but it is better if he learns to enjoy the unadulterated taste of grain. Honey is sometimes contaminated with botulism spores.

What to Do Now about Breastfeeding or Formula-Feeding. Keep offering your baby the breastfeeding or formula-feeding first, before the solids meal. Nutritionally, your baby needs the breastmilk or formula more than he does the cereal.

Fruits and Vegetables. After your baby has gotten to the point that he enjoys eating thick and even lumpy infant cereal, the next step is to begin to offer fruits and vegetables. Here are the signs: Given the stimulation of thicker cereal, your baby will start to keep the food in his mouth rather than sending it straight down his throat. He will use his tongue to push the food between his jaws to mash it in an up-and-down munching motion. At that point, he is ready to begin to learn to eat cooked fruits and vegetables that have been mashed with a fork or put through a baby food grinder, or even very finely diced fruits and vegetables. Your baby may continue to allow you to feed him his fruits and vegetables, but if he has good hand coordination and the need to do it himself, you will be out of a job. Any tender, cooked fruit or vegetable, fork-mashed or milled, is appropriate at this age. Offer them one at a time and wait to add anything else new until you have had 2 to 3 days to wait for reactions such as skin rash, wheezing, stomachaches, or diarrhea.

One or two tablespoons of fruit is a nutritionally adequate serving, although children are generally willing to eat more than that because they like fruit so much. Take it easy at first, as too much can give your baby diarrhea or a stomachache. Use cooked or canned at first because the heating process changes the small amounts of protein in fresh produce to make it less likely to cause allergic reactions. Your choices include fruits canned in juice, water, or syrup, and then drained and milled, mashed, chopped, or chunked, according to your baby's ability to gum and swallow. After fruits have been introduced in their cooked form, it is all right to offer raw fruits such as peaches, pears, and plums, all with skins removed. Many babies are good at sucking on an orange, grapefruit, or even lemon section and, surprisingly, seem to love the sour taste. You can also make apple scrapings: using a carrot peeler, remove and discard the peeling; then keep right on peeling until you have a little pile of scrapings. Cut them up, as some of the strips may be long, and let your child eat them with his fingers, or you may feed them by spoon.

Try to give your baby the cooked vegetable you are having at the family dinner table. Prepare frozen or fresh vegetables or salt-free canned vegetables, and set aside your baby's portion before you add the salt. Until he is well established on table food and eating a variety, it is best to hold back on the salt. Suggestions include mashed peas or potatoes, cut-up cooked green beans, cauliflower or broccoli florets, mixed vegetables, squash, spinach—anything with a texture that he can mush up with his jaws and swallow without choking. After he has successfully tolerated cooked carrots, offer him raw finely grated carrots.

The Nutritional Value of Fruits and Vegetables. Fruits and vegetables are important nutritionally as sources of vitamins C and A in preparation for the day when formula consumption will drop too low to provide these nutrients. Fruits and vegetables also give other nutrients such as trace elements, B vitamins, folic acid, and some nutrients you don't hear much about, like phytochemicals, and diversify your baby's diet to increase his chances of getting all the nutrients he needs.

Fruits and vegetables are low in protein and are primarily sources of carbohydrates; they are relatively low in caloric density (calories per ounce). That's generally not a problem because a baby this age will eat more low-calorie food and get the energy he needs. But if your baby is a particularly slow gainer, you may want to go easy on the fruits and vegetables on the general principle that there is no sense in making it any harder for him

to get enough calories. Fruits and vegetables are quite interchangeable with each other nutritionally and developmentally,
so if your baby lacks interest in one, you can offer the other.
People make up elaborate arguments for starting with one or
the other, but don't worry about them. No particular order is
any better than any other, and there is no particular rush.

Fruits and vegetables lend themselves well to providing the
developmental bridge to pieces of soft food that your child can
finger-feed himself. It is during this stage that you might find
your infant of a couple of months ago sitting up in his high
chair and asking to eat what you eat. He is ready to join in with
the family meal. Pick and choose carefully what you offer, and
modify the texture if necessary to make it safe for him. One of
the most popular segments of my *Feeding with Love and Good
Sense* video is of 8-month-old Elsa, sitting at the table with her
parents, eating pieces of watermelon and green beans. Elsa is
absolutely intent as she chases the food around the high-chair
tray with her awkward little fingers, capturing a green bean
between her palm and fingers and scraping it off the heel of her
hand into her mouth. Sometimes she drops it and has to chase
another piece, and sometimes she gags, but it doesn't bother
her—she keeps right on eating. Elsa's parents keep her company, but they don't interfere, even though they could do it quick-
er and cleaner. Being bigger, stronger, and faster, parents can
take over and snatch the initiative from a child at any moment.
But children, even babies, don't want their parents to simply
smooth the way and accomplish their tasks for them. They want
to do it themselves, whenever they can, because that's the way
they grow and develop good feelings about themselves. With
feeding, and parenting, the developing child requires both support and restraint.

Juice. You don't really need to introduce your baby to juice
at this point, but since so many parents do, we had better talk
about it. Juice is the most abused infant food. Juice in a cup is a
food and a learning device. Juice in a bottle is an abomination.
You may detect that I am a tad touchy about the subject! I wish
I had a nickel for every poorly eating toddler I have evaluated
to find that he was taking 12 or 16 or 20 ounces of juice a day.
And I wish I had a dollar for every toddler I have evaluated
who has diarrhea for the same reason. Often the offending juice
has been apple juice from a bottle, and if that was the case, the

child's teeth were in bad shape as well. Even if it is from a cup, teeth can suffer from too much juice, and so does the overall nutritional quality of the child's diet.

When you offer juice, do it at snack time and put it in a cup, not a bottle. Do not offer a juice bottle. Not ever. The bottle is for formula, and that's all. In preparation for the time when your baby is off formula or breastmilk, make the juice a good source of vitamin C: orange or grapefruit, vitamin C–fortified apple or grape juice. The regular adult varieties—fresh, canned, or frozen concentrate—are all fine and just as nutritious as baby juice. Watch for reactions when you start citrus, because babies sometimes are sensitive to orange or grapefruit juice until they get on toward 1 year of age. Juice is a good breakfast or snack beverage, but get in the habit of giving milk (breastmilk or formula right now, from a cup) for lunch and dinner.

At first put an upper limit on juice of 4 ounces a day, and when your child asks for more, dilute it with water to make the small amount go further. He will ask for more. Children love juice and would drink it all the time if you let them. Parents who get to the point that they give too much juice are being aided and abetted by their children, who point to the refrigerator, beg, and even say "juice" as their first word. That is powerfully difficult to resist, but resist it you must. But I get ahead of myself. Strange though it may seem, given the chance, many times a child would rather drink than eat. While children will push themselves along to learn and grow, they will also take the easy way out if it is offered. Juice is *definitely* the easy way out.

Water. Generally a breastfed or formula-fed baby isn't too interested in extra water to drink. Since both breastmilk and infant formula are relatively dilute, the baby's water needs are satisfied with the nipple-feeding. Certainly it is good to offer, but don't be surprised if you are turned down. Continue to offer water by cup to your baby after you start solid foods. He will likely be more interested now. When you carry him around and have a glass of water yourself, offer him some. Offer him a drink of water to clean out his mouth after he gets finished eating. Water is a wonderful beverage, and getting him in the habit of drinking it now will contribute to his good health for a lifetime.

"I Don't Like It; I Never Tried It." With the introduction of fruits and vegetables, you will begin to notice that there are some foods your baby accepts readily, others he is neutral about, and still others he doesn't seem to like at all. Do not cast about looking for what your baby will eat, but rather keep offering the same foods. It's not cruelty but only giving him an opportunity to learn. I copied the title of this section from a journal article written by Leanne Birch, a Pennsylvania State psychology professor who called this behavior *neophobia:* a fear of the new and, in this case, new food. Even babies notice when they are offered something new and take time to become accustomed to it. However, in most cases their reaction isn't anywhere close to being *phobic,* which implies an extreme fear. It is more like an initial skepticism and caution. Even though a baby doesn't eat much of a new food the first time he tastes it or even the first several times, eventually he will become accustomed to the taste and learn to like it. Breastfed babies are less skeptical than bottle-fed babies, presumably because they have been exposed to the flavors in their mother's breastmilk. Typically, your baby will take a taste of the new food and not want to eat any more of it. In fact, that might be the end of the meal, as I discovered to my chagrin with my granddaughter Emma when I offered her peaches in the midst of a cereal feeding. Since a 7-month-old doesn't have the mental ability to say to herself, "white, cereal; orange, peaches," I couldn't think of any way to convince her that the next bite would be more to her liking! It was tempting to slip a little into her mouth to prove my point, but I knew my limits: mustn't force or trick. Since then, I have learned that putting a bit on a baby's lips is a good way to tell him that the next spoonful will be different.

Children will always do more and dare more with eating if you keep them in control of it. By the next meal, Emma had forgotten about the peaches and was willing to eat again, and a couple of weeks later she was eating peaches enthusiastically. Truth be told, she was also more willing to experiment when her mother fed her than when I did. Children do better with eating when they are fed by someone they know very well. The moral of the story: don't stop offering the rejected food or your baby won't learn. He may need 5 or 10 or as many as 15 tastes in as many meals to become accustomed to the flavor, but he will get so he likes most foods. If you limit his menu to what he readily accepts, he won't get the opportunity to learn to like a variety of foods.

Baby Bowel Movements. When your baby starts eating baby cereals, his stools will begin to change and will likely become thicker and pastier. Don't get excited when pieces of fruits and vegetables and the stains from beets and other foods start to come through in his diaper. Unless someone chews thoroughly, those are the waste products of normal digestion. Stools of older children and adults look the same way; we just don't pay such close attention to them! Once you get to the point of introducing fruits and vegetables, your baby will be able to digest any reasonably bland food that he can gum well. In fact, chewing and swallowing probably represent the major limitation in his digestive system.

Nitrates in Fruits and Vegetables. For the time being, limit potentially high-nitrate vegetables, like beets, carrots, and spinach, to 1 or 2 tablespoons per feeding. Because of low stomach acidity, the young infant may convert nitrate to nitrite, which can displace oxygen in hemoglobin. The rapid breathing, lethargy, and shortage of oxygen that results is called methemoglobinemia, and it can actually be fatal if the dose of nitrate is very large. A while back there was a report of twin boys who were fed bottles of homemade carrot juice made from a batch of carrots that happened to be very high in nitrate. One of the babies refused the bottle, but the other took a large serving of high-nitrate carrots and became very ill from methemoglobinemia.

By age 6 months stomach acidity increases and nitrate overload is less of a problem, but I still wouldn't take chances with carrot juice.

Carotenemia. If you give your baby a lot of dark green and deep yellow vegetables and fruits, like broccoli, sweet potatoes, carrots, squash, apricots, watermelon, and peaches, he might turn yellow. My poor daughter, Kjerstin, turned yellow when she was about 6 months old. The condition is called *carotenemia,* caused by accumulation of the yellow coloring *carotene* in food that the body converts to vitamin A. Carotenemia doesn't hurt your baby, and it goes away if you take him off so many high-carotene vegetables. But there is really no reason why you should let your beautiful baby turn all yellow, so try not to give high-carotene vegetables and fruits more than every other day.

Commercial Baby Foods. I don't have any nutritional qualms about commercial baby foods, but I do find them generally unnecessary, overpriced for what you get, and overused. According to a 1993 report by the Center for Science in the Public Interest, parents in the United States on the average purchased 600 jars of baby food for each child for an average cost of $300. There is nothing nutritionally magical about infant baby foods. They are no better for your baby than what you prepare yourself. By starting solids late and progressing rapidly to table food, you sidestep the whole issue of baby food, as well as the question of whether to make it or buy it, because your baby won't *need* it. European parents use far less baby food than we do, and they feed their babies just as well. Western Europeans purchase 240 jars a year, and in eastern European countries like Poland, parents purchase only 12 jars a year. Rather than getting sidetracked into baby food, I would much rather see you learning to adapt family food for your baby.

If it is convenience you are after, keep in mind that you can buy frozen vegetables or canned vegetables without added salt and fruits canned in light syrup or juice. Then mash or mill them with a baby food grinder. Regular adult applesauce without sugar is ready to eat and is almost as smooth as baby food applesauce. Even sweetened applesauce is not too high in sugar for your baby. When your baby starts eating diced fruits, you can buy canned fruit cocktail (take out the grapes or cut them in half) or investigate the little cans of mixed fruits. Even if fruits are packed in regular syrup they will be all right for your baby—not much sugar soaks into the fruit itself. Drain off the syrup, or rinse it off if you really want to get rid of the syrup. Check out the frozen foods case for fruits and vegetables that you can give your baby with little modification. Regular orange juice or apple and grape juice with added vitamin C are just as nutritious as baby food juice.

While there is nothing special nutritionally about commercial baby foods, there is nothing special developmentally about them either. If your baby is past the stage when he just sends everything from the spoon straight down his throat, baby foods won't give him much help learning to chew and swallow. Using the somewhat lumpier "junior foods" gives a little texture, but not much—junior foods are still pretty thin and smooth. Most brands of baby food are now available in so-called staged forms. That is, stage 1 is super-smooth and contains only a single ingredient, stage 2 has more mixtures, and stage 3 presumably has more texture. With the exception of the Beech-Nut brand, the staged baby foods don't offer much progression in texture. In fact, every stage of the Gerber and Heinz food is very smooth, and it's not until you get to the graduates or toddler level that you get much texture.

Your baby won't get much help with food acceptance from some commercial baby foods either, because they don't taste much like the foods on the family table. A 1993 report by Center for Science in the Public Interest (CSPI) observed that both the second- and third-stage foods put out by both Gerber and Heinz were very dilute.* A fair amount of water was added in the manufacturing, then the food was thickened to a semisolid consistency with modified food starch, tapioca, wheat, rice, or corn flour. Many formulations have changed since then, but read the label to be sure what you are getting. Avoid foods that list water as a main ingredient and foods that contain carbohydrate fillers. The water and starches won't hurt your baby, but keep in mind that when you buy thinned and rethickened bananas, for instance, you are getting only about half bananas and the rest thickened water. That product is not as high in nutrients, it won't taste much like bananas, and your baby won't learn much from it. In their report, CSPI found that Beech-Nut and Earth's Best products used more whole foods and fewer fillers. Earth's Best promotes itself as an organic baby food and is therefore low in pesticides; by law other bottled infant foods also have to be very low in pesticides. Growing Healthy, a Minnesota-based company, markets a line of minimally processed frozen baby foods with no fillers.

While I have made my politics as clear as I can, I will also reassure you that at times baby foods come in handy and it is all right to use them. Commercial baby foods are convenient. You can choose a brand from a company that doesn't mislead you about your baby's care in order to sell their product, or you can keep your usage to a minimum. In some cases, there is a need for commercial baby food. The child under 6 months taking fruits and vegetables may need the silky smooth texture to avoid choking, although I would prefer to see that child wait to

---

*Gerber holds 70 percent of the market; Heinz and Beech-Nut each hold about 14 percent. Earth's Best holds about 2 percent, and Growing Healthy is available only in certain localities.

be introduced to fruits and vegetables until he is more developmentally ready. Children who are very cautious about new tastes and textures, like Elena, the little girl we talked about earlier in the section on oral-motor development, may benefit from baby food. Parents may need the help to work such a child up through flavors and textures of puréed food and gradually introduce thicker, lumpier food. Also, baby foods come in handy when you are traveling and have a hard time getting access to other appropriate foods. And then there is the occasional meal, like salad, that just doesn't work for the baby. When you buy baby food, do make sure the jars are sealed. The dome on the cover will be pulled down by the vacuum inside the jar and you will hear a pop when you open it. Incredible as it seems, shoppers will sometimes open jars, smell or taste, and then close them and put them back on the shelves.

Don't bother with baby food desserts—they don't have that much to offer nutritionally, and your baby doesn't crave the variety. He will learn to eat and enjoy sweets soon enough.

Making Your Own Baby Food. In the section on fruits and vegetables earlier in this chapter I gave you a number of suggestions for making your own baby food. My definition of making baby food is "adapting table food so your baby can eat it." Generally, when people inquire about making their own baby food, they are thinking about puréeing and freezing. Whole books deal with recipes for baby, the art of blending, and techniques for freezing the purée in ice cube trays to provide little blocks of foods that can be thawed and fed. I would prefer to see you put your efforts into planning and preparing family meals so you can adapt and set aside food for your child and so you have a family table waiting when he is ready to eat there. Emphasizing family meals puts the whole solid-foods process in its proper perspective. Unlike the first 6 months, when your baby had to be fed very special food, you no longer have to orchestrate special food for your baby; you are getting him ready to join you at the table.

In general, the infant who still needs the puréeing doesn't need the fruits and vegetables. And the infant who is ready for the fruits and vegetables doesn't need the puréeing. If you are starting your baby early on solid foods, however, or if he for some reason needs puréed food for a long time, and if you have the time and energy to keep your mind on what you are doing with sanitation and storage, then blending and freezing your own may be preferable to buying bottled baby food. I say *may be* because sanitation is absolutely essential, and all the safeguards you learned with respect to storing breastmilk apply here (see pages 181-182). However, don't get so caught up with the fun of puréeing and freezing and thawing that you miss your baby's readiness to eat lumps and pieces of food. Missing those times of developmental readiness makes it harder for your baby to learn and could leave you stuck on puréed food for a long time. When my daughter, Kjerstin, got over being yellow from too much carotene, she got so stuck on baby food applesauce that at age 1 year she wouldn't even *try* regular applesauce. It wasn't her fault—she had an inexperienced mother.

Baby Feeding Pattern: What to Do Now about Breastfeeding or Formula. Cereal made with formula or breastmilk and fruits and vegetables, along with breastmilk or formula to drink, provide an adequate diet for your baby. You can start shaping these foods into meals, offering cereal and fruit for one meal, cereal and vegetable for another. The rest of the time, continue to breastfeed or formula-feed as usual. You may not be able to call "usual," however, your infant who nurses so fast you wonder whether he is getting anything at all and who comes off the breast to crane his neck at anything interesting going on around him! But eat enough he will, and since your child has no nutritional need for more protein, you really don't have to worry about introducing meat until he is ready to go on to table food.

You will hear some made-up rules about "now's the time to start giving the solid foods first." Not really. There are no good reasons to dictate when in your baby's little meal you need to nipple-feed. As with everything else, it depends on your baby. He might love his solid foods so much that he loses patience with the nipple. You might find that you get along better if you give breastmilk or formula in a cup at mealtime. On the other hand, your baby may have little tolerance for being offered solid foods until he gets his nipple hit, and that's fine. If you find he gets so full from the nipple feeding that he has little interest in solid foods, you might consider stopping the nipple-feeding partway through to feed the solid foods, then finishing the nipple-feeding. Although you may have a bit of gummy cereal on your breast, that is otherwise a perfectly acceptable approach. Any cup-feeding you do at this point will help him to learn to drink from a cup and will be good practice, but he won't get much in that way.

Until you add foods from the protein group, breastmilk or formula continue to be the nutritional mainstay of your baby's diet. If your baby is breastfeeding or getting a formula bottle morning and evening and for one or two snacks a day, he will be getting plenty to satisfy his protein needs and provide for his other nutritional requirements as well.

Finger Foods—Breads and Cereals. Once you have gotten so well into the fruits and vegetables stage that your baby is eating pieces of soft cooked vegetables and diced fruits—and even feeding them to himself—it will seem the most natural thing in the world to start giving him dry cereal on his high-chair tray. For the time being, avoid wheat. Use Cheerios, rice crackers, Corn Chex, and Rice Chex, cornflakes, corn tortillas, and the like. Wait to add wheat in the form of crackers and strips of bread or wheat tortillas until he is 7 to 10 months old. This is one of the few strictly age-related considerations in introducing your baby to solid foods. At age 7 months your child's intestine will have matured to the point that he isn't as likely to take into his system the whole protein molecules that cause allergy. Until he is about 2 years old, he will get better and better at digesting protein before he absorbs it, and his risk of an allergic reaction to food will decrease. If either parent has a tendency to allergy no matter what form it takes—skin, respiratory system, digestive tract—and particularly if you both have a *strong* tendency to allergy, delay wheat introduction. Wheat protein (gluten) is one of the most common foods to precipitate allergic reactions. Because wheat is such a common food ingredient, it is far better to avoid a wheat allergy if you can. Read the label and avoid anything that has wheat flour, wheat starch, or wheat gluten in it. Generally, if a label just says "flour," it means *wheat* flour.

Once you start wheat and other grains, however, you will open up a whole new world of possibilities: strips of bread, toast, wheat tortilla, crackers, noodles, and spaghetti cut up into half-inch pieces—ah, the joy of it all! Your baby will have a serviceable grasp by now—either palmar or pincer—and he will delight in clutching pieces of food and gnawing away on them.

(As I've already mentioned, a palmar grasp is holding food between the fingers and the palm, and a pincer grasp is holding it between the thumb and forefinger.) In fact, you will find him being quite territorial about his food and showing the clarion sign of babies this age—he will want to do it *himself.* That need to do it himself will put you out of your spoon-feeding job. If your baby grabs the spoon from you and clams up when you try to feed him, he is giving you a clear message that he is no longer the baby he once was, and you both need to move on. Take the message, unwelcome though it may be. If you try to keep feeding him when he wants to do it himself, he will resist and will likely eat poorly as a result. In that respect he has become a toddler: he would rather not eat than have you impose your will on him.

Put something under the high-chair tray to catch the spills, give him his dish (or put the food on the tray—most dishes end up on the floor), and let him go to it. He will love struggling to pick up the food and finding his mouth with it. You may have to sit on your hands. You could do it far more efficiently and with less mess, but if you try, he will set up a howl that will let you know in no uncertain terms that he prefers to do it *his* way, thank you very much!

You can begin offering a formula or breastmilk from the cup any time during this transitional period from all breast- or formula-feeding to eating table foods.

Meat, Poultry, Fish, Dry Beans, Eggs, and Nuts. By this time we have accumulated quite an array of food: fruits, vegetables, and fruit juices; bread, cereal, rice, and pasta. The only hurdle between your child and table food is the protein group—meat, poultry, fish, dry beans, eggs, and nuts. Peanut butter is a potent allergen, so wait to offer it until age 1 year, and even until age 2 years if you have a strong family history of allergy. However, until now there has been no need for the protein foods. Your baby has been learning to manage textures and accumulating tastes with cereal, fruits, and vegetables, getting iron from infant cereal, and getting plenty of protein from breastmilk or formula.

However, by the time we work our way through those other foods, your child will be somewhere between 8 and 12 months and will be showing a definite interest in what is on the table. Ready or not, we arrive at offering him table foods and, along with that, the protein foods. The problem is texture. Some protein foods, of course, like fish, eggs, and mashed cooked dried beans are no problem—your baby can gum them with aplomb. Cheese is in the milk group, but it's still a protein food, and you will find yourself giving your baby pieces of cheese about this time. However, meat and poultry cannot be gummed well. In fact, when your child gets his molars at about 18 to 24 months, he still won't be able to chew even moist, tender meat or poultry very well. To make meat and poultry more palatable for your baby, cook it using moist heat until it is tender, chop or cut it up very finely across the grain and moisten it a bit with broth or cooking liquid from vegetables. Also consider a well-cooked but still juicy ground beef patty, meatloaf, or a casserole. Because casseroles are moist and easy to chew, they make wonderful baby food—once your baby has been introduced to all the ingredients separately. Cut up noodles to about a half inch in length so your baby can eat them well.

Other possibilities for protein foods include baby meat sticks and eggs. The baby food meat sticks are a low-salt, low-nitrate, convenient (if expensive) meat source for lunches. They give roughly the equivalent of 2 ounces of meat per jar. Because of the salt and nitrate, wait awhile to use lunch meats or hot dogs cut lengthwise in quarters, and then offer them only occasionally. After your baby is 1 year old—or 2 years old, if you have a lot of allergies in your family—peanut butter on toast or a sandwich is okay. Spread it thin and put jelly on it to decrease his risk of choking. Imagine! Your little baby eating a peanut butter and jelly sandwich! Avoid nuts or chop them finely to reduce the risk of choking.

Don't forget eggs. Eggs are the mainstay of feeding children—it's difficult to feed a family without them. Eggs are highly nutritious, easy to like, easy to chew and swallow, easy to keep on hand, and easy to cook in a variety of appealing ways. Unless you have a strong family tendency for allergies, by age 9 to 10 months your baby will be past the high-risk period for egg allergy and ready to eat a scrambled or boiled egg. Don't forget to give him some bread or other starch with it; combine that with a fruit or vegetable and you have a nice meal. Don't worry about the cholesterol in eggs. Cholesterol in egg yolk is unlikely to raise your child's—or anybody else's—

blood cholesterol, so it is safe enough to eat eggs.

The Family Table. When he is somewhere between 8 and 12 months of age your baby is likely to be sitting in the high chair, showing good hand-mouth coordination, developing a pretty dexterous palmar grasp, or perhaps even a pincer grasp, and beginning to show "adult" rotary lateral chewing patterns: side to side movements with his tongue and mashing his food with his jaws. He may be entertaining himself with dry cereal and crackers while you eat your meal. It's time to let him join in; adapt the food and let him feed himself. At this point, his transition to table food is likely to be abrupt and enthusiastic. He will be 8 or 10 or 12 months old—later if he is a cautious or slow developer—and he will *love* joining in with the rest of the family. Pull his high chair as close to the table as you can get it, or even better, take the tray off altogether and push the chair up to the table. Being made so much a part of the family will not be lost on him, and he will watch you eat and take great pleasure in eating the same food you do. This stage is *messy*, and your delighted baby will spread food from ear to ear and up his arms and will scatter it onto the floor. Cover the floor if you can with a waterproof covering that is easy to pick up, dump off, and sluice down. Failing that, let the food dry a bit before you try to sweep!

Once your baby starts eating from the table he will begin to take a main meal, eating the same foods at the same time as the rest of the family. It's best if he continues to get about a half cup of baby cereal a day (after it is mixed), taking it in one or two meals or snacks. I hope that you have long since begun having family dinner meals, so it is a matter of a simple transition. *You must have meals.* At this stage, orchestrating special food for your child is getting the cart before the horse. The meals need to come first, and your child's eating follows. Get the family meal on the table; then adapt that meal for your child. In another of my books, *Secrets of Feeding a Healthy Family*, I give lots of suggestions for what those family meals might be and how you can adapt them for the smallest members of the family. To get some help with your food-management skills, consider tracking down *Secrets*. Including your child at the family table can be an intensely rewarding and entertaining endeavor—he'll love it, and you will love it too.

Putting It All Together. Having worked our way through each of the additions, it is time to take an overall look at the balance of your baby's diet. Maintaining a proper diet is more complicated now than when he was on just breastmilk or formula, because you have the challenge of choosing and cooking a variety of food that is appropriate for your young child. You will learn about this topic in more detail in chapter 8, "Feeding Your Toddler," and I would encourage you to read that right now, even if you aren't ready to start thinking of your baby as a toddler. For now, I will confine my discussion to a few general observations about your baby's overall dietary balance.

At the end of the transition period, anywhere from 9 to 12 months, or even beyond for the cautious or slow-starting baby, all of your baby's daily nutritional requirements will be provided by a mixed table food diet. The *minimum* amount of food from each of the food groups he will need in order to have a nutritious diet are as follows:

Bread, cereal, rice, and pasta group: 6 servings
Fruit group: 2 servings
Vegetable group: 3 servings
    Fruit and vegetable groups put together: 5 servings
Meat, poultry, fish, dry beans, eggs, and nuts group: 2 servings
Milk, yogurt, and cheese group: 2 servings

As you will see from Figure 8.2, "Portion Sizes for Children" (page 339), the serving sizes are tiny. In general, figure that a serving is a tablespoon per year of age, or one-fourth of the adult serving. A fourth of a slice of bread, a tablespoon of applesauce, or a half ounce of meat will be a serving. Your baby will likely eat more than that, and that's fine, but once he has eaten the minimums, you can be secure in the knowledge that he has satisfied his nutritional requirements.

Your baby will vary on a day-to-day basis in the quantities he eats from each of these food groups. Generally that is no problem as long as over a 2- to 3-week period he satisfies his minimum requirement from each of the groups. Babies will often eat disproportionately large amounts of breads and cereals, and that is fine, provided that everything else is there in minimum amounts. However, if he is using a particular food group to the exclusion of the others, it can get to be a problem.

Most often this happens when babies prefer to drink their meals, insisting on more and more milk or juice and showing little interest in solid foods. If that is the case, it would be all right to impose an upper limit on the milk of 3 or even 2 cups a day, to encourage your baby to save some of his hunger for solid foods. Keep on with the juice limit—by now 4 to 6 ounces of juice a day is all right. Be sure to regularly offer water—it may be that you just have an extra-thirsty baby.

Before your child gets really adept at picking up and eating pieces of food, you may find that he enjoys dinner more when you mash or mill the food up for him. As I said earlier, the little hand baby food mills are a great help for managing the texture in food. For meals that are a little too texturally challenging for your baby, here's a recipe for a little milled dinner. This is especially handy when you have a hard-to-chew meat. You will have to cut the meat up rather finely and moisten it a bit to get it through the grinder, but with some persistence it will go. It also helps to mix the finely sliced pieces of meat in with the mashed potatoes, and to keep stirring the mixture as you work it through the grinder. This works as a finger food—if you use our broader definition of a finger food as anything that sticks together long enough to get it from plate to mouth. This concoction is especially helpful for the baby who can grasp well but is still gagging on pieces of food. It is wonderfully messy and dries to the high chair very much like cement.

Recipe for Mixed Dinner
2 tablespoons chopped or ground meat, poultry, fish,
    or grated cheese, *or*
$^1/_2$ egg or $^1/_4$ cup cooked dried beans
$^1/_4$ cup cooked rice, noodles, macaroni, or potatoes
2 tablespoons vegetable: pieces, chopped, or mashed
Liquid to moisten: broth, milk, gravy, white sauce

You may be surprised at the small amount of meat I recommend in the mixed dinner. It is equivalent to a half-ounce serving, and it is enough for a baby. If he has two half-ounce servings of meat per day and continues to take at least 16 ounces of formula or milk per day, that will give him enough protein. The older infant and toddler require roughly 21 grams of protein per day. An ounce of meat and a cup of formula or milk each provides 7 or 8 grams of protein.

Once you get dinner on the table, tomorrow's lunch is well on its way. My favorite and easiest lunch suggestion is leftovers. Cook once, serve twice. Cook a bit extra the night before, put aside enough for the next day, refrigerate it promptly, and reheat it for your baby's (and your) lunch. You could even make him a little dinner, but be sure to refrigerate it promptly and keep it cold until right before the next meal. I will go into meal planning in more detail, and offer more food suggestions, in chapter 8.

Keep in mind at this stage that you are helping your child make the transition from the demand feeding pattern of infancy to the meals-plus-snacks routine of the toddler. In order to allow him to fit into the family meal pattern, you may have to make some adjustments. You may find yourself eating a light breakfast and then having lunch at 11 o'clock so the two of you can eat together before he goes down for his nap. Or you may rely on snacks as a way of tiding him over between meals. If you have a very long afternoon and late dinner, you may want to give him two snacks.

At first, the snacks will be breastfeedings or bottle-feedings. As your baby approaches 1 year of age, however, it is better to begin making those snacks the same that you would feed to an older child: crackers and cheese, cookies and milk, crackers and milk. For more on what foods to offer as snacks, see appendix M, "Nutritious Snacks."

Overall, you will do the best job of selecting food for your child at this age if you stop thinking of him as a baby and start thinking of him as a toddler. How's that for a heart-rending statement? You might not be ready for him to be that grown up, but *he* is ready. Letting go is a regrettable but necessary part of parenting, but it has its rewards—you will be able to enjoy the fun and fascination of what comes next.

What about Fat? Your baby needs fat. As I point out in chapter 8, infants, toddlers, and even preschoolers benefit from having as much as 40 percent of their calories as fat. How do you go about seeing to it that your baby gets enough fat but not too much? Provide meals and snacks that include low-, moderate-, and high-fat foods, and then let your child regulate his actual fat *intake* with his hunger and appetite. He will eat more when he needs it, less when he doesn't need it as much. For more specifics, see Figure 8.3, "Helping Your Child Eat the Right Amount of Fat" (page 352). Keep in mind that your child's stomach is small and his energy needs are high, so he depends on fat to give him access to food that is concentrated in calories. Furthermore, fat will give his food "staying power," because eating fat with a meal retards the emptying time of the stomach and makes energy available to his body more slowly and for a longer time. (See also appendix B, "Select Foods That Help Regulation.")

What about Sugars, Sweets, and Desserts? Now that your baby is eating from the table, the topic naturally shifts to dessert. Sugar is easy enough to avoid while your child is small, and it gives him nothing except calories. As long as your baby doesn't know what he is missing, you might as well keep him away from sweets. Sooner or later someone will come along and give him a cookie, and he will develop a passion for sweets, just like the rest of us. Until then, hold off. There is no reason for you to sweeten his food. He may start eating his cereal sooner if it is sweetened, but it is better for him to get a chance to experience and enjoy the good taste of grain, even if it takes him longer to learn to like it. I think adding sugar to food is different from adding fat. Fat enhances food flavor; sugar disguises it. Your child may like desserts and seem to go for those unnecessary little baby desserts, but he doesn't need the variety. He will be getting plenty of eating challenges in other ways.

Particularly avoid honey in any form for the first year. This includes honey that has been baked into a cookie or bread, in honey graham crackers, or honey for dipping a pacifier. Honey is sometimes contaminated with the spores of *Clostridium botulinum*. If allowed to grow in an airtight place, these spores produce clostridium toxin, which can cause severe illness and even death. Generally this is a problem only in improperly canned, nonacid foods, like green beans. But it can happen in the young infant's intestine, which is also an airtight place. The spores grow, produce the toxin, and poison the infant. Throughout his early months, your baby will be naturally exposed to a variety of harmless bacteria from the environment, and some of those bacteria will take up residence in his colon. By the end of the first year, he will have enough bacteria in his colon to keep the clostridium spores from growing. Clostridium poisoning from spores is generally found only in babies under age 6 months, but be on the safe side and stay away from honey until your child is 1 year old.

For your child, going without honey is no great loss. The practical fact is that honey is no more nutritious than sugar. The same goes for raw sugar and other forms of sugar that are touted as nutritious alternatives to table sugar. The amount of worthwhile nutrients in these foods is so small that if you were to consume enough to give you any significant amount of a nutrient, you would eat way too much sugar.

What about Breastmilk or Formula? Once your child starts eating from the table, his milk intake will start to drop off. He will be more interested in table food than in the breast or bottle, he won't be too handy at drinking from the cup, and he won't be having as many breastfeedings or formula-feedings as before. Don't worry about his milk intake—for most children it drops at about this time, but it recovers later. Wait to substitute pasteurized milk for formula or breastmilk until your baby works up to three meals a day from the table. At that point, at mealtimes it is all right to give whole pasteurized milk in the cup if the amount of milk doesn't exceed the amount of solid food. That is, if he is taking 3 ounces of solid food—about one-third of a cup—his milk intake needs to be roughly 3 ounces or less. He can also have pasteurized whole milk for snacks, provided he is having "big boy" snacks like milk and cookies or milk and crackers. Give the milk in a cup—it's developmentally time for cup drinking, and offering the breast or bottle at mealtime or snack time will only prolong breastfeeding or bottle-feeding unnecessarily. Furthermore, your baby won't be too interested in nipple-feeding. He will love exploring his table food and will be willing to fill up with eating and cup-drinking. Chances are that you can quietly discontinue mealtime nipple-feedings one at a time and he won't even miss them. If you give a nipple-feeding all by itself, have that feeding be formula or breastmilk. The issue is not the nipple *per se* but the amount of undiluted milk your child gets at any one time. If he gets several ounces of pasteurized milk in a bottle, it will set up a tough curd in his stomach, just as when he was an infant. It will be hard to digest and could give him a stomachache.

Keep in mind that he doesn't *have* to change to milk from his formula. If you and your health care advisor think he could use the extra iron or other nutritional support for a while longer, continue to offer him formula rather than pasteurized milk. Keep using the same iron-fortified formula you have been using all along. There is no need to switch to an older baby or toddler formula. In fact, I find these formulas unnecessary. Your baby needs formula to help him finish his nutritional work from the early months, not to substitute for his nutritional work as a toddler. When he is a toddler, it is time for him to learn to eat a variety of table food, not to continue to depend on formula as a primary source of nutrition.

WEANING

Weaning will be easier for you if you think of it as an adding-on process rather than a taking-away process. Generally parents start to wonder what to do about breastfeeding or bottle-feeding when their baby is somewhere between 8 months and 1 year old. Actually, you started weaning when you introduced solid foods. By now, your baby will be eating lots of enjoyable foods and having the wonderful challenges and rewards of tasting, squishing, mashing, munching, and swallowing. He is now a part of the family. While he has had to give up his favored place of being the center of the universe, his compensation is the joy of being a part of the family group. He'll start to take an interest in people and things *other than you*. It may even seem like you aren't as important as you once were. *Not true.* Your presence while he eats—and always—continues to be very important. He will be happier and more secure, and he'll do more and dare more with his eating, when you are there.

You, of course, have to give up thinking of him as being a baby. Depending on whether things have gone well in these first few months, that may be more or less difficult for you. If you have had a slow-starting baby, I do hope you took my earlier advice about delaying starting solid foods and getting in a few more weeks of cuddles. But even if you have given yourself more time, making this shift may be hard for you.

It is, however, time to move on. Getting stuck on the breast or the bottle starts right here. Weaning when your baby loses interest in nipple-feeding is important for a couple of reasons. First and foremost, your baby is ready. Second, excessive and overly prolonged bottle use and breastfeeding can promote some undesirable nutritional habits. He won't eat other foods he needs, and he may develop bad habits, like demanding the bottle or breast instead of eating, and carrying his bottle around. The consequences: he won't learn to eat well, and he will increase his chances of nursing-bottle tooth decay. When nipple-feeding goes on too long, parents and children get into some real struggles as the parent insists on eliminating the bottle or breast and the child begs and cries to have it. Parents ask me, "How am I going to get my child off the bottle?" I always wish they had asked me sooner. The point at which the child arrives at the family table is a window of opportunity for weaning. The process then is one of gradually replacing nipple-feeding with other modes of eating and sources of nourishment. Done at that time, it does not have to become a process of depriving a child of something he holds near and dear. The same principles apply to the juice bottle, but if you followed my earlier advice you haven't ever *introduced* a juice bottle, and now you won't have to cope with it.

Babies generally get ready before their parents do to give up breast or bottle. The baby doesn't drink much formula and parents become alarmed. Or the baby has a bout of teething and loses his appetite for a time and parents run for the bottle. Or parents get in the habit of offering breast or bottle as a way of calming the child down or putting him to sleep. Or, most poignant of all, parents simply don't want to give up this sign of infancy. For whatever reason, missing the naturally presented opportunity to wean increases the likelihood that parent and child will later get into a struggle over it.

You Don't Have to Wean, but Do Avoid Nipple Misuse. Your baby is ready to give up the breast or the bottle—but are you? Letting your baby continue to formula-feed or breastfeed morning and night and at more-or-less scheduled times is fine. Continuing to nipple-feed on demand—breast or bottle—and having it interfere with your child's growing up with respect to eating is not fine. You are misusing nipple-feeding if you let your baby breastfeed or drink from a bottle rather than learning how to eat meals. At the risk of being a broken record, I will remind you: Children will quite willingly drink their meals rather than eat them, and your child won't learn unless you give him opportunities and encouragement to learn. You are misusing nipple-feeding if you use the breast or bottle as a pacifier. Your child needs to learn to express his feelings and find other ways to deal with them rather than just eating. Making the shift to the meals-plus-snacks routine that we have more-or-less evolved and that we will talk about more in the next chapter is an excellent way of squashing that maneuver. Having predictable meals is also an important way of reassuring your child that he *will* be fed. If you can be firm about the feeding routine, you won't fall prey to using food to cope with all the uproar and mishaps of parenting a child this age.

You may find yourself abusing bottle-feeding as a way to get your child to sleep through the night. In a Mt. Pleasant, Michigan, telephone survey, psychologist C. Merie Johnson found that about half of parents gave toddlers bottles in bed to get them to sleep.[5] They said they didn't like the practice, even though they had been warned against it by their physicians and knew that it promoted tooth decay, ear infections, and the possibility of choking. Even a few dental hygienists confessed to giving night bottles. It appears that exhaustion drives us all to use methods we wouldn't otherwise! However, rather than giving bottles in bed, it is more effective to teach children to soothe themselves to sleep—to get in bed drowsy and go to sleep on their own. All children wake up at night, and a child who can self-soothe goes back to sleep again. A child who is nursed, rocked, or comforted to sleep needs the same kind of help in the middle of the night as at bedtime. For parents who were aware of these procedures, crying it out, scheduled wakenings, and progressive delay responding were all effective. Talk with your health care provider about ways to deal with your child's sleep issues—you don't have to suffer, and you don't have to distort feeding to solve them. Consider getting a copy of Richard Ferber's popular and well-known book *Solve Your Child's Sleep Problems* (Simon & Schuster, 1986) to learn the method of progressive delay responding.

Your *child* will misuse nipple-feeding if you let him use breastfeeding as a bid for attention. If you continue to breast-feed your older baby or toddler on demand, he will soon learn that asking to be breastfed is a surefire way of cutting out other children—or adults—and getting you all to himself. It is legitimate for him to find ways to get your attention, but don't reward this one—he's making himself into a baby. That's negative attention, and while children would rather have negative attention than no attention at all, the positive kind is better. You are both misusing nipple-feeding if you let him run around with a bottle. He'll demand too much milk, won't eat his meals, won't get comfortable with other foods, and won't get the other nutrients he needs. Tooth decay is also a concern; he's highly likely to develop *nursing-bottle tooth decay* if you let him carry a bottle around, sipping along through the day. In fact, if you let him have formula, juice, or milk from a cup whenever he asks, he could develop tooth decay. Even nutritious foods like formula and juice can rot teeth if your baby has them continuously.

Now you can give yourself a lovely pat on the back. You have come through the constant changes of the transitional feeding period. From now on, your little one will be polishing his skills—getting better at drinking from the cup, chewing, finally even learning to use a spoon and fork. He'll be interested in his food and pretty accepting of a variety of foods. You can look forward to more of a regular routine as you include him in your family eating pattern and he enjoys trying out new foods. You even get a little breather before your beginning toddler starts to develop the more-limited appetite and contrariness of that age group.

Respecting your child's wishes about food now will pay off when he gets to be a toddler and you'll need to set limits. Babies learn to give back what they get. If you've supported your child's eating, and tried to be sensitive and responsive to his desires, he's more likely to try to go along with *your* wishes later.

CHAPTER 8

FEEDING YOUR TODDLER

12 TO 36 MONTHS

A TODDLER IS CALLED A TODDLER because she—well—toddles. Physically, your baby will become a toddler when she lays hold of the idea that she can get herself where she wants to go and begins to crawl, walk, or scoot on her backside to explore her world. Emotionally, socially, and cognitively she will become a toddler when she begins actively demonstrating to herself and to you that she is separate—she will roam out and come back, say *no*, and test her limits. Relative to her eating, she will become a toddler when her skepticism about and rejection of new food increases. At around age 12 months, your toddler is likely to show a marked increase in her strong food likes and dislikes and become ever more likely to lose interest in a food after only one bite. Furthermore, it is likely to be a change that does not take place gradually. Like much of your child's changing, it may be like night and day.

This is as it needs to be. Your baby of a week or a month or a day ago—the one we left enthusiastically trying new foods, sampling everything that was put before her and reveling in the ability to do it herself, will now begin to direct that passion to asserting herself. Although with food that self-assertion looks like a step in the wrong direction, the toddler's skepticism about food grows out of her mental development. The infant

303

embraced what was put in her path. The toddler is wary, and justifiably so. While she has developed mentally to the point that she can become suspicious of unfamiliar food, she has not yet gotten to the point that she can think and reason about the food or get comfortable with it by talking about it, being reassured about it, helping to cook it, or helping to grow it. When she becomes a preschooler, at around age 3, her worries about food will subside because she will be able do all that.

During her second year, your toddler will continue the process of *separation and individuation* she began when she was around 8 months of age. As you recall, while she was learning to eat solid food she showed her need to be her own little person with her drive to do it herself. Now she will take the initiative in testing her limits and trying out her ability to control. It is vital to help the toddler learn, through experience, to develop autonomy. That can happen only when you neither allow her to control you nor try to control her. What you can do—and must do—is offer structure and limits. Now the division of responsibility in feeding that you learned about with breast- and formula-feeding changes to make you responsible not only for *what* your child is presented to eat but also for *when* and *where* she is allowed to eat by establishing the structure of regular meals and snacks. Within those limits, she continues to be responsible for *how much* she eats and even *whether* she eats at all.

For the toddler and for all ages that follow, the division of responsibility looks like this:

- You are responsible for the *what, when,* and *where,* of *feeding.*
- Your child is responsible for the *how much* and *whether* of *eating.*

When you feed a child observing the division of responsibility, you offer the structure and safety of appropriate opportunities to learn and give choices within limits. Essentially, you make her world small enough so she can handle it. You are not turning her loose in the grocery store or even in the kitchen. You are turning her loose at the family table so she can learn to eat the food that you choose for her. She will test and defy, but that is part of the process. The toddler is like the night watchman, checking all the doors but not really wanting to find any open.

WHAT YOU NEED TO KNOW TO GET STARTED

As with the previous stage, feeding the toddler is like taking a trip that has a destination. Now, our destination is largely behavioral. By the time your child leaves the toddler period, we would like her to have the following eating attitudes and behaviors:

- She is positive about eating.
- She relies on internal cues of hunger and fullness to know *how much* to eat.
- She relies on variations in appetite to know *what* to eat.
- She enjoys many different foods.
- She can try new foods and learn to like them.
- She can politely turn down or ignore foods she doesn't want to eat.
- She can "make do" with less-than-favorite food.

At times during the toddler period, achieving these eating attitudes and behaviors will seem like the impossible dream. But hang in there. Your child *does* want to grow up with respect to eating, and that's what she's all about with her various quirky behaviors. In earlier chapters, I have emphasized the importance of trusting your baby, of assuming that she knows what she is doing and what she is asking for. The same holds true for the toddler, but seeing it requires an educated eye. Furthermore, her behavior will be logical only if you maintain a division of responsibility in feeding. If you cross the lines you will get into struggles for control with your toddler and you won't be seeing trustworthy toddler eating behavior—you will be seeing the struggle. Once again, to get started let's hit the high points, and then we'll go back to each of those points in detail.

What a Toddler Is Like with Respect to Eating. Toddlers are *skeptical:* They don't automatically like new food, but they will gradually experiment with new food and learn to like it, if you let them see it on the table and see you eating it. After a while, they taste it—and take it back out again. They'll do that many times, then eventually they know the food well enough so they swallow it—and like it.

Toddlers are *erratic:* What they like one day, they don't the next. They eat a lot one day and hardly anything the next. They don't eat some of everything at a meal like you do—they eat only one or two foods.

Toddlers are *opinionated:* They know what they do and don't want to do. You can stop them from doing what you don't want, like causing a ruckus at mealtime, but you can't get them to do what you do want—like eat.

How to Feed So Your Toddler Can Eat Well. Eating gives your toddler lots of opportunities to test her limits. To keep yourself out of unproductive skirmishes and to help your child reach the goals that were listed earlier, it is vitally important to maintain the structure of family meals and planned snacks. She needs three meals a day, and planned snacks midway between meals. As I will explain later, snacks are important for nutritional as well as behavioral reasons. Your child will learn and grow, but she will also take the easy way out if it is offered. Here is what you can do to give your child opportunities to learn—and to keep from undermining learning.

- Put yourself in charge of the family menu. Don't give your toddler choices ahead of time.
- Have three meals a day with planned snacks in between.
- Don't allow panhandling for food or beverages (except water) at other times.
- Manage snacks and timing to help your child be calm, well rested, and hungry but not famished at mealtime.
- Include your child in family meals. Don't feed her separately.
- Once you get to the table, let your toddler choose what and how much she wants to eat from what you offer.
- Let your child eat as much or as little as she wants.
- Don't press food on your child or she'll play the toddler's favorite game of turning things down and watching you get desperate.
- Present foods in a way your child can handle relative to form, texture, temperature, and choices.
- Let her eat in her own way. Let her look, feel, mash, and smell to explore—but not just to get a rise out of you.
- Don't make or even entice her to eat anything she doesn't want to eat.
- Don't make her clean her plate. Even adults find it hard to

know ahead of time how hungry they are.
- Make family mealtimes pleasant. Don't argue, fight, or scold at mealtimes.
- Talk and pay attention to your toddler, but don't let her be the center of attention.
- Turn the television off: It distracts your child and other family members from eating and interferes with family social time.

Don't Cater, but Choose Food That Will Help Your Toddler Eat Well. Everybody in the family gets offered the same food, including the toddler. Don't cater to your toddler, and don't get up from the table to make special foods if your toddler won't eat. Make a few modifications to make it easier for her to chew and swallow, but offer her essentially the same food everyone else is served. Your toddler is a novice at eating family meals, but she wants to be successful, so it's all right to help her a little. Offer her a variety of foods at mealtime to increase the chances that she will find something she can manage, but don't cater to her. Variety doesn't mean a buffet but a well-balanced assortment of food. We'll get into the details of that food later. For now, here are some menu-planning strategies that will help your toddler do well at mealtime.

- Serve foods that are generally soft, moist, and easy to chew.
- Serve food that is adequate in its fat content. Low-fat food is neither nutritionally appropriate nor appealing for the toddler.
- Pair new, strange, or disliked food with something that your child generally likes.
- Always put bread on the table. She can eat that if all else fails.
- Offer a second starchy food as well. Children generally do well with foods like potatoes, noodles, tortillas, and rice.
- Have your child's favorite foods sometimes—but not all the time. Other family members have rights too.
- Don't try to force your child to eat anything. She may act stubborn, but she'll feel ashamed when you disapprove of her eating.

Stay Out of Struggles for Control. Since your toddler will be working so hard at being her own person, you are highly likely to get into struggles about control. Check yourself against the following lists. You are being too controlling if you make your child

- Stay at the table to eat her vegetables
- Clean her plate
- Eat everything else before she can have dessert
- Get by on only three meals a day

You aren't providing enough structure and limits if you

- Give your child a snack whenever she wants one
- Let your child behave badly at the table
- Regularly prepare special food for your child
- Short-order cook for her
- Let your child have juice or milk whenever she wants it

Struggles about control are a normal part of this age. But if you feel bad about setting reasonable limits, if the struggles are prolonged or continuous, and if you can't seem to get things to go right with your child, get professional help. An ounce of prevention now is worth many pounds of cure later on.

PARENTS HAVE TROUBLE WITH TODDLER EATING

When I was working in a medical clinic, I could almost write the script for a toddler consult. When parents came to see me with a child 12 to 36 months old, they came with an all-too-familiar list of concerns and frustrations about feeding. They told me that their child was not eating enough, especially not enough meat and vegetables and fruits. They complained that their child would eat only a few foods and that she wanted those foods again and again. They objected to her dawdling with her food or pushing too much into her mouth at one time. Some worried that their child drank too little milk; about an equal number of parents worried that she drank too much.

Now I travel the country doing presentations about eating for parents and professionals, and I hear about the same array of problems. I am accustomed to hearing that toddlers eat like birds, meaning that they eat very small amounts. My daughter said that my granddaughter Emma ate like an air fern, meaning that she existed on no visible nourishment. However, I was mystified when a New Mexico mother said "My daughter eats just like a snake." A snake? Slithering up to the table? Swallowing whole meals at one time? Fortunately for all of us, she elaborated. "She eats a lot one day, and then she doesn't eat again for *days.*" These typical parental laments have everything to do with what is happening to and with the toddler socially, physically, and behaviorally.

RAISING A CHILD WHO EATS WELL

As with any other stage in feeding, your child has to get her emotional needs met in order for her to eat well, feel positive about food, and be proud of her eating capability. Let's consider this eating project from the child's point of view. Keep in mind that "eating well" does not mean sitting down to the table and neatly eating some of everything that is put before her. Rather, it means coming to the table willingly and enjoying being there and being pleasant enough to be allowed to stay there most of the time and not having adults expect anything of you that you can't deliver.

With eating, your toddler *toddles* in the same way she does with everything else. She has a lot to learn, and developing any capacity with food acceptance and mealtime decorum takes time—lots of time. Chances are very good that your toddler's eating will alarm and frustrate you, and it won't stop being alarming and start being gratifying until she becomes a pre-schooler. Between now and then we have roughly 2 years of feeding adventures, pitfalls, and fun—or not fun, depending on your attitude. If you enter this period with the same kind of mind set you had in the earlier stages, with a healthy dose of curiosity about your toddler and the assumption that on some level she knows what's she's doing, then I promise you will have fun. But if you have even the most teensy-weensy of feeding agendas, I promise you won't have fun. A toddler can smell an agenda a mile away, and she will resist. At the opposite extreme, feeding as you did when she was an infant and catering to her every wish and trying to make her happy no matter what won't work either. In fact, it will fail her. You will also not have any fun.

You can't have an agenda, but you *must* have structure and limits. Your structure and limits tell your toddler in a nonverbal way what is appropriate to do and not do. You provide opportunities for your toddler to learn when you maintain the structure of offering appropriate food at appropriate times. You provide limits when you matter-of-factly let her know that she can't get you to offer different food from what you had planned or dole out food between times. At times your toddler will be angry at you, and you will have to withstand her anger and tell her no. She may cry, get upset, or have a tantrum, and you still must hold firm. Many parents have trouble with this part, because they are afraid their child won't like them if they say *no* or impose discipline. Do keep in mind that discipline is not punishment, it is just demonstrating that "no, it isn't all right to do that." Parents who are able to withstand the storm are surprised to discover after it blows over that the toddler is happier and seems to feel more warmly toward them, not less. Keep in mind that we all like and respect other people more when they treat themselves with affection and respect. In setting limits for your toddler, you are treating yourself with respect.

At the same time as you provide structure and limits, you allow your child autonomy within those limits. At meals and snack times, you promote your child's independence by allowing her to pick and choose from what you have made available. She won't eat everything. Some foods won't interest her, and she also has to say no to you in order to prove to herself that she is a separate person. And you need to say no to her to keep her safe and to provide her and yourself with the structure you both need to feel comfortable.

THE TODDLER'S POINT OF VIEW

To get a toddler's eye view of this feeding business, let's start with the table itself. Since the toddler suddenly begins to act as if even foods she has eaten before are new and untried, we can only assume that for her, that is the case. Unlike when she was so celebrating the joys of feeding herself that she was receptive to whatever was put before her, the toddler becomes discriminating. She mentally develops to the point that she can identify the new—and be skeptical about it. Keep in mind, she is merely *skeptical,* not rejecting. In her own way, she will move herself along to learn to eat the food. She will watch you eat it—perhaps for many meals. Then she may allow some of it on her plate—but not eat it—and that may last for many meals. Then she may put some of it in her mouth—and take it out again.

Read this next paragraph slowly because it is so important. To most parents, that taking-out-again maneuver is very discouraging because it looks like food rejection. It is not. It is the toddler's way of gaining comfort with the food. She puts it in her mouth, examines the taste and texture, and then takes it out again, only to do it again at another meal—and another and another. Studies about children and food acceptance say that a toddler will go through this sampling and removing process 5, 10, 15, or even 20 times before she feels comfortable enough to swallow the food. Every toddler knows that putting food in your mouth is one thing and swallowing it is quite another. To understand that, think of the last time you put something in your mouth—say mystery meat—that turned out to taste and feel really weird. How hard was it for you to force yourself to swallow—or did you just slip it into the napkin? Now consider how difficult coping with unknown food must be for your toddler, who has absolutely no context for the food—she doesn't know what it is, where it came from, or how it was prepared. She can't talk about it, she has no way of understanding the food other than looking, touching, and mouthing. Some have speculated that the toddler's routine skepticism is simply a survival mechanism—a way of weeding out food that is likely to be harmful. To read more about the research about food acceptance, see appendix I, "Children and Food Acceptance: The Research."

Now let's take a look at the pitfalls for the toddler in getting to the table and behaving once she gets there. First of all, instead of getting food when she asks for it—having parents drop everything to do a breastfeeding or give a bottle—she now is being asked to go along with someone else's schedule for her eating. "Dinner will be in 15 minutes," we encourage her when she comes around panhandling for a food handout, or "you can play later; now it's dinnertime." Asking her to wait to be fed—and eat at a certain time—is a big change for her, and she needs help with it. While she will be perfectly capable of toddling over to the refrigerator and asking for juice, in whatever language she uses, it will be confusing for her if she gets it. Giving in to her panhandling gives a mixed and misguiding message. You are essentially saying to your toddler, "You need to learn to eat from the table, but you may also eat whatever you want any time you want." I realize that even for some adults not being able to eat on demand—to graze constantly for food—seems like cruel and inhuman punishment. It's not—it's merely making it possible for your child to be successful with eating. You will be offering her food regularly—you won't be forcing her to go hungry. Keep in mind the importance and role of the planned snack in giving your toddler frequent access to food so she can come to the table hungry but not famished. Keep in mind our earlier discussions (and those that follow) about sympathetic and supportive menu planning. Finally, and most important, keep in mind that there are intrinsic rewards embedded in her learning to go along with the structure of family meals and snacks.

The Narcissistic Resolution. Deferring to family mealtimes gives your toddler access to the sociability and socializing that takes place at the family table. Where else does everyone in the family regularly come together to be nurtured and to spend time talking and getting caught up with each other? Your toddler absolutely needs to be a part of it—but only a part, not the focus. As she is struggling with the separation and individuation we talked about earlier, she is going through what the child psychologists call the *narcissistic resolution*. Narcissus, of course, was a Greek demigod who was so self-preoccupied and self-involved that he fell in love with his reflection in a pond. Narcissus didn't resolve things very well—he destroyed himself by pining away for his own reflection. The moral of the story is that you have to give up some behaviors in order to have life turn out well.

Babies are self-centered, and that is as it needs to be. However, children don't benefit from being supported in being self-centered forever. When your child was an infant, you followed her lead with feeding and did what she wanted and needed by dropping everything to feed on her schedule and offer her special food that was catered to her needs. Treating her that way allowed her to tune in on other people and her environment, know that you loved her, and learn to love you back. You show a toddler you love her not by catering to her but by providing guidance and being prompt and neutral about setting limits. Certainly your toddler still requires your undivided attention at times and your expressions of love. However, you will do most of your parenting in the back and forth of your toddler's experimenting and your reacting to those experiments. In the course of those experiments, you will be asking her to give up being the star. Rather than having everything catered to her schedule and preferences, she will learn to partake of what is available to everyone else in the family. The reward is sociability: joining the broader social world of the family and finding out that she doesn't have to be the center of attention to be comfortable and happy. If all goes well, the reward will be far greater than the loss.

You can imagine, however, that she will be a tad ambivalent about it. You will likely be ambivalent as well. After all, who would willingly let go of their baby? However, it must be done, and if you don't do it right away, your child will become an unhappy and obnoxious little princess and you will change your mind. Children do help us to do our own changing and growing! Your child will show her ambivalence about giving up her favored position by taking the easy way out with eating, if you offer it. Let's say you have followed the food selection strategies I have outlined, and you have put together a lovely meal. She had a snack a couple of hours ago, and she will be offered a snack again later. She is at the table and eats in the toddler's typical way: a bite of this, a sip of that, a finger-full of something else. She is doing fine—behaving herself, getting some food in her mouth, making a mess but not deliberately. She may feel a little anxious, because we all do when we are confronted with new situations. But she is not overwhelmingly anxious—your presence makes her feel safe. She is keeping a grip, doing her job, and feeling successful. You are anxious, too, and worried that she is eating so little. Unfortunately, you *lose* your grip, and you say, "Jennifer, here are some noodles. You like those," or, "would you rather have some Goldfish?" and try to put some on her plate.

You have just upped the ante to the point that Jennifer no longer feels successful and she can no longer cope. What happens next is complex and confusing. Jennifer is more than likely to whine, cry, get upset, and cause a fuss. She is likely to feel ashamed, but she shows it by asserting herself—remember her driving need to separate and individuate that we discussed earlier—to be her own little person? She also gets a reward for struggling with you: your undivided attention. Her penalty? She doesn't get to be a big girl and cope with her eating. Do that enough times and she won't even tackle her meal—she will whine for the Goldfish.

Please notice that in the sequence I just described everything was going fine until the parent lost his or her nerve and crossed the lines of division of responsibility. Your child's eating will not go well if you get involved with *her* business of what and how much she eats. If you can stay on your side of that line, your toddler's eating will fall into place and you will be able to trust that what and how much she eats is just right for her. Cross that line, and nothing will be clear, because her eating will get all mixed up with struggles for control and bids for attention. It will all look like your toddler doesn't want to eat. She does, but given the choice between eating and struggling for control and keeping herself center stage, she will choose the latter. As I said before, children want to grow up, but they will also take the easy way out when it is offered.

THE PARENTS' VIEW OF TODDLER EATING

It's not easy staying on the parents' side of the line because toddlers do so much that can pull us in. They eat so little and vary so greatly in the amounts they eat. They accept foods one day and reject them the next. They don't eat a full meal but only 2 or 3 foods. They get distracted and forget all about eating. If your child happens to appear physically vulnerable in any of the ways discussed in chapter 6, it is even harder. When a child is small or has had a rough start, parents remain anxious and are likely to interfere with eating. Struggles around feeding that may have started at birth and perked along at a low and distressing level heighten when a child becomes a toddler. Not only can such struggles make you and your child miserable and feeding unpleasant, but they can make your child eat and grow poorly.

How, then, can you control your own anxiety so you can stay on your side of the feeding line? You need to understand your toddler's behavior, growth, and development and the typical pitfalls parents get into with feeding.

THE TODDLER'S PSYCHOLOGICAL
AND SOCIAL CHANGES

The theme of this chapter is "managing toddler eating behavior." Actually, that is rather a silly theme, because *nobody* manages a toddler. There is a story about a powerful Norse god who was boasting that he could get anyone to do his bidding. A woman responded that she knew of someone whose will and strength were greater than his. She was referring to her 2-year-old daughter. Foolish god, he didn't believe that the toddler's will was stronger than his, and it was left to the girl to prove the truth of the mother's words. And, of course, she did. That mother knew what you and I know: you can prevent a toddler from doing what you *don't* want her to do, but you can't force her to do what you *do* want her to do.

The toddler's task is to establish autonomy—to find out and demonstrate to herself and to you that she is a separate person from you—over and over and over again. She finds out that she is separate by trying to do everything she can and by saying *no* a lot, because whenever she resists what you want she proves to herself that she is separate from you. She also needs to make you stop doing everything for her, even when you can do it far better and faster. She is, after all, not a baby, and she needs the chance to learn. She has a tremendous need to be independent, to be successful, to explore, and to have limits. And she feels altogether ambivalent about it all. She needs to know that she is an individual, but she also needs to know that she can't dominate you. Unless you let her know clearly that the limits exist, she will become more and more provocative, until you finally move in and stop her. She is also impulsive: she has an exuberant and unrestrained curiosity. Dr. Spock called the child this age a "demon explorer." He and Arnold Gesell, another early child development specialist, described toddlers as demanding, assertive, mercurial, pre-cooperative, contrary, obstinate, exasperating, imperious, balky, negativistic, bossy, and fussy. Hardly encouraging. But notice they said *pre-cooperative.* That should give you hope.

Toddler development becomes even more complex when you consider the narcissistic resolution discussed in the previous section. Now we will throw a last concept into the hopper. The toddler is learning *somatopsychological differentiation.* Let's break it down: *somato* means bodily, *psychological* means emotional, and *differentiation* means being able to distinguish between them. Your toddler is learning to recognize her bodily sensations and feelings. She is beginning to consciously tell the difference between being hungry, for instance, and being angry or tired. Her learning to make those distinctions depends on your being able to understand what is ailing her and applying the appropriate solution, at least most of the time. Now before you have one of those parental guilt attacks, let me reassure you that young children are resilient and give us lots of margin for error. The way you learn to parent is by taking a course of action, seeing how it works, and then making any necessary adjustments. If your method repeatedly doesn't work, you think about it, make your best guess about what's wrong, and adjust. Good parents are not the ones who always know the answers and get everything right the first time. They are the ones who are self-possessed enough to realize it when what they are doing isn't working, and they are able to come up with a reasonable alternative.

Now, where was I? Oh yes, understanding your child's signals most of the time. At this age, your child will express pleasure, excitement, protest, rage, aggressiveness, dependency, and affection. She needs you to be able to tolerate those emotions, be matter-of-fact about them, and help sort them out from her sensations of hunger, appetite, and fullness. Ideally, you will be comfortable enough to accept your toddler's aggression and ambivalence and firm enough to set limits when she does something that is unsafe or destructive or interferes with someone else's rights or privileges. You help with the sorting by not feeding her whenever she gets upset and by not giving in to her aggression when she comes around panhandling for food. Children who are offered food whenever they feel upset don't learn to feel their feelings and may eat instead. They can also get turned off by food. It will be far easier for you to stay away from feeding for emotional reasons if you stick to structured meals and snack times. That way, when your child is angry or upset, you won't be as tempted to give a cookie to fix it. Of course, you *will* give a cookie or a cracker at times to entertain your toddler or to calm her down or to get through a grocery store. Remember, however, that this is self-defense feeding, to be reserved for the occasional time when you have really *had* it.

If you do it too often, you will be teaching her to eat instead of tolerate and manage her feelings.

You don't have to tiptoe around your toddler as if she were a little time bomb and try not to upset her. Nor do you have to get angry and punishing when you set limits. You do, as I just said, have to be prompt and unruffled about putting a stop to undesirable behavior. Keep in mind that she is experimenting, not deliberately being bad, and you are teaching her, not retaliating. For instance, if your toddler whines or cries about the food, tell her "no whining," then ignore her until she stops. She will stop in seconds; then promptly pay attention to her again. In those seconds, she will get a grip on herself. Don't continue to scold or explain why she shouldn't be doing what she is doing, because she can't understand it anyway. Your going over and over the rules will only be giving her negative attention, not enlightenment. Ignore her whining. If she steps up the intensity so much that she makes it unpleasant to have her at the table—for instance, if she starts throwing food or trying to tip her high chair—remove her from the table and give her a time out. Again, keep in mind that the intent is not to punish her but to teach her: to be at the table she has to get and keep a grip on herself and behave appropriately. To help you follow through, keep in mind that the family table is a pleasant place to be, and for her to be allowed to participate, she has to make her contribution. It is a privilege to be at the family table. It is not a chore or obligation.

Your role in feeding your child during this special time of exploration, independence, and developmental complexity comes down to one principle: the division of responsibility in feeding. You are responsible for *feeding*, your toddler is responsible for *eating*. Using that principle, you will be setting things up for your child so she can be successful, but at the same time you will not be giving in to unreasonable demands. In getting a meal on the table and eating with your child, you will be remaining present without taking over, and giving her freedom without abandoning her.

The Toddler's Physical and Nutritional Changes. Your child won't eat as much as she did before. She will grow more slowly, and her energy needs won't be as high. Between birth and age 1 year, a child can double and even triple her birth weight.

During her second, third, and fourth years, she gains only about 30 percent of her body weight a year, and her calorie requirement relative to her size drops. The toddler grows in height more quickly than she gains weight, and she doesn't gain as much body fat. She will become slimmer, but she may look fatter because her early efforts at walking give her a sway back and a stuck-out belly. It's not fat, it's just poor posture, and in another year she will look entirely different. Your toddler won't be as hungry, so she will eat less overall. Despite her erratic and sporadic hunger and appetite, she will get the calories she needs by averaging her eating out over several days. She will make up one day for not eating much the previous day—or even the previous week. We adults tend to do the same thing, although we also smooth things out by managing food intake with our heads as well as our bodies. Unlike you, your toddler doesn't tell herself, "I'd better eat now or I will be hungry later," and she pays no attention when you tell her that. She eats according to how hungry and how full she is at the moment, and that can vary a great deal. Have faith: your toddler still knows how much she needs to eat. However, to eat enough and to get a nutritionally adequate diet, she absolutely depends on you to offer nutritious food on a regular and reliable basis.

In my clinical career I have done a great many calculations of toddler food intake. I have been impressed at the bizarre and meager appearance of the meal and snack records: a tablespoon of this, a bite of that, an eighth of something else. However, when I have actually calculated the diets and averaged the nutrients out, I have found almost without exception that children were getting what they needed. They were, that is, as long as they were being offered regular and nutritious meals and snacks. Some children were not getting enough calories, and those children generally were not being allowed to eat enough fat. Since fat carries vitamin E, the vitamin E intake of those children was also low.

In a more systematic fashion, Jean Skinner, at the University of Tennessee, found the same thing. Toddlers ate enough overall, and they got the protein, vitamins, and minerals they needed. The few nutrients that were somewhat low were zinc, vitamin D, and vitamin E. By "a little low" I mean that children were eating less than 100 percent of the Recommended Dietary Allowance (RDA), a standard that has a large enough margin of error that small gaps are unlikely to be a cause for concern. We'll still talk about closing those nutritional gaps later, by being sure to offer your child good sources of zinc, vitamin D, and vitamin E. But the main nutrient that concerned me was *fat*—the percentage of fat calories decreased from more than 40 percent in the first 6 months to as little as 30 percent by age 10 to 24 months. Forty percent of calories from fat is a more desirable figure for toddlers as well as for infants. One-third of the toddlers studied were, inappropriately, given reduced-fat milks at 12 months, and more than half were given them at 24 months.[1] Keep in mind that during the toddler period the brain is still developing rapidly. Also, cholesterol and essential fatty acids are a required component of brain and nervous tissue.

The Toddler's Physical Capabilities. The toddler period is a thrilling and frustrating time of skill building. Your toddler will be learning to crawl, walk, and run, to climb, and to manipulate objects around her. She will be gaining ever more control over the fine muscles in her hands and arms, so she can use her fingers to feed herself, learn to use eating utensils, and drink from a cup. She will spill and drop a lot, won't be able to cut up her food, will have a hard time mouthing certain foods, and won't be able to chew very tough food. She will gag more than an older child, and her risk of choking is still high because she is so inexperienced at chewing and swallowing. She is also still experimenting with how full to fill her mouth. Sometimes she'll get too much food and it will spill out, or she'll gag on it. Be patient. She's not doing it to be impolite, she's just learning.

She needs to feel successful, and sympathetic food selection can help her feel more competent and proud of herself. Providing her with eating utensils that she can manage easily will also help toward that goal—as will ignoring her sloppiness and contrariness. Her skills and interest in feeding herself will vary. At times she will absolutely insist on doing everything herself, and she may even do a rather expert job of it; at other times she will drop things, or want to be fed. She knows how much to eat, but she does need regular meals and snacks in order to do a good job of eating the amount she needs. Given her newfound physical capabilities and her drive to explore and keep going, her excitement and fatigue can get the better of her. She needs regular meals. She needs those predictable feeding times to be *your* idea, and she needs help coming to the table rested and hungry but not famished.

She also needs help staying out of unnecessary struggles. Promptly and dispassionately setting mealtime limits will calm her down. Getting mad or trying to get her to eat will rev her up. Along with any period of rapid change comes emotional upset and frustration. Your toddler will be easily upset, and if eating becomes the stage for struggles, she can become so emotionally worked up and preoccupied with the struggle that it will be difficult or impossible for her to know that she is hungry or how hungry she really is. In the previous edition *of Child of Mine* I made the observation that the toddler would rather fight than eat. Now I can refine that statement: If a struggle emerges about eating, a toddler will get so involved in the struggle and so upset that it overwhelms her need to eat. This observation is just as true of struggles about potty training, what to wear, school work, and so on. Throughout your child's growing-up years, it is important to matter-of-factly set the limits and avoid the emotional fireworks and struggles. Learning to do this with feeding will help you in other areas as well.

FINDING A BALANCE

With food and feeding, your job is to strike a balance: to find the middle ground between rigidity and over-permissiveness. Finding this middle ground is important both for helping your child to develop positive eating attitudes and behaviors and for ensuring that she eats a nutritionally adequate diet. The diets of children of all ages suffer when parents go to the extremes of being controlling on the one hand or failing to provide support and guidance on the other. Children eat poorly when parents criticize, manage, or intrude on eating. Children eat poorly when parents disagree too much about how they should be fed. On the other hand, children also eat poorly if parents ignore food selection or leave too many decisions to children.[2] So how are you going to care nutritionally for this contrary, demanding, mercurial creature?

Give Opportunities to Learn. A planned and structured meal-time, with foods that you have chosen with the preferences of the whole family in mind, provides your toddler with the best—and perhaps the only—appropriate laboratory for learning. Consider these scenarios: You plan a family meal, offering a variety of food, considering what you and the rest of the family like, being considerate of your toddler's preferences and limitations but not catering to them. You put the food on the table, sit down to eat it yourself, and enjoy it thoroughly. Your toddler eats some bread, drinks a few swallows of milk, and squashes the carrots on her plate. How inclined will you be to try to get your toddler to eat? Let's try another scenario: you are having tuna noodle casserole—again—even though by this time both you and your spouse could absolutely barf at the thought of it because you have made it so often. But your child likes it, so you make it yet again. She won't touch it. She eats some bread, drinks a few swallows of milk, and squashes the carrots on her plate—all normal toddler mealtime behaviors. How inclined will you be to try to get her to eat? Let's try a third scenario: You say to your spouse, "she's not eating. What shall we do?" You get up and warm up some of last night's macaroni and cheese. She won't touch it. How likely are you to put pressure on her to eat?

In my experience, the more trouble parents take to make special food for a toddler, the more inclined the toddler is to reject the food. When you ignore your own food needs and defer to your toddler, you are going to put pressure on her to eat whether you realize it or not. In fact, pressure is *inherent* in making special food for a toddler or getting up to make a substitute. Your toddler will sense that, and she will eat poorly. Studies have shown that when children are exposed to even "nice" pressure, like rewards, for their eating, they eat less well, not better. In observations and experiments at a University of Illinois preschool, psychologist Leanne Birch found that children who were rewarded with a trip to the playground for trying a new juice were less likely to sample that juice the next time they were offered it than children who had simply been allowed to experiment with it on their own. What helped with food acceptance? The presence of a trusted adult. When you sit down to eat with your child, she will eat as well as she possibly can. For more about the Illinois and Tennessee studies, and others as well, see appendix I, "Children and Food Acceptance: The Research."

Children want to learn, and they want to grow up. They push themselves along to learn to crawl, walk, talk, and ride a Big Wheel. Why wouldn't they want to learn when it comes to food? Because we won't *let* them, that's why. Somehow we have gotten the idea that children won't eat unless they are somehow pushed or prodded into moving along. A child's eating becomes our investment, and then it loses its appeal for the child.

A lot of people get too pushy with their feeding. In other studies of Tennessee mothers, Jean Skinner showed that 70 percent of mothers of 16-month-olds offered their toddlers alternatives when they didn't eat "enough."[3] You are likely to, also. Being a realist, I know that while I will do everything in my power to dissuade you from short-order cooking or offering special foods to your toddler, chances are all too good that you will. How will you know that it isn't working? Because you will get tired of generating 2 to 3 meals, you will be irritated when your child won't eat, and you will begin to notice that you are putting more effort into your child's eating than she is. Your own feelings are good guides to your relationship with your toddler, and getting tired of doing something is very good corrective feedback! You will definitely know that you have crossed the line of the division of responsibility when the routine gets worse—when you make more and more special foods and your toddler eats less and less. At that point, it's harder to back out because parents start to feel, "if I am doing all this and she still isn't eating, then how will she eat when I don't do all this?" In a word: better.

When you get mad at your toddler for not eating, that tells you something is happening that is not in your best interest. No toddler ever benefited from being allowed to interfere with the rights of others. Use your anger to guide you in being healthier on your own behalf—in the process you will do more for your toddler as well. Don't scold her or take your anger out on her. She is, after all, only doing what you have taught her to do. Don't try to reason with her. She can't reason, it won't help her eating, and your efforts to persuade her will only teach her to use the issue as a bid for attention. Here is a word of encouragement: children change rapidly, and if you change what you do, and keep it changed, your child will change right along with you. Some of the Tennessee mothers learned. By age 20 months, the percentage of parents who offered alternatives to toddlers who didn't eat dropped to 60 percent, and by 2 years it dropped to 45 percent.[3] That's better, but the percentage is still too high. That kind of catering means that children don't really become competent with respect to their eating. Children learn only if they get opportunities to learn. Making special food takes away their opportunities to learn.

Avoid Catering. Parents of finicky preschoolers almost always tell me the same story. "She ate well when she was just starting out on solid foods, but then when she was a toddler she would only eat certain foods. Now she won't even eat what she did when she was a toddler." Typically, parents go on to name a short list of high-sugar, high-fat, easy-to-like foods such as peanut butter and jelly sandwiches, hot dogs, French fries, chicken nuggets, juice, ice cream, and maybe milk. In that phrase describing the toddler, "she would only eat certain foods," the parent is telling me that she was catered to, and in the catering lies the answer.

Children from an upper-middle-class Canadian suburb surveyed by researchers Marcia Pelchat and Patricia Pliner help us to understand how children get to the point that they eat so poorly. Children who were reluctant to try new food had mothers who offered only foods that children readily accepted, or they prepared substitutes when children asked for them. In other words, they did short-order cooking for their children. Mothers complained about their children's poor food acceptance, unwillingness to eat new food, preference for "junk" food, and poor behavior at the table. Many said their child avoided whole classes of foods, like vegetables. Mothers complained that children dawdled or were messy, that they didn't eat enough, they were not interested in food and eating, that they liked junk foods and disliked new foods. Mothers who had a lot of complaints about their children's eating also were more likely to put pressure on children to eat: prodding, rewarding, and punishing. Clearly, parents were using unproductive approaches to feeding, and children were responding predictably.[4]

What Do Children Contribute? Many times, children's characteristics contribute to the evolution of these feeding distortions. What kind of pull do children exert that we find ourselves crossing the lines of division of responsibility, so busily attending to their business of what and how much that we forget to do our own job of holding the line on menu planning? Yes, I am talking about your sweet child, and I am saying that she is contributing to the problem! However, I hasten to add that she is not a bad or awful child; she is simply being a child, and for that we have to make allowances. Catering, no; allowances, yes. Well, for one thing, she is your sweet child. She is small and appealing, and having so recently been an even smaller infant, you are in the habit of making her way smooth. While I can understand the impulse, please allow me to remind you that making her way smooth and her life free of frustration is no longer appropriate. Your job now is to help her grow up to be able to cope with reasonable challenges so she can be comfortable in the world. A vital part of that comfort is being able to eat the food there.

What other pull do children exert to encourage us to cross the line and try to control what and how much they eat? They are so hesitant about trying new food that the overly attentive parent becomes weary and tries to push the process along. They eat so little that it seems it can hardly be enough. They change overnight. This one pulls a lot of parents into feeding struggles: An infant who has been eating with great enthusiasm suddenly turns into a toddler who eats very little. Toddlers pull us into their territory because they are exquisitely sensitive to adult agendas and either fight back or learn to struggle with parents as a way of getting attention. Children who have the "at risk" or "at nutritional risk" characteristics discussed in chapter 6 are especially likely to pull us across the line. The cautious child is likely to be cautious with regard to managing new food and new eating situations as well. The negative or easily upset child is likely to be negative and easily upset in the eating situation as well.

Here's the hard part: The approach for the vulnerable child is the same as for the sturdy, adventurous child. Hang in there with the structure and limits, be friendly and supportive, and give your child the opportunity to learn to manage her own caution, aggression, or upset. Resist the impulse to entice, reward, play games, placate, and make special food. Expecting your child to keep a grip on herself and cope with appropriate food and pleasant mealtimes is not putting intolerable or unrealistic expectations on her, and your doing all the coping won't teach her anything. However, it isn't easy. Dietitian Jane Fowler, who for years has taught parent education classes in Walnut

Creek, California, talks a good bit with parents about understanding their child's temperament as it relates to their eating. She observes, for instance, that cautious, slow-to-warm-up children react so negatively to new food experiences that parents often fall into the trap of not challenging them. "It isn't much fun feeding him," said one mother, who labeled her son's signals as so off-putting that she gave up offering him new food.

Some parents cross the line because they feel or have been told that their child is too fat. Such concerns are exaggerated. The child who is fat at this age is no more likely to grow up fat than the child who is thin. As children get older they tend to get slimmer. Becoming overly concerned at this age that a child will grow up fat is misguided and destructive. It leads parents to take evasive action—to try to restrict the amount the child eats. Such attempts backfire. The Berkeley studies of childhood obesity that I mentioned in chapter 2 showed that the more concerned parents were about keeping their child from being fat, the more likely they were to raise a fat child.[5] Keep in mind that trying to get your child to eat less can interfere with her prerogative with eating just as much as trying to get her to eat more. Given today's preoccupation with fatness and the public health alarm about childhood obesity, many parents hesitate to gratify a child's robust appetite for fear she will get too fat. The results can be tragic. The child becomes preoccupied with food, prone to overeat when she gets the chance, and fatter rather than thinner. If you are concerned about your child's weight, the best thing you can do is feed her in the way I describe in this book. When she gets the support and limits she needs with food and feeding, she will do her very best job of eating the amount that she needs, and she'll grow up to get the body that is right for her.

The Toddler with Allergies. You will have to cater to a certain extent if you have child who has allergies or another health condition like diabetes or an inborn error of metabolism. The trick is catering without it being obvious and without distorting feeding dynamics. At the end of chapter 9 you will find a discussion of children with particular health conditions (pages 414-420). This section will help you to deal with feeding issues that go along with all of those conditions. In my conversations with her, Karen Webber, a British Columbia pediatric dietitian who specializes in helping families with children's food allergies, points out that avoiding distorted feeding dynamics is of particular concern with a child who has allergies. To prevent the child from eating the offending food parents often *have* to cater and make special dishes. Not only that, but because they have seen their child become ill and unhappy with her food allergies, at times they become overprotective and fall into the traps of limiting the menu too much, catering too obviously, and manipulating the child in order to get her to eat. To help parents avoid feeding struggles with children, Webber emphasizes keeping the division of responsibility in place and then putting the emphasis on what the toddler *can* have rather than what she *can't*. Children intuitively learn to avoid foods that make them ill, and it is difficult to tell the difference between the toddler's natural skepticism about new food and the allergic toddler's food avoidance. Webber recommends keeping the toddler in control of food refusal by continuing to make the food available but not pushing it on the child.

Webber has helped many parents of allergic children with their food selection and feeding relationship issues. Here are some of her suggestions:

• Maintain the division of responsibility in feeding.
• Offer a variety of food.
• Adapt the toddler's food to make it look as much as possible like family fare.
• Be matter-of-fact about food limits.
• Respect your child's food preferences. He may like wheat-free pasta even if you don't.

Webber points out that parental attitude is all important, and that is true. In my experience, children who do best in the long run with chronic health conditions are those who are able to take age-appropriate responsibility for themselves and for the condition. Children learn these attitudes and behaviors from parents. I certainly acknowledge that dealing with such health conditions is difficult and represents a loss for the child as well as for the parents. However, with any physical, cognitive, or behavioral attribute, your child will do best if you can be accommodating and matter-of-fact about it. You need to accept her condition, help her out as much as you can, and teach her as she grows up to be increasingly responsible for taking care of herself. If, on the other hand, you feel sorry for her or responsible for the way she is, she won't do as well. You are likely to try to make it up to her by catering with food or not expecting reasonable mealtime behavior. Keep in mind that such behaviors are likely to arise out of your own needs rather than your child's. As far as she is concerned, she is like any other child, and she will act like one. If you give her an opening, she will simply manipulate you and get you to do all sorts of objectionable things in order to get her to eat. Ah, children! They know what the score is, and they help us to know it too!

Be *Appropriately* Unconcerned. A fair percentage of those Tennessee mothers we discussed earlier said they "didn't worry" about food rejection—25 percent of mothers of 16-month-olds, 30 percent of mothers of 20-month-olds, and 40 percent of mothers of 2-year-olds.[3] Not worrying can be positive or negative for you and your child. It can be positive if you provide your toddler with regular opportunities to learn—maintain the structure of meals and snacks, offer appropriately modified food, and enjoy mealtimes with your toddler. Then, when you get to the table, "not worrying" means having the attitude "I can't do anything about what she eats so I may as well not worry about it." When the toddler goes through the long warm-up of 20 meals to learn to eat a vegetable, you won't worry if you understand that this is all part of the learning process, that you need not hold your breath while it goes on, and that your best approach is to help your toddler get served and then pay attention to your own meal. You will be showing a helpful amount of unconcern when you treat her as a mealtime companion, not as the main reason for the meal.

However, not worrying is negative if it means not taking responsibility for the tasks of planning, cooking, and orchestrating pleasant meals. If a parent has given up on offering regular meals and snacks and just lets the toddler have a bottle or panhandle her way through the day, then not worrying amounts to neglect.

Don't Force or Bribe. Fortunately, only 5 percent of surveyed Tennessee mothers of 16-month-olds tried force or bribery to get their child to eat.[3] Since you can't bribe a 16-month-old, we can only assume that those mothers were forcing, a process that is appalling for both parents and children. Parents force when they are afraid their child won't survive unless they do. They also force when they get involved in a struggle for control and can't back out of it. If you are so desperate about your child's eating or so furiously invested in getting her to do your bidding that you feel you must use force, *get help*. Such struggles have physical as well as emotional consequences. Children grow poorly when they struggle with parents about their eating. When parents and children get into pitched battles about eating, they don't like each other very much, and neither gets their needs met. Parents don't feel like good parents, and children don't feel like good children.

According to the Tennessee study, once children were old enough to be bribed, parents bribed them by offering special foods, desserts, or special playtimes. The percentage of parents of 20- to 24-month-olds whose mothers said they forced or bribed held at about around 12 percent. Bribery doesn't work either. It is just a sneaky and devious method of putting pressure on a child's eating. Children sense that pressure, and they eat less well, not better, when they are bribed.

Look again at the destination we set for ourselves on the first page of this chapter, our behavioral goals for the toddler. Having just had this discussion about appropriate parenting with respect to feeding, I think you can begin to see that raising a child who is positive and effective with eating is no longer the impossible dream. Whether your child becomes a competent eater depends on the way you manage feeding. The support and limits you give at mealtime will allow your toddler to come to the table willingly, behave herself, try some foods, reject others, eat still others, and leave the table happily to do it again at snack time or at another meal. Given this frequent and matter-of-fact exposure to a variety of food, she will gradually learn to enjoy many different foods. She will not grow up to be a picky eater. Avoiding pickiness is vital not only for your child's emotional health but for her nutritional health as well.

Before we focus on what to put on the table, let's examine what it takes to keep a toddler comfortable at the table—and how to be comfortable yourself when you have a toddler at the table.

MEALTIME MECHANICS

Managing mealtime mechanics has everything to do with making your toddler a part of the family, helping her to learn and be successful, and giving her structure and limits.

Schedule Meals and Snacks. To do a good job with her eating, and to continue to learn to like a variety of nutritious food, your child needs meals, and she needs snacks between times so that the gaps between feeding times are a length she can manage. Snacks will help you to be firm about expecting your child to eat what is on the table. It will be far easier for you to let her down having eaten little or nothing if you know a snack is coming in 2 or 3 hours. Have your meals and snacks at whatever time works in your household. Don't be too concerned if your family eats at an unusual time—say has the evening meal quite late. The child this age is beginning to fit into the family's routine instead of having the routine fit around her. You can help your child be hungry but not famished for a late dinner by making deliberate use of snacks. You will learn more about this in the section called "Have Planned Snacks" later in this chapter. Having your child at the dinner table is important because one of the most powerful influences on your child's food acceptance is eating with you and seeing you enjoy a wide variety of nutritious food. However, even if your dinner is at the regular time, don't expect her to eat much. She has been eating all day, she is tired and winding down toward bedtime, and dinner meals tend to emphasize adult food that is more challenging for children. As she gets older, she will do better with her dinners. For now, include her and be considerate of her, but don't cater, and do let her eat as much or as little as she can manage.

Before the meal, give some thought to having your child be calm, rested, and ready to eat. She plays hard and has a lot on her mind. The task is getting her mind on food and eating. Give her a 5-minute warning to get ready to come to the meal. Teach her to settle herself down before she eats, giving her time to wash her hands before the meal and even play in the water a bit. If you can find the time, sit down with her to read a book just before the meal. At the table, help interrupt the hurry-up and focus everybody's attention on food by sharing a quiet moment of relaxation, saying grace or singing a little song.

Start Working on Family-Style Meals. Parents are generally startled when I suggest they allow their 2-year-old to serve herself. For some reason this seems to be a large and alarming step. However, on the principle that your child relishes achievement and on the other principle that children always eat better when they feel they have control of the process, go for it. Put the food on the table in serving bowls and let your child help herself as much as she can. Let her pass the dish on after she helps herself. Of course, relatively small serving bowls and spoons work best. I also need not stress that this process will be full of mishaps and adventures, so you may as well hang on to your curiosity and your sense of humor. She may take more than she can eat at first, but that's part of the learning. Your child will love it. As with everything else, she will have a lot to learn. If you help her get served, ask if she wants the food, and then ask how much she wants. If you must serve plates in the kitchen, be sure to reassure your child that she doesn't have to eat what you serve if she doesn't want to and that there is more of everything if she wants more.

Make Seating Arrangements Comfortable. Make any adjustments that help keep everyone comfortable. Your child needs a chair that keeps her high enough to easily reach the table, and she needs help staying put during the meal. A high chair is best—booster chairs tend to wiggle around and are both less safe and less effective at helping settle a child down to eat. Take the tray off the high chair so she can sit up to the table with the rest of the family. When she doesn't need the arms on the high chair anymore, you might consider getting her an adjustable-height junior chair. These chairs have adjustable seat and footrest heights and can grow with your child to keep her comfortable at the table until she is big enough for a regular chair. Your child needs to sit up high enough so she can see what she is eating, use her fingers and utensils well, and reach her glass. She'll do best if her elbows are at table height. Support her feet—it's not comfortable for anyone to have feet dangle.

Give her a child-sized plate and utensils. A plate with a low, vertical edge works well because it gives her a bang-board for pushing the food onto her fork or spoon. A smaller plate will help you regulate your portioning. Junior-sized silverware is great for a child this age, or a broad salad fork and a spoon work well. Give her a cup with handles or a glass with a broad base that sits firmly on the table, and choose one that is small enough so that she can get her little hands around it. You can use a covered junior cup if you want to, but I prefer to see a child this age use an open cup. It is more developmentally appropriate. If you are concerned about your floor, protect it some way, as there will be inevitable spills and dropping food.

Occasionally children ask to be allowed to sit at their own small eating table and chairs. That is fine once in a while and also comfortable for them, as long as they don't abuse the privilege by getting up and running around during the meal. However, doing the little-table routine too often takes away the specialness of it and deprives your child of the opportunity to eat at the table with you.

Be Reasonable about Table Manners. Give your child silverware, but don't insist that she use it. Letting her look, feel, mash, and smell her food helps her get comfortable with it. The Arabs have an expression your toddler understands: "you taste with your fingers." You'll be able to tell if she is truly exploring a new food or just playing or messing around to get you to react because you will feel reactive. Once she stops eating and starts messing around, it is time to let her get down from the table.

Don't worry too much about the mechanics of eating. Table manners will come, and sooner or later your child will begin to imitate your behavior at the table. Do you consider that a promise—or a threat? It will interrupt your child's eating if you get all worked up about table manners and keep reminding her to eat neatly, sit properly, and use the napkin. Nagged children become either rebellious or so preoccupied with the mechanics that they lose interest in food. As your child matures her dexterity will develop, and the spills, dropped food and utensils, and general mess will decrease. Her table manners will improve as she imitates you, but developing wholesome attitudes about eating is more important at this stage than mastering the niceties of table manners. In the meantime, remember that no table is truly set without a roll of paper towels.

Avoid the No-Thank-You Bite. In her comments about this

manuscript, Child Care Food Program (CCFP) consultant
Christine Berman reminded me to include information about
the so-called no-thank-you bite and to stress how vital it is to
use family-style meal service. Berman is one of the authors of
Meals without Squeals: Child Care Feeding Guide and Cookbook (Bull
Publishing, 1997), so you know she has thought and worked a
good deal with these topics. In case you are among the uniniti-
ated, the rule of the no-thank-you bite is that every child has to
take a mouthful of every food on the table. I don't like that rule,
and I don't recommend it. It is a control tactic that interferes
with children's food acceptance. Why? Because it overlooks the
fundamental point that children *want to grow up* with respect to
their eating. While children learn to like new foods only if they
taste them, children do get around to tasting them on their own.
They don't have to be pushed. Children have *within them* the
driving need to experiment and master, and that need pushes
them along to experiment with and master new food. Even the
slowest and most cautious child takes joy, satisfaction, and
pride from mastery. If we make it our business to get a child to
try a food—even just one bite—she gets the message that we
don't trust her to learn and grow, and the lack of trust takes the
joy of accomplishment away from her. If a food is presented
over and over in a neutral fashion, sooner or later a child will
taste it, and in most cases after she tastes it lots of times, she
will like it. If you try to speed up the process, you will in fact
slow it down. In a child's mind, the response is something like
this: "If they have to make me eat that, then it must not be so
good."

FEEDING IN CHILD CARE

Chris Berman also suggested I talk about the CCFP rules, and
she has a good point. For your general information, the Child
Care Food Program is a wonderful federally funded program
that offers financial assistance to help child care and Head Start
programs provide nutritious food for children. Along with the
financial support, of course, come guidelines, inspection, and
training. I have benefited from the latter requirement because I
have had a lot of fun making presentations to child care and
Head Start groups. They are good observers of children and

have much to offer. I have, however, grown to dread the question about the no-thank-you bite. Why? Because right after I answer *that* question, someone *always* asks, "well, what do we do about the food portion requirement? Are we supposed to put that on the child's plate or make her eat it?" Until I finally got smart and put a stop to it, that question would generally signal the end of all productive learning in the presentation. Everyone and her inspecting bureaucrat had a different answer, and everyone was eager to hotly debate the issue. My current solution is to say firmly, "It is not a matter of opinion about what *should* be done. It is a matter of what is best for children. Based on what I know about children and about feeding, let me give you my recommendation. You are obligated to provide a certain amount of food for each child. The food portions for all the children must be put together in the *bowls*. Then the bowls must be passed around and children allowed to take as much or as little as they want." Children will eat well if you use family-style meal service. Sit down and eat with them; have a pleasant conversation and a good time together. No child must be forced to take—or eat—anything that she doesn't want, not even one little, tiny almost invisible *bite*.

If you are a child care provider, this message is for you. Rather than worrying about things like required bites, think about how important you are to the children in your care. Children will eat best when you concentrate on making meal-times pleasant, positive, and supportive. Often in the process of evaluating a child who eats poorly, I visit the child care center to observe the child at feeding time. I have found that when feeding is handled well in the child care setting, children with eating problems eat better at school than they do at home. However, when feeding in the child care setting is handled poorly, children have the same problems at school as they do at home. In the case I am thinking about, I watched a room of about twenty 3-year-olds having their lunch. The children were seated at three low round tables with comfortable chairs that were just their size, and they began eating from pre-proportioned plates of appealing looking food. I would have preferred family-style service, but they did start eating. However, rather than sitting down to eat with the children, the three teachers busied themselves putting out the cots for naps. When they finished their job, they sat down to eat their lunches in the corner of the room away from the children. It was as if those teachers were magnets and the children were iron filings! Every single child in the room turned to face the teachers. Children turned around to sit sideways or backward in their chairs. Every single child forgot about eating. Those children needed the teachers at the tables with them, and until or unless the teachers joined them, the children were not going to continue to eat.

Many child care centers do a good job with family-style meals. They maintain a division of responsibility in feeding, and mealtimes are pleasant social times during which children and adults enjoy being together. In such settings, I have seen poorly eating children eat more, finicky children start to experiment with food, and food-preoccupied and seemingly voracious children revert to eating normal amounts. You do not have to push children or control them to get them to behave better with eating. When children are put in a positive environment, they push themselves along to do well. Serve family-style meals. Teach children to pass the food, but don't make them take any. If they take some, don't make them even taste it. If they taste it, don't make them swallow it. If they swallow it, don't make them eat any more. And don't make them eat everything they have taken. That is so scary for children that they will go hungry rather than experiment. Keep in mind that each time a child sees a food on the table, passes it, or sees someone else eating it, she is learning and getting to the point that she will be able to eat that food. To help you educate parents about your feeding program, give them a copy of the child care feeding policy given in Figure 8.1. You can make copies and use it as long as you leave the copyright statement as it is and don't change anything about it. You can also find a copy of it on my Web site, and you can download it from there (**www.ellynsatter.com**).

If you are a child care worker, know that I respect and admire you, and I have confidence that you will act in the best interests of your small charges. If you feel you are being forced to feed in ways that are uncomfortable for you, think about what is putting pressure on *you* and try to get rid of that pressure. If you have an inspector who insists that you actually *serve* your children the required portions, explain that this approach is counterproductive and that it spoils your feeding relationship with the children. Since the overall goal of the Child Care Food Program is to support children's nutritional welfare, point out

FIGURE 8.1 CHILD CARE FEEDING POLICY

Our child care facility adheres to Ellyn Satter's **division of responsibility in feeding:**

Adults	**Children**
are responsible for	**are responsible for**
what, when, and *where*	*how much* and *whether*
children are fed.	**they eat.**

We provide nutritious, regularly scheduled meals and snacks.

We trust children to manage their eating with respect to both amounts and types of food.

Meals and snacks are an important part of our program day.
- We take time to help children relax and prepare to eat.
- We sit down to eat with children and have good times.
- We help children learn to behave well at meals and snack times.

Children will eat what they need and will learn to eat new foods.
- We let children pick and choose from the food we make available.
- We let children eat as little or as much of the food as they want.

We follow federal and state guidelines to plan meals and snacks.
- We keep in mind the special food needs of small children.
- We offer familiar and popular foods along with unfamiliar foods.
- We let children eat what they like and also try out new foods.

Some days children eat a lot; other days, not so much. But they know how much they need.
- We do not limit the amounts children eat.
- We do not force children to eat certain foods or certain amounts of food.

We follow guidelines on wellness to cook food that is moderate, not low, in fat.
- We use meat, poultry, and fish as well as cooked dried beans.
- We use lean red meats but do not restrict red meat.
- We serve whole or 2% milk.
- We let children help themselves to salad dressings, butter, and margarine.

For more information about the division of responsibility in feeding, see Ellyn Satter's books, *How to Get Your Kid to Eat . . . But Not Too Much, Child of Mine: Feeding with Love and Good Sense,* and *Secrets of Feeding a Healthy Family,* available at your local bookstore or through Ellyn Satter Associates (800-808-7976 or **www.ellynsatter.com**).

that children eat best when the feeding relationship is positive. Then offer the inspector a copy of appendix I, "Children and Food Acceptance: The Research," which will further explain the issues and what's at stake for the children.

PLANNING FAMILY MEALS

Now, at last, we come to the food. It is not by accident that I take up this topic after we have discussed toddler development and feeding dynamics. To do a good job with eating, your toddler needs to have you understand where she is coming from and what she needs. To do a good job with *cooking* and to avoid becoming discouraged about your toddler's skeptical, opinionated, and erratic eating, you need to stay out of the pitfalls of feeding. You must not cater, you must not try to get your child to eat, and you must be realistic about mealtime behavior. You can only offer the food. You must not pin your hopes on getting it into your child.

If you fall into the trap of catering to your child, you are not alone. I am frequently interviewed for magazine and newspaper articles. Often the interviewer approaches me with the topic of getting children to eat a variety of foods and almost without exception begins by assuming that I will give a list of foods that children will eat. I spend the first 5 minutes of the interview going over the ground rules for feeding children. "Adults don't get children to eat," I say firmly and, after hundreds of interviews, no doubt somewhat astringently. "They get *themselves* to eat. Adults put the food on the table and children learn to eat it. Adults are not to cast about looking for something that children will eat. They are to offer a variety of foods and let children pick and choose from what is available."

What Foods to Offer at Family Meals. Adults are the ones who know the most about the food that is in the world. Children grow up to eat what their parents eat. Letting what the child will readily accept dictate the family menu is like letting the child drive the family car. If parents are gourmet cooks, the child will learn to be a gourmet eater. If parents are meat and potato people, the child will be too. If parents like spicy food, children will learn to like spicy food. I was so impressed by a 2-

year-old I watched in a market in Cancun, Mexico, running his finger between the cheese shavings on a taco, dipping into the chili sauce and licking it off. Gourmet or ethnic food is no more challenging to a toddler than any other. After all, what we consider *ethnic* is nothing more or less than someone else's everyday fare, and their children learn to eat it.

Now that your child is eating from the family table, the emphasis of meal planning shifts from planning for your child separate from the family to planning for the family as a whole and *including* your child. While you will still need to make some adaptations and selections to compensate for your child's inexperience with eating, the fundamental shift is the same: we are now talking about the family table. For your child's eating to turn out well, you must have a family table. Put your effort into what you *offer*, not into what your child *eats*. You get your parenting points when it goes on the table. Once you get the meal on the table, it is up to her to decide what and how much she will eat.

Unless you have unlimited money, having meals means that you have to cook, and *that* means a lot of time in the kitchen. Planning, shopping, and cooking all come with the territory of raising children to be competent eaters. Spending time at this task cannot be avoided. You can, however, improve your food management skills to the point of being such a thinking cook that you keep food management time to a minimum. I have written on that topic in detail in *Secrets of Feeding a Healthy Family*, and I have borrowed from that book for writing this section. I do recommend that you read it if you feel you need help with your cooking and with your own eating.

Making Use of Food Guides. In 1992 the *Basic Four Food Plan* that many of us grew up with and learned in school was replaced by the *Food Guide Pyramid*, pictured in appendix O, "Food Guides and Portion Sizes." Since the new guidelines grew out of a concern about *excess* as well as *deficiency*, the pyramid for adults dictates maximums as well as minimums to eat from each of the food groups. There is also a food guide pyramid for children that defines the nutritional minimums. The pyramid can be a helpful guide for getting food on the table. However, don't use it as a guide for how much to get into your child or for limiting how much your child eats—or even for how much to eat yourself. Children eat what they eat, and you don't have any control over that.

In feeding children—or adults for that matter—I find food guidelines to be more helpful and goals more achievable if I use them to define nutritional *minimums,* the nutritional floor, if you will. The nutritional minimum is the amount of food needed from each of the food groups to have a nutritionally adequate diet. Here are the minimum amounts you and your child need to eat on a daily basis to get a diet that is adequate in protein, vitamins, and minerals.

Bread, cereal, rice, and pasta group: 6 servings
Fruit group: 2 servings
Vegetable group: 3 servings
    Fruit and vegetable groups put together: 5 servings
Meat, poultry, fish, dry beans, eggs, and nuts group: 2 servings
Milk, yogurt, and cheese group: 2 servings

This is the same overall eating plan discussed at the end of chapter 7. These same guidelines are appropriate for the toddler. This is what your child will eat averaged over 2 to 3 weeks. On any one day, her food intake will have gaps—big gaps—but she will average out over time to get what she needs, provided that you are faithful about orchestrating nutritious and varied meals and snacks and keeping mealtimes pleasant.

WHAT THE TODDLER NEEDS

Often parents can relax once they know how little food children really need to eat. It is most important to be aware of child-sized portions. Too often we judge what a child "should" be eating by the quantities we ourselves eat. It's easy to put too much on the plate and make the child feel overwhelmed by the amounts, sometimes to the point that she won't even try to eat. Figure 8.2 shows portion sizes for children during the early years. Even at age 8 years, a child's nutritionally adequate portion size is smaller than yours.

Two impressions emerge as you study Figure 8.2. One, your child's little bites and tastes have a pretty good chance of adding up to a nutritionally adequate diet. Two, your child is

FIGURE 8.2 PORTION SIZES FOR CHILDREN

	Ages 1–3 years	Ages 3-5 years	Ages 6-8 years	Ages 8+ years
Meat, poultry, fish	1–2 Tbsp	1 oz	1–2 oz	2 oz
Eggs	$^1/_4$	$^1/_2$	$^3/_4$	1 egg
Cooked dried beans	1–2 Tbsp	3–5 Tbsp	5–8 Tbsp	$^1/_2$ cup
Pasta, rice, potatoes	1–2 Tbsp	3–5 Tbsp	5–8 Tbsp	$^1/_2$ cup
Bread	$^1/_4$ slice	$^1/_2$ slice	1 slice	1 slice
Vegetables	1–2 Tbsp	3–5 Tbsp	5–8 Tbsp	$^1/_2$ cup
Fruit	1–2 Tbsp or $^1/_4$ piece	3–5 Tbsp or $^1/_3$ piece	5–8 Tbsp or $^1/_2$ piece	$^1/_2$ cup or 1 piece
Milk	$^1/_4$–$^1/_3$ cup	$^1/_3$–$^1/_2$ cup	$^1/_2$–$^2/_3$ cup	1 cup
Fats and oils	To appetite	To appetite	To appetite	To appetite
Sugars and sweets	See text	See text	See text	See text

Note: Children may eat more or less, but this is how much you can serve them to start with.

going to eat more than the minimums, especially of some foods. Children generally find starchy foods like pasta, rice, potatoes, and bread easy to like. They often find meat group foods and vegetables more challenging to learn to like. Notice that I am choosing my words carefully. Your child will find some foods more *challenging* to like. She will not find them *impossible* to like. Cookies are not challenging. She will learn to like a new cookie the first time she eats it. Vegetables are challenging. With a new vegetable, it could take 15 or 20 exposures in as many meals before your child decides that she likes it. If you force her to eat it, she will never learn to like it.

The Mother Principle. However, you are not going to plan your family food by what your toddler is supposed to eat in three weeks—or even in a day. You will plan your family meals one meal at a time. In *Secrets of Feeding a Healthy Family*

I emphasized the rituals of good meal planning that, if you were lucky, you learned at your mother's table—what I call the *Mother Principle*. A meal needs to have some protein. It also needs a starch (different cultures have different starches, like grits or potatoes or plantain or rice), a vegetable (or fruit, or both), bread (or tortillas or biscuits), a good source of calcium, like milk, and some fat. At breakfast, milk may do double duty as a source of both protein and calcium, and the fruit/vegetable may be orange juice.

An important part of the *Mother Principle* is enjoyment. Food has to taste good or nobody will want to eat it. Choose foods you like, take your time learning to like new foods, and cook using enough salt and fat to make food pleasant. Your toddler will do better with eating, and you will be more likely to go to the trouble to make meals if you have a good time eating the food you prepare. Put the emphasis on enjoyment, not avoidance. In my view, the best way to ward off disease is to be healthy in the first place. If you are going to cook and keep on cooking, providing your family with nutritious meals day in and day out, food has to be enjoyable and rewarding to plan, cook, serve, and eat.

Don't Make Boring Food. Lest I am not making myself clear, let me say this another way. Do not make boring, nutritionally superior food. Nobody at the table will enjoy it, and the adults will sneak off later to have something better. But children can't sneak off, so the mealtime food has to be pleasant and satisfying to eat. Am I contradicting my earlier statement that you should not cater to your child? I don't think so, but let me tell you the story of 4-year-old Annie. Being a bit older, Annie had found a way to sneak off. Annie would eat only at the neighbor's house. Annie's parents were dedicated to maintaining a low-fat diet. They were confident that their food selection and menu planning were above reproach. They served only broiled poultry and fish, vegetables without added fat, bread with a tiny dab of diet margarine, and nonfat milk. But they were exhausted from fighting with their daughter about food. Why, they asked me, was Annie interested in eating only at a neighbor's house, where they weren't nearly as careful about nutrition? Why didn't Annie appreciate what they were doing for her?

I told them, "You have done what you thought was best for Annie. Unfortunately, it has taken all the fun out of eating for

her. Children won't eat what they are supposed to—they eat
what tastes good. I would guess the neighbors use more fat
than you do, and that makes their food taste better to Annie
than what you make at home. Extremely low-fat food is not
tasty food. Part of the knack wonderful cooks have for making
good food come alive is using some fat. Fat makes food taste
good. Fat also makes food seem more moist. For children, dry
food gets stuck in their mouths."

I encouraged Annie's parents to lighten up on their restrictions. It won't surprise you that I also emphasized the division
of responsibility in feeding and warned them to stop pressuring
Annie to eat. They were loathe to give up their restrictive eating. They weren't the type to sneak off for French fries or a hot
dog. They were proud of their self-discipline, and truth be told,
for them food restriction and avoidance was trendy. But they
loved Annie a lot and wanted her back at dinner time, so they
lightened up. It worked. Annie took more of an interest in what
they had on the table and stopped reminding them how much
better the food was next door. Sometimes Annie ate a little,
sometimes a lot.

Your child will grow up to feel about eating the way you
do. If that gives you a little thrill of dismay and dread, you have
work to do. If you feel conflicted and anxious about eating, it is
not surprising, and you are not alone. Surveys indicate that we
feel that eating nutritious food takes all the pleasure out of eating. Eating "properly" comes loaded with overtones of fear,
control, and dreariness. I am not going to load you down with
the rules. Instead, I will encourage you to celebrate eating. To be
consistent and effective in feeding a family, you must build the
whole structure on enjoyment. Today, far too much is made of
the difficulties of eating: avoiding disease, not getting fat, not
eating fat. The best way to support your child's nutritional vitality and normal growth and to maintain a stable body weight
yourself is to have regular, predictable, and satisfying eating
times. Get a pleasing meal on the table, pay attention while you
eat it, trust your child to take care of her own eating; then forget
about eating until it is time to eat again. For your child's eating
to fall into place, you have to recover eating as one of life's
great pleasures.

While feeding yourself requires sustained effort and discipline, the discipline need not be negative. If the food is good,

the discipline will be positive and joyful and the rewards built right in.

Enjoy Bread, Cereal, Rice, and Pasta. For each meal, include bread and one other complex carbohydrate, like rice, pasta, or potatoes. These high-carbohydrate foods are good foods to fill up on. Children can usually manage to eat the starchy foods when everything else seems just too strange and overwhelming, and children generally get more than enough foods from this group. That's fine. Your child can eat more than the minimum of starchy foods and still eat as much as she needs from the other food groups. Don't worry if she has the rice but skips the stir-fry, or eats the spaghetti but skips the meat sauce. Eventually, she'll get around to having the whole dish, but only if you don't rag on her about it.

Use enriched or whole grain breads and cereal to get B vitamins and iron. Whole grain gives fiber and other nutrients in trace amounts, like zinc. Use whole grain about half the time. Using it all the time will add up to too much fiber for your child, make her too full, and perhaps give her intestinal gas. It can also interfere with the absorption of other nutrients.

Ready-to-eat breakfast cereals are on this list. I would far rather have you depend on the relatively unadorned cereals like Cheerios, Wheaties, Kix, and Oatmeal Squares than the sugar-coated and flavored cereals like Frosted Flakes or Fruit Loops. Those sugared and flavored cereals are nutritious—they give the same B vitamins and iron as the other cereals. In fact, in some cases those cereals are like a vitamin pill—they advertise and really do give 100 percent of the daily requirement of many essential vitamins and minerals. However, the sugar-coated and artificially flavored cereals don't teach children to enjoy the good taste and lovely appearance of grain. Instead, children learn to enjoy the taste and appearance of artificial flavors and colors. By the way, children don't have to depend on a breakfast cereal to give them 100 percent of anything. Cereals need to make only a partial contribution to the overall day's intake. They don't have to carry the full load.

Crackers are on the bread list as well. They are fine for children and can add nutrients, variety, and pleasure to meals and snacks. Given a choice between the low-fat or regular version of crackers, choose the regular. Your child needs fat in her diet to get enough calories, and she won't have a lot of reliable sources of fat. Also keep in mind that bread group foods include buns on hamburgers, pizza crust, burrito wrappers, and bagels. Potato chips aren't on this list, but let's talk about them here anyway. I suppose potato chips would be a vegetable, or maybe a fat. It doesn't matter. They are good, your child will like them, and she is entitled to enjoy them from time to time. Taco chips *could* be here, but they are so hard and tough that toddlers may choke on them. Offer potato chips occasionally at mealtime along with a sandwich, and then let your child eat as many as she wants. If you dole them out they will take on the aura of being an especially appealing food. The salted versions are okay, although I would avoid the brands of chips that are particularly salty. Your child can manage more salt now, so you don't have to be careful to avoid salt as you were earlier.

Enjoy Fruits and Vegetables. Fruits and vegetables are on separate lists on the Food Guide Pyramid, but they give many of the same nutrients. Depending on the survey you consult, children get anywhere from 75 percent to almost 100 percent of their minimums of fruits and vegetables. That's remarkably good, although there is room for improvement, particularly when you realize that white potatoes in French fries and chips and tomatoes in spaghetti sauce, pizza sauce, and salsa make up most of the vegetable choices. Fruit juice consumption is high, and that may or may not be a problem. Toddlers eat best when their juice consumption is kept to a maximum of 6 to 8 ounces a day. Five servings, total, of fruits and vegetables is enough to give the vitamins A and C, B vitamins, fiber, carotene, phytochemicals, and other mysterious and possibly protective ingredients that we need to get from this list. Offer a good source of vitamin C every day and a good source of vitamin A every other day. See appendix P, "Vitamins and Minerals for Children," for a list of good sources of vitamin C and vitamin A.

The more we learn about nutrition, the more we realize how much fruits and vegetables contribute to health and vitality. However, don't let that observation send you on a campaign to get your child to eat them—the campaign will backfire and she will learn to *dis*like them or to play games with you while you struggle to get her to eat them. We don't want to turn our food into medicine. Instead, we must *entice* ourselves and our families with fruits and vegetables. How can you do that? First, make them more interesting. Dress vegetables up with butter and sauces. Make casseroles and soups that have vegetables in them. Bake with fruit: make cobblers and crisps and fruit sauces to serve over ice cream. Consider offering your child dried fruit, like raisins or dried apricots, at meals or for snacks. Do be careful about the chewing-swallowing issue however—dried fruits are tough, and your child might find them beyond her abilities at first. Certainly do not let her wander around eating these or any foods—the risk of choking is increased, and constant munching on sticky, sugary dried fruit increases her risk of tooth decay.

Then, even though the fruit or vegetable will be as delicious as it can possibly be, give your child—and yourself—an out. Again, you get your points when you put it on the table, not when your child eats it. Back off. Generations of parents have somehow been taught that children don't like vegetables, and generations of parents have created that reality by forcing, enticing, and rewarding their children to eat vegetables. Let your child learn to like vegetables at her own speed and in her own way. The same goes for you. If you are just learning to like a food, experiment the way your child does, and always give yourself an out. Look but don't taste; taste but don't swallow; swallow but don't force yourself to take another bite. If you pay attention to whether you really enjoy the food, you, like your child, will be more interested in eating it the next time you have the opportunity. Like a new song, it grows on you. After you eat it enough times, you will like it.

Fresh fruits and vegetables are fine choices for your family, but fruits and vegetables don't have to be fresh to be nutritious. Use canned and frozen vegetables and fruit to cut down on preparation time and to vary the taste. Sweetened applesauce and fruits canned in syrup are fine. If you don't like the syrup, drain it off. Use 100 percent juice. Fruit punches, ades, or fruit-flavored drinks contain only a little juice and lots of sugar water. Apricot and peach nectar are wonderfully tasty and nutritious and are simply fruits in a different form. Raisins and dried apricots or prunes give vitamin A and iron and make a nutritious sweet snack. Consider buying prewashed salads and ready-to-cook or ready-to-eat fresh vegetables and fruits. If they are packaged and labeled "prewashed" or "ready to eat," you can serve them straight out of the bag. Pre-preparation adds some to the expense, but think of it as *help* cost, not as *food* cost. Furthermore, the extra cost may not be as great as you think when you consider that what you buy is all edible. You don't have to pay for anything that gets peeled off or cut away. This pre-preparation may or may not be worth it for you depending on whether you have more time or money. It *certainly* is cheaper than eating out.

Don't forget about breakfast as an opportunity to include fruit and vegetables: An omelet with spinach, fruit on cereal that is dry or cooked, or a dish of peaches can add to the day's offerings. Snacks are a possibility as well: A banana, a few slices of dried apple, raw vegetables with a dip, a pear with some peanut butter, frozen peas eaten frozen like little ice cubes—all can add to the day's offerings. You notice I said *offerings*. I really mean it: Your job is done when you put it on the table.

Lumping fruits and vegetables together and making it your goal to offer five altogether helps when planning meals for children. Sometimes children eat fruits, sometimes vegetables, and there is no predicting which it will be! When you get so you regularly include fruits and vegetables in your menus, try to offer two at each of your main meals to increase the chances that your child—and you—will find one of them appealing enough to eat. This might be a fruit and a vegetable, like corn and peaches; two fruits, like a big fruit salad; or two vegetables, like tomatoes in the lasagna and a vegetable salad or mashed potatoes and broccoli.

You can use all your ingenuity to come up with a variety of fruits and vegetables to put on the table, but, once again, beware: you mustn't try to force your child—or yourself—to eat them. Take it slowly and trust your child—and yourself—to learn to enjoy them. Best intentions aside, you will keep eating fruits and vegetables only if they give you pleasure. Forcing them down either yourself or your child out of duty may work for a while, but eventually you will give it up as a bad job.

Enjoy Meat, Poultry, Fish, Dry Beans, Eggs, and Nuts. Offer two to three servings each day from the protein group. Your child will eat small servings and get enough from this group when she eats about an ounce of meat, poultry, or fish a day, or the equivalent in other high-protein foods. An egg is equal to an ounce of meat, as is half a cup of cooked dried beans or 2 table-spoons of peanut butter. After her first birthday, it is all right to offer your child peanut butter unless you have a strong family tendency to allergies. Then wait until she is 2 years old. As you know, peanut butter sticks to the roof of the mouth, so to cut down on your child's risk of choking, spread the peanut butter thinly or put it on a peanut butter and jelly sandwich. Avoid whole nuts because they present a choking hazard; chop them finely.

Eat red meat if you can, and serve it to your family. People nowadays have the idea that red meat is bad and actually take pride in avoiding it. Wrong, wrong, wrong! Red meat is good for you, and it is particularly good for your child. National sta-tistics on adults that tell what we eat and what nutrients we get from it indicate that from beef alone, on which we spend only about 7 percent of our calories, we get 18 percent of our protein; over 25 percent of our vitamin B12 and zinc; 10 percent of our vitamin B6, iron, and niacin; and significant amounts of thi-amine.[5] These are figures for adults, not children, but the point is the same: meat carries more than its nutritional weight. The iron is especially important for your toddler because she is still in the high-risk period for iron-deficiency anemia. The iron in meat is very well absorbed, far better than the iron in vegeta-bles and grains, and eating meat with a meal improves iron absorption from vegetables and grains as well. Red meat and, to a lesser extent, poultry and fish contain *meat factor*, which improves iron absorption overall. For more about iron nutrition, see appendix L, "Iron in Your Child's Diet." The zinc in meat is also important. If you remember our earlier discussion, zinc is one of the marginal nutrients for toddlers.

When planning the protein part of your meals, consider shortening your preparation time and decreasing your mess by purchasing pre-prepared ingredients, such as lean ground beef; stew meat (plan to cook at a low, moist heat for at least 2 hours), breakfast steaks (thin, quick-cooking steaks), prepared meat patties, chicken thighs, boned chicken breasts or small pieces for stir-fry, canned chicken, frozen fish fillets, canned tuna or salmon, boneless pork chops, cutlets or stir-fry, small ham roasts and slices. Other fast choices from the protein list include canned baked beans, cans or jars of precooked navy beans, garbanzo beans, black beans, or refried beans. Don't forget eggs and all the wonderful ways you can cook them. I already mentioned peanut butter, which is higher in protein than any of the other nut butters.

It is also all right to offer luncheon meats, sausages, and hot dogs once or twice a week—and even bacon. There is lingering worry about such processed meats because they contain nitrate and sodium nitrite. (Nitrates and nitrites are chemically a little different, but nutritionally they are interchangeable.) A couple of decades ago there was a nitrates-and-cancer scare, but the theory has since been disproved. Sodium nitrate used in processed foods retains color and prevents spoilage, and eaten in moderate amounts it won't hurt your toddler.

Parents complain that toddlers don't eat much meat, and toddlers do seem to find meat challenging. It is often more dry than other food, and more chewy. Your toddler won't have molars until she is about 18 months of age at the earliest, and even then she won't chew very well, so it's not a good idea to wait to give her meat. She needs the iron and zinc now. Cook meat and poultry so it is moist and tender, and then cut it into thin slices across the grain. Also consider a juicy ground beef patty, meatloaf, casserole, or hearty soup. Because casseroles are moist and easy to chew, toddlers can generally do better with them than with plain meat.

Vegetarianism. Children can do fine on vegetarian diets, but the diet does need to be well planned and it must include milk, cheese, and eggs. *Vegan* diets that completely omit eggs and dairy products have to be extremely well planned to provide for your child's nutritional needs, and I do not recommend them. Eating a variety of foods is essential to good nutrition. The more food you cut out of your child's diet, the greater her risk of nutritional deficiencies.

If you want your child to be on a vegetarian diet, you must know what you're doing. See a registered dietitian to make sure you give your child what she needs. Learn about vegetarian nutrition by studying reliable cookbooks, such as *Laurel's Kitchen* (by Laurel Robertson and others). In appendix N, "Children and Vegetarian Diets," you'll find recommendations and precautions for following a vegetarian diet. For children, the major challenge with the vegetarian diet is bulk. Unless the cook makes a special effort to include fat with the meals, the vegetarian diet tends to be so low in calories that it is hard for children to eat enough to satisfy their energy needs. Protein can also be a problem. Legumes, seeds, and nuts, in proper combination with grains, provide a high-quality source of protein. However, to get an adequate amount of protein from, for example, a beans and rice dish, a child would have to eat a volume of food that would be four to six times greater than if she were getting her protein from an animal source. The solution, of course, is to be sure each meal includes cheese, eggs, or milk.

Iron nutrition raises another issue. About 3 to 8 percent of the iron in vegetables and grains is absorbed, compared to about 20 percent of the iron in meat, poultry, and fish. Without the well-absorbed iron and the meat factor from meat, poultry, and fish, getting and absorbing enough iron will be more difficult for your child. You can help solve that problem by being sure to include a source of vitamin C with each meal, because vitamin C enhances iron absorption from legumes, vegetables, and grains. Broccoli with a beans and rice meal will increase iron absorption from both the beans and rice. The tomato sauce with a vegetarian lasagna increases iron absorption from both the noodles and vegetables in the lasagna.

Keep in mind that there is nothing about the vegetarian diet that is inherently superior to the omnivorous diet. In fact, unless you have chosen to eat a vegetarian diet for philosophical or aesthetic reasons, you might consider drawing on the best features and enjoyable qualities of both omnivorous and vegetarian diets. Use meat judiciously as a source of protein, iron, zinc, and meat factor. Include a small amount of meat in a largely legume and cereal dish to add flavor as well as nutritional value. Consider Mexican tortillas with shredded chicken and refried beans, Brazilian black beans and rice with small pieces of sausage, and our own navy bean soup with bits of ham and crackers.

Enjoy Milk, Yogurt, and Cheese. Milk is good for children. In fact, I would go so far as to say that milk is essential for children, and for grown-ups as well. A few children are allergic to milk, or can't digest the sugar that milk contains (lactose), but most children benefit from drinking milk, as do grown-ups. Soy milk is generally not the nutritional equivalent of milk, so if your child can't drink cow's milk, continue to offer her soy formula until she is 2 to 3 years old. By that time, her intestine may have matured to the point that she can drink cow's milk. The toddler needs 16 to 24 ounces of milk per day. It won't hurt her to drink more unless she drinks milk instead of eating something else she needs. Milk and milk products contribute important amounts of protein to most children's diets, and they provide everyone's primary source of calcium and vitamin D. Calcium is, of course, necessary for formation of strong teeth and bones, and vitamin D is essential for us to be able to utilize calcium. Children between 1 and 3 years old need 500 milligrams of calcium per day and 200 international units (IU) of vitamin D. A cup of milk gives about 300 milligrams of calcium. One cup yogurt or 1 ½ ounces of cheese do too, but not any vitamin D. Calcium-fortified orange juice gives calcium but not vitamin D and not protein. For more about calcium and vitamin D nutrition, see appendix Q, "Calcium: If Your Child Doesn't Drink Milk."

The rumors (and even press conferences by seeming authorities) that get ballyhooed every so often saying that milk is bad for people in general and for children in particular are simply wrong. Such ideas about milk drinking are based on flimsy evidence by people on crusades. Charges against milk do not hold up to careful examination. Pasteurized milk sold in regular grocery stores is safe and wholesome for your child. It is subject to strict regulation.

By the time your child is 1 year old and is eating big-girl meals and snacks and drinking from a cup, it is all right to make the change from breastmilk or formula to pasteurized whole milk. You don't have to, but you can. If you have doubts about your child's nutrition or she hasn't yet made the transition to table food, it is wise to stay with formula for a while longer. However, *the formula for the most part must be in a cup,* and you have to stay away from the nipple misuse discussed in chapter 7. Why is it all right to give pasteurized milk at age 1 year but not before? Because by that time, the other foods your child eats make up for the nutrients lacking in milk, such as iron and vitamin C; because at meals and snack time other food combines with the milk in your child's stomach to make milk easier to digest; and because by then your child's gastrointestinal tract is more mature. Don't feed unpasteurized milk of any type at any age. Why do I recommend *whole* milk? Because fat is an important source of energy. Younger children especially depend on milk to provide them with fat. After age 2, whole milk is still okay. So is 2 percent, 1 percent, or skim milk, *if* your child likes it and drinks it well and *if* you include other good sources of fat in your child's diet. Many children don't like low-fat milk as well as they like whole milk and consequently don't drink as much of it. Since most parents drink low-fat milk, the main reason for switching the toddler to low-fat milk is to make it possible for everyone in the family to drink the same milk. However, it is easy to get your child's fat intake down too low, so do not use low-fat milk if you use mostly lean meats *or* use low-fat food preparation techniques *or* limit the butter or salad dressing your child uses at the table.[6] If you are in doubt about whether your child is eating enough fat, serve whole milk. If you don't want to purchase whole milk just for your child, put half and half in her milk to increase the fat content. A tablespoon of half-and-half per 4-ounce cup of low-fat milk will turn it into whole milk.

Make milk the family mealtime beverage and offer it in a 3- to 4-ounce glass. Drink it yourself, and if you can't do that, drink water. Don't drink something more appealing like soda or juice, because your child will want that too. Don't push milk, or you will turn it into something your child wants to avoid. Just make it available, and wait. I realize that some cultural traditions don't support milk as a mealtime beverage. If that is the case for you, take special care to get other good sources of calcium and vitamin D in your diet, and be careful about making beverage alternatives too appealing. Water is best. For some reason I do not understand, many young children would rather drink than eat their meals. If you make juice, Kool-Aid, or soda readily available, your child is likely to eat poorly.

It's okay to occasionally put flavorings in milk, but be careful of your attitude. If you are so invested in getting your child to drink milk that you are willing to go to a lot of trouble to make it happen, your child will know that. She will make drinking milk *your* thing, not hers, and she will use it to manipulate you. Even the child who drinks milk will go through periods when she doesn't drink much milk, especially right after she is weaned from the nipple. Don't make a fuss about it; don't try to push milk. Just wait. And drink your milk. She will go back to drinking milk when she's ready. After all, if you drink it, she'll figure out on her own that it must be the thing to do.

Enjoy Fats and Oils. Parents have been alarmed by all the hype about fat avoidance and feel obligated to restrict their child's fat intake for fear they will condemn her to heart disease in later life if they don't. As I pointed out earlier, the current national craze of avoiding fat seems to have—inappropriately—reached the youngest set. Surveys show that, on the average, young children get only about 30 to 33 percent of their calories as fat. That's too low. Children need more fat than adults do. Infants, toddlers, and even preschoolers benefit from having as much as 40 percent of their calories as fat. For young children, unless you have a strong family history of heart disease, taken on a cost-benefit balance, the predictable risks that go along with fat restriction far outweigh the presumed benefits. For young children it is best to make wise and non-restrictive use of fat. Yes, I know the recommendations from all the agencies, large and small, and I still say that. I have read more research than I care to think about, and I still say that. Appendix K, "Children, Dietary Fat, and Heart Disease—You Don't Have to Panic," goes into more detail about the research and my reasoning in arriving at this point of view. However, while I encourage you to ease up on fat restriction, I also want to caution you against the current fad of pushing fat by emphasizing high-fat food and lots of meat at the expense of high-carbohydrate foods. There is nothing to be gained by going to the other extreme. Enough fat gives essential nutrients and enhances the pleasure of food. Too much just wastes calories and unbalances the diet.

How do you go about seeing to it that your toddler gets enough fat but not too much? Provide meals and snacks that include low-, moderate-, and high-fat foods, and then let your child regulate her actual fat intake with her hunger and appetite. She will eat more when she needs it, less when she doesn't need as much. For more specifics, see Figure 8.3, "Helping Your Child to Eat the Right Amount of Fat." Keep in mind that your child's stomach is small and her energy needs are high, so she depends on fat to give her access to food that is concentrated in calories. Furthermore, fat will give her food "staying power" because eating fat with a meal retards the emptying time of the stomach and makes energy available to her body more slowly and for a longer time.

Don't feel you must cook one higher-fat meal for your child and another lower-fat meal for yourself. Giving your child

FIGURE 8.3 HELPING YOUR CHILD EAT THE RIGHT AMOUNT OF FAT

Keep in mind the division of responsibility in feeding.
Put a variety of foods on the table with a variety of fat concentrations and let your child do the translating with her hunger and appetite. Here's what needs to go on the table:

- Offer some foods that are low in fat, like vegetables and fruit prepared with 1 or 2 teaspoons of fat per serving or roasted or broiled low-fat meat.
- Offer some foods that are moderate in fat, like meat, chicken, and fish prepared with added fat, or a fat-containing casserole, scalloped or mashed potatoes.

- Offer some foods that are high in fat, like salad dressings, butter or margarine, gravies and sauces, and whole milk.
- As with all other food, allow your child to pick and choose from the foods you've made available, and let her eat as much or as little as she wants of everything that is on the table.

Your child will use her own signals of hunger, appetite, and fullness to vary the amount of fat she eats, just as she does with everything else. If she is particularly hungry and needs a lot of calories, she will eat more fat. If she isn't so hungry and needs fewer calories, she will eat less fat.

unlimited access to the high-fat table spreads, sauces, and salad dressings will help her to get enough fat. For everyone in the family, be moderate in your fat use, not restrictive. Using butter or a sauce on vegetables makes them more interesting, moister in the mouth, easier to chew, and overall more enjoyable for both you and your child. Fry meat, poultry, and fish occasionally, along with baking, roasting, and stewing. Use some fat in casseroles. For cooking and for making casseroles, you can use even high-fat, high-salt soups like cream of mushroom because the other ingredients dilute the fat and salt to the point of being moderate overall. Notice that while you and your child eat and enjoy some fatty foods, a steady diet of them is not pleasant. The same internal appetite mechanisms that promote eating a variety of foods provides guidance with low- and high-fat food as well. If you pay attention, you will observe that you get enough of even luscious, high-fat food.

Use a variety of fats. I endorse the use of butter, but when I say butter I generally mean butter or margarine. Actual butter has a wonderful taste and greatly enhances flavor, and because it tastes so good, you may use less than if you settle for margarine. You may, in fact, find your toddler eating plain butter, or scraping butter off her bread with her fingers or teeth and asking for more. If she wants it, let her have 2 or 3 tablespoons of butter on her plate at a meal. She may need it to get enough fat and long-lasting calories to run on. Most toddlers go through a phase where they eat a lot of butter.

Most of your child's fat intake will come from your cooking. There, you can hedge your bets against heart disease by emphasizing variety. Monounsaturated fats, like olive, canola, and peanut oils are currently in favor in the heart disease research, so emphasize them in your cooking, frying, and salad dressings. It is okay to include polyunsaturated fats as well, like corn, sunflower, and soybean oils; just don't use them as frequently as the monounsaturated ones. If you use margarine, make sure it adds to the quality and variety of oils in your diet. Ideally, the first listed ingredient of a margarine will be a liquid form of one of the monounsaturated fats. Hardened or hydrogenated oils in vegetable shortenings don't have the nutritional advantages of liquid oils. They work great for baking cakes, but for frying and cooking, the oils are better for you.

Given today's hysteria about fat, I hope you will bear with me while I emphasize this message: *Your child—and you—must have fat.* Many consumers, especially those who are very self-disciplined with their eating and make it a point to read labels, avoid fat in cooking, avoid any food that has fat in it, and set their goals at eating no fat at *all.* That is way out of line and nutritionally dangerous. The greatest nutritional concern of 59 percent of consumers is fat avoidance, while eating an overall healthful diet falls far down the list of concerns. That's backward. In terms of your child's lifelong health, as well as your own, eating an overall healthful diet is far more important than avoiding fat. Fortunately, most consumers can't live up to distorted and nutritionally ludicrous fat-usage standards. When asked about the "quality" of their diets—meaning for most how stringently they were avoiding fat—over 40 percent of consumers said they felt they should be doing better than they were.[7] Many people cycle in and out of fat avoidance, being "good" one day and "bad" another, cooking low-fat at home and taking vacations from low-fat cooking on weekends or during trips to the fast-food emporiums. Such cycling is confusing to children; it is also unnecessary, and in my clinical experience, it appears to contribute to childhood obesity. It is far better to make positive use of fat, day in and day out.

Enjoy Water. Do your child a huge nutritional favor and get her hooked on water. Set up some reminders for yourself to offer her water—when she swings through the kitchen, when she gets up from her nap (and goes down), after you change her pants. You are not trying to force-feed her water but only reminding her to check herself out and notice if she is thirsty. Put a glass of water on the table for her so she can drink water for thirst and milk for hunger. If your tap water doesn't taste good, consider getting a water-treatment unit or a pitcher with a water filter to *make* water taste good. It will be less expensive than soda, fruit beverages, or juice and is far better nutritionally besides. You may want to review the material on water and water-treatment units in chapter 6 (pages 230-233).

Consuming too much soda, fruit-flavored beverages, and even fruit juices is becoming an extremely serious childhood nutritional problem. While the problem is not as pronounced for toddlers as for children around age 5 years and up, it is best to begin heading off that problem while your child is a toddler. Children are drinking these beverages for thirst, and in the process these drinks are replacing other important foods in their diets. Milk consumption is dropping and along with it intake of the calcium your child desperately needs for lifelong bone health. I generally encourage you not to be restrictive, but in this case, I urge you to exercise a good deal of caution. At meals, offer milk. At snacks, offer juice or milk. The rest of the time, give your child water. Save sodas and fruit drinks for the very occasional treat. Withstand your child's begging and pleading and your own guilt trips. Don't regularly make soda and fruit drinks a part of your child's nutritional life.

Putting It All Together. A nutritionally complete meal might contain only two food items, such as a tuna noodle casserole with peas and a glass of milk. Or everything could be separate, as with meat loaf, mashed potatoes, broccoli, bread, and milk.

Vegetables might be part of a combination dish, as in spaghetti and meat sauce or stir-fry with rice. Fruit can be served as part of dessert, as in oatmeal raisin cookies, or given as a juice along with a snack. Here are a few other dinner suggestions from *Secrets of Feeding a Healthy Family:*

- Swiss steak, mashed potatoes and gravy, gingered broccoli
- Chicken and rice, glazed carrots, apple custard
- Spaghetti carbonara (made with eggs and bacon), mixed vegetables, fruit salad
- Braised pork chops with sweet potatoes, chunky applesauce
- Hamburgers on buns, tomato slices, potato chips, fresh fruit
- Mostaccioli with spinach and feta cheese, scalloped corn
- Chicken noodle soup with vegetables, fresh fruit, ice cream
- Black beans and rice, corn pudding, orange rounds with parsley

Although they're not listed here, serve bread of some kind and milk with each meal. The point of this varied list of appealing food? That you don't have to make your menus boring to feed a toddler—your toddler can eat what is on the table. The mostaccioli menu is a little odd—scalloped corn doesn't really go with the main dish—but most toddlers find scalloped corn accessible and can fill up on it if the main dish is too challenging.

Cook once and serve twice—or 3 or 4—times. Each of these menus have features that, with some planning ahead, allow you to get dinner on in a hurry and make good leftovers for lunches and other meals. Many dishes make use of pre-prepared foods or ingredients. To give yourself more help getting meals ready consider convenience foods such as canned or frozen dinners or hearty soups. To evaluate the nutritional quality of the product, look to see if it has vegetable and starch in it, and read the nutrition label to see if it contains enough protein. An adequate level of protein for a toddler will be about 5 grams of protein from a half-cup serving of main dish or hearty soup.

Hamburger, fried chicken, pizza, and taco fast-food restaurants offer nutritious options for an occasional meal. If your child has milk or a milkshake (instead of soda) and some French fries or coleslaw, she can come out quite well in getting a nutritionally complete meal. These fast-food meals have the drawbacks of their lack of fruits and vegetables and their heavy reliance on deep-fat frying. But grilled food is not high in fat like deep-fried food, so if your child has a hamburger and some French fries, she will be having only one deep-fried food and her menu will still be moderate in fat. You can make up the fruits and vegetables at snack time or at another meal.

Using Snacks to Support Meals. We will consider snacks separately, but for now I want to emphasize that they are an essential part of meal planning and we have to take them just as seriously as meals. I am talking about *planned* snacks, not food handouts. Planned snacks are intended to prevent and make you resistant to food panhandling. Resisting food panhandling is, in turn, essential for the success of family meals. Consider this scenario: Your toddler gets down from the table having eaten little or nothing. Five minutes later she is back begging for a cookie. If you know she has a snack coming in a couple of hours, you will be far more ready to firmly say no than if you think she has to wait until the next meal before she can eat again. And if you say no, she will be far more likely to start taking her mealtime eating seriously. We will finish this discussion on pages 361-364, but for now, remember that snacks are an essential part of your child's learning to eat meals.

Catering to Likes and Dislikes. In planning meals for your family, it is best to treat your child like you do everyone else—sometimes she gets lucky, sometimes someone else does. Don't limit your menus to the foods that you know your child likes or she won't learn to like the whole world of other foods. She is growing up to join you at your table; you are not learning to eat off the high-chair tray. However, expecting that she will join you at the table does not mean that it is all right to plan sadistic menus. An alarming meal like liver, boiled potatoes, and boiled cabbage would be a sadistic menu. Putting that meal on the table and then standing over your child and forcing her to eat it would be *truly* sadistic. A more sympathetic meal would be liver and bacon, mashed potatoes, and scalloped corn—and of course bread and milk—and letting your child pick and choose from the menu to eat what she can manage. It may take her *years* to get around to eating the liver, but her chances are pretty good that she will—if you like it. Be sure to include one food she usually likes with each meal; if the vegetable is a less favorite one, have a bread or salad that she seems to like.

I say *usually* likes and *seems* to like because children this age eat a food enthusiastically one time and completely shun it the next, which is frustrating to say the least. You'll run out at one meal and have way too much at the next. And don't ask your toddler ahead of time what she wants you to make. Give your child a choice *at the table*, not when you plan the menu—she isn't mentally developed enough to be able to handle that. When she gets a bit older and has earned the privilege by demonstrating her food-acceptance skills, she can help plan menus occasionally. Also avoid short-order cooking. By getting up to make your child something special you are ignoring your own need to sit down, relax, and enjoy your meal. By catering to her food preferences you are making her more important than anyone else in the family. That's not good for her, and it's not good for others in the family. You aren't forgetting about your child—you are showing her how to join in to be a part of the group and also saying to her, nonverbally, that she is capable of doing so. For her at this stage, supporting her capability is far more important than babying her.

Making Food Easy to Eat. During World War II, dietitian Miriam Lowenberg saw to it that Rosie the Riveter's children got their lunches. Child care centers were set up in the huge Kaiser plant and shipyard in Portland, Oregon, for children of mothers recruited for the World War II manufacturing effort. For the first time, feeding children in a group setting became an issue. Children were from all over the country, with many ethnic backgrounds and all sorts of family foodways. In most cases, their fathers were gone to serve in the military and their mothers were working away from home, some of them for the first time ever, in the war effort. Despite these challenges, the children wanted to grow up, and Lowenberg gave them the opportunity to become more capable with respect to their eating. She did not cater to the children in her care, but she was considerate and helped them as much as she could to be comfortable with the food she served. She found that the children learned to eat the foods they were offered, that they were curious about food, that they wanted to learn, and that certain food-preparation techniques helped them to be successful with eating. Toddlers and even many preschoolers can't chew tough and fibrous food, like meat, and food that is too dry seems to get stuck in their mouths. Here are some of Lowenberg's suggestions, followed by a couple of mine, to help move the learning process along:

- Make some foods soft and moist. If you have dry meat, have creamed peas. Make the mashed potatoes a little softer than you would for adults.
- Allow her to eat her foods at room temperature. Perhaps you can dish hers up in a separate serving bowl so it can cool off or warm up a bit before she tries to eat it.
- Give salad greens without dressing and serve them as finger food. Make soups thin enough to drink from a cup or thick enough to spoon easily.
- To tone down strongly flavored vegetables, such as brussels sprouts, cook them in about an equal volume of cooking water, leave the lid off the pot while you cook, and then throw away the water. You will be throwing away nutrients, but children are more likely to be able to eat them.
- Prepare food well. Children accept foods better when they are properly cooked with natural colors and textures preserved.
- Put a little extra color in foods. Children are interested in a little parsley in the hot dish or some carrot grated into the coleslaw.
- Cut foods into bite-sized pieces, preferably before you serve them. Your child won't be able for some time to handle a knife and is likely to get all upset about not being allowed to try—and upset again when she tries and fails.
- Keep ground beef patties in the freezer to substitute when you have roasts or steaks that your child truly can't eat. Cook patties until all the pink color on the inside goes away, but stop cooking before they are dried out. Meat is hard to eat, even for older children.

While it is worth going to some trouble to make food well pre-pared, attractive, and accessible, don't feel you have to make food cute. You may delight in making little orange section boats and little gingerbread man sandwiches. I think that's fine for a party or special occasion, but not on a regular basis. If you rou-tinely go to a lot of trouble to make food adorable for your child, you are putting more work into it than she is. She will

sense that, and she will eat less well, not better. Regularly
providing cute food tends to confuse food with playthings.
Food needs to look like *food*, not like toys.

What about Dessert? You may feel that no meal is complete
unless you have dessert. On the other hand, you may rarely
have dessert and not miss it. Either way is fine. When you have
dessert, however, you need to know how to manage it.
Generations of parents have learned to put a delay on the
dessert until a toddler has satisfied some obscure requirement
to eat. "Finish your vegetables and then you can have dessert"
say generation after generation of parents, thereby ensuring that
generation after generation of children learn that dessert is far
more desirable than vegetables. Holding out dessert as a reward
for eating pressures a toddler to eat twice—once to eat the meal
to get the dessert and once to eat the dessert when she's already
full from eating the meal. Stay away from the pressure and
make dessert an ordinary part of the meal by putting a single,
child-sized serving of dessert at your child's place when you set
the table. Then at mealtime, let her choose when to eat the
dessert. Keep in mind that only adults mark the end of a meal
with dessert. Your child might eat the dessert first, still feel hungry, and go on to eat the rest of the meal. Or she might eat a bite
of dessert, then a bite of the rest of the meal. Or she might do it
the standard way: eat everything else and save the dessert for
the end. Make dessert something nutritious, like fruit, fruit
crisp or cobbler, oatmeal cookies, or custard. Notice I said a *single* serving. Don't allow "seconds." With dessert you may bend
the rules of the division of responsibility and not allow your
child eat as much as she wants. It goes back to what I have said
more than once before: children push themselves along to learn
and grow, and they also take the easy way out when it is
offered. Being allowed to fill up on dessert is definitely the easy
way out.

   Of course, your toddler will check you out and ask for more
dessert than her single serving. She may feel moved to have a
fit about it. She may even want down after she eats dessert.
There are some things you *can* predict about toddler eating
behavior, and one of them is that she will soon be back, begging
for a food handout. You have to say no, even if she has a
tantrum about it. If you are able to hold firm on these skirmishes

for control, within a couple of days she will have learned that the limits are not going to budge. If you budge, she will have to keep testing and it will take longer for her to learn the limits. Furthermore, she will hang around to keep conducting her tests, and she won't be able to go off and play. Keep in mind that she is truly testing, not being naughty. Her experiments and your consistent matter-of-fact response let her learn.

Many families don't have dessert. That's fine. Just don't try to deprive your child of sweets entirely. Many children who grow up in sugar-free households load up on sugar whenever they have a chance. Better to let your child enjoy an occasional treat. After all, what's a birthday party without cake? For more about sugar, see the discussion "How to Manage Sweets" on page 365.

GAGGING AND CHOKING

Young children gag. The gag reflex is a neurological safety mechanism that, in normally developing children, helps prevent choking. When food slips to the back of their tongues before they are ready to swallow it, the gag reflex shoves the food back out again. Gagging is a normal part of learning to eat and is one sign of a normal swallowing reflex. If you don't react to your child's gagging, she won't either. She'll go right on eating. But if your child continues to gag a lot and doesn't want anything in her mouth, bring it to the attention of your health care provider.

While gagging is to be expected, choking is dangerous. How do you tell the difference? As long as your child is exchanging enough air through her throat to cough, she is probably okay. However, if she is making no sound or only a squeaky, whistling, inhaling sound, she may be choking. A child chokes when she takes in a breath at the same time she swallows. During swallowing, food moves down her throat past the end of her windpipe. Inhaling at the critical moment can make food plug up her windpipe so she can't breathe. Excitement that makes a child laugh or catch her breath while she eats can make her choke. So can getting upset in general during mealtime. Slippery round food like hot dog rounds or grapes are hard for an inexperienced eater to control with her tongue and push between her jaws. Such foods can make her choke if they slip down her throat because they are just the right size and shape to plug up her windpipe. Children have an increased risk of choking on foods that are difficult to chew, like tough meats and hard nuts and candies. Children have also choked on sticky foods, like large wads of peanut butter. To protect your child against choking, take these precautions:

- Build your child's eating skills. Let her work up slowly to more difficult foods.
- For the child under age 3, avoid whole nuts, raw carrots, hard candy, gum drops, and jelly beans.
- Adapt foods that may cause choking hazards. Cut hot dogs lengthwise, quarter grapes, peel and grate raw apples and carrots, and chop nuts finely.
- Always pay attention while your child eats so you can see what she's doing. If she chokes, she can't make noise to attract your attention.
- Have your child sit while she eats. Put in another way, don't let your child wander around the house while she's eating.
- Keep things calm at eating time.
- Have your health care provider teach you how to identify choking and how to do first aid for choking.

HAVE PLANNED SNACKS

People often think that snacking is bad for their children and try to prevent eating between meals. That really isn't necessary or even helpful. The toddler's energy needs are high, and toddlers have a limited capacity for food, so they need to eat every 2 to 3 hours. The important thing is that you keep control of snack times and food selection at snacks.

Consider a snack to be a little meal. It is not a treat. Bring out snacks as matter-of-factly and as neutrally as you do meals. Make snack food as nutritious as meal food. Do not use snacks to put leverage on your child's eating at mealtimes, as in "if you want your snack you had better eat your dinner," or "since you didn't eat dinner, you can't have a snack." No, no, no! A snack just is. It is not a reward or a punishment for anything. Have your child sit up to the table to eat her snacks. Don't let her run around the house to eat: it's dangerous, it's grazing instead of having a planned snack, and it makes a mess. Sit down with her to keep her company. Have something to drink or to eat yourself. Make this a relaxing time for you to have with your child.

Timing. Offer your child a snack midway between meals, long enough after the previous meal so she learns that she will have to go hungry for a while if she refuses the meal. This isn't being punitive; it is allowing your child to experience the logical consequences of her behavior. The snack has to be your idea—your toddler has to know that she can depend on you to remember about food and to bring it out at dependable times. Don't forget to offer a snack even if she seems to forget about wanting one. Having you forget to feed her is scary for her. If she doesn't know you will watch out for her this way, she will become preoccupied with food and will be likely to hang around begging for food. She may even overeat. The planned snack is the ace in the hole of the beleaguered parent. If you know that another feeding is coming up in only 2 or 3 hours, you will be much better at making your *no* stick. Say *no,* explain why *one time,* and then ignore her. It may help you to say no if you acknowledge the request first: "I know you would like a cookie, but now's not the time for it. We'll have cookies later." If you remind her over and over again about the rule and explain over and over again why she can't break the rule, you will be treating her like a dunce and teaching her to use panhandling as a bid for attention. Grazing is a very common eating pattern for today's parents, so making the shift to more-structured eating is not an easy one. If you eat all the time, you must allow your child to do the same thing, and feeding on demand is not a tactic that works with toddlers.

Parents who see their child as fragile for whatever reason—difficult birth, small size, slow growth, or history of illness—are especially easy prey for toddler food panhandling. The parents are so grateful that their child will eat anything at all that they happily dole out snacks, or even follow their child around, offering food. These food handouts can actually make a toddler's eating worse, not better. When children fill up on little scraps and bits of food, they don't work up enough of an appetite to come to the table hungry and ready to do a decent job of eating. If you find yourself caught in this anxious food pushing, you might correct your perceptions. If she has the energy and resources to give you a contest for control, she may not be so fragile after all! I would consider that a very good sign. While some toddlers eat too little when they are allowed to eat on demand, others eat too much. Providing structured meals and snacks helps children to eat the amount they need.

You may have to offer two snacks in a row if you have a particularly long interval between meals. If children have an early lunch and a late dinner, it often works well to have a "heavy" snack (one with protein, fat, and carbohydrate) 2 or 3 hours after lunch and then a carbohydrate snack, such as fruit or crackers, later in the afternoon. A small amount of fruit or juice can help to tide your child over when you are dashing around to get dinner ready.

Keeping Snacks Moderate. Let your child eat as much as she is hungry for at snack time. Have cookies and milk for snacks some of the time, and let her eat as many cookies as she wants. That's different from the dessert strategy at mealtime, because eating cookies—especially nutritious cookies—will be most of the snack, and eating them won't interfere with anything. Furthermore, it will keep cookies from being a *forbidden fruit* that she overeats when she gets the chance. You do not, of course, want her snack to fill her up so that she doesn't eat her meals, but the way to manage that is to keep snack time away from mealtime. Give the snack long enough after the previous meal so she has had time to get hungry but not *too* hungry, and also make it long enough before the next meal so that she will have time to get hungry again. Put another way, the way to regulate snacks is to get there first. If you plan on a reasonably consistent snack time and get the food on the table, you will be able to manage timing, location, and selection. If you feed your child before she is too hungry, she will eat a moderate amount. On the other hand, I will guarantee you a struggle if you wait until she is famished and has already thought about what she wants to eat and where she wants to eat it. You may have to be firm about snacking either way, but at least you won't be asking for more trouble than necessary.

Snack Selection. A snack must be more than an apple or some carrot sticks. A snack has to be big and substantial enough to be filling for a hungry child. A satisfying snack that keeps your child from being hungry for a while needs to contain some protein, some fat, and some carbohydrate, the same as a nutritious meal. Even if an apple or some carrots are filling for the moment, because they are only carbohydrate and don't give too many calories, they won't stay in the stomach long and your child will be hungry too soon. On the other hand, if a snack is only protein and fat, say cheese or peanut butter in celery sticks, it won't be as immediately satisfying, and may tend to be higher in calories. But if the snack contains protein, fat, and carbohydrate, it will be satisfying and will stay with your child but still let her be comfortably hungry in time for the next meal.

Appendix M, "Nutritious Snacks," gives you some suggestions. However, any food that you consider appropriate for a meal is appropriate for a snack. Often at snack time children are more willing to try new foods. Maybe you can work in the servings of vegetables that are still missing in the day's food totals, particularly if you serve them raw or still frozen. The foods that the advertising industry defines as snack foods are all right occasionally, but not as a general rule. Snack cakes, fruit drinks, candies, and Popsicles are great for the occasional treat, but they don't give many nutrients for the calories they contribute. Poor-quality foods rob your child twice—once when she eats them and doesn't get much nutrition and once when the calories replace those of more nutritious food. The main problem is that these foods are low in iron. Nutritional surveys show that while the iron content of toddler meals looks pretty good, the iron content of snacks is poor.

Even though it pains me to say this, even Kool-Aid and snack cakes make some nutritional contribution in the form of calories and a few nutrients. Buy a limited quantity—enough to give a child as much as she wants at a snack but not so much that it forces you to be the gatekeeper in rationing out what is left. Most children are so active that they can satisfy all their nutritional requirements and still have need for more calories, so the extra sugar doesn't hurt. The purist in me, however, feels much more comfortable about giving sugary foods if they are hooked on to something nutritious. For a bunch of hungry and thirsty kids, I like to spike one part orange Kool-Aid with two or three parts orange juice. Ice cream, milkshakes, oatmeal cookies, and carrot-raisin cake are all basically nutritious foods, and they give the extra calories that most children need.

HOW TO MANAGE SWEETS

Children benefit from having some sugar. Their energy needs are high, their stomachs are small, and sugar gives them concentrated energy. But letting your child fill up on sugary foods will deprive her of the other nutrients she needs. How much sugar is "bad" for your child? With the exception of tooth decay, no disease is caused by sugar. Even hyperactivity isn't caused by sugar, although letting a child have a sugar-only snack can soon leave her hungry and cranky and likely to behave poorly. Sweets as part of a meal or snack that also has protein or fat will prevent the sugar high and letdown problem discussed in the section on foods that help regulation in chapter 2 (pages 66-68).

It may help you relax about sugar intake if you have some numbers to work with. Your child will be eating a reasonable amount of sugar if she gets 10 percent or less of her calories from sugar. A child eating about 1,200 calories per day—an average calorie intake for a toddler—has a sugar "allowance" of 120 calories per day. Each teaspoon of table sugar gives about 20 calories. You can figure a reasonable daily sugar allowance at 6 teaspoons (or 24 grams) of sugar (or molasses, jelly, syrup, or honey). A fast way of figuring sugar allowance in teaspoons for your child is to divide calories consumed per day by 200: a child eating 1,200 calories could have 6 teaspoons of sugar. Figure O.3, "Sugar Content of Common Sweet Foods," in appendix O (page 496) gives the sugar content of sweets that your child may like.

MOVES AND COUNTERMOVES

Now that we have assembled all the pieces, we can have some fun talking about the typical skirmishes parents encounter with toddler eating and helping you to learn how best to respond to them. The strategy is to stay on your side of the division of responsibility no matter how tempted you are to cross it. For instance, when my younger son, Curtis, was about 2 years old, he climbed eagerly into his high chair, apparently prepared to do his usual thorough job of eating his dinner. This time, however, he had another idea and he couldn't wait to try it on me.

He sat back in his chair, crossed his arms, and announced, "I won't eat." I don't know where he got the idea that his eating was my project. Since he was my third child, I had long since given up on any such possibility. Maybe he was just running a little research trial to find out what would happen next.

At any rate, I had my cue: I was supposed to say, "Oh, dear, you have to eat." But I could see that little glint in his eye that I recognized as accompanying his opening move in a contest. I did some very quick thinking. It scared me that he might not eat, because when he was hungry he got crabby, impulsive, and super hard to be around. I also realized he could get me to do lots of things, most of them humiliating, to get him to eat: beg, plead, threaten, bribe, play "here comes the airplane." The bottom line was that there was no way I could get him to eat if he didn't want to. So I said, "that's all right, you don't have to eat. Just keep us company for a couple of minutes, then you can go." He looked absolutely crestfallen. It *seemed* like such a good game, and I just wasn't playing. So he sat a minute, and then he said, "I want some of that." He ate it and asked for something else, and so continued until he had eaten his meal.

Curtis gave me an engraved invitation to do *his* job with eating. If I had taken it, that meal would not have turned out well for anyone. Here are some other moves you may encounter.

"I'm Not Hungry." The "I'm not hungry" routine is a slight variation on the previous theme, the difference being in the timing. You call your child to dinner; she is busy playing, doesn't want to be bothered, and probably doesn't even know she is running out of energy. The 5-minute warning may help, but even if you do that, she may say, quite truthfully—or maybe just to get a rise out of you—"I'm not hungry." Now, if you say, "Oh dear, you must be hungry; you haven't eaten for hours," she's got you. You have crossed the line into her territory of *how much* and *whether* she'll eat. She is going to win this one, because there is no way you can persuade her to eat. However, you can get back into your own territory. Your territory is *what, when,* and *where* she eats: structure and limits. That you can implement. You can say, "You don't have to eat, but come and keep us company for a few minutes while we eat." Chances are good that when your child gets to the table, gets her mind off her playing, and settles down a bit she will discover she is interested in eating. But perhaps she won't. Then you have to deliver, and offer to let her down after 2 or 3 minutes. Don't keep her there in hopes that she will eat, or she won't trust you the next time. If it happens often, set a timer. It will be easier for each of you to stay on your own side of the line if you have a clear ending to the meal. When you let her down, say, "Now that's all until snack time." Keep in mind that saying that is more for you than for her. She will probably understand you, because toddlers understand more than we think they do. But she won't believe you. For her, it is just a theory that she has to test.

"*Now* I'm Hungry." Let's say this wily toddler got down from the table and went back to playing. Now, 5 minutes later, she is back wanting to eat. Tough talk aside, you are tempted. Here is your poor sweet little child, large eyes trained on you, wanting another chance. What hard-hearted parent wouldn't give such an appealing waif that chance? Keep in mind that while she is making a move to take over your prerogative of structure and limits, she is not a diabolical and awful child. This is just an experiment for her to see where the limits lie. So you say "No, you said you were done. Now run along and play."

She will not say "Oh, excuse me. I was confused about that." She is likely to whine, cry, get upset, or haul on your arm. That is *your* cue to ignore her until she stops fussing. If you are lucky she will stop in a few seconds and start doing something you can approve of, and you can go back to paying attention again—to something else besides the food. "That looks like a nice book—car—puzzle." If she doesn't stop promptly, tell her "No, you can't do that" and put her in a brief time out. Set her on the floor or on a little chair to give her a chance to calm herself down and interrupt the contest with you. Don't get angry or lecture or scold her. That's attention, and it will reward her for negative behavior. Be matter-of-fact and ignore her until she's quiet; then let her out of time out to play—but not to fuss at you. Be clear, however, that giving her the time out is for *teaching*, not for punishment. Without such teaching, she won't know how you want her to behave.

Chances are very good that you will have to run your own experiments before you will be able to firmly stick to the limits you have set. You may let your toddler back up to the table, and once she gets there she probably still won't eat or she may do something to aggravate and upset you and spoil your meal. If you learn quickly, it won't take too many repetitions of this routine before you are able to hold onto your resolve. If you learn slowly, take heart. You will get there. If you don't learn at *all*, get help. These unproductive struggles can take on a life of their own and spoil eating and feeding relationships.

"Argh! I Don't Like That!" Your toddler will not require language to tell you that she doesn't find something appealing and has no intention of eating it. Your best response is to ignore it. You may also say "You don't have to eat it—there is plenty of other food." It's all right to give your child some encouragement, but be prepared to take no for an answer. My older son, Lucas, would look at a new food and say, "I don't like it." I would say, "Try it. You might like it." He was generally willing to try it, and in many cases he did like it and would eat more. However, he also knew that if he didn't want to try it he didn't have to, and if he didn't like it he didn't have to eat any more. Even that gentle encouragement, however, felt to Curtis like an invasion of his territory. One time I said to him "Try it, you might like it" and he gave me a glare that left no room for misinterpretation. If and when your child tries a new food, you can say "I see you tried it." Do not say "Oh you brave and wonderful child—I am so proud of you—you are Daddy's little angel." Recognition is fine, but praise will take the pleasure of her accomplishment away from her. Praise makes her eating *your* thing, and then she won't take any pride in it.

Unproductive moves you might be tempted to experiment with include saying things like "It's good—you'll like it," "It will make you big and strong," or "You have to take a bite." Such moves involve putting pressure on your child to eat, and they cross the lines of division of responsibility. You are already doing all you can to "get" your child to eat. You are demonstrating that it's good because you are eating it. Giving a nutrition lesson won't help—children don't care if food is good for them—they care if it *tastes* good. Venture forth with the one-bite rule at your own risk. Even dictating one bite interferes with your child's choice with eating. If you happen to have a compliant toddler, you might be able to get away with it, but not if you have a toddler like Curtis was.

The most unproductive response of all to a child who says "Argh! I won't eat that!" is "What would you like?" That amounts to short-order cooking, and it involves you, the weary parent, getting up from table and preparing a substitute—and you, the weary, *irritated* parent, will be plenty disgusted if your child *still* doesn't eat. Which she probably won't. You both lose on this one—you because you don't get to enjoy your dinner and your child because she doesn't get any experience with making a choice and taking the consequence. If your child refuses to eat, the consequence will be that she will be hungry soon after the meal. Make sure that it is *her* consequence and not yours.

"I Want Cereal, Please." Now we come to the toddler who surveys the table, finds it not to her liking, and makes an alternative request. Not only that, but she is using the magic word. So you ask yourself, "What's the matter with a little cereal? I don't have to cook anything; it's right there handy, and not only that, we could just keep cereal on the table in case she doesn't eat." As no doubt you expect, I will tell you what is wrong with it. Making an alternative food so readily available tells your child louder than words can say, "I don't expect you to learn to eat your meals." Remember that your child wants to grow up with respect to eating, but she will also take the easy way out if it is offered. Parents tell me somewhat proudly that they keep the jar of peanut butter on the table in case their child doesn't like the main dish. The logic, of course, is that peanut butter is nutritious and can substitute for meat and the child can get that nutrition if she doesn't eat the main dish. Some make the distinction that the substituted food has to be *plain:* no sugar on the cereal, no jelly on the peanut butter. It doesn't matter: the message is more convoluted but it is the same. Nutritionally, the strategy may be all right, but developmentally it is not. Providing this readily available alternative puts the child in charge of the menu and doesn't hold firm with the expectation that she will learn to eat the variety of nutritious food that she encounters on the family table. There is a certain amount of anxiety for a child in learning to deal with unfamiliar food—for all of us, really. If you don't put pressure on her, your child will manage her anxiety and gradually learn to like the food. If you make an alternative so readily available, she won't grapple with herself and the food and she won't learn. You may wonder why I recommend routinely putting bread on the table but draw the line at peanut butter or cereal. It's because bread can be a part of the meal that anyone can eat and enjoy without replacing other parts of the meal. Peanut butter or cereal is an alternate to the meal.

A variation on the peanut-butter-on-the-table theme is the tactic of slipping vegetables into other food to get the child to eat the vegetables. Proud cooks tell me about their ingenuity in concealing grated carrots in the meatloaf and chopped zucchini in the spaghetti sauce and beets in the chocolate cake. I am impressed by the resourcefulness, but I have to repeat myself: nutritionally such strategies are fine, but developmentally they leave something to be desired. Truth be told, I have tried a few tricks like that myself and found out they didn't work—my children were always on to me. The rule of thumb is that if you are working harder than your child is to get food into her, you are crossing the line. Moreover, like my children, your child will soon figure out that you are lacing her food with vegetables and she will stop eating not only the vegetables but the food itself. The key here is intent. It's fine to put grated carrot in the meatloaf if your child has already mastered undisguised carrots and if carrots add a taste or texture that you like. However, it's not fine if your intent is to trick her into eating carrots. If you are dishonest with children about their food, they become suspicious, cautious, and reluctant to try new food.

"See What a Good Eater I Am?" A mother asked me about her 18-month-old daughter's too-hearty appetite. She and her husband had gone to China to adopt the little girl when she was 4 months old. To their considerable relief, the infant had been very well cared for by her Chinese foster mother and had plenty to eat and plenty of stimulation. From the first, she ate a great deal. She loved her formula, loved solid food when it was time for her to eat it, loved table food, and ate very well. However, now the mother was worrying that her daughter was eating too *much* because her weight was increasing faster than normal. I am accustomed to hearing these stories from parents and foster parents of children who have lived in circumstances in which they may not have gotten enough to eat. At first when these deprived children get in the midst of plenty, they eat enormous quantities of food and never seem to get filled up. If adults are able to reassure the child and tell her over and over again that she may eat all she wants and she will have enough to eat, it generally isn't too long before the child's eating settles down and she stops eating so desperately. However, if adults are alarmed by the child's eating and try to reduce or even restrict the amounts she eats, it further alarms the child and makes her eat all the more.

However, it seemed that this was not what was going on in this situation, so I couldn't attribute the little girl's overeating to restriction. The mother reassured me, in fact, that the whole extended family was so relieved at what good shape the little girl was in and at how well she ate that she got a lot of attention. "Oh, look at how well she eats!" her aunts and uncles and grandparents would exclaim, as they clustered around her, enjoying the gusto with which she attacked her food. I thought I had my answer: that little girl was a pleaser, and she had learned to eat to please her audience. Of course, to really know, I would have had to look at the situation a lot more carefully than just having a brief conversation with the mother. But it is a working theory that has some credibility: children develop a lot of strange behaviors if those behaviors seem to please their parents. Eating a lot is no more far-fetched than a child's throwing up on command or caching so much food in her cheeks that she looks like a chipmunk. At first the vomiting or caching is just a chance behavior, but if the child gets a satisfying response from the parent, she will learn to do it again. What child wouldn't so enjoy watching a parent jump up and grab her out of the high chair and rush her over to the sink that she would be willing to throw up again for the pure joy of it all? How satisfying is it for a toddler who is experimenting with control to stand proud and unbending while a parent wheedles to get food out of her mouth. Being matter-of-fact about wiping up the throw-up and cleaning out the cheek pouches, then ignoring the behavior, will keep it from getting exaggerated and out of control. The message? Be casual and matter-of-fact about your child's eating and about any strange behaviors around eating.

"I Want to Do It *Myself*." In the midst of all these stories about setting limits for toddlers, we must not forget that what fuels it all is the toddler's burning need for autonomy—to be her own person. As I have said before, children must have their emotional needs met in order to do a good job with eating. To remind ourselves of both of those principles, let's close this section with a story about a child who wanted to do it *himself*. Indianapolis public health nutritionist Pam Estes tells about 13-month-old Tobin, a child who needed to be given a chance. Estes works with the special-needs program for 0- to 3-year-old children with developmental disabilities and special health care needs. Every state has one—in Indiana the program is called First Steps. Tobin had been born with cognitive limitations and skeletal malformations. He had done just fine on nipple-feeding, but at age 4 months when his mother tried to introduce solid foods, it went so poorly that she backed off and didn't do much with them after that. At the time Estes met the family, an occupational therapist was working with Tobin to desensitize his mouth, and a physical therapist was helping him with muscle control. It didn't scare him or turn him off to be offered soft table food. He could mouth and swallow, but he just wasn't interested, his mom complained that it was an "all-day job" to feed him, and that during feeding he gagged a lot even on semisolid food. He seemed to enjoy *holding* other food, but it was hard for him to get it in his mouth, and when he did, he gagged. His weight was going down, and he had been put on what Estes calls a "super formula"—a formula containing 30 calories per ounce— on the grounds that the formula was higher in calories than solid foods. Estes doesn't like those formulas, and neither do I. I also don't like Instant Breakfast or other high-calorie liquid formulas. They are a poor substitute for learning how to eat, and they prevent the family from learning how to feed. Tobin didn't seem to like the formula either, because he was taking less and less of it.

When the family had meals, Tobin was in his walker by the table. Tobin was fed separately. Estes suggested they make Tobin a part of what was going on by including him in family meals. His parents were game, so they brought him to the table, propped him up in his high chair, and put small pieces of whatever they were having in front of him. Estes said he looked even smaller with all those pillows around him, but she still warned the parents off pressuring Tobin to eat and pointed out that they were pressuring him with their cheering and clapping when he ate. Imagine their surprise when Tobin's face brightened up, he focused his attention on the food, and he began to struggle to pick it up. At first he just chased food around the tray, but his mother helped by finding the distance for his arm reach that allowed him to most easily grasp the food. It worked like a charm. Tobin quickly developed the increased muscle control he needed to feed himself, chew, and swallow. Gagging stopped being a problem once he was sitting upright in the chair and feeding himself. You can imagine Tobin's breathless audience and how his parents had to positively sit on their hands and zip their lips to keep from interfering. Awed and astonished, they could only admire their determined son as he struggled to *do it himself*. Tobin knew what he needed to do, and once he was allowed, he did a good job of feeding himself.

Estes says she will never forget the tears of joy in Tobin's mother's eyes. She is finding in her work with special-needs children that all children and all parents benefit from understanding that the child has capabilities and that they can help best by looking for and enhancing those capabilities. She says that "having that attitude makes all the difference between handling feeding difficulties with dread, concern, and frustration or with confidence, practicality, and even *joy*. So many children surprise us when we back off and allow them to handle their own eating."

"I wonder what will happen to resolve struggles like this," I mused as I watched my 2$^1/_2$-year-old granddaughter Emma face down her parents on the vital issue of who was to tie her shoelaces. She was absolutely determined but, of course, incapable, and they were frustrated because they knew she was incapable. Being in the enviable bystander position, almost as soon as I thought it I had my answer: the struggle would be resolved when Emma became capable. Right now, she had to get her helpful, concerned, and committed parents to *back off* so she could have opportunities to learn, try herself out, and become her own person. Emma wasn't the only one who was changing: her parents were changing right along with her. They were learning to let her be independent. Someday she would want to try to tie her shoelaces to learn how to do it. Now, tying shoelaces, or at least trying, was just one more way for her to assert herself.

At that point, when she becomes capable and the struggle is

resolved, Emma will be a preschooler. The same is true for your child. Someday you will call your child to dinner and she will come willingly. Someday you will encourage her to taste a new food and it won't precipitate a power struggle. Someday you will be able to leave her in a room without having to worry that she is dismantling either herself or the room. When that day comes, your toddler will have become a preschooler and peace, relatively speaking, will come.

At this point, we have done the important work of establishing the behavioral and nutritional principles of feeding children. They are the same principles that you will use throughout your child's growing-up years. There is, however, one more very important step in laying down the principles of *feeding with love and good sense:* the principle of parenting the cooperative, thinking, independent child. That Norse god we talked about earlier could have gotten a preschooler to do his bidding. Therein lies the opportunity—and the hazard—of the preschool years.

CHAPTER 9

FEEDING
YOUR PRESCHOOLER
3 TO 5 YEARS

IN PREVIOUS CHAPTERS, I assumed that you had a burning need to know how to feed your child. When it comes to the preschooler, however, I don't make that assumption. That says nothing about you, but much about the preschooler. Compared with the ages that have gone before, the preschooler years are easy. You can now leave your preschooler on his own for a while and assume that he will remember what you have told him and keep himself safe. Having asserted his autonomy and found out that he is a separate person, your child now wants to learn and grow and accomplish. His language is better now, and rather than *learning to talk* he is *talking to learn*. Rather than using the toddler's unrelenting process of trial and error, he can talk with you to find out about the world and think about what he will and won't be allowed to do. Most amazing of all, he wants to please you. He thinks you know all the answers, and he wants to be just like you.

You will be all set with feeding your preschooler if you provide him the same structure and limits that you did when he was a toddler. However, your preschooler's new capability and compliance may make you feel that it isn't necessary to be so careful about the structure and limits—you can be lulled into being casual and nonchalant about doing your job with feeding. In addition, your not having to supervise the preschooler *every*

375

single minute, along with his enthusiasm for learning and doing, may make you feel that you aren't as important as you used to be. Not so. Your guidance and support is as important as before—with feeding as with everything else in your preschooler's life. But here's the problem with the preschooler: when you are on the wrong track with feeding, rather than getting immediate feedback as you did earlier, *it takes longer to know.* When your child was an infant, if you didn't read his signals right and give him what he needed, he got fussy and didn't stop being fussy until you got it right. When your child was a toddler, he also gave you lots of help attending to the task at hand. If you erred in the direction of too little or too much control, he became a tyrant or dug his heels in; you discovered the error of your ways and got things back on a more-or-less even keel. The preschooler, though, doesn't put up a fuss but rather shows that feeding is on the wrong track *gradually,* by becoming less and less self-reliant and competent with eating. Often, parents don't realize that there is a problem until that problem is well established.

In my office, I see preschoolers and young children whose feeding has gotten derailed during this early preschool time—they are finicky, appear to eat too much or too little, or have their whole families in an uproar trying to find something they will eat. I remember a 4-year-old girl whose parents were spoon-feeding her bottled baby squash and carrots because that was the only way she would eat vegetables. I remember a 7-year-old whose parents made a trip to Taco Bell every night because the only food he would eat was beef tacos. These problems do not go away. In *How to Get Your Kid to Eat . . . But Not Too Much* I relate the story of a 16-year-old boy on a family vacation in England whose parents felt they had to scope out a steak house every night in order for their son to eat. Would you like to hear about the 23-year-old who would eat only peanut butter, bread, and milk and whose family got in a complete uproar whenever they were invited out to dinner? I could go on, but I won't. The aim is to get your attention, not to traumatize you. My point is that I would rather you didn't show up in my office or anybody else's worrying about your child's eating. Your child will eat, and eat well. You can do your job with providing food and relax in the secure knowledge that he will do his part. However, like the earlier ages, the preschool age has its own particular pitfalls in feeding.

PRESCHOOLERS ARE CHALLENGING TO PARENT

In a funny sort of way, the fact that a preschooler is easier to be around than younger children makes him harder to parent. With the preschooler, the developmental task is initiative: learning and accumulating knowledge and skills. The preschooler wants to learn and get better at all that he does. That puts you in the role of providing your child with guidance and opportunities to learn, and that means you have to know something! The preschool time is formative and pivotal for you as parent. During this time, you need to discover the new and different ways you are important to your child and to grapple with your own upbringing so you can do a good job of parenting with respect to feeding. You need to make your decisions about parenting. With feeding, as with everything else, the task is to raise a child who does well: who is self-reliant, self-controlled, contented, and cooperative. Since your preschooler will no longer give you as much help in knowing whether you are on the right track, and since there are so many common and socially acceptable ways of being on the wrong track with respect to feeding, I will go into more detail in this chapter about what the wrong track looks like. Then we will consider how to get and stay on the right track.

Even the most well-intended, caring, committed parents can get derailed with feeding. Although I speak often to parenting groups, they are generally large groups, and the feedback comes in the form of questions. However, one time I had a special opportunity to speak with a small group of mothers in a parenting support group. The topic, of course, was feeding children. I went through my usual outline of the division of responsibility in feeding, and that went down all right. Then I talked about letting the child be responsible for *what* and *how much* he eats, and they did all right with that. But when I got to the part about encouraging the mothers to make regular meals and snacks and not allow the child to eat between times, they began to avoid my eyes. Suspecting something was afoot, I opened up the topic for discussion. Fortunately, one woman was brave enough to tell me what was on her mind. "I don't think they should have to sit at the table for a long time. I had to do that when I was little, and it was awful. If I try that with my child, he has such a fit that I don't enjoy my meal." It hadn't occurred to her that she could let him down when he finished his meal.

Another said, "My 4-year-old gets so busy playing, and it is so much trouble to get her to come for meals, that I just don't bother. And besides, mealtime is more pleasant when she isn't around." It hadn't occurred to her to teach her daughter how to behave at the table. Even the group leader, who ran a parenting class and had said earlier in the evening that she thought children needed clear limits, waffled when it came to setting those same clear limits with respect to eating. She said she did make meals for the family, but she did not expect her 4-year-old to come to the table and to participate in the meal. She let him come if he wanted to and even let him take something from the table and eat it elsewhere, but she did not expect that he sit there while he ate. I pointed out the contradiction and asked her why she felt limits were necessary in one area and not in the other, and she said she didn't know. However, she came up to me afterward with tears in her eyes and said that her mother had shamed her when she wouldn't eat and had told her that she was an ungrateful girl who was lucky to have such nice food. She had been so upset about it that when it came time to have her child at the table, she didn't do it. It hadn't occurred to her that she could make the table pleasant for her son by *not* manipulating and belittling him.

FINDING THE MIDDLE GROUND

Parenting becomes the issue in the preschool years, and the way we have been *parented* comes up and has to be dealt with. You have, of course, been parenting all along. However, with all the commotion of the toddler period, the issues of maintaining structure, setting limits, and preserving life and limb have been primary. Now that the preschooler is such a settled and capable little being, the fine points of parenting emerge. Since our subject is feeding, our focus will remain there. However, I will emphasize good *parenting* with feeding and draw on the parenting literature as a whole. For the most part, parents act the same with feeding as they do with everything else, and children behave in other areas the way they behave with respect to eating. Children who are competent in their eating tend to be competent in other areas as well. Children who have a lot of problems with eating act out more and are more fearful. Children who are cautious in general tend to be cautious with eating as well.

The mothers in the parenting support group had grown up being fed with too much control, and they were avoiding behaving the same way by using too little control. Like a lot of us, they were resolving their parenting issues by doing the opposite of what they had grown up with, and in the process they had gone to the other extreme. Because the issue of control is so important, let me remind you of what it looks like when you're being too controlling. You are being too controlling if you make your child

- Stay at the table to eat his vegetables
- Clean his plate
- Eat everything before he can have dessert
- Get by on only three meals a day

You aren't setting strong enough limits if you

- Give your child a snack whenever he wants one
- Let your child behave badly at the table
- Regularly produce special food for your child
- Short-order cook for him
- Let your child have juice or milk whenever he wants it

The definition of *control* in its most negative sense is imposing your will on another person, as in the examples of too much control given in the above list. You may feel that setting strong limits for your child is also too controlling, but in that case you are controlling the *situation,* not your *child.* In the examples from the parent support group, the mothers weren't offering their children any limits or guidance. They were reacting to what *their* parents in turn had done to them with feeding, and earlier generations, of course, had only done what *they* thought was right. Like holding a mirror in front of a mirror, it goes back forever. Traditional wisdom said that a child had to be made to eat or he wouldn't, that a child had to be forced to eat vegetables or he wouldn't, and that wasting food was worse than wasting a child. We know a lot more about feeding now than when you were a child, and you can make use of that knowledge by feeding your own child better than you were fed.

PARENTING WITH RESPECT TO FEEDING

It's always most difficult to find the gray area: the place between being overly controlling and not controlling enough, between being domineering and being neglectful—between, at the one extreme, forcing your child to eat and, at the other extreme, throwing open the refrigerator door. The division of responsibility in feeding defines that gray area between the extremes.

• The parent is responsible for the *what, when, where* of *feeding*.
• The child is responsible for the *how much* and *whether* of *eating*.

There is plenty of research to back up the wisdom of the division of responsibility in feeding, and I have outlined that research in appendix I, "Children and Food Acceptance," and appendix J, "Children and Food Regulation." Children eat well when they are given structure, opportunities to learn, and limits. They eat the amount they need and learn to like a variety of healthful food. The wisdom of finding that gray area between the extremes is supported by the parenting research as well. Children who grow up in families that give them both love and limits are most likely to become successful, happy with themselves, and generous with others. Children whose parents are overly strict are likely to be obedient but unhappy; those whose parents are overly lenient are likely to lack self-control because parents have provided insufficient guidelines for them.

Diane Baumrind, a child development specialist at the University of California, Berkeley, called these three approaches to parenting *authoritative, authoritarian,* and *permissive.* In an original, often-quoted and often-confirmed piece of work, she observed 134 three- and four-year-old children in nursery school to see how comfortable they were with themselves and how well they did with other people. She then observed them with their parents at home and in the nursery school to see how they were parented.[1] I know the words *authoritative* and *authoritarian* are much alike, but since they are standard usage in the child development world, I will use them. Keep in mind that the word *authoritative* means *decisive* and *reliable. Authoritarian* means *dictatorial* or *overbearing.*

Parenting Styles. The *authoritative* parents, the ones who held

the middle ground, were good leaders. They set limits and
enforced rules, but they were also willing to listen receptively to
children's requests and questions and support them in survey-
ing and mastering their world. They were matter-of-fact about
making use of power and reason, rather than guilt or fear, to
make and enforce rules. If children disobeyed, parents disci-
plined promptly, calmly, and matter-of-factly and kept control
of the situation. The division of responsibility in feeding is an
authoritative approach. Children raised using an authoritative
approach were self-reliant, self-controlled, inquisitive, curious,
and content.

The *authoritarian* parents were overly strict and too controlling. They were haphazard and arbitrary in what they expected
from their children—they didn't explain why they expected a
particular behavior of the child, and they weren't consistent
about following through. They expected immediate and
unquestioning compliance and punished for anything less.
Children of authoritarian parents were likely to be obedient but
unhappy. They were belligerent, anxious, withdrawn, and distrustful and not as curious, independent, or achievement-orient-
ed as other children. The authoritarian parent is likely to insist
that a child eat a certain amount or type of food and not let the
child leave the table unless or until he has eaten that amount.
The child's distress and trauma will be lost on the authoritarian
parent: the main concern is obedience to the parent, not how
the child feels. "Eat that or you will get a spanking" threatened
the authoritarian father I had the misfortune to witness. "Finish
your corn. You're not going to blow up are you?" Bite after bite,
food after food, the father persisted in his tyranny from the
beginning to the end of the meal. His unhappy child grudging-
ly, reluctantly, painfully pushed down each mouthful.

The *permissive* parents were overly lenient. They were
unclear about appropriate behavior for their child and were
unable to lay out any consistent expectations. They placed no
expectations or limits on the child's eating behavior, bedtime
schedule, or contribution to the family. If they did lay out an
expectation for the child, it tended to be offhand and they did
not follow through to be sure the child did what they wished.
They concealed their disapproval of their child's behavior or
tried to control the child with guilt or pleas for consideration.
In most cases they simply went along with the child's demands

until their patience was exhausted and then punished him, sometimes very harshly. Children of these permissive parents learned little from their parents' disciplinary techniques. Children were likely to be aggressive and to lack self-control, and they were often openly disobedient or disrespectful. The mothers in the parenting group I just described were parenting in a permissive fashion: they weren't being controlling enough. In fact, they seemed to be a self-selected group of permissive mothers. Little wonder they needed outside support. It is certainly not pleasant or reinforcing to be around such disobedient and disrespectful children, and keeping that sort of permissiveness going requires energy from somewhere.

Other studies of children at this and other ages focusing on issues ranging from latchkey after-school situations to adjustment to divorce have used these same categories (although sometimes different names) in describing parenting styles. And they have reached the same conclusions: to do well, children need appropriate guidance and limits. In their textbook *The Developing Person through Childhood and Adolescence*, Kathleen Berger and Ross Thompson observed, "authoritative parenting . . . is most likely to produce a happy child rather than a distrustful puppet or an uncontrolled little devil."

Authoritative Parenting Requires Leadership. The advantages are so many, one wonders why we don't all parent in an authoritative fashion. It won't surprise you that I have some ideas about that. Authoritative parenting takes more time, energy, judgment, and nerve than either being dictatorial or being permissive. Authoritative parenting requires leadership, making judgments about appropriate behavior, the willingness to set limits and to take a stand and the ability to tolerate and manage the child's anger and aggression. Authoritative feeding takes more knowledge, understanding, and energy than does simply laying down the law about eating or letting children graze for food. Furthermore, if you have not had a positive upbringing with respect to food, it will be harder for you to provide your child with food, positive eating examples, and pleasant mealtimes.

Of course, we can't overlook the child's part in inducing a certain parenting style. Your child's ease and willingness to develop self-control and self-reliance may let you be a more relaxed and flexible parent than you otherwise would be. A child who comes readily to the table, takes an interest in the food there, and makes it his business to learn how to eat will give you lots of reinforcement for providing meals and will make you seem like a stellar parent. An aggressive child who constantly tests his limits may cause you to be more authoritarian than you really want to be. And a cautious child who reacts strongly and negatively to new food experiences may make you feel like such a tyrant when you expect reasonable behavior that you back down and cater to him. On the other hand, you may have precipitated those extremes of behavior by being too permissive or too authoritarian. When I evaluate distorted feeding, I often find it hard to tell where the cycle of feeding distortion started, but frequently it appears to grow out of a particular vulnerability or characteristic of the child. Of course, being the parent, you are the one who has to stop the cycle. In stopping it, you give your child the opportunity to behave better—and in the process to feel better about himself.

ENTICING YOUR CHILD TO EAT IS CONTROLLING— AND PERMISSIVE

Of course, parenting doesn't always fit into these neat categories. In my experience, some parents manipulate to achieve control rather than directly tyrannizing their children. These same parents can also be permissive at times and not give their children reasonable limits and expectations. In the process they cross the lines of division of responsibility and take away their child's initiative with eating. I was amazed when I listened to a public radio talk show featuring the author of a book of recipes that was promoted as "tempting even the pickiest eater." The host of the show was delighted, apparently because she was in the business of trying to get her own children to eat and was looking for new ideas. Callers were eager to share their tactics of getting children to eat. By the way, when you hear that phrase, "getting children to eat," know that the adult is trying to control the child. Keep in mind that if you start trying to control another person, that person will respond by trying to control you. You will see in the stories that follow that the parents were trying to control their children and that their children were controlling them right back by being reluctant and incompetent with their eating.

One mother who called the radio talk show said her child ate best when foods were covered with barbecue sauce, so she covered everything with barbecue sauce. Her child was getting her to jump an increasing number of hurdles in order to get him to eat. Another said she would let her child have cereal or peanut butter if he wouldn't eat, but only plain: no jelly, no sugar. Undoubtedly, she will find that there are more and more days when her child resorts to the peanut butter and cereal. A father reported putting himself in his child's shoes and realizing that children are regularly expected to eat what adults pick out. So his solution was to turn menu planning over to the children half the time. Since the parents made it a point to eat what the children planned, the children were more willing to eat what the parents planned. That one is a little harder to see through, but think of the attitude: it was that the children's eating was an *obligation* and a *chore*, not a pleasure. Parents and children were taking turns obligating each other to eat.

One mother got delighted and somewhat vicious approval from the host and author when she told about her tactic of serving a new vegetable but not offering it to her children. "It's for us," she would announce. "I don't think you will like it, and it is too expensive to throw away." She claimed that it made the children want the vegetable and that now they ate those vegetables readily. She was not only controlling them, she was tricking them. And she reveled in her trickery because they were making her mad. The word that comes to mind for me is resentment. How must those parents feel when they go to all that trouble to feed their children and then the children are so fickle about their eating? And what of the children? Surely they know they are being manipulated, but the parents' disguising that manipulation so skillfully as indulgence makes it hard to know what is going on. So they fight back by behaving badly. Of course, everyone loses. Children know on some level that they are behaving badly, and therefore they don't feel as good about themselves. There are several books that take this approach to helping you trick or otherwise coerce children into eating, and you can find them if you want to go that route. However, it is not good parenting, and I can predict that if you resort to such coercion you will be painting yourself into a corner.

RAISING CAPABLE CHILDREN

The figure of speech "painting yourself into a corner" comes from the days when people painted their floors. Choosing to tackle this arcane task required some planning to be sure the last strokes took the painter out the door rather than into the corner. If the painter wasn't careful, she would end up either trapped by a wet floor or having to spoil her work to get out. Likewise, if you make it so much your business to "get" your child to eat that you are willing to go to great efforts to feed him, including trickery and giving away your job with family menu planning, your efforts will create more problems than they solve. Your child will become more and more demanding and less and less capable with eating, until eventually you will be going to such monumental lengths that you get fed up with it. Your child will consequently not be as curious or interested in achieving, he will be likely to lack self-control, and he will be disrespectful of the limits. In other words, he will have forgotten how to keep a grip on himself and take responsibility for his own eating. By that time, it will take a major overhaul to get feeding to go well.

While preparing good-tasting, appealing food is important for everyone at the table, preschoolers do not need to be catered to or enticed. In fact, preschoolers in particular seek reasonable expectations, opportunities to learn, and limits. They do not seek the easy way out. A preschooler will taste a new vegetable because *inside* of him he has a burning need to learn and grow and do everything that you do. On the other hand, if you make his eating your business, it will take all of the joy and accomplishment out of it for him.

Is Your Preschooler a Good Eater? Someday you will be able to include your child in family menu planning, but he has to *earn* that privilege by demonstrating that he takes responsibility for his eating. To be a good eater, your preschooler does not have to eat everything that is put before him. He has to know how to behave at the table, mind his manners, and have some good food approach and food refusal skills. The following list outlines what you are working toward with preschooler eating behavior. Your preschooler is a good eater if you can answer yes to the following questions:

- Does your child like eating and feel good about it?
- Is he interested in food?
- Does he like being at the table?
- Can your child wait a few minutes to eat when he is hungry?
- Does he rely on internal cues of hunger and fullness to know how much to eat?
- Does he rely on variations in appetite to know what to eat?
- Does your child enjoy many different foods?
- Can he try new foods and learn to like them?
- Can he politely turn down foods he doesn't want to eat?
- Can he be around new or strange food without getting upset?
- Can he "make do" with less-than-favorite food?
- Does he have pretty good table manners?
- Can your child eat in places other than home?

With feeding, your role as parent broadens from providing structure and limits to teaching and guiding. A couple of suggestions made on the radio talk show gave good examples of teaching and guiding. One mother said she had encouraged her child to try new foods by pointing out that "if you had never tried ice cream or corn on the cob, you wouldn't know how good it was. You might like this too. If you don't taste it, you could miss something you would enjoy." Whether or not that mother's approach was positive depends on her motives. If she was trying to help her son to be more competent with his eating, it was positive. If she was just trying to get food into him, however, it was negative. Clean tools in dirty hands are detrimental.

Another parent on that same talk show recalled putting a stop to her teenagers' saying at the table, "Oh, yuck, that looks terrible!" She asked them, "how would you feel if you had worked really hard on a project and then someone came along and said, 'Oh, yuck, that looks terrible!' Well, that's how I feel when you react that way after I have worked hard to make a meal." I did wonder, however, why she had waited until her children were teenagers to have that conversation. It is a conversation that you can quite reasonably have with a preschooler. And you can go on to say, "you don't have to eat the food, but you do need to be polite about turning it down. There is plenty of other food on the table. You can eat some of that if you don't feel like trying this. All you have to say is 'no, thank you.'" If you can say that, *mean* it, *and* take no for an answer, such a statement will actually free your child to do *more*, not *less*. Children—and the rest of us—do more and dare more when we feel we have an out. Not only that, but in teaching your child to politely turn down food you are empowering him in his relationships with other people.

A Child Who Wasn't Capable. One more story about the don'ts of feeding, then we will get down to the dos. A mother called me because she was desperate about her 4-year-old son John's eating. John was a finicky child. He had a very short list of foods he would accept, a list you may recognize: breakfast cereal, chocolate milk, eggs scrambled hard, white bread lightly toasted with jelly, hot dogs, cheese pizza, hamburgers from McDonald's, French fries, chicken nuggets, noodles. You get the idea; all the foods were familiar, easy-to-like foods. Until then, John's limited food acceptance hadn't bothered his mother; she was quite happy to provide him with what he liked. She gave him a vitamin pill and didn't worry about his lack of fruits and vegetables. Now, however, it was time for her to return to paid employment outside the home, and John was to be cared for at a child care center. John was in a panic; he was frightened about what they would feed him and afraid that he wouldn't be able to eat. John had already encountered problems with his eating. When he played at a friend's house, he got very upset at mealtime if he wasn't offered exactly what he got to eat at home. In fact, John no longer even *wanted* to play at his friends' homes because he was so worried that he would be offered something that he couldn't eat. John's dilemma illustrates all too clearly what I said in chapter 8: a vital part of a child's comfort in the world is being able to eat the food there.

How had John become so incapable with his eating? His mother had worked so hard to make his way smooth that he hadn't had opportunities to learn. If John didn't eat what she prepared the first time she offered it, she immediately made him an alternative. Eventually she made only the foods that John liked and ate readily. While it seemed she was being very good to John in catering to him, she was actually not teaching him what he needed to know about learning to like new food. Children learn to like new food by seeing it on the table again and again. Eventually they taste it, and then they taste it again and again. By making John special food, that mother took away not only his opportunities to learn but also his learning about how to learn. John forgot what every child knows, that you learn to like a new food by putting it in your mouth, sampling its taste and texture, and then taking it out again—and again—and again.

How Children Become Incapable. Children who don't do well with food acceptance get too few opportunities to learn or have too much pressure put on their eating. For John, both were true, although the pressure is harder to see. Inherent in making special food for a child is the message "it is desperately important that you eat." Refusing food is no longer an option. John had learned that he *had* to eat, and he didn't know how to go about it. Little wonder that when he was presented with unfamiliar food he felt so upset and overwhelmed. Not eating was not an option.

I didn't try to solve that mother's problem—I never do on the telephone. I gave her the standard advice about feeding preschoolers—advice I will be giving you. If I had investigated further, I suspect I would have found that she had had a rather poor upbringing with eating herself and that she had some of her own issues with eating. She did say in passing that she could understand John's feelings because there were only a few foods she liked herself, which seemed a clue to her own negative experiences with eating.

Clearly, the way adults behave with feeding has everything to do with the way children behave with—and feel about—eating.

WHAT THE PRESCHOOLER IS LIKE WITH RESPECT TO EATING

Your preschooler takes *initiative*. He has a great deal of energy and now takes on new tasks and play activities for the sake of being active and on the move, rather than for the purpose of asserting his independence as he did earlier. He has a lot of resilience that will keep him going if his efforts don't pan out. However, he will also feel guilty and critical of himself if you make an issue of his failures or criticize his efforts. He wants to explore and achieve in all areas of his life—including eating.

However, keep in mind that *initiative* is different from *industry*—the desire to accomplish—which will come along in the next developmental stage. Your preschooler will be more interested in starting tasks than finishing them. When he's hungry, he attends strictly to his eating, working at mastering the foods you present. But when he gets full, he completely loses interest in eating.

The preschooler is *self-aware*. After all of his struggles for autonomy as a toddler, he has emerged able to identify his own emotions, thoughts, and intentions and to distinguish his own from those of others. Rather than learning about new food strictly by trial and error, he can talk about it, cook it, and study it. As a consequence, he is less suspicious of new food and is more ready to taste it than when he was a toddler. It will still take a lot of tastes, however, before he learns to like it. He can think ahead and be deliberate about what he does, rather than barreling along over anything in his path. It is possible to talk with your preschooler about mealtime rules and expectations and to find out from him how he thinks and feels. However, you can't expect him to enforce or even *remember* the rules, even if you have agreed upon them together, because he is still developing his self-control.

The preschooler wants to *please* and *imitate* you. He becomes aware of how you see him and feel about him, so your praise and blame, reinforcements, and punishments become powerful in a way they weren't earlier. He feels bad if you are unhappy with him. Because he thinks that you are great and that you know all the answers, when he sees you eating green beans he reasons that eating green beans must be the thing to do. You don't have to say another word. All you have to do is enjoy your green beans. Observing that, your child will assume that someday he, too, will eat green beans.

The preschooler is *playful*. Play is his work, and his self-centered way of looking at the world will give you some surprises. A preschooler can ask in all seriousness, "Why do they put a pit in every cherry? We just have to throw it away." It is this same self-centered thinking that temporarily puts a preschooler off beef or chicken when he discovers that it comes from a living animal. He will invest the animal with his own thoughts, feelings, and fears. He is not saying he wants to be a vegetarian, any more than the child in the previous example is saying he doesn't want to eat cherries. He is just getting accustomed to the idea. The preschooler will eat well if the table is a pleasant place to be. He will make mountains of mashed potatoes, create trails between his string beans, and have some quirky ways with his eating, like a girl I observed in a child care center who could spit her celery out between her lower lip and cup while she drank her soup. Your child's quirky behavior is not intended to get a rise out of you; he is just being himself.

HAVE STRUCTURED MEALS AND SNACKS

The idea is to *eat with* your child, not just to *feed* him. You must have meals to give your child predictable opportunities to be with you, to learn and to grow. Without family meals and structured, planned snacks between times, your child's eating will simply not turn out well. Meals and snack times must be pleasant social times, not spoiled by imposing outside expectations on what and how much your child will eat. Meals give your child love, food, and mastery expectations; they show him what he has to learn and support him while he's learning. Children depend on structured feeding times to know that they are going to be fed and to learn to like a variety of nutritious food. Children depend on meals to have reliable access to their parents and to the love and sociability of the family table. Children depend on meals to learn social skills for life—how to behave at the table, how to make conversation, how to be pleasant so other people can have a good time, how to pass and serve food, how to say "yes, please," and "no, thank you."

The parents mentioned earlier who let their children run with food rather than asking them to be at the family table were selling themselves short and selling what they had to teach short. They didn't realize that for the child the primary importance of the family table is not getting *fed* but being with the *parent*. Your preschooler loves you and wants to be with you. Certainly he is hungry and needs to eat, but he is far more interested in your attention and companionship than in the food. If his need for pleasant attention and companionship is satisfied, he will eat, and eat well.

Chapter 8 lists many suggestions about what foods to serve for family meals. You can find many more ideas in my book

Secrets of Feeding a Healthy Family, and there you will also learn many time-saving ways to sharpen your cooking, planning, and shopping skills. When you are raising children, like it or not, you have to cook, so you may as well be efficient and effective at it. Like any task we master, you may even find that getting good at food management helps you to like it!

Parents are the menu planners and gatekeepers of the food that comes into the home. You are the ones who know the most about the food that is in the world, and you are giving your child the opportunity to learn to like all the foods that you like, and more besides. He will start to have some ideas about what he wants on the table, and you can take those ideas into account when you plan your menus, but no more or less than you do for the rest of the family. He may have had a new vegetable at child care or at a friend's house and ask you to make it, or he may have seen some hard sell on television for the latest snack atrocity and beg you for it. There is certainly nothing wrong with honoring these requests at times, as long as you are comfortable with them, but don't put your child in charge of the family menu. He is still too young for that. He doesn't have the experience and mastery with a variety of food and he doesn't have the intellectual maturity to make value judgments about food. While he will enjoy learning about food and nutrition, he won't apply that learning to his eating. As I pointed out in my discussion of nutrition education in *Secrets of Feeding a Healthy Family,* while preschoolers and even children as old as ages 12 or 13 years can recite nutrition lessons and even arrange foods on the Food Guide Pyramid, they don't have the intellectual maturity to make value judgments about food.

Be Honest about Your Preferences. You do not have to make excuses for your preferences, but you do have to take responsibility for them. A friend who fancied herself a gourmet cook and was committed to using only fresh ingredients and only the most respectful of cooking techniques was appalled when her son came home from a play date thrilled because Chris's dad had made a wonderful new food: boxed macaroni and cheese dinner. She knew she was a food snob, and to her credit she managed to remain positive. "Good for you," she said. "It sounds like you found something new to eat!" She didn't deal with the issue of whether they would have that food at home because he didn't ask her. It did, however, come up later, and then she had her answer ready. "I don't make the boxed macaroni and cheese dinner because I don't like it and I'm not comfortable making it. But it's fine if you eat it at Chris's house." To understand why that's important, consider how disrespectful and even shaming a parent might be when she doesn't take responsibility for her own preferences: "That stuff is awful! How can you even like it?" Also keep in mind that a parent taking responsibility for her own preferences serves as a model for her child. If the parent is respectful of the child's preferences, the child is more likely to be respectful of the parent's.

The issue is the same with other foods. You do not have to buy your child sugar-coated cereals if you don't want to, even if he has seen them on his favorite television program and puts pressure on you to buy them. You do not have to serve hot dogs if you are not comfortable with them, and you do not have to serve meat if you are a vegetarian. You must not, however, condemn your child for *wanting* those foods, even if you find them reprehensible, and you mustn't try to keep him from eating them when he goes to someone else's house or eats at child care. The distinction is between *feeding* and *eating*. You can say to your child, "I don't buy sugar-coated cereals because they have too much sugar and not enough cereal. I know Timmy's mother buys them, and if you want to eat them when you're there, it's up to you." Taking responsibility for your own choices will give you the courage of your convictions, and your child will take your *no* for an answer. If you are ambivalent about saying no, or if you try to talk your child out of wanting those foods, he will keep after you in hopes he can wear you down.

You have made nutritional decisions and value judgments about the foods you serve, and you are entitled to those values and choices. It is reasonable to hope and expect that your child will grow to value and choose the foods that you do. Even though he will be exposed to "contaminating" outside influences, you have the advantage. If you are casual and accepting about the occasional food or meal that you consider substandard, your child will be casual about it as well. It won't take on the aura of forbidden fruit, and over time, your child will become most comfortable with the foods you serve day in and day out. He will also become comfortable with eating—or turning down—the food he is offered when he is away from home.

MAKE MEALTIMES PLEASANT

Turn off the television. Family mealtime is for connecting with each other, and if the television is on you won't be able to pay attention to each other. Certainly, an occasional meal in front of a family video is a special treat that everyone can enjoy, but as a regular rule television at mealtimes spoils meals. It is distracting for children so they don't eat as well, and it keeps children from getting what they crave most of all—their parents' attention.

Include your child in the mealtime conversation, but don't make him the center of attention. Ask about his day, and make it a general, open-ended question: "What have you been up to today?" is better than "Did you have a good day?" because the answer to that is "yes" or "no." "What went on in school today?" is better than "How was school today?" because the answer to the latter question is "fine," or "okay." Then take an interest when he tells you, as you do with anyone else. Conversation with your preschooler will give you a glimpse into his delightful mind and his surprising ways of looking at the world. What counts even more than what you talk about is that you truly take an interest. If you don't understand something your child tells you, say it in your own words and let him straighten you out. Don't criticize or judge what he says to you, and don't seize on the opportunity to give a lesson or try to fix his problems. Just acknowledge what he says, find out how he feels about whatever happened, and accept his feelings. "Sounds like that really made you mad" will do, or "I would have felt the same way." *Even if your child's feelings are negative, you don't have to make him feel better. Just accept his feelings and assume that he will be able to handle whatever it is that is bothering him.*

Bring a topic of conversation to the table and be prepared to share it with your child at a level he can understand. Make it clear that you thought about your child when you heard it or saw it. "I heard something today that I thought you might be interested in. They have a new elephant over at the zoo." Also expect your child to listen or at least be quiet and not interfere when the adults at the table are talking. Don't ignore him completely, but don't feel he has to understand every single thing you say. It is, after all, part of being a child to not understand everything and to assume that you will find out sometime. Your child will still be included if you look at him and smile and perhaps throw in a few words now and then to explain what's going on. "Daddy is having trouble with the sewer system for that new building they are putting up," or "Mommy's telling me about her new computer program." Being quiet and listening to adult conversation is a wonderfully entertaining learning opportunity for a child. Children nowadays don't do this as much, but I can remember as a child loving to lie on the floor and listen to my parents and their guests make conversation.

Don't entertain your child, play games, or sing songs together as a way to make the table pleasant. Those are ways for you to take way more responsibility for your child's mealtime behavior than he does, and they are distracting besides. Most people who take such approaches to mealtimes don't trust that children will eat and are trying to keep them there in hopes that they *will* eat. It might work in the short run, but in the long run children don't take responsibility for their own eating and they eat less well, not better.

Teach Your Child to Behave at Meals. A part of making mealtimes pleasant is teaching your child to behave in a way that makes the table pleasant for everyone else in the family as well. You don't have to put up with your child's whining, eating in sloppy ways that are deliberately provocative, crying, being sullen or belligerent, acting out physically, or whatever unpleasant behavior your child comes up with. You can say, "you are whining—now stop" and then ignore him. Ignoring is usually enough to squash the behavior, but if he doesn't stop it, whatever it is, in 5 or 10 seconds, excuse him from the table. Don't let him come back, and don't let him make a doggie bag. This is not as heartless as it sounds. Rather, it says to the child, "you are important, and the way you behave affects everyone else at the table." In fact, when your child settles down, you can put that message in words and have a little conversation with him. "The table is a special place for all of us, and you need to do your part to make it pleasant. When you cry and whine, it makes it unpleasant for everyone." Have the conversation only *one time,* and do not expect your child to act on it right away. You still have to enforce the rule, but having had that conversation, you can expect that your child will remember why the rule exists. He does take seriously what you say. He will remember it, and so will you, and it will be easier for you to be firm and to follow through on the limits you set.

Take a look at your own behavior, however, and be sure not to do anything to cause your child's behavior. If you push food on your child and don't take no for an answer, he will be rude about refusing. If you limit the amount that your child can eat, he will beg you for second and third helpings. If you say, "no dessert until you eat your vegetables," he will bargain with you. "How many bites? That's too many!" If you have an investment in getting food into your child, you will put up with negative behavior in hopes that he will eat something, and his behavior will get worse and worse.

Cooking with Your Child and Growing a Garden. Your child will love being in the kitchen with you and being allowed to help, and he will love growing a garden with you. Keep in mind, however, that the main point of the activity is to have an enjoyable time together—it is not to get the child's help or even to teach him anything. Some parents cook or grow gardens with their children in hopes that doing so will make them eat better. It won't work. If that is your motive, your child will be on to you in a flash and will be less, not more, likely to eat even the food he grew with his own hands. If, on the other hand, you grow the garden and cook the food for the sheer joy of it, then your child probably will take more of an interest in the food and will be more likely to eat. Preschoolers can learn about a new food by talking about it, studying it, cooking it, and growing it. Their learning, however, only makes them more willing to *taste* it. It still takes many tastes to learn to like it.

Eating in Restaurants. Seventy percent of families eat out at least once a week. If you can afford it, eating out is a way of having pleasant and relaxed family time and getting that all-important family meal. Keep in mind that the first priority is *having* a meal. The second is the *nutritional quality* of the meal—but you can have both. If you eat out only rarely, you can afford to throw nutritional considerations to the winds and let your child order only what he likes. If you eat out a lot, it's worth setting up some simple guidelines to encourage nutritious eating without having him load up on fat and sugar. Here are some suggestions:

- Have at least two food groups. You'll probably find that this happens automatically anyway. A hamburger and a bun would qualify, as would pizza. By the time your child has the crust and the topping, he's covered at least two and probably three or four food groups. A salad and bread would work; so would bread and ice cream.
- Limit sweets to one per meal. If your child has a milkshake or soda for his beverage, that counts as his sweet. However, if he has milk or water to drink, he can still have a sweet.
- Keep it down to one fried food per meal. For example, if your child has French fries and a hamburger, a fried apple pie for dessert would add up to too many fried foods. To have the apple pie, he would have to skip the French fries, and to fill up he might need a second hamburger. Grilled foods like burgers don't count as fried foods because they aren't so greasy. It's the starch in French fries and the starchy coating on chicken nuggets and fish sandwiches that tend to soak up the grease.
- Keep dessert portions child-sized, just as you would at home. That might mean splitting a dessert with someone else at the table, or ordering a sundae rather than a banana split.

The children's menus in restaurants are extremely limited. They are made up of uninformed adults' ideas of what children like and can master easily. If you give him some help, your child can order from the wider range of foods on the adult menu. Consider ordering a la carte, or take a look at the list of appetizers. Split meals with your child, or plan for tomorrow's dinner by taking home leftovers. Keep in mind that in a restaurant, as at home, your child isn't going to know ahead of time how food will taste to him and how much he will be able to eat. Have in mind ahead of time what you are willing to pay for, and give your child some guidelines. Don't let your child order lavishly and then waste food, but don't expect him to eat all of everything he has ordered either. He might order something and not like it. It's hard not to get mad about food refusal when you're paying the bill, but keep your cool, and let your child figure out this problem for himself. Don't try to force him to eat the food, or he'll get upset and behave badly. Have some options available, just as you do at home: the restaurant can give you a basket of bread, and he can fill up on bread and milk. Then sit back and see what he figures out. Will he eat it, even though it doesn't taste as good as he hoped? Will he try to get you to share your dinner? Keep in mind that you don't have to share if you don't want to. Also keep in mind that whining and complaining is no more appropriate in a restaurant than at home. Your preschooler needs to do his part to make mealtime pleasant for other diners.

BE REALISTIC ABOUT MEALTIME ETIQUETTE

Your preschooler will enjoy serving himself from the serving dishes and pouring his own milk from a small pitcher. He may even eat more and be more experimental with food when he serves himself, but that is not the point. Letting him learn how to do it and have the feeling of accomplishment is the point.

As with everything else, he will have a lot to learn. He may serve himself way more than he can reasonably eat at first, but that is just because his eye hasn't been trained yet. You can encourage him to take a small serving and show him how to do that; then reassure him that you have made plenty and he can have more if he wants it. The point here is to avoid wasting a lot of food or depriving someone else in the family of their share, not having your child clean his plate. In fact, don't expect him to clean his plate. He won't know how much he needs to eat to be satisfied until he eats it, and that is likely to mean that he leaves food. *Food waste is an unavoidable part of feeding young children.* Even adults can't always estimate ahead of time how hungry they are, and encouraging your child to clean his plate will teach him to ignore his hunger and fullness.

Use Serving Bowls. Put the food on the table in serving bowls and let your child help himself. That will give him the most control over what and how much he eats, and he will eat better when he has that control. If you serve your child, ask him ahead of time if he wants the food, and check as you serve to find out how much he wants. If you must serve plates in the kitchen, be sure to reassure your child that he doesn't have to eat what you serve if he doesn't want to and that there is more of everything if he wants more. And deliver on your promise. You will not be able to trick or fool your child into letting you do his job of *what* and *how much* he eats, and if you try it will backfire.

Your child will likely want only part of a dish that you think goes together—he will be interested in only the spaghetti from the spaghetti and meat sauce, and that is fine. Eventually he will get around to eating the meat sauce, but only if you don't make a fuss. He will take only the rice from the stir-fry and rice, and that is fine. Eventually, he will take a small serving of the stir-fry, and chances are that he will eat only the parts that are familiar, and that is fine. Then he will want to dig through the dish of stir-fry and take out the parts that he likes. That is not fine. That is depriving someone else of the pleasure and enjoyment of their meal.

By the same token, it is fine for your child to have several helpings of something he really enjoys, as long as it doesn't deprive someone else of their share. Eating is a social activity, and sharing the food is part of that sociability. Do have enough food to go around, and have enough so there is something popular or acceptable left over. That is the only way you can be sure that everyone gets enough to eat. You may not feel you can afford to serve enough shrimp, asparagus, or fresh strawberries so that everyone can eat their fill. That is fine. Serving those foods and making clear that there isn't a lot of them will encourage everyone to savor them. However, be sure to make plenty of rice or noodles, and put lots of bread on the table. Some parents of chubby children "run out" of food as a way of cutting down on the amount their child eats. Don't do it. You are not fooling anyone. Your child will feel deprived and preoccupied with food—and hurt that you are trying to trick him.

Mealtime Behaviors. Your child will likely eat with his fingers or use his fingers to load his silverware, then eat with his silverware. That's fine. He will likely enjoy his food more if it is lukewarm rather than hot and will do better with salad without dressing so he can pick it up with his fingers. The suggestions for toddlers in the section on making food easy to eat (chapter 8, page 307) are appropriate for the preschooler as well. Keep in mind that when you follow those recommendations, you are setting up the meal to help your preschooler to be successful. You are not catering to him or trying to get him to eat. Also keep in mind that while your child's chewing and swallowing abilities are better than they were when he was a toddler, they are still not as good as those of an older child or an adult. He can still lose track of food in his mouth and choke more easily, so he has to be seated, supervised, and calm when he eats. His swallowing will still be somewhat immature. Instead of using an up-and-back motion of his tongue to propel the food to the back of his mouth like he will when he gets older (try it), he uses his cheeks as if he were drinking from a straw (try that, too). As a result, it will be hard for him to chew and swallow meat, and he may just take the cud out of his mouth and slip it under the edge of his plate. That's fine. Make the meat as moist as you can and offer to cut it up for him. Unlike when he was a toddler, he may even *let* you.

He will squirm. If he doesn't now, he will soon. Squirming seemed to strike each of my children in turn when they were about 6 years old. They would be interested in the meal and the conversation and eat well, but they would squirm. Back and forth on their chair they would go, side to side, leaning on the table, leaning back in the chair, doing pull-ups, first one arm and then the other, stretching first one leg and then the other. Amazing. As closely as I could tell, it had to do with excess energy, and since they were doing their job with eating and not hurting anything, I didn't try to get them to sit still. When they got a bit older, the squirming went away—mostly.

Your child will learn to behave nicely at the table. "A trip of a thousand miles," said the Chinese philosopher, "begins with a single step." Head Start teachers know this very well. Among other school-readiness skills, Head Start teaches preschoolers appropriate behavior at family-style meals. At the beginning of the year, meals are chaotic and lessons are basic: sit on your chair; eat off your plate—your *own* plate; use the serving spoon; say "no, thank you;" use words to ask and tell (don't whine and cry); keep your hands to yourself. Barbara Turner, Health and Nutrition Coordinator of Broome County Head Start in Binghamton, New York, reminds us to give children recognition not for eating but for all the contributions they make to a pleasant mealtime. "I like having you at the table" is good recognition for a child who isn't ready to eat anything. "Nice passing" or "I like hearing you talk about that" are ways of recognizing the child's positive mealtime behaviors and getting the pressure *off* eating. When children feel comfortable and accomplished at the table, they will eat. Turner says that teachers have a hard time in September when new children come in. For instance, they have to make sure they are on guard with clean serving spoons. Often children who are not used to passing and serving lick the serving spoon. The teachers have to be quick before that licked spoon goes back in the bowl! By the end of the year, teachers can relax. Children set the table, pass food to one another, enjoy being at the table, attend to their own eating, make conversation, and clear away their dishes. Turner points out that children's self-esteem is built on their accomplishments and that they take pride and have good feelings about themselves when they are successful with mealtime behaviors. Achievement and a positive atmosphere give them confidence to accomplish even more.

Turner asked me what I thought about encouraging but not forcing children to try foods. I said it is okay to encourage, but only if the adult *clearly* knows the different between encouraging and forcing. I have worked with so many child care people who think that a *no-thank-you bite* is encouraging that I am skeptical about whether most people can make that distinction. The obligatory taste of the so-called no-thank-you bite isn't encouraging; it is forcing. (See chapter 8, pages 331-332, for more on the no-thank-you bite.) To be truly encouraging, the child must be allowed to say "no, thank you" before he ever puts the food on his plate. "Why don't you try some spinach? You might like it" is encouraging, but only if you are prepared to take no for an answer. I am not singling out child care providers in making this criticism. I don't think they are particularly prone to being controlling. When it comes to children and food, I have observed that almost everybody can easily become controlling. Not only that, but so many children have been controlled with eating that they have become extremely sensitive to adult maneuvers that feel anything *like* pressure. Being controlling with children's eating is so counterproductive and even destructive that it is important to bend over backward to avoid feeding behaviors that come anywhere *close* to control.

Stay on Your Side of the Line. A major part of your job with feeding is staying on your own side of the line—not getting into your child's business of what and how much he eats. If you do your job with feeding—but no more—your child will eat. If you review our discussions on mealtime mechanics and planning meals and snacks in chapter 8 (pages 329-336 and 336-338), you will see that you still have plenty to do. Sit down, enjoy your child, and enjoy your own food. Your child will eat well. I can't overemphasize the importance of your being there and enjoying the meal with your child. A mother complained to me about her preschooler's poor eating—she felt she had to lean on him to get him to eat his cereal and toast before they went off to the child care center. Then it hit her why it was happening. Every morning she parked him in the kitchen to eat his breakfast while she ran around, putting on her makeup, finding her keys, rushing to get ready to leave the house. Reluctantly, she decided to get up 15 minutes earlier so she could sit down to have breakfast with her child. He ate better, and they both felt better beginning the day having had a few pleasant minutes with each other.

In the preschooler segment of the videotape *Feeding with Love and Good Sense,* the vignette with Adam has made a particular impact on parents. Adam is eating his spaghetti in first-rate preschooler fashion—spearing his spaghetti with his fork, slurping it into his mouth, and helping it along with his fingers. Meanwhile he is clearly enjoying making conversation with his parents, telling them about the events of his day. He runs out of spaghetti and asks his mother, "can I have some more?" In the grand tradition of generations of parents, his mother responds, "yes, but first you have to eat the rest of your food." Adam eats his way bravely through his peas and grapes and drinks his milk. He even manages to choke down two slices of the hated cucumbers, although we viewers hold our breath, noticing his difficulty swallowing and wondering if he will simply throw up on his plate. Having the advantage of being outside observers, we can feel for Adam. The longer he eats, the more glum and discouraged he becomes. He loses interest in the mealtime conversation, leans back in his chair, pulls his knees up to his chest, and watches his fist as he throws it into the air. His father scolds him, "sit up straight, Adam." Words couldn't say it more clearly: as far as Adam is concerned, this meal is a real bust. Finally, his father gives him more spaghetti. Adam perks up and undergoes a complete personality transplant in front of our eyes. He goes back to being a happy, companionable boy who enjoys being with his family. Adam's parents have gotten so caught up in getting food into him that they have spoiled their time together.

I don't think that Adam's parents enjoyed making him miserable. However, they felt obligated to make him jump over his fruit and vegetable hurdles before they would let him eat what he wanted. They are not alone. Adam's misery has been responsible for a lot of parental reform with feeding. However, parents still worry, and they still ask me, sometimes in an exasperated, how-can-you-let-that-kid-get-away-with-that voice, "Well, what would you do? Just let him have more spaghetti?" My answer? "Yes. Adam's eating is not a chore that he *has* to do. It is a pleasant and rewarding behavior that he *gets* to do." Sooner or later—if not at this meal then the next or the one after that—Adam will get filled up on spaghetti and take an interest in peas. Or grapes. But probably not cucumbers. We all are entitled to some likes and dislikes, and it appears that Adam and cucumbers will never be close. It takes a long time to learn to like a variety of food, and if Adam's parents back off, he will make it his business to push himself along and learn. If his parents continue to force him to eat, they will take away all his initiative and he will eat vegetables only because his parents make him. When they stop pushing him, he will stop eating them altogether—or just eat them out of obligation, not because he really likes them.

Adam's parents are already doing a wonderful job getting an attractive, varied meal on the table. They have laid out and exercised the expectation that he will be at the table with the rest of the family. It is clear that he is hungry, so they likely haven't let him eat before the meal. They make conversation with Adam and make him an important part of the family at mealtime. They are already doing a great deal! Why in the world do they sign up for more work by taking it upon themselves to do his job of getting food into him?

I can't answer that question, but I will tell you that Adam's parents behave in a way that is more typical than atypical. In the Western Massachusetts Growth Study researchers found that parents of preschoolers provided children with structured meals and snacks. However, when the children came to the table, the parents controlled what and how much children ate of the food that parents offered. To visualize that control, think of the hurdles Adam's parents made him jump before he could

have a second helping of spaghetti. Think of the last time you
said to your child "You must eat your vegetables before you can
have dessert" or the last time you asked "Don't you think
you've had enough?" Despite being overly controlling at mealtimes, between times, the Massachusetts parents weren't controlling enough: Children were allowed to help themselves
between meals with no limits to the refrigerator and cupboards.
They could eat whatever they wanted, whenever they wanted
it.[2] The implications to nurturing and child development of this
approach to feeding are grave. Children love their parents and
want them around. They do more and dare more when their
parents are nearby. However, when the Massachusetts parents
were around, they spoiled eating. The only way children could
eat without interference was by going off on their own to do it.
The learning? That to be your own person, you have to be by
yourself. That kind of eating is just eating—it's not about love
and companionship and getting your needs met.

YOUR CHILD WILL EAT WHAT HE NEEDS

Trust your child's capabilities with eating. If you do your part
with feeding, your child will eat. Your child knows how much
he needs to eat, and he will continue to know that throughout
his growing-up years. Given the support of regular and predictable meals and snacks, your child will come to the table
hungry and eat with focus and attention until he is full. Then he
will stop, knowing another meal or snack is coming later and he
can do it all over again. He will eat more or less depending on
how active he has been and how fast he is growing. He will eat
the right amount to get the body that is right for him.

Given the support of regular and varied meals and snacks,
he will eat the variety he needs to get a nutritionally adequate
diet. If you serve a variety of food, over time he will learn to
like a variety of food and will maintain the dietary variety he
needs. In his tasting experiments, he will develop a skill for a
lifetime: he will be prepared to learn to like the new food he
encounters.

Your child will learn to behave nicely at the table. If you
have pleasant family mealtimes and have reasonably good table
manners yourself, your child will become a pleasant companion

at the table and, over time, develop more and more positive eating behaviors. Preschoolers take real pleasure in the accomplishment of eating in grown-up ways, in getting to the point that they can comfortably eat in a restaurant and at a friend's house.

The key phrase is *over time*. Clara Davis, a researcher whose work is cited in appendix I, did a famous experiment in which she found that toddlers who are offered a variety of nutritious food self-selected a nutritious diet and grew well. Davis did another, but lesser known, study that was just as helpful. Davis observed children's temperament and reactions to new foods and their food acceptance overall, and she observed how their food acceptance changed over time. She identified three classes of children: the enthusiastic, the steady accumulator, and the late bloomer.[3] I raised one of each. Curtis was the enthusiastic one. He was interested in new food, and even when he was a toddler he would taste it readily and learn to like new foods quickly. However, as I told you before, encouraging him to try something that he had decided not to try was simply out of the question. He would push himself along, but no one else was to push him! Lucas, on the other hand, was a steady accumulator. He was skeptical of new food, but with a little encouragement he would take a taste and would keep tasting until he learned to like the food. Kjerstin was a late bloomer. She ate a limited assortment of food throughout grade school and would on no account let a vegetable past her lips. However, in the pattern that Davis pointed out, when she got into the late grades she seemed to discover that she was missing out on quite a lot and made it her business to learn to like more food. Now she loves vegetables.

If your child is a late bloomer, there is nothing you can do about it. You can't make a child eat foods he doesn't want. If you try, or if you do a lot of catering or short-order cooking, you will simply rule out the possibility for ever after that someday he will make it his job to learn.

CHILDREN NEED POSITIVE FEEDING TO EAT AND GROW WELL

As you will discover in appendix I, "Children and Food Acceptance," and appendix J, "Children and Food Regulation,"

it is estimated that as many as 35 percent of children have
some sort of eating difficulty. Some children have trouble eating
and growing properly because they have medical conditions,
neuromuscular problems with chewing or swallowing, developmental delays, or because the food they are being offered isn't
right for them. However, *to the limits of their ability,* once medical
and nutritional issues are resolved, children are able to push
themselves along to learn to do a good job with their eating.
Parents can learn to present food and adjust their expectations
of their child so they can have a satisfying feeding relationship
and children can do a good job with eating.

If you are able to feed well, you have every reason to expect
that your child will grow up to get the body that nature intended for him. In my judgment, much of the current increase in
childhood obesity can be explained by distortions in the feeding
relationship. Current economic and social trends in eating as
well as current attitudes about food and weight have conspired
against children and families and have distorted feeding to the
point that children don't get the support they need to eat and
grow properly. More children than ever before live in poverty.
While it's not only the poor who are unable to keep their children safe, poor parents have particular difficulty providing, and
it is children who live in limited social and economic circumstances who show the greatest increase in childhood obesity.
When parents are unable to keep their children safe, those children have a greatly increased risk of eating and growing poorly.
We all absolutely depend on nurturing and reliable access to
food to be able to do a good job with eating.

It is beastly difficult in today's world to provide positive
and reliable access to food. As I have pointed out in *Secrets of
Feeding a Healthy Family,* there are so many barriers of time,
skills, and money; weight and health concerns that make food
seem like medicine or, worse, the enemy; lack of food traditions
that guide us in fitting food into our ever-changing lifestyles.
Parents are told that the way to prevent childhood obesity is to
"get" children to eat less and exercise more, so parents try to do
what they think is right, but in the process they promote the
very thing they are trying to prevent. If there is a meal, parents
feel obligated to interfere with children's prerogative of what
and how much they eat. It doesn't work. In my clinical experience, when parents are overly controlling about what and how

much children eat or erratic about providing, children grow up incapable of managing what and how much they eat. As I indicate in appendixes I and J, the research backs me up.

The key, of course, is maintaining the division of responsibility in feeding, making sure to execute your feeding tasks and not crossing into your child's area of what and how much he eats. However, while feeding and growth problems grow out of too much pressure or lack of support with feeding, those problems can also begin when a child's characteristics overwhelm the parent's ability to cope. As I have pointed out before, when children display certain eating attitudes and behaviors, it is extraordinarily difficult to stand your ground with your feeding tasks and to stay out of the child's area of deciding what and how much he will eat. Of course, the possibilities can be endless, but let's take a look at some of those attitudes and behaviors that might make it hard for you to stick to your job with feeding.

The Child Who Is Cautious about Food. A young mother was very concerned about her 4-year-old son's poor food acceptance. Adrian would eat only from the usual short list of food, plus infant cereal, and that only after a lot of hassle getting him to the table. Despite the fact that the mother went through the cupboard with Adrian ahead of time, choosing what he would be offered to eat, Adrian was reluctant to go to the table and, once he got there, he was even more reluctant to consume anything but his milk. He got most of his food by grazing and panhandling. His growth was fine, and his nutritional status was fine, but his mother still worried about whether he was going to be all right.

Adrian had always been cautious about trying new food, the mother explained. Was it possible that he was just born finicky? There were a lot of foods she didn't like. For instance, just looking at butter on bread made her feel like throwing up. I agreed that Adrian, like a lot of children, could be an extra-cautious child who takes a long time to warm up to new food. He could have been born with a particular sensitivity to the taste, texture, and smell of food. Being so tuned in can be positive or negative. Such children can enjoy food a lot, or they can be so upset by the appearance or smell of food that they can hardly bear to have it around. However, I also pointed out that the

finicky eater can be *created*. Parents will often pass their fussiness along to their children by not making foods they don't like
and by not giving their children experience with certain foods.
At the other extreme, parents can pressure the cautious child to
get him to eat and thereby make the problem worse. It
appeared with Adrian that the problem was *both*. From the time
his mother introduced him to solid foods, Adrian had been
reluctant to eat, and she felt she had to force him to eat. His
mother made a limited number of foods for family meals, but
Adrian wouldn't even eat what she cooked. The parents, worried that he would develop the mother's food aversions, had
bribed, overencouraged, persuaded, pushed, threatened, and
punished. Through it all, he held steadfast. He wouldn't eat
anything he didn't want to eat.

It won't surprise you that I taught the parents the division
of responsibility in feeding. Then I told them that the main task
with a finicky eater was not to get him to accept more food but
to keep his eating from being an issue. Adrian needed to learn
to cope with his sensitivities and to behave nicely at the table.
The parents established the structure of meals and snacks, put
on one or two of the foods that he loved the best at each feeding
time, and let him eat those foods or anything else on the table
until he got full. They didn't ask him what he wanted to eat,
they just put it on the table. Then they said to him, "You don't
have to eat if you don't want to, but you do need to come and
keep us company for a couple of minutes while we eat." Then
they taught him to be polite about refusing food and let him
down when he had finished.

At first, it was a big accomplishment for Adrian to stay at
the table without making a fuss. Gradually he learned to
behave at the table, and after a week or two, he started to sneak
up on new food. He didn't want any spaghetti, but he did ask
his parents to leave the serving dish near his plate. Then he
wanted a little spaghetti on his plate, and his mother was wise
enough to reassure him and she helped him serve it saying,
"You don't have to eat it if you don't want to." By the fourth
week, he occasionally tasted a mouthful of food, then took it
out again. His parents reassured him, "That's all right. You
don't have to swallow it if you don't want to." Adrian made
rapid progress because his parents really meant what they told
him: "It's up to you to choose what you eat."

Eventually, Adrian learned to behave himself at the table, to drink his milk and eat his bread and to make do with what the rest of the family was eating. He learned not to make a fuss and was proud of that, and proud of himself for behaving nicely at the table. He was successful with his mealtime *behavior* and what he did and didn't eat took on far less importance. As his parents held steady, over the next couple of years he learned to eat more and more foods and eventually mastered a pretty good assortment of food. He keeps learning. Given his history with eating and his cautious nature, he might not get to the point that he is a robust or enthusiastic eater, but he will do a good job to the extent that he is able. In my experience, when children have trouble with eating early on, their eating tends to be somewhat fragile and easily disrupted. When they are stressed or excited or preoccupied with some wonderful new life experience, they may not eat too well for a while. However, when the upset blows over, they go back to eating as well as ever and make up for lost time.

The Child Who *Loves* to Eat. Parents prefer it when a child *loves* to eat. Well, they do and they don't. Like other behavioral extremes, a child's passion for food can make parents take evasive action. Given the normatively distorted—that is, generally screwed up—eating attitudes and behaviors in our culture, parents might assume that if a child loves to eat, he will eat too much and he will be too fat. Not so. Children are such good regulators that if you truly maintain a division of responsibility in feeding, your child will stop in the middle of a bowl of ice cream when he gets enough. However, your child will respond to his passion for food by overeating if you are so alarmed by his gusto that you take evasive action and try to get him to eat less. He will be afraid that he won't get enough to eat and will be prone to overeat when he gets the chance. He has to manage this—you can't do it either directly or indirectly. If you react to your child's passion for food by giving him only food that doesn't *inspire* passion, then he will be all the more ardent about the forbidden food.

In *Secrets of Feeding a Healthy Family* I told the story of Joshua, who couldn't wait for Friday night. Joshua's parents hailed from the "I know I should but . . . " group of people who have trouble getting their shoulds and wants to come together when it comes to eating. They tried to follow what they thought were the eating rules to prevent disease, but they kept getting ambushed by their fat cravings. Their strategy was to plan for the ambush. They ate drab food all week and then gave themselves weekends off to enjoy their food. For the parents, it seemed to work. They ate a few—well, all right, quite a few—foods they had been craving, then buckled down again on Monday morning. The problem was that Joshua, their 8-year-old, was too interested in food. Joshua ate what his parents prepared—and then some. It seemed that Joshua couldn't get filled up. During the week he seemed to be constantly hungry and begged for snacks. On the family's Friday trips to the movies, Joshua was up and down all evening—visiting the snack bar to buy nachos, ice cream, buttered popcorn, and all the treats his parents wouldn't let him have any other time. At his grandmother's house, Joshua couldn't get enough of her fried chicken, mashed potatoes with gravy, and salad with blue cheese dressing.

I encouraged Joshua's parents to lighten up. I taught them some meal-planning strategies and warned them against being so restrictive with their food that they had to take a vacation from it. I pointed out that Joshua's energy needs were high and his stomach was still relatively small. He needed some higher-calorie foods throughout the week to have the energy to go on. The new strategy worked. Joshua settled down with his eating. On Friday nights his parents let him have one treat at the movies, and that was all he wanted. After all, now he could get those foods at home. His grandmother worried at first that he didn't like her fried chicken anymore, but he reassured her that now his mom made it sometimes, too.

Joshua was on the right track with his passion for good food. If your child truly enjoys eating, he will have the best chance of growing up to be healthy and well nourished and maintaining a consistently healthy weight. People who are positive and trusting of their sensations and feelings about eating are able to tune in accurately to their hunger, appetite, and satiety and eat the amount and type of food they need. All food is wonderful. Children can't be passionate about vegetables if they aren't allowed to be passionate about ice cream or boxed macaroni and cheese dinner.

But here is a word of warning: don't go off in the other

direction either. In some families, a child gets a lot of positive attention for being a hearty and robust eater. Grandparents and aunts and uncles will say, "Bobbie is such a good eater! I wish my little Jeffrey ate that well!" Bobbie, of course, basking in the praise and attention, will eat all the more, and in the process he'll lose track of his own feelings of hunger and fullness. Unless they are subjected to outside interference, even children who *love* to eat still have a reliable stopping place.

The Fat Child. Four-year-old Toni's parents had recently been told by her pediatrician, albeit reluctantly, that Toni was too fat. Toni was a big girl and had always been big. Her growth had consistently been at the 95th percentile and her height at the 50th percentile, which meant that she was relatively heavy for her height. While the parents were somewhat uneasy about her size and shape, they had hung in there with a division of responsibility in feeding, and the pediatrician had consistently advised taking a wait-and-see approach. Toni was an active girl and very physically coordinated, so her parents couldn't understand why she should be so fat. Recently, however, with all the dire warnings in the media about childhood obesity, they had become alarmed and had pressed their pediatrician for some answers. As he told me when we talked about it, he was reluctant to make an issue of it with them because he was afraid the parents would start to restrict Toni's food intake and precipitate an eating disorder. However, he too was concerned about all the recent alarm and public health warnings about child obesity, so he had finally told them they should do something about Toni's weight.

So the parents had begun to restrict Toni, limiting the amount she could have at meals to a single serving, cutting way down on the fats and sweets and limiting her snacks to an apple or some carrot sticks. It wasn't long before Toni let them know that they were on the wrong track. Toni couldn't get her mind off food. This was new for her—in the past she had eaten well but not a lot, at least compared with some of her thinner friends, and she had seemed to forget all about eating between times. Now Toni thought about food all the time, constantly pleaded for food handouts, snuck into the kitchen to eat, and cried when they refused her food. To their embarrassment, her parents heard themselves saying to her, "No, you have had enough—that's all for now. Why do you want to eat so much?"

They could tell that Toni felt ashamed of herself for wanting so much, but they didn't know what to do about it.

Fortunately, the next stop was my office, and we were able to get some things straightened out. First of all, I told them that there was nothing wrong with Toni's size and shape. She wasn't stylishly thin and she was above the 95th percentile for size and shape, but that was the way she had always been. Furthermore, she had demonstrated with her consistent growth that her weight was normal for her and that she was a good regulator— she was capable of eating what she needed. Not only that, but it was apparent that her parents had given her the support she needed to do a good job with her eating. I told them my recommendation was to go back to doing what they had done before: feeding Toni well and letting her develop the size and shape that was right for her.

Weight and Health. Toni's parents were relieved about the feeding part, but they were still concerned about her weight and her health. What about all the research that says that obesity is unhealthy? I reassured them that despite the media reports, and despite current public health recommendations, the answers about the connections between weight and health are far from being clear. In general, people who seem to suffer negative health consequences connected with weight are those who are very thin or very fat. Toni didn't qualify for either category. Furthermore, people who seem to have the most medical consequences of high body weight are those who became fat as adults, those whose weight has fluctuated, and those who didn't maintain other positive health behaviors like being active and taking good care of themselves with respect to eating. The bottom line, however, was that even in the unlikely prospect that Toni's size and shape persisted into her adult life and in the equally unlikely event that her adult weight was bad for her, in my view there was *nothing we could do to change it*. In fact, if we tried to slim her down, we would make matters worse, not better. As they had demonstrated in their brief experiment, when they restricted Toni she became preoccupied with food and was prone to overeat.

I am happy to say that Toni's parents took my advice, and I am even happier to say that after a week or two of eating quite a bit more than she had in the past, Toni figured out that she could really trust her parents to feed her and she settled right down with her eating. To start with they had a little conversation with her to explain that they were going back to their old ways. However, Toni still had to find out for herself that they really meant it. They said to her, "Toni, we talked with someone who told us that you know how much you need to eat. We have been trying to get you not to eat so much, but that was wrong. From now on, we will do it like we always did before. We will put the food on the table for meals and snacks and you can eat as much as you want."

Now Toni, being a child of rare perception, saw an immediate opportunity. "Does that mean I can have all the cookies I want?" she asked.

"No," said her parents. The answer *is* no, the same for a fat child as for a thin child. The rules are the same. You won't traumatize her with restrictive feeding or make her preoccupied with food by adhering to the rules on dessert or on anything else. "We'll do like we always did before. We'll put your serving of dessert at your plate and you can eat it when you want it. But you can't have seconds on dessert."

Parents Need Support. I was clear with Toni's parents that I wouldn't be able to change her size and shape. There was, however, much that I could do to help Toni and her parents. I could support the parents in going back to feeding her using a division of responsibility. Mostly they needed *moral* support. It is hard for parents of chubby children to be positive and trusting in feeding their children. Taking a chubby child to the ice cream parlor requires steady nerves and a thick skin, because in the parent's mind it goes something like, "they must be thinking, 'why is he letting that fat child have an ice cream cone? No wonder she is fat!'" They needed situational support as well. I went back over the structure and limits of good feeding with them and reassured them that those guidelines were appropriate for Toni. "In fact," I told them, "Toni absolutely depends on the structure and predictability of family meals and predictable snacks to be able to do a good job with her eating."

They had some trouble finding and staying in the middle ground with feeding, but it was only when something happened to undermine their trust in Toni's ability to regulate her food intake. When Toni's grandfather confronted them about Toni's chubbiness, for instance, they briefly revisited their anxieties. However, they were able to explain their philosophy to him, and even though he didn't accept it, he agreed to stop making an issue of Toni's eating and weight. They again became concerned about her weight when they read a news release from the Centers for Disease Control about the "alarming increase in childhood obesity" and had to reassure themselves all over again that they were on the right track. "Are we supposed to put any limits on her at all?" asked the mother one day after they had been to a potluck. When I asked her to be more specific, she continued her story. "When we put the desserts out, all the kids lined up to fill their plates, and they were all hitting on some really gooey looking brownies with thick frosting. Should I have made her stop?"

"How would you have handled it if Toni hadn't been chubby?" I asked her.

She thought a minute, and then got this delighted expression her face. "I would have made her stop," she said. "I would have made them all stop. Those kids were eating up all of those great-looking brownies, and I wanted some for myself!" Great answer! *Superb* answer! Children generally get the best parenting when parents can be honest about their own needs.

Toni's pediatrician, of course, was both relieved and skeptical about my recommendations for Toni's parents. I gave him the summary of my philosophy, and followed it up with a copy of one of my professional journal articles.[4] If I had had this book by then, I would have given him a copy of it and encouraged him to read chapter 2, "Your Child Knows How to Eat and Grow." He was able to see the merit in the approach and be supportive of what Toni's parents were doing. They were relieved. They liked him very much and respected his medical capability, but they were prepared to go elsewhere if he had pressured them to continue to try to get her weight down. They didn't feel they could withstand his skepticism and still hold steady with feeding Toni.

Children Need Reassurance. Children who have been traumatized by feeling that they may have to go without, even briefly, need a lot of reassurance to trust that they will get enough to eat. If the trauma has gone on for a long time, it doesn't take much to make them scared all over again. With Toni, it was a reasonably quick fix because her parents had seen right away that they were on the wrong track. A 6-year-old who had been restrained from birth took longer. Her mother had to be very consistent about offering her meals and snacks and reassuring her she could have as much as she wanted at those times. Rather than dishing up the child's plate in the kitchen as she had always done before, it seemed far more reassuring to her daughter to put the food on the serving dishes on the table and let the child help herself. "Are we going to have the dishes on the table?" her daughter would ask her.

"Yes, we are," answered the mother. "The dishes will be on the table, and you can have as much as you want." It became a mantra that they repeated to each other at every meal. This little girl took longer to settle down, and her mother was pretty anxious in the meantime. It made it harder that the mother was a long-term dieter who had only recently begun to trust her own internal regulators.* But they got through it, and both mother and daughter are doing fine.

Children who grow up with food insecurity often show the same preoccupation with food and likelihood of overeating when they get the chance. A mother who adopted a child from another country said that at first her daughter's response to being presented food was to put her hands behind her back. She had been taught to restrain herself. Once her new parents had reassured her that she could have all she wanted, the child got very excited about food and began to eat huge quantities. The mother wisely reassured her that she would get enough to eat and, far more important, made sure the little girl had plenty of food. After a few weeks her daughter's eating calmed down and she developed a very good sense of when she was full and hungry.

The Vulnerable Child. Children who are small or ill, have medical problems, are developmentally delayed, or simply eat poorly present particular challenges with feeding and parenting. Studies have shown that, compared with children who are not ill, there are consistently more mealtime difficulties in families of

---

*She had worked with me using a method I call *How to Eat.* I have trained other nutrition, health, and mental health professionals in my methods in a workshop called *Treating the Dieting Casualty.* There may be one of these professionals near you. Call the nutrition services department at your local hospital or medical clinic and ask whether they have a trained *How to Eat* specialist.

children with chronic illness, including inflammatory bowel disease, sickle-cell anemia, cancer, and cystic fibrosis. Negative mealtime interactions in all illnesses tend to reflect overall patterns of family functioning.[5] The stress of having a special-needs child can make families compensate in counterproductive ways. It is difficult to adhere to clear limits and set firm expectations with a child you see as being fragile. Parents may show their concern through pressing the child to eat, or by giving him special treats. Ill children are children first and ill second. Being the resourceful little creatures that they are, even the ill child is not above using his parents' concern to his own advantage: "If you don't let me do that, I won't eat." Then, of course, the parent is truly over a barrel—how can you get angry at such a vulnerable child? The answer? Easily! Furthermore, that anger is a good guide that things are out of whack and need to be adjusted.

At times parents' efforts to feed can turn to brute force as they resort to increasingly desperate measures. The parents I met after my presentation in Louisiana were feeding their son in the bathtub. He was truly small. He had been tiny from the time he was born—it seemed not just ordinarily small but the kind of particular smallness that affected little Alice, whose story I told in chapter 2. The boy's doctor had reportedly said to the parents, "Feed him. I don't care how you do it." I am sorry to say that is a piece of advice I have heard all too often, and it never fails to be destructive. I can understand where a physician is coming from in giving such advice—he or she is charged with preserving life, and a physician who doesn't know much about feeding dynamics wouldn't realize how counterproductive such instructions would be. But that advice gives no credit to the child for managing his own eating. It turns parents into force feeders, desperate to get food into their child, fearing for his very life. Those parents were pushing so hard to get food into their child and he was fighting back so hard that among them they made a terrible mess. After the meals, they simply rinsed him down.

It seemed such a desperate situation that it fairly took my breath away, and no way was I going to be able to solve it in 5 minutes after a talk. I offered to do a thorough evaluation with them and asked in passing if at any time their child willingly ate. "Yes," they said, "he eats his breakfast in front of the television, and he eats well at child care." Clearly, this child was capable with his eating when his parents backed off. However, in their desperation and, yes, anger, they had not recognized his capability and continued to torture their son and themselves with feeding. I gave them some advice, being extravagantly careful to point out that without an evaluation I couldn't make it specific to their situation: Establish a division of responsibility in feeding and stop crossing into their son's area of what and how much he will eat. I doubt if they took it, because they were too scared. In my experience, for parents to make such a drastic change they have to be sure I clearly understand them and their situation, and they need some step-by-step follow-up.

Without looking at that child's growth records from birth, I don't know his particular problem. If he is like other children I have evaluated, his growth would have started out low—say around the 5th percentile—then dropped down even further with all the forcing and the resultant poor eating. However, some children truly can't eat enough to preserve themselves—children who have neuromuscular difficulties and can't sustain the energy and muscle control to take in food, children who have heart defects and are too worn out to eat enough, children who are in cancer treatment and don't have the appetite to maintain the nutrition they need to support therapy. In all cases, parents carry a tremendous burden. They feel and are often given responsibility for doing what they simply can't do—get food into the child. Feeding the ill or physically incapable child is like feeding any other child: you maintain a division of responsibility. Providing a range of appropriate food is your responsibility; eating it remains the child's. Children almost invariably eat more, not less, when parents are able to back off with the forcing and put the emphasis on maintaining an appropriate feeding relationship.

Tube-Feeding. If the problem is a physical and medical one and not distorted feeding dynamics, it is far better to tube-feed as an adjunct to family meals than to spoil the feeding relationship with forcing. Dietitian Ellen O'Leary, who coordinates nutrition services in the pediatric oncology unit at Children's Healthcare of Atlanta, has been successful at routinely and matter-of-factly recommending tube-feeding for children who are in cancer treatment. Chemotherapy and radiation therapy may distort children's hunger and fullness cues by slowing down the function of the stomach and intestine. As a consequence, the child may not be hungry enough to eat what he needs to keep his body strong during the chemotherapy. Forcing the not-hungry child to eat is miserable for both parents and children and can permanently spoil the way a child feels about eating. Using supplemental tube-feedings—through either a nasogastric tube or gastrostomy tube—allows the child to eat as little as interests him and lets parents stop trying to get more food into their child than he wants. Children continue to feel good about eating, and parents continue to feel good about feeding. So when the child gets better, they can all go back to normal feeding and eating.

A nasogastric tube goes in through the nose, down the throat, and into the stomach. A gastrostomy tube is placed directly into the stomach through the abdominal wall in a simple surgical procedure. For a young child who won't be self-conscious about having the tube coming out of his nose and taped to his cheek, O'Leary recommends a nasogastric tube. She says they use small, soft Silastic feeding tubes. For children with normal chewing and swallowing, the tubes are comfortable and are not irritating, and they don't complicate swallowing. She has talked with her young patients, about ages 8 years and up, and they have told her that the tubes are comfortable but that they simply don't like the way they look. For older children and for tube-feeding that lasts longer than a couple of months, she recommends a gastrostomy tube. O'Leary generally encourages parents to tube-feed the child at night and gives careful guidance for what and how much goes into the tube-feeding.

O'Leary recently told me that just the other day a toddler was admitted for a bone marrow transplant, and before she could even say "hi" the mother burst out with "we are so, so grateful that Isaac was started on tube-feedings. I know I was resistant, but I just can't tell you what a relief it was when we got home and I did not have to worry about getting food into him every minute of the day!" O'Leary was so pleased with the mother's response, and she was also delighted that he was in such great nutritional shape at the beginning of his procedure. O'Leary's encouragement and matter-of-fact approach is important, because in some settings tube-feeding is viewed as a negative and undesirable step of last resort. In fact, parents are threatened: "If you don't get that child to eat, we will have to put in a tube." A father from New Orleans called me just the other day from a pay phone outside the hospital, desperately opposed to "letting them cut on my kid." I wasn't able to give him any specific advice, but I did reassure him that installing a feeding tube is not major surgery but a simple procedure. Temporarily having the tube-feeding to fall back on could help them get things back on an even keel with feeding.

Colorado speech-language pathologist and swallowing therapist Gretchen Hanna goes on to point out that she often recommends tube-feedings when children are limited to certain textures. For instance, a child born with low muscle tone can have a severely delayed swallow. It may be hard or impossible for him to chew the food, then gather it up in his mouth to propel it down his throat. He may be able only to mouth and swallow puréed foods. Based on a team conference with the family, dietitian, and physician, Gretchen often encourages tube-feeding as a way of relieving pressure on feeding. A child can enjoy a few bites of ice cream or pudding or food of whatever consistency he can manage, and parents can enjoy giving it to him. When parents stop having to worry about the child's overall nutrition, it frees both them and their child to focus on the pleasure of the feeding interaction. Hanna goes on to express her preference for the gastrostomy tube. She points out that for children with swallowing difficulties, unlike children with normal chewing and swallowing, nasogastric feeding irritates the mouth and throat and can further complicate swallowing. The child not only must cope with the difficulties of chewing and swallowing but also must adapt neurologically to a new stimulus (the tube) in the back of his throat. Unless there is a particular reason for using the nasogastric tube, or if it will be needed only briefly, Hanna has found that installing the gastrostomy tube is relatively easy and worth the effort.

Using the tube-feeding as a way of *preserving, restoring,* and *supporting* the pleasure of normal feeding, rather than as an *alternative* to feeding, is the key. A 1998 study showed that mothers of children requiring gastrostomy-tube-feeding initially resented the decision as "unnatural," but immediately after placement of the tube most experienced relief that their child was receiving adequate nourishment. However, as time passed, all mothers felt growing concern about additional changes that tube-feedings brought to their lives and viewed the gastrostomy-tube placement as a "mixed blessing."[6] Of course, being able to use tube-feeding in a knowledgeable and skillful way requires careful guidance—for that I would recommend that you seek out an experienced pediatric dietitian working in a team with a physician and a pediatric speech-language pathologist or occupational therapist. In managing your child's tube-feeding, keep in mind this little-known fact: children experience hunger and fullness when they are tube-fed, just as they do when they feed themselves orally. Except for children with certain medical conditions like cancer and other complicated medical and neurological conditions, hunger and fullness continue to provide accurate guides to energy needs.

Developmental Disabilities. Katelyn had spina bifida, and after many surgeries she was able to get around reasonably well using her braces and crutches. Katelyn was plump and getting plumper, and her parents were concerned about it. They had long ago been warned that children with spina bifida can easily get too fat, and they were trying to be careful: limiting the amount she ate at meals, not letting her have between-meal snacks. But Katelyn was not willing to go with the program. She protested and complained at mealtime until they would let her have a little more—and a little more after that. Between meals, she managed to get the candy and potato chips she wanted, no matter how her parents tried to hold out against her pleading. In fact, if they wouldn't give them to her, she simply helped herself. Katelyn seemed to be the victim of a self-fulfilling prophecy. There is no evidence that children with spina bifida are incapable of regulating their food intake, and the same holds true for children with Down's syndrome, who presumably are also prone to eat too much and get too fat. The only children who truly can't regulate are children who have Prader Willi syndrome. These children have developmental delays as well as a voracious and boundless appetite with a seemingly tremendously thrifty metabolism.

Predicting to parents that their child will be fat puts a type of curse on the child and on the feeding relationship. Parents begin withholding food, and like any self-respecting and self-preserving child anywhere, special-needs children become preoccupied with food and prone to overeat when they get the chance. They truly get fatter, not because of any innate defect, but because of distortions in feeding dynamics. For Katelyn, the solution was the same as for any other child: restoring a divi-

sion of responsibility in feeding. It was as important and necessary for her parents to be firm with Katelyn as with any other
child, but the firmness had to be realistic. It is realistic to expect
a child to come to the table and cope with what parents have
chosen for the meal or snack. It is not realistic to expect a child
to go hungry.

Given that medical treatments are beyond the scope of this
book, I won't go into the details of managing children with special health care needs, nor even try to touch on most or even
many of those conditions. My intention in writing this section is
to point out that fundamentally your ill or special-needs child is
still a child and that the same principles of feeding apply. Much
about your child is simply normal, and maintaining normal
feeding and preserving your child's normal eating attitudes and
behaviors is all-important. Your child's eating does not have to
be medicalized or spoiled. Neither does your child's experience
of being a child. Authoritative parenting is as important for the
vulnerable or special-needs child as it is for the child without
such challenges. In fact, in some ways it is *more* important.
Children with disabilities require emotional maturity and
particularly good social skills to deal with the emotional and
social challenges that are sure to come. It is all too natural to
feel sorry for a child with special needs and to try to protect
him. However, such protection doesn't really help. To feel good
about themselves, children need to feel they are capable. When
you struggle to determine whether you are being realistic in
your limits and expectations with your special child, ask yourself the same question that Toni's parents asked themselves:
"How would I handle this if he were just a regular child without this problem?"

YOU AND *YOUR* EATING

As I said earlier, you will need to grapple with your own
upbringing with regard to eating in order to do a good job of
feeding your preschooler. It may be that having read the previous pages, you will feel considerable anxiety, wondering if you
are up to the task. Take heart. The fact that you are asking the
question and reading this book is a good sign. As I have said
before, the parents who examine themselves and what they are

doing are the healthy ones. The ones who are likely to be in
trouble are the ones who don't feel uneasy or question themselves but just blame the problem on the child: "What's the matter with that kid? He has to eat!" The blunt truth is that you
can't take your child any further than you have taken yourself.
The encouraging truth is that in feeding your child, you have
the possibility of doing some learning and growing yourself.
The opportunity for our own personal maturation is, after all,
one of the fringe benefits of having children.

As you have read *Child of Mine,* I hope you have been reflecting on your own upbringing with respect to eating and getting
some insight into why you think and feel the way you do. Look
again at the section earlier in this chapter called "Is Your
Preschooler a Good Eater?" This time apply the questions listed
in that section to yourself. You may find, as many do, that you
feel ashamed of your positive feelings about eating. You may
condemn your eating based on your dissatisfaction with your
weight or your blood cholesterol—or even your hips. But eating
isn't something you manipulate to get your body to turn out a
certain way. Eating just *is.* You eat to keep yourself alive and to
give yourself joy. The robust enjoyment of wonderful food is definitely out of fashion and may even seem to be somewhat indecent. Asceticism is decidedly *in,* and those few who can successfully deprive and overcome their base impulses to eat what and
how much they want are regarded with admiration and even
awe by the rest of us. The truth of the matter, however, is that
those truly capable of self-denial are in the minority. Know it or
not, they are paying an enormous price for their self-deprivation
in comfort and emotional and physical well-being.

As I pointed out in *Secrets of Feeding a Healthy Family,*

> current eating attitudes and behaviors are negative.
> The specifics of the advice may vary, but from the
> latest government directives about the "healthy
> diet," to articles in the media about nutrition
> research, to food advertisements everywhere, it
> seems the official attitude about eating is "don't."
> Don't eat too much fat, too much sugar, too much
> salt, too much food, period. Lose weight, eat more
> fiber. It has gotten to the point where we worry
> more about *avoiding* than we do about *eating.*

That negativity doesn't work. It doesn't work with feeding yourself, and it doesn't work with feeding a family. Again, quoting from *Secrets:*

> To feed yourself and your family well, you must build the whole structure on enjoyment. Today, far too much is made of the difficulties of eating: avoiding disease, not getting fat, not *eating* fat. I hope by the time you finish reading this . . . you will have a more positive vision. Put the emphasis on feeding yourself, not on avoiding. Get a satisfying meal on the table, pay attention while you eat it, trust yourself to eat as much or as little as you need, then forget about eating until it is time to eat again. To have your eating fall into place, you have to make it important and gratifying.

The division of responsibility works for feeding yourself as well as for feeding your child. Instead of having someone else do the *what, when,* and *where* for you, however, you do it for yourself. Eat your vegetables—but only if they taste good to you. Learn to like new foods, not by forcing but by sneaking up on them just as your child does: Look but don't taste. Taste but don't swallow. Swallow but don't feel you have to take another bite.

To do the topic of you and your eating justice, I will have to write another book. I have been promising that book for a long time, and for those who have been waiting for it, I can only reassure you: it is coming. I won't say when, but it is coming! For now, I will choose two topics that I have found to be key for adults in realigning their thinking about eating—and lightening up.

Restrained Eating. It is unnatural to deprive, either with amounts or types of food. The blithe assumption that we should be able to eat less and weigh less is embedded in all the messages, from the public health recommendations to the pitches of the weight-loss businesses to the attitudes about body weight in situation comedies and novels. Certainly we will benefit from learning to eat in a way that we don't continually *gain* weight, but that is a different matter. It is absolutely unrealistic to expect a person to maintain an artificially low body weight, because the internal pressure to maintain a consistent and biologically preferred body weight is simply enormous. Anyone who has starved knows that *food* becomes the central issue in life, and that all else pales by comparison. If wisdom and experience aren't enough to make the point, there is research to back it up. Ancel Keys's Minnesota World War II starvation studies with conscientious objectors demonstrated beyond a doubt that starvation is physically debilitating and emotionally life-limiting. Young men who ate half their usual food intake for 6 months and lost 20 percent of their body weight became physically, emotionally, and socially handicapped.[7]

Self-deprivation to lose weight is starvation, and depending on the degree to which you attempt to deprive yourself, you will experience the symptoms of starvation to a greater or lesser degree. People who sustain significant food deprivation make it their life's work and sacrifice enormously to do so. Those people are in the minority. Most people try and fail, often over and over again, in a pattern that the eating disorders people have come to call *restraint and disinhibition.* Joshua's parents showed this pattern by taking weekend vacations from low-fat eating, as did Toni's mom in her attempts and periodic failures to restrict her daughter's food intake. As I point out in appendix J, "Children and Food Regulation," that pattern in parents is associated with excess weight gain in children, and it is associated with unstable body weight in adults.

Going without and then periodically making up for lost eating opportunities has become such a part of our eating culture that it seems normal. It is not. Restraint and disinhibition are built into our current preoccupation with fat avoidance, as people restrict themselves on high-fat food, then throw away all eating controls and eat a great deal when they think the food is low in fat. Advertising panders to our need to periodically throw away control by promoting tanker sizes of soft drinks and monster sandwiches. Such contradictory and inconsistent approaches do not work with feeding children, and they don't work with feeding ourselves either. Find the middle ground. You don't have to give in to every eating impulse, but you do need to eat the foods you like and tune in while you eat them.

Emotional Eating. I may have to stop listening to public radio. Yesterday, the topic that had me grinding my teeth was

"Avoiding Emotional Eating." According to the author of the day, emotional eating is bad—we aren't supposed to eat for emotional reasons, and if we do it will make us fat, unhealthy, and ugly. The guest was condemning the way we use food to make ourselves feel better, help us celebrate, and grease the wheels of social events. Well of *course* we use food in all those ways, and more besides, and there is nothing wrong with it! That's what nurturing is all about—taking good care of our children with food, taking good care of ourselves with food. Feeding ourselves is more than putting fuel in a car or throwing wood on a fire. It is love and joy and feeling soothed and uplifted when we have had a good meal. There is nothing wrong with using food for emotional reasons, and doing so will not disrupt our ability to regulate our body weight or eat a healthy diet. It doesn't follow that if we eat for emotional reasons we will overeat, and even if we do, our body's weight regulation capability is too sophisticated to be so easily overwhelmed. If we overeat today, we won't be as hungry tomorrow or next week, and we will eat less. Or we will be hot and have to take off a few clothes or turn down the thermostat. The body will compensate.

The problem with emotional eating is that most people do it poorly. They feel they shouldn't eat to help lift their spirits or to celebrate, but they do it anyway and then cut loose and do it chaotically or guiltily. They get into the pattern of restraint and disinhibition. It doesn't have to be that way. Let me use myself as an example. Like everyone else, occasionally I feel down, discouraged, and even fed up with the pressure of the moment. Yesterday was one of those days. I have been working far too hard to meet a writing deadline and have no choice in the matter. One of the ways I take care of myself is to make a delicious meal. I had meatloaf, mashed potatoes, and some wonderful gingered broccoli (all recipes from *Secrets of Feeding a Healthy Family*), accompanied by a glass of cold Wisconsin milk. I savored the cooking; I savored the eating and felt uplifted and comforted afterward. Why did it help me? Because I was absolutely dead certain why I was doing it—I was feeling sorry for myself and needed some uncomplicated pleasure. I was also clear about *what* I wanted. It wasn't a walk. I had already walked a lot. It wasn't getting together with friends and family. I had been doing that, too. It wasn't a nap. Ditto. It might have been a month off, but that was out of the question. It was that wonderful meal.

Emotional upset will make you go off your *diet* and eat chaotically, but that is quite a different matter than comforting yourself with food. Continuing to undereat despite all the physical and emotional symptoms I mentioned earlier takes a lot of energy. Stress takes away the energy for sustaining starvation and disinhibits food restriction. It doesn't make you overeat.

Rather than getting caught in this pattern of restraint and disinhibition, be dependable about feeding yourself. Have satisfying meals that include foods you enjoy. Don't make yourself sneak to get your potato chips—include them with your sandwich for lunch. Then eat until you truly feel like stopping— when your mouth has had enough as well as your stomach. Interpret for yourself the division of responsibility in feeding, playing both the role of the parent and that of the child.

Get a good meal on the table, arrange to be hungry for it, eat what tastes good, and continue eating until you truly feel like stopping. Then stop—you'll be able to, because another meal or snack is coming later and you'll be able to do it all over again.

NUTRITIONAL ISSUES FOR THE PRESCHOOLER

In this book, as in raising children, our task is to continually weave together the themes of child development, parenting, and nutrition. At this point, we have accumulated most of the nutritional, feeding, and parenting information you will need to do a good job of feeding your child. However, there are still a few issues to consider, and I have pulled them together here. The issues of more general interest will come first. Here is a list of the topics covered on the next few pages:

- Activity
- Sweets, with particular attention to Halloween
- Fat in your child's diet
- Eating and behavior
- Vitamin and mineral supplements
- Dietary fiber and bowel habits

- Lactose intolerance
- Managing food allergies
- Feeding the child with diabetes

Activity. I consider activity a nutritional topic because your child needs a certain minimum level of activity in order to be able to do a good job regulating his food intake. This topic is covered in more detail in chapter 2, "Your Child Knows How to Eat and Grow" (pages 72-76). In my view, helping your child remain active demands a division of responsibility. You are responsible for providing your child with opportunities to be active and for providing him with a safe place to move and play. He is responsible for deciding what and how much he wants to do. Along with providing your child with opportunities for active play, develop your own tolerance and judgment for a child's normal level of activity and risk taking. Seek out active recreation with your child—bouncing a ball, playing Frisbee, riding a bike or tricycle, going for walks—all of these will reinforce your child's respect and pleasure in his body. However, do it for fun, not because it is good for your child. Don't force activity, and don't feel you have to be your child's training coach or companion in all his physical activity. The point is to set up the situation so that your child can remember that he likes to move and discover what activities he truly enjoys. It is not to make him physically fit or to burn calories or to lose weight. If you become controlling in "getting" your child to be active, it will simply take all the fun out of it for him.

The little research we have on children's physical activity comes in the context of weight-management interventions. However, if we set aside the goal of slimming children down, those studies give us some good information about what helps children to be more active. The greatest impact on children's overall activity level came when their sedentary activity was reduced, not when they were encouraged or even rewarded for being more active.[8] What does that mean? Turn off the television! The American Academy of Pediatrics recommends keeping television watching down to two hours or less a day.[9] Even if children turn to another seemingly sedentary activity like reading or coloring, they are more active and not so sedated as when they are watching television, and it appears to make a significant difference in their overall activity levels. I am not sure that it is as important to limit overall screen time as it is to limit television. The studies haven't been done, so I can only speculate. It certainly seems that children are more actively engaged and not as hypnotized by the computer or video games as they are by television. But neither are they being very creative, and that can have something to do with whether their emotional needs are being met. As I have said before, to do a good job with eating and growth, children need to have their emotional needs met.

Don't worry if your child is bored, and don't try to rescue him from his boredom. It is lovely if you can spend time with your child, but your child also benefits from spending time with himself and from learning to entertain himself. For children, as for adults, boredom can be motivating. Your child will come up with ways to keep himself happily occupied if you aren't too quick to do it for him.

Sweets, with Particular Attention to Halloween. I am writing this in late October. Each year, at least one enterprising writer or reporter approaches me for my views on Halloween candy. The night before Halloween last year a local television station made an emergency visit to my home to consider this critical issue. I had been speaking at a conference all day, and the last thing I wanted to do was to talk with a reporter, but I agreed to do it since they promised they would make it easy for me. It was worth the trouble, because the interview gave me my very first disclaimer. "The views of this interview are not necessarily those of the station management," they wrote across the bottom of the screen as I was holding forth. What had I said that was so alarming and revolutionary? I said that trick-or-treating and eating Halloween candy was a part of being a child and that children needed to be allowed to eat their candy without a lot of interference from their adults. Then I suggested a routine: when the child comes home from trick or treating, let him lay out his booty, gloat over it, sort it, and eat as much of it as he wants. Let him do the same the next day. Then have him put it away and relegate it to snack time and mealtime: a couple of small pieces at meals for dessert and a couple of small pieces for snack time won't crowd out other food and will give him a way of using up the precious stuff.

The interviewer was a tad appalled, but still game about

trying to herd me into what she considered safer pathways. "That's pretty liberal advice," she skeptically pointed out. "Couldn't anything bad happen if parents follow that advice?"

After a moment's reflection I said, "Well, I suppose if children were allowed to eat too much candy they would lose their taste for it, and I think that would be too bad. Candy eating is a wonderful part of being a child." I am not sure if that is the part that got the disclaimer, or whether it was what I said next: "If parents are doing a good job of feeding, even a few days of candy eating aren't going to impair a child's nutritional health. If they aren't, all the candy restriction in the world is not going to make any difference." I stand by that advice, but remember—those aren't the views of the management! Your child needs to learn to manage eating sweets, and to keep sweets in proportion to the other food he eats. Halloween candy presents a learning opportunity. Work toward having your child be able to manage his own stash.

Keep Sugar in Proportion. The only malady caused by sugar is tooth decay. The longer and more often sugar is in contact with the teeth, the more likely it is to cause tooth decay. If your child sips soda or fruit juice or eats candy all the time, he's bathing his teeth in sugar and promoting tooth decay. As a matter of fact, eating crackers or bread all the time will do the same thing—the mouth bacteria learn to grow on whatever is available, and they can learn to survive on complex carbohydrate as well as on sugar. Maintaining structure is the key. For the most part, allowing your child access to food or caloric beverages only at set times will help protect his teeth from decay.

With sugar use in general, the issue is keeping a balance, and balancing is always harder than going to one extreme or the other. Children are born with a sweet tooth. Children need sweets to get the concentrated calories they need. Chapter 8 (page 365) outlines how to keep sweets in reasonable proportion to everything else in the diet and gives a rough guide for doing that, and Figure O.3 in appendix O gives you the sugar content of common sweet foods. The preschooler eats 1,200 to 1,800 calories a day, so his sugar allowance would be 6 to 9 teaspoons of sugar a day. That guideline is intended to help you *relax*, not to make you slavish about adding up your child's sugar intake. If you give your child his serving of dessert with meals, have cookies for snacks now and then, bring home an occasional candy bar, and look the other way on Halloween, your child will get about the right amount of sugar.

You don't have to worry about the sugar you use in cooking and what comes along with other nutritious foods, like the sugar syrup on canned fruit. The fact that a food contains sugar doesn't somehow negate the other nutrients it contains and make it a "bad food." Good cooks use a *little* sugar to make food taste better—not enough to disguise it, just to enhance it. A teaspoon of sugar in a tomato dish takes the harsh edge off the tomato taste and makes the dish more acceptable, especially to younger taste buds. A teaspoon of sugar in the frozen peas gives them a "just-picked" flavor. Some desserts and sweets are very nutritious. Custards, puddings, oatmeal or peanut butter cookies, and pumpkin pie are all good choices. If your child likes sugar on his low-sugar breakfast cereal, or enjoys flavoring in milk, or jam on toast, those are valid uses of sugar.

I object to sugar-coated cereals, and their advertising, primarily because they teach kids that food has to be sweet to be good. Highly sweetened breakfast cereals dyed vivid colors disguise the delicious flavors of grains and promote a substitute food that is more like candy than cereal. When my children were small, I would buy a few boxes of sugar-coated cereal a year for them to eat when we went on camping trips. That was the time we often ate weird food that didn't interest us any other time. They thought it was a big treat and they would wolf it down for snacks. They told me they thought I was being too strict when I wouldn't buy it all the time. I told them I couldn't stand it. But the last laugh was on me—I discovered years later that friends we went camping with thought I gave them presweetened cereals all the time!

Fat in Your Child's Diet. In chapter 8 I pointed out that for young children it is best to make wise and nonrestrictive use of fat. To allow your preschooler to eat enough fat but not too much, provide meals and snacks that include low-, moderate-, and high-fat foods; then let your child regulate his actual fat *intake* with his hunger and appetite. He will eat more when he needs it, less when he doesn't need as much. For more specifics, review Figure 8.3, "Helping Your Child Eat the Right Amount of Fat" (page 352). I am comfortable with those recommendations even for children beyond the preschool years. Until they get through the rapid growth of puberty, children need adequate calories to support their growth.

Don't restrict your child's dietary fat in an attempt to get or keep him slim. The tactic doesn't work, and it will make him overeat on high-fat foods whenever he gets the chance. Correctly realizing that weight-reduction diets are bad for children, many health providers resort to recommending reduction of dietary fat in the chubby child's diet as a presumably indirect tactic for slimming him down. It doesn't work. Unless they are administered with religious zeal and unwavering control, low-fat diets don't slim children down. Telling a child he needs to be on a low-fat diet because of his "health" makes him feel just as bad about himself as being put on a weight-reduction diet. Weight-reduction diets give children the message "you're not all right the way you are." Even if the message is disguised by saying "it's for your health," the child will still know that it is his weight that is the issue. If you are concerned about your child's weight, hang in there with feeding. Follow the guidelines you have learned in this book—offer well-planned, structured meals and snacks and maintain the division of responsibility in feeding. That will give your child his very best chance of growing up to get the body that is right for him.

The Child with Inherited Elevated Blood Lipids. Some very few children may benefit from being started early on a special dietary regimen to control their blood cholesterol and triglycerides. These children have what we call "familial hyperlipidemia." They have inherited a marked susceptibility to heart disease and may benefit from a carefully controlled diet to hold down their levels of blood cholesterol and triglycerides. Children are at risk of having this trait if they have a close relative who has severe heart disease, particularly at a young age. The dietary modifications for a child with familial hyperlipidemia are specific, difficult to administer, and easy to do incorrectly. If the diet is managed incorrectly, it won't do any good.

If your physician determines that your child has familial hyperlipidemia, see a dietitian specializing in this area for instruction and follow-up. Do not attempt to follow the diet on your own. It is too complicated, and you will likely be more rigid and restrictive than you have to be. Furthermore, you will need help maintaining the division of responsibility in feeding. Whenever a child is on a restricted diet, it is far too easy to start making yourself responsible for what and how much he eats. In the long run, you could precipitate eating problems that could worsen his condition.

Eating and Behavior. There are a number of pseudoscientists selling books that say that food allergies cause behavioral problems such as irritability, contrariness, sleeplessness, rebelliousness, and general nastiness. Allergy can have an impact on behavior, not because particular foods directly affect the nervous system but because particular foods can precipitate allergic reactions that, in turn, make a child miserable and crabby. A child with severe dermatitis, stomachaches, intestinal cramps, and headache is likely to be an irritable child and may have trouble sleeping besides, which exacerbates his negative behavior. For the embattled parent, it is tempting to believe that some external, definable, controllable force can be responsible for all these maddening traits. It is extremely difficult to prove, or disprove, a food-allergy basis for a behavioral problem. To prove that a particular behavior is caused by dietary intolerance, you have to keep the environment the same and change only the diet. Since behavior is so complex and changes so rapidly, it is difficult to know whether any improvement is due to a change in diet or a change in other factors. A child may behave better after he is taken off Kool-Aid because he is sensitive to something in the Kool-Aid—or he may behave better because he is impressed by his mother's firmness in refusing to give in to his demands.

People try to use nutritional supplements to solve problems such as hyperactivity, mental retardation, and learning disabilities. They aren't successful. To have a nutritional solution, you must have a nutritional problem. That is, a person can be made better by nutritional supplementation only if the symptoms are caused in the first place by a nutritional deficiency. There is no evidence that any of these conditions is caused by nutritional deficiency. They are often *treated* with massive doses of nutrients, but the treatment doesn't work; in fact, at times it *causes* serious nutritional and physical problems. Deficiency of almost any vitamin or mineral is likely to make someone behave differently because he will be physically weak and susceptible to disease. People with iron-deficiency anemia are lethargic and irritable. Some nutrients, such as niacin and thiamine, are particularly important for a steady and well-functioning nervous system. But if your child is eating a variety of foods and growing well, he is unlikely to be deficient in any nutrient.

Food calories are the one nutritional factor that is likely to have a direct impact on your child's behavior. A child who is hungry is likely to be tired, irritable, and contrary. Sometimes a hungry child is so contrary that he won't eat. The child who is very physically active and enthusiastic will often get so busy and involved that he won't notice that he's getting hungry until it is too late. For a time, he will go on nerves and excitement alone, but he will eventually collapse before your eyes into a cranky, unmanageable heap, or become even more frantically active in response to hunger. The busy and active child is a likely candidate for a pattern of sugar jags because he will want something he can get down in a hurry that doesn't interrupt his schedule too much. Stand firm. Insist that he calm down and come to the table and spend some time eating. Once he finds out that you mean business and gets to the table, he will likely eat just as enthusiastically as he plays. Be particularly careful to choose snacks for him that have a balance of protein, fat, and carbohydrate. He needs to have his food stay with him long enough so he can get some of his playing done. It's such a chore for him to get himself settled down and ready to eat; it may work out better for both of you if you provide food that will last him a while.

Can dietary restriction in general, or of artificial colors and artificial flavors in particular, help control hyperactivity in children? Perhaps, but only for a few. Carefully controlled studies have shown that a fraction of one percent of very young hyperkinetic children in controlled experiments show a mild decrease in hyperactive behavior as the result of dietary restrictions.[10,11]

Vitamin and Mineral Supplements. If your water is inadequately fluoridated, your child may need to take a fluoride supplement. For more specific information about fluoride supplements, see appendix P, "Vitamins and Minerals for Children." Beyond that, if you are preparing a nutritionally adequate diet, eating it yourself, and presenting it in a neutral and matter-of-fact fashion, your child will not need to take vitamin-mineral supplements. Sooner or later he will eat well and will provide himself with an adequate diet.

Nutrients that have been shown by nutritional surveys to possibly be low in children's diets include iron, zinc, vitamin A, vitamin D, vitamin E, folic acid, and vitamin B6. For children as young as 6 years of age, calcium is increasingly a problem if they are drinking sodas and juice rather than milk. Good food choices, of course, can ensure that your child gets as much as he needs of these nutrients. Meat is a good source of zinc, iron, and vitamin B6. Milk is a good source of calcium, vitamin A, and vitamin D. Dark green and deep yellow vegetables give vitamin A, and the dark green ones give folate as well. Folate is also in whole grains, and enriched flour is now routinely supplemented with folic acid. Read your bread, roll, or breakfast cereal label to be sure the flour used is enriched flour. Vitamin E is in vegetable oils. Don't get too caught up in evaluating your child's diet; put your emphasis on what goes on the table; then *pay attention to whether he seems energetic and is growing well.* If observing his food intake and assessing it for nutritional adequacy is making you nervous, stop. He is probably doing okay. When I actually sit down to calculate nutrient intake in detail, I am always surprised at what odd diets add up to nutritional adequacy. Pay more attention to what you are offering (and the way you are offering it) than you do to what he is eating. Overall that will reflect his nutritional status much more clearly than any analysis of what he happens to accept on a few isolated days.

Specific Supplement Recommendations. However, if you just *can't* relax until you give your child a supplement, read on. Use one of the standard brands. Choose a broad-spectrum vitamin-mineral supplement that contains at least all the nutrients listed above as possibly lacking, in quantities no greater than 100 percent of the DV (daily value) of most nutrients. Centrum for children is a good brand and is superior to some of the cute supplements, both because it has a wide variety of nutrients *and* because it doesn't disguise itself as candy. Cute supplements tempt children to sneak around and take too many, and that can be toxic, especially if the supplement contains iron. To save a little money, compare the label on the children's broad-spectrum store brand in your pharmacy with the Centrum label. It could very well be almost identical. I have recommended Centrum because it contains a variety of trace elements like copper, chromium, and selenium as well as the run-of-the-mill vitamins and minerals. Supplementing with one nutrient can impair the absorption or use of another, so taking the broader range of nutrients is a good idea. Taking too much iron, for instance, can impair the use of zinc and copper.

It's not a good idea, with children or with anyone else, to supplement with a little of this and a little of that—or, for that matter, a *lot* of this or that. For instance, children require 40 to 45 milligrams of vitamin C per day, but some health professionals recommend—and even sell—vitamin C in doses as large as 500 milligrams per day to their small patients on the grounds that it will prevent colds. It won't. Careful and extensive research shows that dosing with vitamin C in large amounts produces only a drug effect—it acts like a mild decongestant that relieves some of the cold symptoms. It would be better to use a decongestant, because vitamin C dosing is not without its dangers. Some people develop diarrhea or low blood sugar when they take too much vitamin C, and vitamin C overdosing can give a false positive result for urine sugar.

Natural Supplements, Nutraceuticals. Nutraceuticals are nutrients or other natural substances that are marketed for their health or medicinal value. A nutraceutical might be high doses of vitamin C, Echinacea from flowers, or chamomile tea. Because they are marketed as nutrients, not medications, they escape the scrutiny of the Food and Drug Administration and are subject to neither safety testing nor standards of purity and potency. Many people who resort to nutraceuticals are those who are suspicious of medicine or the food supply and are looking for low-cost, do-it-yourself cures. I find the burgeoning popularity of these products to be downright alarming. They have great potential for harm, both from the point of view of injury from taking in toxic levels of unknown substances *and* the associated assumption that the food supply is lacking or even detrimental. Contrary to popular assumption, nutritional supplements *can* have negative side effects. Furthermore, regular food from the regular grocery store *is* nutritious. With very few exceptions, like iodine, no matter how crops are grown, they can't help but contain the vitamins, minerals, and trace elements we depend on them for. While modern farming methods may be hard on the land, the fertilizers and most pesticides used in growing can be washed off in the harvesting process and in your kitchen.

Avoid nutraceuticals for your child. They are untested for safety with children and anyone else, and they are not subject to outside controls for safety and potency. Even if it is labeled as "natural," a nutrient taken in large quantities is no longer a *nutrient*, it is a *drug*. The effect it gives is not a nutrient effect, it is a drug effect.

Dietary Fiber and Bowel Habits. While the jury is still out about whether eating a high-fiber diet can prevent bowel cancer, that is not really the point of eating fiber. Getting enough fiber is a side benefit of eating a nutritionally adequate diet that includes whole grains, legumes, seeds, nuts, and raw fruits and vegetables. For children as well as adults, a moderate amount of fiber in the diet promotes good bowel function. The large intestine seems to work best when it has a certain amount of filling from a diet that has some indigestible residue. If a diet has a reasonable amount of fiber, it gives a stool that is formed, soft, and somewhat bulky and is easy to pass without a lot of straining. Stools from a highly refined diet tend to be smaller, harder, and more formed. If your child's stool is small and hard, it may hurt to go to the bathroom, and it could give him intestinal cramps and make him afraid to go to the bathroom.

To provide your child with enough fiber, offer an adequate amount of fruits and vegetables, especially raw and unpeeled, use whole grains at least part of the time, and make regular use of cooked dried beans and peas. Read the label on whole grain bread, tortillas, and cereals to make sure the first listed ingredient listed is whole wheat or whole grain. For instance, "wheat flour" is not whole wheat, nor is unbleached wheat flour. It has to say *whole* wheat. Other sources of whole grain include graham crackers, dry and cooked cereals, brown rice, or oatmeal cookies. Bran and bran cereals are high in fiber but not necessary if you are offering fruits, vegetables and whole grains. Don't overdo the whole grains, though. If your child eats too much whole grain, it could backfire and give him diarrhea. Further, an extremely high-fiber diet, such as a vegetarian diet with a lot of legumes, seeds, and nuts as well as whole grains can cause nutritional problems.

Constipation. Before I launch into the topic of constipation, let me remind you that your child's toileting habits require a division of responsibility: you provide the toilet and he makes

use of it. Children are capable of withholding their bowel movements if they get the message that you are making it too much
your business. As with eating, if you get in a struggle about
your child's bowel habits, your child will be more invested in
the struggle with you than he will be in taking care of the job
himself.

Normal bowel habits are extremely variable. One child will
go to the bathroom more than once a day, another not for several days. Both can be normal, and neither can hurt your child or
cause problems as long as you are casual and accepting of his
normal pattern. Drinking enough water and the way he eats
will have an effect on his bowel habits. If he eats quite a lot of
fiber, he is likely to have more frequent and softer stools. Less
fiber may give him a harder stool that is more difficult to pass.
Water that is being offered as a beverage can help. You can only
offer him water and higher-fiber food and give him the information—once. You can't affect his willingness to drink water,
eat, or not eat by reminding him over and over again. He might
take it upon himself, but it's not likely. Preschoolers don't apply
those associations even after we tell them.

For some children, constipation can be a medical as well as
a behavioral and nutritional concern. Some children have
underactive muscles in the intestinal tract, and children with
irritable bowel can have periods of alternating diarrhea and
constipation. If your child's bowel habits are of ongoing concern to you, consult your health professional.

Diarrhea. Appendix S, "Diarrhea and Dehydration," gives
details of managing the *medical* condition of diarrhea caused by
gastroenteritis. In most cases, though, loose stools aren't diarrhea at all but simply a change in bowel habits. However, some
toddlers and preschoolers develop what is often called chronic
nonspecific diarrhea. These are bowel movements so urgent
that a child has trouble getting to the bathroom on time and has
stools so runny that when he has an accident you have to
change his socks as well as his pants. That is a *social* disease, not
a physical ailment. The child isn't ill, and the diarrhea doesn't
seem to indicate that he is absorbing nutrients poorly. If a child
has an extremely high-fiber diet, it could give him loose stools.
However, the main culprit seems to be too much juice—especially juice that has a lot of *fructose* and *sorbitol* in it, like prune,
pear, peach, and apple juice. Peach juice has sorbitol but not so

much fructose. Fructose is fruit sugar. Most children (and many adults) poorly digest and incompletely absorb fructose. Like a sponge, leftover fructose in the large intestine attracts water and can make the stools extremely liquid. Fructose can also feed intestinal bacteria and, in turn, cause gas and irritation. Sorbitol can't be digested or absorbed but attracts water, makes the stools loose, and can also contribute to intestinal gas. Of course, eating a lot of those *fruits* could do the same thing. A low-fat diet can also indirectly cause loose stools. Children who get too little fat in their diets eat too much sugar to make up for it and have trouble digesting all the sugar. Any undigested sugar in the colon can draw water in the same way that fructose and sorbitol do.[12]

Lactose Intolerance. *Lactose* is milk sugar. People who can't digest lactose don't make *lactase* in their small intestine and have *lactose intolerance*. It's *not* the same as being allergic to milk. Among adults, lactose intolerance affects about 70 percent of the world's population. If your ancestors came from Northern Europe, you can probably digest lactose. If you're of African, Asian, Mediterranean, Hispanic, or Native American ancestry, your chances of being lactose-intolerant are greater. But even in groups of people who are extremely likely to become lactose-intolerant, it doesn't appear before ages 4 or 5. It's possible that when children refuse milk, it's because they have experienced some discomfort from drinking it. Children who are lactose-intolerant get intestinal gas, loose stools, or explosive diarrhea (uncontrolled and accompanied by gas) from drinking milk, and they may have stomach cramps. These symptoms appear within 12 hours after they drink milk.

Even if a child is lactose intolerant, it doesn't necessarily follow that he should give up drinking milk and miss out on its important contributions of calcium and vitamin D. Drinking some milk will not harm the lactose-intolerant child who's feeling well. How much milk that child can drink depends both on his individual sensitivity to lactose and on what other foods he eats along with the milk. Almost everyone makes at least a small amount of lactase and can digest some lactose, and a moderate amount of gas from lactose is not a problem.

What your child eats with the milk makes a difference. If your child drinks milk with a meal containing fat, it will cause fewer problems than when he consumes only milk. Whole or 2 percent milk will cause fewer problems than skim milk. Solid food or fat with milk slows down the emptying time of the stomach. The lactose gets to the intestine more slowly and doesn't cause as much of an overload.

Managing Food Allergies. Pronounced food allergies can be very serious indeed and must be attended to medically with a pediatric allergist and with careful dietary management by a dietitian who is experienced with the management of allergies. True allergy can be serious for the few children who react significantly to certain foods. Allergic reactions include abdominal pain, nausea, vomiting, and diarrhea; cough, runny nose, wheezing, and pronounced breathing difficulties; skin rashes from mild to extreme; headache and irritability; and shock. For some few children, ingestion of even a small amount of an offending food can be life-threatening. Those children must be under a doctor's care, and parents must know emergency procedures. Some children have multiple reactions to many foods and require very skillful management. If you have a child with multiple allergies, do seek the help of a dietitian who specializes in food allergy. The most useful tool for diagnosing food allergy is removing, then challenging with, the offending food. Skin tests are only partially successful in diagnosis. Challenging must be done with a physician *present* if the child has had marked reactions to food. For milder reactions, you can challenge at home by keeping the diet constant, reintroducing the suspected food, and watching for symptoms. Children's food allergies can also be transient. As they get past age 2 years and older, the allergic condition often resolves itself and the offending food may be reintroduced into the diet. If an allergy *starts* after age 3 years, however, it is likely to persist.

Severely allergic children are the exception. In most cases, what parents think are food allergies are not allergies at all but simply physical reactions to food or coincidences: a child reacts physically or emotionally about the same time he eats a particular food and the food is named as the culprit. Don't put yourself through the hassle of catering to a food allergy unless it is really necessary. Many times when children who are assumed to be allergic are challenged with an offending food, it is discovered that they aren't even sensitive to it. Reactions to foods may come and go with bowel disturbances, so they really fall in the category of sensitivities rather than allergies. For instance, gastroenteritis will often leave a child temporarily intolerant of the lactose in milk. Occasionally someone who has had an infection will become sensitive to the protein in milk. If all goes well and these substances are removed for a few weeks, the ability to tolerate them can be regained.

Feeding Dynamics for the Child with Allergies. The tendency with the child with allergies is to hover and to become a dietary policeman. Don't. You know after reading this far that if you hover, your child will become incapable with his eating. Be as matter-of-fact as you can about telling your child what he can and can't eat. Be equally matter-of-fact about teaching him to be responsible for keeping his limitations in mind when he eats at a friend's house or at school. You can say, "you can't eat peanut butter, so when we have peanut butter at home I will give you tahini instead. But when you go to someone else's house and they have peanut butter and jelly sandwiches, they won't have tahini. So when you are there, just say, 'no, thank you,' and ask for plain bread and jelly. If your friend's mother insists, you can say you're allergic, but you don't have to make a big deal out of it."

Certainly you must talk with the family, child care, schools, and other parents about your child's allergies, but you won't always be able to run interference. My friend Rosie told me about still another trip to the emergency room with her severely citrus-allergic son when he ate a lemon drop at a neighbor's house. The neighbor felt terrible, but Rosie was sympathetic and philosophical about it. "I guess we all learned," she said. "One more thing he knows to look out for." Rosie didn't make it her life's work to chase around after her son to keep him safe or to try to purge his life of everything that might make him sick. *Saying* that, of course, is far more easily done than *doing* it. Severe allergy can be a life-threatening condition, and it is entirely natural to be overprotective when a child is at such serious risk. Try to remember, though, that your child will be the safest in the long run if he learns to take responsibility for his own condition.

Feeding the Child with Diabetes. I won't advise you about managing your child's diabetes. For that, you need a knowledgeable health care team, including both a physician and a dietitian. I do, however, want to reassure you that you don't have to settle for distorted feeding dynamics with your diabetic child, and I will give you some ideas about how you can manage both good diabetic control and a positive feeding relationship. The way your child's diabetes is managed will determine whether you will cross the lines of division of responsibility in feeding and whether you will be set up for problems with eating. The traditional approach to managing diabetes is to give a child an injection of insulin and then have the child eat to cover the insulin. The injected insulin, of course, forces down the child's blood sugar and makes it imperative that he eat, or else his blood sugar will go too low and he may even lose consciousness. It is certainly understandable that parents are so desperate to get their children to eat that they get into major struggles and contests of manipulation with them. I talked with a group of parents in Arizona who said they were *paying their children to eat*. Unless something happens to change them, the distorted eating attitudes and behaviors that begin when children are small do not go away. A study in Edinburgh, Scotland, showed a high incidence of eating disorder symptoms in adolescents and young adults with diabetes.[13]

Based on her concern about impairments in the feeding relationship between children with diabetes and their parents, dietitian Edie Applegate, coordinator of the Nutrition Clinic at Rockford Health System in Illinois, collaborated with the medical staff to change their diabetic protocol. Applegate set aside the defined diet and exchange system and instead emphasized the same principles of feeding that have been outlined in this book. Making it clear that the principles of feeding children with diabetes need be no different from feeding any other children, Applegate established the priority of helping parents with the practicalities of feeding rather than administering the mechanics of following a defined diet.

With the development of forms of insulin that start to work in 15 minutes, at-home blood sugar testing, multiple daily injections, or even insulin pumps, the Rockford team is turning the insulin-injection-and-eating sequence around the other way. Children are allowed to eat, then the insulin injection is given *after* the meal to cover the food the child has eaten. That way, whether the child eats a little or a lot isn't so critical because the insulin dose can be adjusted to compensate for a little or a lot of food. Parents are taught a system for counting the carbohydrates in the child's meal and adjusting the insulin to cover for that amount of carbohydrate.[14]

Furthermore, allowing the target level of blood sugar to be somewhat higher than the "physiological" level—the level you would see in a child without diabetes—is important in freeing children and parents from struggles about eating. A child whose blood sugar is kept relatively low is at greater risk of having an insulin reaction. A child in the early stages of an insulin reaction may not know he needs food but only *shows* it by looking tired and crabby or acting stubborn. In the later stage of reaction, the child passes out. Little wonder that parents feel they have to keep an eagle eye on their child and be prepared to press food on him if he seems to be running out of energy. Also little wonder that the child in the early stages of a reaction is too stubborn to eat. To a great extent, the pressure on the parent to hover depends on the target levels for the child's blood sugar. Some practitioners feel strongly that keeping blood sugars low protects diabetic children from the long-term, degenerative consequences of the disease. Practitioners who make target blood sugars somewhat higher make avoiding reactions a priority and point out that the reactions themselves contribute to degenerative consequences.

Although I won't try to resolve the medical arguments, I will register my conviction that preserving positive eating attitudes and behaviors is all-important. The Edinburgh study showed that people who had distorted eating attitudes and behaviors had poorer diabetic control.[13] In my experience, preventing eating disorders, preserving a child's capabilities with eating, and achieving a positive diabetic control are one and the same thing. Any regimen that keeps parents in their own arena of preparing and offering food and out of the child's arena of what and how much he eats best positions the child for lifelong management of his condition.

If you feel your current approach to managing your child's eating and diabetes is distorting your feeding relationship and making your child less capable with eating, talk with your health care team. They may be willing to experiment with you.

We have come to the end. Thank you for taking this journey with me, and best wishes to you and your child as you continue on your way. You now have the information you need to finish raising your child with respect to food and feeding: the division of responsibility in feeding, the basis for family food selection and meal planning, a clear sense of your own importance, and a thinking approach to parenting. As your child gets older, these tools will continue to be important. The school-aged child and the teenager still depend on you to maintain the structure of family meals. As he gets older, your child will do more and more of his own food selection outside the home, but you will still be the gatekeeper and the one who takes responsibility for family food preparation and nurturing. If your children is a capable eater, he can take a role in planning the family menus and can even cook once in a while. Your child has a very good chance of carrying the positive eating attitudes and behaviors you have taught him in these early years into his older life. Certainly, when he is a teenager he will experiment and even be rebellious with his food selection as with everything else. But he will settle down. You have started him in the right direction, and sooner or later he will return to what you have taught him in these first few years.

In the meantime, I hope you have learned to take feeding *yourself* more seriously and to lighten up with your own eating as well. Eating well is one of life's great pleasures. It is too important to turn it into a hassle. Enjoy your child, and celebrate eating.

APPENDIXES

SELECTED REFERENCES

INDEX

APPENDIXES

WHAT IS NORMAL GROWTH?

Your child has a natural way of growing that is right for her, and she knows how much she needs to eat to grow that way. If you let her decide how much she wants to eat, you generally don't need to worry about normal growth—it will happen.

There are many different normal shapes and sizes. Some children are short and stocky; some are tall and slender. Your child's body shape and size is determined mostly by heredity: the size and shape of her mother and father.

Charting Your Child's Growth. When you take your child to the health clinic for regular checkups, she's weighed and measured. These numbers are plotted on growth charts and become part of her records. Keeping track of the rate your child grows can be fun and interesting. But don't get compulsive and overreact to every little variation. It's important to have a health care provider help you interpret your child's growth charts.

Growth Curves. Children may be taller or shorter, heavier or lighter, but usually they grow in height (or length) and weight in a predictable pattern. Reference growth curves, as shown for girls in Figures A.1-A.3), show typical patterns of children throughout the country (a growth curve for a boy is shown in Figure 2.1 on page 35). These curves are helpful in assessing an individual child's growth.

It doesn't matter how your child's growth compares with that of other children in your neighborhood. Just compare her with herself: Is she growing consistently? Do her heights and weights show a consistent pattern? If so, her growth is fine. To understand how these reference curves work, let's try plotting some figures on them. Imagine we have a little girl whose weights in pounds and lengths in inches at her routine health visits are below.

	Weight	**Length**
Birth	7.75	19.5
1 month	9.5	21
2 months	11.25	22.25
4 months	14.5	24.25
6 months	17	26
9 months	20.25	27.75
12 months	22.5	29.25
15 months	24	30.5

Weight Charts. As we plot her weights against her age on the weight chart in Figure A.1, a pattern emerges. Notice that her dots follow pretty closely along the 75th percentile curve. That means if we took an average group of 100 baby girls, 25 of them would weigh as much or more than this baby; 75 would weigh less. Don't get caught up in treating growth curves like grades in school. A child growing at the 95th percentile curve isn't doing any better than one growing at the 5th percentile curve. Children vary enormously from one another in the way they grow—*that's* normal. But you can compare her with *herself:* Her growth is showing a consistent pattern that follows the 75th percentile curve. She's growing well and predictably.

Length Charts. Plotting our imaginary baby's length measurements against her age in Figure A.2, you will notice that her length measurements fall near the 50th percentile. She's shorter than half the babies her age and longer than the rest.

Weight-for-Length Charts. There's more. When we plot her weights against her lengths on Figure A.3, we see that her weight-for-lengths follow along near the 80th percentile curve. She is a relatively heavy baby for her length. She is totally normal; she's growing consistently and predictably. She's just built differently—perhaps with heavier bones and muscles or a little more fat—than another baby. The baby who follows along at the 50th percentile curve has an average build. The one who follows below the 50th percentile curve has a relatively light build.

Accurate Measurements Are a Must. To get accurate measurements, your child must be weighed using a table model scale checked periodically for accuracy and precision. Her length must be measured using a measuring board with a fixed vertical head and movable vertical foot piece. Accurately measuring length requires two people: one to hold her head straight against the head piece (you may be asked to do this), the other to straighten out her legs and hold her feet flat against the foot piece.

Smaller and Larger Children. Some children consistently plot at or below the 5th percentile curve. These children are shorter or lighter. Some other children consistently plot at or above the 95th percentile curve. These children are taller or heavier. Generally, a growth pattern following a particular percentile curve is considered normal, even if it is at the extremes of the reference growth curves. A child consistently

FIGURE A.1 GIRLS' WEIGHT FOR AGE

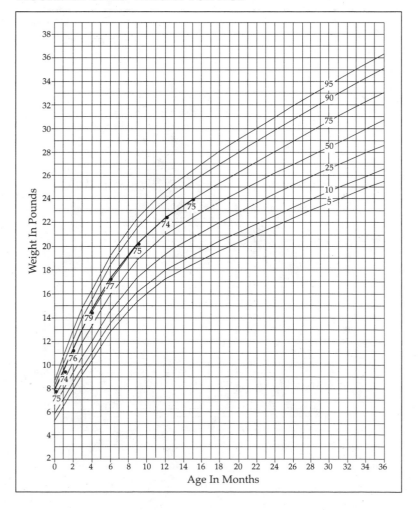

growing above the 95th percentile or below the 5th percentile on any of the charts is probably growing normally. However, these extremes of growth can raise concerns if your child is plotted for the first time and her growth is above the 95th or below the 5th percentile. Then your health care provider may want to monitor her growth for a while to be sure she grows consistently.

Changes in Growth. As your child gets older, she'll probably continue to show the same growth pattern. She may also show moderate shifts.

FIGURE A.2 GIRLS' LENGTH FOR AGE

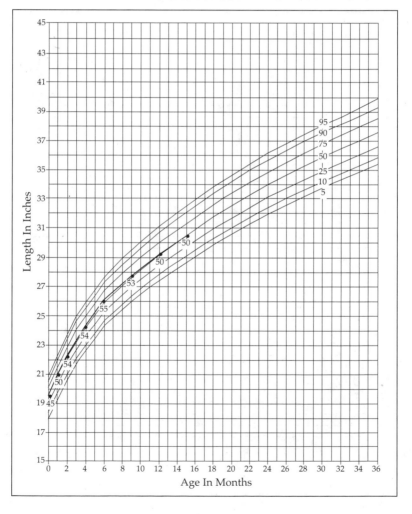

She could gradually go up or down to a different percentile curve on her weight and/or height chart. Then, once she's established in her new pattern, she's likely to stay there. If the adjustment in weight and/or height is smooth and involves only one percentile curve over several months or two percentile curves over a year, it's probably normal. Breastfed babies may shift downward by as much as a percentile curve in weight between 3 and 12 months.

Small shifts in growth are generally nothing to worry about, although it is a good idea to review your food selection and feeding

FIGURE A.3 GIRLS' WEIGHT FOR LENGTH

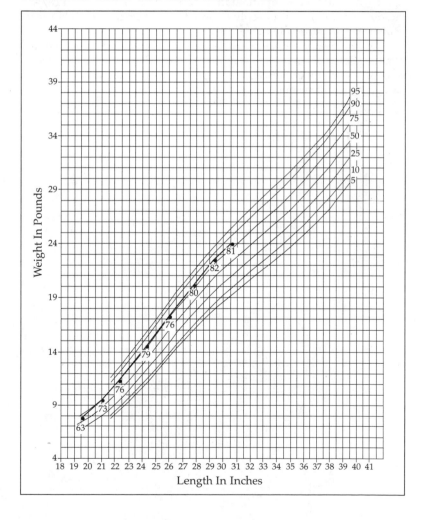

methods. But if your child veers away from her usual growth pattern and continually and rapidly shifts up or down across percentile curves on her chart, something may be disrupting her growth. Your health care provider will work with you to figure out what's going on.

Babies Need Extra Body Fat. In addition to growth charts, you'll evaluate your child's growth the same way parents always have: by looking at her. During the first year, she gets longer and heavier; her body and arms and legs fill out. Her stomach sticks out; her face gets rounder. That's fine. It's normal and desirable for your child to increase her body fat during the first year: from 11 percent at birth to 24 percent by age 1. This extra fat is important in her little body as a source of calories in case of illness. Fat is only a cause for concern if your child veers off her weight percentile curve.

During the second and third years, your child's body continues to change a lot as she moves through the chubbiness of the toddler stage to become a slimmer preschooler. Body fat drops to about 21 percent by age 2 and 18 percent by age 3.

APPENDIX **B**

SELECT FOODS THAT
HELP REGULATION

A well-selected meal, with a good distribution of protein, fat, and carbohydrate, can help your child regulate his food intake. Each of these
nutrients has a role to play in inducing some of the many satiety factors that let your child know that he has had enough to eat and give
him sustained energy between eating times. The pattern of satisfaction
from consuming each separately appears to be different from the pattern of satisfaction from all of them consumed together.

Food Composition. Before we can get to the fun part, we have to have a
little lesson in food composition. There are three major sources of calories in the diet: protein, fat, and carbohydrate—sugar and starch). The
only other nutrient that gives calories is alcohol. Figure B.1, "Protein, Fat,
and Carbohydrate Content of Foods," illustrates which foods are good
sources of which major nutrients. The capital Xs indicate that the food
contains a lot of the nutrient; the lowercase ones indicate that the food
contains some but not a lot.

As you can see from the figure, you get protein from the meat
group as well as from milk and milk products. You also get protein
from cooked dried beans and peas and in small amounts from breads
and cereal products. Fat is often a separate food such as butter or oil,
but it is often also contained *in* foods, where it may not be noticeable.
Cookies, cakes, and ice cream have fat in them. Most meats have fat in
them, as do many dairy products. Skim milk, fat-free yogurt, and cottage cheese would be exceptions. Fat is often used in food preparation,
as in frying or in buttering or creaming vegetables. Fat is also used as a
spread or as a dressing on other foods.

Carbohydrate comes in two forms: the *simple,* or sugar, form, and
the *complex,* or starch, form. The basic chemical structure of both forms
is sugar, and starches are essentially made up of many molecules of
sugar, linked together. The important difference, metabolically, is that

451

FIGURE B.1 PROTEIN, FAT, AND CARBOHYDRATE CONTENT OF FOODS

Food	Protein	Fat	Complex Carbohydrate: Starch	Simple Carbohydrate: Sugar
Milk	X	X (if not skim)		X
Vegetables	X		X	
Fruit; fruit juice				X
Breads and cereals	X		X	
Meat, fish, poultry, eggs, cheese, peanut butter	X	X (unless fat-free)		
Cooked dried beans	X		X	
Butter, margarine, salad dressing, cooking oils		X		
Cookies, chocolates, cakes	X	X	X	X
Jelly candies, soda, fruit drinks				X

starch has to be broken down chemically before it can be made available to the body, whereas sugar is virtually ready to be absorbed, as is, from the intestine. Sugar can be transported into the blood stream very promptly with very little digestive action. You get starch in cereal products, like noodles, rice, and breakfast cereals and anything made with flour. Starchy vegetables such as potatoes, corn, and lima beans are also good sources of carbohydrate. Sugar is found in nature in fruits and honey, and in sugar cane and sugar beets. Of course, the last two are usually refined and used mainly as brown or white sugars. Fruits and fruit juices, as well as cookies, cakes, candies, soda pop, and sweetened fruit-flavored beverages are all major sources of sugar in the diet.

Satisfaction from Carbohydrate, Protein, and Fat. Following is a series of figures that illustrate what happens to sensations of hunger and fullness and to the "staying power" from eating when the food is high in sugar, starch, protein, fat, and all four. Take a look now at the figures. Each of the charts measures *satisfaction* on the left-hand side, or vertical axis; it has no specific number on it because it is really a general sort of feeling that is made up of several components. It is hard to calibrate because it is so subjective. On the horizontal axis is time, which is also given as an approximation. How quickly a child feels satisfied after

FIGURE B.2 SATISFACTION FROM CONSUMING SUGAR

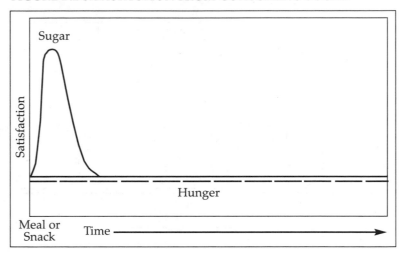

eating has something to do with bodily state (including mental state), the amount eaten, and the food itself—so these lines will have to be imprecise.

Sugar. Figure B.2 demonstrates the kind of satisfaction response a child would get if he were at a fasting or hungry level and consumed only sugar. That sugar might be fruit or fruit juice. It might also be some kind of "sweet," like jelly beans or hard candy, or soda pop or a sweetened fruit drink.

Notice that the satisfaction response to sugar is quite fast. In this case, the feeling of satisfaction probably comes from an increase in blood glucose, which is apparently one of many signals to the body that it has been fed. But since the curve drops off just as fast as it went up, the sugar doesn't have much staying power. Once it is used up, the child who has had a sugar-only meal or snack will again be hungry and may even be cranky and unmanageable because of it. The sugar didn't *make* him cranky; it just let him down before he got too far.

Starch. Now let's take a look at Figure B.3. A meal like orange juice and dry toast might produce the effect shown in the figure. The addition of the starch helps make the satisfaction from the meal last longer. The starch has to be digested before it can be absorbed, and it can't be digested all at one time, so the nutrients get into the bloodstream more slowly and over a more extended time. The nutrient that enters the blood is still glucose, because when starch is digested it is absorbed and carried in the bloodstream as glucose. The sugar from starch is burned up by the body cells just as fast as that from refined sugar, but because

FIGURE B.3 SATISFACTION FROM CONSUMING SUGAR AND STARCH

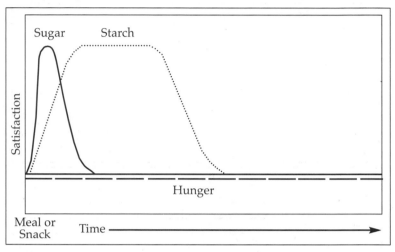

it gets to the blood more slowly, it is likely to last longer.

With bread and starchy foods like cereals we are also adding other components of satisfaction: bulk and chewing. Bread is solid and it is bulky, so it gives the stomach a feeling of having something in it. Depending on the kind of bread, it will require a greater or lesser amount of chewing. Some people depend heavily on chewing to let them feel that they have had enough to eat, so a tougher bread, like toast or bagels, is likely to give them a greater feeling of satisfaction than they get from squishy sandwich bread. Finally, bread adds pleasure. People generally like bread, and we all depend on pleasure to feel satisfied after a meal.

Protein. But let's say we know better than to have just juice and dry toast. We have been watching television and have seen an ad for a high-protein breakfast cereal, and that is what we are going to have: a protein-fortified cereal, juice, and also some skim milk. In adding protein to our breakfast, we are likely to get a response to our breakfast that looks like the one shown in Figure B.4. The protein helps make our breakfast last longer. It takes a while for the protein to be satisfying because it has to be broken down in the intestine into amino acids before it can be absorbed into the blood stream.

Eating a source of protein adds still another component of satisfaction to the diet: that of circulating amino acids in the blood stream. As with increases in blood sugar, it appears that the body is able to sense increases in blood amino acids and uses that as one of the bits of information supporting a sense of satisfaction. Skim milk

FIGURE B.4 SATISFACTION FROM CONSUMING SUGAR, STARCH AND PROTEIN

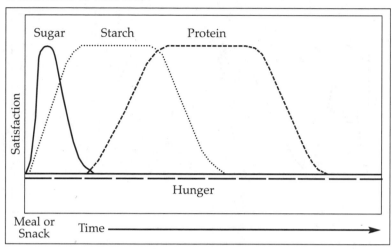

is one of the few sources of protein in the diet that doesn't also have some fat associated with it. Egg white, tofu, and fat-free cottage cheese are all sources of fat-free protein, and some very lean fish is almost fat free, but most sources of protein come associated with varying amounts of fat.

Fat. Adding fat to an otherwise fat-free meal gives quite a different picture of satisfaction. Let's consider the same cereal-and-milk-and-juice breakfast; only now let's add a source of fat with it, like 2 percent or whole milk on the cereal instead of skim milk. Now take a look at Figure B.5. You will notice that the curve goes out even longer before it starts to drop. Fat is digested and absorbed slowly, so fatty acids from fat digestion get into the blood stream after sugar and amino acids, and fat is released to the blood stream over a more extended period of time than the other nutrients. But more important, the presence of fat in the meal slows down the rate at which the whole meal is used. Fat retards the emptying time of the stomach. It keeps food in the stomach where it is released more slowly to the intestine. Once there, it is digested and absorbed at a moderate rate, so that accompanying carbohydrate and protein are also available to the body more slowly and over a more extended time. Fat mixed with a meal makes the meal stay around considerably longer.

Including fat in the meal adds on a couple of other components of satisfaction. One of them is simple pleasure. Fat carries the flavor in food; addition of fat allows you to taste the food better and more acutely. You can taste the cereal more when you have 2 percent milk

FIGURE B.5 SATISFACTION FROM CONSUMING SUGAR, STARCH, PROTEIN AND FAT

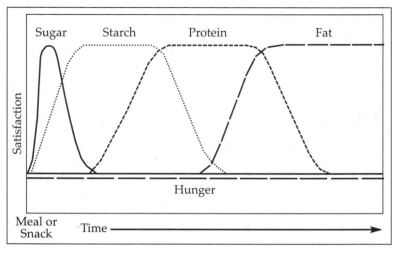

rather than skim milk. A little butter on the vegetables improves their flavor considerably. And it isn't just because butter tastes so wonderful—somehow fat makes taste buds more appreciative of what they are getting and improves satisfaction from the rest of the meal.

Fat has a metabolic effect on satisfaction as well. Fatty acid level in the bloodstream is probably another of the indicators that the body uses to know that it has enough and, like increased blood sugar, helps to turn off the desire to eat.

Omitting Starch. It's clear that trying to go without fat can seriously decrease the satiety value of the meal. But what if you try to go without carbohydrate? Carbohydrate is popular right now, but as faddish as we are about our eating, it is just a matter of time before carbohydrate becomes the evil nutrient. If you look at the best-seller list, in fact, you will see that the extremely high-protein, high-fat diets are back, recommending cutting down carbohydrate and emphasizing fat and protein. Aside from the fact that those diets are nutritionally reprehensible, what happens to satiety if we omit sugar and starch? Take a look at Figure B.6. You can see that there is an increase in the lag time before this meal starts to feel satisfying. The protein breaks down slowly, and fat more slowly still. When the diet lacks carbohydrate, the body does still manufacture its essential blood glucose from protein. However, the process takes a while, and that slows down the blood glucose response. Furthermore, without the bulk of starch the meal won't feel very filling.

FIGURE B.6 SATISFACTION FROM CONSUMING PROTEIN AND FAT

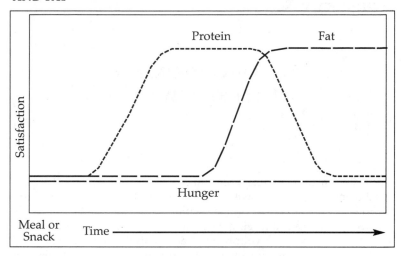

Applications. To help your child—and yourself—with food regulation, plan meals to include carbohydrate, protein, and fat. Consuming these major nutrients together lets them work best nutritionally, makes meals more satisfying and lasting, and makes it easier to regulate food intake. Knowing something about the metabolic responses from carbohydrate, protein, and fat also gives you some help with planning snacks. If you want a snack to keep your child comfortable and satisfied for 2 or 3 hours, choose all three major nutrients. If, however, it is five o'clock and dinner is at six and your child is desperate from hunger, a small glass of juice or a small apple might be a better choice. The fruit sugar will satisfy him quickly and have a good chance of allowing him to be hungry a short time later.

What else can you do with this information? Some children in particular will benefit from carefully planned meals that include carbohydrate, protein, and fat. The extremely active child who is too busy to eat—or even think about being hungry—will benefit from meals and snacks that provide long-lasting energy. The child with diabetes needs a more sustained release of nutrients in order to cover injected insulin and give a slower, smoother release of glucose. In fact, knowing this strategy can even let the diabetic child eat a modest amount of sweets with a meal or with a well-balanced snack. The other food slows down the release of sugar to his blood stream and keeps from having a spike of blood glucose that insulin can't cover.

APPENDIX C

HELPING YOURSELF
WITH LETDOWN

These tips are more to quiet your mind than because you are likely to need them. Few women have trouble with letdown, but most everyone worries about it. You help yourself with letdown by maintaining a relaxed, positive attitude. Have your goal be a warm and close breast-feeding experience with your baby. That is definitely an achievable goal and puts less pressure on you than if you feel you have to provide your baby with a certain amount of breastmilk. You will learn over and over as your baby gets older that if the feeding relationship is positive, nutrition has a way of falling into place. Relax, and enjoy your baby.

Letdown is a conditioned reflex. Pavlov's dogs learned to salivate when they heard the dinner bell go off. You learned to relax before labor and delivery by breathing in a certain way. Do you automatically yawn when you start your deep breathing? Setting up a little routine for yourself will condition your letdown in the same way you condition your relaxation.

You won't need all the suggestions I am giving you, so pick and choose what is helpful. Chances are you'll be letting down nicely before you ever get to the massaging suggestions at the bottom of the list. You will be letting down if you hear your baby's long, rhythmic suck and swallow when she is getting milk instead of her short, choppy jaw movements when she is not.

- Maintain a relaxed enough lifestyle so you can tune in on your baby. For those dogs to salivate, they had to give the food their full attention. Particularly at first when you are establishing letdown, don't let yourself get rushed, overtired, or distracted from your baby.
- Pick up your baby; watch and hold her at times when you don't feel pressure to nurse so you can be aware of the satisfaction of sharing that time.
- Pay attention to letdown that takes place at odd times and give

yourself the reassurance that the system is working. If you have leaking, you are probably having a letdown. Pick up your baby and feed her if you think she is likely to be hungry enough to cooperate. Early feeding signs are if your baby is mouthing, rooting, or making feeding sounds, or if she has her hands clenched and her arms and legs pulled up over her body.

- Set up a little routine to condition yourself. Get your nursing pillow and something to drink (but limit alcohol to one drink maximum) and eat, round up your portable telephone, and go to your special nursing chair.
- Keep yourself comfortable. Sit well supported so you're not strained—get a stool to support your feet at a comfortable angle.
- Start your routine a few minutes before your baby is ready to eat so you can tune in and let yourself enjoy her. That will probably be when she is just waking up from being drowsy or beginning to be quietly alert.
- Relax yourself. Take a couple of slow, deep breaths, or use the breathing pattern that you used during labor and delivery.
- Read a book or watch television, if that helps you relax. This is contradictory to the earlier advice about focusing attention on the baby. However, it may work for you to turn your attention away in a relaxed fashion and trust your body to take care of the process by itself. It probably will!
- Before you nurse, apply moist heat to your breasts and massage gently in a circular pattern the area over the alveoli (see Figure 5.1 on page 140 for an illustration of a lactating breast) for a few minutes. This does externally what the letdown reflex does internally—moves the milk from the alveoli to the ducts and sinuses, where it can be readily removed. Or better still, take a warm shower and let the water pressure do the massaging!
- Using the same technique, massage your breasts as your baby nurses, emptying first one quadrant and then another.
- If you have cracked or sore nipples, attend to them between times and take a pain reliever a few minutes before nursing.
- If you are not hearing your baby's long, steady swallow after several feedings, have someone skilled in breastfeeding watch you and your baby at a feeding. This could be a lactation consultant, nurse, peer counselor, or physician.

APPENDIX D

BREASTFEEDING WHILE WORKING

There are a number of ways of continuing to breastfeed after you return to work or school. I will list the possibilities, but also keep in mind that your baby will have ideas of his own. Because of your baby's contribution and because you can't fully anticipate how the process will work or how you will feel until you get there, be prepared to take a wait-and-see attitude. Begin by reflecting on and recalling the pleasure, rewards, and real contributions your breastfeeding has made up until now. Whatever happens, those rewards will remain. Here are some of the ways women have continued breastfeeding after they go back to work:

- Taking your baby to work. Oh fabulous day! This requires an extremely cooperative employer—and baby.
- Breastfeeding fully, pumping the breasts 2 or 3 times during the day and having the child care provider give it in a bottle. This approach is most likely to allow breastfeeding fully on weekends and days off.
- Breastfeeding fully and going to child care to breastfeed the baby at lunches and even during breaks. This requires a cooperative and fairly predictable baby.
- Breastfeeding fully and having the baby brought in during breaks. This also requires a cooperative and predictable baby.
- Breastfeeding evenings, nights, and mornings and giving the baby formula during the day.
- Working or going to school part time and breastfeeding fully or with occasional support from bottles of expressed breastmilk or formula.

Here are supports that can help you continue to breastfeed after you go back to work or school:

- Taking care of yourself. Getting enough to eat—including breakfast and lunch.
- Getting enough rest. You will be tired with all your responsibilities

and likely continuing to get up at night, so you will need extra sleep.

- An extended maternity leave. Six to eight weeks is essential for establishing milk supply—as well as a strong bond between you and your baby. If you can manage 16 to 20 weeks, your breastmilk supply and your feeding relationship may be so well established that you can maintain your breastmilk supply by nursing only evenings, nights, and mornings.
- Nursing often during off hours. Nurse right away when you get to the child care center, several times during the evening, a time or two at night, and in the morning.
- Nursing times that are calm and unhurried.
- Moral and situational support. Someone to help with the housework, the other children, getting the evening and morning meal ready.
- Relaxed opportunities to pump during the day.
- A flexible work schedule so you can take as long as you need in the morning to get your baby—and yourself—fed and settled before you leave.
- A supportive child care provider who is willing and resourceful about helping you continue your breastfeeding.

To maintain your breastmilk supply at a level that is the same or near what you have when you are nursing full time, you will need to express milk during the time you are working. The electric breastmilk pumps work well—there are portable options that you can purchase as well as hospital-grade machines that you can rent. Pumping breastmilk at work, of course, raises the issue of having a private place where you can do that. Best of all is a private room with a lock on the door. Some employers provide lactation support for their employees with a private room, a lock on the door, comfortable chairs, refrigeration for expressed breastmilk, electrical outlets for breast pumps, and even a breast pump. Employees have to bring only their own reusable attachment kit with collection bottles, tubing, and breast shields.

Your Baby Will Influence Your Feeding Choice. The wild card in all of this, of course, is your baby. Your baby may be so predictable that 2 or 3 breastmilk bottles during the day or nursing during breaks works well. On the other hand, he may need to eat so irregularly and so often that it is difficult to keep up with his needs or to predict when he will need to eat. He may need less or more breastmilk, and you may or may not be able to express enough to provide for him in your absence. If he is a little older, he may simply refuse the bottle and wait for you to show up to feed him. Such babies apparently can comfortably go for extended times without eating and continue to grow well on such a pattern of eating. He is likely to need two night feedings and may get his nights and days turned around for a time. An older baby who is ready for solid foods can eat his solids during the day and have sips of breastmilk or formula from the cup, then do most of his breastfeeding evenings, nights, and mornings. However, don't rush your baby into solid foods to prolong your breastfeeding. Wait until he is ready to have solid foods, even if it means you have to supplement with formula for a while.

Your Own Feelings and Reactions Will Influence Your Feeding Choice. You may be comfortable with expressing breastmilk, or you may not. You may be able to get a significant amount of breastmilk when you express, or you may not. Start experimenting with equipment and learning to express several weeks before you return to work. That will give you time to find out how you react—both emotionally and physically. Do consider this as you make your plans for your maternity leave dates and for breastfeeding your baby when you return to work. Your feelings are all-important in your feeding relationship with your baby. Breastfeeding needs to help you as well as your baby. The potential rewards during the day are lowering your stress level and giving you time-outs when you can rest, express breastmilk, and think about your baby. The reward of breastfeeding comes, of course, in the off hours. It's a balance, and you must be honest with yourself—is your approach to breastfeeding while working rewarding for you? Is it decreasing your stress level—or increasing it? Be prepared to adjust.

There Will Be Night Feedings. To maintain your breastmilk supply and your baby's nutritional needs, you will need to get up at night to feed your baby, perhaps even twice. Many working mothers value these night feedings as a way of squeezing in a little extra time with their baby. Unless you enjoy socializing at night, keep the feedings quiet, dimly lighted, and businesslike and put both of you back to bed drowsy. Try to catch up with your sleep by taking a nap at some point during the day.

Maintain a Positive and Flexible Attitude. Keep in mind that any amount of breastfeeding is a success. It is all a grand experiment. Do your thinking, planning, and providing to set yourself up as well as you can to breastfeed while you work. Then let go of it. You can't control the outcome. Given your particular physiology, circumstances, and baby, you may or may not be able to achieve your goals with breastfeeding. The bottom line is feeding your baby and supporting his growth and development. Achieving your goals in breastfeeding need not contradict that, but if it does, your baby's growth and development comes first.

However long you breastfeed your baby, sooner or later you will have to stop. For most breastfeeding mothers, stopping is a loss whether you are at home full time or working full time. Keep in mind that no matter what happens, you are special to your baby, and that won't change.

APPENDIX E

RELACTATION AND
INDUCED LACTATION

Resuming breastfeeding after it stops or decreases significantly is called *relactation*. Women attempt to relactate if they have been ill or away from their baby for a while. Or they may have started out formula-feeding and discovered their baby doesn't tolerate any formula and has a chance of being able to tolerate breastmilk better. Some women attempt to induce lactation when they adopt. To accomplish either requires time, patience, and a cooperative baby. Babies under 3 months are generally more willing to cooperate with the required sucking than older babies. The limited studies of breastmilk composition with relactation or induced lactation show that the colostrum phase is skipped—the milk is mature milk.[1]

Both relactation and induced lactation use the same principles of supply and demand covered in chapter 5, "Breastfeeding Your Baby." Stimulating your breasts, either manually or with your baby's suckling, activates prolactin release, which, in turn, promotes breast tissue development and milk manufacture.

Start stimulating your nipples and breasts manually about 4 to 6 weeks before you expect your baby; then add on mechanical pumping after 2 to 3 weeks of manual stimulation. Milk production can be stimulated within 2 weeks with manual stimulation or infant sucking, with or without the administration of hormones such as oxytocin. Nurse your baby frequently, on demand, 8 to 12 times per 24-hour period. Avoid rubber nipples, pacifiers, and nipple shields.

The trick is to provide for your baby's nutritional needs while you wait for your mammary tissue to be generated and get started functioning. Don't delay supplemental feeding while you wait for your milk to come in. You may want to breastfeed and then offer a bottle afterward. The exceptional baby may be able to take a good amount of formula from a cup. Or you may want to use the Supplemental Nursing System or Lact-Aid nursing trainer. These devices have the advantage of nourishing the baby at the breast, eliminating prolonged feeding times, and stimulating the proper suckling reflex. A nursing trainer appears to be a very helpful part of the process. The Lact-Aid trainer is essentially a milk pouch or other container with a thin feeding tube that ends just above the nipple. You hang the container on your bra or around your neck, tape the tube to your breast, and put your baby to your breast to nurse. You can tell by the character of the baby's stool when breastmilk is being produced (it gets less formed and less smelly on breastmilk), and you can gradually decrease the amount of formula, until you are providing your maximum amount of breastmilk—which may or may not satisfy all of your baby's need.

Success Rates. A study in Nebraska of 366 women who attempted relactation or lactation induction showed varying degrees of success. Fifteen percent of women needed to supplement breastmilk with formula for no more than a month, 30 percent for a month or longer, and 54 percent supplemented for the entire nursing period. Forty to 50 percent of relactating women and 15 percent of adoptive mothers were able to stop supplements after one month. Between 54 and 64 percent of adoptive mothers supplemented during their entire nursing career. Breastfeeding an adoptive child, without benefit of the priming of pregnancy, is a more difficult process. Most women who went through the process felt positive about it, and their good feelings really had very little to do with either the length of time they nursed their baby or with their baby's need for supplementary formula. Most mothers stressed as important the impact that nursing had on their relationship with their baby. When the mother stressed milk production itself as a goal, she was less likely to have been satisfied with her lactation experience. In fact, striving to produce a certain amount of milk was more likely to present a barrier to her in increasing her milk supply.[2]

APPENDIX F

NUTRITIONAL PRINCIPLES FOR BABY FORMULA

This appendix could also be titled "why formula and why not cow's milk." I hope you are convinced of the importance of using infant formula, and I hope you will continue to use formula during your baby's first year. However, the pressure to use pasteurized milk for infant feeding comes and goes. Right now, it has gone—it seems that health care workers and parents are headed in the right direction—toward routinely using formula for babies. However, when you plunk down that price per can at the grocery store, you may find yourself wondering whether it is really necessary. Once your baby starts eating solid foods, you'll wonder again. Unfortunately, you may get advice from health care workers or other parents to start feeding pasteurized milk long before your baby is ready for it. You may even encounter one of the worst bits of advice ever given about infant feeding and that is the recommendation to put a chubby 3- to 4-month-old on 2 percent milk. Read on—here is your ammunition.

Digestibility. If your newborn were to drink a bottle of pasteurized milk, the milk would mix with the acid in her stomach to set up such a tough, cheeselike curd that she would have trouble digesting it, and her ability to absorb protein and fat from her food would go way down. Pasteurized milk would give her an upset stomach, and it could throw off her body chemistry. Infant formulas have been treated to set up a soft custardlike curd that is easy to digest when it is mixed with the acid in the baby's stomach. Protein and fat absorption are excellent.

Satisfy All the Baby's Nutritional Requirements. The milk feeding must carry the whole nutritional load for your baby until about age 6 months. Because of that, it must be absolutely appropriate and adequate for her needs. Breastmilk and standard formulas are both balanced, so a given volume will provide the proper proportion of calories, water, pro-

465

tein, fat, carbohydrate, vitamins, and minerals. When a baby's calorie needs are high, other nutrient needs are also high. The infant automatically eats more to satisfy her calorie needs and at the same time gets increased amounts of the other nutrients she needs.

Give the Proper Calories per Ounce. Breastmilk and standard infant formulas each give 20 calories per ounce. Some formulas for special needs are concentrated to give 24 calories per ounce, but since some of those formulas may challenge your baby's ability to maintain her body chemistry, use them only under the close supervision of your doctor. Prepare formula exactly according to package directions. *Do not* concentrate or dilute your baby's formula without careful supervision from your doctor.

Overconcentrated formula can overload your baby's kidneys. Overdiluted formula gives the baby too much volume for the calories she needs and makes it harder for her to grow and gain properly. Pasteurized 2 percent, 1 percent, and skim milk give less than 20 calories per ounce and are wrong for babies for a lot of other nutritional reasons as well.

Give a Balance of Protein, Fat, and Carbohydrate. Protein, fat, and carbohydrate each have a nutritional role to play in your baby's diet. Since each contributes a percentage of total calories, varying one will alter another. Standard formulas have a distribution of calories that is as close to breastmilk as possible: 7 to 10 percent as protein, 50 to 55 percent as fat, and 40 to 45 percent as carbohydrate. To properly support your child nutritionally, it is important to roughly maintain these proportions of protein, fat, and carbohydrate. Protein builds body tissue. Too little protein can cause nutritional inadequacy; too much gives excess nitrogen breakdown products. Fat carries essential nutrients, provides long-lasting energy, and keeps your baby from being hungry again right away. Too little fat makes it hard for a baby to gain and grow properly; too much could cause *ketosis,* a biochemical imbalance. The carbohydrate in formula provides quick energy, spares protein for building and repair, and helps burn dietary fat. Too much carbohydrate makes formula unsatisfying and too little allows ketosis to develop.

All standard infant formulas have a good proportion of protein, fat, and carbohydrate. However, pasteurized milk, whether it is whole, 2 percent, or skim, is far too high in protein and low in carbohydrate. The low-fat milks are far too low in fat.

Don't Hurt Your Baby. Feeding cow's milk to your baby may actually undermine iron nutrition. Some young infants (up to 5 months old) who consume large amounts of pasteurized milk bleed a little from the gastrointestinal tract. Although the amount is small (about 3 milliliters per day in some cases—less than a teaspoon—which means the loss of 0.9 milligrams of iron per day), it could undermine iron nutrition and make your baby anemic.

Feeding cow's milk can undermine your baby's body chemistry. Pasteurized, 2 percent, or skim milk are all too concentrated in both protein and sodium. They can draw too much water out of her body and make her dehydrated, especially if she is losing more water than usual in other ways—if she is sweating a lot, is vomiting, or has diarrhea.

APPENDIX G

FORMULAS OFF
THE BEATEN PATH

Babies who need these special formulas have a tendency to allergy, have trouble eating enough to satisfy their nutritional needs, or have a particular health condition that can be managed only by careful nutritional manipulation of their diets.

Partially Protein Predigested Formulas. The protein, fat, or carbohydrate, or all three, in predigested formulas are modified to make them more manageable to the infant with allergies or with digestive problems. The three major formulas that have a low likelihood of causing or aggravating allergies are Alimentum, Nutramigen, and Pregestimil. Alimentum has predigested protein and MCT oil, Nutramigen predigested protein and carbohydrate, and Pregestimil has predigested protein and carbohydrate and MCT oil. The partially predigested protein in all three is casein hydrolysate (predigested cow's milk protein) with added amino acids (protein building blocks). MCT oil is a fat made up of medium-chain triglyderides, a special fat that doesn't require the usual digestion before it can be absorbed. MCT oil makes up only a portion of the fat in the formulas—its purpose is to provide a form of fat that needs no digestion and is well absorbed by the infant who has more difficulty managing other kinds of fat, such as an infant who has had part of the intestine removed, has cystic fibrosis, or for some unknown reason gets diarrhea from other dietary fat.

The carbohydrate in Pregestimil comes from corn syrup solids and modified tapioca starch, both of which can be digested by most babies who have trouble digesting other sugars such as lactose (milk sugar) or sucrose (table sugar).

To summarize, Alimentum, Nutramigen, and Pregestimil have important, if limited, uses:

- For babies who are allergic to cow's milk and soy protein. (See chapter 8, pages 325-327, for a more detailed discussion on allergies.)

468

- As a supplemental feeding for breastfed babies who have a good chance of being allergic.
- For babies who have had a severe reaction to cow's milk formula—breathing difficulties, severe diarrhea, lots of mucus or blood in the stools, serious skin rashes. These babies are also likely to react adversely to soy protein.

Nutrient-Dense Formulas. Designed for children age 1 year and older, nutrient-dense formulas give 30 calories per ounce and are intended to provide for at least two-thirds of the child's nutritional needs. They are most often used as an oral supplement to feeding for children who can't—or won't—eat enough to support their nutritional needs. Often they are fed by tube and one, Compleat Pediatric Blenderized, is intended only for tube-feeding. Compleat Pediatric is made from puréed foods and provides the nutrients as well as the fiber of its food sources. All the nutrient-dense formulas are lactose-free and contain cow's milk casein as a major ingredient. The formulas come in flavored as well as unflavored forms. The flavoring, of course, is to make them more appealing to children. However, if formulas are used for tube-feeding it is important to choose the unflavored. The flavorings put an unnecessary load on the kidneys.

Special-Needs Formulas. Special-needs formulas are intended to provide complete nutritional support for children who are least 1 year old who have particular health conditions. Children who have impairment of the gastrointestinal tract in conditions such as chronic diarrhea, malabsorption, short gut syndrome, Chrohn's disease, and HIV/AIDS. The formulas may be the partially or almost wholly predigested formulas and include: Good Start, Alimentum, Nutramigen, Pregestimil, or Neocate. Some of these formulas are adapted for infants over the age of 1 year under slightly different names. Whether a child needs to be changed to these formulas from the infant versions is a medical decision. The special-needs formulas provide 24 to 30 calories per ounce and may put more of a load on the child's kidneys, and a child may or may not be medically ready to make the change. Ask your pediatrician and/or pediatric dietitian for guidance about choosing a formula for your child.

APPENDIX H

FEEDING YOUR
PREMATURE BABY

Your child might have had a rough start. Maybe she had to stay in the hospital for a while after she was born. She may still be small, ill, and growing slowly. You may have been advised to get your baby to eat more or to get her to gain weight. Of course, you would like to do that: We worry less about a baby's eating and growing if she has a bit of extra weight to go on. The question is, *how* do you help your baby eat well so she can gain weight?

Your Baby Has Special Nutritional Needs. Continue to work with your health care team during your baby's early weeks. They will advise you about how to manage breastfeeding for your baby or which formula to use. They will help you evaluate your baby's suck and tell you if she is doing a good job coordinating her suck and swallow. Also ask if you are holding your baby properly for feeding. To eat well, she needs to be comfortable, have her head, neck, shoulders and hips lined up, and have her head straight ahead or tilted back slightly.

Your Baby Will Eat. Trying to force your baby to eat is not the answer. Babies do better when you let them do their part in the feeding. Three-pound babies in premature nurseries who were allowed to feed on demand ate less—but grew better—than babies who were given a calculated amount of formula and fed on a schedule.[1] Both you and your baby are better off when you trust her to eat.

Give Your Baby Early Experience with a Nipple. Try to see to it that your tiny newborn gets a chance to nipple-feed while she is still in the hospital. She may eat only a little bit, or nothing at all. But if she gets to suck on a nipple—even if she doesn't get any food that way—she'll have an easier time learning to eat when the time comes and she will do better nutritionally. Babies who get even tiny amounts of feedings by mouth early have better digestive functioning than babies who don't.

Your Baby Will Be Cautious. Even after you take your baby home, her mouth may be touchy because of what happened to her in the hospital. If your baby had tubes and respirators put in her mouth, she may expect anything unfamiliar that happens to her mouth to hurt her. A new nipple, a new formula, or a new method of eating may scare her. It's important to settle on *one* nipple and *one* formula and stick with it, working with her slowly and persistently until she gets the hang of it.

Your Baby Knows How Much to Eat. Even the tiniest baby knows how much she needs to eat. However, if your baby was fed on a schedule in the hospital, she might not have had a chance to know what it feels like to be hungry and full, and to be fed in response to those sensations. Now that she's home, it's important that she learn to eat on demand. Study her to figure out her hunger and fullness cues and how she tells you when she wants to be with you and when she needs a break.

Premature Babies May Show Hunger in Unusual Ways. Premature babies, and other children who have been ill and had their feeding disrupted early in life, often don't show in clear ways that they want to eat. Instead, your baby's signs may be more subtle. She may get tired, irritable, or sleepy rather than mouthing when she's hungry. Hunger might make her lose interest in talking and interacting with you, becoming so remote that it's hard to attract her attention. She could become rigid or squirmy.

At first, you'll have to make the connection between the signs and your baby's hunger. Eventually, your baby will start to figure out for herself what it feels like to be hungry. She'll develop more direct signals to tell you that she wants to eat.

Learn Your Baby's Sleep Habits. For your baby to eat well, you need to go along with her sleep habits. Wait for her to wake up before you try to feed her. When she's sleeping soundly, it's almost impossible to wake her up. When she stirs, it might mean she's waking up, or it might mean she's in a light part of her sleep cycle and will go back to sleeping deeply again. It's only when she stirs around quite a bit, or even fusses a little, that she is really awake enough so that with your help she can wake up the rest of the way and do a good job with eating.

She Needs Help Waking Up. Pick your baby up when she starts to wake up, but wait for her to become fully awake before you start to feed her. "Fully awake" is the time after *still-drowsy* and before *upset*. Many premature babies have a lot of trouble waking up fully without getting upset, so you might have to work on it. To help her wake up and get organized so she can eat, talk to your baby. Change her diaper. Hold her close to your face (about 9 inches away) and let her study you. Be slow and steady as you quietly imitate her sounds and expressions. Experiment with your tone of voice and with stroking different parts of her body, watching her to see what helps her to wake up without getting upset.

Take it slowly, and be gentle in your talking and handling. Don't tickle or jiggle her, because that could just make her upset and so flustered she can't eat well. You don't want her to get upset so she has trouble paying attention to eating. Let her wake up enough to indicate she's hungry before you try to feed her. She needs a little time to anticipate being fed. That's how she learns what hunger feels like and what to do to make hunger go away.

Help Her to Stay Awake and Calm While She Eats. It's better, over the long run, if your baby doesn't go to sleep while she's eating. Using eating to fall asleep won't help her learn about being full or about putting herself to sleep. Eventually, you will want her to be able to sleep well, and going to bed drowsy but still awake will help her learn to do that. Help her to stay awake during feeding by holding her close enough so she can see your face. Talk with her gently while she eats.

Keep the feeding smooth and continuous. Avoid interruptions, jiggling, and burping (unless your baby seems like she's uncomfortable). If she fusses, be slow and gentle while you soothe her; then give her another chance to eat. If she shows she doesn't want to, stop trying to feed her.

Know When to Quit. It may be tempting to try to get your baby to keep on eating after she acts like she's full, but it isn't a good idea. If you want her to learn to pay attention to when she's hungry, *you'll* have to pay attention to when she's full. Otherwise, when she gets hungry she'll feel like something bad is going to happen to her—like being disrespected, made to eat more than she wants, and feeling stuffed and uncomfortable.

When your baby has had enough, she'll let you know by slowing down her sucking, turning away from the nipple, relaxing all over or sealing her lips. Her rooting reflex will go away. Some babies drift off, gradually losing interest in sucking. Others stop all of a sudden.

When your baby stops eating, give her a chance to rest and look at you. Talk with her quietly. She might start to act hungry again. Offer the nipple, but don't force. You're just giving her a chance to let you know.

Be Sure You Know Whether You Are Making Progress. Because prematurely born babies are so small, it is hard to tell when they are making progress with their growth. You need the encouragement of knowing your baby is growing well, but it is hard to tell that on the standard growth charts. Ask your health care provider about a special growth chart for a premature baby, about rate of gain charts, or about plotting your baby's Z scores.*

Don't Be in a Rush to Start Solid Foods or to Stop Formula. Always go by what your baby can *do* rather than by how old she is to make decisions about when to start and progress to solid foods. Even corrected age may not be a good guide for when to start solid foods. Work with her slowly and gently to help her learn to like solids—you will probably find that she is as cautious about new tastes and textures as she was earlier about learning to take the nipple. Take your time. She will eventually get so she eats a variety of foods. Keep her on formula until she is well established on solid foods. At the earliest, that will be 1 year corrected age. Even later is just fine—give her formula in a cup so she can learn cup drinking and not get stuck on the nipple.

---

* For information about a free program for calculating growth percentiles and Z scores, see the Centers for Disease Control Web site: **www.cdc.gov/epo/epi/intro/manual/manchp23.htm**

CHILDREN AND
FOOD ACCEPTANCE:
THE RESEARCH

Children will learn to eat the foods that appear on the family table, and they will automatically eat a variety. However, typical childhood eating behaviors and poor information about feeding lead parents to feed in ways that hinder, rather than foster, competent eating. What do we know about children's ability to eat a variety of food? What do we know about productive and counterproductive approaches to feeding?

Some of the earliest research on child feeding was reported in 1928 by physician Clara Davis, a New York Mt. Sinai Hospital physician. At the time, pediatricians dictated precisely the amounts, types, and frequencies of foods for children from 7 months to 3 years of age, and the belief was that the transition from suckling to adult food was to be made over 3 or 4 years. Furthermore, it was assumed that infants lacked the ability to regulate their own food intake. Davis set out to test that assumption in feeding experiments with three boys ages 8, 9, and 10 months and lasting from 6 to 12 months. She and her team demonstrated that infants could be healthy and grow well on self-selected diets of a variety of natural, healthy foods. At first babies chose foods and spit them out again, but after the first few meals they promptly recognized and chose what they wanted, no matter the location on the tray, and they stopped spitting out foods. It was impossible to predict what a child would eat at a given meal. An infant might eat from 1 to 7 eggs a day or 1 to 4 bananas. Milk consumption ranged from 11 to 48 ounces. Infants even ate salt occasionally, crying and spluttering but not spitting it out, then going back for more.[1] At the time he was enrolled in the study, one infant had rickets caused by vitamin D deficiency. He was offered cod liver oil in one of his little dishes—cod liver oil is a rich source of vitamin D. Over the first several months of the experiment he voluntarily consumed almost 9 ounces of the strong-tasting cod liver oil overall. Although he continued to be offered the cod liver oil after the rickets had healed and his diagnostic tests indicated his vitamin D status to be corrected, he stopped taking it. Davis's study is often misquoted and used to rationalize letting children freely graze for food, but essentially the researchers maintained a division of responsibility in feeding. They chose a variety of simple, single-ingredient, healthful foods for the infants and then let them pick and choose from what the adults had made available.

Pennsylvania State researcher Barbara Rolls freshened up the Davis research and gave it a new name. Rolls found that through a process she called *sensory specific satiety,* children and other people tire of even favorite food and choose otherwise.[2] Like the Mt. Sinai babies, children's variations in appetite will lead them over time to eat a variety of food and maintain a nutritionally adequate diet. Studies at the University of Illinois preschool under the direction of psychologist Leanne Birch illustrated that children are particularly equipped to make use of these internal cues. Children are tuned in to the taste of food and are far more likely than adults to eat in response to how food tastes to them at any given time. Furthermore, they considered food to taste good at one time and not good at another.[3]

Children generally like what is familiar. Nutrition professor Jean Skinner found Tennessee mothers in her surveys complained that at age 12 months their infants markedly increased their strong food likes and dislikes and that, far more than before, they were likely to lose interest in a food after one bite.[4] This is a typical food behavior that the Illinois preschool researchers called *neophobia:* the dislike of new food. However, the Illinois researchers found that children would taste new food, and the more often they tasted it, the more they liked it. Children might take 10, 15, or 20 tastes in as many meals before they learned to like a new food. This skepticism about new food appears in infants as young 4 to 6 months old, when they are first introduced to solid foods. The solution for the infants is the same as for older children: repeated exposure. Babies learned to like new foods when they had the opportunity to taste them over and over again. Breastfed infants, presumably because they were accustomed to tastes from their mother's milk, were more receptive to new foods than formula-fed infants.[3]

However, to move successfully and willingly through the transition period from nipple-feeding to semisolid, an infant has to have oral-motor readiness. Colorado public health nutritionist Virginia Beal found that babies under age 4 months old resisted taking solid foods and got into feeding struggles with their mothers. Babies first cheerfully accepted solid foods at around age 4 months.[5] Many parents offer solid foods far too early to their infants and apparently engage in struggles similar to those Beal observed. A 1998 survey done by the Beech-Nut baby food company found that spoon-feeding was a least favorite activity of up to 40 percent of surveyed parents, second in undesirability only to changing diapers.[6] It is unclear what long-term impact these early feeding struggles have on food acceptance.

In addition to waiting for developmental readiness and serving the foods repeatedly, it helps children learn to like new foods if they are allowed to try the food on their own initiative. Preschoolers who had been offered a new juice and allowed to experiment with it on their own were more likely to try the juice the next time they were offered it than the children who had been rewarded for trying it with a trip to the playground. Eating with a friend who likes the food helps. Eating with a trusted adult who is simply being companionable, friendly, and supportive, but not talking about the food, also helps.[3] Nebraska nutrition professor Kaye Stanek found that preschoolers did better with food acceptance when they ate with their parents and/or siblings, when they were given enough time to eat, when they were allowed to help with preparing foods or setting the table, and when they were allowed to take small portions of new foods.[7]

What Gets in the Way of Food Acceptance? As is apparent from the previous discussion, children need exposure to the food, they need the support of trusted adults, and they need *not* to be pressured in any way to eat. Even seemingly positive pressure, like a reward, decreases children's food acceptance. In contrast, children have trouble learning to like new food if they have either too few opportunities to learn or too much pressure on their learning. What does the research have to say about what goes wrong with feeding? In brief, children eat poorly when parents pressure and persuade, limit menus to food that children readily accept, and fail to provide regular and reliable opportunities to eat.

Many parents make the mistake of making alternatives too readily available and then at the same time put pressure on children to eat. Skinner's Tennessee studies showed that 70 percent of mothers of 16-month-olds offered alternatives when their toddlers didn't eat "enough," and over 10 percent acknowledged using force or bribery to get children to eat.[4] In Toronto, Marcia Pelchat and Patricia Pliner found that children who were reluctant to try new food had mothers who offered only foods that children readily accepted and short-order cooked for their children. Those mothers complained that their children were finicky, unwilling to try new foods, avoided whole classes of foods like vegetables, ate too little, liked junk food, or were simply not interested in food and eating. The same mothers prodded, rewarded, and punished to get children to eat.[8] Researchers in the Western

Massachusetts growth study found parents to behave at both extremes at the same time. They provided children with structured meals and snacks but controlled food choices and portion sizes at those times. Between times, children were allowed to help themselves with no limits to the refrigerator and cupboards.[9]

Feeding problems are common, as are negative feeding behaviors. While we can't answer the question of which came first, without a doubt the two are connected. A 1986 review of the literature indicated that at least 25 percent of the pediatric population presents with feeding problems, with a 33 percent incidence in specialized centers dealing with developmental disabilities. Problems included bizarre food habits, mealtime tantrums, delays in self-feeding, difficulty in accepting various food textures, and multiple food dislikes, as well as other feeding disorders such as infant rumination, childhood obesity, and anorexia nervosa.[10] Stanek found that typical negative food-related behaviors of parents with 2- to 5-year-old children included bargaining, bribing, and forcing; promising a special food, such as dessert, for eating a meal; withholding food as punishment; rewarding good behavior with food; persuading children to eat; playing a game to get children to eat; taking over and feeding children who refuse to eat; threatening punishment for not eating; and making children clean their plates.[7]

What conclusion can we reach from all this research? Children are born with food acceptance capability, but they need help from adults if they are to act on and retain that capability. Children watch their parents eat certain foods and assume, even if they don't eat them, that "someday I will eat that." Their assumption and their desire to grow up can be squashed by adults' behaving at either, or both, of the two extremes: by being too demanding or too protective. Children need adults to be supportive and companionable, to show them what it means to grow up with respect to food, and to give them opportunities to experiment and master. They don't need to be motivated—being motivated comes with the territory of being a child.

APPENDIX J

CHILDREN AND FOOD REGULATION: THE RESEARCH

Children know how much they need to eat, and virtually from birth they are resilient and resourceful regulators. University of Iowa physician Sam Fomon showed that when infants over age 6 weeks were fed either overconcentrated formula or overly dilute formula, they simply ate less of the concentrated or more of the dilute and grew consistently.[1] From age 1 week to 9 months, Houston anthropologist Linda Adair followed the formula- and solid-food intake of a little boy who was fed on demand. She found that, although the infant ate three times as much some days as others, and even though his food intake was lower than 90 percent of other babies, his growth was consistent and his size and shape were average. When he started eating solid foods, he took less formula and continued to regulate well.[2]

From birth, to do well with food regulation, children depend on tuned-in and responsive feeding. In an Edinburgh, Scotland, study with normal, well-born infants, bottle-feeding parents of small babies were more active in feeding and their babies grew less well than breastfeeding mothers of small babies, who were not overactive. Average-sized breast- and bottle-fed babies were fed similarly and grew equally well.[3] With children suffering from growth problems serious enough to be diagnosed as Nonorganic Failure to Thrive (NOFTT), in many if not most cases disruptions in the feeding relationship are at the root of the problem. Clinicians in a Buffalo, New York, hospital found that half of infants hospitalized with growth failure had feeding problems.[4] Feeding problems that can contribute to NOFTT range from undersupport of feeding to overcontrol. Supporting the child in achieving developmental tasks is important in allowing normal eating and

---

growth. In her work with infants and toddlers, Washington, D.C., Children's Hospital psychiatrist Irene Chatoor found that disorders of homeostasis, attachment, and separation/individuation can contribute significantly to NOFTT.[5]

The considerable food-regulation capability of children throughout their growing-up years depends on an appropriate division of responsibility in feeding. Both overcontrol of the child's prerogative in eating and undersupport of the child's access to food can cause disruptions in food regulation and growth. Fima Lifshitz, a physician in a pediatric nutrition clinic on the upper east side of New York, has documented over 300 young patients who have eaten and grown poorly when their parents have restricted their food intake. Parents were doing what they thought was right based on scientific warnings about obesity or heart disease.[6] Letting children graze for food can *inadvertently* underfeed them as they fill up on small amounts and don't work up a good appetite for meals. Denver Children's Hospital psychologist Kay Toomey found in her clinical work with poorly eating toddlers that structured feedings allowed toddlers to voluntarily eat 50 percent more than when they were allowed to graze for food.[7] With grazing, the expectation is that children can be mobile and vocal enough to get food for themselves and see to it that they get fed. In an extreme cultural example of toddler grazing, Texas A&M anthropologist Katherine Dettwyler observed New Guinea toddlers roaming the village in groups and eating only if they happened to be present in a home when food was available. Adults did not, in any systematic way, see to it that toddlers got fed. Growth rates of children in New Guinea were very slow.[8]

Research in the University of Illinois preschool laboratories demonstrated that the amount children ate varied throughout the day. Furthermore, children were able to compensate for variations in the amounts they ate at meals and snack times. Most children who got snacks before meals automatically ate less at mealtimes.[9] Colorado Public Health studies that followed children from year to year found that the amounts they ate as well as the composition of their food intake varied considerably. Some years, for instance, they ate far less fat, and other years they ate far more.[10] Even premature babies can regulate. A study conducted by newborn intensive-care unit nurses showed that medically stable babies weighing as little as 3 1/3 pounds were able to give signs to their care providers indicating when they were hungry and when they were full. They grew well when they were fed on demand and, in fact, consumed fewer calories than schedule-fed babies and still grew well.[11]

It is impossible to predict how much children will eat. Children of all ages who look alike and act alike may vary from one another in their calorie requirement by as much as 40 percent.[12] This is a result of the children's constitutional endowment, not because of distorted patterns of food consumption or activity. Activity patterns, like food regulation and body size and shape, appear to be predominantly determined by genetics. Studies of young infants by Harvard nutritionist Jean Mayer showed that the fattest babies tended to eat the least and were the least active, the leanest babies ate the most and were the most active.[13] The point? Being constitutionally determined, these tendencies can be changed only with extreme effort and at a high risk of destructive consequences.

Although children are good regulators, the way they are fed can undermine their ability to regulate and make them too fat. In my own clinical experience, children can *overeat* as well as undereat when they are allowed to graze for food and beverages. However, most of the research focuses on the negative consequences of *restricting* children's food intake. Most children given pre-meal snacks compensated by eating less at lunchtime, but some did not. Those who didn't adjust their intake were children whose eating was overcontrolled at home: parents and other adults controlled how much they ate by limiting quantities or by enforcing a clean-plate policy.[9] Sometimes this overcontrol is documented indirectly. A 16-year longitudinal study conducted in the San Francisco bay area in California tried to identify differences between infants who became fat as teenagers and those who remained slim. There were no differences between the two groups with respect to family composition, calorie intake, early feeding patterns, and typical food selection, to name a few. However, children who became fat as teenagers were more likely to have had eating problems as preschoolers and they were more likely to have had parents who were worried that their children would grow up fat.[14] From my clinical experience, I reason that these early eating problems came about when parents were overcontrolling and children were reacting to that control. Parents and children often have feeding struggles when parents try to manage the amounts children eat. Eating struggles with parents can be so upsetting for children that they lose track of their internal regulators and have trouble eating the amount of food that is right for them.

The tactics parents use to control their own food intake rub off on children, for good or ill. Parents who overcontrol their own eating, with either amount or type of food, tend to throw away all controls from time to time and be fatter than if they ate consistently. Studies at Pennsylvania State University show that children of parents who show this restraint and disinhibition pattern tend to overeat when they are given free access to "forbidden" food. Daughters of mothers who show this pattern are relatively fat.[15] Even without parental patterns of restraint and disinhibition, when children are not regularly allowed access to high-fat or high-sugar snack foods, they tend to overeat on those foods when they get the chance.[16] To head off this feast-and-famine pattern and still retain control of the family menu, serve high-fat foods like chips with the occasional meal or high-sugar foods like cookies for the occasional snack. Let children have as much as they want at those structured times.

Whether an underfed child eats too little, as in the Lifshitz reports,[6] or too much, as in the Pennsylvania State studies,[15,16] depends on who gets the upper hand. The submissive child of a controlling parent may get underfed. A more aggressive child who is able to beat down the parents' limits—at least at times—will likely be fed in a more erratic and inconsistent fashion and be at risk of gaining too much weight.

The point? Children know how much they need to eat, but they need help from adults if they are to act on and retain that capability. Children need to be able to tune in on what goes on inside of them and be aware of how hungry or how full they are. If adults give them insufficient support—don't offer food regularly or fail to offer appropriate emotional support at feeding times—children can have trouble knowing how hungry or how full they are and can eat too little or too much. If adults are too active and controlling in feeding, children experience so much static and interference from the outside that they can't tune in on their own sensations. Sometimes children go along with pressure from the outside and eat more or less than they really want. Sometimes they fight against that pressure and, again, eat more or less than they really want. Either way they lose sight of how much they need and make errors in regulation. They eat too much or too little and get too fat or too thin.

APPENDIX K

CHILDREN, DIETARY FAT, AND HEART DISEASE— YOU DON'T HAVE TO PANIC

At this writing, there are no generally accepted dietary guidelines for children about fat intake. There is a movement in that direction, though, and the arguments have begun. The enthusiasts say to reduce fat in children's diets by the time they are 2 years old[1]; the compromisers say by 5 years old,[2] and the moderates say not until after puberty.[3-5] The justification given for extending the guidelines to young children is that fat restriction is effective in preventing heart disease in adults and that it will be even more effective if it is started at age 2 years. This argument leaves something to be desired since, as I pointed out elsewhere,[6] dietary changes are only marginally effective.

The atherosclerotic process begins in childhood, warn the enthusiasts. Well, yes and no. Almost all children, regardless of national origin, diet, and sex, do develop fatty streaks in their major arteries.[7] Since children everywhere, on every kind of diet, develop fatty streaks, it is unclear what can be done to avoid them. These fatty streaks are reversible and do not necessarily progress to the hardening and plaque formation that is characteristic of heart disease. It is only after puberty that the hardening process continues and then only for some people, and only after age 30 does the process become significant.[8]

If hardening of the arteries starts in childhood, it must be slow. Heart disease, for the most part, is a disease of aging. Eighty percent of deaths from heart disease occur after age 65.[9] The alarming and often-repeated figure that "53 percent of people over age 50 die of heart disease" implies that heart disease presents a great risk of *premature* death. However, when you break the numbers down by age ranges, it appears that old people are the ones who are most likely to die of heart disease. Only 1 percent of women aged 50 to 59 die of heart disease, 2 percent at 60 to 69, 6 percent at 70 to 79, 20 percent at age 80 to 89, and 45 percent over age 89.[10]

People who develop heart disease when they are young are, for

482

the most part, people born with errors in fat metabolism, called *familial hyperlipidemia*, which give them early hardening of the arteries. Their disease process is quite different from that of other people. The someone we know who died of a heart attack at age 30 was probably a victim of familial hyperlipidemia. Even children who have high blood cholesterol are not likely to be at risk because most children who have high blood cholesterol grow out of it.[11]

The Canadians are much more sensible than we are about dietary guidelines for children. They say that adult fat recommendations should be applied only after puberty. The Canadian Pediatric Society/Health Canada report pointed out what even the enthusiasts acknowledge: that there is no clear evidence. No long-term testing has been done to see if modified-fat, low-cholesterol diets in childhood reduce heart disease in adults, nor, given the complexity and expense of such studies, is it likely to be done. As a consequence, the Canadians decided it was impossible and even risky to set rigid guidelines for what and how much children should eat.[3]

The safety of applying the Dietary Guidelines to young children is a major point of contention in the United States. The moderates say that it is dangerous to try to restrict children's fat intake and show clinical evidence of poor growth in many children put on such regimens by parents who were trying to do the "right" thing.[12] The enthusiasts say it is only overzealous parents who cause such problems and that if the diet is intelligently applied, children will grow just fine. For their evidence, enthusiasts show intensively supervised clinical interventions in which parents and children were provided with laborious instruction and follow-up.[13] The truth of the matter is that applying the Dietary Guidelines with all the complicated fat instructions is complex, difficult to do, and easy to screw up. If you screw up, your efforts don't do any good and may even do harm.

Children are already eating only 33 percent of their calories as fat.[14] Getting them to eat 30 percent or less without interfering with their intake of energy or other nutrients involves a significant increase in precision, attention to detail, and risk of error. Pennsylvania State researchers doing computer modeling of children's diets found that using more than one fat-lowering strategy produced deficient diets, particularly for children under age 2. Strategies included using low-fat meat and milk, doing low-fat cooking, and avoiding added fats at the table.[15] If your child has a particularly high risk of heart disease, and if you and your doctor have determined that he needs a special diet, get careful and informed dietary guidance from a registered dietitian to avoid the likelihood of nutritional deficiencies and poor growth.

Most people, however, are not in that category. Most of us are simply trying to be responsible and practical in feeding our children. For the most part, neither the moderates nor the enthusiasts are too practical about children and how they eat. They argue about the formula for managing the fat in children's diets, but neither group seems to realize that no child ever ate according to a formula. The moderates have the edge, however, because they are more flexible, which is always a good idea when dealing with children.

I am sad to say it, but current nutritional politics being what they are, when the Dietary Guidelines for children come out, they are likely to reflect the enthusiast camp. Right now, there are many sets of guidelines. The United States Department of Agriculture has already gone ahead on its own and is recommending fat restriction after age 2 in the Child Care Nutrition Program. In January 1999, the American Dietetic Association published its position paper on children and dietary fat; it is from the enthusiast camp. The American Academy of Pediatrics is meeting to reconsider theirs, and early signs indicate it is likely to be from the enthusiast camp as well.

The National Cholesterol Education Program has long taken the position that children's diets should be restricted, and they are making a lot of noise with their Eat Smart school curriculum for teaching low-fat nutrition classes. The American Heart Association, with its huge advertising budget, has been in the fat-modification business since the 1960s. When the Dietary Guidelines for children are released to the media, their introduction will seem like news, it will be announced with great fanfare, and it could scare you. Don't worry; it won't be news. It will be a political event, not a nutritional event. Stay calm. Be positive. Feed your child well. Emphasize variety. Wait to see what happens next. If something you hear about "eating for health" makes you and your child afraid of food, it won't help.

APPENDIX L

IRON IN YOUR
CHILD'S DIET

Iron in red blood cells carries oxygen to all parts of the body. When children don't get enough iron, they may look pale, act cranky, and not have much energy. Iron-deficiency anemia is one of the most common nutritional problems in children. You can, however, prevent anemia without much trouble by doing the following:

- Breastfeeding or using iron-fortified formula.
- Starting your baby by age 6 months on iron-fortified infant cereal. By 6 months, the natural supply of iron your baby had at birth is becoming depleted.
- Teaching your child to eat solid foods so she doesn't get stuck on milk.
- Having regular meals and taking some moderate care in menu planning.
- Serving nutritious food at snack time. Snacks shouldn't be just "treat" foods, because those have mostly calories and few other nutrients.

Strategies for Improving Iron Nutrition. When you think about your child's iron nutrition, you have to think not only about the amount of iron in her food but also about how much iron she can absorb from the food into her body. For both adults and children, only a small percentage of iron in food is absorbed. Your child will absorb iron much better from meat, poultry, and fish than from vegetables or grains. But she'll absorb the iron in vegetables or grains better when she eats them at the same time she eats meat, poultry, or fish.

Vitamin C helps iron absorption, too. Eating a good vitamin C food along with a meal improves iron absorption from the whole meal. Vitamin C is in many vegetables and fruits, such as oranges, strawberries, spinach, and broccoli. If your child gets meat, poultry, or fish and vitamin C at the same meal, she'll absorb even more iron from all the food in the meal. Examples of these combination meals (with meat, vitamin C, grain, and vegetable sources of iron) include hamburgers and coleslaw, spaghetti with meat-tomato sauce, hot dogs and orange wedges, and chicken with broccoli.

Eggs, Milk, and Liver. Although an egg yolk contains 1 milligram of iron, that iron is poorly absorbed. In fact, unless your child gets vitamin C at the same time, egg yolk actually cuts down on the iron she absorbs from other foods. Milk is low in iron—anemic children used to be called "milk babies."

Liver is an excellent source of iron, but eating a lot of liver gives too much vitamin A. If you serve liver, keep it down to twice a month.

Helping Your Child to Eat Iron-Rich Foods. Have regular meals and snacks, keep control of the menu, offer a variety of good foods, make eating times pleasant, and then wait. If you try to *force* your child to eat nutritious food she doesn't like, she probably won't eat.

Typically, iron-rich foods are challenging for children. Green leafy vegetables, for example, have a strong flavor. Eat and enjoy them yourself, and after a while your child will try them and maybe even learn to like them. Meat may be hard for her to chew and swallow, so make it moist and tender. Remember that even eating a *little* meat, fish, or poultry helps her body absorb more iron from *all* the food in her meal.

Iron Content of Selected Foods. Children need 6 to 10 milligrams iron per day. The foods listed in Figure L.1 provide significant amounts of iron.

FIGURE L.1 FOODS HIGH IN IRON

Food	Amount	Iron (in milligrams)
Meat and other protein		
Beef, pork, lamb	1 ounce	1.0
Poultry	1 ounce	0.5
Beef or chicken liver	1 ounce	3.0
Calf liver	1 ounce	5.0
Pork liver	1 ounce	8.0
Clams	1 ounce	2.0
Oysters	1 ounce	4.0
Other fish, shellfish	1 ounce	0.5
Nuts, average	2 Tbsp.	1.0

APPENDIX M

NUTRITIOUS SNACKS

Here are some suggestions for nutritious snacks that will tide your child over from one meal to the next. All of these foods will contribute to iron nutrition (see Appendix L).

Grain Products

- Bread products: Use whole wheat about half the time. Read the label to make sure the flour is enriched or whole grain—the first ingredient listed should be *enriched* or *whole wheat*. Try a variety of yeast breads and quick breads, including enriched or whole wheat, rye, oatmeal, and mixed grains. Try rye crisps, enriched or whole grain flat bread, and crackers. Serve bread and crackers with cheese, peanut butter, or a glass of milk to give protein and fat.
- Dry cereals: Many breakfast cereals make good snacks for children. Check the box label to choose varieties with less than 5 grams of sugar per usual-size serving. Serve with milk to give protein and fat. Add fresh or dried fruits, nuts, and seeds for variety and increased nutrients. *Don't give seeds and nuts to your child until she has her molars and can chew and swallow well.* Cereals with sugar-coated flakes, or sweet bits mixed in with the flakes, contain 12 to 20 grams of sugar per serving—about 3 to 5 teaspoons of sugar per serving.
- Popcorn: Try using grated cheese instead of salt and butter. Serve with milk or cocoa to give protein and fat. Wait to give popcorn until children can chew and swallow well.
- Cookies: Bake your own, substituting one-half whole wheat flour for

white flour. Try oatmeal, peanut butter, or molasses cookies. Serve cookies with milk to give protein—cookies already have fat.

Beverages

- Offer water for thirst between meal and snack times; offer your child a glass of water at snack time along with other beverages.
- Use fruit juices and vegetable *juices* rather than powdered, canned, or frozen fruit *drinks*. Fruit drinks lack folate, fiber, and other nutrients provided by real juices.
- Milk: Serve plain with bread, crackers, cereal, and so on. Mix milk in a blender with banana, other fruit, or orange juice for a healthy milkshake. Try adding vanilla extract, honey, molasses, or sugar. Use chocolate and strawberry flavorings for an occasional treat.

Vegetable Snacks

Depending on your child's chewing and swallowing ability, cut up fresh, raw vegetables. Serve frozen vegetables, like peas, still frozen. Serve with peanut butter, cheese, cottage cheese, or milk to get protein and fat. Whole or 2 percent milk give fat. Skim milk doesn't give fat, and 1 percent doesn't give very much. If you use skim or 1 percent milk, offer your child some other good source of fat. Add crackers or fruit juice to get carbohydrate. Make a dip with sour cream to give fat, a few extra nutrients, and some taste appeal.

Broccoli	Celery	Green peas
Carrots	Cucumber	Turnip sticks
Cauliflower	Green beans	Zucchini

Fresh Fruit Snacks

Slice or serve whole. Serve with peanut butter, cheese, cottage cheese, yogurt, ricotta cheese or milk to give protein and fat. Again, guide your food selection by considering your child's ability to chew and swallow.

Apples	Grapefruit	Oranges
Apricots	Grapes	Peaches
Bananas	Melons	Pears
Berries	Nectarines	Pineapple

Frozen blueberries make good snacks—thaw them for young children.

Dried Fruit Snacks

Serve with nuts (almonds, cashews, peanuts) or with seeds (pumpkin, squash, sunflower) to give protein and fat. *Wait to give seeds and nuts to young children until they can chew and swallow well.*

Apples	Dates	Pears
Apricots	Figs	Prunes
Bananas	Peaches	Raisins

Nuts and Seeds

Peanuts, pumpkin and squash kernels, sunflower seeds. Again, wait to give seeds and nuts to young children.

APPENDIX N

CHILDREN AND
VEGETARIAN DIETS

If you want your child to be on a vegetarian diet, you need to know what you're doing. See a registered dietitian to make sure you give your child what she needs. Take these precautions:

- Follow the recommended food plan in Appendix O, offering eggs, legumes, nuts, and seeds instead of meat, poultry, or fish. (Dried peas, dried beans, lentils, and peanuts are legumes.) Wait to give young children whole or chopped nuts or seeds until they can chew and swallow well—they could choke. Mash beans for young children.
- Use vitamin D–fortified milk to provide calcium, vitamin D, and a concentrated source of high-quality protein. You can use soy formula instead of cow's milk. However, soy or nut beverages (that you buy or make yourself) don't substitute for cow's milk. They generally don't have as much calcium as cow's milk and don't have vitamin D.
- Keep an eye on iron nutrition. Cutting out meat, poultry, and fish makes it hard for your child to get enough iron. About 3 to 8 percent of the iron in vegetables and grains is absorbed (depending on what's in the rest of the meal), compared to about 20 percent of the iron in meat, poultry, and fish. Without the well-absorbed iron and the "meat factor" from meat, poultry, and fish to improve absorption of plant iron, it's difficult for your child to get and absorb enough iron from his diet. Try to give a good source of vitamin C (citrus fruits or juices, green leafy vegetables, green pepper, tomato) along

with at least two of his meals every day to help him absorb plant iron.

- Use whole grains only about half the time, enriched refined grains the rest. If your child gets too much fiber, he'll fill up before he eats as much as he needs. Too much fiber can also interfere with iron, copper, and zinc nutrition. Enriched white flour, white rice, and white macaroni products give some of the advantages of grain without overloading your child with fiber.
- Make sure you include enough fat. Vegetarian diets tend to be low in fat because foods like beans, grains, fruits, and vegetables are mostly fat-free or low in fat. Children need fat. It's nearly impossible for children, with their small stomachs and high energy needs, to eat enough low-fat food to get the calories they need. To provide food that is moderate in fat, fry occasionally, use butter or margarine on vegetables, have the occasional sauce or gravy, and use 2 percent or whole milk. Fat makes food taste better, too. If you include more fat with your vegetarian food, your child may find it more appealing.

APPENDIX

FOOD GUIDES AND PORTION SIZES

In 1992, the *Basic Four Food Plan* that many of us grew up with and learned in school was replaced by the *Food Guide Pyramid,* shown in Figure O.1.

The Children's Food Guide. Recently, a pyramid for young children was published **(www.usda.gov/cnpp/KidsPyra/)**. Essentially, the children's version defines the minimums only, rather than the

---

FIGURE O.1 THE FOOD GUIDE PYRAMID

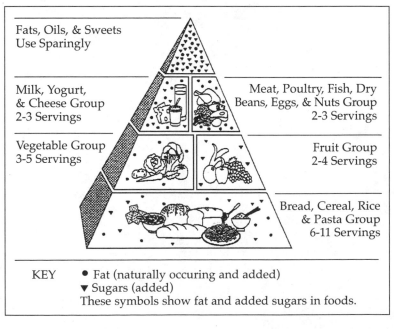

Fats, Oils, & Sweets
Use Sparingly

Milk, Yogurt,
& Cheese Group
2-3 Servings

Meat, Poultry, Fish, Dry
Beans, Eggs, & Nuts Group
2-3 Servings

Vegetable Group
3-5 Servings

Fruit Group
2-4 Servings

Bread, Cereal, Rice
& Pasta Group
6-11 Servings

KEY   • Fat (naturally occuring and added)
           ▼ Sugars (added)
           These symbols show fat and added sugars in foods.

minimums and maximums defined in the adult version. With the exception of fats, my recommended minimums from each of the food groups are the same as those of the pyramid–they are outlined below. I do not agree, however, with the pyramid's recommended "in moderation" notation on fat intake for young children because that *means* limiting fat to 30 percent of calories. In my view, for children that is *low*, not moderate. As a consequence, I have changed the fat recommendation to read, "to appetite." For my reasoning, see Appendix K; for my recommendations on managing fat in your child's diet, see pages 429-430.

> Bread, cereal, rice and pasta group: 6 servings
> Fruit group: 2 servings
> Vegetable group: 3 servings
> > Fruit and vegetable groups put together: 5 servings
> Meat, poultry, fish, dry beans, eggs & nuts group: 2 servings
> Milk, yogurt, and cheese group: 2 servings
> Sugars and sweets: In moderation
> Fats and oils: To appetite

Portion Sizes. To translate the food guide for your child, you need some help figuring out portion sizes. Keep in mind that portion sizes are nothing more or less than a unit of measurement, like a gallon of gas. A gallon of gas costs a certain amount, a half cup of orange juice gives certain amounts of nutrients. When I fill up my car, I buy 14 gallons of gas or more. When I fill up on milk, I drink 12 ounces or more. Simply because the label on a carton of milk says a portion is 8 ounces, that doesn't mean I have to stop at a cup. That would be as silly as running by the gas station every time I need a gallon of gas. With eating, as with buying gas, a *portion* and a *fill-up* are two different things.

You can use portion sizes to get a feeling for how your child is doing nutritionally. When I assess the nutritional quality of a child's diet, I use portion sizes as a basis for my nutrient calculations. Children's portion sizes are quite different from adult portions. Figure O.2 shows portion sizes for children during the early years. Even at age 8 years, a child's nutritionally adequate portion size is smaller than yours.

Food Equivalents from Food Groups. The last piece you'll need for figuring out the nutrition puzzle is a list of foods that belong in the groups. Foods are grouped according to their nutritional contributions, and one food within a group can substitute for another.

Bread, Cereal, Rice, and Pasta Group. Breads and cereals are good sources of B vitamins and iron and, if they are whole grain, fiber and

FIGURE O.2 PORTION SIZES FOR CHILDREN

Food	Ages 1–3 years	Ages 3–5 years	Ages 6–8 years	Ages 8+ years
Meat, poultry, fish	1–2 Tbsp	1 oz	1–2 oz	2 oz
Eggs	$^1/_4$	$^1/_2$	$^3/_4$	1 egg
Cooked dried beans	1–2 Tbsp	3–5 Tbsp	5–8 Tbsp	$^1/_2$ cup
Pasta, rice, potatoes	1–2 Tbsp	3–5 Tbsp	5–8 Tbsp	$^1/_2$ cup
Bread	$^1/_4$ slice	$^1/_2$ slice	1 slice	1 slice
Vegetables	1–2 Tbsp	3–5 Tbsp	5–8 Tbsp	$^1/_2$ cup
Fruit	1–2 Tbsp or $^1/_4$ piece	3–5 Tbsp or $^1/_3$ piece	5–8 Tbsp or $^1/_2$ piece	$^1/_2$ cup or 1 piece
Milk	$^1/_4$–$^1/_3$ cup	$^1/_3$–$^1/_2$ cup	$^1/_2$–$^2/_3$ cup	1 cup
Fats and oils	To appetite	To appetite	To appetite	To appetite
Sugars and sweets	See text	See text	See text	See text

Note: Children may eat more or less, but this is how much you can serve them to start with.

trace elements. Children generally like breads and cereals and have little trouble getting enough to eat from this group. Use whole grain about half the time to get trace elements and fiber. Don't feel you have to use whole grain all the time. Too much fiber from whole grain can interfere with trace element absorption. On the following list are adult-serving equivalents of breads and cereals. To convert to your child's serving size, go by Figure O.2.

Bread: white, whole wheat, rye, raisin	1 slice
Bagel	$^1/_2$
Biscuit, dinner roll, muffin	1
Buns, hamburger, hot dog	$^1/_2$
Cereal, cooked	$^1/_2$ cup
Cereal, dry	$^3/_4$ cup
Crackers	5–7 average
English muffin	$^1/_2$
Macaroni, spaghetti, noodles	$^1/_2$ cup cooked
Pancake, waffle	1 average
Rice, grits	$^1/_2$ cup
Taco shell, tortilla	1 average

Fruits and Vegetables. Fruits and vegetables are the primary sources of vitamins A and C in the diet. They also contain other nutrients such as calcium, B vitamins, iron, trace elements, and phytochemicals. However, in selecting fruits and vegetables we look particularly for the ones that are good in vitamins A and C. If you get these two nutrients from natural foods and in adequate amounts, you can generally assume that you will get enough of the other nutrients you need. Consult the list in appendix P, "Vitamins and Minerals for Children."

Below are adult-serving equivalents of fruits and vegetables. To convert to your child's serving size, go by Figure O.2.

Fruit: ³/₄ cup or a piece as commonly served, like a banana
Vegetable: ³/₄ cup

Meat, Poultry, Fish, Dry Beans, Eggs, and Nuts Group. Foods from the meat, poultry, and fish group are good sources of protein, iron, B vitamins, and trace elements. To help estimate portion sizes and think of alternatives, here are some examples of one-ounce portions of meat and meat substitutes or the equivalent. Don't give nuts or seeds to small children as they might choke. Children like hot dogs and luncheon meats because they are soft and easy to chew, and using them once or twice a week is fine. Dairy products give protein but they do not give the same iron and trace elements as meat, poultry and fish.

1 egg
2 tablespoons chopped chicken, beef, or pork
A piece of meat half the size of an audio cassette
1 slice (1 ounce) of cheddar-type cheese
¹/₂ cup cooked dried beans, dried peas, lentils
2 to 3 tablespoons nuts or seeds
¹/₄ cup cottage cheese
2 tablespoons peanut butter
2 slices bologna
1 hot dog
¹/₈ cheese pizza

Milk, Yogurt, and Cheese Group. The following foods each give the calcium and at least the protein of an 8-ounce glass of milk (only fluid milk gives vitamin D):

1 cup buttermilk or skim milk
1 cup chocolate milk or malted milk
1 cup yogurt
1 ¹/₂ ounces cheddar-type cheese
1 cup custard or milk pudding
1 ¹/₂ cup ice cream
1 ¹/₂ cup cottage cheese
¹/₄ cheese pizza

Fats and Oils. I don't recommend fat portion sizes for children. Food guides that dictate amounts of fat automatically impose outside limits on the child's food intake and remove trust in the child's ability to regulate food intake. As I said in the text, offer children foods with a variety of fat contents and then let them pick and choose from those foods, including foods that are high in fat, like butter, margarine, salad dressings, and gravies.

Sugars and Sweets. A child eating a reasonable amount of sugar will get 10 percent or less of calories from sugar. That means a toddler eating about 1,200 calories per day has a sugar "allowance" of 120 calories per day and a preschooler eating 1,800 calories a day has a sugar allowance of 180 calories per day. Those are average calorie intakes for children those ages. Since each teaspoon of table sugar (or honey, syrup, or molasses) gives about 20 calories, figure a reasonable daily sugar allowance at 6 teaspoons for a toddler, 9 for a preschooler. A fast way to figure sugar allowance in teaspoons for your child is to divide calories consumed per day by 200: a child eating 1,200 calories could have 6 teaspoons of sugar.

Fun Foods That Make Nutritional Sense. You don't have to be a puritan about good nutrition. "Snack" food, franchise food, and convenience food can all be nutritious if you eat it along with a variety of other nutritious foods. Figure O.4 on the next page lists foods that can perk up your food selection and also tells you what the foods give you. Once you get the idea, you will have more ideas of your own.

FIGURE O.3 SUGAR CONTENT OF COMMON SWEET FOODS

Food	Teaspoons of Sugar
Candy bar, 1 ounce	7
Cereal, sugar-frosted, 1 cup	3–5
Chocolate milk, 1 cup	3
Cookie, one 3-inch	1–2
Doughnut	2
Frosted cake, 2-layer, $^1/_{16}$	7
Gelatin dessert, $^1/_2$ cup	4
Ice cream, $^1/_2$ cup	3
Kool-Aid soft drink mix, 8 ounces	6
Milkshake, 10 ounces	9
Soda, 12 ounces	6–9

FIGURE O.4 FOODS THAT CAN PERK UP YOUR FOOD SELECTION

Food	Meat	Milk	Fruits and Vegetables	Bread
Chili	•		•	•
Tacos, burritos	•	•	•	•
Pizza	•	•	•	•
Spaghetti and meatballs or meat sauce	•		•	•
Lasagna	•	•	•	•
Beans: Bean soup, bean salads, refried beans, pork and beans	•			
Sandwiches: Hamburgers, hot dogs, peanut butter	•			•
with cheese	•	•		•
with lettuce, tomato, etc.	•		•	•

APPENDIX P

VITAMINS AND MINERALS FOR CHILDREN

- Eating a variety of foods is the best way to ensure good nutrition.
- If your child eats a varied diet, he probably doesn't need to take a vitamin or mineral supplement.
- He gets the nutrients he needs from the good foods you offer him.
- If you choose to use a supplement, be wise and cautious about selecting it.

Vitamin/Mineral Risks. You may hear lots of claims in advertisements about the benefits of certain vitamins and minerals. Be careful, and remember the following:

- Don't give too much of *any* vitamin, especially vitamins A, D, and B6. Too much can make children sick.
- Do provide iron in food or supplements by the time your baby has used up the natural supply of iron he was born with—age 6 months for term babies, 2 months for premature babies.
- To get enough calcium, your child needs to have at least 2 cups of milk a day.
- Supplement your infant's diet with vitamins or minerals only during his first year if they're recommended by your physician. Give only the prescribed dose and keep the bottle out of reach of children.
- After the first year, if you want to supplement, look for a children's brand that offers nutrients at levels of 100 percent or less of the DV (daily value).

Copyright by and reprinted with permission from *ELLYN SATTER'S NUTRITION AND FEEDING FOR INFANTS AND CHILDREN: Handout Masters.* Ellyn Satter Associates, Madison, Wis., 1997. For ordering information call 800-808-7976 or see **www.ellynsatter.com**

Don't Supplement Trace Elements Individually. Chromium, copper, fluoride, iodine, manganese, molybdenum, selenium, and zinc are called trace elements because they're needed in very small amounts in the body. Deficiencies are rare and it's easy to get too much from supplements. While *adequate* levels of trace elements are essential for good health, *too much* is dangerous for your child. It's easy to get too much, so don't give trace element supplements without specific recommendations from your health care provider.

Vitamins as Drugs. Recently, a research report claimed that Vitamin E, taken in large doses, could ward off heart attacks. Large doses of Vitamin A are used to treat some types of skin disease. Niacin (a B vitamin) taken in large doses is used to lower blood cholesterol. These are examples of nutrients being used as *medicines,* not for their nutritional effect.

As nutrients, vitamins are used in small amounts as essential components of the body's structure and functioning. As medicines, vitamins are used in large amounts and do something to the body that has little if anything to do with the nutritional effect. Because high doses of *even "natural"* vitamins can be toxic, particularly after prolonged use, using vitamins as medicines should be done only under careful and ongoing medical supervision.

B Vitamins. Children usually get enough B vitamins (thiamine, riboflavin, niacin) because they like vitamin B–rich foods like breads, cereals, and pasta. Your physician may recommend a vitamin B12 supplement if your child follows a pure vegetarian (vegan) diet.

Vitamin C. Vitamin C strengthens bones, cartilage, and other connective tissues and helps the body absorb iron. Babies under 1 year old need about 35 milligrams (mg) of vitamin C per day. If you're breastfeeding, drinking 4 to 6 ounces of orange juice per day allows you to pass along at least that amount to your baby. Commercial formulas provide about 35 mg of vitamin C per quart. Children age 1 to 10 need about 45 mg of vitamin C daily. Excess vitamin C does not protect against colds. At most, it acts as a mild decongestant to relieve cold symptoms. That is another example of a nutrient being used in excess for its drug effect. However, since excess vitamin C dosing may contribute to diarrhea and kidney stones, it is better to avoid giving it to your child in amounts above the daily value.

Almost all fruits and vegetables have some vitamin C, so eating a variety ensures good vitamin C nutrition. But because it's water soluble, vitamin C is not stored well in the body. Serve your child one excellent or two good sources of vitamin C *every* day. See Figure P.1 for

FIGURE P.1 VITAMIN C IN FRUITS AND VEGETABLES

Excellent Sources	Good Sources
Broccoli, brussels sprouts	Asparagus
Cabbage, cauliflower, kohlrabi	Chard
Cantaloupe	Honeydew melon
Grapefruit and juice	Potato
Mango, papaya	Tangerine
Oranges and juice	Tomatoes and juice
Peppers, spinach	Puréed baby fruits
Strawberries	
Vitamin C–fortified adult and infant juices	

excellent and good sources of vitamin C in fruits and vegetables.

Children generally like fruit juice and are willing to drink more than they need. But children fill up from too much and aren't hungry for meals. Overdoing juice can also cause stomachache or diarrhea. Limit juice to 3 to 6 ounces per day, and give it from a cup, not a bottle. You can dilute juice with water to make it go further. If your child is simply thirsty, offer water.

Vitamin A. Vitamin A is important for the growth and health of cartilage, bone, membranes and skin, and for good night vision. From birth to age 3 years, children need about 2,000 international units (IU) of vitamin A per day; older children need a bit more. A quart of formula or breastmilk contributes about 2,000 to 2,600 IU of vitamin A, a quart of cow's milk about 1,000 IU. Your child's greatest need for nonmilk sources of vitamin A comes after the transition to cow's milk, when milk consumption drops to 2 or 3 cups per day. Then he gets only about 500 to 750 IU of vitamin A from milk, and you'll have to depend on vegetables and fruits to provide the other 1,250 to 1,500 IU.

Fruits and vegetables contain beta-carotene, which the body converts to vitamin A. Figure P.2 tells relative amounts of vitamin A that can be made from the beta-carotene in the foods listed. The excellent sources can be eaten every *other* day. Vitamin A is a fat-soluble vitamin and is stored in the body.

Other Fruits and Vegetables. Fruits and vegetables like peas, beets, bananas, potatoes, and apples don't have enough vitamins A and C to appear on the lists given in Figures P.1 and P.2. However, they contribute other nutrients to the diet. For example, bananas have folic acid, and fruits and vegetables in general are good sources of potassium.

FIGURE P.2 VITAMIN A IN FRUITS AND VEGETABLES

Excellent Sources	Good Sources	Fair Sources
Apricots, dried	Apricot nectar	Apricots
Cantaloupe	Asparagus	Brussels sprouts
Carrots	Broccoli	Peaches
Mixed vegetables	Nectarine	Peach nectar
Mango	Purple plums	Prunes
Pumpkin		Prune juice
Spinach, other greens		Tomatoes
Squash		Tomato juice
Sweet potatoes		Watermelon

Most will give some trace elements like zinc and copper. All have fiber. Other nutrient and protective substances are less well defined, like phytochemicals. Once your child gets enough vitamins A and C, these other fruits and vegetables make worthwhile choices to round out his diet.

Vitamin D. Vitamin D helps the body absorb calcium and phosphorus to form strong bones and teeth. A deficiency of vitamin D causes *rickets,* a softening and malformation of the bones that results in bowed legs and other deformities. Commercial infant formulas are fortified with vitamin D, so formula-fed babies receive adequate amounts of the vitamin. However, breastmilk contains only small amounts of vitamin D. Some breastfed babies may need a supplement (200 IU per day) if they have dark skin or limited exposure to sunlight. Children who drink very little milk, or who consume milk not fortified with vitamin D, must have a supplement of 200 IU of vitamin D daily. But don't give too much vitamin D or it can make your child very ill.

There are a few foods that contain vitamin D naturally (egg yolks and salmon, for example), but our best source is vitamin D–fortified pasteurized milk. Our bodies also *make* vitamin D when the skin is exposed to sunlight. The amounts we produce depend on many factors, like age and skin color (dark skin reduces vitamin D production). Generally, a child who plays outdoors and drinks his milk is likely to get enough vitamin D.

Fluoride. Children who get recommended amounts of fluoride from birth have an average of 60 to 65 percent fewer cavities than children who do not get recommended amounts. However, too much fluoride even before the teeth erupt can cause fluorosis: white mottling of the tooth enamel or even colored mottling in extreme cases. Fluoride in your baby's diet comes from fluoridated drinking water, from formula made with fluoridated water, from foods and drinks that use processing water—both tap and bottled—from fluoridated municipal water supplies and from fluoridated toothpaste. Properly treated water is fluoridated to a level of somewhere between 0.3 and one part per million (ppm). Water is supplemented at a lower level in hot climates where water consumption is higher. Call your city water department to find out the fluoride level in your water, or have it tested. Your home water treatment system will remove fluoride only if uses a process called *reverse osmosis*. Figure P.3 shows the supplemental recommendations of the American Academy of Pediatrics and American Academy of Dentistry.

Vitamin and Mineral Supplements. If you decide to give your child a "vitamin," make it a multivitamin mineral preparation. Use a brand from a reputable manufacturer. Since *no* nutritional supplements are tested for safety and potency, the brand name is your best safeguard. Choose a broad-spectrum vitamin-mineral supplement in quantities no greater than 100 percent of the DV—daily value—of most nutrients. Centrum for children is a good brand, and superior to some of the toy-like supplements, both because it has a wide variety of nutrients *and* because it doesn't disguise itself in a form that your child will find attractive. Cute supplements tempt children to sneak around and take too many. If you purchase a store brand, compare the label with the Centrum label and look for one that is very similar. I have recommended Centrum because it contains a variety of trace elements like copper, chromium, and selenium at safe levels as well as the run-of-the-mill vitamins and minerals. Supplementing with one nutrient can impair the absorption or use of another, so taking the broader range of nutrients is a good idea. Taking too much iron, for instance, can impair the use of zinc and copper.

It's not a good idea, with children or with anyone else, to supplement with a little of this and a little of that—or, for that matter, a *lot* of this or that.

FIGURE P.3 SUPPLEMENTAL FLUORIDE DOSAGE SCHEDULE

Age	Drinking Water Fluoride Concentration		
	< 0.3 ppm	0.3 to 0.6 ppm	> 0.6 ppm
Birth to 6 months	0	0	0
6 months to 3 years	0.25	0	0
3 to 6 years	0.50	0.25	0
6 to 16 years	1.0	0.50	0
American Academy of Pediatrics, Com. on Nutr., *Pediatrics* 95: 777, 1995.			

APPENDIX Q

CALCIUM: IF YOUR CHILD DOESN'T DRINK MILK

Children from age 1 to 3 years need 500 milligrams of calcium per day, and children from 4 to 8 years of age need 800 milligrams of calcium per day. If your child doesn't drink enough milk because she is allergic, lactose intolerant, or doesn't like it, she might not be getting enough calcium and vitamin D for her bones. To help her to get enough calcium, you can substitute other calcium-rich foods. If she tolerates milk but won't drink it, you can incorporate more dairy products or high-calcium vegetables in your cooking. Here are some suggestions for incorporating calcium into your child's diet.

Use Dairy Products

- Make fortified milk: combine 2 cups fluid milk with a half cup powdered milk. Refrigerate before using. Substitute wherever you use milk. One cup fortified milk = 1 ½ cups regular milk.
- Add flavorings to milk: strawberry, chocolate, soft-drink powders. Make eggnog, cocoa, milkshakes.
- Make a "smoothie." Blend milk with fruit to make a milkshake-like beverage.
- Use milk in some cooking instead of water: cooked cereal, soups, gravies.
- Put powdered milk in baking. Add 2 tablespoons of powdered milk to each cup of flour. Store and use for all baking.
- Put powdered milk in other cooking. Ground beef: a half cup per pound. Add 2 tablespoons of water. Patties will be juicier. Casseroles:

2 tablespoons per cup. Powdered milk will make the casserole firmer and less watery. Vegetables: make cream sauce.

- Make desserts (use fortified milk): custard, pudding, rice pudding, bread pudding, pumpkin custard.
- Use cheese in cooking: macaroni and cheese, lasagna, tacos, grilled cheese sandwiches, cheeseburgers, pizza.
- Use high-calcium vegetables. Legumes: bean or split pea soup, chili, three-bean salad, pea-pickle-cheese salad, kidney beans with cheese. Greens: in salads, soups, as a vegetable in casseroles.
- If you use tofu, select the calcium-precipitated varieties.

Supplemental Calcium for Children Who Don't Consume Milk Products. Supplementing calcium can be done, but it is difficult. If at all possible, it's better to try for food sources. Supplements in the form of calcium lactate or calcium carbonate are reasonably well absorbed. Supplements may be syrup (one brand is Neo-Calglucon), chewable tablets (two brands are Caltrate Jr. and Calci-Chew), or wafers (one brand is Dical-D). The dose and calcium content will be on the label. If your child has to have several tablets, they should be spread throughout the day so she can absorb the calcium better. Avoid bonemeal and dolomite: They may be contaminated with lead and other trace elements.

Calcium-Fortified Food. Calcium-fortified orange juice is a good source of calcium. Ounce for ounce, it has the same calcium as milk. However, even this calcium-fortified orange juice is not a good substitute for milk because it doesn't have milk's vitamin D and protein. Your child may need a supplement to get enough vitamin D. To get more protein, she'll need more foods from the meat, poultry, fish, dry beans, eggs, and nuts group.

In some areas of the country, bread or other products are fortified with extra calcium. Read the label to find out how much calcium there is in a serving. Bread generally has about 25 milligrams of calcium per slice. Does the fortified bread have more?

Vitamin D. Calcium supplements come with or without vitamin D. Which is better for you to use depends on whether your child is getting vitamin D from other sources. Our bodies make some vitamin D when we expose our skin to sunlight, but the amount varies with skin color (dark skin reduces vitamin D production) and other factors. Vitamin D is also found in a few foods besides milk, including egg yolks, certain fortified cereals (check the labels), and salmon. Too much vitamin D can cause toxicity. The recommended daily intake throughout childhood is 200 IU (international units).

FIGURE L.1 CALCIUM CONTENT OF FOODS

Food	Amount	Calcium (mg)
Dairy products		
Milk, fluid	1 cup	300
Milk, powdered	1 Tbsp	60
Cheese, natural or processed	1 ounce	200
Cottage cheese	¼ cup	40
Yogurt	1 cup	300
Ice cream	½ cup	110
Cream cheese	1 Tbsp	10
Meat and other protein sources		
Meat, poultry, fish	3 ounces	10–20
Canned fish with bones	3 ounces	250
Egg	1	30
Cooked dried beans	½ cup	45
Nuts and seeds	2 Tbsp	20–40
Peanut butter	2 Tbsp	20
Tofu with calcium lactate (brands vary—check label)	4 ounces	50–250
Bread, cereal pasta		
Bread	1 slice	25
Biscuits, rolls	1	25
Corn tortillas	1	60
Cooked and dry cereals	1 serving	15
Noodles, macaroni	½ cup	15
Vegetables and fruits		
Vegetables, average	½ cup	20–40
Green leafy vegetables, average	½ cup	100
Fruits, average	½ cup	20–40
Calcium-fortified orange juice	½ cup	160

APPENDIX R

FOOD SAFETY

Food scientists agree that the most serious health threat from our food supply is contaminated food. You are entitled to depend on your grocer and producers to supply you with clean and wholesome food. However, much of the potential for contamination is in your own kitchen, and much of the responsibility falls on you for keeping your food safe.

- Keep hot foods hot and cold foods cold. Bacteria grow most rapidly at temperatures between 40°F and 140°F. Adjust your refrigerator to keep it at 40° or below. When you hold hot food, keep the temperature above 140°.
- Never leave perishable food out of the refrigerator for more than 2 hours, including preparation and standing times. At room temperature, bacteria grow quickly and the food can become unsafe. If you can't go home right after you shop, take along an ice chest to keep your food cold.
- Freeze fresh meat, poultry, or fish immediately if you can't use it within a couple of days after you buy it. Freezing food doesn't destroy bacteria. If food is contaminated going into the freezer, it will be contaminated coming out.
- Thaw food in the refrigerator, not on the kitchen counter.
- Most fresh vegetables, opened canned foods, meat, eggs, and dairy products should be kept in the refrigerator. It is all right to cover the can and put it in the refrigerator. Ketchup and mayonnaise go in the refrigerator after opening.
- Thoroughly wash your hands—and the hands of anyone who will

help—before starting to prepare food.

- Bacteria live in kitchen towels, sponges, and cloths. Use a clean dish towel and cloth every day; wash them in hot, soapy water. Sanitize sponges, kitchen brushes, and nylon scrubbers every day by soaking them for five minutes in a solution of 1 teaspoon of chlorine bleach (like Clorox) per cup of water. Unless you have a special sanitizing cycle, washing brushes, scrubbers and sponges in the dishwasher doesn't sanitize them—the temperature isn't hot enough. Rinse them out with clear water. Be careful not to get bleach on your clothes or it will take out the color.

- Keep raw meat, poultry, and fish (and their juices) away from other food when you shop, store, and cook. Bag raw meats separately in an extra plastic bag. Wash your hands, cutting board, and knife in hot, soapy water after cutting up these foods, *before* handling other foods. Take a clean dish cloth or sanitize your sponge after washing up from working with chicken.

- Cook meat, poultry, fish, and eggs thoroughly to kill bacteria. Cook ground meat to uniform internal temperature of 160°, poultry to 170°, pork to 160°, unground meat such as roasts to 145°, and eggs to 150° (the point at which the white is set and the yolk is starting to set). When microwaving, let food stand covered for the full number of minutes recommended to finish cooking and equalize the temperature in the whole dish.

- Rinse all fresh fruits and vegetables thoroughly with cold water before you start working with them, even the rinds and peels you plan to throw away. You have to assume the rinds have bacteria on them and take precautions to keep from cutting the bacteria into the fruit. As a knife slices through a contaminated rind, it carries bacteria into the fruit. Wash mushrooms, even through the gourmets say not to.

- Refrigerate produce after you slice it.

- Don't use detergent to wash produce. It can soak into the produce, and detergent ingredients have not been deemed safe for consumption. There is, however, a new fruit and vegetable rinse on the market that helps remove residues and wax.

- Avoid any fruit or vegetable juice that hasn't been pasteurized.

- Don't use sprouts, especially for children. The temperature and humidity necessary for sprouting seeds is also ideal for culturing bacteria, and some alfalfa sprouts have been contaminated.

APPENDIX S

DIARRHEA AND DEHYDRATION

Diarrhea is a medical condition that can make your child dehydrated. It is a symptom of an illness caused by a virus or bacteria, or by food contamination. That is quite different from the loose stools that are caused by a change in dietary habits, routine, or teething. Your child may have diarrhea if he seems ill and has a sudden increase in the number of loose or watery stools. Poor appetite combined with fluid loss through watery stools and perhaps even vomiting increases the danger that a child will become dehydrated. Taking in too little fluid at the same time he puts out too much will deprive him of the fluid and minerals he needs to maintain his body chemistry. If his dehydration becomes severe, he may have to be hospitalized.

Your health care provider will have specific advice and guidelines for you in identifying and managing your child's diarrhea. Here are the guidelines for managing childhood diarrhea compiled from recommendations of the World Health Organization, the National Oral Rehydration Therapy Project, and the American Academy of Pediatrics.[1]

- Keep oral rehydration solutions on hand. You can purchase these at any grocery store or drugstore. Brand names include Pedialyte, Infalyte, Nutramex, and Rehydralyte. You can also purchase the solutions made into flavored ices.
- If your child is under 2 years old, give a half cup every hour in sips using a small spoon or cup. Call your health care provider.
- If your child is over 2 years old, give $1/2$ to 1 cup every hour in sips.
- Keep giving the oral electrolyte solution until the diarrhea stops.
- If your child vomits, continue to give sips of the oral electrolyte solution. Give one teaspoon every 2 to 3 minutes until the vomiting stops. Then give the regular amount.
- Do not give sugary drinks such as Gatorade, soda pop, cola drinks, or apple juice. They can make your child's diarrhea worse.

While he is ill, your child is likely not to be hungry or interested in food. To find out, offer him food and let him turn it down. Feed him if and when he is hungry, and feed him as usual. If he isn't at all interested in food within 24 hours, call your doctor.

- If you are breastfeeding, continue as usual.
- If you are formula-feeding, continue to offer the same formula.
- If your baby is eating solid foods, continue to offer him what he is accustomed to eating.

Your child may need medical help if the diarrhea is more serious than usual. Be prepared to call your health care provider if the following occurs:

- The diarrhea and/or fever lasts more than 24 hours.
- Vomiting lasts more than 12 hours.
- The diarrhea gets worse.
- There are any signs of dehydration.
- There is blood in the stools.
- He has severe stomach pain or a swollen stomach.

Figure S.1 lists the signs of dehydration. Oral rehydration therapy will likely prevent these symptoms but knowing what they are will help

FIGURE S.1 DEGREES AND SIGNS OF DEHYDRATION IN CHILDREN

Mild dehydration	Slightly dry mouth Increased thirst Decreased urination
Moderate dehydration	Sunken eyes Sunken fontanelle (the soft spot) Skin not as smooth or elastic Dry mouth Few tears when child cries
Severe dehydration	Signs of moderate dehydration plus— Rapid light pulse Unusually blue skin Rapid breathing Cold hands and feet Listlessness, drowsiness Loss of consciousness

you to know whether you are being successful. If your child shows any signs of moderate dehydration, immediately get in touch with your health care provider. Severe dehydration can develop quickly in infants, and as you can see by the description, it is such a serious condition that it is a medical emergency.

This oral-rehydration, early refeeding approach is well tested and has become standard throughout the world. It has been responsible for saving the lives of countless babies because not only does it protect babies from dehydration, but it also protects them against nutritional depletion from prolonged food restriction. Until this method had been developed and tested, the standard approach to childhood diarrhea was to "rest the gut" by withholding food or by giving various dietary concoctions, the most common of which was the highly inadequate BRAT diet: bananas, rice, applesauce, and toast. Babies got hungry, and parents hesitated to feed them for fear they would do them harm.

Like all major changes in medical practice, this major shift in the management of childhood diarrhea has taken time to become standard practice. A 1991 report in the professional journal *Pediatrics* indicated that only a third of physicians regularly recommended the oral rehydration solutions. Furthermore, the majority incorrectly recommended withholding feedings until the second day or later.[2]

APPENDIX T

BOOKS AND RESOURCES BY ELLYN SATTER

Secrets of Feeding a Healthy Family Kelcy Press, Madison, WI, 1999 **877-844-0857**. Satter thoughtfully and responsibly stows the nutritional finger-wagging as she tells parents, "the secret of feeding a healthy family is to love good food, enjoy eating–and teach children to do the same." A perfect companion to *Child of Mine*, this book tells adults how to feed themselves joyfully, appealingly and wisely and how to get family meals on the table. Recipe, planning and shopping chapters entertainingly offer the reader a kitchen primer: food preparation for the "thinking cook," fast tips, night-before suggestions, in-depth background information, ways to involve kids in the kitchen and guidelines for adapting menus for young children. For singles, couples and parents as well as nutritionists, educators and mental health professionals, this is a must resource for anyone who works with families and/or food. Quantity discounts available.

How to Get Your Kid to Eat...But Not Too Much. Bull Publishing Co., Palo Alto, CA, 1987. After more than 10 years, this readable and authoritative resource for parents and professionals remains *the* book about solving childhood feeding problems. Satter's writing is firmly grounded in clinical experience as well as research in the areas of nutrition, feeding dynamics, parenting and child development. Adults struggling with eating issues have found this book invaluable in forgiving themselves for their own distorted eating attitudes and behaviors as well as in understanding their child's eating. An indispensible resource for anyone concerned about or working with nutrition, feeding or eating.

ELLYN SATTER'S FEEDING WITH LOVE AND GOOD SENSE: Video and Teacher's Guide. Ellyn Satter Associates, Madison, WI, 1995. These live action videotapes of real situations touch, move, startle, upset and

511

inform parents and child care workers and help them take a look at their own feeding behavior. Sometimes feeding goes well, sometimes it doesn't. The hour-long videotape shows what makes the difference and teaches nutrition and feeding by observation and experience. Available as the videotape only or as part of a teacher's guide including lesson plans, audio scripts and reproducible masters. The information on these tapes is based on Ellyn Satter's teaching and books.

The Infant. Babies know how much they need to eat, and parents read their messages.

The Older Baby. Babies learn to eat solid foods and talk to parents.

The Toddler. Toddlers need to explore, but they also need support and limits.

The Preschooler. Preschoolers want to get better at everything—eating included.

ELLYN SATTER'S NUTRITION AND FEEDING FOR INFANTS AND CHILDREN: Handout Masters. Ellyn Satter Associates, Madison, WI, 1995. Distilled from Ellyn Satter's philosophies and teaching and the pages of both *Child of Mine* and *How to Get Your Kid to Eat*, these informative, readable and engaging handouts are ready for copying and distribution to parents in nutrition, health and education settings. Equally valuable for training nutrition workers, each of the 56 handout masters is two 8 $1/2$ by 11 pages long. Topics have been selected on the basis of questions most often raised by parents about growth, feeding and nutrition. Feeding behavior is emphasized with nutrition information embedded in the question driven format. Indexed and cross referenced, these handout masters provide an accessible road map to the complexity of feeding infants and young children. Titles include *Being a Role Model for Your Child's Eating, If Your Baby Doesn't Eat Enough, What is Normal Growth? Weaning Your Baby, If Your Child is Finicky, If Your Preschooler Seems Fat, If Your Child Won't Eat Vegetables, Should Your Child Drink Milk?* Registered purchasers may make up to 300 copies of each master. Subsets available.

Ellyn Satter's Montana FEEDING RELATIONSHIP Training Package. Ellyn Satter Associates, Madison, WI, 1997. For agencies and professionals working with child feeding, Ellyn Satter's popular one-day primary interventions feeding dynamics workshop on videotape. Staff training on feeding interactions, child development as it relates to feeding, developmentally appropriate feeding practices, and preventing and managing feeding problems. Includes five hours of professional quality videos of lecture, demonstration and audience participation. Handouts include a multi-page training outline and materials, references and informational handouts for parents.

FEEDING WITH LOVE AND GOOD SENSE: Intensive Workshop
Ellyn Satter Associates, Madison, WI. Using Ellyn Satter's approach,
established feeding problems can be effectively treated in general practice on an outpatient basis. Training for professionals in evaluating and
solving childhood feeding problems integrates the principles of nutrition, feeding, child development and parenting. Specific problems covered in the workshop are: the child who eats poorly; the finicky child;
and the obese child. For health, education, child care and mental health
professionals.

FEEDING WITH LOVE AND GOOD SENSE: Training Manual Ellyn
Satter Associates, Madison, WI, Updated annually. This 125+ page
training manual for the *Feeding with Love and Good Sense* intensive
workshop provides essential information and tools for the practitioner
working with parent/child feeding interactions and solving childhood
feeding problems. Includes guidelines for assessment and treatment,
examples of written evaluations, letters to parents and physicians,
teaching materials and annotated bibliographies.

TREATING THE DIETING CASUALTY: Intensive Workshop The
missing piece for treating those with disordered eating, this powerful,
step-by-step approach resolves inner conflicts about eating and teaches
positive, competent eating based on internal regulators. There is far
more to normal eating than not dieting! This workshop teaches an
in-depth, theoretically sound understanding of eating attitudes and
behaviors and approaches to treatment. For health, education and
mental health professionals.

TREATING THE DIETING CASUALTY: Training Manual Ellyn Satter
Associates, Madison, WI, Updated annually. This 150+ page training
manual for the *Treating The Dieting Casualty* intensive workshop gives
an overview of Satter's unconventional and remarkably successful
approach to treating distorted eating attitudes and behaviors. This
manual serves as an in-depth resource handbook for working with
adults whose eating is out of control. Included in the manual are evaluation and treatment protocols, guidelines for communicating with
other professionals, standard eating and eating disorders tests, outlines
of principles of cognitive and behavioral management and annotated
bibliographies.

For a current catalog and price list, call Ellyn Satter Associates, 800-
808-7976 or see Ellyn Satter's website at **www.ellynsatter.com**

SELECTED REFERENCES

Preface

1. Cone T. *Two Hundred Years of Feeding Infants in America*. Columbus, Ohio: Ross Laboratories, 1976.
2. Davis CM. Self selection of diet by newly weaned infants: An experimental study. *American Journal of Diseases of Children*. 1928; 36(4): 651–679.
3. Council on Foods. Strained fruits and vegetables in feeding of infants. *Journal of the American Medical Association*. 1937; 108: 1259–1260.
4. Gesell A, Ilg FL. *Feeding Behavior of Infants*. Philadelphia: J. B. Lippincott, 1937.
5. American Academy of Pediatrics, Committee on Nutrition. On the feeding of solid foods to infants. *Pediatrics*. 1958: 685–692.
6. Beal VA. On the acceptance of solid foods and other food patterns of infants and children. *Pediatrics*. 1957; 20: 448–456.
7. American Academy of Pediatrics, Committee on Nutrition. On the feeding of supplemental foods to infants. *Pediatrics*. 1980; 65: 1178–1181.
8. American Academy of Pediatrics, Committee on Nutrition. The use of whole cow's milk in infancy. *Pediatrics*. 1992; 89(6): 1105–1108.
9. Satter E. A moderate view on fat restriction for children. *Journal of the American Dietetic Association*. 2000; 100: 32–36.
10. Satter E. Internal regulation and the evolution of normal growth as the basis for prevention of obesity in childhood. *Journal of the American Dietetic Association*. 1996; 9: 860–864.

Chapter 1

1. Linscheid TR. Disturbances of eating and feeding. In *New Directions in Failure to Thrive: Implications for Research and Practice*, ed. Drotar D. New York: Plenum, 1986: 191–218.
2. Pelchat ML, Pliner P. Antecedents and correlates of feeding problems in young children. *Journal of Nutrition Education*. 1986; 18(1): 23–28.
3. Skinner JD, Carruth BR, Houck K, Moran J, Reed A, Colletta F, Ott D. Mealtime communication patterns of infants from 2 to 24 months

of age. *Journal of Nutrition Education.* 1998; 30: 8–16.

4. Stanek K, Abbott D, Cramer S. Diet quality and the eating environment of preschool children. *Journal of the American Dietetic Association.* 1990; 90: 1582–1584.

5. Stayton DJ, Hogan R, Ainsworth MDS. Infant obedience and maternal behavior: The origins of socialization reconsidered. *Child Development.* 1971; 42: 1057–1069.

6. Satter EM. Childhood eating disorders. *Journal of the American Dietetic Association.* 1986; 86: 357–361.

7. Satter EM. *How to Get Your Kid to Eat . . . But Not Too Much.* Palo Alto: Bull Publishing, 1987.

8. Satter EM. The feeding relationship. *Journal of the American Dietetic Association.* 1986; 86: 352–356.

9. Satter EM. The feeding relationship: Problems and interventions. *Journal of Pediatrics.* 1990; 117: S181–S189.

10. Satter E. Internal regulation and the evolution of normal growth as the basis for prevention of obesity in childhood. *Journal of the American Dietetic Association.* 1996; 9: 860–864.

11. Satter EM. *Secrets of Feeding a Healthy Family.* Madison, Wis.: Kelcy Press, 1999.

12. Ikeda JP, Hayes D, Satter E, Parham ES, Kratina K, Woolsey M, Lowey M, Tribole E. A commentary on the new obesity guidelines from NIH. *Journal of the American Dietetic Association.* 1999; 99: 918–919.

13. Satter E, Sharkey PB. *Ellyn Satter's Feeding with Love and Good Sense: Video and Teacher's Guide.* Madison, Wis.: Ellyn Satter Associates, 1995.

14. Satter E, Sharkey PB. *Ellyn Satter's Nutrition and Feeding for Infants and Children: Handout Masters.* Madison, Wis.: Ellyn Satter Associates, 1995.

15. Satter EM. *The Montana Feeding Relationship Training Package.* Madison, Wis.: Ellyn Satter Associates, 1996.

16. Satter EM. *Feeding with Love and Good Sense: Intensive Workshop on Treating Childhood Feeding Problems.* Madison, Wis.: Ellyn Satter Associates, 2000.

17. Satter EM. *Treating the Dieting Casualty: Intensive Workshop on Treating the Chronic Dieter.* Madison, Wis.: Ellyn Satter Associates, 2000.

18. Nature of concern about nutritional content, 1989–1998. Research Department. *Trends in the United States: Consumer Attitudes and the Supermarket.* Washington, D.C.: Food Marketing Institute, 1998: 72.

Chapter 2

1. Serdula MK, Mokdad AH, Williamson DF, Galuska DA, Mendlein JM, Heath GW. Prevalence of attempting weight loss and strategies for controlling weight. *Journal of the American Medical Association.* 1999; 282: 1353–1358.

2. American Dietetic Association. *Nutrition and You: Trends 2000.* Chicago: The American Dietetic Association, 2000.

3. Hamill PVV, Drizd TA, Johnson CL, Reed RB, Roche AF, Moore

WM. Physical growth: National Center for Health Statistics percentiles. *American Journal of Clinical Nutrition.* 1979; 32: 607–629.

4. Lifshitz F, Tarim O. Nutrition dwarfing. *Current Problems in Pediatrics.* 1993; 23: 322–336.

5. Crawford PB, Shapiro LR. How obesity develops: A new look at nature and nurture. In *Obesity and Health,* ed. Berg FM. Hettinger, N.Dak.: Healthy Living Institute, 1991; 5: 40–41.

6. Serdula MK, Ivery D, Coates RJ, Freedman DS, Williamson DF, Byers T. Do obese children become obese adults? A review of the literature. *Preventive Medicine.* 1993; 22: 167–177.

7. National Research Council. *Recommended Dietary Allowances,* 10th ed. Washington, D.C.: National Academy Press, 1989.

8. Gesell A, Ilg FL. *Feeding Behavior of Infants.* Philadelphia: J.B. Lippincott, 1937.

9. Purvis GA. Infant nutrition survey. *Gerber Products Company,* 1979.

10. Rose HE, Mayer J. Activity, calorie intake, fat storage, and the energy balance of infants. *Pediatrics.* 1968; 41: 18–29.

11. Ainsworth MDS, Bell SM. Some contemporary patterns of mother-infant interaction in the feeding situation. In *Stimulation in Early Infancy,* ed. Ambrose A. New York: Academic Press, 1969: 133–170.

12. Fisher JO, Birch LL. Restricting access to food and children's eating. *Appetite.* 1999; 405–419.

13. Cutting TM, Fisher JO, Grimm-Thomas K, Birch LL. Like mother, like daughter: Familial patterns of overweight are mediated by mothers' dietary disinhibition. *American Journal of Clinical Nutrition.* 1999; 69: 608–613.

14. Mayer J, Roy P, Mitra KP. Relation between caloric intake, body weight, and physical work. *American Journal of Clinical Nutrition.* 1956; 4(2): 169–175.

15. Anderson RE, Crespo CJ, Bartlett SJ, Cheskin LJ, Pratt M. Relationship of physical activity and television watching with body weight and level of fatness among children: Results from the Third National Health and Nutrition Examination Survey. 1998; 279: 938–942.

16. Klesges RC, Shelton ML, Klesges LM. Effects of television on metabolic rate: Potential implications for childhood obesity. *Pediatrics.* 1993; 91(2): 281–286.

17. Epstein LH, Saelens BE, Myers MD, Vito D. The effects of decreasing sedentary behaviors on activity choice in obese children. *Health Psychology.* 1997; 16: 107–113.

Chapter 3
1. Ryan AS. The resurgence of breastfeeding in the United States. *Pediatrics.* April 1997; 99: e12.

2. American Academy of Pediatrics Work Group on Breastfeeding. Breastfeeding and the use of human milk. *Pediatrics.* 1997; 100: 1035–1039.

3. Anderson JW, Johnstone BM, Remley DT. Breast-feeding and

cognitive development: A meta-analysis. *American Journal of Clinical Nutrition.* 1999; 70: 525–535.

4. de Boissieu D, Matarazzo P, Dupont C. Allergy to extensively hydrolyzed cow milk proteins in infants: Identification and treatment with an amino acid–based formula. *Journal of Pediatrics.* 1997; 131: 744–747.

Chapter 4

1. Stayton DJ, Hogan R, Ainsworth MDS. Infant obedience and maternal behavior: The origins of socialization reconsidered. *Child Development.* 1971; 42: 1057–1069.
2. Crow RA, Fawcett JN, Wright P. Maternal behavior during breast- and bottle-feeding. *Journal of Behavioral Medicine.* 1980; 3(3): 259–277.
3. Brazelton TB. *Neonatal Behavioral Assessment Scale.* London: Spastics International Medical Publications, 1984.
4. Barnard K. *Keys to Caregiving: Self-Instructional Video Series.* Seattle, Wash.: NCAST Publications, University of Washington, 1990.
5. Sander L. The regulation of exchange in the infant caregiver systems. In *Interaction and Conversation and the Development of Language,* ed. Levins M, Rosenblum L. New York: John Wiley & Sons, 1977: 133–156
6. Chess S, Thomas A. *Know Your Child: An Authoritative Guide for Today's Parents.* North Vale, N.J.: Jason Aronson Publishers, 1996.
7. Johnson CM. Infant and toddler sleep: A telephone survey of parents in one community. *Journal of Developmental and Behavioral Pediatrics.* 1991; 12: 108–114.

Chapter 5

1. Pridham KF. Meaning of infant feeding issues and mothers' use of help. *Journal of Reproductive and Infant Psychology.* 1987; 5: 145–152.
2. Worthington-Roberts BS. Lactation: Basic considerations. In *Nutrition in Pregnancy and Lactation,* ed. Worthington-Roberts BS, Williams SR. Boston: WCB McGraw-Hill; 1997: 316–346.
3. Dettwyler KA, Fishman C. Infant feeding practices and growth. *Annual Review of Anthropology* 1992; 21: 171–204.
4. Victoria CG, Behague DP, Barros FC, Olinto MTA, Weiderpass E. Pacifier use and short breastfeeding duration: Cause, consequence, or coincidence? *Pediatrics.* 1997; 99: 445–453.
5. Food and Nutrition Board, Institute of Nutrition, National Academy of Sciences. *Nutrition during Lactation.* Washington, D.C.: National Academy Press; 1991.
6. Isolauri E, Tahvanainen A, Peltola T, Arvola T. Breast-feeding of allergic infants. *Journal of Pediatrics.* 1999; 134: 27–32.
7. Fomon SJ. *Nutrition of Normal Infants.* St. Louis, Mo.: Mosby-Year Book, 1993.
8. Dewey KG, Heinig MJ, Nommsen LA, Peerson JM, Lonnerdal B. Growth of breast-fed and formula-fed infants from 0 to 18 months:

The DARLING study. *Pediatrics.* 1992; 89(6): 1035–1041.
9. American Academy of Pediatrics Work Group on Breastfeeding. Breastfeeding and the use of human milk. *Pediatrics.* 1997; 100: 1035–1039.
10. Schanler RJ, O'Connor KG, Lawrence RA. Pediatricians' practices and attitudes regarding breastfeeding promotion. *Pediatrics.* 1999; 103: (e) 35.
11. Lawrence RA, Lawrence RM. *Breastfeeding: A Guide for the Medical Professional,* 5th ed. New York: Mosby, 1999.

Chapter 6

1. Stayton DJ, Hogan R, Ainsworth MDS. Infant obedience and maternal behavior: The origins of socialization reconsidered. *Child Development.* 1971; 42: 1057–1069.
2. Price G. Sensitivity in mother-infant interactions: The AMIS scale. *Infant Behavior and Development.* 1983; 6: 353–360.
3. Nadasdi M. Tolerance of a milk-based formula by infants. *Clinical Therapeutics.* 1992; 14(2): 242–246.
4. Adair LS. The infant's ability to self-regulate caloric intake: A case study. *Journal of the American Dietetic Association.* 1984; 84(5): 543–546.
5. Mackin ML, Medendorp SV, Maier MC. Infant sleep and bedtime cereal. *American Journal of Diseases in Childhood.* 1989; 143: 1066–1068.
6. Chandra RJ. Five-year follow-up of high-risk infants with family history of allergy who were exclusively breast-fed or fed partial whey hydrolysate, soy, and conventional cow's milk formulas. *Journal of Pediatric and Gastroenterological Nutrition.* 1997; 24: 380–388.
7. Setchell KD, Zimmer-Nechemias L, Cai J, Heubi JE. Exposure of infants to phyto-oestrogens from soy-based infant formula. *Lancet.* 1997; 350: 23–27.
8. American Academy of Pediatrics, Committee on Nutrition. Soy protein–based formulas: Recommendations for use in infant feeding. *Pediatrics.* 1998; 101: 148–153.
9. Boulton TJC, Rowley MP. Nutritional studies during early childhood. III. Incidental observations of temperament, habits and experiences of ill health. *Australian Paediatrics Journal.* 1979; 15: 87–90.
10. Zeigler RS, Sampson HA, Bock SA, Burks AW, Harden K, Noone S, Martin D, Leung S, Wilson G. Soy allergy in infants and children with IgE-associated cow's milk allergy. *Journal of Pediatrics.* 1999; 134: 614–622.
11. Fein SB, Falci CD. Infant formula preparation, handling, and related practices in the United States. *Journal of the American Dietetic Association.* 1999; 99: 1234–1240.

Chapter 7

1. Mackin ML, Medendorp SV, Maier MC. Infant sleep and bedtime cereal. *American Journal of Diseases in Childhood.* 1989; 143: 1066–1068.

2. American Academy of Pediatrics, Committee on Nutrition. *Pediatric Nutrition Handbook.* Elk Grove Village, Ill.: American Academy of Pediatrics, 1998.
3. Beal VA. On the acceptance of solid foods and other food patterns of infants and children. *Pediatrics.* 1957; 20: 448–456.
4. Parmelee AH, Wenner WH, Schulz HR. Infant sleep patterns from birth to 16 weeks of age. *Journal of Pediatrics.* 1964; 65: 839–848.
5. Johnson CM. Infant and toddler sleep: A telephone survey of parents in one community. *Journal of Developmental and Behavioral Pediatrics.* 1991; 12: 108–114.

Chapter 8
1. Skinner JD, Carruth BR, Houck KS, Coletta F, Cotter R, Ott D, McLeod M. Longitudinal study of nutrient and food intakes of infants aged 2 to 24 months. *Journal of the American Dietetic Association.* 1997; 97(5): 496–504.
2. Satter EM. The feeding relationship. *Journal of the American Dietetic Association.* 1986; 86: 352–356.
2. Skinner JD, Carruth BR, Houck K, Moran J, Reed A, Coletta F, Ott D. Mealtime communication patterns of infants from 2 to 24 months of age. *Journal of Nutrition Education.* 1998; 30: 8–16.
3. Pelchat ML, Pliner P. Antecedents and correlates of feeding problems in young children. *Journal of Nutrition Education.* 1986; 18(1): 23–28.
4. Subar AF, Krebs-Smith SM, Cook A, Kahle LL. Dietary sources of nutrients among U.S. adults, 1989 to 1991. *Journal of the American Dietetic Association.* 1998; 98: 537–547.
5. Sigman-Grant M, Zimmerman S, Kris-Etherton PM. Dietary approaches for reducing fat intake of preschool-aged children. *Pediatrics.* 1993; 91: 955–960.
6. American Dietetic Association. *Nutrition and You: Trends 2000.* Chicago: American Dietetic Association, 2000.

Chapter 9
1. Baumrind D. Current patterns of parental authority. *Developmental Psychology Monograph.* 1971; 4(1 pt.2): 1–103.
2. Anliker JA, Laus MJ, Samonds KW, Beal VA. Mothers' reports of their three-year-old children's control over foods and involvement in food-related activities. *Journal of Nutrition Education.* 1992; 24(6): 285–291.
3. Davis CM. Feeding after the first year. In *Brennaman's Practice of Pediatrics,* ed. Brennaman. Hagerstown, Md.: W.F. Prior, 1957.
4. Satter E. Internal regulation and the evolution of normal growth as the basis for prevention of obesity in childhood. *Journal of the American Dietetic Association.* 1996; 9: 860–864.
5. Davies HW, Behrens D, Miller T, Splaingard M, Davies CM, Combs LD, Noll RB. Mealtime interactions and family characteristics in CF.

Eighth Annual North American Cystic Fibrosis Conference. Orlando: 1994.
6. Spalding K, McKeever P. Mothers' experiences caring for children with disabilities who require a gastrostomy tube. *Journal of Pediatric Nursing.* 1998; 13: 234–243.
7. Keys A, Brozek J, Henschel A, Mickelsen O, Taylor H. *The Biology of Human Starvation.* Minneapolis: University of Minnesota Press, 1950.
8. Epstein LH, Saelens BE, Myers MD, Vito D. The effects of decreasing sedentary behaviors on activity choice in obese children. *Health Psychology.* 1997; 16: 107–113.
9. American Academy of Pediatrics Committee on Communications. Children, adolescents, and television. *Pediatrics.* 1990; 85: 1119–1120.
10. Consensus Development Conference National Institutes of Health. Defined diets and hyperactivity. *Journal of the American Medical Association.* 1982; 248: 290–292.
11. Rowe K. Synthetic food coloring and behavior: A dose-response effect in double-blind, placebo-controlled, repeated measures study. *Journal of Pediatrics.* 1994; 125: 691–698.
12. Lifshitz F, Ament ME, Kleinman RE, Klish W, Lebenthal E, Perman J, Udall JN. Role of juice carbohydrate malabsorption in chronic nonspecific diarrhea. *Journal of Pediatrics.* 1992; 120(5): 825–829.
13. Steel JM, Young RJ, Lloyd GG, Macintyre CCA. Abnormal eating attitudes in young insulin-dependent diabetics. *British Journal of Psychiatry.* 1989; 155: 515–521.
14. Applegate E. Nondiet counseling for diabetes in medical nutrition therapy. *Healthy Weight Journal,* ed. Berg FM. Hamilton, Ontario: Decker; 1998; 12: 6–8.

Appendix E

1. The nutritional value of breast milk from non-pregnant mothers. *Nutrition Reviews.* 1981; 39: 308–309.
2. Auerbach KG, Avery JL. Relactation: A study of 366 cases. *Pediatrics.* 1980; 65: 236–242.

Appendix H

1. Saunders RB, Friedman CB, Stramoski PR. Feeding preterm infants: Schedule or demand? *JOGNN.* 1990; 20: 212–218.

Appendix I

1. Davis CM. Self selection of diet by newly weaned infants: An experimental study. *American Journal of Diseases of Children.* 1928; 36(4): 651–679.
2. Rolls BJ. Sensory specific satiety. *Nutrition Reviews.* 1986; 44: 93–101.
3. Birch LL, Fisher JA. Appetite and eating behavior in children. *Pediatric Clinics of North America.* 1995; 42(4): 931–953.
4. Skinner JD, Carruth BR, Houck K, Moran J, Reed A, Colletta F, Ott

D. Mealtime communication patterns of infants from 2 to 24 months of age. *Journal of Nutrition Education.* 1998; 30: 8–16.

5. Beal VA. On the acceptance of solid foods and other food patterns of infants and children. *Pediatrics.* 1957; 20: 448–456.

6. Public Relations Department. *Beech-Nut Baby Survey.* St. Louis, Mo.: Beech-Nut Nutrition Corporation, 1998.

7. Stanek K, Abbott D, Cramer S. Diet quality and the eating environment of preschool children. *Journal of the American Dietetic Association.* 1990; 90: 1582–1584.

8. Pelchat ML, Pliner P. Antecedents and correlates of feeding problems in young children. *Journal of Nutrition Education.* 1986; 18(1): 23–28.

9. Anliker JA, Laus MJ, Samonds KW, Beal VA. Mothers' reports of their three-year-old children's control over foods and involvement in food-related activities. *Journal of Nutrition Education.* 1992; 24(6): 285-291.

10. Linscheid TR. Disturbances of eating and feeding. In *New Directions in Failure to Thrive: Implications for Research and Practice.* ed. Drotar D. New York: Plenum, 1986: 191–218.

Appendix J

1. Fomon SJ, Filer LJ Jr., Thomas LN, Anderson TA, Nelson SE. Influence of formula concentration on caloric intake and growth of normal infants. *Acta Paediatrica Scandanavica.* 1975; 64: 172–181.

2. Adair LS. The infant's ability to self-regulate caloric intake: A case study. *Journal of the American Dietetic Association.* 1984; 84(5): 543–546.

3. Crow RA, Fawcett JN, Wright P. Maternal behavior during breast- and bottle-feeding. *Journal of Behavioral Medicine.* 1980; 3(3): 259–277.

4. Sills RH. Failure to thrive: The role of clinical and laboratory evaluation. *American Journal of Diseases of Children.* 1978; 132: 967–969.

5. Chatoor I, Schaefer S, Dickson L, Egan J. Non-organic failure to thrive: A developmental perspective. *Pediatric Annals.* 1984; 13(11): 829–843.

6. Lifshitz F, Tarim O. Nutrition dwarfing. *Current Problems in Pediatrics.* 1993; 23: 322–336.

7. Toomey KA. Caloric intake of toddlers fed structured meals and snacks versus on demand. *Verbal Communication.* 1994.

8. Dettwyler KA. Styles of infant feeding: Parental/caretaker control of food consumption in young children. *American Anthropologist.* 1989; 91: 696–703.

9. Birch LL, Fisher JA. Appetite and eating behavior in children. *Pediatric Clinics of North America.* 1995; 42(4): 931–953.

10. Beal VA. Dietary intake of individuals followed through infancy and childhood. *American Journal of Public Health.* 1961; 51(8): 1107–1117.

11.Saunders RB, Friedman CB, Stramoski PR. Feeding preterm infants: Schedule or demand? *Journal of Obstetric, Gynecologic, and Neonatal*

Nursing. 1990; 20: 212–218.
12. National Research Council. *Recommended Dietary Allowances,* 10th ed. Washington, D.C.: National Academy Press, 1989.
13. Rose HE, Mayer J. Activity, calorie intake, fat storage, and the energy balance of infants. *Pediatrics.* 1968;41:18-29
14. Crawford PB, Shapiro LR. How obesity develops: A new look at nature and nurture. In *Obesity and Health,* ed. Berg F.M. Hettinger, N. Dak.: Healthy Living Institute, 1991; 5: 40–41.
15. Cutting TM, Fisher JO, Grimm-Thomas K, Birch LL. Like mother, like daughter: Familial patterns of overweight are mediated by mothers' dietary disinhibition. *American Journal of Clinical Nutrition.* 1999; 69: 608–613.
16. Fisher JO, Birch LL. Restricting access to food and children's eating. *Appetite.* 1999: 405–419.

Appendix K

1. NCEP expert panel on blood cholesterol levels in children and adolescents. National Cholesterol Education Program (NCEP): Highlights of the report of the expert panel on blood cholesterol levels in children and adolescents. *Pediatrics.* 1992; 89(3): 495–501.
2. American Academy of Pediatrics, Committee on Nutrition. Statement on Cholesterol. *Pediatrics.* 1992; 90(3): 469–473.
3. Canadian Paediatric Society, Health Canada. Nutrition Recommendations Update . . . Dietary Fat and Children. *Report of the Joint Working Group of the Canadian Paediatric Society and Health Canada,* 1993.
4. Newman TB, Garber AM, Holzman NA, Hulley SB. Problems with the report of the expert panel on blood cholesterol levels in children and adolescents. *Archives of Pediatric and Adolescent Medicine.* 1995; 149: 241–247.
5. Olson RE. The dietary recommendations of the American Academy of Pediatrics. *American Journal of Clinical Nutrition.* 1995; 61: 271–273.
6. Satter EM. Dietary fat and heart disease: It's not as bad as you think. In *Secrets of Feeding a Healthy Family.* Madison, Wis.: Kelcy Press, 1999: 211–213.
7. Tejada CJ, Strong JP, Montenegro MR, Restrepo C, Solberg LA. Distribution of coronary and aortic atherosclerosis by geographic location, race and sex. *Laboratory Investigation.* 1968; 18: 509–526.
8. Pathobiological Determinants of Atherosclerosis in Youth (PDAY) Research Group. Relationship of atherosclerosis in young men to serum lipoprotein cholesterol concentrations and smoking. A preliminary report. *Journal of the American Medical Association.* 1990; 264: 3018–3024.
9. Harper AE. Dietary guidelines in perspective. *Journal of Nutrition.* 1996; 126(supplement): 1042S–1048S.
10. Bush TL. The epidemiology of cardiovascular disease in postmenopausal women. *Annals of the New York Academy of Science.* 1990; 592: 263–271.

11.Lauer RM, Clarke WR. Use of cholesterol measurements in childhood for the prediction of adult hypercholesterolemia: The Muscatine study. *Journal of the American Medical Association*. 1990; 264: 3034–3038.

12. Lifshitz F, Tarim O. Nutrition dwarfing. *Current Problems in Pediatrics*. 1993; 23: 322–336.

13. The Writing Group for the DISC Collaborative Research Group. Efficacy and safety of lowering dietary intake of fat and cholesterol in children with elevated low-density lipoprotein cholesterol. *Journal of the American Medical Association*. 1995; 273: 1429–1435.

14. Lytle LA, Ebzery MK, Nicklas T, Montgomery D, Zive M, Evans M, Snyder P, Nickaman M, Kelder SH, Reed D, Busch E, Mitchell P. Nutrient intakes of third graders: Results from the Child and Adolescent Trial for Cardiovascular Health (CATCH) baseline survey. *Journal of Nutrition Education*. 1996; 28: 338–347.

15. Sigman-Grant M, Zimmerman S, Kris-Etherton PM. Dietary approaches for reducing fat intake of preschool-aged children. *Pediatrics*. 1993; 91: 955–960.

Appendix S

1. American Academy of Pediatrics, Committee on Nutrition. *Pediatric Nutrition Handbook*, 4th ed. Elk Grove Village, Ill.: American Academy of Pediatrics, 1998.

2. Snyder JD. Use and misuse of oral therapy for diarrhea: Comparison of U.S. practices with American Academy of Pediatrics recommendations. *Pediatrics*. 1991; 87(1): 28–33.

INDEX

References to the major treatment of topics are printed in bold.